T0338729

Intelligent Analytics With Advanced Multi-Industry Applications

Zhaohao Sun
Papua New Guinea University of Technology, Papua New Guinea

A volume in the Advances in Data Mining and
Database Management (ADMDM) Book Series

Published in the United States of America by
IGI Global
Engineering Science Reference (an imprint of IGI Global)
701 E. Chocolate Avenue
Hershey PA, USA 17033
Tel: 717-533-8845
Fax: 717-533-8661
E-mail: cust@igi-global.com
Web site: http://www.igi-global.com

Library of Congress Cataloging-in-Publication Data

Names: Sun, Zhaohao, editor.
Title: Intelligent analytics with advanced multi-industry applications / Zhaohao
  Sun, editor.
Description: Hershey, PA : Engineering Science Reference, an imprint of IGI
  Global, [2021] | Includes bibliographical references and index. |
  Summary: "This book conveys the foundations, technologies, thoughts, and
  methods of intelligent analytics with multi-industry applications to
  scientists, engineers, educators and business, service and management
  professionals, who have interest in big data, big information, big
  knowledge and big intelligence and wisdom, can be applied in data
  science, information science, and knowledge science"-- Provided by
  publisher.
Identifiers: LCCN 2020026655 (print) | LCCN 2020026656 (ebook) | ISBN
  9781799849636 (hardcover) | ISBN 9781799877806 (softcover) | ISBN
  9781799849643 (ebook)
Subjects: LCSH: Operations research--Data processing. | Industrial
  management--Data processing. | Quantitative research. | Big data. | Data
  mining.
Classification: LCC T57 .I58 2021 (print) | LCC T57 (ebook) | DDC
  658.4/034--dc23
LC record available at https://lccn.loc.gov/2020026655
LC ebook record available at https://lccn.loc.gov/2020026656

This book is published in the IGI Global book series Advances in Data Mining and Database Management (ADMDM) (ISSN: 2327-1981; eISSN: 2327-199X)

British Cataloguing in Publication Data
A Cataloguing in Publication record for this book is available from the British Library.

For electronic access to this publication, please contact: eresources@igi-global.com.

Advances in Data Mining and Database Management (ADMDM) Book Series

David Taniar
Monash University, Australia

ISSN:2327-1981
EISSN:2327-199X

MISSION

With the large amounts of information available to organizations in today's digital world, there is a need for continual research surrounding emerging methods and tools for collecting, analyzing, and storing data.

The **Advances in Data Mining & Database Management (ADMDM)** series aims to bring together research in information retrieval, data analysis, data warehousing, and related areas in order to become an ideal resource for those working and studying in these fields. IT professionals, software engineers, academicians and upper-level students will find titles within the ADMDM book series particularly useful for staying up-to-date on emerging research, theories, and applications in the fields of data mining and database management.

COVERAGE

- Cluster Analysis
- Profiling Practices
- Predictive Analysis
- Association Rule Learning
- Heterogeneous and Distributed Databases
- Customer Analytics
- Data Analysis
- Database Security
- Data Mining
- Enterprise Systems

IGI Global is currently accepting manuscripts for publication within this series. To submit a proposal for a volume in this series, please contact our Acquisition Editors at Acquisitions@igi-global.com or visit: http://www.igi-global.com/publish/.

701 East Chocolate Avenue, Hershey, PA 17033, USA
Tel: 717-533-8845 x100 • Fax: 717-533-8661
E-Mail: cust@igi-global.com • www.igi-global.com

Table of Contents

Section 3
Applications of Intelligent Analytics

Detailed Table of Contents

Section 1
Foundations of Intelligent Analytics

Intelligent analytics is an emerging paradigm in the age of big data, analytics, and artificial intelligence (AI). This chapter explores the nature of intelligent analytics. More specifically, this chapter identifies the foundations, cores, and applications of intelligent big data analytics based on the investigation into the state-of-the-art scholars' publications and market analysis of advanced analytics. Then it presents a workflow-based approach to big data analytics and technological foundations for intelligent big data analytics through examining intelligent big data analytics as an integration of AI and big data analytics. The chapter also presents a novel approach to extend intelligent big data analytics to intelligent analytics. The proposed approach in this chapter might facilitate research and development of intelligent analytics, big data analytics, business analytics, business intelligence, AI, and data science.

Chapter 2

Analytics is a key success factor for any business in the competitive and fast-changing world we live in. Using analytics, people, business, social, and government organizations become capable of understanding the past, including lessons from faults and achievements; realize current strengths, weaknesses, opportunities, and threats; and predict the future. Intelligent analytics allow doing these more effectively and efficiently. Modern analytics uses many advanced techniques like big data, artificial intelligence, and many others. This chapter aims to introduce the hybrid intelligence approach by focusing on its unique analytical capabilities. The state-of-the-art in hybrid intelligence—symbiosis and cooperative interaction between human intelligence and artificial intelligence in solving a wide range of practical tasks—and one of the hybrid intelligence frameworks—a human-centered evaluation approach and monitoring of complex processes—have been considered in this chapter. The chapter could be interesting for analysts and researchers who desire to do analytics with more intelligence.

Chapter 3

Andrew Stranieri, Federation University, Australia
Zhaohao Sun, Papua New Guinea University of Technology, Papua New Guinea

This chapter addresses whether AI can understand me. A framework for regulating AI systems that draws on Strawson's moral philosophy and concepts drawn from jurisprudence and theories on regulation is used. This chapter proposes that, as AI algorithms increasingly draw inferences following repeated exposure to big datasets, they have become more sophisticated and rival human reasoning. Their regulation requires that AI systems have agency and are subject to the rulings of courts. Humans sponsor the AI systems for registration with regulatory agencies. This enables judges to make moral culpability decisions by taking the AI system's explanation into account along with the full social context of the misdemeanor. The proposed approach might facilitate the research and development of intelligent analytics, intelligent big data analytics, multiagent systems, artificial intelligence, and data science.

Chapter 4

Li Chen, University of the District of Columbia, USA
Lala Aicha Coulibaly, University of the District of Columbia, USA

Data science and big data analytics are still at the center of computer science and information technology. Students and researchers not in computer science often found difficulties in real data analytics using programming languages such as Python and Scala, especially when they attempt to use Apache-Spark in cloud computing environments-Spark Scala and PySpark. At the same time, students in information technology could find it difficult to deal with the mathematical background of data science algorithms. To overcome these difficulties, this chapter will provide a practical guideline to different users in this area. The authors cover the main algorithms for data science and machine learning including principal component analysis (PCA), support vector machine (SVM), k-means, k-nearest neighbors (kNN), regression, neural networks, and decision trees. A brief description of these algorithms will be explained, and the related code will be selected to fit simple data sets and real data sets. Some visualization methods including 2D and 3D displays will be also presented in this chapter.

Section 2
Technologies for Intelligent Analytics

Chapter 5

Vladimir Mic, Masaryk University, Brno, Czech Republic
Pavel Zezula, Masaryk University, Brno, Czech Republic

This chapter focuses on data searching, which is nowadays mostly based on similarity. The similarity search is challenging due to its computational complexity, and also the fact that similarity is subjective and context dependent. The authors assume the metric space model of similarity, defined by the domain of objects and the metric function that measures the dissimilarity of object pairs. The volume of contemporary data is large, and the time efficiency of similarity query executions is essential. This chapter investigates transformations of metric space to Hamming space to decrease the memory and computational complexity of the search. Various challenges of the similarity search with sketches in the Hamming space are addressed, including the definition of sketching transformation and efficient search algorithms that exploit sketches to speed-up searching. The indexing of Hamming space and a heuristic to facilitate the selection of a suitable sketching technique for any given application are also considered.

Chapter 6

Umut Can Çabuk, Ege University, Turkey
Mustafa Tosun, Ege University, Turkey
Vahid Akram, Ege University, Turkey
Orhan Dagdeviren, Ege University, Turkey

Drone technologies have attracted the attention of many researchers in recent years due to their potential opportunities. Fleets of drones integrated with widely available relatively short-range communication technologies have various application areas such as wildlife monitoring, disaster relief, and military surveillance. One of the major problems in this manner is maintaining the connectivity of the drone network. In this chapter, the authors study the connectivity management issues in drone networks. Firstly, movement, communication, and channel models are described by the authors, along with the problem definition. The hardness of the problem is investigated by proving its NP-Hardness. Various algorithms proposed to solve the connectivity management problem and their variants are evaluated in detail. Lastly, for future directions, the authors present mathematical methods to solve the emerging problem in drone networks.

Chapter 7

Jiwen Fang, The University of Hong Kong, Hong Kong
Dickson K. W. Chiu, The University of Hong Kong, Hong Kong
Kevin K. W. Ho, University of Guam, Guam

Social media has become a popular communication platform and aggregated mass information for sentimental analysis. As cryptocurrency has become a hot topic worldwide in recent years, this chapter explores individuals' behavior in sharing Bitcoin information. First, Python was used for extracting around one month's set of Tweet data to obtain a dataset of 11,674 comments during a month of a substantial increase in Bitcoin price. The dataset was cleansed and analyzed by the process documents operator of RapidMiner. A word-cloud visualization for the Tweet dataset was generated. Next, the clustering operator of RapidMiner was used to analyze the similarity of words and the underlying meaning of the comments in different clusters. The clustering results show 85% positive comments on investment and 15% negative ones to Bitcoin-related tweets concerning security. The results represent the generally bullish environment of the cryptocurrency market and general user satisfaction during the period concerned.

Faiz Maazouzi, Department of Mathematics and Computer Science, University of Souk
Ahras, Algeria
Hafed Zarzour, LIM Research, Department of Mathematics and Computer Science,
University of Souk Ahras, Algeria

With the increased development of technology in healthcare, a huge amount of data is collected from healthcare organizations and stored in distributed medical data centers. In this context, such data quantities, called medical big data, which include different types of digital contents such as text, image, and video, have become an interesting topic tending to change the way we describe, manage, process, analyze, and visualize data in healthcare industry. Artificial intelligence (AI) is one of the sub-fields of computer science enabling us to analyze and solve more complex problems in many areas, including healthcare. AI-driven big healthcare analytics have the potential to predict patients at risk, spread of viruses like SARS-CoV-2, spread of new coronavirus, diseases, and new potential drugs. This chapter presents the AI-driven big healthcare analytics as well as discusses the benefits and the challenges. It is expected that the chapter helps researchers and practitioners to apply AI and big data to improve healthcare.

Priyank Jain, Indian Institute of Information Technology, Bhopal, India
Meenu Chawla, Maulana Azad National Institute of Technology, Bhopal, India
Sanskar Sahu, Indian Institute of Information Technology, Bhopal, India

Identification of a person by looking at the image is really a topic of interest in this modern world. There are many different ways by which this can be achieved. This research work describes various technologies available in the open-computer-vision (OpenCV) library and methodology to implement them using Python. To detect the face Haar Cascade are used, and for the recognition of face eigenfaces, fisherfaces, and local binary pattern, histograms has been used. Also, the results shown are followed by a discussion of encountered challenges and also the solution of the challenges.

Section 3
Applications of Intelligent Analytics

Desmond Narongou, National Airports Corporation (NAC), Papua New Guinea
Zhaohao Sun, Papua New Guinea University of Technology, Papua New Guinea

Smart airport management has drawn increasing attention worldwide for improving airport operational efficiency. Big data analytics is an emerging computing paradigm and enabler for smart airport management in the age of big data, analytics, and artificial intelligence (AI). This chapter will explore big data analytics for smart airport management from a perspective of PNG Jackson's International Airport. More specifically, this chapter first provides an overview of big data analytics and smart airport management and then looks at the impact of big data analytics on smart airport management. The chapter discusses how to apply big data analytics and smart airport management to upgrade PNG Jackson's International Airport in terms of safety and security, optimizing operational effectiveness, service enhancements, and customer experience. The approach proposed in this chapter might facilitate research and development of intelligent big data analytics, smart airport management, and customer relationship management.

Chapter 11

Wentao Gao, The University of Hong Kong, Hong Kong
Ka Man Lam, The University of Hong Kong, Hong Kong
Dickson K. W. Chiu, The University of Hong Kong, Hong Kong
Kevin K. W. Ho, University of Guam, Guam

A movie's economic revenue comes mainly from the movie box office, while the influencing factors of the movie box office are complex and numerous. This research explores the influencing factors of China's commercial movie box office by analyzing the top 100 box office movies released in Mainland China between 2013-2016, with a total of 400 movies. The authors analyzed the data collected using correlation analysis and decision tree analysis using RapidMiner, respectively. Based on the analysis results, they put forward suggestions for improving the box office of the movie industry.

Chapter 12

Burak Efe, Necmettin Erbakan University, Turkey
Ömer Faruk Efe, Afyon Kocatepe University, Turkey

In recent years, with the development of the internet, there has been an increase in interest in the internet thanks to other technological developments. In the face of increased user demand, hotel webpages have to maintain high quality of service for a sustainable success. The authors present the Pythagorean fuzzy TOPSIS method to evaluate the hotel webpages. In this study, the most suitable hotel web page has been selected among the five hotel web page alternatives based on 13 criteria according to three experts' opinions. In contrast to precise numbers in TOPSIS method, the merit of fuzzy TOPSIS method is to handle the fuzzy numbers to evaluate the alternatives. Experts cannot express certain evaluations explicitly when using precise values during making decisions. However, the use of linguistic variables provides great success in decision making under uncertain environments. Pythagorean fuzzy number is used to define the weights of the criteria according to three experts' opinions. Five alternative hotel web pages are ranked by using Pythagorean fuzzy number.

Chapter 13

Poshan Yu, Soochow University, China
Zhenyu Xu, Independent Researcher, China

In data analytics, the application of text analysis is always challenging, in particular, when performing the text mining of Chinese characters. This study aims to use the micro-blog data created by the users to conduct text mining and analysis of the impact of stock market performances in China. Based upon Li's instance labeling method, this chapter examines the correlation between social media information and a public-private partnership (PPP)-related company stock prices. The authors crawled the data from EastMoney platform via a web crawler and obtained a total of 79,874 language data from 10 January 2017 to 28 November 2019. The total material data obtained is 79,616, which the authors use for specific training in the financial corpus. The findings of this chapter indicate that the investor investment sentiment has a certain impact on the stock price movement of selected stocks in the PPP sector.

Chapter 14

Burak Efe, Necmettin Erbakan University, Turkey

Material handling refers to the processes of loading materials onto a material handling equipment, moving from one location to another location with the help of material handling equipment, and unloading the material from the transportation equipment to the relevant location. Non-ergonomic material handling equipment for the employee causes the increment of cycle time that does not add value to the product during transportation within the enterprise. The increase in cycle time causes an increase in fatigue and inefficiency in the employee. This study evaluates five material handling equipment based on eight ergonomic criteria by using interval type-2 fuzzy TOPSIS method. Interval type-2 fuzzy number provides to examine the fuzziness and the uncertainty more accurately than type-1 fuzzy number, which handles only one crisp membership degree. The opinions of experts are aggregated by employing interval type-2 fuzzy number operators.

Chapter 15

Cataldo Zuccaro, University of Quebec in Montreal, Canada
Michel Plaisent, University of Quebec in Montreal, Canada
Prosper Bernard, University of Quebec in Montreal, Canada

This chapter presents a preliminary framework to tackle tax evasion in the field of residential renovation. This industry plays a major role in economic development and employment growth. Tax evasion and fraud are extremely difficult to combat in the industry since it is characterized by a large number of stakeholders (manufacturers, retailers, tradesmen, and households) generating complex transactional dynamics that often defy attempts to deploy transactional analytics to detect anomalies, fraud, and tax evasion. This chapter proposes a framework to apply transactional analytics and data mining to develop standard measures and predictive models to detect fraud and tax evasion. Combining big data sets, cross-referencing, and predictive modeling (i.e., anomaly detection, artificial neural network support vector machines, Bayesian network, and association rules) can assist government agencies to combat highly stealth tax evasion and fraud in the residential renovation.

Chapter 16

Maria Ndapewa Ntinda, University of Namibia, Namibia
Titus Haiduwa, University of Namibia, Namibia
Willbard Kamati, University of Namibia, Namibia

This chapter discusses the development of a virtual laboratory (VL) named "EduPhysics," an assistive software tailored around the Namibian Physical Science textbook for Grade 8 learners, and examines the viability of implementing VL in education. It further presented reviews on the role of computer simulations in science education and teachers' perspective on the use of EduPhysics in physical science classrooms. The chapter adopted a mixed method with an experimental research design and used questionnaires and interviews as data collection tools in high school physical science classes. The analysis found that there are limited resources in most physical science laboratories. Computer laboratories, however, are well equipped and have computing capacities to support the implementation of VL. It was concluded that virtual laboratories could be an alternative approach to hands-on practical work that is currently undertaken in resource-constrained physical science labs. For future work, augmented reality and logs will be incorporated within EduPhysics.

Preface

We are living in an age of intelligent analytics. Intelligent analytics is an emerging paradigm in the age of big data, analytics, and artificial intelligence (AI). Intelligent analytics is an integration intelligence that integrates artificial intelligence, analytics, data, information, knowledge, intelligence, and wisdom using advanced ICT computing to provide smart services for improving business, management, and governance. Intelligent analytics has been revolutionizing our work, life, business, management, and organization as well as healthcare, finance, e-commerce, and web services. It becomes disruptive technology for healthcare, web services, service computing, cloud computing, the Internet of Everything (IoE), and social networking computing.

More specifically, intelligent analytics (IA) is science and technology about collecting, organizing, and analyzing big data, big information, big knowledge, and big intelligence as well as big wisdom to discover and visualize patterns, knowledge, and intelligence as well as other information within the big data, information, knowledge, and intelligence based on big analytics, artificial intelligence (AI), and intelligent systems. Intelligent analytics at least includes intelligent data analytics, intelligent information analytics, intelligent knowledge analytics, and intelligent wisdom analytics, all of them are underpinned by intelligent statistical modeling, machine learning, intelligent visualization, and intelligent optimization. Intelligent data analytics further includes big data, intelligent big data analytics, intelligent data analysis, intelligent data warehousing, intelligent data mining, and intelligent data visualization. Intelligent information analytics at least includes big information, intelligent information analysis, intelligent information warehousing, intelligent information retrieval, and intelligent information visualization. Intelligent knowledge analytics at least includes big knowledge, intelligent knowledge analysis and engineering, intelligent knowledge systems, intelligent knowledge retrieval and warehousing, and intelligent knowledge visualization. Intelligent wisdom analytics at least includes big wisdom, intelligent wisdom analysis and engineering, intelligent wisdom systems, intelligent wisdom retrieval, and intelligent wisdom visualization.

Currently, intelligent analytics can be classified into intelligent descriptive analytics, intelligent diagnostic analytics, intelligent predictive analytics, and intelligent prescriptive analytics for big data, information, knowledge, intelligence, and wisdom. Intelligent big data analytics has made remarkable achievements thanks to the dramatic development of big data and big data analytics. Intelligent information analytics, intelligent knowledge analytics, and intelligent wisdom analytics have not yet drawn significant attention in academia and industry, because we are still indulged in the age of big data, and ignore the dawning age of big information, big knowledge, big intelligence, and big wisdom. Big data is a foundation of big information, big knowledge, and big intelligence or wisdom. Therefore, we are still at the foundational stage and scare about the emerging age of big information, big knowledge, big intelligence, and big wisdom.

Intelligent analytics is an emerging intelligent technology and becomes a mainstream market adopted broadly across industries, organizations, and geographic regions and among individuals to facilitate big data-driven, big information-driven, big knowledge-driven, big intelligence-driven, and big wisdom-driven decision making for businesses and individuals to achieve desired business outcomes. However, there are only three books on "Intelligent analytics" available based on Amazon.com search (retrieved on 19 December 2020). The first is Andrew Minteer, 2017, Analytics for the Internet of Things (IoT): Intelligent analytics for your intelligent devices, Packt Publishing. Another is R. Anandan, G. Suseendran, et al. (2021) Industrial Internet of Things (IIoT): Intelligent Analytics for Predictive Maintenance. The third is Celeste Fralick and Sarah Kalicin (2015) Intelligent Analytics: Bringing Analytics to the Internet of Things, Apress. All these three books can be considered as applications of intelligent analytics in the Internet of Things (IoT). Many fundamental theoretical, technological, and managerial issues surrounding the development and implementation of intelligent analytics within multi-industry applications remain unsolved. For example: What is the foundation of intelligent analytics? What are the elements of intelligent analytics? What is the nature of intelligent analytics? What are the relationships between intelligent analytics and big data analytics? How can we apply intelligent analytics to improve explainable AI, healthcare, mobile commerce, web services, cloud services, and digital transformation? What are the implications of intelligent analytics on business, management, IoT, blockchain, service, and society? What are the real big characteristics of intelligent analytics? All these mentioned challenges should be addressed through theoretical, technological, and methodological development to meet the social, economic, marketing, commercial, scientific, and technological demands from different parties or individuals for intelligent analytics with applications. As a follow-up to the book entitled *Managerial Perspectives on Intelligent Big Data Analytics*, this book addresses these issues by exploring the cutting-edge theories, technologies, and methodologies of intelligent analytics with multi-industry applications, and emphasizes the integration of artificial intelligence, business intelligence, analytics intelligence, and intelligent big data analytics from a perspective of computing, service, and management. This book also provides a creative and innovative understanding of and insight into how the proposed theories, technologies, and methodologies of intelligent analytics can improve e-SMACS (electronic, social, mobile, analytics, cloud, and service) commerce and services, healthcare, IoE (the Internet of everything), sharing economy, blockchain, 5G technology, cybersecurity, and Industry 4.0 in the real world. The proposed approaches will facilitate research and development of intelligent analytics, big data analytics, data science, digital transformation, e-business, web service, service computing, cloud computing, and social computing, and more.

This book includes foundations, technologies, and applications of intelligent analytics. The foundations of intelligent analytics mainly include core foundations and supporting foundations. The core foundations include intelligent warehouses, intelligent mining, intelligent statistical modeling, machine learning, intelligent visualization and optimization for big data, information, knowledge, intelligence, and wisdom. The supporting foundations include artificial intelligence (AI), explainable AI, machine learning, natural language processing, mathematics and statistics, data science, and optimization, domain sciences including business, management, and service science. The topics for this part include fundamental concepts, models/architectures, frameworks/schemes or foundations for planning, designing, building, operating or evaluating, managing intelligent analytics.

Technologies of intelligent analytics in this book include intelligent technology, computational technology, web technology, Internet technology, social networking technology, cloud technology, management technology, big data technology, and IoE technology, to name a few. The topics for this part include all the mentioned technologies for developing intelligent analytics.

Applications of intelligent analytics in this book cover all the applications and case studies of intelligent analytics in e-commerce, social networking, big data, digital transformation, SMACS computing, IoT, 5G systems, intelligent drones, healthcare, smart cities, and other real-world problem solving. The topics for this part include cases and applications for using foundations and technologies in Part I, II for planning, designing, building, managing and operating or evaluating intelligent analytics in the various domains such as digital transformation, SMACS computing, commerce and services, financial services, legal services, healthcare services, educational services, and military services taking into account intelligent descriptive, diagnostic, predictive, and prescriptive analytics. This book also includes emerging technologies, methodologies, and applications for intelligent analytics.

In order to develop this book, we released the Call for book chapter (CFP) with a large number of topics for foundations, technologies, applications at the website of IGI-Global (https://www.igi-global.com/publish/call-for-papers/call-details/4539), wikiCFP (http://www.wikicfp.com), AIS world (aisworld@lists.aisnet.org), and researchgate (https://www.researchgate.net/project/Intelligent-Analytics-with-Applications) to appeal the worldwide scholars for contributions. It is certainly impossible for a book to cover each of these topics, although the editor has tried to do his best to use various media and research social networking platforms. We received 34+ book proposals based on CFP and 22 full book chapter manuscripts' submission. Based on the double-blinded peer review, 16 book chapters out of them are selected from the book chapter manuscripts' submission, and published in this book, each of them aligns with one or few of the mentioned topics. In what follows, we will overview each of the chapters published in this book.

SECTION 1: FOUNDATIONS OF INTELLIGENT ANALYTICS

Section 1 consists of the following four chapters.

Chapter 1, contributed by Zhaohao Sun and Andrew Stranieri, titled "The Nature of Intelligent Analytics," identifies the foundations, cores, and applications of intelligent big data analytics based on the investigation into the state-of-the-art scholars' publications and market analysis of advanced analytics. Then it presents a workflow-based approach to big data analytics and technological foundations for intelligent big data analytics through examining intelligent big data analytics as integration of AI, big data, and analytics. The chapter presents a novel approach to extend intelligent big data analytics to intelligent analytics. Finally, this chapter examines the theoretical, technical, and social implications of the research and development of intelligent analytics, big data analytics, business analytics, business intelligence, AI, and data science.

Chapter 2, contributed by Alexander Ryjov, titled "Hybrid Intelligence Framework for Augmented Analytics," looks at the hybrid intelligence approach by focusing on its unique analytical capabilities. The state-of-the-art hybrid intelligence-symbiosis and cooperative interaction between human intelligence and artificial intelligence in solving a wide range of practical tasks and one of the hybrid intelligence frameworks–a human-centered evaluation approach and monitoring of complex processes are examined in this chapter. The chapter could be appealing to analysts and researchers for analytics intelligence.

Chapter 3, contributed by Andrew Stranieri and Zhaohao Sun, titled "Only AI Can Understand Me? Big Data Analytics, Decision Making, and Reasoning," addresses an interesting question: Can AI understand me? and looks at the relationship between appropriate and intelligent actions to illustrate that decisions about moral culpability in an era of AI systems learning from big data are social constructs. This chapter examines explanation-oriented reasoning as a foundation of explainable AI, overviews intelligent agents, multiagent systems, and discusses delegation intelligence, mind, intention, and responsibility as a foundation of artificial agency. Then the chapter presents a framework for regulating AI agents as a multiagent system, which enables AI agents to be regulated by socio-legal structures designed for AI agents. The key elements of the framework consist of the assignment of an agency to an AI System, the introduction of a human sponsor responsible for certifying the AI agent with regulatory boards, and a hierarchy of courts with human judges to make socially meaningful decisions about moral culpability. The framework has been elaborated on by a proposed AI system for regulating AI agents in this chapter.

Chapter 4, contributed by Li Chen and Lala Aicha Coulibaly, titled "Data Science and Big Data Practice Using Apache-Spark and Python," addresses the challenges of real data analytics to the students and practitioners when they use programming languages such as Python and Scala, especially when they attempt to use Apache-Spark in cloud computing environments-Spark Scala and PySpark. This chapter provides a practical guideline to different users in this area. It covers the main algorithms for data science and machine learning including principal component analysis (PCA), support vector machine (SVM), k-Means, k-nearest neighbors (kNN), regression, neural networks, and decision trees. A brief description of these algorithms is explained, and the related code is selected to fit simple data sets and real data sets in this chapter. Some visualization methods including 2D and 3D displays are also presented in this chapter.

SECTION 2: TECHNOLOGIES FOR INTELLIGENT ANALYTICS

Section 2 consists of the following five chapters.

Chapter 5, contributed by Vladimir Mic and Pavel Zezula, titled "On the Similarity Search With Hamming Space Sketches," focuses on similarity-based data searching and investigates transformations of metric space to Hamming space to decrease the memory and computational complexity of the search. It addresses various challenges of the similarity-based search with sketches in the Hamming space, which includes the definition of sketching transformation and efficient search algorithms that exploit sketches to speed-up searching. This chapter also looks at the indexing of Hamming space and a heuristic to facilitate the selection of a suitable sketching technique for any given application.

Chapter 6, contributed by Umut Can Çabuk, Mustafa Tosun, Vahid Akram, and Orhan Dagdeviren, titled "Connectivity Management in Drone Networks: Models, Algorithms, and Methods," examines the connectivity management issues in drone networks. Firstly, movement, communication, and channel models are described by the authors, along with the problem definition. Then the hardness of the problem is investigated by proving its NP-Hardness. Various algorithms proposed to solve the connectivity management problem and its variants are evaluated in detail. Lastly, for future directions, the authors present mathematical methods to solve the emerging problem in drone networks in this chapter.

Chapter 7, contributed by Jiwen Fang, Dickson K. W. Chiu, and Kevin K. W. Ho, titled "Exploring Cryptocurrency Sentimental With Clustering Text Mining on Social Media," explores individuals' behaviors in sharing Bitcoin information. First, Python was used for extracting around one month's set of

Tweet data to obtain a dataset of 11,674 comments during a month of a substantial increase in Bitcoin price. The dataset was cleansed and analyzed by the process documents operator of RapidMiner. A word-cloud visualization for the Tweet dataset was generated. Next, the clustering operator of RapidMiner was used to analyze the similarity of words and the underlying meaning of the comments in different clusters. The clustering results show 85% positive comments on investment and 15% negative ones to Bitcoin-related tweets concerning security. The results represent the generally bullish environment of the cryptocurrency market and general user satisfaction during the period concerned.

Chapter 8, contributed by Faiz Maazouzi and Hafed Zarzour, is titled "AI-Driven Big Healthcare Analytics: Contributions and Challenges." With the increasing development of technology in healthcare, a huge amount of data is collected from healthcare organizations and stored in distributed medical data centers. In this context, such data quantities, called medical big data, which include different types of digital contents such as text, image, and video have become an interesting topic tending to change the way we describe, manage, process, analyze and visualize data in the healthcare industry. Artificial intelligence (AI) can be used to analyze and solve more complex problems in many areas, including healthcare. AI-driven big healthcare analytics have the potential to predict patients at risk, the spread of viruses like SARS-CoV-2, the spread of new coronavirus, diseases, and new potential drugs. This chapter presents the AI-driven big healthcare analytics as well as discusses the benefits and the challenges. It is expected that this chapter helps researchers and practitioners to apply AI and big data analytics to improve healthcare.

Chapter 9, contributed by Priyank Jain, Meenu Chawla, and Sanskar Sahu, titled "Face Recognition and Face Detection Using Open Computer Vision Classifiers and Python," looks at various technologies available in the Open-Computer-Vision (OpenCV) library and methodology to implement identification of a person by looking at the image. It looks at detecting the face using the Haar Cascade and the recognition of face Eigenfaces, using Fisherfaces and local binary pattern, histograms. The research results shown are followed by a discussion of encountered challenges and also the solution of the challenges.

SECTION 3: APPLICATIONS OF INTELLIGENT ANALYTICS

Section 3 consists of the following seven chapters.

Chapter 10, contributed by Desmond Narongou and Zhaohao Sun, titled "Big Data Analytics for Smart Airport Management," explores big data analytics for smart airport management from the perspective of PNG Jackson's International Airport. More specifically, this chapter first overviews big data analytics and smart airport management and then looks at the impact of big data analytics on smart airport management. This chapter also discusses how to apply big data analytics and smart airport management to upgrade PNG Jackson's International Airport in terms of safety and security, optimizing operational effectiveness, service enhancements, and customer experience. The approach proposed in this chapter might facilitate research and development of intelligent analytics, smart airport management, and customer relationship management.

Chapter 11, contributed by Wentao Gao, Ka Man Lam, Dickson K.W. Chiu, and Kevin K.W. Ho, titled "A Big Data Analysis of the Factors Influencing Movie Box Office in China," explores the influencing factors of China's commercial movie box office by analyzing the top 100 box office movies released in Mainland China between 2013-2016, with a total of 400 movies. It analyzes the data collected using correlation analysis and decision tree analysis using RapidMiner, respectively. Based on the analysis results, the research puts forward suggestions for improving the box office of the movie industry.

Chapter 12, contributed by Burak Efe and Ömer Faruk Efe, titled "Evaluation of Hotel Web Pages According to User Suitability," presents the Pythagorean fuzzy TOPSIS method to evaluate the hotel webpages. In this study, the most suitable hotel web page has been selected among the 5 hotel web page alternatives based on thirteen criteria according to three experts' opinions. In contrast to precise numbers in the TOPSIS method, the merit of the fuzzy TOPSIS method is to handle the fuzzy numbers to evaluate the alternatives. Experts cannot express certain evaluations explicitly when using precise values during making decisions. However, the use of linguistic variables provides great success in decision making under uncertain environments. The Pythagorean fuzzy number is used to define the weights of the criteria according to three experts' opinions. Five alternative hotel web pages are ranked by using Pythagorean fuzzy numbers.

Chapter 13, contributed by Poshan Yu and Zhenyu Xu, titled "The Impact of News on Public-Private Partnership Stock Price in China via Text Mining Method," uses the micro-blog data created by the users to conduct text mining and analysis of the impact of stock market performances in China. Based on Li's instance labeling method (Li et al., 2014), this chapter examines the correlation between social media information and a public-private partnership (PPP) related company's stock prices. The authors crawled the data from the EastMoney platform (http://stock.eastmoney.com/) via a web crawler and obtained a total of 79,874 language data from January 10, 2017 to November 28, 2019. The total material data obtained is 79,616, which the authors use for specific training in the financial corpus. The findings of this chapter indicate that the investor's investment sentiment has a certain impact on the stock price movement of selected stocks in the PPP sector.

Chapter 14, contributed by Burak Efe, titled "Ergonomic Criteria-Based Material Handling Equipment Selection," evaluates five material handling equipment systems based on eight ergonomic criteria by using interval type-2 fuzzy TOPSIS method. Interval type-2 fuzzy number provides to examine the fuzziness and the uncertainty more accurately than a type-1 fuzzy number, which handles only one crisp membership degree. The opinions of experts are aggregated by employing interval type-2 fuzzy number operators. The research demonstrates that non-ergonomic material handling equipment for the employee causes the increment of cycle time that does not add value to the product during transportation within the enterprise.

Chapter 15, contributed by Cataldo Zuccaro, Michel Plaisent, and Prosper Bernard, titled "A Preliminary Framework to Fight Tax Evasion in the Home Renovation Market," presents a preliminary framework to tackle tax evasion in the field of residential renovation. This chapter proposes a framework to apply transactional analytics and data mining to develop standard measures and predictive models to detect fraud and tax evasion. The research demonstrates that combining big datasets, cross-referencing, and predictive modeling (i.e., anomaly detection, artificial neural network support vector machines, Bayesian network, and association rules) can assist government agencies to combat highly stealth tax evasion and fraud in residential renovation.

Chapter 16, contributed by Maria Ndapewa Ntinda, Titus Haiduwa, and Willbard Kamati, titled "Development and Analysis of Virtual Laboratory as an Assistive Tool for Teaching Grade 8 Physical Science Classes," discusses the development of a virtual laboratory (VL), named "EduPhysics", an assistive software tailored around the Namibian Physical Science textbook for Grade 8 learners, and examines the viability of implementing VL in Education. It further presents the role of computer simulations in science education and the teachers' perspective on the use of EduPhysics in Physical Science classrooms.

The chapter adopts a mixed method with an experimental research design and uses questionnaires and interviews as data collection tools in high school physical science classes. The analysis demonstrates that there are limited resources in most physical science laboratories. Computer laboratories, however, are well equipped and have computing capacities to support the implementation of VL. The research shows that virtual laboratories could be an alternative approach to hands-on practical work that is currently undertaken in resource-constrained physical science labs. For future work, augmented reality and logs will be incorporated within the EduPhysics.

This book is the first book on "Intelligent analytics" which focuses on intelligent big data analytics, intelligent big information analytics, intelligent big knowledge analytics, intelligent big wisdom analytics in the age of big data, analytics, and artificial intelligence. This book titled "Intelligent Analytics with Advanced Multi-industry Applications" is the first book to reveal the cutting-edge theory, technologies, methodologies, and applications of intelligent analytics in the emerging age of intelligent analytics in an integrated way. This is also the first book demonstrating that intelligent analytics is an important enabler for developing intelligent data analytics, digital transformation, business, management, governance, and services in the digital age.

This book's primary aim is to convey the foundations, technologies, thoughts, and methods of intelligent analytics with multi-industry applications to scientists, engineers, educators and university students, business, service and management professionals, policymakers, decisionmakers, and others who have an interest in big data, big information, big knowledge, big intelligence and big wisdom, intelligent analytics, AI, digital transformation, SMACS intelligence and computing, commerce, service and data science. Primary audiences for this book are undergraduate, postgraduate students, and a variety of professionals in the fields of big data, data science, information science and technology, knowledge technology and engineering, intelligence science, analytics, AI, ICT, computing, commerce, business, services, management, and government. The variety of readers in the fields of government, consulting, marketing, business, and trade, as well as the readers from all the social strata, can also be benefited from this book to improve understanding of the cutting-edge theory, technologies, methodologies, and intelligent analytics with multi-industry applications in the digital age.

ACKNOWLEDGMENT

The publication of this book entitled Intelligent Analytics with Advanced Multi-Industry Applications reflects the integration of intelligence, wisdom, and perseverance of many researchers and friends worldwide. I would like to express my sincere gratitude to all the members of the Editorial Advisory Board (EAB) for their erudite comments and guidance. I heartily thank all the contributors for their time and submission of manuscripts, they have made this book possible and transformed our initiatives into reality. I would also like to thank all the contributors who have submitted book chapter proposals, drafts, ideas to this book although the proposals have not been changed into accepted book chapters for publication because of the worldwide coronavirus pandemic. My special thanks go to the international team of reviewers for blindly reviewing the book chapters and submitting review reports on the paper selflessly, timely, and professionally. These review reports include their erudite comments on the book chapters included in this book. Without such selfless and professional contributions, most books in general and this book in particular would not have been published. I must express my sincere thanks to PNG University of Technology, Federation University Australia, and Hebei University of Science and Technology for their excellent research environment that I have used to develop my ideas, books, and research papers effectively. I express extreme thanks to WikiCFP, ResearchGate, IS World, and other social networking platforms for their timely and tirelessly sharing of our CFP on the platform. My heartily thanks also go to researchers for accessing WikiCFP, ResearchGate, and IS World, and caring for our CFP. My sincerest thanks go to my good friends Ms. Lindsay Wertman, Ms. Jan Travers, Ms. Crystal Moyer, Ms. Nicole Hagan, and Mr. Eric Whalen of IGI-Global for their outstanding and continuous support and patience throughout the book development process. Finally, I would like to express my deepest appreciation for the support and encouragement of my wife, Dr. Yanxia (Monica) Huo. Without her lasting support and patience as well as academic comments, authoring and editing this book would not have been possible.

Zhaohao Sun
Papua New Guinea University of Technology, Papua New Guinea
December 2020

Acknowledgment

The publication of this book entitled Intelligent Analytics with Advanced Multi-Industry Applications reflects the integration of intelligence, wisdom, and perseverance of many researchers and friends worldwide. I would like to express my sincere gratitude to all the members of the Editorial Advisory Board (EAB) for their erudite comments and guidance. I heartily thank all the contributors for their time and submission of manuscripts, they have made this book possible and transformed our initiatives into reality. I would also like to thank all the contributors who have submitted book chapter proposals, drafts, ideas to this book although the proposals have not been changed into accepted book chapters for publication because of the worldwide coronavirus pandemic. My special thanks go to the international team of reviewers for blindly reviewing the book chapters and submitting review reports on the paper selflessly, timely, and professionally. These review reports include their erudite comments on the book chapters included in this book. Without such selfless and professional contributions, most books in general and this book in particular would not have been published. I must express my sincere thanks to PNG University of Technology, Federation University Australia, and Hebei University of Science and Technology for their excellent research environment that I have used to develop my ideas, books, and research papers effectively. I express extreme thanks to WikiCFP, ResearchGate, IS World, and other social networking platforms for their timely and tirelessly sharing of our CFP on the platform. My heartily thanks also go to researchers for accessing WikiCFP, ResearchGate, and IS World, and caring for our CFP. My sincerest thanks go to my good friends Ms. Lindsay Wertman, Ms. Jan Travers, Ms. Crystal Moyer, Ms. Nicole Hagan, and Mr. Eric Whalen of IGI-Global for their outstanding and continuous support and patience throughout the book development process. Finally, I would like to express my deepest appreciation for the support and encouragement of my wife, Dr. Yanxia (Monica) Huo. Without her lasting support and patience as well as academic comments, authoring and editing this book would not have been possible.

Zhaohao Sun
Papua New Guinea University of Technology, Papua New Guinea
December 2020

Section 1
Foundations of Intelligent Analytics

Chapter 1
The Nature of Intelligent Analytics

Zhaohao Sun
ⓘ https://orcid.org/0000-0003-0780-3271
Papua New Guinea University of Technology, Papua New Guinea

Andrew Stranieri
Federation University, Australia

ABSTRACT

Intelligent analytics is an emerging paradigm in the age of big data, analytics, and artificial intelligence (AI). This chapter explores the nature of intelligent analytics. More specifically, this chapter identifies the foundations, cores, and applications of intelligent big data analytics based on the investigation into the state-of-the-art scholars' publications and market analysis of advanced analytics. Then it presents a workflow-based approach to big data analytics and technological foundations for intelligent big data analytics through examining intelligent big data analytics as an integration of AI and big data analytics. The chapter also presents a novel approach to extend intelligent big data analytics to intelligent analytics. The proposed approach in this chapter might facilitate research and development of intelligent analytics, big data analytics, business analytics, business intelligence, AI, and data science.

1 INTRODUCTION

Big data, analytics, Artificial Intelligence (AI) and their integration are at the frontier for revolutionizing our work, life, business, management, and organization as well as healthcare, finance, e-commerce, and web services (Henke & Bughin, 2016) (Lohr, 2012 February 11) (John, 2013) (Sun & Huo, 2019) (Chen & Zhang, 2014) (Laney & Jain, 2017) (Russell & Norvig, 2010). Big data and its emerging technologies including big data analytics have been not only making big changes in the way the business operates but also making traditional data analytics and business analytics bring forth new big opportunities for academia and enterprises (Sun, Sun, & Strang, 2016; Sun, Zou, & Strang, 2015; McAfee & Brynjolfsson, 2012). Big data analytics has big market opportunities. For example, International Data Corporation

DOI: 10.4018/978-1-7998-4963-6.ch001

(IDC) forecasts that big data and business analytics (BDA) revenue will be $274.3 billion BY 2022 with a five-year compound annual growth rate (CAGR) of 13.2% from 2018 to 2022 (IDC, 2019).

AI and business intelligence (BI) have penetrated into modern analytics that at least includes augmented analytics, embedded analytics, mobile analytics, and cloud analytics (Eiloart, 2018) (Howson, Richardson, Sallam, & Kronz, 2019). For example, Amazon Web Services (AWS): Amazon QuickSight is a cloud analytics and BI service for performing ad hoc analysis and publishing interactive dashboards (Howson, Richardson, Sallam, & Kronz, 2019). Gartner predicts that 30% of new revenue growth from industry-specific solutions will include AI technology by 2021 (Laney & Jain, 2017). AI-derived business value is forecasted to increase to $US3.9 trillion in 2022 from $US1.2 trillion of 2018 (Pettey & van der Meulen, 2018), 325% jump! IDC predicted global spending on AI systems will more than double to $79.2 billion in 2022 with a compound annual growth rate (CAGR) of 38.0% over the 2018-2022 forecast period (IDC, 2019).

Intelligent big data analytics is an emerging science and technology based on AI (Russell & Norvig, 2010), and is becoming a mainstream market adopted broadly across industries, organizations, and geographic regions and among individuals to facilitate decision making for businesses and individuals to achieve desired business outcomes (Laney & Jain, 2017) (Sun, Sun, & Strang, 2018) (Sun Z., 2019) (INFORMS, 2014). Intelligent big data analytics in particular and intelligent analytics in general have become a disruptive technology for effective innovation and decision making in the digital age (Holsapplea, Lee-Postb, & Pakath, 2014) (Davis, 2014). However, the following issues have still been ignored to some extent in academia, industries, and governments.

1.   What are fundamentals of intelligent analytics?
2.   What is the relationship between big data analytics and intelligent analytics?
3.   How can we integrate big data analytics and AI?

This chapter will address these three research issues through exploring the nature of intelligent analytics. More specifically, this chapter identifies the theoretical and technological foundations, cores, and applications of intelligent big data analytics through an investigation into the state-of-the-art scholars' publications and market analysis of advanced analytics. Then it examines intelligent big data analytics as an integration of AI and big data analytics through presenting a workflow-based approach to big data analytics and technological foundations for intelligent big data analytics. The chapter uses a multidisciplinary approach to significantly extend intelligent big data analytics to intelligent analytics and looks at augmented analytics as a kind of intelligent analytics.

The remainder of this chapter is organized as follows: Section 2 identifies foundations, cores, applications as fundamentals of intelligent big data analytics. Section 3 argues that intelligent big data analytics = big data analytics + AI. This is a basis and motivation for Section 4. Section 4 presents an inclusive approach to intelligent analytics. Section 5 examines augmented analytics as intelligent analytics. It is an example of intelligent analytics taking into account the state-of-the-art advanced analytics in the global market of analytics. Sections 6 provides discussion and implications as well as future research directions of this research. The final section ends this chapter with some concluding remarks and future work.

From a viewpoint of research methodology, this chapter has used a multidisciplinary approach consisting of business, logical, algebraic, and systematic, research as a search method. For example, in order to identify foundations, cores, applications of intelligent big data analytics based on the principle of "research as a search", this chapter uses Scopus indexed publications search, which reflects the state-of-the-art research of the scholars on intelligent big data analytics worldwide. Then it uses the market analysis provided by Gartner, which reflects the start of the art research and development of the modern analytics industry. Both are excellent complements for understanding the state-of-the-art intelligent big data analytics. This chapter also uses business, logical, algebraic, and systematic approach to examine intelligent big data analytics as an integration of AI and big data analytics and proposes the technological foundation of intelligent big data analytics as a hierarchical structure. This chapter uses logical, algebraic, and systematic (software engineering) approach to extend intelligent big data analytics to intelligent analytics inclusively and proposes a novel system architecture of intelligent analytics as an intelligent system.

2 FOUNDATIONS, CORES, AND APPLICATIONS OF INTELLIGENT BIG DATA ANALYTICS: THE STATE-OF-THE-ART

This section presents foundations, cores, applications of intelligent big data analytics based on the principle of "research as a search".

We searched Scopus (https://www-scopus-com.ezproxy.federation.edu.au/) for "intelligent big data analytics" (for short, hereafter, IBA) using search strategy: TITLE (intelligent AND big AND data AND analytics) (22 January 2020) and found 44 document results. In order to analyze the related work of the found 44 document results, we classify each title of them into three categories based on

1. What is for IBA?
2. What is deep exploration to IBA?
3. What is IBA for?

The answer to the first question is the theoretical and technological foundations for developing IBA. The answer to the second question is the theoretical and technological development of IBA. The answer to the third question is the applications of IBA. From a viewpoint of research methodology, such a classification is significant for developing intelligent analytics in general, and intelligent big data analytics in particular.

The mentioned 44 research publications are summarized as follows, based on the above three categories,

1. 10 out of 44 research publications address what is for IBA. These publications cover ontology-based workflow generation, intelligent multi-engine resource scheduler, ontology-based service discovery, intelligent interfaces, intelligent computing, semantic data ingestion, intelligent data traffic adaptation, software architecture design, intelligent query placement strategy, and intelligent technologies and applications. This implies that only a few strong theoretical and technological enablers for developing IBA. More theoretical and technological foundations are required to develop IBA.
2. 10 out of 44 research publications address what deep exploration is to IBA. These research publications cover model design, intelligent health data analytics, data-less big data analytics, adaptive e-commerce website ranking, big data management, a managerial framework, a theoretical framework, dynamic big data analytics. This implies that deep explorations into IBA have not been reflected very much by quality research publications.

3. 24 out of 44 research publications address the third question. These research publications cover the following applications of IBA: intelligent manufacturing, intelligent transportation, teaching, prediction of driver's intent, prediction of air pollution, predictive enterprise, intelligent process prediction, e-Commerce metasearch and ranking system, sustainable retail environment, knowledge discovery, surgery risk assessment, intelligent management of autonomous vehicles, intelligent mobile service provisions of customer relationship management (CRM), big video data, intelligent urban transport, cloud computing, travel, intelligent automation, and surveillance video system. This implies that the applications of IBA are still very isolated based on the quality research publications.

44 research publications indexed by Scopus demonstrate that

1. The number of publications (intelligent big data analytics is a part of the title of article) indexed by Scopus has been dramatically increased from 2016 to 2020 (5/2016, 6/2017, 11/2018, 10/2019, 5/2020, accessed on 23 01 2020). Only seven articles were published before 2016.
2. Where is "intelligent" in research and development of intelligent big data analytics? We find from the mentioned 44 research publications that "intelligent" has been used in the foundation of intelligent big data analytics, and deep exploration into intelligent big data analytics and applications of intelligent big data analytics. For example, intelligent technologies/techniques (as foundations) for intelligent big data analytics, and intelligent technologies/techniques in intelligent big data analytics and intelligent applications of intelligent big data analytics.
3. Among 44 founded results, only 13 publications use "intelligent big data analytics" as a key word in their titles, 31 publications use "big data analytics" as a key word in their titles.

Now we turn to marketing analysis on intelligent big data analytics. The annual magic quadrant for analytics and BI platforms of Gartner (Howson, Richardson, Sallam, & Kronz, 2019) has a significant impact on the market of intelligent analytics and also their research and development. 2019's Magic Quadrant for analytics and BI platforms includes 21 software vendors, they have been classified into four categories: leaders, challengers, visionaries, and niche players. The leaders are Microsoft, Tableau, ThoughtSpot, Qlik. The challenger is MicroStrategy. The following Table 1 is the summary of leaders and challenger based on the mentioned three questions and (Howson, Richardson, Sallam, & Kronz, 2019). The detailed analysis of these 21 software vendors is available to the readers, if required.

The above discussion demonstrates that

1. Modern analytics and BI innovations around visual-based exploration have become mainstream since 2017 (Howson, Richardson, Sallam, & Kronz, 2019).
2. Decentralized analytics and agile centralized BI provisioning are main applications of big data analytics
3. Big data analytics, advanced analytics, and modern analytics have drawn increasing attention in academia, industry, and government (IDC, 2019) (Howson, Richardson, Sallam, & Kronz, 2019) (Sun Z., 2019) (IDC, 2019). They have successfully applied to many industries including finance, banking, marketing, health care, and enterprise management. Many vendors in the modern analytics and BI market have double-digit revenue growth (Howson, Richardson, Sallam, & Kronz, 2019).

Table 1. Foundations, cores and applications of leading analytics and BI platforms

Software vendors	What is for big data analytics?	What are Functions of big data analytics?	What is big data analytics for?
Microsoft, Power BI	data preparation, visual-based data discovery, interactive dashboards, augmented analytics, Azure Machine Learning, text, sentiment and image analytics. agile, self-service analytics, conversational analytics	A platform of integrating data preparation, visual-based data discovery, interactive dashboards, augmented analytics, complex data models with integrated advanced analytics	Self-service, analytics and BI tool, decentralized analytics, agile, centralized BI provisioning
MicroStrategy	Augmented analytics, semantic graph, data manipulation, enterprise-grade security and an in-memory columnar data store, cloud BI and augmented analytics	A platform combining data preparation, visual-based and NLQ-based data discovery and exploration, dashboards and mobile capabilities with enterprise analytics and BI	Decentralized analytics Agile, centralized BI provisioning, governed data discovery
Qlik, Qlik Analytics Platform	data management, conversational analytics, multicloud deployments, big data, data preparation, data cataloguing and embedded analytics, augmented analytics, social media analytics	Qlik Sense, cognitive engine, business-value-based messaging, Data Literacy Project campaigns, and multiple conference	Decentralized analytics, agile centralized BI provisioning
Tableau	data preparation and profiling, visual exploration and data manipulation	augmented analytics	Decentralized analytics, agile, centralized BI provisioning
ThoughtSpot	augmented analytics, NLP, R, data preparation, visual exploration, dashboards and architecture	Search-based interface with augmented analytics	Decentralized analytics, agile, centralized BI provisioning.

3 INTELLIGENT BIG DATA ANALYTICS = AI + BIG DATA ANALYTICS

The interrelationship among big data, analytics, and AI have drawn increasing attention (Sun Z., 2019). Intelligent big data analytics is similar to analytics intelligence mentioned in (Wang, 2012). The difference between them is that the latter is limited to the data in cyberspace or the Web. The similarity between them is that incorporating AI into analytics is a huge global and social need in the near future (Wang, 2012). The intelligent big data analytics discussed in this section is an answer to such global and social needs.

3.1 Big Data Analytics: A Workflow Centric Framework

First, we describe two use cases below.

Peter feels not well today. He visits Dr Paul. Paul provides a description on Peter's illness based on descriptive analytics. Paul diagnoses Peter's symptoms based on diagnostic analytics. Paul provides a prediction for Peter's illness based on predictive analytics. Finally, Paul provides a prescription on Peter's illness based on prescriptive analytics.

ABBA (it is an imaginary name) is a global system company. Its enterprise system ASSA is well known in the big data industry. However, recently, the enterprise system has not been running well. The CEO of ABBA invites a global system service company (BAAB) for help. BAAB system engineer, Dr Weber visits ABBA and investigates the enterprise system ASSA. Weber first diagnoses ASSA based on the diagnostic analytics of BAAB. Weber provides a description on ABBA's malfunction based on the descriptive analytics. Then Weber provides a prediction of ASSA's malfunction based on the predictive analytics of BAAB. Finally, Weber provides a prescription on how to fix ASSA's malfunction based on the prescriptive analytics of BAAB.

The above two cases have a lifecycle of the workflow: Description → diagnosis→ prediction → prescription. As well-known, data analytics has been classified into four categories: Descriptive analytics, diagnostic analytics, predictive analytics, and prescriptive analytics (Kumar, 2015) (Sun Z., 2019) (INFORMS, 2014) (Sharda, Delen, & Turba, 2018) (Gartner-diagnostic analytics, 2020) (LaPlante, 2019), briefly,

Data analytics: = data descriptive analytics + data diagnostic analytics + data predictive analytics + data prescriptive analytics (1)

The above use cases and the classification of data analytics leads to a workflow-based lifecycle of data analytics, illustrated in Figure 1.

The proposed workflow-based lifecycle of analytics demonstrates that data analytics has penetrated into each of a lifecycle of the business workflow (Sathi, 2013) (Howson, Richardson, Sallam, & Kronz, 2019). One stage of the lifecycle corresponds to one analytics (one-to-one correspondence), as illustrated in Figure 1. Descriptive analytics, diagnostic analytics, predictive analytics, and prescriptive analytics form a workflow centric analytics platform. In order to improve the effectiveness and efficiency of all the mentioned analytics, the platform has a central mechanism, called analytics engine (Sathi, 2013). The analytics engine manipulates a centralized database, information base, knowledge base, and wisdom base. It processes analytical algorithms, models, tools and transforms the input to the output. One of analytical tools is online analytical processing (OLAP), massively used in business and e-Commerce industry (Laudon & Laudon, 2016).

Figure 1. A workflow-based lifecycle of analytics

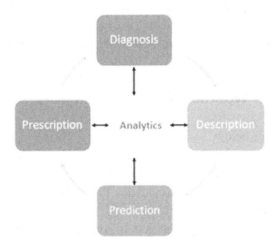

These four analytics can share the same data, information, knowledge, and wisdom. Therefore, an integrated analytics platform (system) consists of descriptive analytics, diagnostic analytics, predictive

Figure 2. An integrated analytics platform

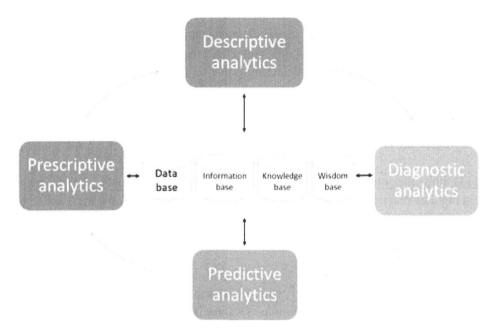

analytics, and prescriptive analytics, which have the centralized database, information base, knowledge base, and wisdom base (DIKW base), as shown in Figure 2.

The integrated analytics platform is a kind of analytics integration. It is also a kind of data integration, because any data, information, knowledge, and wisdom (DIKM) can be considered as the input for the integrated analytics platform.

Big data analytics can be defined as a process of collecting, organizing and analyzing big data to discover, visualize, and display patterns, knowledge, and intelligence within the big data (Sun & Huo, 2019). Similarly, big data analytics can be defined as techniques used to analyze big data, acquire and visualize knowledge and intelligence from big data (Gandomi & Haider, 2015). Applying big as an operation to both sides of equation (1) (Sun & Wang, 2017), we have

Big data analytics = big data descriptive analytics + big data diagnostic analytics + big data predictive analytics + big data prescriptive analytics (2)

This conforms with "the main components of big data analytics include big data diagnostic analytics, big data descriptive analytics, big data predictive analytics, and big data prescriptive analytics" mentioned in (Minelli, Chambers, & Dhiraj, 2013) (Gandomi & Haider, 2015) (Howson, Sallam, & Richa, 2018) (Gartner-diagnostic analytics, 2020) (LaPlante, 2019).

3.2 Intelligent Big Data Analytics

Intelligent big data analytics is AI-driven big data analytics (Sun, Sun, & Strang, 2018) (Sun & Wang, 2017) (Sun Z., 2019). Therefore, intelligent big data analytics can be represented as

Intelligent big data analytics = Big data analytics + AI (3)

Where + can be explained as "and". Equation (3) means that intelligent big data analytics includes big data analytics and AI and their integration (Wang, 2012) (Sun Z., 2019). Intelligent big data analytics can be represented as follows through extending Equation (3), applying intelligent as an operation to both sides of (2).

Intelligent big data analytics = intelligent big descriptive data analytics + intelligent big data diagnostic analytics + intelligent big predictive data analytics + intelligent big prescriptive data analytics (4)

Equation (4) shows that intelligent big data analytics consists of intelligent big data descriptive analytics, intelligent big data diagnostic analytics, intelligent big data predictive analytics, and intelligent big data prescriptive analytics. Equation (4) is an extension of existing data analytics (Delena & Demirkanb, 2013) by integrating AI with big data (Sun Z., 2019).

- Intelligent big data descriptive analytics is intelligent descriptive analytics for big data (Delena & Demirkanb, 2013; Kantardzic, 2011) (Sun, Sun, & Strang, 2018). It is used to discover new, nontrivial information based on AI techniques (Kantardzic, 2011, p. 2), and explain the characteristics of entities and relationships among entities within the existing big descriptive data (Coronel & Morris, 2015, p. 611). It addresses the problems such as what and when happened, and what is happening (Delena & Demirkanb, 2013) (Kumar, 2015) (LaPlante, 2019). For example, intelligent business reports with dashboards for global COVID-19 pandemic is a result from intelligent big data descriptive analytics on big data of the global COVID-19.
- Intelligent big data diagnostic analytics is intelligent diagnostic analytics for big data (Sun, Sun, & Strang, 2018). It is used to examine data or content to answer the question "Why did it happen?" (After one knows what happened, one wants to know why (LaPlante, 2019)), from the historical and current diagnostic data based on AI techniques such as drill-down, data discovery, data mining, and correlations (Gartner-diagnostic analytics, 2020). For example, diagnostic analytics available on the cloud belongs to intelligent big data diagnostic analytics.
- Intelligent big data predictive analytics is intelligent predictive analytics for big data (Sun, Zou, & Strang, 2015). It focuses on forecasting future trends by addressing the problems such as what will happen next? what is going to happen? what is likely to happen? and why it will happen? based on historical and current big data (Kumar, 2015) (Sun Z., 2019) (LaPlante, 2019). Intelligent big data predictive analytics uses techniques of data mining (predictive mining), statistical modelling, mathematics and AI to create intelligent models to predict future outcomes or events (Delena & Demirkanb, 2013) (Coronel & Morris, 2015, p. 611) (Sharda, Delen, & Turban, 2018). For example, intelligent big data predictive analytics can be used to predict where might be the next attack target of terrorists smartly (Sun, Sun, & Strang, 2018).
- Intelligent big data prescriptive analytics is intelligent prescriptive analytics for big data (Sun, Zou, & Strang, 2015). It addresses the problems such as what we should do, why we should do and what should happen with the best outcome under uncertainty (Minelli, Chambers, & Dhiraj, 2013, p. 5) (Delena & Demirkanb, 2013) (LaPlante, 2019). Intelligent big data prescriptive analytics uses intelligent algorithms to determine optimal decisions for the future actions (Delena &

Demirkanb, 2013). For example, intelligent big data prescriptive analytics can be used to provide an optimal marketing strategy for an e-commerce company.

3.3 Technological Foundation of Intelligent Big Data Analytics

The fundamentals of intelligent big data analytics consist of AI and machine learning (ML), mathematics, statistics and data mining, human interface, computer science, operations research, data science and systems (Chen & Zhang, 2014) (INFORMS, 2014) (Sun & Huo, 2019). The techniques for intelligent big data analytics encompass a wide range of mathematical, statistical, modeling and algorithm techniques (Coronel & Morris, 2015, p. 590) (Sun Z., 2018). Big data analytics always involves historical or current data and data visualization (LaPlante, 2019) (Sathi, 2013). This requires big data analytics to use data mining (DM) to discover knowledge from a data warehouse (DW) or a big dataset in order to support decision making (Turban & Volonino, 2011) (Holsapplea, Lee-Postb, & Pakath, 2014; Davis, 2014). DM employs advanced statistical and analytical tools to analyze the big data available through DWs and other sources to identify possible relationships, patterns and anomalies and discover information or knowledge for business decision making (Coronel & Morris, 2015, p. 590; Kantardzic, 2011) (Delena & Demirkanb, 2013). In DM, regression and classification are usually used for prediction, predictive mining and analytics, while clustering and association are used for description or descriptive mining and analytics (Fan, Lau, & Zhao, 2015). DW extracts and obtains the data from operational databases and external open sources, providing a more comprehensive data pool (Coronel & Morris, 2015, p. 590; Holsapplea, Lee-Postb, & Pakath, 2014). Big data analytics also uses statistical modeling (SM) to discover knowledge through descriptive analysis that can support decision making (Sun, Zou, & Strang, 2015). Visualization technologies including display technologies as an important part of big data analytics make knowledge patterns and information for decision making in a form of figure or table or multimedia. In summary, big data analytics can facilitate business decision making and realization of business objectives through analyzing existing data and future trends, creating predictive models to forecast future threats and opportunities, and optimizing business processes to enhance organizational performance using the mentioned techniques (Delena & Demirkanb, 2013; Chen, Chiang, & Storey, 2012). Therefore, big data analytics can be represented technically below (Sun, Zou, & Strang, 2015; Holsapplea, Lee-Postb, & Pakath, 2014; Chen, Chiang, & Storey, 2012).

Big data analytics = Big data + data analytics + DW + DM + SM + ML+ visualization+ optimization (5)

Equation (5) reveals the fundamental relationship between big data, data analytics, and big data analytics, that is, big data analytics is based on big data and data analytics. It also shows that computer science, data science, AI, and statistics play a dominant role in the development of big data analytics through providing latest techniques and tools of DM, DW, ML and visualization (Sun Z., 2018; Davis, 2014). SM and optimization still play a fundamental role in the development of big data analytics (Minelli, Chambers, & Dhiraj, 2013) (Sun & Huo, 2019).

Equations (3), (4), and (5) are a concise representation for the technological components of intelligent big data analytics. Figure 3 illustrates these equations on intelligent big data analytics and their interrelationships (Sun, Sun, & Strang, 2018).

Apache Hadoop is a platform of big data analytics (Reddy, 2014). As an open source platform for storing and processing large datasets using clusters and commodity hardware, Hadoop can scale up to hundreds and even hundreds of nodes (Sun & Huo, 2019).

The current leading DW includes Amazon's Redshift, Google's BigQuery, Microsoft's Azure SQL Data Warehouse, and Teradata (Tableau, 2015).

Apache Spark is one of the most popular big data analytics services. It is a big data analytics platform for several enterprises (Tableau, 2015; Reddy, 2014). Spark provides dramatically increased large-scale data processing compared to Hadoop, and a NoSQL database for big data management (Coronel & Morris, 2015; Reddy, 2014). Apache Spark has provided Goldman Sachs with excellent big data analytics services (Tableau, 2015).

Figure 3. An ontology of intelligent big data analytics

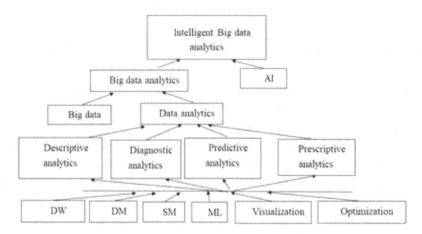

Applying intelligent as an operation to both side of Equation (5) (Sun & Wang, 2017), we have

intelligent big data analytics = intelligent big data + intelligent data analytics + intelligent DW + intelligent DM + intelligent SM + intelligent ML+ intelligent visualization+ intelligent optimization   (6)

Where intelligent big data can be considered as big data. Equation (6) means that intelligent big data analytics at least includes big data, intelligent data analytics, intelligent data warehousing, data mining, intelligent statistical modelling, ML, intelligent visualization and intelligent optimization (Delena & Demirkanb, 2013) (Sun & Wang, 2017) (Sun, Sun, & Strang, 2018) (Sun Z., 2019), because data mining and ML are themselves intelligent techniques. Equation (6) demonstrates that AI plays a central role in transforming big data analytics to intelligent big data analytics through penetrating into each component of big data analytics.

4 INTELLIGENT ANALYTICS: AN INCLUSIVE PERSPECTIVE

This section extends intelligent big data analytics to intelligent analytics based on an inclusive approach.

Intelligent analytics is an emerging paradigm in the age of big data, analytics, and AI (Sun Z., 2019). Incorporating AI into big data analytics have become a hotspot in many research fields such as business, information systems, operations research, data science, and computer science (INFORMS, 2014) (Sun Z., 2019). However, the following issues are still significant for academia, industries and governments.

1. Is intelligent big data analytics the unique form of intelligent analytics?
2. What are fundamentals of intelligent analytics?
3. How can we apply mathematical methods and thinking to intelligent analytics?

This section will address these three issues.

Data, information, knowledge, and wisdom (for short, DIKW) have played a significant roles in computing and ICT in the past few decades and led to data computing, information computing, knowledge computing, and wisdom computing (for short, DIKW computing) (ACM/IEEE/AIS, 2019). For example, data computing includes data science, technology, engineering, management and systems, and so on (Sun & Huo, 2020). DIKW computing covers almost all the aspects of current ICT with applications. Therefore, data, information, knowledge, and wisdom are elements for the digital age in general and for intelligent analytics in particular. Therefore, all science in the digital age is like a tree of which four elements, namely, data, information, knowledge, and wisdom are the roots, mathematics and computing the trunk, and all the other sciences the branches that grow out of this trunk, inspired by the work of (Descartes, 1637) (Wiki-Descartes, 2020).

Furthermore, data analytics can be defined as the "art of examining, summarizing, and drawing conclusions from data". (Norusis, 1997). Let x be a variable, then, this definition of data analytics can be extended below.

x analytics is the "art of examining, summarizing, and drawing conclusions from x." (7)

When x is information, knowledge, and wisdom respectively, we have information analytics, knowledge analytics, and wisdom analytics.

Data analytics can also be defined as a method that "uses data to learn, describe and predict something" (Turban & Volonino, 2011, p. 341). Let y be a variable, this definition of analytics can be extended below.

y analytics is a method that "uses y to learn, describe and predict something" (8)

When y is information, knowledge, and wisdom respectively, we have information analytics, knowledge analytics, and wisdom analytics.

Combining (7) and (8), we have

x analytics is the art of examining, summarizing, and drawing conclusions from x to learn, describe and predict something. (9)

Where x is an element of {data, information, knowledge, wisdom}. We have information analytics, knowledge analytics, and wisdom analytics. Data, information, knowledge and wisdom can be considered as an input for an analytics system for processing. The processing of this analytics system is to examine, summarize, and draw conclusions from x. The goal of this analytics is to learn, describe and predict something (Sun Z., 2019).

The above discussion demonstrates that data analytics is not all forms of analytics. Information analytics, knowledge analytics, and wisdom analytics are extended forms of data analytics. In such a way, data analytics, information analytics, knowledge analytics, and wisdom analytics (for short, DIKW analytics) can be considered as the basic form of analytics, taking into account DIKW (Sun & Huo, 2020). Briefly,

Analytics: = data analytics + information analytics + knowledge analytics + wisdom analytics   (10)

In other words, analytics consists of data analytics, information analytics, knowledge analytics and wisdom analytics, at a fundamental level. At a higher level, analytics can be a system of integrating a few analytics at the fundamental level. If we consider data analytics, information analytics, knowledge analytics, and wisdom analytics as the atomic level, then we have three levels of integrated analytics. The top (4th) level of analytics is the analytics integrating data analytics, information analytics, knowledge analytics and wisdom analytics. From a Boolean structure viewpoint (Sun & Xiao, 1994) (Lang, 2002) (Johnsonbaugh, 2013), there are 16 (2^4) different kinds of analytics based on equation (10).

As well-known, big data is significant for innovation, competition, and productivity in the digital age (McKinsey, 2011) (Sun & Huo, 2019), then big information, big knowledge, big wisdom are also significant for effective management, decision making and innovation for development of economy, society and even nations, because many governments and organizations have carried out a number of initiatives on development of information industry (e.g. China, China has the Ministry of Information Industry), knowledge economy (e.g. Australia) and wisdom cities (e.g. China, China has launched many national projects for developing wisdom cities). Therefore, big information analytics, big knowledge analytics, and big wisdom analytics should have played same significant role as that of big data analytics in the digital age, although currently some of academia, industries and governments have technically ignored them, just as they ignore the rules of lockdown and social distancing in the age of coronavirus pandemic. Therefore, applying big as an operation (Sun & Wang, 2017) to both sides of equation (10), we have

Big analytics: = big data analytics + big information analytics + big knowledge analytics + big wisdom analytics   (11)

Equation (11) have extended the result on big analytics in (Sun, Strang, & Li, 2018), in which big analytics is a representation of big data analytics.

Now, let intelligent analytics be intelligent big analytics, apply intelligent as an operation to both sides of equation (11), we have

Intelligent analytics = Intelligent big data analytics + intelligent big information analytics + intelligent big knowledge analytics + intelligent big wisdom analytics.   (12)

Similarly, we can use Boolean structure to have 4 levels of integrated analytics and have 16 (2^4) different kinds of intelligent analytics based on equation (12).

Equations (9) to (12) forms an inclusive approach on intelligent analytics. We searched Google.com and scholar.google.com for each component of intelligent analytics listed in (12) on 15 August 2020. The searched number of websites or scholarly publications demonstrates that academia and industries are still focusing either intelligent analytics or intelligent big data analytics. Intelligent big information (or knowledge or wisdom) analytics are not yet appealing to the mainstream in the analytics and BI market though data, information, knowledge and wisdom have a very close relationship.

5 AUGMENTED ANALYTICS AS INTELLIGENT ANALYTICS

This section will examine augmented analytics as intelligent analytics.

Augmented analytics is data analytics that uses "enabling technologies such as ML and AI to assist with data preparation, insight generation and insight explanation to augment how people explore and analyze data in analytics and BI platforms" (Gartner-augmented analytics, 2020). It can be also defined as "a technology that automates the selection and preparation of data, the generation of insights, and the communication of thosc insights" (LaPlante, 2019, p. 5)

The features of augmented analytics include automated data preparation, automated insight generation and explanation, NLQ and natural language narration, as well as content creation (Howson, Richardson, Sallam, & Kronz, 2019).

Augmented data preparation on multistructured data is the need to profile, enrich and infer relationships (to automatically generate a model for analysis), and to make recommendations to improve or enhance insights from data, it will stimulate differentiating innovations.

Insight generation is automated for identifying significant segments, clusters, drivers, outliers, and anomalies. Augmented alerting and anomaly detection are new trends in augmented analytics although only a few smaller vendors offer these functions (Howson, Richardson, Sallam, & Kronz, 2019).

NLQ, NLP, NLG and (natural language query, processing and generation) are used to access data and to interpret findings (Howson, Richardson, Sallam, & Kronz, 2019). With the use of voice- and search-based interfaces, the query process (NLQ) changes from a primarily drag-and-drop query-building process into a more search-like experience. NLP includes conversational analytics that integrates chatbots and virtual assistants into the workflow for analytics. NLP allows nontechnical users to easily ask questions from source data (LaPlante, 2019, p. 6). NLG automates the process of translating complex data into text with intelligent recommendations, thereby accelerating analytic insights (LaPlante, 2019). NLG aims to generate explanations of charts, and insights enhance data literacy. NLG uses ML to explain findings that may have been either manually or automatically generated (Howson, Richardson, Sallam, & Kronz, 2019). Natural language narration includes narration of findings and prescriptive actions. These include understanding of data distribution and correlations.

Content creation includes augmented data discovery, augmented alerting, search, and NLP for voice and text, as well as conversational analytics. Conversational analytics represents the convergence of several technologies, including personal digital assistants, smartphones, bots, and ML (Howson, Richardson, Sallam, & Kronz, 2019). Virtual reality and augmented reality support for a broad range of content analytics and text analytics for use on unstructured data.

Oracle analytics has implemented augmented analytics capabilities across its platform (LaPlante, 2019). Augmentation is a kind of intelligence. Augmented analytics will be a dominant driver of new purchases of analytics and AI, data science, ML platforms, and embedded analytics in the years ahead (Howson, Richardson, Sallam, & Kronz, 2019).

Augmented analytics is a kind of intelligent big data analytics, because it has embedded AI and ML into the data analytics (LaPlante, 2019, p. 2), also because it includes ML-enabled analytics, AI-driven analytics in all phases of the data workflow for analytics, from data preparation to data modeling, insight generation and insight explanation. Augmented analytics is a kind of intelligent data predictive analytics because it assists with insight generation and insight explanation (Kumar, 2015). However, not only big data, but also big information, big knowledge, and big wisdom are required to generate and explain hindsight, insight, and foresight for smart decision making and business solutions. Therefore, how to manage and process big data, big information, big knowledge, and big wisdom based on AI is significant for the future of both augmented analytics and intelligent analytics. We will address it in the future work.

6 DISCUSSION AND IMPLICATIONS

We have mentioned several scholarly researches on data analysis, big data analytics, AI and intelligent analytics. In what follows, this section will discuss the related work, examine theoretical and technical implications of this research as well as limitations and future research directions.

6.1 Discussion

Intelligent analytics has drawn some attention in academia and industries. For example, Rose provides a conceptual framework for defining analytics (INFORMS, 2014). He mentioned analytics can be classified two categories: data centric and decision centric. The former uses data to find interesting insights and information to predicate what might happen. The latter understands the business problem, and determines the specific methodologies and information needed to solve the specific problem. Our workflow-based approach to big data analytics is an important complement to the above classification, because it creates a one-to-one correspondence between a stage in the (business) workflow and data analytics. Therefore, the proposed workflow-based approach to data analytics can be workflow centric, which covers the conceptual framework of analytics (INFORMS, 2014). Furthermore, this research demonstrates that intelligent analytics is a big DIKW centric, AI driven analytics. Therefore, the research of this chapter provided a better understanding of data analytics, big data analytics, intelligent big data analytics, and intelligent analytics.

Chen et al consider intelligent big data analytics as a big data system and use the collective intelligence model and multiagent paradigm to propose a collective intelligence framework to solve the system integration problem in the big data environment (Chen, Li, & Wang, 2015). However, few have discussed the fundamental problems of intelligent big data analytics nor provided an inclusive approach on intelligent analytics. This research identifies theoretical and technological foundations, cores and applications of intelligent big data analytics based on the investigation into the state-of-the-art scholars' publications and market analysis of advanced analytics. It also presents the technological foundations for intelligent big data analytics through examining intelligent big data analytics as an integration of AI and big data analytics. This research demonstrates that intelligent big data analytics is not the unique form of intelligent analytics, which in fact consists of intelligent big data analytics, intelligent big information analytics, intelligent big knowledge analytics, intelligent big wisdom analytics at a fundamental level.

Gartner uses advanced analytics, modern analytics, and augmented analytics to analyze AI and BI, big data, and analytics and their impacts (Laney & Jain, 2017) (Howson, Richardson, Sallam, & Kronz, 2019). With the further development of analytics, either advanced analytics or modern analytics or augmented analytics or intelligent analytics will be selected by the customers, because the general customers hope to use the simple concept to cover what they perceive just as smartphones to intelligent phones are accepted in the world. Industries and governments also prefer simple terms to jargon words, just as they like big data rather than massive data in the past decade.

From an evolutionary viewpoint, intelligent analytics is a more general form of data analytics (Kantardzic, 2011). Data analytics is an extended form of data mining (Gandomi & Haider, 2015), because data analytics is considered as the whole data mining process or process of knowledge discovery in databases (KDD) (Tsai, Lai, Chao, & Vasilakos, 2015). Therefore, the relationships among data mining, intelligent big data analytics and intelligent analytics can be represented as

Data mining $\in$ intelligent big data analytics $\in$ intelligent analytics.

This means that data mining as an intelligent technique is a foundation of intelligent analytics. However, the difference between intelligent analytics and data mining is that the former discovers AI-driven knowledge and wisdom not only from big data but also from big information, big knowledge and big wisdom.

6.2 Theoretical and Technical Implications

The theoretical implication of this research is that it provides an inclusive approach for understanding the interrelationship among big data, information, knowledge, wisdom, analytics, and AI and their integration. Intelligent analytics is not only intelligent big data analytics. Fundamentally, intelligent analytics consists of intelligent big data analytics, intelligent big information analytics, intelligent big knowledge analytics and intelligent big wisdom analytics. This inclusive approach will pave a new way for developing intelligent analytics with applications.

The technical implication of this research is that the proposed approach on intelligent analytics in general and intelligent big data analytics, intelligent big information analytics, intelligent big knowledge analytics, intelligent big wisdom analytics in particular can attract more researchers and practitioners to undertake the research and application of intelligent analytics for more effective management decision making in business workflow.

6.3 Limitations

A limitation of this chapter is that it should consider intelligent descriptive, diagnostic, predictive and prescriptive analytics as one dimension, and the technological components of intelligent analytics as another dimension. Therefore, one of future research directions is to provide the matrix analysis for intelligent analytics.

Another limitation of the chapter is that it should have provided more practical examples for readers to better understand proposed theoretical discussion.

6.4 Future Research Directions

Intelligent analytics is an integrated analytics paradigm of big data, big information, big knowledge, big wisdom, analytics and AI. It provides smart solutions to business, marketing and services through intelligent analytical technologies, methodologies, tools, and applications embedded in workflow-driven intelligent analytics systems. Intelligent analytics is a term that embodies the realization of a historic and current vision of how big data, big information, big knowledge, bid wisdom, analytics and AI will revolutionize the world of business, organizations, society and our lives to create a society of analytics intelligence, forever and irrevocably (Davis, 2014) (Sun Z., 2019). Therefore, one of the future research directions is to address systems integration among intelligent analytics, augmented analytics and modern analytics (Howson, Sallam, & Richa, 2018).

Analytics thinking and analytics intelligence will play a critical role in research and development of big data analytics and intelligent analytics, just as computing thinking has played a significant role in computing in the past two decades. However, how can analytics thinking and analytics intelligence influence research and development of intelligent analytics with applications? This is a significant issue. Therefore, another future research direction is to address this issue through theoretical and technological research with real-world examples.

7 CONCLUSION

The objective of this chapter is to propose a unified nature for intelligent analytics as an integration between analytics and AI. This chapter presents an inclusive approach to intelligent analytics, which treats many aspects of intelligent analytics and business analytics using mathematical methods and AI in a unified way. The main three contributions of this research to intelligent analytics with applications are 1. It identified the theoretical and technological foundations, cores of intelligent big data analytics with applications; 2. It integrated AI techniques with big data analytics through proposing a workflow-based approach to big data analytics and technological foundations for intelligent big data analytics; 3. It demonstrates that intelligent analytics is an integration between analytics and AI taking into account big data, big information, big knowledge and big wisdom and their close relationships. This research also demonstrates that 1. Data, information, knowledge, and wisdom are four elements underpinning the digital age. 2. Intelligent analytics has analytical tools and techniques including DM, DW, SM, and ML. Therefore, the proposed approach in this chapter might facilitate research and development of intelligent analytics, intelligent big data analytics, analytics intelligence and AI.

In the future work, as an extension of future research directions and our research of Section 4, we will investigate 2D analysis for big data, big information, big knowledge and big wisdom as a dimension, and descriptive analytics, diagnostic analytics, predictive analytics, prescriptive analytics as another dimension based on AI and ML to form a unified framework of intelligent analytics. We will also develop a unified theory for analytics thinking and analytics intelligence.

REFERENCES

ACM/IEEE/AIS. (2019). *Computing Curricula.* Retrieved from https://computingcurricula.com/

Chen, C. P., & Zhang, C.-Y. (2014). Data-intensive applications, challenges, techniques and technologies: A survey on Big Data. *Information Sciences, 275,* 314–347. doi:10.1016/j.ins.2014.01.015

Chen, H., Chiang, R., & Storey, V. (2012, December). Business intelligence and analytics: From big data to big impact. *Management Information Systems Quarterly, 36*(4), 1165–1188. doi:10.2307/41703503

Chen, K., Li, X., & Wang, H. (2015). On the model design of integrated intelligent big data analytics systems. *Industrial Management & Data Systems*, *115*(9), 1666–1682. doi:10.1108/IMDS-03-2015-0086

Coronel, C., & Morris, S. (2015). *Database Systems: Design, Implementation, and Management* (11th ed.). Cengage Learning.

Davis, C. K. (2014). Viewpoint Beyond Data and Analytics- Why business analytics and big data really matter for modern business organizations. *Communications of the ACM*, *57*(8), 39–41. doi:10.1145/2602326

Delena, D., & Demirkanb, H. (2013). Data, information and analytics as services. *Decision Support Systems*, *55*(1), 359–363. doi:10.1016/j.dss.2012.05.044

Descartes, R. (1637). Discourse on the Methods of the Rightly Conducting the Reason, and Seeking Truth in the Sciences. *GlobalGrey 2018*. Retrieved from https://www.globalgreyebooks.com/index.html

Eiloart, J. (2018, Dec 2). *Top five business analytics intelligence trends for 2019*. Retrieved from https://www.information-age.com/business-analytics-intelligence-123477004/

Fan, S., Lau, R. Y., & Zhao, J. L. (2015). Demystifying Big Data Analytics for Business Intelligence Through theLens ofMarketing Mix. *Big DataResearch*, *2*, 28–32.

Gandomi, A., & Haider, M. (2015). Beyond the hype: Big data concepts, methods, and analytics. *International Journal of Information Management*, *35*, 137–144.

Gartner. (2020a). *Augmented analytics*. Retrieved August 13, 2020, from Gartner Glossary: https://www.gartner.com/en/information-technology/glossary/augmented-analytics

Gartner. (2020b). *Diagnostic Analytics*. Retrieved August 12 2020, from Gartner: https://www.gartner.com/en/information-technology/glossary/diagnostic-analytics

Henke, N., & Bughin, J. (2016, December). *The Age of Analytics: Competing in a Data Driven World*. McKinsey Global Institute.

Holsapplea, C., Lee-Postb, A., & Pakath, R. (2014). A unified foundation for business analytics. *Decision Support Systems*, *64*, 130–141. doi:10.1016/j.dss.2014.05.013

Howson, C., Richardson, J., Sallam, R., & Kronz, A. (2019). *Magic Quadrant for Analytics and Business Intelligence Platforms*. Retrieved 7 7, 2019, from Gartner: https://cadran-analytics.nl/wp-content/uploads/2019/02/2019-Gartner-Magic-Quadrant-for-Analytics-and-Business-Intelligence-Platforms.pdf

Howson, C., Sallam, R. L., & Richa, J. L. (2018, Feb 26). *Magic Quadrant for Analytics and Business Intelligence Platforms*. Retrieved Aug 16, 2018, from Gartner: www.gartner.com

IDC. (2019). *IDC Forecasts Revenues for Big Data and Business Analytics Solutions will Reach $189.1 Billion This Year with Double-Digit Annual Growth Through 2022*. Retrieved 1 23, 2020, from IDC: https://www.idc.com/getdoc.jsp?containerId=prUS44998419

IDC. (2019, March 11). *Worldwide Spending on Artificial Intelligence Systems Will Grow to Nearly $35.8 Billion in 2019*. Retrieved August 11, 2020, from New IDC Spending Guide: https://www.idc.com/getdoc.jsp?containerId=prUS44911419

INFORMS. (2014). Defining analytics a conceptual framework. *ORMS Today, 43*(3). Retrieved August 12, 2020, from INFORMS: https://www.informs.org/ORMS-Today/Public-Articles/June-Volume-43-Number-3/Defining-analytics-a-conceptual-framework

John, G. (2013). *The Age of Artificial Intelligence.* Retrieved from TEDxLondonBusinessSchool: https://www.youtube.com/watch?v=0qOf7SX2CS4

Johnsonbaugh, R. (2013). *Discrete Mathematics* (7th ed.). Pearson Education Limited.

Kantardzic, M. (2011). *Data Mining: Concepts, Models, Methods, and Algorithms.* Wiley & IEEE Press. doi:10.1002/9781118029145

Kumar, G. B. (2015). An encyclopedic overview of 'Big Data' Analytics. *International Journal of Applied Engineering Research: IJAER, 10*(3), 5681–5705.

Laney, D., & Jain, A. (2017, June 20). *100 Data and Analytics Predictions Through.* Retrieved August 04, 2018, from Gartner: https://www.gartner.com/events-na/data-analytics/wp-content/uploads/sites/5/2017/10/Data-and-Analytics-Predictions.pdf

Lang, S. (2002). *Algebra, Graduate Texts in Mathematics 211* (Revised third ed.). Springer-Verlag.

LaPlante, A. (2019). *What Is Augmented Analytics? Powering Your Data with AI.* Boston: O' Realy. Retrieved from https://go.oracle.com/LP=84622

Laudon, K. G., & Laudon, K. C. (2016). *Management Information Systems: Managing the Digital Firm* (14th ed.). Pearson.

Lohr, S. (2012, February 11). The Age of Big Data. *The New York Times*, 1-5.

McKinsey. (2011, May). *Big data: The next frontier for innovation, competition, and productivity.* Retrieved from McKinsey Global Institute: https://www.mckinsey.com/business-functions/business-technology/our-insights/big-data-the-next-frontier-for-innovation

Minelli, M., Chambers, M., & Dhiraj, A. (2013). *Big Data, Big Analytics: Emerging Business Intelligence and Analytic Trends for Today's Businesses* (Chinese Edition 2014). Wiley & Sons. doi:10.1002/9781118562260

Norusis, M. J. (1997). *SPSS: SPSS 7.5 Guide to Data Analytics.* Prentice Hall.

Pettey, C., & van der Meulen, R. (2018, April 25). *Gartner Says Global Artificial Intelligence Business Value to Reach $1.2 Trillion in 2018.* Retrieved August 04, 2018, from Gartner: https://www.gartner.com/newsroom/id/3872933

Reddy, C. K. (2014). A survey of platforms for big data analytics. *Journal of Big Data (Springer), 1*(8), 1–20.

Russell, S., & Norvig, P. (2010). *Artificial Intelligence: A Modern Approach* (3rd ed.). Prentice Hall.

Sathi, A. (2013). Big data analytics: Disruptive technologies for changing the game. Boise, ID: MC Press, IBM Corporation.

Sharda, R., Delen, D., & Turba, E. (2018). *Business Intelligence and Analytics: Systems for Decision Support* (10th ed.). Pearson.

Sun, Z. (2018). 10 Bigs: Big Data and Its Ten Big Characteristics. *PNG UoT BAIS, 3*(1), 1–10. doi:10.13140/RG.2.2.31449.62566

Sun, Z. (2018). Intelligent Big Data Analytics. *Foundations and Applications., 3*(4). Advance online publication. doi:10.13140/RG.2.2.11037.41441

Sun, Z. (2019). Intelligent Big Data Analytics: A Managerial Perspective. In Z. Sun (Ed.), *Managerial Perspectives on Intelligent Big Data Analytics* (pp. 1–19). IGI-Global. doi:10.4018/978-1-5225-7277-0.ch001

Sun, Z., & Huo, Y. (2019). A Managerial Framework for Intelligent Big Data Analytics. In *ICBDSC 2019, January 10-13, Proceedings of ICBDSC 2019*. Bali, Indonesia: ACM.

Sun, Z., & Huo, Y. (2019). The spectrum of big data analytics. *Journal of Computer Information Systems*. doi:10.1080/08874417.2019.1571456

Sun, Z., & Huo, Y. (2020). Intelligence without Data. *Global Journal of Computer Science and Technology C, 20*(1), 25–35. doi:10.34257/GJCSTCVOL20IS1PG25

Sun, Z., Strang, K., & Li, R. (2018). Big data with ten big characteristics. In *Proceedings of 2018 The 2nd Intl Conf. on Big Data Research (ICBDR 2018), October 27-29* (pp. 56-61). Weihai, China: ACM.

Sun, Z., Sun, L., & Strang, K. (2018). Big Data Analytics Services for Enhancing Business Intelligence. *Journal of Computer Information Systems, 58*(2), 162–169. doi:10.1080/08874417.2016.1220239

Sun, Z., & Wang, P. (2017). Big Data, Analytics and Intelligence: An Editorial Perspective. *Journal of New Mathematics and Natural Computation, 13*(2), 75–81. doi:10.1142/S179300571702001X

Sun, Z., & Wang, P. P. (2017). A Mathematical Foundation of Big Data. *Journal of New Mathematics and Natural Computation, 13*(2), 8–24.

Sun, Z., & Xiao, J. (1994). *Essentials of Discrete Mathematics, Problems and Solutions*. Hebei University Press.

Sun, Z., Zou, H., & Strang, K. (2015). *Big Data Analytics as a Service for Business Intelligence. I3E2015, LNCS 9373*. Springer.

Tableau. (2015). *Top 8 Trends for 2016: Big Data*. Retrieved from www.tableau.com/Big-Data

Tsai, C., Lai, C., Chao, H., & Vasilakos, A. (2015). Big data analytics: A survey. *Journal of Big Data, 2*(1), 31–62. doi:10.118640537-015-0030-3 PMID:26191487

Turban, E., & Volonino, L. (2011a). *Information Technology for Management: Improving Performance in the Digital Economy* (8th ed.). John Wiley & Sons.

Turban, E., & Volonino, L. (2011b). *Information Technology for Management: Improving Strategic and Operational Performance* (8th ed.). Wiley & Sons.

Wang, F.-Y. (2012). A big-data perspective on AI: Newton, Merton, and Analytics Intelligence. *IEEE Intelligent Systems, 27*(5), 2-4.

Wiki-Descartes. (2020). *Rene_Descartes.* Retrieved August 05, 2020, from Wikipedia: https://en.wikipedia.org/wiki/Rene_Descartes

ADDITIONAL READING

Abidi, S. S. R., & Abidi, S. R. (2019). Intelligent health data analytics: A convergence of artificial intelligence and big data. *Healthcare Management Forum, 32*(4), 178–182. doi:10.1177/0840470419846134 PMID:31117831

Al Janabi, S., Yaqoob, A., & Mohammad, M. (2020). Pragmatic method based on intelligent Big Data analytics to predict air pollution. *Lecture Notes in Networks and Systems, 81*, 84–109. doi:10.1007/978-3-030-23672-4_8

Chen, K., Li, X., & Wang, H. (2015). On the model design of integrated intelligent big data analytics systems. *Industrial Management & Data Systems, 115*(9), 1666–1682. doi:10.1108/IMDS-03-2015-0086

Debattista, J., Attard, J., & Brennan, R. (2018) Semantic data ingestion for intelligent, value-driven big data analytics. *Proceedings-2018 International Conference on Big Data Innovations and Applications, Innovate-Data, 8500063*, pp. 1-8. 10.1109/Innovate-Data.2018.00008

Dong, F., Wu, C., & Gao, S. (2019). Cloud computing–based big data processing and intelligent analytics. *Concurrency and Computation, 31*(24), e5531. doi:10.1002/cpe.5531

Ghavami, P. (2019). Big Data Analytics Methods: Analytics Techniques in Data Mining. In Deep Learning and Natural Language Processing (2nd ed.). de Gruyter.

Iyer, L. S., & Raman, R. M. (2011). Intelligent Analytics: Integrating Business Intelligence and Web Analytics. *International Journal of Business Intelligence Research, 2*(1), 31–45. doi:10.4018/jbir.2011010103

Kumara, B. T. G. S., Paik, I., Zhang, J., Siriweera, T. H. A. S., & Koswatte, K. R. C. (2015) Ontology-based workflow generation for intelligent Big Data analytics. *IEEE International Conference on Web Services, ICWS 2015, 7195607*, 495-502. 10.1109/ICWS.2015.72

Lv, Z., Song, H., Basanta-Val, P., Steed, A., & Jo, M. (2017) Next-Generation Big Data Analytics: State of the Art, Challenges, and Future Research Topics. *IEEE Transactions on Industrial Informatics, 13*(4), 1891-1899.

Malhotra, D., Verma, N., Rishi, O. P., & Singh, J. (2017) Intelligent big data analytics: Adaptive e-commerce website ranking using apriori Hadoop-BDAS-based cloud framework. Maximizing Business Performance and Efficiency Through Intelligent Systems, 50-72.

Mashingaidze, K., & Backhouse, J. (2017). The relationships between definitions of big data, business intelligence and business analytics: A literature review. *International Journal of Business Information Systems, 26*(4), 488–505. doi:10.1504/IJBIS.2017.087749

Verma, S. (2017). Big data and advanced analytics: Architecture, techniques, applications, and challenges. *International Journal of Business Analytics*, *4*(4), 21–47. doi:10.4018/IJBAN.2017100102

Xu, Z., Liu, Y., Li, Z., & Mei, L. (2016). The intelligent big data analytics framework for surveillance video systems. *Lecture Notes in Electrical Engineering.*, *375*, 1147–1152. doi:10.1007/978-981-10-0539-8_115

KEY TERMS AND DEFINITIONS

Artificial Intelligence (AI): Is science and technology concerned with imitating, extending, augmenting, automating intelligent behaviors of human beings.

Big Data: Is data with at least one of the ten big characteristics consisting of big volume, big velocity, big variety, big veracity, big intelligence, big analytics, big infrastructure, big service, big value, and big market.

Data Mining: Is a process of discovering various models, summaries, and derived values, knowledge from a given collection of data. Another definition is that it is the process of using statistical, mathematical, logical, AI methods and tools to extract useful information from large databases.

Data Science: Is a field that builds on and synthesizes a number of relevant disciplines and bodies of knowledge, including statistics, informatics, computing, communication, management, and sociology to translate data into information, knowledge, insight and intelligence for improving innovation, productivity and decision making.

Intelligent Analytics: Is science and technology about collecting, organizing and analyzing big data, big information, big knowledge and big wisdom to transform them to intelligent information, intelligent knowledge, and intelligent wisdom based on artificial intelligence and analytical algorithms and technologies.

Intelligent Big Data Analytics: Is science and technology about collecting, organizing and analyzing big data to discover patterns, knowledge, and intelligence as well as other information within the big data based on artificial intelligence and intelligent systems.

Intelligent System: Is a system that can imitate, automate some intelligent behaviors of human beings. Expert systems and knowledge-based systems are examples of intelligent systems.

Machine Learning: Is concerned about how computers can adapt to new circumstances and to detect and extrapolate patterns.

Chapter 2
Hybrid Intelligence Framework for Augmented Analytics

Alexander P. Ryjov
Lomonosov Moscow State University, Russia

ABSTRACT

Analytics is a key success factor for any business in the competitive and fast-changing world we live in. Using analytics, people, business, social, and government organizations become capable of understanding the past, including lessons from faults and achievements; realize current strengths, weaknesses, opportunities, and threats; and predict the future. Intelligent analytics allow doing these more effectively and efficiently. Modern analytics uses many advanced techniques like big data, artificial intelligence, and many others. This chapter aims to introduce the hybrid intelligence approach by focusing on its unique analytical capabilities. The state-of-the-art in hybrid intelligence—symbiosis and cooperative interaction between human intelligence and artificial intelligence in solving a wide range of practical tasks—and one of the hybrid intelligence frameworks—a human-centered evaluation approach and monitoring of complex processes—have been considered in this chapter. The chapter could be interesting for analysts and researchers who desire to do analytics with more intelligence.

INTRODUCTION

Organism and organization are words with the same root. Both of them survive in a complex environment and try to achieve their goals. Both of them have particular organs and structures for surviving and being effective and efficient. In this analogy, analysts are a brain for any organization. The analytical structure is people and tools. Analytical tools had evolved from simple models and standard software like Excel to specialized tools based on advanced complex models and methods. The more intelligent analytical structure organizations have, the more effective organization is. An intelligent analytical structure means intelligent analysts and intelligence tools. Analytical talents are a limited resource; therefore, improvement of analytical tools' intelligence level is a topical and requested task.

Which analytical tool is suitable for a particular organization? There is no universal recommendation; all organizations are unique. But it is possible to present a general picture (Figure 1). Any organization

DOI: 10.4018/978-1-7998-4963-6.ch002

Figure 1. Technology stack

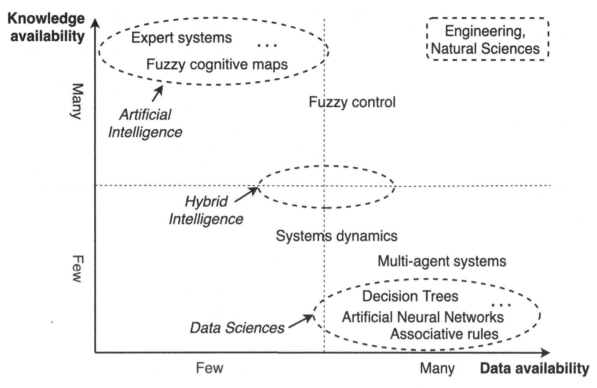

accumulates data and expertise (or knowledge) during its lifetime. If the organization has a large amount of data, suitable tools could be Big Data-based analytics like Data Mining, Artificial Neural Networks, etc. The examples could be retail, telecom, government (smart city). If the principal asset is knowledge (for example, consulting companies), suitable tools could be Artificial Intelligence (AI)-based analytics. Both these situations (left-top and right-bottom corners in Figure 1) are well-studied. The left- bottom corner is when only intuition could help analysts; the right-top corner is engineering tasks (like calculating the reliability of a bridge or building).

This chapter focuses on the situation when an organization has some mix of data and knowledge. This situation is typical for many organizations and is not so well-studied, like analytics based on Big Data or AI.

BACKGROUND

The idea of intelligent systems as a tool for augmenting human intelligence was first proposed in the 1950-s and 1960-s by cybernetics and early computer pioneers. The term *Amplifying intelligence* was introduced by William Ross Ashby in his classical work (Ashby, W.R., 1956, p. 271). At the end of his fantastic book, he wrote: "*Intellectual power, like physical power, can be amplified. Let no one say that it cannot be done, for the gene-patterns do it every time they form a brain that grows up to be something better than the gene-pattern could have specified in detail. What is new is that we can now do it synthetically, consciously, deliberately.*" (Ashby, 1956, p. 272). The idea of a symbiosis of human and computer was formulated by psychologist and computer scientist Joseph Carl Robnett Licklider: *"Man-computer symbiosis is an expected development in cooperative interaction between men and electronic computers. It will involve very close coupling between the human and the electronic members of the partnership. The main aims are 1) to let computers facilitate formulative thinking as they now facilitate the solution of formulated problems, and 2) to enable men and computers to cooperate in making decisions and controlling complex situations without inflexible dependence on predetermined programs. In the anticipated symbiotic partnership, men will set the goals, formulate the hypothesis, determine the criteria, and perform the evaluations. Computing machines will do the routinizable work that must be done to prepare the way for insights and decisions in technical and scientific thinking. Preliminary analyses indicate that the symbiotic partnership will perform intellectual operations much more effectively than man alone can perform them."* (Licklider, 1960, p. 4). This idea was specified and studied by Douglas Carl Engelbart: *"By "augmenting human intellect" we mean increasing the capability of a man to approach a complex problem situation, to gain comprehension to suit his particular needs, and to derive solutions to problems. Increased capability in this respect is taken to mean a mixture of the following: more-rapid comprehension, better comprehension, the possibility of gaining a useful degree of comprehension in a situation that previously was too complex, speedier solutions, better solutions, and the possibility of finding solutions to problems that before seemed insoluble. And by "complex situations" we include the professional problems of diplomats, executives, social scientists, life scientists, physical scientists, attorneys, designers—whether the problem situation exists for twenty minutes or twenty years. We do not speak of isolated clever tricks that help in particular situations. We refer to a way of life in an integrated domain where hunches, cut-and-try, intangibles, and the human "feel for a situation" usefully co-exist with powerful concepts, streamlined terminology and notation, sophisticated methods, and high-powered electronic aids."* (Engelbart, 1962).

After this romantic period, we had some tens of years of stagnation for human-computer systems. One of the fundamental problems from the author's point of view was a vast difference between perception, manipulation of information, reasoning, etc., for a human being and for a computer. Boolean 0/1 logic is natural for computers but very artificial for people; work with uncertain information is natural for people but very complicated for computers. How can we organize the symbiosis of such two completely different subsystems?

A mathematical tool capable of being an interface between human beings and computers - fuzzy logic - was introduced by Lotfi Zadeh (Zadeh, 1965). In (Zadeh, 1975, p. 200), he wrote: *"The main applications of the linguistic approach lie in the realm of humanistic systems-especially in the fields of artificial intelligence, linguistics, human decision processes, pattern recognition, psychology, law, medical diagnosis, information retrieval, economics and related areas"*. His definition of the humanistic system is: *"By a humanistic system we mean a system whose behavior is strongly influenced by human judgement, perception or emotions. Examples of humanistic systems are: economic systems, political systems, legal systems, educational systems, etc. A single individual and his thought processes may also be viewed as a humanistic system"* (Zadeh, 1975, p. 200). Fuzzy logic allows us to use perception-based descriptions of objects and manipulate them in a human-like reasoning manner in computer models. It is a base for cognitive computing and Augmented Intelligence as defined by IBM (2018): *"At IBM, we are guided by the term "augmented intelligence" rather than "artificial intelligence". It is the critical difference between systems that enhance and scale human expertise rather than those that attempt to replicate all of human intelligence. We focus on building practical AI applications that assist people with well-defined tasks, and in the process, expose a range of generalized AI services on a platform to support a wide range of new applications"*.

The chapter's mission is to discuss the analytical capabilities of a hybrid (human + computer) intelligence. A subclass of hybrid systems - human-computer systems for evaluating the status and monitoring of complex processes' progress (Ryjov, 2013) is discussed in detail. These systems allow "assist people with well-defined tasks" in the management of complex processes in a partnership manner. In an ideal case, it becomes possible to combine the strengths of a human being (for example, intuition) and a computer (for example, computation power) in an optimal way.

From a business perspective, these systems are close to the "Automation of knowledge work" set of technologies in McKinsey Global Institute terms (McKinsey Global Institute, 2013, p. 41): *"These capabilities not only extend computing into new realms ..., but also create new relationships between knowledge workers and machines. It is increasingly possible to interact with a machine the way one would with a coworker"*. McKinsey estimated potential economic impact across sized applications in 2025 from $5.2 trillion to $6.7 trillion per year (McKinsey Global Institute, 2013, p. 44).

The final remark in this section is about AI and Hybrid Intelligence. The last decade could be named as the time of AI and Big Data. Both AI and Big Data have a broad spectrum of definitions; they cast themselves as many technologies that span across many different things and can be described in different ways. It is not a good situation for science and engineering. A formal criterion like the Turing test has been successfully passed (University of Reading, 2014), informal criteria like playing chess or Go have been passed, too. So, even specialists do not understand what AI is; as a result, opinions like "Artificial intelligence has accrued some very bad reputation over the years" (Dickson, 2017) or "Some industry experts believe that the term artificial intelligence is too closely linked to popular culture, causing the general public to have unrealistic fears about artificial intelligence and improbable expectations about how it will change the workplace and life in general" (Rouse, 2017), etc. becomes popular. The author would not like to participate in such discussions: without a common criterion like the Turing test, it is a matter of taste. Autonomous adaptive self-learning and self-sufficient intelligent systems seem like a future (the question is how far is this future?), a more realistic way to solve intelligent tasks, for now, is a symbiosis of human and computer intelligence. Note that this direction is becoming recognized by science and technology experts as an essential part of the future technology landscape:

- USA National Science Foundation presented NSF's 10 Big Ideas - pioneering research and pilot activities areas (NSF, 2019 a)); the Big Idea #1 is "Future of Work at the Human-Technology Frontier" (NSF, 2019 b))
- USA Defense Advanced Research Projects Agency announced a multi-year investment of more than $2 billion in new and existing programs called the "AI Next" campaign with a focus on "research and development in human-machine symbiosis sets a goal to partner with machines" (DARPA, 2018);
- The USA President approved The National Artificial Intelligence Research and Development Strategic Plan: 2019 update where Strategy 2 is "Develop Effective Methods for Human-AI Collaboration" (WH, 2019).

EVALUATING THE STATUS AND MONITORING THE PROGRESS OF COMPLEX PROCESSES: MAIN ISSUES, BASIC PRINCIPLES, AND THEORETICAL FOUNDATIONS

Many organizations and specialists are trying to achieve their goals in a complex environment using some understanding of a current status (where are we?) and possible ways to achieve the expected level or the objective (where would we like to be?). There are many different types of processes (a journey from current status to the expected one) from well-defined (for example, manufacturing processes) to very uncertain (for example, political processes). Many people and institutions are involved in understanding these processes and finding actions that allow achieving the goal via some acceptable (or optimal in the ideal case) path.

The following way can classify the processes from the point of view of the ability to control (or controllability):

a. assuredly control in automatic mode (computer only) – technical processes; examples are manufacturing, mechanics, robots.
b. reliably controlled in automated mode (computer + expert) – sociotechnical processes; examples are social processes, politics, management.
c. control in expert mode only (some selected/unique persons can control) – "art" processes; examples are ballet, writing poetry, creativity.

It is not possible to automate or computerize unique and not systematically reproducible "art" processes. Let us compare technical and sociotechnical processes; top 3 differences are collected in Table 1. The conclusion is classical mathematics is not suitable for describing and modeling socio-economic, political, etc. processes due to huge complexity, uncertainty, and vagueness. Only the right mix of computer intelligence and human intelligence can solve these problems.

Table 1. Features of the processes

Technical processes	Sociotechnical processes
We have adequate and proven mathematical models of the processes (in the form of equations, automata, etc.).	We have a description of the processes in the form of natural language texts, diagrams, parametric dependencies, etc.
Information about the parameters' values is measurable and has unambiguous interpretation (we have measuring devices).	Information about the parameters' values is available in the form of evaluations (the measuring device is a human being); evaluations for the same parameter could be different.
Repeatability and reproducibility of the processes. It is possible to run experiments (for example, for gathering statistics).	Uniqueness of the processes. Impossible to run a series of independent experiments.

The evaluation and monitoring task includes evaluating some process' current status and modeling possible ways of its development based on real information. System for Evaluation and Monitoring (SEM) is a human-computer system that provides a solution to the evaluation and monitoring task. There are many evaluations and monitoring tasks in business (marketing, management, strategic planning, etc.), politics (elections, control of bilateral and multilateral agreements, terrorism, etc.), and many other areas of our life. A significant share of analysts focuses on evaluation and monitoring tasks, and SEM is a tool for automation of their work.

Human-Centric Systems for Evaluation of the Status and Monitoring the Progress of Complex Processes

From the systems point of view, SEM relates to a class of hierarchical fuzzy discrete dynamical systems. The theoretical base for this class of systems is provided by the fuzzy sets theory, discrete mathematics, methods of the analysis of hierarchies, which was developed in works of L.A. Zadeh (1965, 1975), M.D. Mesarovich et al. (1970), T.L. Saaty (1980), and others. The analytic hierarchy process (AHP) was developed in the 1980s by (Saaty, 1980). It is a systematic decision-making method that includes both qualitative and quantitative techniques. It has been widely used in many fields for a long time. J.J. Buckley (1985) incorporated the fuzziness into the AHP, called the FAHP. Hierarchical fuzzy systems have attracted considerable attention in recent years. V. Torra (2002) summarized the related recent research work in this domain. Detailed FAHP literature review is also presented in (Anvary et al., 2012).

SEM allows uniformly process diverse, multi-level, fragmentary, unreliable, and varying in time information about some processes. Based on this type of information, SEM can monitor the process's status evaluation and work out strategic plans for process development. These capabilities open a broad area of applications in business (for example, (Ryjov, 2004)), politics (Ryjov et al., 1998; Ryjov, 2014a), health care (Ahkmedzhanov et al., 2003), engineering (Lebedev, 2009), social systems (Ryjov, 2014a).

There is a growing interest in such systems (The Economic Times, 2016). These systems could be one of the automation of knowledge work technologies defined by McKinsey as a disruptive technology number 2 (McKinsey Global Institute, 2013). This chapter could help people who work in this extremely exciting and important area of development of optimal systems.

Basic Elements of SEM

Let's name a task of evaluating a current state of the process and elaborating the forecasts of its evolution as an evaluation and monitoring task, and human-computer systems are ensuring support of a similar sort of information tasks – systems for evaluation and monitoring.

Basic elements of SEM at the top level are the process, the information space, in which information about the state of the process circulates, and analysts, working with this information and making conclusions about the state of the process and forecasts of its progress. Basic elements of IMS and their interaction are presented in Figure 2.

The *information image* represents a set of various information elements, which can be characterized as follows:

- Diversity of the information carriers, i.e., presentation of the information in articles, newspapers, electronic documents, audio-, and video- data, etc.;
- Fragmentary. The information most often related to any fragment of a problem, and the different fragments may be differently "covered" with the information;
- Multi-levelled. The information can concern the whole problem, some of its parts, or a particular element of the process;

Figure 2. Basic elements of SEM and their interaction

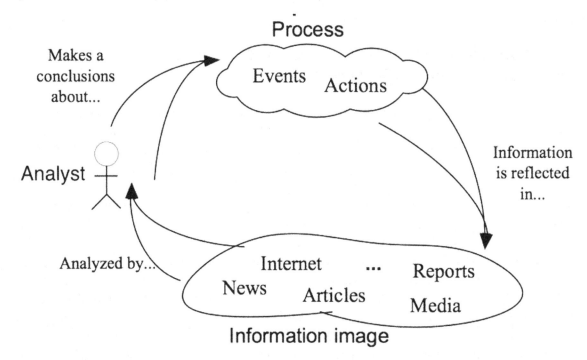

- Various degrees of reliability. The information can contain data points with various degrees of reliability, indirect data, results of conclusions on the basis of reliable information or indirect conclusions;
- Possible discrepancy. The information from various sources can coincide, differ slightly or be contradictory;
- Varying in time. The process develops over time; therefore, the information about the same element can be different between two different moments in time;
- Possible bias. The information reflects the specific interests of the source of information; therefore, it can have a tendentious character.

The *analysts* are an active element of the monitoring system. They observe and study pieces of the information space and make conclusions about the state of the process and prospects of its development while considering the information space's above-listed properties.

Basic Principles of Technology for Evaluation and Monitoring of Complex Processes

Taking into account the given features of the information and specific methods of its processing is possible to declare the main features of the technology for evaluation and monitoring of complex processes as follows:

- The system provides the facility for taking into account data conveyed by different information vehicles (journals, video clips, newspapers, documents in electronic form, etc.). Such a facility is

Figure 3. Typical structure of a model for SEM

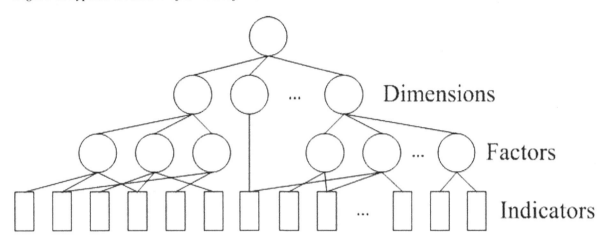

provided through storage in a database of references to an evaluated piece of information if it is not a document in electronic form. If the information is a document in electronic form, then both the evaluated information (or part thereof) and a reference thereto are stored in the system. Thus, the system makes it possible to consider and use in analysis all pieces of information, which have a relationship to the subject area, irrespective of the information vehicle.

- The system makes it possible to process fragmentary and/or multi-level information. For this purpose, a considerable part of the model is represented in the form of a tree or graph (Figure 3).

- Information with different degrees of reliability, possibly biased, can be processed in the system. This is achieved by assessing the influence of a particular piece of information on the model's elements' status using fuzzy linguistic values.
- Time is one of the parameters of the system. This makes it possible to have a complete picture of the variation of the model's status with time.

SEM workflow is presented in Figure 4:

Thus, the systems constructed based on this technology allow having the model of the process developing in time. It is supported by the references to all information materials chosen by the analysts, with general and separate evaluations of the process's status. Using the time as one of the system's parameters allows the retrospective analysis and building the forecasts of development of the process. There is the opportunity to allocate "critical points", i.e., element(s) of the model for which a small change can cause significant changes in the whole process's status. The knowledge of such elements has immense practical significance. It allows to reveal "critical points" of the process, work out the measures on blocking out undesirable situations or promote the desirable ones, i.e., somewhat guide the development of the process in time in the desirable direction.

Figure 4. SEM workflow

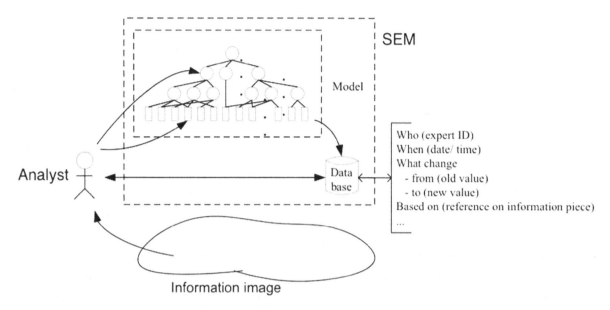

Information image

Theoretical Base of SEM

For effective practical application of the proposed technological solutions, it is necessary to tackle a series of theoretical problems.

It is assumed that the expert describes the degree of inconsistency of the obtained information (for example, the readiness or potential for the readiness of certain processes in a country (Ryjov et al., 1998)) in the form of linguistic values. The subjective degree of convenience of such a description depends on the selection and the composition of such linguistic values (Ryjov, 2003).

It is assumed that the system tracks the development of the problem, i.e., its variation with time. It is also assumed that it integrates the evaluations of several different experts. This means that different experts may describe one object. Therefore, it is desirable to have assurances that the different experts describe the same object in the most "uniform" way.

Based on the above, we may formulate the first problem as follows:

Problem 1 (perception-based descriptions of physical objects). Is it possible, considering certain features of the man's perception of objects of the real world and their description, to formulate a rule for selecting the optimum set of values of characteristics based on which these objects may be described? Two optimality criteria are possible:

Criterion 1. We regard as optimum those sets of values through which one experiences the minimum uncertainty in describing objects.
Criterion 2. If a certain number of experts describes the object, then we regard as optimum those sets of values that provide the minimum degree of divergence of the descriptions.

It is shown that we can formulate a method of selecting the optimum set of values of qualitative indications (scale values). Moreover, it is shown that such a method is robust, i.e., the natural small errors that may occur in constructing the membership functions do not significantly influence the selection of the optimum set of values. The sets which are optimal according to criteria 1 and 2 coincide. The results obtained are described in (Ryjov, 1988). Following this method, we may describe objects with minimum possible uncertainty, i.e., guarantee optimum operation of the systems for evaluation and monitoring from this point of view.

Below we shortly describe the main ideas of formalization and a summary of the method's main results.

The model of estimating real object's properties by a person as a procedure of measuring in fuzzy linguistic scale (FLS) has been described in (Ryjov, 2003). The set of scale values of some FLS is a collection of fuzzy sets defined on the same universum.

Let us consider t fuzzy variables with the names a_1, a_2, ..., a_t, specified on one universal set (Figure 5). We shall call such a set the scale values set of a FLS s_t.

Figure 5. The scale values set of a FLS

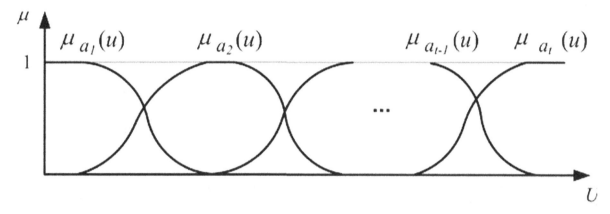

Let us introduce a system of limitations for the membership functions of the fuzzy variables comprising s_t. For the sake of simplicity, we shall designate the membership function a_j as μj. We shall consider that:

1. $\forall \mu_j \left(1 \le j \le t\right) \exists U_j^1 \ne \varnothing$ where $U_j^1 = \left\{u \in U : \mu_j\left(u\right) = 1\right\}$ is an interval or a point;

2. $\forall j (1 \le j \le t) \mu j$ does not decrease on the left of U_j^1 and does not increase on the right of U_j^1 (since, according to 1, U_j^1 is an interval or a point, the concepts "on the left" and "on the right" are determined unambiguously).

Requirements 1 and 2 are quite natural for membership functions of concepts forming scale values set of an FLS. The first one signifies that at least one object for any concept is used in the universal set, which is standard for the given concept. If there are many such standards, they are positioned in a series and are not "scattered" around the universe. The second requirement signifies that, if the objects are "similar" in the metrics sense in a universal set, they are also "similar" in the sense of FLS.

Henceforth, we shall need to use the characteristic functions as well as the membership functions, and so we shall need to fulfill the following technical condition:

3. $\forall j (1 \leq j \leq t) \mu j$ has no more than two points of discontinuity of the first kind.

For simplicity, let us designate the requirements 1-3 as *L*.

Let us also introduce a system of limitations for the sets of membership functions of fuzzy variables comprising s_t. Thus, we may consider that:

4. $\forall u \in U \exists j \left(1 \leq j \leq t\right): \mu_j \left(u\right) > 0$;

5. $\forall u \in U \sum_{j=1}^{t} \mu_j \left(u\right) = 1$.

Requirements 4 and 5 also have quite a natural interpretation. Requirement 4, designated the completeness requirement, signifies that for any object from the universal set, there exists at least one concept of FLS to which it may belong. This means that in our scale values set, and there are no "holes". Requirement 5, designated the orthogonality requirement, signifies that we do not permit the use of semantically similar concepts or synonyms, and we require sufficient distinction of the concepts used. Note also that this requirement is often fulfilled or not fulfilled depending on the method used for constructing the membership functions of the concepts forming the scale values set of a FLS (Ryjov, 2003).

For simplicity, we shall designate requirements 4 and 5 as *G*.

We shall term the FLS with scale values set consisting of fuzzy variables, the membership functions that satisfy the requirements 1-3, and their populations the requirements 4 and 5, a *complete orthogonal FLS* and denote it *G(L)*.

Different FLS have a different degree of internal uncertainty. Let us explain this in a model example.

Example. Let it be required to evaluate the height of a man. Let us consider two extreme situations.
Situation 1. It is permitted to use only two values: "short" and "tall".
Situation 2. It is permitted to use many values: "very short", "not very tall", ..., "not short and not tall", ..., "very tall".

Situation 1 is inconvenient. In fact, for many men, both the permitted values may be unsuitable, and, in describing them, we select between two "bad" values.

Situation 2 is also inconvenient. In fact, in describing the height of men, several of the permitted values may be suitable. We again experience a problem, but now due to the fact that we are forced to select between two or more "good" values.

Is it possible to measure this degree of uncertainty? For complete orthogonal FLS, the answer to this question is yes. To prove this fact and derive a corresponding formula, we need to introduce additional concepts.

Let there be a certain population of *t* membership functions $s_t \in G(L)$. Let $s_t = \{\mu 1, ..., \mu t\}$. Let us designate the population of t characteristic functions $\hat{s}_t = \left\{h_1, \cdots, h_t\right\}$ as t*he most similar population of characteristic functions,* if $\forall j (1 \leq j \leq t)$

$$h_j \left(u\right) = \begin{cases} 1 & , \quad \text{if } \mu_j \left(u\right) = 1 \\ 0 & , \quad \text{otherwise} \end{cases}$$

It is not difficult to see that if the complete orthogonal FLS consists not of membership functions but characteristic functions, then no uncertainty will arise when describing objects. The expert unambiguously chooses the term a_j if the object is in the universal set's corresponding region. Some experts describe the same object with the same term. This situation may be illustrated as follows. Let us assume that we have scales of certain accuracy and we have the opportunity to weigh a certain material. Moreover, we have agreed that, if the material's weight falls within a certain range, it belongs to one of the categories. Then we shall have the situation accurately described. The problem lies in the fact that there are no such scales for our task, nor do we have the opportunity to weigh on them the objects of interest to us.

However, we can assume that, of the two FLS, the one having the least uncertainty will be most "similar" to the space consisting of the populations of characteristic functions. In mathematics, distance can be a degree of similarity. Is it possible to introduce distance among FLS? For complete orthogonal FLS, it is possible.

First of all, note that the set of functions L is a subset of integrable functions on an interval so that we can enter the distance in L, for example, $\rho(f,g) = \int_U |f(u) - g(u)| du$, $f \in L$, $g \in L$.

Let consider two population of t membership functions $s_t = \{\mu 1, ..., \mu t\}$ and $s_t' = \{\mu_1', \cdots, \mu_t'\}$. The following lemma holds (Ryjov, 1988).

Lemma 1. Let $s_t \in G(L)$, $s_t' \in G(L)$, $\rho(f,g)$ - some distance in L. Then $(s_t, s_t') = \sum_{j=1}^{t} \rho(\mu_j, \mu_j')$ is a distance in $G(L)$.

The semantic statements formulated above may be formalized as follows.

Let $s_t \in G(L)$. For the measure of uncertainty of s_t, we shall take the value of a functional $\xi(s_t)$, determined by the elements of G(L) and assuming the values in [0,1] (i.e., $\xi(st)$ G(L)→[0,1]), satisfying the following conditions (axioms):

A1. $\xi(st) = 0$, if st is a set of characteristic functions;

A2. Let $s_t, s_{t'}' \in G(L)$, t and t' may be equal or not equal to each other. Then $\xi(s_t) \leq \xi(s_{t'}')$, if

$$d(s_t, \hat{s}_t) \leq d(s_{t'}', \hat{s}_{t'}').$$

Does such functional exist? The answer to this question is given by the following theorem (Ryjov, 1988).

Theorem 1 (theorem of existence). Let $s_t \in G(L)$. Then the functional

$$\xi(s_t) = \frac{1}{|U|} \int_U f\left(\mu_{i_1^*}(u) - \mu_{i_2^*}(u)\right) du,$$

where $\mu_{i_1^*}(u) = \max_{1 \leq j \leq t} \mu_j(u)$, $\mu_{i_2^*}(u) = \max_{1 \leq j \leq t, j \neq i_1^*} \mu_j(u)$, f satisfies the following conditions:

F1: $f(0)=1, f(1)=0$; F2: f does not increase – is a measure of uncertainty of s_t.

There are many functional satisfying the conditions of Theorem 1. They are described in sufficient detail in (Ryjov, 1988). The simplest of them is the functional in which the function f is linear. It is not difficult to see that conditions F1 and F2 are satisfied by the sole linear function $f(x)=1-x$. Substituting it in $\xi(st_j$, we obtain the following simplest measure of uncertainty of the complete orthogonal FLS:

$$\xi(s_t) = \frac{1}{|U|} \int_U \left(1 - \left(\mu_{i_1^*}(u) - \mu_{i_2^*}(u)\right)\right) du.$$

We can provide the following interpretation of the simplest measure of uncertainty (Ryjov, 1988). Let us consider the process of a description of real objects by a person. We do not have any uncertainty in providing a linguistic description of an object with the "physical" value of the attribute u_1 (Figure 6).

Figure 6. Interpretation of degree of fuzziness of a FLS

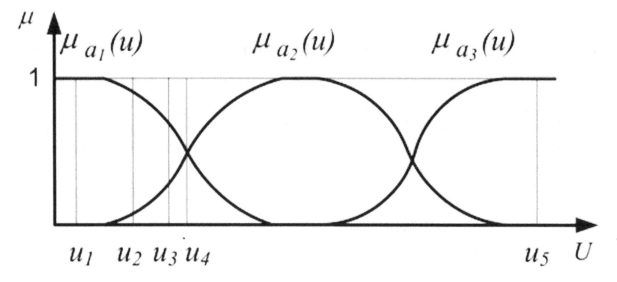

We attribute it to term a_1 with complete certainty. We can repeat this statement about an object whose "physical" value of the attribute is u_5. We choose the term a_3 for its description without fluctuations. We begin to experience difficulties in choosing a suitable linguistic significance in describing an object with the physical value of attribute u_2. These difficulties grow (u_3) and reach the maximal significance for an object with the physical value of attribute u_4: for such objects, both linguistic significances (a_1 and a_2) are equal. If we consider the significance of the integrand function $\eta(s_t, u) = 1 - \left(\mu_{i_1^*}(u) - \mu_{i_2^*}(u)\right)$ in these points, we can say, that

$$0 = \eta(s_t, u_5) = \eta(s_t, u_1) < \eta(s_t, u_2) < \eta(s_t, u_3) < \eta(s_t, u_4) = 1.$$

Thus, the integral $\xi(s_t)$ value can be interpreted as an average degree of human doubt while describing some real object.

It is also proved that the functional has natural and good properties for fuzziness degree (Ryjov, 1988).

Finally, we present the results of our model's analysis, when the membership functions that are members of a given collection of fuzzy sets are not given with absolute precision, but with some inaccuracy not exceeding δ (Figure 7). Let us call this particular situation the δ - *model* and denote it by $G\delta^{(L)}$.

Figure 7. Presentation of $G^\delta(L)$.

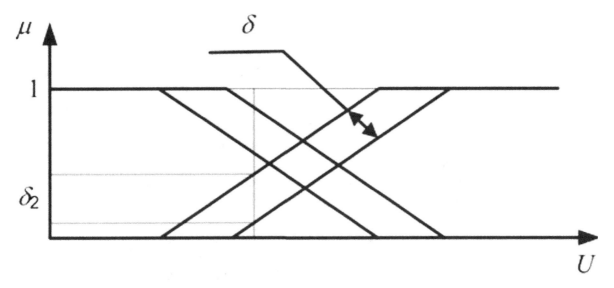

In this situation, we can calculate the top ($\overline{\xi}(s_t)$) and the bottom ($\underline{\xi}(s_t)$) valuations of the degree of fuzziness $\xi(s_t)$. The following theorem holds (Ryjov, 1988).

Theorem 2. Let $s_t \in G^\delta(L)$. Then $\underline{\xi}(s_t) = (1 - \delta_2)^2 \xi(s_t)$, $\overline{\xi}(s_t) = (1 + 2\delta_2)\xi(s_t)$.

Therefore, we can use our estimation technique of the degree of fuzziness in practical tasks since we have shown it to be robust.

Based on these results, we can propose the following method for selection of the optimum set of values of characteristics:

1. All the "reasonable" sets of linguistic values are formulated;
2. Each of such sets is represented in the form of $G(L)$;
3. For each set, the measure of uncertainty $\xi(s_t)$ is calculated;
4. As the optimum set minimizes both the uncertainty in the description of objects and the degree of divergence of users' opinions, we select the one with minimal uncertainty.

Following this method, we can describe objects with minimum possible uncertainty, i.e., guarantee that different users will describe the objects for SEM in the most unified manner possible (see Criterion 2 in Problem 1). This means that the number of situations when one real object has more than one image in SEM, or different real objects have the same image in SEM, will be minimal. Accordingly, we will have maximal possible adequacy of the SEM as a model of the real world from this point of view. Robustness of the measure of uncertainty (Theorem 2) allows us to use this method in practical applications.

Evaluation and monitoring technology assumes the storage of information (or references to it) and its linguistic evaluations in a system database. In this connection, the following problem arises.

Problem 2 (information retrieval for perception-based descriptions). Is it possible to define metrics of quality of information retrieval in fuzzy (linguistic) databases and formulate a rule for selecting such a set of linguistic values that would maximize information retrieval quality?

It is shown (Ryjov, 2004) that it is possible to introduce such quality metrics of information retrieval in fuzzy (linguistic) databases and formalize them. It is possible to formulate a method of selecting the optimum set of values of qualitative indications, which maximizes the quality metric of information retrieval. Moreover, it is shown that such a method is robust, i.e., the natural small errors in the construction of the membership functions do not significantly affect the selection of the optimum set of values. The results obtained are shown in (Ryjov, 2004; Ryjov, 2012). It ensures that the offered methods can be used in practical tasks and guarantees optimal systems for evaluation and monitoring of complex processes.

Like for Problem 1, below, we shortly describe main ideas of formalization and summarize the main facts for Problem 2. As well as in analysis of Problem 1, we shall consider that the set of the linguistic meanings can be submitted as $G(L)$.

In our study of the process of information searches in databases whose objects have a linguistic description, we introduced the concepts of information loss ($IL_X(U)$) and information noise ($IN_X(U)$). These concepts apply to information searches in these databases, whose attributes have a set of values X, which are modeled by the fuzzy sets in s_t. The meaning of these concepts can informally be described as follows. While interacting with the system, a user formulates his query for objects satisfying certain linguistic characteristics and gets an answer according to his search request. If he knows the real (not the linguistic) values of the characteristics, he would probably delete some of the objects returned by the system (information noise), and he would probably add some others from the database, not returned by the system (information losses). Information noise and information losses have their origin in the fuzziness of the linguistic descriptions of the characteristics.

These concepts can be formalized as follows (Ryjov, 2004):

$$IL_X(U) = IN_X(U) = \frac{1}{|U|} \sum_{j=1}^{t-1} (p_j + p_{j+1}) \int_U \mu_j(u)\mu_{j+1}(u)N(u)du,$$

where $X = \{a_1, \ldots, a_t\}$, $p_i(i = 1, 2, \ldots, t)$ - the probability of request offering in i- meaning of the characteristic X, $N(u)$ is the number of objects, the descriptions of which are stored in the database, that possess a real (physical, not linguistic) value equal to u.

The following theorems hold (Ryjov, 2004; Ryjov, 2012).

Theorem 3. Let $s_t \in G(L)$, $N(u)=N=Const$, $p_i = \frac{1}{t}(i = 1, 2, \cdots, t)$. Then

$$IL_X(U) = IN_X(U) = \frac{c}{t}\xi(s_t),$$

where c is a constant with depends on N only.

This theorem shows that the volumes of information losses and information noise arising when searching for information in SEM are proportional to the degree of uncertainty of objects' description. It means that by optimally describing objects (concerning minimizing the degree of uncertainty), we also provide the optimal search of information in SEM.

Similarly to the analysis of Problem 1, we can construct the top ($\overline{IL}_X(U) = \overline{IN}_X(U)$) and the bottom ($\underline{IL}_X(U) = \underline{IN}_X(U)$) valuations of the $IL_X(U)$ and $IN_X(U)$.

Theorem 4. Let $s_t \in G^{\delta}(L)$, N(u)=N=*Const*, $p_i = \frac{1}{t}(i = 1, 2, \cdots, t)$. Then

$$\underline{IL}_X(U) = \underline{IN}_X(U) = \frac{c}{t}(1 - \delta_2)\underline{\xi}(s_t)$$

$$\overline{IL}_X(U) = \overline{IN}_X(U) = \frac{c}{t(1 + 2\delta_2)}\left(\frac{(1 - \delta_2)^3}{3} + 2\delta_2\right)\overline{\xi}(s_t).$$

This theorem shows us that for small significances δ our model of information retrieval's main laws is preserved. Therefore, we can use our estimation technique of the degree of uncertainty and our model of information retrieval in fuzzy (linguistic) databases in practical tasks since we have shown it to be robust.

Since we model processes as hierarchical structures (see Figure 3), choosing and selecting (tuning) of aggregation operators for the nodes of the model is another important issue in the development of SEM. We may formulate this problem as follows:

Problem 3. (aggregation in fuzzy hierarchical dynamic systems) Is it possible to find the operators of information aggregation in fuzzy hierarchical dynamic systems that allow us to minimize contradictoriness in the model of process in SEM?

It is shown that it is possible to propose the following approaches based on different interpretations of aggregation operators: geometrical, logical, and learning-based. The latter includes learning based on genetic algorithms and learning based on neural networks. These approaches are described in detail in (Ryjov, 2001).

Analytical Capabilities of SEM

Having set up an SEM, we can solve two types of problems: direct and inverse.

The direct problem is to find all "critical ways" of the process. It means to reveal those elements of the process, the small change of which status may qualitatively change the process's status as a whole. For a big class of aggregation operators, we can calculate the degree of criticality for any element of the model; for all aggregation operators, we can use universal algorithms (like backtracking algorithms) to calculate the degree of criticality for any element of the model. That means that we can understand and

Figure 8. Example of the Model

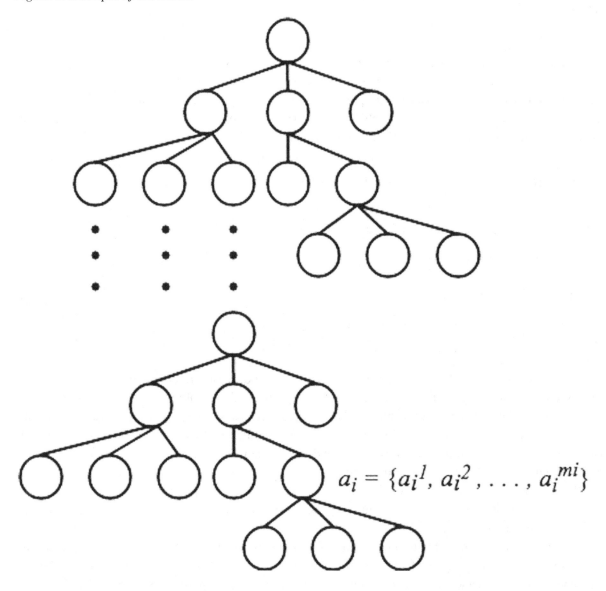

$$a_i = \{a_i^1, a_i^2, \ldots, a_i^{mi}\}$$

measure the strengths and weaknesses of any element of the current process. This understanding is a base for developing a strategic plan for optimally controlling the process.

The inverse problem is finding elements of the model, which must be changed for reaching some given status of the model's target element. For example, we can understand how we can reach a maximal effect for a given budget or reach a given effect for a minimal budget.

We can formalize this in the following way. Let's use notations:

N – number of nodes in the Model;
m_i – number of values for node i;
$a_i = \left\{a_i^1, a_i^2, \cdots, a_i^{m_i}\right\}$ – values for node i (i=0,1,..., N–1) – see Figure 8;

Figure 9. Analytical capabilities of SEM

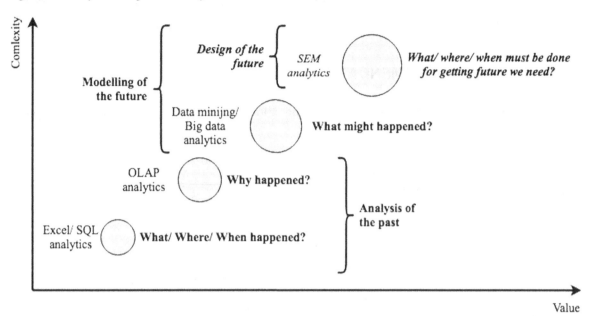

X – budget;

c_i – cost of changing for node i ($a_i^k \rightarrow a_i^{k+1}, k = 1, \cdots, m_i - 1$); for simplicity assume that c_i is the same for all k;

Δa_i - the "power of changing" for node i; $\Delta a_i = q$ for changing $a_i^k \rightarrow a_i^{k+q}$.

Task 1. To find a set of nodes $\left\{ a_{i_1}, a_{i_2}, \cdots, a_{i_n} \right\}$: $\Delta a_0 \rightarrow max, \sum_{j=1}^{N-1} c_{i_j} \leq X$.

It is a task to reach the maximal effect for a given budget.
We can also formulate a dual task:

Task 2. To find a set of nodes $\left\{ a_{i_1}, a_{i_2}, \cdots, a_{i_n} \right\}$: $\sum_{j=1}^{N-1} c_{i_j} \rightarrow min, \Delta a_0 \geq q$.

It is a task to reach the given effect for a minimal budget.

Examples of such tasks could be evaluation and increasing capitalization for startups, increasing an investment's attractiveness for companies and/or regions, increasing the sustainability of a business, etc.

We can solve these tasks if we have the model (structure and tuned aggregation functions), the nodes' actual status, i.e., a working system for evaluation and monitoring of the process. Comparison analysis of these capabilities with other analytical tools is presented in Figure 9.

The current level of almost all companies – Excel/ SQL or OLAP Analytics; only a few companies use Big Data Analytics; analytical tools of systems of evaluation and monitoring used in selected international and governmental organizations, and large international high-tech business. The use of analytical systems capabilities of SEM is a natural evolutionary stage in the development of analytical tools and frameworks for the Automation of knowledge work.

SOLUTIONS AND RECOMMENDATIONS

SEMs can solve the task of evaluation and monitoring, allow user input of all available information in a "natural manner", and capable of:

- saving the history of process development,
- evaluating the current status,
- modeling the future of process development.

SEMs are effective when:

- we do not have (cannot develop) a mathematical model of the process in the form of equations, automata, etc.
- we have experts who perform the monitoring task.

We can develop SEM with minimal requirements for the task when:

- it is possible to develop a "semantic model" of the process in the form of a set of concepts and their inter-dependencies
- we work with real information (we can learn or tune the system)

We can develop an optimal system in terms of:

- how easy it is for the user to input information
- coordination of estimations of users
- information support of processes of input information and modeling.

Based on the methods described above, several systems for evaluation and monitoring were developed: a system for evaluation and monitoring of peaceful nuclear activities (DISNA) for the department of Safeguards International Atomic Energy Agency (Ryjov, et al., 1998), a system for evaluation and monitoring of risks of cardiovascular disease for Federal State Institution "National Research Center for Preventive Medicine" of the Ministry of Healthcare of the Russian Federation (Ahkmedzhanov et al., 2003), a system for evaluation and monitoring design team capability and project progress in microelectronics for Cadence Design Systems (Lebedev, 2009) and others.

Analytical capabilities of SEM allow us not only to analyze the past, even not only to model the future like Big Data analytics, but they also allow us to design the future and answer questions like "What, where and when we need to change to get the future we need?".

Figure 10. Task-driven information granulation (Ryjov, 2015)

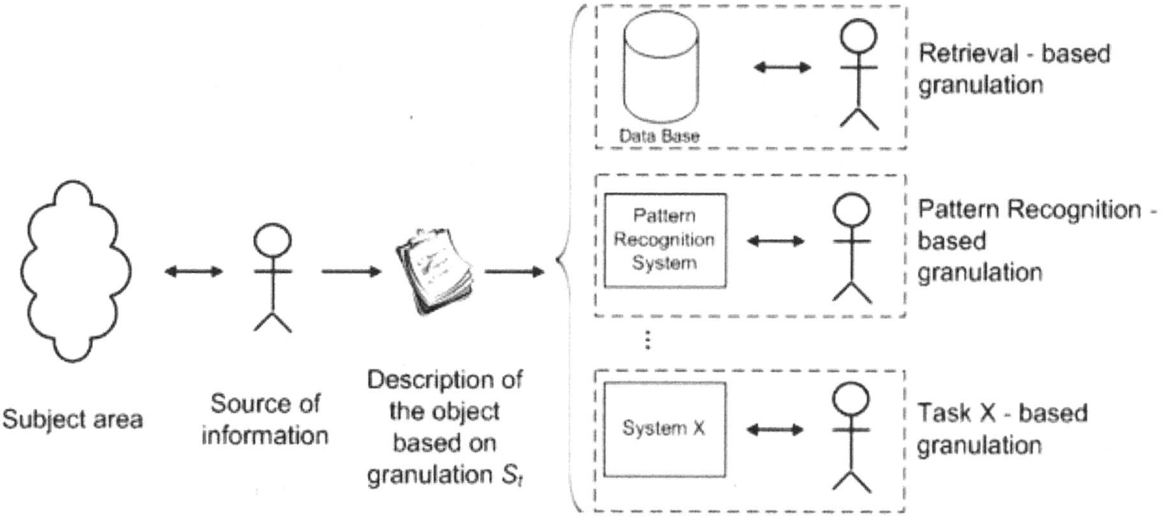

FUTURE RESEARCH DIRECTIONS

Because we have solved fundamental theoretical problems needed to develop human-centric systems to evaluate the status and monitor the progress of complex processes, we see future research directions in an expansion into new application areas.

For problem 1, we see perspectives in the personalization of a person's interaction with the digital world. The digital world - social networks, e-government, digital services, etc. - has become an essential part of our everyday life. However, our interaction with it is still not so comfortable and personalized as with the physical world. The first steps in this direction are described in (Ryjov, 2014b).

Generalization of problem 2 is task-driven information granulation. When solving this problem, we have proposed an optimal and robust information granulation for information retrieval. Can we do the same for other tasks like pattern recognition, data mining, reasoning, etc.? The general picture for this direction is presented in Figure 10 (Ryjov, 2015).

The technology of evaluation and monitoring of complex processes is a framework for a big part of the automation of knowledge work tasks. Many analysts work every day in this paradigm (Figure 2), and automating their work based on the described results will dramatically increase their effectiveness and efficiency.

Fuzzy logic is a natural mathematical foundation for Hybrid Intelligence. Described solutions for problems 1-3 are the solution of fundamental issues for developing optimal Hybrid Intelligence systems.

CONCLUSION

A big part of "tasks that rely on complex analysis, subtle judgments, and creative problem solving" (McKinsey Global Institute, 2013, p. 41) is evaluation of the status and monitoring the progress of processes in business, economy, society, etc. Modeling and control for these processes are very different from physical and technical ones. These processes are unique in the physical sense – a series of independent experiments is not possible; we cannot measure parameters like in physics – "measuring device" is a human being; we do not have adequate models like heat transfer equation – processes are described in natural language or the form of parametric dependencies, etc. As a result, we can conclude that classical mathematics is not suitable for describing and modeling socio-economic processes due to colossal complexity, uncertainty, vagueness. Only the right mixes of computer intelligence and human intelligence can solve these problems.

ACKNOWLEDGMENT

The author would like to express his deep appreciation to professors V.B. Kudrjavtcev and A.S. Stogalov from Lomonosov Moscow State University (Russia); professors N.M. Ahkmedzhanov and R.G. Oganov from Federal State Institution "National Research Center for Preventive Medicine" of the Ministry of Healthcare of the Russian Federation (Russia); professor L.A. Zadeh from Berkeley, California (USA); professors E. Kerre and G. de Cooman from Gent University (Belgium); professor Y. Nishiwaki from Osaka University (Japan); Mr. A. Fattah from IAEA (Austria); Mr. W.-E. Matzke from Cadence Design Systems (Germany) for fruitful work on projects based on technology to evaluate and monitor complex processes.

REFERENCES

Ahkmedzhanov, N. M., Zhukotcky, A. V., Kudrjavtcev, V. B., Oganov, R. G., Rastorguev, V. V., Ryjov, A. P., & Stogalov, A. S. (2003). System for evaluation and monitoring of risks of cardiovascular disease [in Russian]. *Intelligent Systems*, 7, 5–38.

Ashby, W. R. (1956). *An Introduction to Cybernetics*. Chapman and Hall. doi:10.5962/bhl.title.5851

Buckley, J. J. (1985). Fuzzy hierarchical analysis. *Fuzzy Sets and Systems*, 17(3), 233–247. doi:10.1016/0165-0114(85)90090-9

DARPA. (2018). *AI Next Campaign*. Retrieved from https://www.darpa.mil/work-with-us/ai-next-campaign

Dickson, B. (2017) *What is the difference between artificial and augmented intelligence?* Retrieved from https://bdtechtalks.com/2017/12/04/what-is-the-difference-between-ai-and-augmented-intelligence/

Engelbart, D. C. (1962). *Augmenting human intellect: a conceptual framework*. Retrieved from https://www.dougengelbart.org/pubs/augment-3906.html

IBM. (2018). *Cognitive computing. Preparing for the Future of Artificial Intelligence*. Retrieved from https://research.ibm.com/cognitive-computing/ostp/rfi-response.shtml

Lebedev, A. A., & Ryjov, A. P. (2009). Design team capability and project progress evaluation based on information monitoring technology. In *Proceedings of the 5th International Conference on Soft Computing, Computing with Words and Perceptions in System Analysis, Decision and Control*. Famagusta, Cyprus: IEEE. 10.1109/ICSCCW.2009.5379492

Licklider, J. C. R. (1960). Man-Computer Symbiosis. *IRE Transactions on Human Factors in Electronics, HFE-1*, 4-11. Retrieved from http://groups.csail.mit.edu/medg/people/psz/Licklider.html

McKinsey Global Institute. (2013). *Disruptive technologies: Advances that will transform life, business, and the global economy.* Retrieved from https://www.mckinsey.com/insights/business_technology/disruptive_technologies

Mesarovich, M. D., Macko, D., & Takahara, Y. (1970). *Theory of hierarchical multilevel systems.* Academic Press.

NSF. (2019 a). *NSF's 10 Big Ideas.* Retrieved from https://www.nsf.gov/news/special_reports/big_ideas/index.jsp

NSF. (2019 b). *NSF's 10 Big Ideas. Future of Work at the Human-Technology Frontier.* Retrieved from https://www.nsf.gov/news/special_reports/big_ideas/human_tech.jsp

Rostamy, A. A. A., Meysam, S., Behnam, A., & Bakhshi, T. F. (2012). Using fuzzy analytical hierarchy process to evaluate main dimensions of business process reengineering. *Journal of Applied Operational Research, 4*(2), 69–77.

Rouse, M. (2017, July). *Augmented intelligence.* Retrieved from https://whatis.techtarget.com/definition/augmented-intelligence

Ryjov, A. (1988). *The principles of fuzzy set theory and measurement of fuzziness* [in Russian]. Dialog-MSU Publishing.

Ryjov, A. (2001). On information aggregation in fuzzy hierarchical systems [in Russian]. *Intelligent Systems, 6*, 341–364.

Ryjov, A. (2003). Fuzzy Linguistic Scales: Definition, Properties and Applications. In L. Reznik & V. Kreinovich (Eds.), *Soft Computing in Measurement and Information Acquisition* (pp. 23–38). Springer. doi:10.1007/978-3-540-36216-6_3

Ryjov, A. (2004). *Models of information retrieval in a fuzzy environment* [in Russian]. MSU Publishing.

Ryjov, A. (2004). Information Monitoring Systems as a Tool for Strategic Analysis and Simulation in Business. In *Proceeding of the International Conference on Fuzzy Sets and Soft Computing in Economics and Finance.* Saint-Petersburg, Russia: RFSA.

Ryjov, A. (2012). Modeling and Optimization of Information Retrieval for Perception-Based Information. In F. Zanzotto, S. Tsumoto, N. Taatgen, & Y.Y. Yao (Eds), *Proceedings of the International Conference on Brain Informatics 2012* (pp. 140-149). Berlin: Springer. 10.1007/978-3-642-35139-6_14

Ryjov, A. (2013). Systems for evaluation and monitoring of complex processes and their applications [in Russian]. *Intelligent Systems, 17*(1-4), 104–117.

Ryjov, A. (2014a). Human-centric systems for evaluating the status and monitoring the progress for socio-political processes. In *Proceedings of the 8th International Conference on Theory and Practice of Electronic Governance.* New York: ACM Conference Publications. 10.1145/2691195.2691285

Ryjov, A. (2014b). Personalization of Social Networks: Adaptive Semantic Layer Approach. In W. Pedrycz & S.-M. Chen (Eds.), *Social Networks: A Framework of Computational Intelligence* (pp. 21–40). Springer International Publishing Switzerland. doi:10.1007/978-3-319-02993-1_2

Ryjov, A. (2015). Towards an optimal task-driven information granulation. In W. Pedrycz & S.-M. Chen (Eds.), *Information Granularity, Big Data, and Computational Intelligence* (pp. 191–208). Springer International Publishing Switzerland.

Ryjov, A., Belenki, A., Hooper, R., Pouchkarev, V., Fattah, A., & Zadeh, L. A. (1998). Development of an Intelligent System for Monitoring and Evaluation of Peaceful Nuclear Activities (DISNA). Vienna: IAEA, STR-310.

Saaty, T. L. (1980). *The analytic hierarchy process*. McGraw-Hill.

The Economic Times. (2016). *Human-machine super-intelligence may tackle world's problems*. Retrieved from http://articles.economictimes.indiatimes.com/2016-01-01/news/69448299_1_systems-hci-problems

Torra, V. (2002). A review of the construction of hierarchical fuzzy systems. *International Journal of Intelligent Systems*, *17*(5), 531–543. doi:10.1002/int.10036

University of Reading. (2014). *Turing test success marks milestone in computing history*. Retrieved from http://www.reading.ac.uk/news-and-events/releases/PR583836.aspx

WH. (2019). *The National Artificial Intelligence Research and Development Strategic Plan: 2019 update*. Retrieved from https://www.whitehouse.gov/wp-content/uploads/2019/06/National-AI-Research-and-Development-Strategic-Plan-2019-Update-June-2019.pdf?fbclid=IwAR3QZaL_1w3Y4I7pEva8J8qIfjc_azzbSnyBjD63dZO5xqMAwYUA_dQ1IQ0

Zadeh, L. A. (1965). Fuzzy set. *Information and Control*, *8*(3), 338–353. doi:10.1016/S0019-9958(65)90241-X

Zadeh, L. A. (1975). The concept of a linguistic variable and its application to approximate reasoning. Part 1,2,3. Information Sciences, 8, 199-249. doi:10.1016/0020-0255(75)90036-5

ADDITIONAL READING

IBM. (2017). Augmented Intelligence, NOT Artificial Intelligence! Retrieved from https://www.ibm.com/blogs/collaboration-solutions/2017/01/31/augmented-intelligence-not-artificial-intelligence/

Padmanabhan, G. (2018). Industry-Specific Augmented Intelligence: A Catalyst For AI In The Enterprise. *Forbes*. Retrieved from https://www.forbes.com/sites/forbestechcouncil/2018/01/04/industry-specific-augmented-intelligence-a-catalyst-for-ai-in-the-enterprise/#31d1eac31748

Technologies, D. (2017). Dell Technologies 2018 Predictions – Entering the Next Era of Human Machine Partnerships. Retrieved from https://www.delltechnologies.com/en-us/perspectives/dell-technologies-2018-predictions-entering-the-next-era-of-human-machine-partnerships/

Zadeh, L. A. (1997). Towards a theory of fuzzy information granulation and its centrality in human reasoning and fuzzy logic. In: Fuzzy sets and systems vol. 90, 111 - 127. doi:10.1016/S0165-0114(97)00077-8

Zadeh, L. A. (1999). From computing with numbers to computing with words. From manipulation of measurements to manipulation of perceptions. *IEEE Transactions on Circuits and Systems. I, Fundamental Theory and Applications, 46*(1), 105–119. doi:10.1109/81.739259

Zadeh, L. A. (2012a). *Computing with Words: Principal Concepts and Ideas*. Springer Publishing Company. doi:10.1007/978-3-642-27473-2

Zadeh, L. A. (2012b). Fuzzy logic-a personal perspective. *Fuzzy Sets and Systems, 281,* 4–20. doi:10.1016/j.fss.2015.05.009

Zadeh, L. A. (2015). The Information Principle. *Information Sciences, 294,* 540–549. doi:10.1016/j.ins.2014.09.026

KEY TERMS AND DEFINITIONS

Artificial Intelligence (AI): AI is the simulation of human intelligence processes by computer systems. Particular applications of AI include text and speech recognition, machine vision, learning by examples, etc.

Augmented Intelligence: Human-computer systems allow us to combine human intelligence strengths (for example, intuition) and computer's computational power. Augmented intelligence enhances and scales human expertise; AI systems attempt to replicate human intelligence.

Evaluation and Monitoring: It is a process that helps improve performance and achieve results for particular processes. Its goal is to improve current and future management of outputs, outcomes, and impact. It establishes links between the past, present, and future actions.

Fuzzy Logic: Fuzzy Logic is a form of mathematical logic in which the truth values of variables may be any real number between 0 and 1. It is employed to handle the concept of partial truth, where the truth value may range between completely true and completely false. By contrast, in Boolean logic, the truth values of variables may only be the integer values 0 or 1.

Fuzzy Sets: It is a set of elements that have no strict boundaries. Examples of such sets are sets of "young people", "expensive cars", "successful companies", etc.

Hierarchical Systems: It is a special type of systems where elements (objects, names, values, categories, etc.) are represented as being "above", "below", or "at the same level as" one another. A hierarchy can link elements either directly or indirectly, and either vertically or diagonally.

Measurement: Measurement is the assignment of a value (number, symbol, etc.) to a characteristic of an object or event, which can be compared with other objects or events.

Chapter 3
Only Can AI Understand Me?
Big Data Analytics, Decision Making, and Reasoning

Andrew Stranieri
Federation University, Australia

Zhaohao Sun
ⓘ https://orcid.org/0000-0003-0780-3271
Papua New Guinea University of Technology, Papua New Guinea

ABSTRACT

This chapter addresses whether AI can understand me. A framework for regulating AI systems that draws on Strawson's moral philosophy and concepts drawn from jurisprudence and theories on regulation is used. This chapter proposes that, as AI algorithms increasingly draw inferences following repeated exposure to big datasets, they have become more sophisticated and rival human reasoning. Their regulation requires that AI systems have agency and are subject to the rulings of courts. Humans sponsor the AI systems for registration with regulatory agencies. This enables judges to make moral culpability decisions by taking the AI system's explanation into account along with the full social context of the misdemeanor. The proposed approach might facilitate the research and development of intelligent analytics, intelligent big data analytics, multiagent systems, artificial intelligence, and data science.

INTRODUCTION

For decades since its inception in the 1950's, the field of artificial intelligence has included active research in the development of models and algorithms where real-world knowledge is represented explicitly. This is known as symbolic reasoning, and contrasts with models and algorithms where knowledge is indirectly learnt by repeated exposure to data or real-world environments, known as sub-symbolic reasoning (Stranieri & Zeleznikow, 2006). Although, hybrid models including abductive case based reasoning (Sun, Finnie, & Weber, 2005a) and argumentation based neural networks (Stranieri, Zeleznikow, Gawler, &

DOI: 10.4018/978-1-7998-4963-6.ch003

Lewis, 1999) proved useful, in recent years, machine learning based sub-symbolic reasoning has risen in prominence to disrupt AI practice (Kaplan, 2016).

High profile applications in driverless cars (Raviteja, 2020) have raised concerns about who takes responsibility for misdemeanors or errors that vehicle autopilots, trained with machine learning, may make. The degree of machine learning is so high in many driverless cars that the software developers who designed the learning system cannot be held responsible for poor decisions made by the systems that have learnt from long term exposure to traffic environments (Dixit, Chand, & Nair, 2016). Drivers who guide the autopilot's learning similarly ought not be blamed for relying on the autodriving.

Concerns regarding decision making responsibility with reference to automated systems has led to calls, surveyed by (Payrovnaziri et al., 2020) for AI systems to be able to explain their reasonings. The concept of explanation is far from straight forward particularly when AI systems attempt to make decisions in law (Atkinson, Bench-Capon, & Bollegala, 2020). Doshi-Velez, et al, highlights that it is not sufficient for the AI and law programs to arrive at the correct outcome but it must also explain its reasonings properly (Doshi-Velez et al., 2017). Logic based AI and law systems do this by reproducing a trace of the logical statements that were proven during inference chains. Case based reasoning is a kind of experience-based reasoning(Sun & Finnie, 2007). Its principle is that similar problems have similar solutions. In Case-based reasoning, a case is a representation of an experience, which consists of the problem entered in the past and its corresponding solution. The special similarity mentioned here is equality and equivalence. The Case based reasoning systems explain its reasoning by referencing the way in which a case is similar to some past cases and different to others (Ashley, 1991; Sun, Han, & Dong, 2008). Other AI and law programs generate an explanation for an inferred outcome by drawing on knowledge organized in argument schemas. Arrieta, et al, survey explainable artificial intelligence research in recent years to offer a definition (Barredo Arrieta et al., 2020):

Given an audience, an explainable Artificial Intelligence is one that produces details or reasons to make its functioning clear or easy to understand.

In this chapter, we follow (Doshi-Velez et al., 2017) and assume that AI systems will increasingly be required to explain their reasonings and increasingly sophisticated ways for generating explanations will be discovered (Turek, 2020). Secondly, we assume that machine learning algorithms underpinning AI systems will continue to learn more and more sophisticated ways to make decisions or perform actions, particularly as they have increased access to big data (Sun, Strang, & Li, 2018). Our third assumption is that AI agents ought to make morally good decisions and actions (Turek, 2020). Approaches therefore need to be developed to assess the extent to which an AI system has performed, or will perform, appropriate actions for appropriate reasons.

In this chapter, we advance the proposition that a framework that regulates AI systems must involve AI systems that can offer explanations for their actions, but this is not enough. A regulatory framework must also include processes where humans operating through social institutions intervene in the judgement of moral culpability of AI systems. The framework presented in this chapter integrates explainable AI with concepts from jurisprudence and address the following questions:

- How to use feedback from the AI program (system) to discover errors the AI system has made.
- What are the key elements of a framework that can be used to assess the extent to which an AI system may have erred?

- How can decisions regarding appropriate actions to take once an AI system has erred, be made?

This chapter is organized as follows. Section 2 will look at explanation-oriented reasoning as a foundation of explainable AI. Section 3 overviews intelligent agents, multiagent systems, and discusses delegation intelligence which can be considered the foundation of artificial agency. Section 4 looks at mind, intention and responsibility. Section 5 addresses whether AI can understand me and looks at the relationship between terms appropriate and intelligent. Sections 6 and 7 discuss regulations and social behaviors as well as stare decisis. Section 8 presents a framework for regulating AI agents as a multi-agent system. Sections 9 and 10 provide discussion and implications and then end this chapter with some concluding remarks and future work.

EXPLANATION ORIENTED REASONING

Explainable AI has become a hot topic in the past decade thanks to the dramatic development of big data, intelligent analytics, multiagent systems, autonomous vehicles as well as algorithmic trading and medical diagnoses ("Explainable artificial intelligence," 2020; Samek & Müller, 2019; Turek, 2020). This section looks at explanation-oriented reasoning as a foundation of explainable AI.

Explainable AI (XAI) refers to methods and techniques in the application of AI technology such that the results of the AI solution can be explainable and understood by humans ("Explainable artificial intelligence," 2020). XAI can improve the user experience of an AI system, product, and service by helping end users trust that the AI provides a good service. XAI will be essential if human users can understand, appropriately trust, and effectively manage an emerging generation of AI systems such as artificially intelligent machine partners (Turek, 2020). XAI aims to create a suite of intelligent techniques that:

- Produce more explainable models and algorithms, while maintaining a high level of learning performance (prediction accuracy); and
- Enable human users to understand, appropriately trust, and effectively manage the emerging generation of artificially intelligent partners such as AI systems and intelligent agents.

The core of XAI is explanation of every reasoning conducted by AI systems, the latter must explain their rationale. Therefore, explanation-oriented reasoning is the foundation of XAI to realize its aims.

Abduction is a basic explanation-oriented reasoning paradigm (Sun, Finnie, & Weber, 2005a). Abduction is becoming an increasingly popular term in many fields of AI, such as system diagnosis, planning, natural language processing, motivation analysis, and logic programming.

The general form of abduction or abductive reasoning is as follows.

$$\frac{Q}{P \to Q}$$
$$\therefore P \tag{1}$$

where P and Q represent compound propositions in a general setting. P is sometimes called an explanation; thus, abduction provides a reasoning paradigm for explanation-oriented reasoning. For example, Q

represents "fever", P represents "flu", $P \rightarrow Q$ represents: "if fever then flu". Now we have a hypothesis, that is, patient x has flu, then we check if the patient has fever, Based on equation (1). We can explain that patient x has fever, then patient x has suffered the flu, because of the rule, $P \rightarrow Q$. Therefore, abduction based on equation (1) is an explanation-oriented reasoning.

Abductive case-based reasoning is a more practical explanation-oriented reasoning paradigm based on past experience(Sun et al., 2005a). Its general form is as follows.

$$
\begin{array}{c}
Q' \\
\underline{P \rightarrow Q} \\
\therefore P'
\end{array}
\qquad (2)
$$

where P' and Q' represent compound propositions in a general setting, but they are similar to P and Q respectively. P' is sometimes called an explanation; thus, abductive case-based reasoning provides a reasoning paradigm for explanation-oriented reasoning. For example, Q represents "fever, dry cough and fatigue", P represents coronavirus, $P \rightarrow Q$ represents: if coronavirus then fever, dry cough and fatigue. Now we have a patient x in a clinic, x suffered fever, dry cough, and fatigue. Then based on the above abductive reasoning paradigm (2), we have an explanation for this patient. x has been infected with coronavirus.

Furthermore, Q' represents "fever and very dry cough", P' represents possible coronavirus. Now we have a patient y in a clinic, y suffered fever and very dry cough. Then based on above abductive case-based reasoning, we have an explanation for this patient. y might infect coronavirus based on the clinic experience in the past a year since early 2020.

The influential layout of arguments advanced by (Toulmin, 1958) sets out to depict elements that are invariant when arguments are actually generated in practice to support a claim. In doing so, the Toulmin's argument structure focuses less on abduction as an inference rule and more on providing the wider context inherent in an explanation. Figure 1 illustrates an argument that makes a claim that the driver is not culpable given the **data** that he ran over the dog to avoid a pedestrian. The Toulmin **warrant** provides a reason to connect the **data** to the **claim** and the backing provides supporting evidence for the **warrant**.

Stranieri, et al, created a legal knowledge based system that predicted the judgement in a property dispute following divorce by embedding neural networks into the a tree of Toulmin's argument structure (Stranieri et al., 1999). The inferences were made by the neural networks but explained with recourse to the warrant, backing and rebuttal components from the structure. As (Atkinson et al., 2020) points out research into systems where the explanation primitives are tightly coupled, but not identical to, the inference primitives, is in its infancy.

Many AI systems are not monolithic, self-contained systems but involve communication between numerous agents, each performing inferences on their own. A framework for regulating AI systems must accommodate architectures that involve intelligent agents and multi-agent systems. These are discussed next.

INTELLIGENT AGENTS AND MULTIAGENT SYSTEMS

This section overviews intelligent agents, multiagent systems, and looks at delegation intelligence.

Figure 1. Toulmin Layout of Arguments

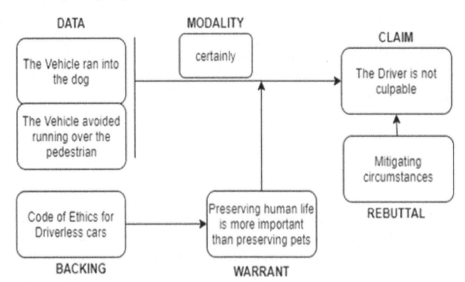

Intelligent Agents

Agent research crosses many disciplines and has been influenced by areas such as artificial intelligence (AI), distributed computing, cloud computing, big data analytics, software engineering, sociology, economics, object-oriented systems, artificial life, and game theory(Herrera, Pérez-Hernández, Kumar Parlikad, & Izquierdo, 2020; Russell & Norvig, 2010).

Currently, one only uses a click of a web browser to retrieve information with a search engine such as Google's Chrome and Baidu. One can also click an app using smartphone to search hotels, cinemas, restaurants, petrol stations, and parks around where one is. Behind all these is the support of intelligent agents or multiagent systems (MAS). At least they have used ideas, principles, and technologies of intelligent agents and MAS (Russell & Norvig, 2010). Intelligent agent technology has become important in both AI and mainstream computer science (Weiss, 2013). It is now making the transition from the information era to the digital era.

Generally speaking, an agent is: "an entity which acts for or in the place of another by authority from him, either as a representative or as an instrument by which a guiding intelligence achieves a result" (Sun & Finnie, 2004; 2010). An intelligent agent (IA) can be defined as an autonomous computerized system which acts, directing its activity towards achieving goals ("Intelligent agent," 2020). In other words, an intelligent agent is a self-contained program capable of controlling its own decision making and acting, based on its perception of its environment, in pursuit of one or more objectives (Sun & Finnie, 2004; 2010; Weiss, 2013).

Intelligent agents have several important characteristics (Sun & Finnie, 2004; 2010; Wooldridge, 2002):

Autonomy: An intelligent agent will perceive, learn, decide, and act on their own (Turek, 2020). An intelligent agent at least is partially independent, self-aware, autonomous. An autonomous agent is a system situated within and a part of the environment that senses that environment and acts on it, over time, in pursuit of its own agenda and to effect what it senses in the future (Sun & Finnie, 2004; 2010).

The environment here can be computer operating systems, a computer screen or its memory, databases, networks or the Internet, etc. The agents live in all these artificial environments.

Local views: No agent has a full global view, or the system is too complex for an agent to exploit such knowledge. Some agents require that an agent "can be viewed" as sensing and acting in an environment; that is, there must exist an environment in which an agent lives.

Decentralization: No agent is designated as controlling (or the system is effectively reduced to a monolithic system).

Different from 'traditional' software/programs, intelligent agents are personalized, semi-autonomous, proactive, adaptive, and so on (Sun & Finnie, 2004; 2010). In this chapter, intelligent agents are considered as autonomous and adaptive ICT programs operating within software environments such as databases or the Internet. They are the computerized counterpart of human agents existing in the society and business as well as on the cloud. Typical tasks performed by intelligent agents could include collecting, filtering, and processing information, scheduling appointments, locating information, alerting to commerce opportunities and making travel arrangements, etc. (Kamdar, Paliwal, Kumar, & Computers, 2018). For example, information agents filter and coherently organize unrelated and scattered data; and autonomous agents can accomplish unsupervised actions.

Multiagent Systems

Multiagent systems (MASs) have been studied for a few decades, and various types of such systems have been developed (Sun & Finnie, 2004; 2010; Weiss, 2013). This subsection looks at the fundamentals and features of MASs.

MAS technology is now one of the most important, exciting, and fast-moving areas of information communications technology (Weiss, 2013; Wooldridge, 2002). For example, cloud computing provides various services on the web. MAS provides airline tickets and package tours consisting of plane flight and hotel stays online. Recently, the term MAS is now used for all types of ICT systems composed of multiple agents showing the following characteristics (Sun & Finnie, 2004; 2010; Weiss, 2013):

- Each agent has incomplete capabilities to solve a problem,
- There is no global system control over agents,
- Data and information are decentralized,
- Computation is asynchronous.

One of the more important factors fostering MAS development is the increasing popularity of the Internet, the Internet of things (IoT), and cloud computing, which provide the basis for an open environment where agents interact with each other to reach their individual or shared goals through machine to machine communications.

MASs have the following four vitally important characteristics: Coordination, cooperation, communication, and negotiation(Sun & Finnie, 2004; 2010).

- Coordination is a property of a system of agents performing some activities in a shared environment. The degree of coordination is the extent to which they avoid extraneous activity by reducing resource contention, avoiding deadlock, and maintaining applicable safety conditions.

- Cooperation is coordination among nonantagonistic agents and arises as they plan and execute their actions in a trustworthy way to achieve their goals. Cooperation among agents, in this case algorithms and humans, depends on trust ("Explainable artificial intelligence," 2020).
- Communication forms the basis of the cooperation, collaboration, and coordination, and is conducted following the communication protocols and the resulting communication methods.
- Negotiation means a compromise for both parties and causes a degradation of their results. The overall aim of all negotiation activities is to permit constructive cooperation from within the group of independently operating agents that have their own goals, based on the win-win principle.

For a single intelligent agent, these characteristics are not important as it could do all the work on its own. However, their importance becomes obvious in the MASs; standards-based mechanisms and means to coordinate, cooperate, and communicate with all kinds of agents are at the root of the MASs. For detail, see (Sun & Finnie, 2004; 2010, pp. 80-96).

MASs have been successfully applied in computer games, films, automatic and dynamic load balancing, high scalability and self-healing networks ("Multi-agent_system," 2020). Generally speaking, all AI systems are MASs (Russell & Norvig, 2010), because they are all used for delegating human beings to complete the requirements and needs of individuals, society and the nations around the world smartly, taking into account the advantage of value and interest. For example, one likes to borrow a book from a library. However, one can use a MAS, search engine, to get it online. This saves one's energy, time, and petrol, because the MAS delegated one's job and completed it optimally.

Delegation Intelligence

Delegation is a core for any modern business, trade, and management as well as communications (Daft & Marcic, 2008, p. 384; Sun, 2017a). Any business process is a delegation process. Supply chain from supplier through organization to customer (Chaffey, 2009) is, in essence, a delegation chain from upstream to downstream. Intelligent agents, apps, and robots are real delegators for delegating our tasks from one to another. One of the main functions of intelligent systems is delegation. Facebook, Google, eBay, JD.com, and WeChat are excellent delegators that provide delegations services to end users. When chatting on any social media, one really does not know that interactions occur with another person, a bot or a delegator. Therefore, modern life, work, and social interaction involves delegation (Sun, 2017a).

Like business intelligence (BI), delegation intelligence (DI) has a few different definitions from different perspectives. For example,

- DI is a framework that allows a delegation business or service to transform data into information, information into knowledge, and knowledge into wisdom (Coronel & Morris, 2015, p. 560). DI has the potential to positively affect a company's culture by creating "business wisdom" and distributing it to all users in an organization. This business wisdom empowers users to make sound business decisions based on the accumulated knowledge of the delegation as reflected on recorded historic operational data (Coronel & Morris, 2015, p. 560)
- DI refers to a collection of information systems (IS) and technologies that support managerial decision makers of operational control by providing information on delegation operations (Turban & Volonino, 2011)

- DI is defined as providing decision makers with valuable information and knowledge by leveraging a variety of sources of data as well as structured and unstructured information on delegation (Sabherwal & Becerra-Fernandez, 2011)

The first definition of DI emphasizes that DI is a framework and creates business wisdom for decision makers through business data, information, knowledge, and their transformations. The second definition stresses "a collection of ISs and technologies" while specifying the decision makers to "managerial decision makers of operational control", and information to "information on delegation operations". The last definition emphasizes that DI provides "decision makers with valuable information and knowledge". Based on the above analysis, DI can be defined as a framework that consists of a set of theories, methodologies, architectures, systems and technologies that support business decision making with valuable data, information, knowledge, and wisdom on delegation from delegators to delegates. This definition reflects the evolution of DI and its technologies from BI (Sun, 2017a).

The key of an intelligent agent as a computerized agent of human agents is its delegation (Sun, 2017a). That is, an intelligent agent must work based on the delegation of human agents, to delegate the human agent to work, to see, to listen to, to read, to think and to make decisions smartly and effectively (Sun, 2017a). In this sense, intelligent agents aim to realize delegation intelligence of human agents more completely in the decades to come. The human beings will be completely liberated from intelligent activities of themselves. Delegation is the core of AI systems that have performed, or will perform, appropriate actions for appropriate reasons with appropriate explanations.

MIND, INTENTION, AND RESPONSIBILITY

Cromzigt notes that the concept of agency implies the concepts of mind, intention and responsibility (Cromzigt, 2016). A human agent consciously uses their mind to choose to perform an action and by so doing, takes responsibility for the action. The notion of responsibility has been widely discussed by philosophers and scholars of business and management as well as computing. They identify attributes of an agent or an object when performing an action in a context of agency. However, arguments to do with AI systems having minds, and taking responsibility are interesting metaphysically but don't help in regulating the actions of AI systems in general and intelligent agents in particular. The approach formulated by (Strawson, 1962) provides the foundation for a framework for regulating AI systems to be presented in the late section of this chapter.

The elements of a framework for regulating the actions of AI agents presented here is motivated by the moral responsibility philosophy of (Strawson, 1962). (Strawson, 1962) side steps debates about the features that define the responsibility an agent possesses by declaring that moral responsibility is better described as a social construct than attributes of an agent. This renders questions about whether an agent intended to perform an action or not as irrelevant. Strawson first outlines the position held by many moral philosophers he categorized as *pessimists*, that if actions are largely pre-determined and not subject to free will, then responsibility for the actions is reduced and people who commit bad actions are not to blame. The opposing view, held by philosophers he called *optimists,* refutes determinism, thereby attributing responsibility for bad actions to the perpetrator who can therefore be rightly blamed and punished. The key purpose for making the distinction between *optimists* and *pessimists*, is to highlight that the distinction is of interest to no-one except moral philosophers. In practice, decision makers involved in determining responsibility and blame;

"..the attitudes and reactions of victims and beneficiaries; of such things as resentment, forgiveness, love, and hurt feelings" ((Strawson, 1962) p5)

Once the attitudes and reactions are considered the decision maker determines that the agent caused the hurt accidentally or unintendedly, or it is inappropriate to apply the judgement, as it is for example with children. Alternatively, the decision maker takes attitudes and reactions into account and determines the agent is culpable. In both cases, the decision maker's reasoning occurs in a social context making the exercise a social construction. This allows Strawson to take the stance that the assignment of moral culpability requires institutions sanctioned by society to support the decision-maker.

In the next section, the regulation of AI systems is broadened to describe some of the social context that is relevant in the relationships between AI systems and human agents. This is a precursor to the subsequent section that provides an overview of regulation of social agents.

CAN AI UNDERSTAND ME?

Explainable AI, whether the AI system is realized through multi-agent architectures or not, aims to advance approaches so that humans can understand an AI system's actions, decisions and behaviors. As AI systems increase in capability, it is reasonable to expect that the AI systems will be able to understand a human's actions, decisions and behaviors. This section will look at the relationship between artificial and human intelligent agents. This is the foundation of addressing whether only AI can understand me. The authors' perspective, in the first person, is offered as follows:

We are academic staff members at university. We have at least four roles at work. Firstly, we have to teach undergraduate students and postgraduate students appropriately and with high quality based on the codes of conduct and expectations, set by the university, wider community and government departments. Can AI understand me? If AI can understand me appropriately, then AI must first understand my social context including the codes of conduct, competing obligations we have to our students, spouses, friends, and others, and then use it to judge if we have taught our students appropriately. To our knowledge, no AI system has been used to understand our social context including our teaching activities, although lots of data and digital images from cameras installed in classrooms existing somewhere or sometimes.

Secondly, we undertake research and aim to publish quality research papers with international visibility. To this end, we have to keep abreast of the state-of-the-art big data analytics, cloud computing, business intelligence, data science, and artificial intelligence, and other disciplines. First of all, we must observe the ethics of ACM and the ethics of AI (Bostrom & Yudkowsky, 2018). Can AI understand me? If yes, AI systems must understand the ethics of ACM and the ethics of AI. Then they understand whether I have undertaken research appropriately. To my knowledge, no AI systems have been used to understand my research activities, although my research manuscripts have been screened by advanced AI systems and check whether my manuscript has plagiarized a lot or have a number of typo errors or grammatical errors. However, AI systems cannot understand whether my research idea is original, the abstract of my research manuscript is creative, and the basic structure of my research manuscript is creative. Furthermore, no AI systems can create original ideas towards changing the impossible to possible and make the unimaginable imaginable, because idea discovery is still not a matured research area in AI and machine learning in particular, computer science, data science and big data analytics in general.

Thirdly, we are citizens of a developed country, my ordinary behaviors must observe the national law and regional regulations appropriately. Otherwise, I would face the court and might be sentenced to jail if I would breach the law and regulations. Can AI understand me? If yes, AI systems must first understand the laws and regional regulations appropriately. Then the AI systems can advise me whether I might breach the laws or regulations timely and appropriately. However, no AI systems as a part of artificial brain embedded into our natural brains to advise us timely and appropriately, although a smartphone and a laptop have been indispensable tools to augment our cognition in terms of intelligence development and knowledge base systems.

Fourthly, different from the knowledge instinct (Mayorga & Perlovsky, 2018), as scholars and researchers, we have our own idea instinct. That is, I have recorded my journey of intuition, imagination, creation, formation, and publication for my research careers over the past two decades. All this is an innovative and creative force for us to undertake research activities in the past, present, and in the coming decade. Can AI understand me? If, yes, AI systems must first understand my idea instinct based on my research career development appropriately. Then the AI systems should have an idea engine, not only a knowledge base and inference engine (Russell & Norvig, 2010). The idea engine is a mechanism for initiating and manipulating intuition, imagination, creation, formation, and publication. So far, this is still one of the most difficult topics in AI and artificial mind. There is little practical progress in this area. We will advance AI system designs that consist of an idea engine, a model engine and a knowledge engine as future research.

In fact, we have played more roles as a natural individual living in this global village. If AI can understand me, then AI systems must also understand my environment surrounding my living area and help me to make appropriate decisions timely as the instant message reminds me "you have a new instant message, darling."

More generally, if AI can understand me. AI systems should first make appropriate decisions just as I have done during my working and engaging in public affairs. However, AI systems may also learn inappropriate rules, for example, if people consider the rule to be "cheating" or "unfair". Then cheating and unfair implied inappropriate ("Explainable artificial intelligence," 2020). AI systems can also deceive humans often. For example, if one plays a computer game, one knows that there are a lot of deception algorithms and strategies that make the player into a pit, and finally conceded that one has been defeated by the computer game armed by AI deception strategies and algorithms.

A human can audit if the rules in an XAI are appropriate. However, not every reasoning is appropriate. For example, from a fundamental viewpoint, only three reasoning paradigms are appropriate and valid from a logical viewpoint, whereas other five reasoning paradigms are not appropriate nor valid (Sun, 2017b). Each of them will easily lead to inappropriate results. This implies that all the reasoning chains based on these five reasoning paradigms are inappropriate and invalid. The above discussion on the question: Can AI understand me? and the appropriate reasoning also implies that explainable AI is a hard problem, even if we do not consider the combinatorial complexity of big data, machine learning, data mining from big data (Mayorga & Perlovsky, 2018).

AI systems will continue to learn more and more sophisticated ways to make decisions or perform actions, particularly as they have increasing access to big data, and embedded with big data analytics in particular and intelligent analytics in general. Our third assumption is that AI agents ought to make morally good decisions and actions ("Explainable artificial intelligence," 2020). Approaches therefore need to be developed to assess the extent to which an AI system has performed, or will perform, appropriate actions for appropriate reasons. Broersen approaches this with a proposal to build intelligent systems that model the responsibilities an AI agent has so that its execution of actions can be formally tested (Broersen, 2014). But, as Prakken points out that this assumes complete knowledge of the legal and situational knowledge of a world that doesn't change an unrealistic expectation (Prakken, 2017).

"AI system has performed, or will perform, appropriate actions for appropriate reasons with appropriate explanations".

Now a research problem is raised: What is the relationship between terms appropriate and intelligent? We can argue it as follows.

That is, a system has performed, or will perform, appropriate actions for appropriate reasons with appropriate explanations, then this system is intelligent. Vice versa, an intelligent system should perform appropriate actions for appropriate reasons with appropriate explanation. In this sense. we can claim that in explainable AI,

appropriate » intelligent

Human users should be able to determine when to trust the AI system and when the AI system should be distrusted ("Explainable artificial intelligence," 2020). However, this might be unsolvable, just as Turing test (Turing, 1950). However, this assertion implies that it is important for us to look at regulating the behaviors of intelligent agents in particular and AI systems in general.

Fairness, accountability, and transparency are the basis for explainable AI, for example, I am a world class AI scholar. In the traditional world, this claim might be fake. However, in the web world, this can be verified and recognized easily, because WoS (the web of science), Scopus, Google scholar, Semantic scholar, and Researchgate can be used to verify if one is a world class AI scholar. Appropriate, explainable and trustworthy are the consequence of global fairness, accountability, and transparency (Sample, 2017).

REGULATIONS AND SOCIAL BEHAVIORS

With the development of XAI, regulation of intelligent agents in particular and AI systems in general become increasingly important. For example, The EU (European Union) has carried out a right to explanation in General Data Protection Right (GDPR) to deal with the potential problems stemming from the rising importance of algorithms since 2018 (Wachter, Mittelstadt, & Floridi, 2017).

Lessig identifies four types of mechanisms that regulate social behaviors; the law, market forces, social norms, and natural phenomena (Lessig, 2009). A simple example illustrates these mechanisms. Motor vehicle speed along suburban streets may be regulated using the law by the implementation of an ordinance that sets a maximum speed, appropriate signage to inform drivers, speed detection mechanisms, and appropriate penalties for offenders. Motor vehicle speed may also be regulated with the installation of speed humps. In this case, no ordinance needs to be passed, no signage is needed, and penalties are not relevant as the humps provide a natural barrier to speed. Similarly, the regulation of individual smoking could be realized by a legislative ban on smoking. However, experience with prohibition of alcohol suggests that the black market and other side effects of such an attempt are undesirable. Instead, smoking is more aptly regulated by market forces, by ensuring that the price of cigarettes is kept extremely high in conjunction with extensive advertising campaigns that aim to alter social norms so that smoking becomes socially undesirable. Bans on advertising tobacco at point of sale implemented in many countries are further examples of economic type constraints.

Natural barriers are very strong mechanisms for regulation. As Lessig points out there is no need for laws prohibiting the theft of skyscrapers because of the physical impossibility of stealing an entire building (Lessig, 2009). In the physical world natural barriers such as humps on roads or immoveable buildings are typically obvious. In cyberspace, natural barriers are implemented by software and are not so obvious. Lessig uses an example about chat rooms organized by a large, global internet service provider (Lessig, 2009). The number of participants in a chat room is regulated by software that admits users up to the maximum number and displays a message inviting others to try later. The regulation of participants in chat rooms using software restricting access is not as transparent as it would be if the regulation was implemented with laws, market incentives or social norms.

The four types of mechanisms that realize the regulation of activity are applied in conjunction with each other. A campaign to reduce addiction to tobacco involves legislation to restrict direct advertising together with encouraging greater awareness of the effects of smoking to change social norms. A focus on a single type of constraint can lead to regulation attempts that are too specific. According to (Liu et al., 2020), the response in some states in the United States to DeepFakes, deep learning based image generation, that produces fake images and videos, has resulted in legislation that has been criticized by many commentators as dangerously specific.

The framework for regulating AI systems described below involves the four types of constraints as central concepts. However, another concept that is also relevant is that of Stare Decisis, described next.

Stare decisis is a fundamental principle in common law legal systems. The principle dictates that the reasoning, used by decision-makers in new cases must follow the reasoning used by decision-makers in courts at the same or higher level in the hierarchy. The principle is not absent in civil law jurisdictions but only applied differently (Fon & Parisi, 2006). Wasserstrom identifies three types of stare decisis; traditional, personal, and local stare decisis (Wasserstrom, 1961). The principle of stare decisis presumes a hierarchy of courts. Under traditional stare decisis, a court is bound by prior decisions of courts of equal or higher level as illustrated in **Figure 2**, Personal stare decisis illustrated in **Figure 3** reflects the tendency that judges exhibit to make current decisions in a similar manner to past decisions where facts are similar. Personal stare decisis is not absolute as there are many factors that could influence a decision maker to arrive at a different outcome given the same fact scenarios. Local stare decisis reflects the principle that judges tend to make decisions consistent with their peers as illustrated in **Figure 4**.

The vast majority of cases that come before the courts are not extraordinary in that they do not involve extraordinary facts, and do not lead to unexpected outcomes. They are commonplace cases and are distinct from cases that set a precedent for the future, generally regarded as landmark cases (Stranieri &

Figure 2. Traditional Stare Decisis

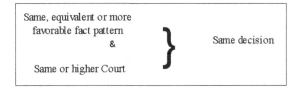

Figure 3. Personal Stare Decisis

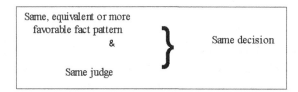

Zeleznikow, 1998). In jurisdictions where traditional stare decisis is emphasised, any case that is currently viewed as commonplace could be used in the future as a landmark case. This blurs the distinction between landmarks and commonplace cases. However, in domains where traditional stare decisis is not strongly followed, if a case is regarded as commonplace at the time of decision, it is extremely unlikely to be invoked in the future as a landmark case. An ordinary case impacts by adding to the body of cases for personal and local stare decisis.

Our traditional, local, and personal stare decisis conceptualisation also has ramifications relating to the way in which we evaluate explanations generated by computer systems that use knowledge from a KDD process (Laudon & Laudon, 2016). In domains characterised with traditional stare decisis, reasons for a first instance decision often involve principles laid down by appellate courts. In the absence of traditional stare decisis, explanations cannot be rigidly derived from principles, because none have been specifically laid down by appellate courts. Explanations must necessarily be further removed from the sequence of reasoning steps used to infer an outcome.

FRAMEWORK FOR REGULATING AI AGENTS

To motivate the framework for regulating AI agents advanced in this chapter, we outlined the Strawson approach (Strawson, 1962). Following that, some comments were made about the social nature of the relationship between humans and agents and four types of regulation in general. The concept of stare decisis from jurisprudence was then advanced. These elements underpin before describing our regulatory framework. In the penultimate section we apply our framework to a hypothetical AI system action and discuss ramifications arising from our framework.

The key elements of a framework advanced for the regulation of AI agents are:

- **AI System has agency.** Defining an AI agent as an actor with complete agency over its actions. A process is defined by law for registering a program as an AI agent.

Figure 4. Local Stare Decisis

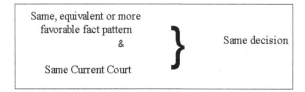

- **AI System has a human sponsor.** Defining a sponsor as a human agent who is responsible for maintaining the AI agent's registration and enacting any sanctions imposed on the agent.
- **Explainable AI is a registration requirement.** Technologies for enabling an agent to explain its actions are required to be built into the agent as a pre-requisite for registration.
- **Hierarchy of courts with stare decisis.** A hierarchy of courts is established to hear complaints about AI agents.

Defining an AI agent as an actor with agency entails a registration and approval process in a manner analogous to that currently imposed on medical devices. Certifying authorities such as the Federal Drugs Administration (FDA) follow a process to approve devices as medical equipment. Deployment options are limited by regulation unless the device is certified. For instance, hospitals in most jurisdictions are bound to use only certified devices. Similarly, AI agents can be certified, and legal regulations passed that prohibit the deployment of uncertified agents.

The role of an AI agent sponsor is defined as a legal entity (individual or organization) that is associated with the AI agent. The sponsor is required to adhere to sanctions applied to the AI agent. The most extreme sanction is the de-registration of the AI agent, but other forms of sanctions may include re-training or other modifications.

Technological mechanisms that enable an AI agent to explain its actions as appropriate are required to be built into an AI agent that seeks to be certified.

A legal system that includes a hierarchy of courts is constituted to hear cases of AI agency misdemeanor. The AI agent is the actor that has agency over their actions and is on trial over the actions. A first instance court, composed of a judicial decision maker must ascertain the facts, by hearing an explanation from the AI agent and other human or non-human agents. The decision maker must then deliberate and ultimately reach a judgement following principles of stare decisis set out in previous cases. The sponsor is required to ensure the sanctions ordered in the judgement are carried out. Penalties include de-registration of the agent and fines. The sponsor has the capacity to appeal the decision to a higher court.

These elements ensure that an AI agent's actions are regulated by drawing on each of the four types of constraints presented by (Lessig, 2009). Technological constraints apply because the AI agent is required to exhibit technological sophistication in its capacity to draw inferences and generate explanations for its actions in order to pass regulation requirements. Social constraints are incorporated into the framework because decisions by regulators, or courts will need to be publicly accessible and any that depart from social norms will attract complaints and influence the decision makers.

Economic constraints are enabled with the introduction of a sponsor role. The AI agent sponsor invests in an AI agent initially by funding its registration. The sponsor has a vested interest in maintaining the agent's viability. Any sanctions imposed on the agent by courts must be carried out by the sponsor and impact economically on the sponsor.

In what follows, we propose an AI system for regulating AI agents to further elaborate what we discussed above.

The AI system for regulating AI agents is a multi-agent system to raise a cardiovascular incident alarm given an ECG trace from wearable sensors. The multi-agent system comprises four different AI systems, each receiving data from a patient's wearable sensors, processing it independently and forwarding the alarm inference to a multi-agent Ensemble system. Here, an agent in the ensemble multi-agent system represents each one of the inference systems and negotiates with the agents representing the other inference systems, using an argumentation-based communication protocol. The result of the negotiation is a decision to raise an alarm or not. Each of the four different AI systems that perform independent inferences about whether to raise an alarm or not, has been registered as a medical AI System by respective human sponsors Xiao, Jill, Mustafa, and Guillermo. The ensemble multi-agent system has been sponsored by Hiroto. All five AI systems have been registered as AI agents with an international regulatory authority.

Andrea had been feeling unwell from a minor hospital heart procedure. Doctors recommended that she rest at home monitored with an ECG linked to the AI systems. The AI System had not raised alarms when Andrea had a myocardial infarction and died. Her husband advanced a civil lawsuit against the sponsors demanding they supply the ECG traces and their reasons for not raising an alarm. Under the conditions of the AI System registration, each AI system supplied the ECG trace and a rationale to explain its actions. Each AI System has agency, so it responded to the demand, not the human sponsor, who is not responsible for the AI's actions.

The AI system Xiao sponsored used deep learning and had in-fact raised an alarm as did the system Guillermo had sponsored. However, the other systems did not raise an alarm. Their explanation was that, the prior ECG trace, did not reveal abnormal ECG patterns. Both systems reproduced training data from recent months. The ensemble system sponsored by Hiroto explained that it had relied on an algorithm that was heavily influenced by the majority viewpoints.

Andrea's family restricted their civil action to Hiroto's ensemble system, Jill's backpropagation system and Mustafa's recurrent neural network system. The matter was heard in the first instance court where a judge followed previous cases that were similar and ruled that the ensemble AI system was at fault, but not the others. The backpropagation and recurrent neural networks erred but, they could not reasonably be expected to never err, that was why they fed their alarm output to the ensemble. The judge ruled that the ensemble AI system be decommissioned and that the other two systems be permitted to resume operations as feeder systems to other ensemble AI systems.

The Ensemble AI system appealed to a higher Court on the grounds that it cannot be expected to overturn incorrect suggestions from feeder AI systems. This time, the judge, taking into consideration that the error had caused death and great suffering, overturned the first instance judge and ordered that the Ensemble AI system, the backpropagation and recurrent network system be decommissioned. This was largely done to send a strong signal to other AI systems and sponsors that the Courts will not tolerate life-threatening errors by AI Systems.

DISCUSSION AND IMPLICATIONS

The elements of a framework for regulating the actions of AI agents presented here is motivated by the moral responsibility philosophy of (Strawson, 1962). (Strawson, 1962) side steps debates about the features that define the responsibility an agent possesses by declaring that moral responsibility is better described as a social construct than attributes of an agent. This renders questions about whether an agent intended to perform an action or not as irrelevant. The assumption that responsibility is a social phenomenon, which also aligns with the notion that agent's actions should be regulated in a civil society and thus enables us to formulate a social process for judging whether an AI agent's actions are within the bounds of acceptability or bounds of appropriateness. This has the additional benefit of situating the regulation within the confines of existing legal systems with their hierarchy of courts.

The role of sponsor is carefully crafted in our framework so that a human, who can be easily motivated by financial gain, and coerced by the threat of legal sanction, is aligned to the AI agent in a role that is more like the human owner of a wild animal than the creator of an autonomous agent. Few would blame a wild animal who escapes captivity and harms people, but most will sanction the animal's owner for failing to ensure that the animal cannot escape. In the same way, the sponsor does not assume any sort of responsibility for the AI agent's actions but instead assumes the role of the person who maintains the AI agent's registration.

The framework presented in this chapter can conceivably be subverted if unregistered AI agents are deployed in many settings. The incentives for registering an AI agent needs to be carefully engineered as they are in regulation of current medical devices. Manufacturers of medical devices seek out registration because social norms exist in most jurisdictions that frown on backyard devices, regulations requiring registration exist and are strictly enforced and sales are likely to be more plentiful with a registered device. The same rationale for enticing registration of AI agents can readily be imagined.

The proposed AI system for regulating AI agents paints a picture of the full range of complex, socially defined components that are considered by a judge making decisions about moral culpability. It intended to reaffirm Strawson's claim that philosophical constructs of determinism and responsibility are not so pertinent in the reaching decisions in practice.

CONCLUSION

This chapter looked at explanation-oriented reasoning as a foundation of explainable AI, overviewed intelligent agents, multiagent systems, and discussed delegation intelligence, mind, intention and responsibility; these can be considered a foundation of artificial agency. This chapter addressed an interesting question: Can AI understand me? and looked at the relationship between appropriate and intelligent actions to illustrate that decisions about moral culpability, particularly in an era of AI systems learning from big data, are social constructs. As such, the way in which other phenomena are regulated in social communities are described. This resulted in the description of a framework to regulate AI Systems where AI regulations and social behaviors as well as stare decisis and presented a framework for regulating AI agents. The key elements of the framework included the assignment of agency to an AI System, the introduction of a human sponsor responsible for certifying the AI agent with regulatory boards and a hierarchy of courts with human judges to make socially meaningful decisions about moral culpability.

The need to regulate the actions of AI agents becomes more pressing as these agents increase in sophistication driven by the confluence of big data, big data analytics, IoT (the Internet of things) and collaborative decision making that characterizes the modern era according to (McAfee & Brynjolfsson, 2017). However, the regulation of AI agents is challenging partly because ensuring these agents act morally and explain their reasoning is difficult to achieve. In this chapter, we followed the philosophy of (Strawson, 1962) in declaring responsibility to be a social construct and not an attribute of an agent. This enabled us to define elements of a framework for the regulation of AI agents. Taken together, the elements of the framework combine to posit a workable, scalable, solution to the problem of regulating AI agents.

In the future work, we will develop the proposed AI system for regulating AI agents and apply it to a real-world medical incident processing, taking into account our framework for regulating agents and explainable AI.

REFERENCES

Ashley, K. D. (1991). Reasoning with cases and hypotheticals in HYPO. *International Journal of Man-Machine Studies*, *34*(6), 753–796. doi:10.1016/0020-7373(91)90011-U

Atkinson, K., Bench-Capon, T., & Bollegala, D. (2020). Explanation in AI and law: Past, present and future. *Artificial Intelligence*, *289*, 103387. Advance online publication. doi:10.1016/j.artint.2020.103387

Barredo Arrieta, A., Díaz-Rodríguez, N., Del Ser, J., Bennetot, A., Tabik, S., Barbado, A., Garcia, S., Gil-Lopez, S., Molina, D., Benjamins, R., Chatila, R., & Herrera, F. (2020). Explainable Explainable Artificial Intelligence (XAI): Concepts, taxonomies, opportunities and challenges toward responsible AI. *Information Fusion*, *58*, 82–115. doi:10.1016/j.inffus.2019.12.012

Bostrom, N., & Yudkowsky, E. (2018). The Ethics of Artificial Intelligence. In *Cambridge Handbook of Artificial Intelligence*. Cambridge University Press.

Broersen, J. (2014). Responsible intelligent systems. *KI-Künstliche Intelligenz*, *28*(3), 209–214. doi:10.100713218-014-0305-4

Chaffey, D. (2009). *E-business and E-commerce Management*. Prentice Hall.

Coronel, C., & Morris, S. (2015). *Database Systems: Design, Implementation, and Management* (11th ed.). Cengage Learning.

Cromzigt, L. (2016). Strawson's take on responsibility applied to AI. *Student Undergraduate Research E-journal!*, *2*.

Daft, R., & Marcic, D. (2008). *Management: The New Workplace*. China Cengage Learning.

Dixit, V. V., Chand, S., & Nair, D. J. (2016). Autonomous vehicles: Disengagements, accidents and reaction times. *PLoS One*, *11*(12), e0168054. doi:10.1371/journal.pone.0168054 PMID:27997566

Doshi-Velez, F., Kortz, M., Budish, R., Bavitz, C., Gershman, S., O'Brien, D., . . . Wood, A. J. a. p. a. (2017). *Accountability of AI under the law: The role of explanation*. Academic Press.

Explainable artificial intelligence. (2020). In *Wikipedia*. https://en.wikipedia.org/wiki/Explainable_artificial_intelligence

Fon, V., & Parisi, F. (2006). Judicial precedents in civil law systems: A dynamic analysis. *International Review of Law and Economics*, *26*(4), 519–535. doi:10.1016/j.irle.2007.01.005

Herrera, M., Pérez-Hernández, M., Kumar Parlikad, A., & Izquierdo, J. (2020). Multi-Agent Systems and Complex Networks: Review and Applications in Systems Engineering. *Processes (Basel, Switzerland)*, *8*(3), 312. doi:10.3390/pr8030312

Intelligent agent. (2020). In *Wikipedia*. https://en.wikipedia.org/wiki/Intelligent_agent

Kamdar, R., Paliwal, P., & Kumar, Y., & Computers. (2018). A state of art review on various aspects of multi-agent system. *Journal of Circuits. Systems*, *27*(11), 1830006.

Kaplan, J. (2016). *Artificial intelligence: What everyone needs to know*. Oxford University Press. doi:10.1093/wentk/9780190602383.001.0001

Laudon, K. G., & Laudon, K. C. (2016). *Management Information Systems: Managing the Digital Firm* (14th ed.). Pearson.

Lessig, L. (2009). *Code: And other laws of cyberspace*: ReadHowYouWant. com.

Liu, H.-Y., Maas, M., Danaher, J., Scarcella, L., Lexer, M., & Van Rompaey, L. (2020). Artificial intelligence and legal disruption: A new model for analysis. *Law, Innovation and Technology*, *12*(2), 1–54. doi:10.1080/17579961.2020.1815402

Mayorga, R. V., & Perlovsky, L. (2018). Sapience, Consciousness, and Knowledge Instinct. In Toward artificial sapience. Principles and methods for wise systems (pp. 1-24). Academic Press.

McAfee, A., & Brynjolfsson, E. (2017). *Machine, platform, crowd: Harnessing our digital future*. WW Norton & Company.

Multi-agent system. (2020). In *Wikipedia*. https://en.wikipedia.org/wiki/Multi-agent_system

Payrovnaziri, S. N., Chen, Z., Rengifo-Moreno, P., Miller, T., Bian, J., Chen, J. H., Liu, X., & He, Z. (2020). Explainable artificial intelligence models using real-world electronic health record data: A systematic scoping review. *Journal of the American Medical Informatics Association: JAMIA*, *27*(7), 1173–1185. doi:10.1093/jamia/ocaa053 PMID:32417928

Prakken, H. (2017). On the problem of making autonomous vehicles conform to traffic law. *Artificial Intelligence Law. Innovation and Technology*, *25*(3), 341–363.

Raviteja, T. (2020). An introduction of autonomous vehicles and a brief survey. *Journal of Critical Reviews*, *7*(13), 196–202.

Russell, S., & Norvig, P. (2010). *Artificial Intelligence: A Modern Approach* (3rd ed.). Prentice Hall.

Sabherwal, R., & Becerra-Fernandez, I. (2011). *Business Intelligence: Practices, Technologies, and Management*. John Wiley & Sons, Inc.

Samek, W., & Müller, K.-R. (2019). Towards explainable artificial intelligence. In *Explainable AI: interpreting, explaining and visualizing deep learning* (pp. 5–22). Springer. doi:10.1007/978-3-030-28954-6_1

Sample, I. (2017). Computer says no: why making AIs fair, accountable and transparent is crucial. *The Guardian*.

Stranieri, A., & Zeleznikow, J. (1998). *The Role of Open Texture and Stare Decisis in Data Mining Discretion*. Academic Press.

Stranieri, A., & Zeleznikow, J. (2006). Knowledge discovery from legal databases—Using neural networks and data mining to build legal decision support systems. In *Information Technology and Lawyers* (pp. 81–117). Springer. doi:10.1007/1-4020-4146-2_4

Stranieri, A., Zeleznikow, J., Gawler, M., & Lewis, B. (1999). A hybrid rule–neural approach for the automation of legal reasoning in the discretionary domain of family law in Australia. *Artificial Intelligence and Law, 7*(2-3), 153–183. doi:10.1023/A:1008325826599

Strawson, P. F. (1962). Freedom and Resentment in Free Will. Oxford UP.

Sun, Z. (2017a). *Delegation intelligence-The Next Frontier for Making Business Success* (BAIS No. 17007). https://www.researchgate.net/publication/318813383_Delegation_Intelligence_The_Next_Frontier_for_Making_Business_Success

Sun, Z. (2017b). A logical approach to experience-based reasoning. *Journal of New Mathematics and Natural Computation, 13*(1), 21–40. doi:10.1142/S179300571750003X

Sun, Z., & Finnie, G. (2007). A fuzzy logic approach to experience based reasoning. *International Journal of Intelligent Systems, 22*(8), 867–889. doi:10.1002/int.20220

Sun, Z., & Finnie, G. (2010). Intelligent Techniques in E-Commerce: A Case-based Reasoning Perspective. Berlin: Springer-Verlag.

Sun, Z., Finnie, G., & Weber, K. (2005a). Abductive case-based reasoning. *International Journal of Intelligent Systems, 20*(9), 957–983. doi:10.1002/int.20101

Sun, Z., Han, J., & Dong, D. (2008). *Five Perspectives on Case Based Reasoning.* Paper presented at the ICIC2008, Shanghai, China. 10.1007/978-3-540-85984-0_50

Sun, Z., Strang, K., & Li, R. (2018). Big data with ten big characteristics. *Proceedings of 2018 The 2nd Intl Conf. on Big Data Research (ICBDR 2018), Weihai, China, Oct. 27-29, 2018, ACM International Conference Proceeding Series,* 56-61.

Toulmin, S. (1958). *The Uses of Argument.* Cambridge University Press.

Turban, E., & Volonino, L. (2011). *Information Technology for Management: Improving Strategic and Operational Performance* (8th ed.). Wiley & Sons.

Turek, M. (2020). Explainable Artificial Intelligence (XAI). *DARPA.* https://www.darpa.mil/program/explainable-artificial-intelligence

Turing, A. (1950). Computing Machinery and Intelligence. *Mind, 49*(236), 433–460. doi:10.1093/mind/LIX.236.433

Wachter, S., Mittelstadt, B., & Floridi, L. (2017). Why a right to explanation of automated decision-making does not exist in the general data protection regulation. *International Data Privacy Law, 7*(2), 76–99. doi:10.1093/idpl/ipx005

Wasserstrom, R. A. (1961). *The judicial decision: Toward a theory of legal justification.* Stanford University Press.

Weiss, G. (2013). *Multiagent systems* (2nd ed.). MIT Press.

Wikipedia-EAI. (2020, November 5). *Explainable artificial intelligence.* Retrieved November 13, 2020, from Wikipedia: https://en.wikipedia.org/wiki/Explainable_artificial_intelligence

Wikipedia-IA. (2020, November 11). *Intelligent agent.* Retrieved November 13, 2020, from Wikipedia: https://en.wikipedia.org/wiki/Intelligent_agent

Wikipedia-MAS. (2020, November 9). *Multi-agent system.* Retrieved November 13, 2020, from Wikipedia: https://en.wikipedia.org/wiki/Multi-agent_system

Wooldridge, M. (2002). *An Introduction to MultiAgent Systems.* John Wiley & Sons.

ADDITIONAL READING

Delena, D., & Demirkanb, H. (2013). Data, information and analytics as services. *Decision Support Systems, 55*(1), 359–363. doi:10.1016/j.dss.2012.05.044

Finnie, G. R., & Sun, Z. (2003). R5 model for case-based reasoning. *Knowledge-Based Systems, 16*(1), 59–65. doi:10.1016/S0950-7051(02)00053-9

Howson, C., Richardson, J., Sallam, R., & Kronz, A. (2019). *Magic Quadrant for Analytics and Business Intelligence Platforms.* Retrieved 7 7, 2019, from Gartner: https://cadran-analytics.nl/wp-content/uploads/2019/02/2019-Gartner-Magic-Quadrant-for-Analytics-and-Business-Intelligence-Platforms.pdf

Sabherwal, R., & Becerra-Fernandez, I. (2011). *Business Intelligence: Practices, Technologies, and Management.* John Wiley & Sons, Inc.

Sample, I. (2017, November 5). Computer says no: why making AIs fair, accountable and transparent is crucial. *The Guardian.*

Sun, Z. (2019). Intelligent Big Data Analytics: A Managerial Perspective. In Z. Sun (Ed.), *Managerial Perspectives on Intelligent Big Data Analytics* (pp. 1–19). IGI-Global. doi:10.4018/978-1-5225-7277-0.ch001

Sun, Z., & Huo, Y. (2020). Intelligence without Data. *Global Journal of Computer Science and Technology C, 20*(1), 25–35. doi:10.34257/GJCSTCVOL20IS1PG25

Sun, Z., & Wang, P. (2017). Big Data, Analytics and Intelligence: An Editorial Perspective. *Journal of New Mathematics and Natural Computation, 13*(2), 75–81. doi:10.1142/S179300571702001X

KEY TERMS AND DEFINITIONS

Artificial Intelligence (AI): Is science and technology concerned with imitating, extending, augmenting, and automating intelligent behaviors of human beings.

Big Data: Is data with at least one of the ten big characteristics consisting of big volume, big velocity, big variety, big veracity, big intelligence, big analytics, big infrastructure, big service, big value, and big market.

Case-Based Reasoning: It is a kind of experience reasoning. It is based on the principle of "similar problems have similar solutions" A case is an experienced problem and its solution. Abductive case-based reasoning is a more practical explanation-oriented reasoning paradigm.

Data Mining: Is a process of discovering various models, summaries, and derived values, knowledge from a large database. Another definition is that it is the process of using statistical, mathematical, logical, AI methods and tools to extract useful information from large databases.

Intelligent Big Data Analytics: Is science and technology about collecting, organizing, and analyzing big data to discover patterns, knowledge, and intelligence as well as other information within the big data based on artificial intelligence and intelligent systems.

Intelligent System: Is a system that can imitate, automate and augment some intelligent behaviors of human beings. Expert systems and knowledge-based systems are examples of intelligent systems.

Machine Learning: Is concerned about how computers can adapt to new circumstances and to detect and extrapolate patterns and knowledge.

Stare Decisis: The requirement that a decision maker in a court makes decisions consistent with his or her past decisions, decisions of courts at the same level and those of higher courts.

Chapter 4
Data Science and Big Data Practice Using Apache Spark and Python

Li Chen
University of the District of Columbia, USA

Lala Aicha Coulibaly
University of the District of Columbia, USA

ABSTRACT

Data science and big data analytics are still at the center of computer science and information technology. Students and researchers not in computer science often found difficulties in real data analytics using programming languages such as Python and Scala, especially when they attempt to use Apache-Spark in cloud computing environments-Spark Scala and PySpark. At the same time, students in information technology could find it difficult to deal with the mathematical background of data science algorithms. To overcome these difficulties, this chapter will provide a practical guideline to different users in this area. The authors cover the main algorithms for data science and machine learning including principal component analysis (PCA), support vector machine (SVM), k-means, k-nearest neighbors (kNN), regression, neural networks, and decision trees. A brief description of these algorithms will be explained, and the related code will be selected to fit simple data sets and real data sets. Some visualization methods including 2D and 3D displays will be also presented in this chapter.

1. INTRODUCTION

Data science is about to solve problems for massive data sets even through the size of the data sets is not the only key factor in this area. Machine learning and deep learning become the centralized focus due to the tremendous success in image processing, computer vision, voice recognitions and natural processing, data classification, and social network applications (Goodfellow et al., 2016; LeCun et al., 2015).

DOI: 10.4018/978-1-7998-4963-6.ch004

Since we still could not find more solid mathematical or computational approaches that are better than existing ones especially deep learning neural networks. Two basic environments researchers and data engineers are using today are the following: (1) Standalone applications that mainly use Python or R Language in addition to traditional C++ and Java, (2) Cloud based applications that involve Apache-Spark as in AWS, Azure, Google Cloud. Some professional software packages such as SAS or MatLab also contain these functionalities.

For individual or small companies, Python and Spark-based Python are the most convenient and economic tools for solving problems in data science. Even though there are many books and web-based sources that provide excellent tutorials, learners still must spend a considerable amount of time to learn the basic techniques in the relatively short time. In this paper, we try to condense the whole learning procedure into this educational article for both aspects of understanding for methods and the practical coding. For mathematics of the methods covered in this paper, see (Chen et al., 2015; Géron, 2019).

The purpose of this paper is to provide practical basics to students and professionals in data science research and industry. These basics include methods often used and the code samples. We first introduce the simple examples using essential tools in data science and big data technology. Then, we present some important algorithms and code samples of applying these algorithms to data science. Those algorithms are mainly related to machine learning and deep learning. Finally, we provide case studies to explain how to deal with real problems in practices.

2. BASIC DATA SCIENCE AND BIGDATA ANALYTICS: BACKGROUND AND TOOLS

A common problem to solve in data science is usually associated with big data and cloud computing under a special infrastructure involving the huge number of computers with software supporting systems called Hadoop and Spark. The algorithmic part is highly related to machine learning and artificial intelligence. Data science today influences everyone's life due to the usage of smartphones, social networks, and business services. Everyone could meet data science problems constantly.

Before we focus on Python, we need to first discussion the cloud computing methodology along with Hadoop and Spark.

2.1 Apache-Spark and the Cloud Computing Methodology

The key to a system for BigData is to be able to handle the petabyte sized problem. It means that the problem needs to be partitioned into smaller pieces so that we can run it on hundreds even thousands of computers in parallel. *Apache Hadoop* and *Apache-Spark* are such open-source systems that enables applications to work with thousands of computation-independent devices.

Hadoop was developed based the parallel computing model of MapReduce. The concept of Mapreduce was introduced in Google for bigTable and cloud computing in 2003. The main idea of Mapreduce is to split (the action of "map") the tasks to many computers/machines, then collect the results from each computer to union them (the action of "reduce"). This realizes the parallel computation. See Figure 1 (Forge, n.d.).

That makes the Python language becoming the most popular in data science.

Figure 1. Map-reduce Computing Model (Forge, n.d.)

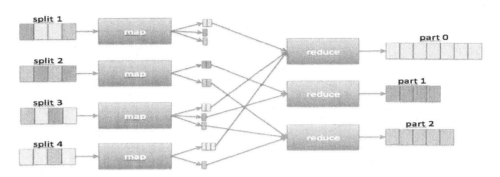

At the time of Google's scientists J.Dean and S. Ghemawat developing Map-reduce (Dean & Ghemawat, 2008), D. Cutting was working on cloud computing as well. He tried to search for a mathematical or logical way to form his structure. When Cutting read the paper (Dean & Ghemawat, 2008), he immediately realized that Mapreduce is the one he needs. Hadoop was developed for users in 2006. However, Hadoop was too hard to use for none-computer science professionals since it uses HDFS the distributed file system that is much slower than memory. Therefore, based on Hadoop, Apache Spark (Spark) was developed at Berkeley in 2010 for the purposed of easiness for users to simplifying the Hadoop. Spark also supports cloud computing especially cluster computing environments. Spark provides high-level library functions for Java, Scala, Python and R.

Apache Spark (Spark) now has renewed its latest version at v3.01. However, Spark v2.3.2 and v2.4.4 is still widely used in public.

From a user's point of view, Cloud Computing refers the virtualized pool of resources. Cluster computing uses multiple computer stations as nodes to complete the complex or massive task. So, cloud computing is usually supported by a cluster of computers (called cluster computing)(Geeks for Geeks, n.d.). The best examples would be Amazon's AWS, Microsoft's Azure, and Google Cloud. Codebricks has the personalized free account to help individuals to learn Spark-based programming. Now, *Google Colab* also made efforts to install *Jupyter Notebook* looking system that can run spark code as well.

What does Spark do? Spark is a software system that provides an operational management for cluster computing (Apache, n.d.).

According to the specification of Spark, "Spark applications run as independent sets of processes on a cluster, coordinated by the ***SparkContext*** object in your main program (called the *driver program*)." (Apache, n.d.) The details for how ***SparkContext*** sends application code and tasks to each executor can be skimmed or glanced in the following figure (Apache, n.d.):

2.2. Python and PySpark

Python is a general-purpose interpreted, interactive, object-oriented, and high-level programming language (Tutorials Point, n.d.). It combines the advantages of many languages including C++, Java, Basic, even Fortran due to Python's powerful packages of computing, graphics, computer vision, and artificial intelligence. MIT and many universities choose Python as the first computer language to teach CS students nowadays.

Figure 2. The Structure of Spark. Source of this diagram is at: https://spark.apache.org/docs/latest/ cluster- overview.html

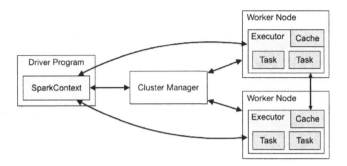

On the other hand, in order to fit the needs of cloud-based computing, Apache-Spark provides PySpark for cloud computing users specially in Python. As we described above Spark is based on MapReduce, so PySpark is one along with other Spark languages such as Java, Scala, and R in the Spark system.

Spark also supports other tools including *Spark SQL* for databases, *MLlib* for machine learning, *GraphX* for graph related computation, and *Structured Streaming* for stream data. See Figure 3. (Apache Spark, n.d.)

2.3 Examples of Data Processing in Python and PySpark

As the most popular computer language today, there are many online compiler and interpreter for Python languages. For the beginning learners, we like to introduce you TutorialPoint (https://www.tutorialspoint. com/python/index.htm). It provides an excellent resource for new learners. For intermediate and experienced professionals, the Jupyter Notebook is the best (https://jupyter.org/). Google Colab has adopted Jupyter Notebook online. So, the user can use it directly. We will give examples in this section.

The following is an example by clicking on https://www.tutorialspoint.com/python/index.htm, and input some line you like.

The first PySpark code usually use the **wordcount** example that contains explicit map-reduce actions in the code. The code means that mapping each line and splitting(map) a line into words with a number for return (splitting is based on a " " space in the code). The reduce function is to add the word together by the numbers accumulated. You can see that each line will be map to different computer node to

Figure 3. Apache Spark Structure (Apache Spark, n.d.) (see https://spark.apache.org/)

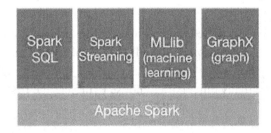

Figure 4. Jupyter Notebook Online Version

Figure 5. An Online Python environment for easy coders

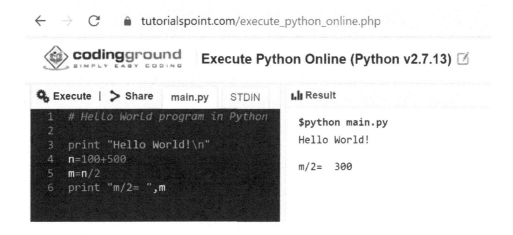

calculate with return of words with just "1" as the associated number count. But in reduce function the machine will add them together if the same words were encountered.

The following shows the modified code for local files, and output file shows the frequency of each word from the input file:

Figure 6. The Code is from PySpark official website (Apache Spark, n.d.)

```
text_file = sc.textFile("hdfs://...")

counts = text_file.flatMap(lambda line: line.split(" ")) \
        .map(lambda word: (word, 1)) \
        .reduceByKey(lambda a, b: a + b)
counts.saveAsTextFile("hdfs://...")
```

```
1.  # Modified PySpark Code for WordCount
2.  #
3.  text_file = sc.textFile("file:///home/chen/myPython/text.txt")
4.  counts = text_file.flatMap(lambda line: line.split(" ")) \
5.          .map(lambda word: (word, 1)) \
6.          .reduceByKey(lambda a, b: a + b)
7.  counts.saveAsTextFile("file:///home/chen/myPython/out1")
8.
9.  ---------------------------------------
10. #Input file: text.txt
11. this is a test file for python
12. this is a test second
13. this third line
14.
15. ---------------------------------------
16. # Output file
17. /out1/part-00000
18.
19. (u'a', 2)
20. (u'third', 1)
21. (u'for', 1)
22. (u'this', 3)
23. (u'is', 2)
24. (u'python', 1)
25. (u'second', 1)
26. (u'file', 1)
27. (u'test', 2)
28. (u'line', 1)
```

3. MACHINE LEARNING AND DEEP LEARNING IN DATA SCIENCE: SCIENCE, TECHNOLOGY, AND EDUCATION

Due to the fact of most concerns for data science issues in programming is about machine learning, we will focus on the machine learning and AI problems in this paper. In this section, we attempt to give the effective introduction to each of the most popular algorithms or methods used in data science as well as related Python coding examples. We include Regression, Principal Component Analysis, Classification, Clustering, and Neural Networks. We will also discuss the deep learning and Tensorflow in Python as well.

What is machine learning? In short, machine learning is to use a computational machinery to build a mathematical or algorithmic model (formula or procedure) based on some data collected beforehand. These collected data are called samples. There are two major categories of machine learning: supervised learning and unsupervised learning (Chen et al., 2015).

For *supervised learning*, the collected data samples contain the input data as well as the target data. For instance, we like to get a model for evaluating the ranks of universities. The input data could be a set of vectors where each of the vector is like *X=(Research, Teaching, Faculty, Students, Funding)*. We also know value *y* (the target data) from 1 to 5 for each *X* where the highest score is *5*. The purpose of supervised learning is to find the general function *f* such that *f(Xi)=yi* (or *f(Xi) is near yi* for each samples *(Xi,yi)*. When a new input data comes, we can use *f(X$_{new}$)* to get the value of *y$_{new}$*.

For *unsupervised learning*, the collected data samples contain only input data *X*. The purpose is to find the similarity among the samples in the data collected and provide a partition or categorization of the sample data set. When a new data comes, the completed learning model may tell us which category this new data is mostly belong to.

Since machine learning is usually for classification purpose. Therefore, we have *supervised classification* and *unsupervised classification* where unsupervised classification is also called *clustering*.

In this paper, we will also talk about when and where we shall use a specific algorithm. Please note that for the mathematical principle of the methods and algorithms we cover in this section, we refer to our previous writings and other related books (Chen et al., 2015; Géron, 2019). This paper is only focus on coding samples. (Many of them were collected and modified from difference sources.)

Before we start the course for algorithms and coding, we like to first introduce how to prepare the data set for our tasks in data science.

3.1 Preparing Data Sets for Classification or Machine Learning.

Students or learners often ask the question about how we prepare data sets for classification or/and machine learning?

As we discussed here are two types of classifications: supervised classification and unsupervised classification(clustering), for supervised classification, the datasets must contain the data for target results. This is because that we need to use target results for training. Here is an example: if we have GDP data, Stock data, Real-estate data. We want to find the relation to people's buying-power in 100 countries. We could use people's Purchasing-Power in 100 countries as target data. Even though we might not have 100 instances for 100 countries for family Purchasing Power. We still can continue to use them. For instance, GDP data, Stock data, and Realestate data can be used as input data. Called feature vectors *X={S1,...,S100}* where Si=(GDP,Stock,Realestate) for Country-i. *Y={R1,...,R100}* where Ri=(Purchasing Power) for country-i. Something like the following

```
==== Input X===========
(GDP1,GDP2, ...., GDP100)
(AvgHomePrice1,AvgHomePrice2,…,AvgHomePrice100)
(Stock1,Stock2,          ...          Stock100)
X must be formed as numerical vectors      .
===Target data y (Purchasing Power) ====
(PPower1,PPower2,.          ,PPower100)
y can be numerical data or symbolic data such as the following:
y=(0.1,0.85,0.95,., 0.7)
y=(bad,good,good,., OK)
```

In order to make a computing model to be trusted, we need to use some of the data collected to build the model or system, then use some of the data (pairing (Xi,yi)) to do the test. So, we could split 100 countries to two sets: 70 samples for training and 30 for testing. However, one could randomly decide how to split them as well. It is quite typical in machine learning.

If we just want to do unsupervised classification, we usually do not need to separate the target data *y*. We can just add it to the input data.

In the first author's data science class, the first author used public GDP data as examples. It showed the students how to read and process the real data sets using machine learning methods. After we discuss the coding for each method in machine learning, we also list the code piece for the real data.

3.2 Linear Regression and Logistic Regression

Linear Regression is to find a line or a hyper plane according to X and y where X is the set of samples that could be multi-dimensional, and y is a set of samples that is single valued. So, this method can be regarded as a supervised method. For instance, when X is just one-dimensional, we can get

$$y = \beta 0 + \beta 1 \mathrm{x}$$

By using the training data.

Logistic Regression is like Linear Regression. The only difference is that used a sigmoid (logistic) function to determine a clip-level that is easy to split 0 or 1.

$$s(y) = \frac{1}{1 + e^{-y}}$$

In the following, we just show a sample code for linear regression using the *sklearn* package:

```
1. # Linear Regression with plot
2. #
3. from sklearn import linear_model
4. Y = [10,15,21,12,13,14,15,14,15,15,14,15,14,10,14,16]
5. X = [[15,12,33,11,5,14,15,16,7,14,12,9,18,8,16,16]]
6. clf = linear_model.LinearRegression()
7. clf.fit([[X[i][j] for i in range(len(X))] for j in range(len(X[0]))],Y)
8. print("coef:", clf.coef_)
9. print("intercept:", clf.intercept_)
10. [X_cord]=X
11. from matplotlib import pyplot as plt
12. plt.plot(X_cord,Y,'o') # can use plt.scatter(x, y, marker='o');
13. plt.plot([0,25], [clf.intercept_, clf.intercept_+clf.coef_*25])
14. plt.title("L.R. Visualization")
15. plt.ylim(0, 30);
```

Figure 7. Linear Regression

```
coef: [0.26663185]
intercept: 10.504647519582246
[15, 12, 33, 11, 5, 14, 15, 16, 7, 14, 12, 9, 18, 8, 16, 16]
```

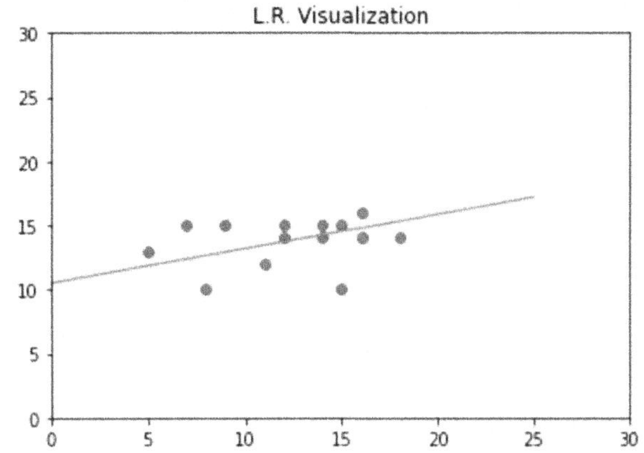


```
plt.xlim(0, 30);
plt.show()
```

The code for real data could be different from the testing data. One of the most significant part is to get the data in the format that a programmer can use. We usually use CSV format that is also text readable file. The package ***Pandas*** was used to read the data from a file. The following is the example of GDP data downloaded. With a little modification we will be able to use Python to read the data.

```
import pandas as pd
import numpy as np
import math
import matplotlib.pyplot as plt
%matplotlib inline

#setting figure size
```

Figure 8. GDP data set in the CSV format

	A	B	C	D	E	F	G	H	I	J	K	L	M	N	O
1	Country Na	Country Co	Indicator N	Indicator C	1960	1961	1962	1963	1964	1965	1966	1967	1968	1969	1970
2	Aruba	ABW	GDP (curre	NY.GDP.MKTP.CD											
3	Afghanista	AFG	GDP (curre	NY.GDP.M	5.38E+08	5.49E+08	5.47E+08	7.51E+08	8E+08	1.01E+09	1.4E+09	1.67E+09	1.37E+09	1.41E+09	1.75E+09
4	Angola	AGO	GDP (curre	NY.GDP.MKTP.CD											
5	Albania	ALB	GDP (curre	NY.GDP.MKTP.CD											
6	Andorra	AND	GDP (curre	NY.GDP.MKTP.CD											78619206
7	Arab World	ARB	GDP (curre	NY.GDP.MKTP.CD									2.58E+10	2.83E+10	3.19E+10
8	United Ara	ARE	GDP (curre	NY.GDP.MKTP.CD											
9	Argentina	ARG	GDP (curre	NY.GDP.MKTP.CD			2.45E+10	1.83E+10	2.56E+10	2.83E+10	2.86E+10	2.43E+10	2.64E+10	3.13E+10	3.16E+10
10	Armenia	ARM	GDP (curre	NY.GDP.MKTP.CD											
11	American S	ASM	GDP (curre	NY.GDP.MKTP.CD											
12	Antigua an	ATG	GDP (curre	NY.GDP.MKTP.CD											
13	Australia	AUS	GDP (curre	NY.GDP.M	1.86E+10	1.97E+10	1.99E+10	2.15E+10	2.38E+10	2.59E+10	2.73E+10	3.04E+10	3.27E+10	3.66E+10	4.13E+10
14	Austria	AUT	GDP (curre	NY.GDP.M	6.59E+09	7.31E+09	7.76E+09	8.37E+09	9.17E+09	9.99E+09	1.09E+10	1.16E+10	1.24E+10	1.36E+10	1.54E+10
15	Azerbaijan	AZE	GDP (curre	NY.GDP.MKTP.CD											

TestGDP2

Figure 9. An example of reading a real data and plot the partial data set

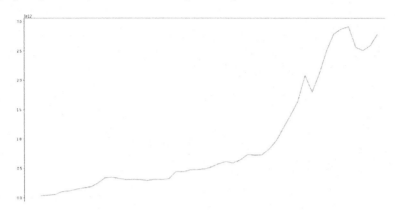

```
8.  from matplotlib.pylab import rcParams
9.  rcParams['figure.figsize'] = 20,10
10.
11.           #for normalizing data
12.           from sklearn.preprocessing import MinMaxScaler
13.           scaler = MinMaxScaler(feature_range=(0, 1))
14.
15.           #read the file
16.           df = pd.read_csv('TestGDP2.csv')
17.
18.           #print the head
19.
df.head()
20.
21.
plt.plot(df.iloc[5,15:63])
#
line
5
col
from
15
to
63
```

The plotting result shows the growth of a country in GDP in Figure 3.2. This data set will be used later.

The Practice Problem for learners: The above data looks like not a perfect fit for linear regression. However, it does not stop one to learn how to apply the linear regression algorithm to real data. Learners could merge the two programs above together to try to run linear regression over the GDP data. A hint here would be to try to form a small set of *X* and *y* as years and GDP values.

3.3 Principal Component Analysis

The principal component analysis (PCA) method is usually a unsupervised method. For 2D data points, PCA is used to ðnd the major direction of the data. For higher dimensional data, it can be used to determine the most important subspace---based on the most significant eigen-vectors of its covariance matrix. (See [3] page 23) This method is essential to data processing especially for data compression since most of time we only need to find the most important components of the data. Once we find the data components identified by these eigen-vectors, we can just map the whole data sets to the sub-space. The method is also related to regression analysis.

The following code shows you the calculation of PCA using the same data in Section 3.2. Other PCA examples can be found at https://scipy-lectures.org/packages/scikit-learn/auto_examples/plot_pca.html.

Figure 10. The example of using PCA on the same data set as shown in Figure 7

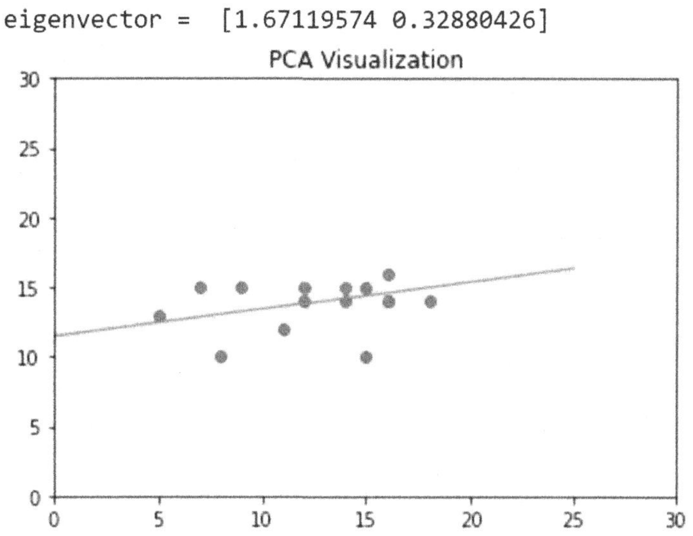

```
eigenvector =  [1.67119574 0.32880426]
```

3.3 kMeans

The k-means method is one of the most popular methods in data science today. It is an unsupervised classiðcation method. Given a set of vectors X, we might want to partition the data set into two or more categories. kMeans is to ðnd two or k-centers such that the total summation of the distances of each data point to its center to reach the minimum (Chen et al., 2015). To do this, we can first select the k-centers randomly, then use an iterated process to update these k-centers until the centers do not change or just change a little. The following figure explains the process (Chen et al., 2015).

This method is particularly useful in clustering. It is usually a very fast method, but it could reach an exponential time for some special case. Therefore, users can setup an interaction limits to the algorithm.

Here is the example of the code in Python (Stack Exchange, n.d.). In this example, five data groups are generated randomly, but we only try to group 3 data clusters. The result shows correctly.

Figure 11. kMeans: (a) data samples, (b) randomly selected centers and its data points, and (c) updated centers and its data points

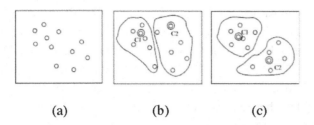

(a)   (b)   (c)

```
1. # 2D k-Means
2. # Code was modified from:
3. # https://dsp.stackexchange.com/questions/23662/k-means-for-2d-point-clus-
tering-in-python
4.
5. import numpy as np
6. import matplotlib.pyplot as plt
7. from sklearn.cluster import KMeans
8. from sklearn.datasets.samples_generator import make_blobs
9.
10. ########################################################################
####
11. # Generate sample data
12. np.random.seed(0)
13. batch_size = 45
14. centers = [[1, 1], [-1, -1], [1, -1],[-2,-5],[2,6]]
15. n_clusters = 3
16. X, labels_true = make_blobs(n_samples=3000, centers=centers, cluster_
std=0.7)
17.
18. ########################################################################
####
19. # Compute clustering with Means
20.         k_means = KMeans(n_clusters=3, n_init=10)
21.         k_means.fit(X)
22. k_means_labels = k_means.labels_
23. k_means_cluster_centers = k_means.cluster_centers_
24. k_means_labels_unique = np.unique(k_means_labels)
25.
26. ########################################################################
####
27. # Plot result
28. #colors = ['#4EACC5', '#FF9C34', '#4E9A06']
```

```
29. colors = ['#4EACC5', '#FF9C34', '#4E9A06','#009C34', '#8E9A06']
30. #colors = ['#4EACC5', '#FF9C34']
31. plt.figure()
32. print(n_clusters)
33. for k, col in zip(range(n_clusters), colors): # zip make a tuple for k,
color
34.        my_members = k_means_labels == k
35.        cluster_center = k_means_cluster_centers[k]
36.        plt.plot(X[my_members, 0], X[my_members, 1], 'w',
37.        markerfacecolor=col, marker='.')
38.        plt.plot(cluster_center[0], cluster_center[1], 'o',
markerfacecolor=col,
39.        markeredgecolor='k', markersize=6)
40. plt.title('KMeans')
41. plt.grid(True)
42. plt.show()
```

Figure 12. The plot in kMeans for the example above

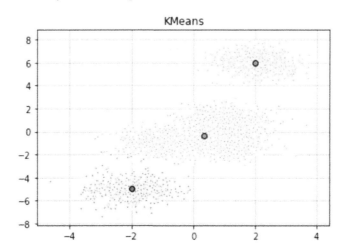

In the first author's data science class, we added another data set for food consumption. With two data sets, we can do a 2D k-means. However, we could use k-means to single data set as well. For instance, we could find the groups of countries that has the similar GDP values. Here is the example the first author showed to students. The code was not polished but it was real classroom development while communicating with students.

It is very important in learning programming; some strategy is to learn the simple logic of coding first meaning that to make the road of learning easier not just focusing on the beautiful code in length that could be referring to find a great way to solve a problem. We sometime want to first find an easy way to solve a problem for students. Then let students to find a better way that could improve the instructor's code. The following code shows we obtained five centers from the two data sets.

```
1. # Insert import code here as shown above......
2.
3. #read the file
4. df = pd.read_csv('FoodConsumptionNutrients_en_test.csv')
5.
6. # Combine two data sets to do 2D kMeans for the same year. with interpola-
tion.
7.
8. # v=[x1,x2] x1--gdp x2--Food
9.  # set of data: [v0,v1,v2           ]
10. df2 = pd.read_csv('API_NY_GDP_MKTP_CD_DS2_en_csv_v2_219924_test.csv')
11. plt.plot(df2.iloc[:,10])
12.
13. X1=df2.iloc[:,60] # data for 2015?
14. X2=df.iloc[:,2]        # data for 2015?
15.
16. V= np.zeros((len(X1),2))
17. for i in range(len(X2)):
18.        V[i][0]=X1[i]
19.        V[i][1]=X2[i]
20.
21. for i in range(len(X1)):
22.        if math.isnan(V[i][0]):
23.        V[i][0]= 0
24.
25. for i in range(len(X2)):
26.        if math.isnan(V[i][1]):
27.        V[i][1]= 0
28.
29. kmeans1 = KMeans(n_clusters=5, random_state=0).fit(V)
30. kmeans1.cluster_centers_
31.
32. Result from the above code:
33. #kmeans1 = KMeans(n_clusters=5, random_state=0).fit(V)
34. #kmeans1.cluster_centers_
35. #array([[4.19800562e+11, 4.69590164e+01],
36. #        [4.73341015e+13, 0.00000000e+00],
37. #        [2.29009106e+13, 5.48000000e+01],
38. #        [7.61028312e+13, 0.00000000e+00],
39. #        [1.28456528e+13, 7.10000000e+01]])
```

3.4. kNN and Decision Trees

k-Nearest Neighbors(kNN) and Decision trees are typical computer science method for data processing. They are very efficient and easy to understand in basic terms. They are both supervised methods. For decision trees, iterative dichotomiser 3 (ID3) and classiðcation and regression tree (CART) are popular methods to determine when will be the best time to split a tree node.

A code sample for kNN can be found at . (Cory Maklin, K Nearest Neighbor Algorithm In Python, Jul 21, 2019, https://towardsdatascience.com/k-nearest-neighbor-python-2fccc47d2a55.)

The Python code example for decision trees can be easily found at https://www.geeksforgeeks.org/decision-tree-implementation-python/. We here provide an example for PySpark code

```
1. #The Code example for Decision-Tree. The code source is from
2. #https://spark.apache.org/docs/latest/mllib-dccision-tree.html
3.
4. from pyspark.mllib.tree import DecisionTree, DecisionTreeModel
5. from pyspark.mllib.util import MLUtils
6.
7. # Load and parse the data file into an RDD of LabeledPoint.
8. data = MLUtils.loadLibSVMFile(sc, './dt_libsvm_data.txt')
9. # Split the data into training and test sets (30% held out for testing)
10. (trainingData, testData) = data.randomSplit([0.7, 0.3])
11.
12. # Train a DecisionTree model.
13. # Empty categoricalFeaturesInfo indicates all features are continuous.
14. model = DecisionTree.trainClassifier(trainingData, numClasses=3, categoricalFeaturesInfo={},
15.         impurity='gini', maxDepth=5, maxBins=32)
16.
17. # Evaluate model on test instances and compute test error
18. predictions = model.predict(testData.map(lambda x: x.features))
19. labelsAndPredictions = testData.map(lambda lp: lp.label).zip(predictions)
20. testErr = labelsAndPredictions.filter(
21.         lambda lp: lp[0] != lp[1]).count() / float(testData.count())
22. print('Test Error = ' + str(testErr))
23. print('Learned classification tree model:')
24. print(model.toDebugString())
25.
26. # Save and load model
27. model.save(sc, "./dt_tmp/myDecisionTreeClassificationModel")
28. sameModel = DecisionTreeModel.load(sc, "./dt_tmp/myDecisionTreeClassificationModel")
```

The result of the learned decision tree is:

```
1.  #======Learned model ====================
2.
3.  Learned classification tree model:
4.  >>> print(model.toDebugString())
5.  DecisionTreeModel classifier of depth 2 with 5 nodes
6.          If (feature 0 <= 1.0)
7.          Predict: 1.0
8.          Else (feature 0 > 1.0)
9.          If (feature 1 <= 0.0)
10.          Predict: 0.0
11.          Else (feature 1 > 0.0)
12.          Predict: 2.0
```

The training data set has three categories:

```
1.  #===============Data Set: dt_libsvm_data.txt
2.  0 1:10 2:-5
3.  1 1:-5 2:5
4.  2 1:10 2:5
5.  0 1:10 2:-2
6.  1 1:-5 2:2
7.  2 1:10 2:2
8.  0 1:1 2:-5
9.  1 1:-2 2:5
10. 2 1:12 2:5
11. 0 1:4 2:-2
12. 1 1:-3 2:2
13. 2 1:10 2:22
14. 0 1:10 2:-15
15. 1 1:-5 2:15
16. 2 1:10 2:15
17. 0 1:10 2:-12
18. 1 1:-5 2:12
19. 2 1:10 2:12
20. 0 1:1 2:-15
21. 1 1:-2 2:15
22. 2 1:12 2:15
23. 0 1:4 2:-12
24. 1 1:-3 2:12
25. 2 1:10 2:25
```

3.5 Support Vector Machines SVM

The Support Vector Machine algorithm is supervised machine learning model. It is an advanced method. The theory behind this method is complex. However, its philosophy is simple. It is to get a separation line or high dimensional plane between two classes (sample points belong to two classes). The method is to find a best middle line or plane to separate these two classes such that the distance from each class to the line reaches maximum.

Figure 13. Separation based on support vector machines(Chen et al., 2015)

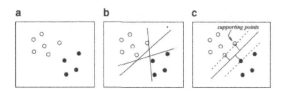

Fig. The support vector machine: (a) a training set with two classes, (b) three possible classifiers shown as three lines, and (c) the best separation line supported by three points.

Here is the example of the code in SVM, the author of this great piece of code is not clear. The confusion_matrix shows the correctness of the linear separation. *Google Colab* was use to run this application.

```
1. #3D SVM, Code sample source:
2. # https://stackoverflow.com/questions/36232334/plotting-3d-decision-boundary-from-linear- svm
3.
4. import numpy as np
5. import matplotlib.pyplot as plt
6. from mpl_toolkits.mplot3d import Axes3D
7. from sklearn.svm import SVC
8.
9. rs = np.random.RandomState(1234)
10.
11. # Generate some experimental data.
12. n_samples = 200
13. # X is the input features by row.
14. X = np.zeros((200,3))
15. X[:n_samples//2] = rs.multivariate_normal(np.ones(3), np.eye(3), size=n_samples//2)
16. X[n_samples//2:] = rs.multivariate_normal(-np.ones(3), np.eye(3), size=n_samples//2)
17. # Y is the class labels for each row of X.
18. Y = np.zeros(n_samples); Y[n_samples//2:] = 1
19.
```

```
20. # Fit the data with an svm
21. svc = SVC(kernel='linear')
22. svc.fit(X,Y)
23.
24. #just use training data for correctness check
25. y_pred = svc.predict(X)
26. cm=confusion_matrix(Y, y_pred)
27. print("confusion_matrix\n",cm)
28.
29.
30. # The equation of the separating plane is given by all x in R^3 such that:
31. # np.dot(svc.coef_[0], x) + b = 0. We should solve for the last coordinate
32. # to plot the plane in terms of x and y.
33.
34. z = lambda x,y: (-svc.intercept_[0]-svc.coef_[0][0]*x-svc.coef_[0][1]*y) /
svc.coef_[0][2]
35.
36. tmp = np.linspace(-2,2,51)
37. x,y = np.meshgrid(tmp,tmp)
38.
39. # Plot
40. fig = plt.figure()
41. ax = fig.add_subplot(111, projection='3d')
42. ax.plot_surface(x, y, z(x,y))
43. ax.plot3D(X[Y==0,0], X[Y==0,1], X[Y==0,2],'ob')
44. ax.plot3D(X[Y==1,0], X[Y==1,1], X[Y==1,2],'sr')
45. plt.show()
```

3.6. Neural Networks and Deep-Learning

The most popular neural network is called the feed forward neural network today [1]. It was called back-propagation neural network before since it used back-propagation for training. See Figure 3.9.

Each small circle is called a neuron that performs the calculation. Each arrow will carry with a wight that was assigned randomly. The training process is to update the weights on the arrow until weights do not change much.

A code example of Neural Networks is listed as follows.

```
1. #The Code example for Neural Networks. The code source is mainly from
2. #https://scikit-learn.org/stable/modules/generated/sklearn.neural_network.
MLPClassifier.html
3. #
4. from sklearn.neural_network import MLPClassifier
5. from sklearn.datasets import make_classification
```

Figure 14. 3D display of the result from support vector machines [12]

```
confusion_matrix
[[99  1]
 [ 2 98]]
```

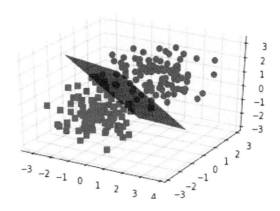

```
6. from sklearn.model_selection import train_test_split
7.
8. #make random sets for NN ; 100 samples with 5 features. Can try 20 samples.
9. X, y = make_classification(n_samples=100, n_features=5, random_state=1)
10.
11. #seplit the set into two: training and testing
12. X_train, X_test, y_train, y_test = train_test_split(X, y,
stratify=y,random_state=1)
13.
```

Figure 15. A feed forward neural network with back-propagation training [1,3]

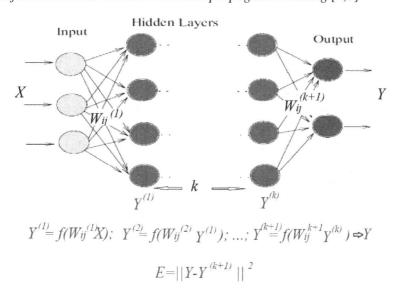

$$Y^{(1)} = f(W_{ij}^{(1)}X); \quad Y^{(2)} = f(W_{ij}^{(2)} Y^{(1)}); \quad ...; \quad Y^{(k+1)} = f(W_{ij}^{k+1} Y^{(k)}) \Rightarrow Y$$

$$E = ||Y - Y^{(k+1)}||^2$$

```
14. #use training data to get the model, here for NN is weights for arrows
from one layer to another.
15. clf = MLPClassifier(random_state=1, max_iter=500).fit(X_train, y_train)
16. # In this sentence, the randomly assign weights first and then iterate for
300 times
17.
18. #Testing the model using testing data, "Predict using the multi-layer per-
ceptron classifier"
19. # for 1 element
20. Proba=clf.predict_proba(X_test[:1]) #Probability estimates for just 1 ele-
ment in the testing set.
21. print("test result for the first element:\n ",Proba,y_test[:1])
22. # for 10 element
23. Proba=clf.predict_proba(X_test[:5]) #Probability estimates for just 1 ele-
ment in the testing set.
24. print("test result for the first 5 element:\n",Proba,"\n", y_test[:5])
25. #output layers has two neurons, the first is for categroy "0" and the sec-
ond one determines catego ry "1",
26. #So third test is wrong
27.
28. #just predict the category for the first 5 elements (not probablity); com-
pare with the testing classif ication
29. Predict=clf.predict(X_test[:5,:])          #X_test[:5,:]=X_test[:5]
30. print("predict the category for the first 5 element:\n",Predict,"\n",y_
test[:5])
31. #The third one is wrong
32.
33. #Return the mean accuracy on the given test data and labels. Predict(X_
test) vs. y_test, the ratio
34. #This is for entire testing set. It run several times. Report its mean
35. Accuracy=clf.score(X_test, y_test)
36. print("Accuracy for entire testing set= \n",Accuracy)
```

Recently, researchers focused on convolutional Neural Networks and recurrent Neural Networks for deep learning. The idea of deep learning is to make special hidden neurons for the calculation to reduce the size of the hidden layers. In such a way, the training would be much faster. This is a central idea of Tensorfollow that was developed by Google. This is a feed forward NN that tries to perform a calculation for an image. See Fig.

For recurrent Neural Networks, LSTM is the most popular. We will write introductions for this method in in another article [1].

Figure 16. TensorFlow (This figure is from Google)

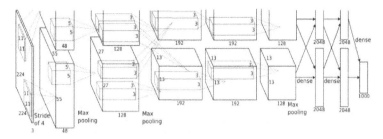

4. CASE STUDY: GDP ANALYSIS USING PYTHON

This section shows several aspects of programming work that use Python to do analysis on GDP and related data. This section mainly contains the code and results visualization. More details can be found in [13].

Global population growth (GDP) will drive a significant increase in demand that will present a growing challenge in the next two decades [13]. Population growth rhymes with the evolution of Food consumption. It might be challenging for countries to meet the growing demand in food supply due to the increase of the population. Will the countries meet the demand? Is the Food consumption of a country related to its Gross Domestic Product? How significant is this correlation? For reference Gross Domestic Product (GDP) is the overall market value of all the finished services and goods that have been produced in a country during a specific period.

Our objective here is to analyze the two data and use the k-means algorithm to see how they cluster.

The first step in each Data Science project is Data Gathering. Finding meaningful and useful data in quantity can be a difficult task.

Figure 17. GDP data format

```
1 import pandas as pd
2 import numpy as np
3 food= pd.read_csv('FoodConsumptionNutrients_en_test2.csv')
4 food
```

	Country Code	Country Name	1990-92	1995-97	2000-02	2005-07
0	3	Albania	68.0	83	83	92
1	4	Algeria	72.0	68	70	67
2	7	Angola	41.0	36	39	46
3	8	Antigua and Barbuda	101.0	75	74	83
4	9	Argentina	106.0	113	110	108
...	...	...	...	...	...	...
169	236	Venezuela (Bolivarian Republic of)	70.0	66	70	74
170	237	Viet Nam	28.0	35	44	59

Figure 18. The head information of the data set

```
1 food.head()
```

	Country Code	Country Name	1990-92	1995-97	2000-02	2005-07
0	3	Albania	68.0	83	83	92
1	4	Algeria	72.0	68	70	67
2	7	Angola	41.0	36	39	46
3	8	Antigua and Barbuda	101.0	75	74	83
4	9	Argentina	106.0	113	110	108

Step 1: Get the Data

The data imported should be in csv (comma separated values) format. We need to import pandas in order to read our csv files. Pandas is a popular data manipulation package in python programming language.

Pandas loads 2-dimensional data into data frame type.

In Figure 17, we are loading our first file which is the food consumption data. The code used to read the file is on line 3. The output is the data frame. It is also possible to view only the 5 first rows (Figure 18).

To view dimension of the data frame (how many rows and how many columns), the code used is dataframe.shape. In this case:

This code returns a tuple, the first value is the number of rows and the second value is the number of columns.

We keep going by loading the second file, The GDP data (Figure 20) and merging the two files (Figure 21).

On Figure 4.5, line 3 is the code that is used to merge two data files. The merge function might have parameters like how, on, sort, left_on, right_index etc. In our case the merge function only has two parameters which are how and on. *How* is inner by default but can be left, right, outer, inner. Inner use a common key of intersection from both data frames. *On* is used for the column on which to join on. The two data files must have the same column name present in both data file in order to merge, in this case that column name is 'Country Name'.

We read third data file, the Human Consumption file using the code:

HDI = pd.read_csv('HDI_test3.1.csv')

Next, we merge the third data file with the two previously merged file:

Figure 19. The Shape indicates there are 174 countries in the data set

```
1 food.shape
```

```
(174, 6)
```

Figure 20. Files alignment

```
1 GDP = pd.read_csv('API_NY.GDP.MKTP.CD_DS2_en_csv_v2_247793_test.csv')
2 GDP
```

	Country Name	Country Code	Indicator Name	Indicator Code	1960	1961	1962	1963	1964
0	Aruba	ABW	GDP (current US$)	NY.GDP.MKTP.CD	NaN	NaN	NaN	NaN	NaN
1	Afghanistan	AFG	GDP (current US$)	NY.GDP.MKTP.CD	5.377778e+08	5.488889e+08	5.466667e+08	7.511112e+08	8.000000e+08
2	Angola	AGO	GDP (current US$)	NY.GDP.MKTP.CD	NaN	NaN	NaN	NaN	NaN
3	Albania	ALB	GDP (current US$)	NY.GDP.MKTP.CD	NaN	NaN	NaN	NaN	NaN
4	Andorra	AND	GDP (current US$)	NY.GDP.MKTP.CD	NaN	NaN	NaN	NaN	NaN

new_data = pd.merge(HDI, data, how='inner', on ='Country Name')

GDP contains data up to year 2018 and Human consumption contains data up to year 2017 but unfortunately, we observed that the highest year that the food consumption data contains is 2007, therefore we will focus on that specific year. Let us create a new data frame that only has data from year 2007. The code for that is:

data_2007 = new_data[['Country Name', '2007_x', '2007_y', '2005-07']]

Figure 21. Data Merge

```
1 #Merge two data based on the country name
2 data = pd.merge(GDP, food, how='inner', on ='Country Name')
3 data
```

	Country Name	Country Code_x	Indicator Name	Indicator Code	1960	1961	1962	1963	1964
0	Angola	AGO	GDP (current US$)	NY.GDP.MKTP.CD	NaN	NaN	NaN	NaN	NaN
1	Albania	ALB	GDP (current US$)	NY.GDP.MKTP.CD	NaN	NaN	NaN	NaN	NaN
2	United Arab Emirates	ARE	GDP (current US$)	NY.GDP.MKTP.CD	NaN	NaN	NaN	NaN	NaN

Figure 22. Data are cleaned by deleting some empty spots

```
1 #DataFrame with only the columns of the values
2 data_values = data_2007[['X1','X2','X3']]
3 data_values
```

	X1	X2	X3
0	0.72	1.067732e+10	92
1	0.707	1.349771e+11	67
2	0.492	6.526645e+10	46
3	0.778	1.311401e+09	83
4	0.792	2.875305e+11	108
...	...	...	...
137	0.762	2.341057e+10	77
138	0.646	2.231139e+10	69
139	0.582	5.264283e+08	93
140	0.503	1.405696e+10	35
141	0.442	5.291950e+09	58

142 rows × 3 columns

Note: 2007_x from the HDI file, 2007_y is from the GDP file, those names were automatically generated after merging and finally 2005-07 is from the Food consumption file. We might replace these names by names of our choice like so:

data_2007.columns=['Country Name', 'X1', 'X2', 'X3']

Now that we finished uploading all our files and we have the data frame we need; we have completed the first part of our work.

Step 2: Clean the Data

Cleaning the data consists of dealing with missing data. We get to decide if we are willing all rows or all columns with a missing value or replacing the missing value with 0 in case dropping the entire row or columns might have an impact on the whole project thus leading to false interpretation. For this particular task, we first need to get to know your data. This might be the longest part of the project.

Figure 23. Data normalization

```
1 data_values['X1'].dtypes

dtype('O')


1 data_values['X2'].dtypes

dtype('float64')


1 data_values['X3'].dtypes

dtype('int64')
```

To drop all rows with missing values we use: data_2007=data_2007.dropna()

dropna() is a function that drop all rows with null, NaN values.

At this point, we only need the values, let us regroup the data excluding the country names.

Figure 6 shows the data frame with only the values for year 2007 excluding the countries name themselves. Let us verify the types of data we have.

data_values['X3']= data_values['X3'].astype(np.float64)

We can see that the HDI values are objects type, while the GDP values are float type and Food consumption values are integer type. To manipulate these data we must convert them all to the same data type. We are going to convert them into float data type.

The above code changes the integer data type into float data type.

The above line of code changes the dots to value 0 and at the same time changes values from object type to float type.

Step 3: Normalize the Data

After loading the three data, we noticed that the values are not similar, and they have different range. When features have different value range, it is important to convert them to the same range which is why we normalize. Normalization consists of changing the values of the columns in the data frame to a common scale.

MinMaxScaler() is a function that changes values of a dataset by scaling each of them to a given ranges. The default range is (0,1).

From figure 23, we can observe are all values are within the range 0 and 1.

Figure 24. Code for kMeans

```
1 #rescale data range
2 from sklearn.preprocessing import MinMaxScaler
3 scaler=MinMaxScaler()
4 data_scale=scaler.fit_transform(data_values)
5 data_scale

array([[7.67590618e-01, 2.33540240e-03, 5.23178808e-01],
       [7.53731343e-01, 2.98650008e-02, 3.57615894e-01],
       [5.24520256e-01, 1.44256652e-02, 2.18543046e-01],
       [8.29424307e-01, 2.61062053e-04, 4.63576159e-01],
       [8.44349680e-01, 6.36521472e-02, 6.29139073e-01],
       [7.67590618e-01, 2.00960465e-03, 3.04635762e-01],
       [9.75479744e-01, 1.88912968e-01, 8.60927152e-01],
       [9.39232409e-01, 8.60570161e-02, 9.93377483e-01],
       [7.55863539e-01, 7.29052289e-03, 2.58278146e-01],
       [5.54371002e-01, 1.76028562e-02, 1.05960265e-01],
       [8.28358209e-01, 1.00541433e-03, 5.56291391e-01],
       [8.07036247e-01, 9.99854038e-03, 6.42384106e-01],
       [9.58422175e-01, 1.04468363e-01, 1.00000000e+00],
       [7.45202559e-01, 2.56442303e-04, 3.70860927e-01],
       [4.85074627e-01, 1.29273377e-03, 2.64900662e-01],
       [7.59061834e-01, 3.46525782e-03, 3.97350993e-01],
       [6.66311301e-01, 2.39337012e-03, 2.71523179e-01],
```

Step 4: Apply k-Means Algorithm to Find Clusters

The kMeans algorithm is used to cluster data by separating samples into x groups of equal variances. The kMeans algorithm requires the number of clusters to be precise before head. Each data point after the kMeans clustering will belong to only one group. kMeans algorithm cluster groups together in a way that the sum of the squared distance between the data points and the cluster centroid is at the smallest value it could get. The data points are more likely to be in the same cluster if there is not much variation within clusters. More variation within clusters means that data points are less similar. The steps are KMeans algorithm follow are:

1. Clusters the data into k groups after specification of k
2. Shuffle dataset, initialize centroid by selecting randomly k points as centroid (cluster centers)
3. Based on *Euclidean distance function*, assign data points to their closest centroid
4. Compute the centroid of all data point in each cluster.
5. Keep iterating by repeating the last three steps until there is no change in the assignment of data points to clusters

Figure 25. Result for classification of each country (Three classes)

```
1 #Cluster into # groups using Kmenas and find centroids
2 from sklearn.cluster import KMeans
3 kmeans=KMeans(n_clusters=3).fit(data_scale)
4 centroids=kmeans.cluster_centers_
5 centroids

array([[0.5083511 , 0.01210474, 0.2434388 ],
       [0.91968728, 0.22259416, 0.82671082],
       [0.78082494, 0.02532371, 0.47933318]])
```

On Figure 24, the 2 imports the kMeans package, line 3 applies the kMeans algorithm by specifying the number of cluster (n_clusters=3), line 4 get the centroids of the kMeans clusters and line 5 print the three centroids value as an array.

On Figure 25, line 1 gets the labels of all the different data points and line 2 prints them. We can observe that some data points belong to group 2, some other belong to group 0 and others to group 1, The different group are the different clusters.

We can view which countries belong to which group. For example to view the countries that belong to group 1 we write the line of code on line 2. And line 3 prints all countries of present in group 1.

We can do the same to view countries that belong to group 0 and group 2 by just changing 1 to 0 or 2.

We use the describe function to find the summary of the statistics of a data frame. Figure 11 shows summary description of all the statistics of group 1. We can do the same for the remaining group in order to find relevant information on the different cluster and make differs them apart.

Plt.scatter plots the data points in a 2D format.

After kMeans algorithm, the graph help visualize the relationship between the Gross Domestic Product of 145 countries, the food nutrient data and human development index for year 2007. Each dot represents a country based on the score it received and in the group (it belongs to). We can therefore state that there is a significant positive relationship between growth in food consumption and growth

Figure 26. Scatter display of the data points

```
1 labels=kmeans.labels_
2 labels

array([2, 2, 0, 2, 2, 2, 1, 1, 2, 0, 2, 2, 1, 2, 0, 2, 0, 1, 2, 2, 0, 0,
       0, 0, 1, 0, 0, 2, 1, 2, 0, 2, 2, 2, 1, 1, 0, 2, 2, 2, 2, 0, 2, 0,
       2, 1, 1, 0, 2, 1, 0, 1, 2, 0, 0, 0, 0, 0, 0, 1, 1, 0, 0, 1, 1, 1,
       2, 1, 2, 2, 0, 2, 2, 2, 2, 0, 0, 2, 1, 0, 0, 2, 2, 0, 2, 0, 2, 2,
       2, 0, 0, 0, 0, 1, 1, 0, 0, 0, 1, 0, 2, 2, 0, 0, 1, 1, 2, 2, 0, 1,
       0, 2, 0, 2, 0, 1, 0, 2, 1, 2, 0, 2, 1, 1, 2, 0, 2, 0, 0, 2, 2, 2,
       0, 0, 2, 2, 1, 2, 2, 2, 0, 0], dtype=int32)
```

in GDP for all countries. There is some indication that growth in food consumption declines with GDP per capita, for any given growth in GDP [13].

5. CONCLUSION

In this paper, the authors showed a comprehensive description for using Python in data science. In this concise article, the reader could learn Python and PySpark in an effective manner. The authors would like to thank various writers for code samples using Python in machine learning. We are very sorry for sometimes not able to find their names of the owners of the code. We also thank the website that provide the Mircrosoft word converting from text code [14].

REFERENCES

Apache. (n.d.). https://spark.apache.org/docs/latest/cluster-overview.html

Apache Spark. (n.d.). https://spark.apache.org/docs/latest/index.html

Chen, L. M., Su, Z. X., & Jiang, B. (2015). *Mathematical Problems in Data Science*. Springer. doi:10.1007/978-3-319-25127-1

Dean, J., & Ghemawat, S. (2008). Map-Reduce: Simplified data processing on large clusters. *Communications of the ACM, 51*(1), 107–113. doi:10.1145/1327452.1327492

Forge. (n.d.). https://forge.fiware.org/plugins/mediawiki/wiki/fiware/index.php/FIWARE.OpenSpecification.Data.BigData

Geeks for Geeks. (n.d.). https://www.geeksforgeeks.org/difference-between-cloud-computing-and-cluster-computing/

Géron, A. (2019). *Hands-on machine learning with Scikit-Learn, Keras, and TensorFlow: Concepts, tools, and techniques to build intelligent systems*. O'Reilly Media.

Goodfellow, I., Bengio, Y., & Courville, A. (2016). *Deep Learning*. MIT Press.

LeCun, Y., Bengio, Y., & Hinton, G. (2015). Deep learning. *Nature, 521*(7553), 436–444. doi:10.1038/nature14539 PMID:26017442

Planetb. (n.d.). http://www.planetb.ca/syntax-highlight-word

Stack Exchange. (n.d.). https://dsp.stackexchange.com/questions/23662/k-means-for-2d-point-clustering-in-python

Stack Overflow. (n.d.). https://stackoverflow.com/questions/36232334/plotting-3d-decision-boundary-from-linear-svm

Tutorials Point. (n.d.). https://www.tutorialspoint.com/python/index.htm

Ukeneru-Steve & Coulibaly. (2019). *Application of K-Means Clustering Algorithmic for the Classification between Gross Domestic Product and Food Consumption in the World*. University of The District of Columbia.

Section 2
Technologies for Intelligent Analytics

Chapter 5
On the Similarity Search With Hamming Space Sketches

Vladimir Mic
Masaryk University, Brno, Czech Republic

Pavel Zezula
Masaryk University, Brno, Czech Republic

ABSTRACT

This chapter focuses on data searching, which is nowadays mostly based on similarity. The similarity search is challenging due to its computational complexity, and also the fact that similarity is subjective and context dependent. The authors assume the metric space model of similarity, defined by the domain of objects and the metric function that measures the dissimilarity of object pairs. The volume of contemporary data is large, and the time efficiency of similarity query executions is essential. This chapter investigates transformations of metric space to Hamming space to decrease the memory and computational complexity of the search. Various challenges of the similarity search with sketches in the Hamming space are addressed, including the definition of sketching transformation and efficient search algorithms that exploit sketches to speed-up searching. The indexing of Hamming space and a heuristic to facilitate the selection of a suitable sketching technique for any given application are also considered.

INTRODUCTION

The ability to produce and store vast volumes of data has brought new challenges to data processing. We focus on the problem of efficient searching in big complex data such as images, videos, sounds, movements and biometrics. Many real-life applications of searching in these domains require efficient processing based on a pairwise similarity of data objects instead of the exact matching. This is caused by the narrow applicability of exact match in real-life scenarios. A typical example of searching that has to utilise similarity instead of the identity is given by the identification of people based on biometric data, e.g. fingerprints, body motions and images of irises, faces and retinas. The biometric data are slightly different when taken repeatedly (Jafri et al., 2009, Hua et al., 2011, Daugman, 2003, Mehrotra et al.,

DOI: 10.4018/978-1-7998-4963-6.ch005

2013) and therefore exact matching cannot be exploited to identify people according to biometrics. We illustrate this by Figure 1 that contains two images of the same iris. Even though both images show the same iris, they are not identical but just quite similar. The appearance of the iris is inferred mainly by the illumination, blinking and even by a particular camera that took the image. Therefore, photos of the same iris are not identical in general.

Figure 1. Two images of the same iris: identification of a person based on the iris image illustrates the need for search based on the similarity. Images are reprinted from Mehrotra et al., 2013.

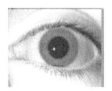 

Searching based on similarity is also advantageous when searching for general images, sounds, time series, videos, movements, and other complex data, e.g. datasets in biology and chemistry. The complexity of all these data types leads to a usual need to search for *similar* items instead of the *identical*. For instance, event detection in videos from surveillance cameras is a nice example of application of a similarity search in these domains, as it is usually implemented as matching scenes similar to given patterns (Turaga et al., 2008). Also, recommender systems (Adomavicius & Tuzhilin, 2005) usually find people who make similar choices as a given person and then recommend the choices of these *similar people*. Customers can also exploit a similarity search actively to find goods or items. This use-case includes for example the finding of images for websites or wallpapers for electronic devices as illustrated by Figure 2.

Figure 2. A similarity search may be also exploited to find wallpaper for an electronic device

This chapter is focused on a particular approach to efficient similarity search in complex data domains, such as in multimedia. It targets big data processing, data and information science, and technology. Presented techniques are applicable in services, management, as well as in the government.

The pairwise similarity of complex multimedia objects is not usually evaluated directly using the raw data. Instead, the characteristic features are extracted to describe objects from a specific point of view. We denote these features *descriptors*, and we assume the *global descriptors* that describe the whole data objects. The similarity of descriptors thus expresses the similarity of original data objects. We consider these similarities to be the same unless we do not have to distinguish them. This allows us to use term *object* to denote both, the data object and its descriptor. The ability of descriptors to capture properties and semantics of complex objects has rapidly increased in recent years. With it, the descriptors have grown as well, which has made their efficient processing more difficult. Our goal is not to define new and better descriptors. Our research is motivated by the need to search efficiently in big volumes of data.

A selection of the similarity model is the only theoretical assumption limiting the applicability of this work. We assume that the function d which expresses the similarity of descriptors is a metric function, and therefore the domain of descriptors D and the function d form the *metric space*. Therefore, the higher the value $d(o_1, o_2)$, $o_1, o_2 \in D$, the less similar descriptors o_1, o_2. We further denote d as the distance function and value $d(o_1, o_2)$ as the *distance*. Metric space is one of the most general similarity models and thus its adoption ensures wide applicability of investigated techniques.

This chapter considers the *queries by example*: Having a dataset $X \subseteq D$ and an arbitrary query object $q \in D$, the goal is to efficiently find the most similar objects $o \in X$ to q. Usually, it is acceptable to allow some pre-processing of the dataset X to allow efficient similarity queries execution. We focus on techniques that support searching efficiency by the transformation of the metric space to Hamming space, which is then exploited to discard some dissimilar objects during the search. More specifically, we focus on techniques that transform each descriptor $o \in X$ to the binary string $sk(o)$ that we call *sketch*. The dissimilarity of sketches is expressed by the Hamming distance function that evaluates the number of different bits in two sketches. The sketches, compared by the Hamming distance, approximate the similarity relationships as defined by the metric space (D, d). The size of sketches $sk(o)$ is significantly smaller than the size of original objects $o \in X$, and the Hamming distance is very efficient to evaluate. Therefore, despite an inaccuracy caused by the transformation of objects to sketches, the transformed space can be exploited to speed-up a high-quality similarity search significantly and to mitigate problems of computational and memory complexity of the searching.

This chapter provides an overview of various aspects of the similarity search with sketches. At first, we focus on the quality of sketches and discuss techniques to transform objects to sketches (*sketching technique*s). Then we discuss ways to employ sketches to speed-up the similarity search. We reveal that the contribution of the sketches to the efficiency of the similarity search is more significant when the sketches are employed as an additional filter of the promising (*candidate*) objects identified by a similarity index. Then we describe an approach that enables efficient selection of a suitable sketching technique for given data. This research is motivated by the dependency of the quality of sketching techniques on statistical properties of the metric space (D, d). Finally, we focus on the indexing of sketches. We use the recently proposed index for efficient searching in Hamming space, which is called the *Hamming weight tree* (*HWT*), and we present modifications of Hamming space that preserve pairwise Hamming distances and tighten the lower-bounds on the Hamming distances exploited by the HWT.

The chapter is organised as follows: Section *Similarity Search* provides the formalization of the similarity searching. Section *Challenges & Problem Formulation* presents the main challenges of the similarity search. A brief discussion about the extraction of descriptors, similarity measures, and a related research about the searching in metric spaces is provided in Section *Background & Preliminaries*, and the remaining sections address particular challenges of the searching with sketches: *Transformations of Metric Spaces into the Hamming space, Similarity Search with Sketches, Selection of Sketching Technique, and Statistical Analysis of Sketches to Facilitate their Indexing.*

SIMILARITY SEARCH

We focus on the similarity searching using metric space similarity model and queries by example. This section formalizes such searching.

Similarity Queries

We focus on the similarity *queries by example* (Zezula et al., 2006). Formally, we assume arbitrary data objects and the domain of their descriptors D. Having a dataset $X \subseteq D$, we want to be able to efficiently find the most similar descriptors $o \in X$ to an arbitrary query object $q \in D$. We assume the *similarity function* $d : D \times D \mapsto R$ that expresses the pairwise similarity of objects $o \in X$ in a way, that the bigger the value $d(o_1, o_2)$, the less similar objects o_1, o_2. There are two basic types of these similarity queries:

- The range query is assigned by the query object q and the distance d_q. Its goal is to find objects $o \in X$ such that $d(q,o) \leq d_q$.
- The k nearest neighbour query (kNN) is given by the query object q and a number $k \in N$. Its goal is to find k closest objects $o \in X$ to q.

We often denote the similarity query just by the query object q, as our findings are applicable on both these query types.

In practice, the kNN queries are of greater interest, as setting the distance d_q in the case of range queries requires non-trivial knowledge about the similarity function d and the dataset X. Moreover, usual differences in density of objects $o \in X$ around particular query objects $q \in D$ lead to big differences in numbers of objects $o \in X$ within a given distance d_q to q (Mic et al., 2018a). Knowledge of the suitable range d_q is as fundamental that the execution of the range queries is significantly more efficient using some indexing structures than the execution of the k NN queries (Mic et al., 2018b).

The execution of the similarity queries in complex domains where the data objects are characterised by the descriptors requires two stages: the pre-processing of the raw data in which we want to search and the actual similarity search. Figure 3 illustrates these stages using the example of searching in images: In the pre-processing phase, the descriptors of images are extracted and stored in a database to form the dataset X. When evaluating the similarity queries, the descriptor $q \in D$ of the query image is extracted and the closest descriptors o from the dataset X are identified to return the images associated with these descriptors.

An efficient similarity search cannot afford to evaluate all the pairwise distances $d(q,o)$, $o \in X$ for current large datasets, so techniques to prune the search space are being developed to speed up the

Figure 3. The similarity search for the most visually similar images

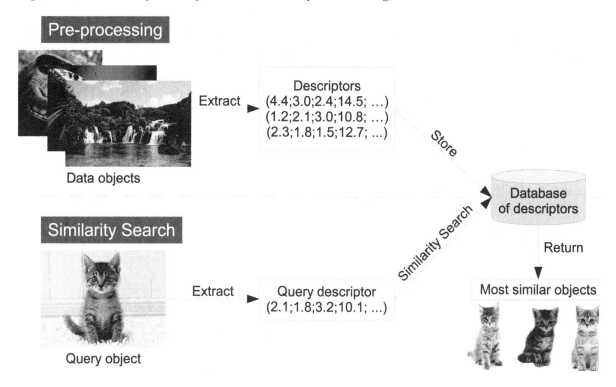

query evaluation. We focus on the transformation of the search space to Hamming space to support the efficiency of similarity searching in big datasets.

Quality of the Query Result

The similarity search does not have to return precise results in many real-life applications. Conversely, a more efficient search that returns answers of sufficient quality is usually preferred. Moreover, precise searching can be even unfeasible in some cases, due to rapidly changing datasets, geographical distances of particular storages, and insufficient network speed. In general, users usually want a *relevant* and *quickly* delivered query result.

We describe the quality of searching via the intersection of the returned and the precise query answer. We denote $Prec(q,k) \subseteq X$. the k most similar objects to q, and $Ans(q,k) \subseteq X$ the answer rerned by the searching. The *recall* of the query answer is then defined:

$$recall(q,k) = \frac{\left| Prec(q,k) \cap Ans(q,k) \right|}{k}.$$

Therefore, $recall(q,k) \in [0,1]$ and the bigger the recall, the better the searching quality.

Metric Space Similarity Model

Descriptors of complex data objects are usually proposed with some properties that allow their efficient processing. We assume the similarity of objects modelled by metric space, which is one of the most generic models that enables efficient searching using sophisticated similarity indexes. Metric space (D,d) is defined by a domain of objects D, which, in our case, is the domain of descriptors, and the distance function d with the following properties. For all objects $o_1, o_2, o_3 \in D$:

- $d(o_1,o_2) \geq 0$ (non-negativity),
- $d(o_1,o_2) = 0 \Leftrightarrow o_1 = o_2$ (identity),
- $d(o_1,o_2) = d(o_2,o_1)$ (symmetry),
- $d(o_1,o_2) + d(o_2,o_3) \geq d(o_1,o_3)$ (triangle inequality).

The advantage of the metric space similarity model is its robustness, since it treats data objects as black boxes and it does not limit their structure or properties.

CHALLENGES AND PROBLEM FORMULATION

This section summarises the challenges of an efficient similarity search in domains modelled by metric space. It also specifies the problems addressed in this chapter.

Similarity Search as a Challenge

Data Volume Many applications require efficient searching in big data. For instance, surveillance cameras produce huge volumes of data, and the efficacy of video processing is crucial for reactions to the scene on time. The volume of searched data is increasing due to both: increasing data production and the size of descriptors. The descriptors have grown significantly along with their ability to describe the raw data more precisely. State-of-the-art descriptors from neural networks consist of thousands of float numbers. As a result, e.g. 100 million of the *DeCAF* visual descriptors of images (properly described later) occupy 1.5 TB on hard-drive after the compression. Despite the volume, whole datasets must be often searched. For example, social media have to prevent the uploading of malicious or other restricted content to their websites. Since the volume of the data is enormous, datasets do not fit into main memory. Similarity search techniques thus have to take into account the cost of the accessing particular descriptors in secondary or distributed storage to evaluate their distances to the query descriptor.

Similarity Function Complexity Another challenging aspect of the similarity search is the complexity of similarity functions. Many distance computations are usually needed to evaluate the similarity query, so even small differences in the complexity of the distance functions are important. Various metric indexes have been proposed to reduce the number of distance computations, but the number of accessed descriptors and distance evaluations usually still determine the query execution time.

Data Complexity A lot of similarity search techniques degrade to sequential evaluation of too many distances when applied to state-of-the-art descriptors. This is caused by the phenomenon called *the curse of dimensionality*: The volume of search spaces has increased significantly in recent years, due to the increasing dimensionality of descriptors. On the other hand, datasets have grown significantly less than domains. As a consequence, the spaces of the state-of-the-art descriptors are getting sparse, the mean of distances is growing, and their variance is relatively shrinking (Skala, 2005, Kraus, 2019). Therefore, it is hard to distinguish *"close"* and *"far"* descriptors by an efficient simple estimation, since the distances are similar. Searching in high dimensional data thus figures an important challenge for all newly developed searching techniques.

Additional Requirements Some applications require another challenging properties of the search engines such as the minimum query throughput. Such requirements can further limit the computational power available for the query executions. Therefore, it is suitable to do a fine-tuning of searching engines for particular use cases. A typical example is given by the surveillance cameras operated by a limited number of servers.

Chapter's Goals

We address the challenges of the similarity search by the transformation of the metric search space (D,d) to Hamming space $(\{0,1\}^\lambda, h)$, where h is the Hamming distance function, and λ is the length of sketches. This transformation should provide an approximation of the similarity relationships of objects as described by the metric space (D,d) using just a small amount of memory and a cheap distance function. We address the following topics in this chapter:

- Definition of the sketching technique that transforms the metric space to Hamming space.
- Proposal of searching algorithm that uses sketches to speed-up the similarity search.
- Since many different sketching techniques exist, we discuss efficient selection of an appropriate sketching technique for particular data.
- The search in the Hamming space may also be time-consuming in the case of very big datasets. Thus, the indexing of sketches is also important and we discuss properties of sketches that facilitate their indexing.

BACKGROUND AND PRELIMINARIES

This section describes the background and context of the chapter. It also provides an overview of the similarity distance functions and related work.

Content Based Descriptors and their Extraction

Originally, *content-based* searching was based on user-defined keywords (Yoshitaka & Ichikawa, 1999). However, this approach cannot involve many demanded use cases, as keywords cannot describe complex multimedia thoroughly. State-of-the-art content-based retrieval thus exploits features extracted from data objects that are adapted to specific usage. These extracted features are called descriptors, and they are usually high dimensional vectors compared by a similarity function. This similarity of descriptors then expresses the similarity of original data objects.

Designing extractors of descriptors required considerable domain expertise before the boom of deep learning techniques. The state-of-the-art methods are fed with the raw data to automatically discover the representations suitable for the further processing. The deep learning use *multiple levels of representation, obtained by composing simple but non-linear modules that each transform the representation at one level (starting with the raw input) into a representation at a higher, slightly more abstract level* (LeCun et al., 2015).

These deep learning methods have been achieving the state-of-the-art results since 2012. First, they brought a revolution to image classification (Krizhevsky et al., 2012) and speech recognition (Dahl et al., 2012). Currently, they dominate machine learning in various domains such as the understanding and translation of natural languages, recommender systems, image post-processing, video classification, and face recognition. While the deep neural networks have usually been proposed to solve classification problems, the values from the last hidden layer of the networks are often high-quality descriptors of the raw data objects.

We also reproduce experiments to illustrate various features of discussed methods, and we use visual descriptors of images. Specifically, we use two types of descriptors.

DeCAF descriptors are image visual descriptors made for the *Profiset image collection*[1] (Donahue et al., 2013, Oquab et al., 2014). They are 4,096-dimensional vectors of float numbers taken as an output from the last hidden layer of a deep convolutional neural net (Krizhevsky et al., 2012). They are usually compared by the Euclidean distance.

MPEG-7 descriptors are also the image visual descriptors made as a combination of five visual descriptors. They are provided by the CoPhIR2[2] data collection (Batko et al., 2009). Each descriptor is accompanied with a suitable metric function, and all five descriptor spaces are combined into a single metric space (*D,d*) by a weighted sum of particular distances (Batko et al., 2010). In total, this image representation can be viewed as a 280-dimensional vector, which occupies about 600 B in a main memory.

Similarity Measures

In the following section, we provide an overview of often used similarity functions together with examples of the research fields where they are traditionally applied. We emphasise the complexity of distance functions, as the transformation of descriptors to sketches is particularly advantageous for expenve distance functions. All the described functions are metrics unless otherwise stated (Deza et Deza, 2009, Zezula et al., 2006).

Descriptors of complex multimedia objects are often vectors of real numbers. The Minkowski distance is probably the most often used function to expresses the similarity of vectors. Given a value $p \in N$ and vectors of length Λ, the Minkowski distance is defined as:

$$d_{Minkowski}\left(\overrightarrow{o_1}, \overrightarrow{o_2}\right) = \sqrt[p]{\sum_{i=0}^{\Lambda-1} |o_1[i] - o_2[i]|^p}$$

Examples of the Minkowski distances are the Euclidean distance ($p=2$) and the Manhattan distance ($p=1$). The length of vectors that describe complex multimedia objects has increased in the last decades, which makes the Minkowski distance function more expensive. The transformation of descriptors to sketches thus improves the searching efficiency in Minkowski spaces significantly.

A possible generalisation of the Euclidean distance is the *Quadratic form distance*. It enhances the Euclidean distance with the positive semi-definite matrix $M=[m_{i,j}]$ that expresses the interconnection between particular coordinates i and j of vectors $\overrightarrow{o_1}, \overrightarrow{o_2}$.

$$d_{QFD}\left(\vec{o_1}, \vec{o_2}, M\right) = \sqrt{\left(\vec{o_1} - \vec{o_2}\right)^T \cdot M \cdot \left(\vec{o_1} - \vec{o_2}\right)}$$

The Quadratic form distance is expensive to evaluate due to matrix multiplication. Note that the unit matrix M implies the Euclidean distance. The Quadratic form distance was originally proposed to search for similar images (Faloutsos et al., 1994).

A traditional and well-developed field of searching is the text search. The *Edit distance* expresses the dissimilarity of strings, and it is defined as the minimum number of *editing operations* needed to transform string o_1 to string o_2. Its most often used variant is the *Levenshtein distance* that uses editing orations *insert*, *delete* and *replace*, all applied to one character. Formally, operation *insert* adds a character to a given position and shifts all the remaining characters. Operation *delete* removes a character from a selected position and also shifts the rest, and operation *replace* changes one character in a given position to another one. The complexity of the Levenshtein distance is $\mathcal{O}\left(l\left(o_1\right) \cdot l\left(o_2\right)\right)$ where $l(o)$ is the length of string o. The *Tree Edit Distance* defined on trees also exists, with the operations *insert*, *delete* and *rename*. The complexity of this distance evaluation is $\mathcal{O}\left(\max\left(s\left(o_1\right), s\left(o_2\right)\right)^3\right)$ where $s(o)$ is the size of the tree o.

The generalisation of the Edit distance is the *Earth mover's distance* (EMD) (Rubner ert al., 2000). It is based on a *transportati problem*. Specifically, it evaluates the least-expensive flow between the *producers* and *customers* that satisfies the consumer's demand. The name of this distance is inspired by an example of several workers filling holes with the ground. The EMD is often applied to express the similarity of colour distributions in images, i.e. histograms. It is the metric function iff the *ground distance* that describes the flow between points is the metric function. Its complexity is $\mathcal{O}\left(N^3 log N\right)$ for N-bin histograms (Shirdhonkar and Jacobs, 2008).

The similarity of texts based on their content needs to be expressed in many real-life applications, for which the Edit distance is not suitable as it works on a low level of particular letters. The similarity of sets is often exploited to overcome this issue as it may express the similarity of texts from a higher information level. The sets usually consist of groups of letters so-called *shingles* (Manber, 1994).

The *Jaccard distance* is a typical measure to express the dissimilarity of two sets A and B:

$$d_{Jaccard}\left(A, B\right) = 1 - \frac{|A \cap B|}{|A \cup B|}$$

its variant called the *Tanimoto distance* expresses the dissimilarity of two bit strings that often denote the presence of subparts in a structure. The Tanimoto distance considers the ordering of particular bits, and it evaluates the dissimilarity of two bit-strings in length Λ:

$$d_{Tanimoto}\left(\vec{o_1}, \vec{o_2}\right) = 1 - \frac{\sum_{i=0}^{\Lambda-1}\left(o_1[i] \wedge o_2[i]\right)}{\sum_{i=0}^{\Lambda-1}\left(o_1[i] \vee o_2[i]\right)}$$

Figure 4. Example of distance densities. In black: $d(o_1,o_2)$, $o_1,o_2{\in}X$, in grey: $d(q,o)$, $o{\in}candSet(q)$ for a selected query object q; solid double line: 72 smallest distances $d(q,o)$, $o{\in}X$

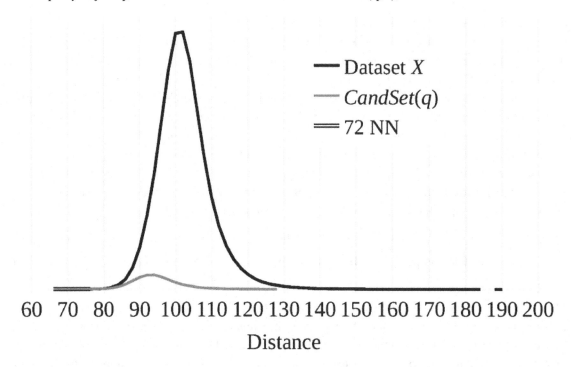

This distance is suitable to express the similarity of structured objects, and it is widely used, e.g. in chemistry to express the similarity of molecules (Kosman and Leonard, 2005).

New domains that require searching based on a similarity have also arisen, and they sometimes use their own proprietary and expensive distance functions. For instance, the similarity of protein sequences is studied for their classification. The evaluation of the *Q-score* that expresses the similarity of two protein structures (Krissinel, 2012) takes approximately 0.03 s on average according to our experiments. However, the variance is as huge, as some distance evaluations take tens of seconds. Therefore, 500,000 evaluations of this function take more than 4 hours.

Similarity models are also combined to achieve better fidelity of the perceived similarity description (Kittler et al., 1998). These approaches often increase the computational complexity of the similarity search, memory requirements or both.

The Hamming distance is the special case of the Manhattan distance. It is defined on vectors of binary numbers instead of the real numbers; therefore, it evaluates the number of different bits in two bit-strings. The Hamming distance is usually implemented using the XOR of two bit-strings and the sum of bits set to 1 in the result vector. It is thus one of the most efficient distance functions, and moreover, it can be efficiently evaluated on GPUs in parallel.

Metric Similarity Search

Techniques for efficient searching in metric space are of particular interest and also form the background of the sketching techniques, as the Hamming space is also a metric space. Moreover, these techniques can be used as an inspiration or basis of the sketching transformation, or they can be used together with the sketches, as sketches can form an additional filter incorporated into the similarity indexes.

All the similarity indexes, seen from a high-level view, split the search space to partitions. When the query object comes, they efficiently identify the partitions that are likely to contain similar objects to the query, and process them to return the query answer. This identification of promising partitions must be efficient and thus simple, as it is performed during the query execution. Having complex high dimensional spaces, the partitions identified to contain the most similar objects contain a lot of irrelevant objects as well. An example is given in Figure 4. The black curve depicts the density of distances in the dataset X which consists of 1 million DeCAF image visual descriptors. The two remaining curves depict the distances between one selected query object $q \in D$ and other objects: The short double curve depicts the 72 smallest distances $d(q,o)$, $o \in X$. All these distances are less than or equal to 76. The grey solid curve shows the density of distances $d(q,o)$, $o \in CandSet(q)$, where the $CandSet(q)$ consists of the partitions selected by the metric index M-$Index$ (Novak et al., 2011) to contain 50,000 objects $o \in X$, i.e. 5% of X. This $CandSet(q)$ contains just 66 out of 72 closest objects depicted by the double curve, i.e. approximately 92%. But at the same time, it contains even object o with the distance $d(q,o)=128$, its one half is formed by objects with $d(q,o)>92$, and 90% of it consists of objects with $d(q,o)>86$. This illustrates a lot of space for further filtering of this candidate set $CandSet(q)$. The accuracy of candidate sets generally decreases with the data complexity, which is a consequence of the dimensionality curse.

The space partitionings and the identification of the candidate set $CandSet(q)$ can be done in many ways, using different approaches. In the following paragraphs, we summarise the most significant ones.

Indexes can exploit the already evaluated distances to determine bounds on distances between the query object and objects from the dataset. Such pruning is usually based on triangle inequality. Examples are given by the *M-tree* (Ciaccia et al., 1997), *PM-tree* (Skopal, 2004), first version of the *M-Index* (Novak et al., 2011), and the *NOBH-tree* (Pola et al., 2014). Space pruning based on triangle inequality is not efficient in high dimensional spaces due to the dimensionality curse. Recently, Mic & Zezula, 2020 proposed a generic enhancement of triangle inequalities to define tighter bounds on unknown distances in metric spaces, and also a novel type of lower-bounds on distances. Their enhancement can be exploited in all these indexes with no additional time nor memory overhead.

The object positions in the search space can also be approximated by the *pivot permutation* (Chávez et al., 2008). It is defined by the ordering of the pre-selected reference points (*pivots*) sorted according to their distance to the object. For instance, the *PPP-codes* (Novak and Zezula, 2016) perform a multi-step filtration of the identified partitions to increase the precision of the similarity filtering.

Richard Connor et al. study the so-called *N-simplex projection* (Connor et al., 2017a) of complex metric spaces to the finite-dimensional Euclidean spaces where the specialised similarity search techniques can be applied for efficient search. They also propose a pruning mechanism that provides geometric guarantees stronger than the triangle inequality (Connor et al., 2017b) and is applicable in a large class of metric spaces.

Locality sensitive hashing (LSH) is a special type of hashing that assigns the same hash to two objects $o_1,o_2 \in X$ with probability that increases with their similarity (Leskovec et al., 2014, Novak et al., 2010). LSH techniques usually consist of several more or less independent instances of a simple LSH function, that are aggregated together. This aggregation allows the probability of assigning the same hash to two objects to be tuned according to their distance. The *Min-Hashing* is an example of the LSH that approximates the Jaccard similarity (Broder, 1997, Chiu et al., 2010).

TRANSFORMATIONS OF METRIC SPACES INTO THE HAMMING SPACE

We address transformations of the search space to Hamming space. These transformations are popular due to the efficiency of Hamming distance evaluations and a small size of bit string sketches. They are thus often applied to facilitate efficient searching in big datasets.

Formally, sketching technique is a function $sk : D \mapsto \{0,1\}^\lambda$. Sketches $sk(o)$, $o \in D$ compared by the Hamming distance should approximate the similarity as described by the metric space (D,d). Therefore, in an ideal case holds for all $q \in D$, $o_1, o_2 \in X$:

$$d(q,o_1) < d(q,o_2) \Rightarrow h\big(sk(q), sk(o_1)\big) < h\big(sk(q), sk(o_2)\big). \tag{1}$$

In practice, however, this implication is often violated even due to a different range of functions d and h. The distance function d is often continuous and the Hamming distance h. is a discrete function with range $[0,\ldots,\lambda]$ where λ is the length of sketches. In this case, many different distances $d(q,o)$ must be pjected to the same Hamming distance.

We do not consider the equality

$$h\big(sk(q), sk(o_1)\big) = h\big(sk(q), sk(o_2)\big)$$

in Equality 1, as in that case the trivial transformation of all objects $o \in D$ to the one-bit sketch $sk(o)=(0)$ would be defined as the perfect.

Related Work on Sketching

According to our best knowledge, Moses S. Charikar was the first author that proposed a transformation of the search space to Hamming space to speed-up similarity searching (Charikar, 2002). He used random hyperplanes to split vectors in multi-dimensional spaces in a way that the resulting bit strings approximate the cosine distance. This pioneering work does not contain experiments with real-life descriptors. The thesis of Kraus, (Kraus, 2019) however reveals, that the sketching technique GHP_50 which we describe in detail later, approximates the cosine space much better than Charikar's, despite it is widely applicable.

Lv et al. proposed their sketching technique for vectors compared by the (weighted) L_1 distance (Lv el al, 2004). It is based on thresholding; a threshold is determined for each dimension of the original space. Individual bits of the sketches are set according to values in corresponding dimensions and compressed. Wang et al., 2007, used these sketches and proved that they have the binomial distance distribution. It allows them to propose a probabilistic model to estimate the recall values to be achieved by simple sketch-based filtering. However, their experiments show significantly higher recall than predicted, with the difference up to 0.15.

After these pioneering studies, dozens of sketching techniques have been proposed (Cao et al., 2018). For instance, Mitzenmacher et al., 2014, proposed the sketching technique that exploits the min-hashing to approximate the Jaccard space by the Hamming space. This sketching technique, as well as the Min-

Hashing, are efficient in case of queries with the nearest neighbours within relatively small distances and thus strongly suffer from the dimensionality curse.

John Daugman, 2003, investigates statistical properties of bit-strings in Hamming space. He proposes the encoding of images of human irises to bit-strings that are exploited to identify persons. Despite a different research area, these bit-strings have the same properties as sketches proposed by Muller-Molina and Shinohara, 2009. The work of Daugman is extended by Mic et al. towards generic sketching techniques, and we describe it more in detail in this chapter.

Current approaches often rely on deep neural networks (Cao et al., 2018), which is advantageous as an ability of the sketching techniques to approximate the search space is data dependent. Moreover, sketches can be of various lengths, and sketching transformations use various parameters. This makes the fair comparison of sketching techniques difficult – see for instance the discussion provided by Vadicamo et al., 2019. In general, there is no clear winner and many different approaches have been shown to provide a reasonable search space approximation using a specific data.

Sketching techniques are also of a different applicability. Often, they are restricted to the vector spaces or subclasses of metric spaces. This is the case of techniques proposed in articles Charikar, 2002, Lv et al., 2004, Lv et al., 2006, and Mitzenmacher et al., 2014. Other techniques, like those proposed by Muller-Molina and Shinohara, 2009, Mic et al., 2016, Mic et al., 2017, Higuchi et al., 2018, Higuchi et al., 2019 are applicable in generic metric spaces and treat descriptors as black boxes. Generic metric-based techniques usually require a learning phase that is often time-consuming. It usually contains a selection of reference objects, so-called pivots, exploited to transform objects to sketches. Sketching techniques specialised for particular spaces approximates them often more precisely than the generic metric-based approaches (Cao et al., 2018, Vadicamo et al., 2019).

Figure 5. The Generalised hyperplane partitioning

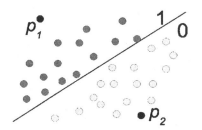

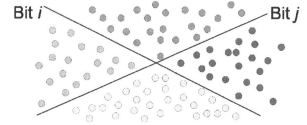

(a) GHP to set values in one bit   (b) Two GHPs to set values in two bits

Generic Sketching Techniques and Properties of Sketches

Further, we describe sketching techniques applicable in an arbitrary metric space, which try to produce sketches with specific statistical properties. Such properties can be further exploited when building a complex similarity search engine, which is a challenge described in following sections.

Muller-Molina and Shinohara, 2009, emphasize that each bit i, $0 \leq i < \lambda$ of sketches $sk(o)$, $o \in X$ divides the dataset X into two parts. They propose to use this fact conversely, and use a simple partitioning of the metric space to define the sketching technique *sk*. Specifically, they use the *Generalised hyperplane partitioning* (*GHP*) to define bits of sketches *sk(o)*, $o \in X$ (see Figure 5): a pair of pivots $p_{i1}, p_{i2} \in D$ is selected for each bit *i* of sketches *sk(o)*, $o \in X$, and the value of bit *i* expresses which of these two pivots is closer to *o*. Therefore, one instance of GHP determines one bit of all sketches *sk(o)*, $o \in X$. Muller-Molina and Shinohara propose to select pivots p_{i1}, p_{i2} to define sketches with approximately *balanced bits:*

Balanced bits: each bit *i* of sketches *sk(o)*, $o \in X$ is set to 1 in one half of sketches *sk(o)*.

Figure 6. The Ball partitioning

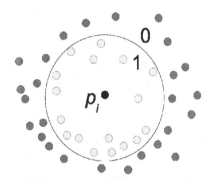

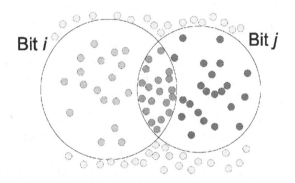

(a) BP to set values in one bit   (b) Two BPs to set values in two bits

Mic et al. further elaborate on the statistical properties of sketches (Mic et al., 2016, Mic et al., 2017), and they investigate both basic types of the metric space partitioning – beside the GHP also the *Ball partitioning* (*BP*) – see Figure 6. Sketching techniques based on the BP use one pivot p_i and a selected radius rad_i to determine values of bit *i* in all sketches *sk(o)*, $o \in X$: if $d(p_i, o)$ is smaller than rad_i, then the *i*th bit of *sk(o)* is 1, otherwise it is 0. To select suitable pivots p_{i1}, p_{i2} for the GHPs, and p_i and radii rad_i for the BPs, respectively, Mic et al. experimentally verify an influence of various statistical properties of sketches on their ability to approximate the original metric space (*D,d*).

Specifically, these authors investigate the influence of the properties of sketches *sk(o)*, $o \in X$ on their ability to approximate the original metric space (*D,d*) to support the efficiency of the similarity search. The first investigated property is same as addressed by Muller-Molina and Shinohara, i.e. the property of the Balanced bits. The other two properties are:

Independent bits: all pairs of bits *i* and *j*, $i \neq j$ of sketches *sk(o)*, $o \in X$ should be independent, i.e. uncorrelated. Authors use the Pearson correlation coefficient.

Bits clarity: considering that each bit *i* divides the objects $o \in X$ into two sub-spaces, these sub-spaces should be as far from each other, as possible.

While the properties of the balanced and independent bits support the potential of sketches to well approximate original distances, the *bits clarity* brings additional problems since such bits are usually highly correlated. Generally, big bit correlations are also the reason why the quality of sketches made by the Ball partitioning suffer from the high (intrinsic) dimensionality of data. Authors thus propose a heuristic that selects λ pivots pairs

$$\left(\left(p_{i1}, p_{j1}\right), \left(p_{i2}, p_{j2}\right), ..., \left(p_{i\lambda}, p_{j\lambda}\right)\right)$$

for λ GHP instances to produce sketches with approximately balanced and low pairwise correlated bits. This sketching technique is denoted as *GHP_50,* where suffix "_50" denotes balanced bits. The GHP instances can be also modified to define precisely balanced bits, e.g. by a technique described by Dohnal et al., 2001. Nevertheless, this infer the quality of space approximation just negligibly (Mic et al., 2017) and does not solve the problem of pivot selection by itself.

Articles of Mic et al., 2018b, and Mic et al., 2017, explain the meaning of the signum of the Pearson correlation coefficient. Having arbitrary lists of binary values *I* and *J*, e.g. values in the *i*th and *j*th bit of sketches $o \in X$, and list $\neg I$ of the negated values from *I*, the following holds for the Pearson correlation coefficient *corr* of two lists:

$$corr(I,J) = -corr(\neg I,J) \tag{2}$$

The proof is provided in Mic et al., 2018b. Since flipping arbitrary bit *i* of all sketches *sk(o)*, $o \in X$ does not infer the pairwise Hamming distances of sketches, just the absolute value of the Pearson correlation coefficient matters when focusing an ability of sketches to approximate the search space *(D,d)*.

Sketching technique GHP_50 tries to maximise the *entropy* of sketches with respect to their length λ (Cao et al., 2018). However, it also maximizes the *intrinsic dimensionality (iDim)* of sketches, which is a measure expressing the difficulty of metric-based indexing (Skala, 2005). The *iDim* of metric data is often estimated by the formula of Chávez et al., 2001:

$$iDim \approx \frac{\mu^2}{2 \cdot \sigma^2} \tag{3}$$

where μ is the mean of distances d(o1 o2$_j$), o1 o2 $_{\in}$D and $\sigma2$ is their variance. Therefore, the main drawback of sketches with balanced bits and low pairwise bit correlations is related to their further processing. Despite of the efficiency of the Hamming distance evaluation, the indexing of sketches is required to speed up their searching in the case of very big datasets (Ong el al., 2016). This drawback motivates further investigation of the pairwise bit correlations and balance of bits.

Mic et al., 2017, relax the property of the balanced bits and introduce sketches with b*its balanced to* β:

Bits Balanced to β:
Bit i is balanced to β, $\beta \in [0,1]$ with respect to dataset X, *i*ff it is set to 1 in $\beta \cdot |X|$ s*k*etches sk(o), $o \in X$.

Authors analyse these sketches to reveal, that their iD*im decreases* with increasing $\beta \in [0.5,1]$, under the assumption of the same bit correlations. The opposite case $\beta \in [0,0.5]$ is symmetric, so the iDim *is* maximised in case of balanced bits, i.e. $\beta = 0.5$. Specifically, the iDim *of* s*k*etches balanced to $\beta = 0.5$

and $\beta = 0.8$ differs by one third in the experiments. On the other hand, the quality of sketches with bits balanced to $\beta \in [0.5, 0.8]$ is practically the same on condition of sufficient length of sketches λ.

These results confirm a better trade-off concerning quality, indexability and length λ provided by sketches with unbalanced bits. Experiments that confirm theoretical analysis from the article of Mic et al., 2017, are conducted in the article of Mic et al., 2018b. Authors recommend to use sketches with balanced bits on the condition, that the evaluation of all the Hamming distances h(sk(o), *sk(q)*), o∈X *is* sufficiently efficient.

The Length of Sketches

Sketching techniques usually require the length of sketches λ to be set in advance, and thus its selection is another natural challenge to address. Many authors that propose techniques of dimensionality reduction claim: ideally, *the reduced representation should have a dimensionality that corresponds to the intrinsic dimensionality of the data (Van De*r Maaten et al., 2009, Journaux et al., 2008). Mic et al., 2016 reveal, that the sketches sk(o), o∈X *m*ade by the sketching technique GHP_50 have a similar

Figure 7. Sketch length λ and average pairwise correlation of bits of sketches c that implies the intrinsic dimensionality of sketches 30

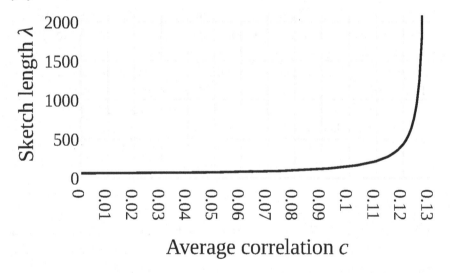

intrinsic dimensionality as the dataset X. They *p*rovide an analysis of the Equation 3 that estimates the iDim of *the* data, and derive an estimation of the iDim of *sket*ches based on their length λ and an average pairwise bit correlation c:

$$iDim \approx \frac{\mu^2}{2 \cdot \sigma^2} \approx \frac{\lambda}{2 \cdot \left(1 + (\lambda - 1) \cdot c^2\right)} \quad (4)$$

Assuming that we know the iDim *of s*ketches, we can express the dependency of the sketch length λ and the average pairwise correlation c that induce this iDim. *An e*xample of such dependency for iDim

= *30* is given in Figure 7. The consequence of the Equation 4 is just a finite iDim *of the* sketches that have correlated bits, i.e. c>0:

$$\lim_{\lambda \to \infty} iDim = \frac{1}{2 \cdot c^2}$$

This is also illustrated by Figure 7. Sketches with the iD*im 30* cannot have an average pairwise bit correlation

$$c > 1/\sqrt{60} \approx 0.1291$$

Mic et al., 2016, experimentally verify that the ability of sketches to approximate the metric space (D,d) increases with their length, however, the contribution of additional bits is negligible from some length λ. They propose to identify this length via a tangent of the curve depicted in Figure 7, made for the *iDim* of the dataset X. More specifically, they recommend selecting a sufficiently steep tangent of this curve and to adopt a corresponding sketch length λ which provides a suitable trade-off between the length λ and the memory occupation.

SIMILARITY SEARCH WITH SKETCHES

Sketches are compared by the Hamming distance which brings the drawback of a relatively narrow range of possible distances. This does not allow to distinguish sketches within the same distance h*(sk(*q*),* s*k(*o*))* to the query sketch s*k(*q*)*. Some authors propose to overcome this issue with the weighted Hamming distance. Others motivate their research by the possibility of a better approximation of the distance d*(*q*,*o*)* using the precise position of the query object q. In that case, sketches s*k(*o*)* are created for objects o∈X and they are somehow compared directly with the query object q∈D. We further insist on the most common approach, i.e. comparing the sketches purely by the Hamming distance to exploit its efficiency.

Related Work on Similarity Search with Sketches in the Hamming Space

Another challenge is figured by the searching mechanism, i.e. how to use sketches to speed-up similarity searching. The naive searching algorithm implements a paradigm *filter and refine*:

1. Having the similarity query (*k*NN or *range* query), the sketch $sk(q)$ of the query object q is created.
2. Some fixed number k' of sketches $sk(o)$, $o \in X$ with the minimum Hamming distances $h(sk(q)$, $sk(o))$ is selected (*filtering phase*).
   ◦ Candidate set $CandSet(q) \subseteq X$ cosists of objects that correspond to these most similar sketches $sk(o)$.
3. All distances $d(q,o)$, $o \in CandSet(q)$ are evaluated to return the most similar objects $o \in CandSet(q)$ as the query answer (refinement phase).

This algorithm does not address the main searching challenges. The selection of the candidate set size k' requires non-trivial knowledge. Moreover, it should be selected for each query object $q \in D$ independently, since real-life datasets X usually form a subspace of the domain D with in-homogeneous

Figure 8. Example of the distances d(q,o) and Hamming distances h(sk(q), sk(o)) on corresponding sketches

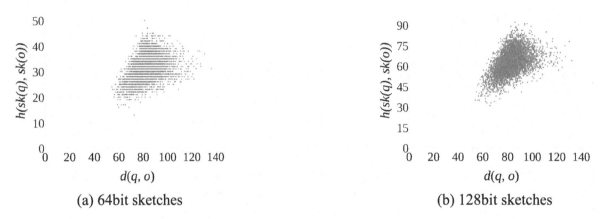

(a) 64bit sketches   (b) 128bit sketches

density. Therefore, the k' needed to achieve a search of sufficient quality differs significantly for particular query objects $q \in D$.

The candidate set size k' must be quite big, usually in orders of percentages of the dataset X, to achieve sufficient searching quality. This is caused by a rather low correspondence of the Hamming distances $h(sk(q), sk(o))$, $q \in D$, $o \in X$ and original distances $d(q,o)$, as we show in Figure 8. It depicts 5,000 distances $d(q,o)$ for a selected query object $q \in D$ and 5,000 randomly selected objects $o \in X$ (see x-axis), and the corresponding Hamming distances $h(sk(q), sk(o))$ (y-axis). The Pearson correlation coefficient is +0.36 in case of 64bit sketches (Figure 8a), and +0.47 in case of 128bit sketches (Figure 8b). We used sketches created by the sketching technique GHP_50 and dataset DeCAF in these experiments.

Jegou et al., 2008 propose gradual two step similarity filtering. The authors focus on the search for similar images represented by local descriptors organised by the *bag-of-features (BOF)* (Sivic and Zisserman, 2003). The BOF considers the image local descriptors quantized by the k-means algorithm into visual words, which are the centroids of Voronoi cells. An image is then represented by a frequency histogram of the visual words. Jegou et al. propose to use sketches to refine the matching based on the visual words. Sketches, called *binary signatures* in this article, encode the locations of high dimensional descriptors within their Voronoi cell. Signatures are integrated within the inverted file and efficiently exploited to skip some comparisons of high dimensional descriptors during the query executions. Jegou et al. do not solve the main task of such additional filtering, however, which is figured by the setting of the Hamming distance threshold for the filtering with sketches. They provide experiments with a few fixed values selected manually, always picking one for all query objects $q \in D$. Such an approach does not exploit the main potential of the additional filtering, which can adaptively react to the nature of particular query objects.

Additional Similarity Filtering with Sketches in Metric Spaces

Mic et al., 2018a, elaborate on searching that uses sketches together with some similarity index, and propose a more generic algorithm for an arbitrary metric space. More specifically, these authors consider an arbitrary index for similarity searching in metric spaces that works on the filter and refine principle. Having a query object $q \in D$, the index identifies the candidate set $CandSet(q) \subseteq X$, and then when the distance $d(q,o)$, $o \in CandSet(q)$ is to be evaluated, authors propose first to evaluate the Hamming distance $h(sk(q), sk(o))$ on corresponding sketches to decide whether the evaluation of the $d(q,o)$ pays off or the chance of o to be included in the query result is too small.

The key contribution of this secondary filtering consists of the possibility of a *dynamic* skipping of distance evaluations according to already evaluated distances $d(q,o)$, $o \in CandSet(q)$. The article of Mic et al., 2018a, contains a probabilistic model that enables to efficiently decide the filtering threshold t on the Hamming distance $h(sk(q), sk(o))$, $o \in CandSet(q)$ during the refinement of the $CandSet(q)$ to fully exploit already known information.

Figure 9. Example of the Tukey box-plot

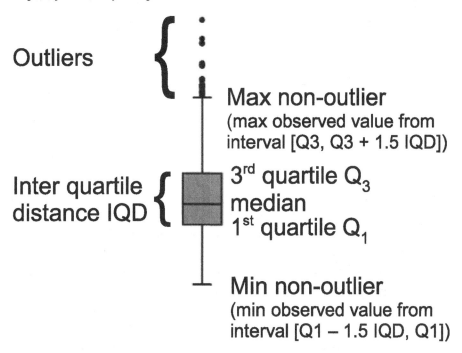

Specifically, authors model the correspondence between the distances $d(o_1,o_2)$, $o_1,o_2 \in X$ and the Hamming distances $h(sk(o_1), sk(o_2))$. Having this correspondence, a fixed probability π is selected to create a mapping of the Hamming distances b: $0 \le b \le \lambda$ to the distances x= $d(o1,o2)$, $o1,o2 \in_x$ such that π expresses the probability that the sketches of two objects $o1,o_2$: $_d(o1,o_2)= x$ are within the Hamming distance $h(sk(o1), sk(o2))_= b$. When the refinement of the $CandSet(q)$ is performed and the distance $d(q,o)$, $o \in CandSet(q)$ is to be evaluated, authors check the distance x= $d(q,ok)$ $_t$o the currently found kth nearest neighbour ok t_o q and select the minimum filtering threshold t such that:

$$P\left(h\left(sk\left(o_1\right), sk\left(o_2\right)\right) \ge t \mid d\left(o_1,o_2\right) = x\right) \ge \pi$$

This t is searched in a table that contains a mapping of distances x and b, $0 \le b \le \lambda$ and thus contains just $\lambda+1$ records. Therefore, this secondary filtering is very efficient since all the expensive information

Figure 10. Secondary filtering with sketches, = 205, DeCAF dataset, primary filtering with the M-Index, = 150,000 objects out of 1M

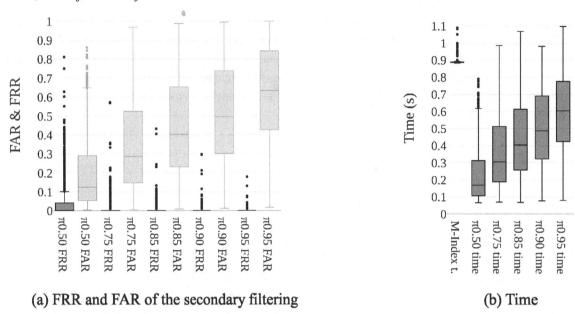

(a) FRR and FAR of the secondary filtering   (b) Time

is pre-computed during the pre-processing time and just this table is exploited during the query execution time. We reproduce a few experiments described properly by Mic et al., 2018a, to illustrate the power of the secondary filtering with sketches. We use Tu*key box-plots t*o depict the variance of the results of particular query objects. This type of the box-plot is described in Figure 9.

Figure 10 describes results of the secondary filtering with sketches of length λ=205, applied to the DeCAF dataset of size |X|=1 million descriptors. In this scenario, 1,000 query objects q∈*D a*re selected in random, and 100NN queries are evaluated, i.e. we are searching for 100 most similar objects to each q. The metric index called the M-*Index (*Novak et al., 2011) is used to identify 150,000 most promising objects C*andSet(q)* from the dataset X, i.e. 15%, to each query object q∈*D.* This C*andSet(q)* contains 99 out of 100 true nearest neighbours to q, on median. Figure 10a depicts the f*alse reject rate (*FRR) and f*alse accept rate (*FAR) of the secondary filtering with sketches, for various values of the probability π. Specifically, the FRR expresses the relative number of the true nearest neighbours that are in the C*andSet(q) a*nd have been wrongfully filtered out by sketches. This FRR is zero for the majority of queries (see the dark-grey box-plots in Figure 10a). The FAR expresses the ratio of objects from the C*andSet(q) w*hich are not the true nearest neighbours and thus can be filtered out by sketches, and they have been not filtered out (see the light-grey box plots in Figure 10a). The FRR thus infers the quality of the query result, FAR infers the searching time, which is depicted in Figure 10b. The secondary filtering with sketches speed-up the searching 2.9 times on median (from 886 ms to 306 ms) while preserving the quality of searching for more than 75% of the query objects, in these experiments.

An intuitive question about the size of the C*andSet(q)* arises: What is the contribution of the secondary filtering if a significantly smaller C*andSet(q)* is selected? And moreover: since the secondary filtering decreases the quality of the search in general, is it possible to achieve similar quality of the searching just by a selection of a smaller C*andSet(q)?* A big C*andSet(q)* in the previous example is selected to cover 99 out of 100 true nearest neighbours for median query object q. If a smaller C*andSet(q)* is selected, its

Figure 11. Secondary filtering with sketches, λ = 160, MPEG7 1M dataset, primary filtering with the PPP-codes, |CandSet(q)| ∈ {500, 1000, 2000, 4000, 6000, 8000, 10000, 12500, 15000}, π=0.75

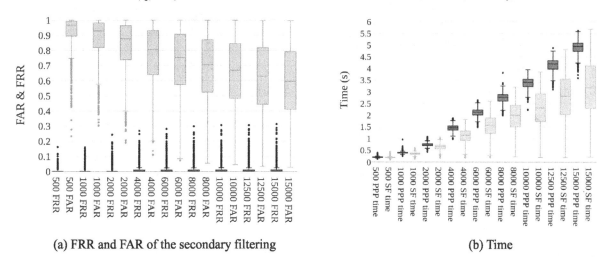

(a) FRR and FAR of the secondary filtering   (b) Time

quality is lower and it contains less clearly irrelevant objects, assuming a meaningful primary filter. We illustrate this with the experiments conducted on the dataset of 1 million MPEG7 descriptors in Figure 11. In this case, the PP*P-codes a*re used as the primary index (Novak & Zezula, 2016). Figure 11a confirms a decreasing FAR with increasing size of Ca*ndSet(q)*, while the FRR is still zero for the vast majority of the query objects. Figure 11b depicts the searching times of the PPP-codes without and with the secondary filtering, in the dark-grey and light grey colours, respectively. Beside the overall speed-up of the similarity search, Figures 10 and 11 also illustrates a fundamental contribution of the secondary filtering. The variance of the FAR with respect to different queries is large and the variance of FRR is marginal, for π≥0.75. This testifies to the well-known fact that the using the same size of Ca*ndSet(q) f*or all query objects is in principle wrong. The secondary filtering behaves dynamically considering different query objects q∈D, *a*s the filtering threshold t i*s* given by the distance to the current kth nearest neighbour. Therefore, it significantly reduces the number of distance d(q,o*), o*∈C*andSet(q) e*valuations in case of unnecessarily big Ca*ndSet(q) a*nd conversely, it allows to fully exploit the Ca*ndSet(q) s*ize in case of queries that need it to achieve a high quality search. This feature makes the secondary filtering useful especially for indexing techniques which use a Ca*ndSet(q) of* a fixed size for all query objects q∈D.

SELECTION OF SKETCHING TECHNIQUE

Many sketching techniques that transform the search space to Hamming space exist, and the selection of a technique suitable for a particular dataset *X* is challenging due to a dependency of the quality of sketches on data (Tiberio & Zezula, 1993). Practitioners usually evaluate a sufficient number of similarity queries using the filter and refine algorithm described in Section "*Related Work on Similarity Search with Sketches*". This testing is, however, quite time consuming, and has several drawbacks, as pointed out by Mic et al., 2018c:

- The results are affected by a selection of query objects *q*∈*D*.

Figure 12. Means and standard deviations of the Hamming distances for a given

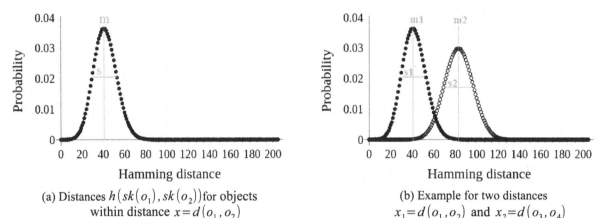

(a) Distances $h\left(sk\left(o_1\right), sk\left(o_2\right)\right)$ for objects within distance $x=d\left(o_1,o_2\right)$

(b) Example for two distances $x_1=d\left(o_1,o_2\right)$ and $x_2=d\left(o_3,o_4\right)$

- A representative number of queries q must be evaluated on a representative sample of the dataset X.
- Sketches $sk(o)$ for all objects o from a sample of X and query objects must be created, which can be time consuming.
- An evaluation of precise answers for each query object q must be performed.
- The quality of approximate evaluations is strongly influenced by the candidate set size k'.
- A selection of k' with no prior knowledge of the sketching technique is difficult.

Therefore, the selection of a suitable sketching technique for a particular dataset X based on this testing is expensive and influenced by variables that are hard to set.

Mic et al., 2018c, propose a heuristic to efficiently estimate the quality of sketches using only a very small sample of a dataset X. This estimation can be efficiently evaluated using many sketching techniques to select the promising ones for any given data. In the following paragraphs, we briefly describe the basics of this proposal.

The heuristic is based on a comparison of a set of distances $d(o_1,o_2)$, $o_1,o_2 \in X$ and the Hamming distances $h(sk(o_1), sk(o_2))$ on corresponding sketches. It does not use any query objects, so the estimation of the quality of sketches is not influenced by their selection. Having an arbitrary distance $x=d(o_1,o_2)$, $o_1,o_2 \in X$, authors analytically estimate the mean m and the variance s^2 of the Hamming distance $h(sk(o_1),$ $sk(o_2))$ between corresponding sketches. Figure 12a provides an example: The black points express the probability that the Hamming distance $h(sk(o_1), sk(o_2))$ of objects within a fixed distance $x=d(o_1,o_2)$ is equal to the value on the horizontal axis. Then, authors consider a pair of distances $x_1=d(o_1,o_2)$ and $x_2=d(o_3,o_4)$ such that $x_1 \leq x_2$ (see Figure 12b), and extend the concept of the *separation* (Daugman, 2003). The *separation* $sep_{sk}(x_1,x_2)$ of distances x_1,x_2 after the transformation of objects o_1,o_2,o_3,o_4 to their sketches is defined as:

$$sep_{sk}\left(x_1,x_2\right) = \frac{m_2 - m_1}{\sqrt{\dfrac{s_1^2 + s_2^2}{2}}} \tag{5}$$

Assuming that the distance function d is continuous in range $[0,\Gamma]$, an ability of the sketching technique sk to approximate the distance function d is expressed by the double integral of Equation 5 over this range of distances x_1 and x_2. Since we consider the application of sketches for the similarity search, it is meaningful to describe their ability to distinguish *"small"* distances from the rest. For this reason, Mic et al., 2018c, propose to evaluate the integral using a threshold t: $0 < t \ll \Gamma$:

$$quality\left(sk,t\right) = \int_0^t \int_{x_1}^{\Gamma} sep_{sk}\left(x_1,x_2\right) \partial x_2\, \partial x_1$$

The value *quality(sk,t)* thus describes an ability of sketches to correctly distinguish the distances with a stress on the distances $d(o_1,o_2) \leq t$. To estimate the quality of sketches, the proposed technique only requires a set of distances $d(o_1,o_2)$, corresponding Hamming distances of sketches, and the optional parameter t. The estimation is unsupervised and takes just tens of seconds per sketching technique. Authors present the correspondence of their estimations with the recall of the simple sketch-based filtering. The Pearson correlation coefficient between the recall of various sketching techniques and the estimations is from +0.93 to +0.98, using various settings.

STATISTICAL ANALYSIS OF SKETCHES TO FACILITATE THEIR INDEXING

Sketch-based similarity search usually assumes that the efficiency of the Hamming distance calculations allows for the evaluation of all the Hamming distances between the query sketch and sketches $sk(o)$, $o \in X$, or $sk(o)$, $o \in CandSet(q)$. However, as the size of datasets grows, the sequential evaluation of all the Hamming distances is sometimes too demanding for real-life purposes, as it takes minutes in the case of datasets with billions of sketches (Ong et al., 2016). Techniques specialised for an indexing and pruning of the Hamming space exist, and also generic metric indexes can be applied to prune the space of sketches. However, similarity indexes and pruning mechanisms are efficient only in cases that near neighbours exist. In the case of sketches, it means that there must be sketches within relatively small Hamming distances for each query sketch $sk(q)$, $q \in D$. The sketches are required to be short, despite the fact that they usually approximate complex search spaces. This leads to a high information density and poor indexability of sketches (Skala, 2008). Eghbali et al., 2017, proposed the *Hamming Weight Tree (HWT)* to index Hamming spaces, and we describe, how the statistical analysis of sketches summarised in this chapter enables to push the searching in sketches further towards real-life requirements.

The HWT is based on the lower-bound that uses the number of bits set to 1 in each sketch $sk(o)$. We denote this number as the *weight* $w(sk(o))$ of sketch $sk(o)$, and the lower-bound holds:

$$h\left(sk\left(o_1\right), sk\left(o_2\right)\right) \geq \left| w\left(sk\left(o_1\right)\right) - w\left(sk\left(o_2\right)\right) \right|$$

Eghbali et al. propose to exploit this lower-bound in a trie structure, which we depict in Figure 13. It has an artificial root with up to $\lambda+1$ children. Each of these children covers the sketches $sk(o)$ with a specific weight $w(sk(o))$, and only non-empty nodes are stored to reduce the memory occupation. Level 2 of the HWT considers the weights of the halves of sketches. In general, level θ of the HWT consider

Figure 13. The structure of the Hamming Weight Tree

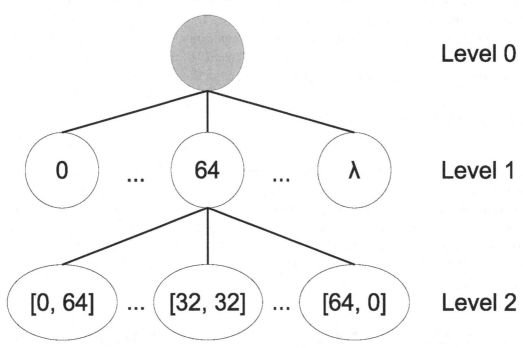

sketches sk(*o*) split into $b = 2^{\theta-1}$ disjunctive parts, and each node covers the sketches with the same

Figure 14. The difference between the actual Hamming distance of 128bit sketches and the lower-bound defined in the specific level of the HWT. Dark-grey colour: sketches created by the GHP_80 technique, light-grey colour: sketches updated by the distance preserving heuristic.

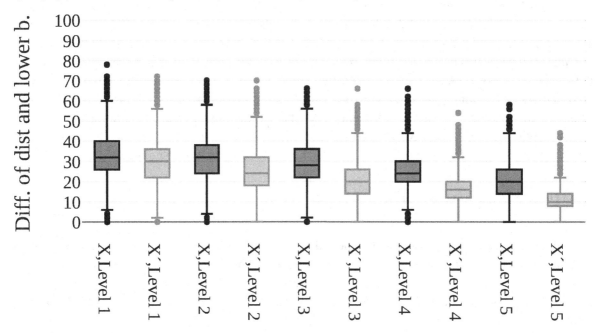

weights in all these subparts. The lower-bound on the Hamming distance is given:

$$h\big(sk\left(o_1\right),sk\left(o_2\right)\big) \geq \sum_{i=0}^{\frac{\lambda}{b}-1} \Big| w\big(o_1\big[i\cdot b,\dots,(i+1)b-1\big]\big) - w\big(o_2\big[i\cdot b,\dots,(i+1)b-1\big]\big)\Big| \tag{6}$$

The HWT searches for the most similar sketches to $sk(q)$ in an incremental manner and from the root to leaves. It starts with the nodes that provide the lower-bound equal to 0, and then increases the searching radius until the lower-bounds prevent remaining sketches from being in the precise query answer. This algorithm is formalised in Mic et al, 2018b.

The statistical properties of sketches can be exploited to propose modifications of sketches that preserve all the pairwise Hamming distances $h(sk(o_1), sk(o_2))$, $o_1, o_2 \in D$ and tighten the lower-bound defined by Equation 6. Mic et al. clarify that the bits of sketches within the same subparts examined in Equation 6 should be positively correlated, using the Pearson correlation coefficient, to make the lower-bounds as tight as possible. Pairwise bit correlations within the subparts of sketches can be increased by the *flipping* of bits, as described by Equation 2. These authors also propose a heuristic to select bits to flip in conjunction with the second proposed modification.

Since the tightness of the lower-bound defined in Equation 6 is influenced by the pairwise bit correlations within the subparts of the sketches, authors propose to permute bits of sketches to put the correlated bits to the same subparts. Their heuristic evaluates all the pairwise correlations of bits of sketches, identifies bits to flip and defines their permutation to maximise the lower-bounds exploited by the HWT. Its contribution is illustrated in Figure 14. It these experiments, 128bit sketches of the MPEG7 descriptors created by the GHP_80 sketching technique are exploited. For instance, the difference between the actual Hamming distance of sketches and the lower-bound provided by level 5 of the HWT decreases from 20 to 10, on median. This improvement of the lower-bounds speeds-up the nearest neighbour search in 100 million sketches 10.5 times, from 2.237 s to 0.214 s on median. Just thanks to these modifications, the HWT significantly outperforms the sequential evaluation of all the Hamming distances, which takes 1.503 s. In case of 20 million 128bit sketches of the DeCAF descriptors created by the GHP_80 technique, the 1NN search with the HWT is sped-up 5.3 times by the proposed sketch modifications (from 1.218 s to 0.229 s, on median). Again just thanks to the proposed modifications, the HWT outperforms the sequential evaluation of all the Hamming distances, which takes 0.300 s per query.

FUTURE RESEARCH DIRECTIONS

Our chapter provides a broad discussion about transformations of metric spaces into the Hamming space, and their usage to speed-up a high-quality similarity search. We discussed several consecutive steps that must be addressed when building a retrieval system that uses sketches. Despite the popularity and many proposed sketching techniques, just minor attention is paid to consequences of their properties and features that infer their further usage. For instance, sketching transformations of original descriptors are usually addressed independently of their specific usage to speed-up searching. Similarly, indexing of sketches is usually not considered when proposing a sketching technique, and vice versa.

Studies of the statistical properties of sketches and their consequences are important especially for a stringing of particular steps when building a searching engine. A natural continuation of this research is to study various indexing techniques for Hamming space to build a retrieval system that exploits all the addressed areas of the searching with sketches. Also, a distributed environment figures a possibility to support the efficiency of the similarity search in big datasets. The described results allow for a focus on bigger datasets (i.e. more than tens or a hundred of millions of objects) rather than to improve effectiveness and efficiency of searching in datasets of these and smaller sizes. Also, the context dependent and data-dependent similarity models that correspond better to human perception than traditionally used geometric based models figures an emerging research field, and sketches could be applied even in this field to support the efficiency of the searching.

CONCLUSION

This chapter considers similarity searching in data domains modelled by metric space. To speed-up searching, we consider the transformation of the metric space to Hamming space. We use the term *sketches* to denote the produced bit strings. The chapter clarifies the pros and cons of the sketching transformations and usage of sketches in similarity searching. We gave many examples of how sketches can speed-up the similarity search. While the contribution to the searching efficiency forms the main advantage of the search space embeddings to the Hamming space, the main drawback is given by numerous tasks that must be solved to develop the search engine. This includes a selection of a proper algorithm that uses sketches to speed up the actual search, the setting of all parameters, and also a selection of a particular sketching transformation technique. While a perfect synergy of all these steps is necessary to develop an efficient and high-quality searching engine, all the individual tasks are usually addressed independently of each other in the literature. This usually leads to their poor mutual compatibility. This chapter provides an overview of issues of searching with sketches. Many examples of their state-of-the-art solutions are given with an emphasis on their consequences and requirements. The main covered topics are:

- Transformation (sketching) techniques based on the investigation of the statistical properties of sketches. These properties include the balance of bits of sketches, pairwise bit correlations and intrinsic dimensionality of sketches. We emphasize techniques that are applicable in general metric spaces as they treat objects as black boxes and use just the pairwise object distances.
- Usage of sketches as an additional (secondary) filter of objects when evaluating the similarity queries by a *filter and refine* paradigm. This approach is thus applicable together with various similarity indexes that we propose to enhance with sketches to decrease the number of accessed objects $o \in X$ during the query execution.
- Approaches to efficiently estimate the quality of sketches $sk(o)$, $o \in X$ to facilitate the selection of a suitable sketching technique for given data.
- Investigation of the properties of sketches that influence their *indexability*, i.e. performance of indexes built upon the sketches.

ACKNOWLEDGMENT

This research was supported by ERDF "CyberSecurity, CyberCrime and Critical Information Infrastructures Center of Excellence" (No. CZ.02.1.01/0.0/0.0/16_019/0000822).

REFERENCES

Adomavicius, G., & Tuzhilin, A. (2005). Toward the next generation of recommender systems: A survey of the state-of-the-art and possible extensions. *IEEE Transactions on Knowledge and Data Engineering*, *17*(6), 734–749. doi:10.1109/TKDE.2005.99

Batko, M., Falchi, F., Lucchese, C., Novak, D., Perego, R., Rabitti, F., Sedmidubsky, J., & Zezula, P. (2010). Building a web-scale image similarity search system. *Multimedia Tools and Applications*, *47*(3), 599–629. doi:10.100711042-009-0339-z

Batko, M., Gennaro, C., Savino, P., & Zezula, P. (2004). *DigitalLibrary Architectures: Peer-to-Peer, Grid, and Service-Orientation, Pre-proceedings of the Sixth Thematic Workshop of the EU Network of Excellence DELOS*. Edizioni Libreria Progetto.

Batko, M., Kohoutkova, P., & Novak, D. (2009). Cophir image collection under the microscope. In *Second International Workshop on Similarity Search and Applications* (pp. 47-54). IEEE. 10.1109/SISAP.2009.25

Broder, A. Z. (1997). On the resemblance and containment of documents. Proceedings of Compression and Complexity of SEQUENCES 1997, 21-29.

Cao, Y., Qi, H., Zhou, W., Kato, J., Li, K., Liu, X., & Gui, J. (2018). Binary hashing for approximate nearest neighbor search on big data: A survey. *IEEE Access: Practical Innovations, Open Solutions*, *6*, 2039–2054. doi:10.1109/ACCESS.2017.2781360

Charikar, M. S. (2002). Similarity estimation techniques from rounding algorithms. *Proceedings on 34th Annual ACM Symposium on Theory of Computing*, 380-388.

Chávez, E., Figueroa, K., & Navarro, G. (2008). Effective Proximity Retrieval by Ordering Permutations. *IEEE Transactions on Pattern Analysis and Machine Intelligence*, *30*(9), 1647–1658. doi:10.1109/TPAMI.2007.70815 PMID:18617721

Chiu, C. Y., Wang, H. M., & Chen, C. S. (2010). Fast min-hashing indexing and robust spatio-temporal matching for detecting video copies. *ACM Transactions on Multimedia Computing Communications and Applications*, *6*(2), 1–23. doi:10.1145/1671962.1671966

Ciaccia, P., Patella, M., & Zezula, P. (1997). M-tree: An Efficient Access Method for Similarity Search in Metric Spaces. *Proceedings of the 23rd VLDB Conference*, 426-435.

Connor, R., Cardillo, F. A., Vadicamo, L., & Rabitti, F. (2017b). Hilbert exclusion: Improved metric search through finite isometric embeddings. *ACM Transactions on Information Systems*, *35*(3), 1–27. doi:10.1145/3001583

Connor, R., Vadicamo, L., & Rabitti, F. (2017a). High-dimensional simplexes for supermetric search. In *Similarity Search and Applications – 10th International Conference, SISAP 2017, Proceedings*, 96–109.

Dahl, G. E., Yu, D., Deng, L., & Acero, A. (2011). Context-dependent pre-trained deep neural networks for large-vocabulary speech recognition. *IEEE Transactions on Audio, Speech, and Language Processing*, 20(1), 30–42. doi:10.1109/TASL.2011.2134090

Daugman, J. (2003). The importance of being random: Statistical principles of iris recognition. *Pattern Recognition*, 36(2), 279–291. doi:10.1016/S0031-3203(02)00030-4

Deza, M. M., & Deza, E. (2009). Encyclopedia of distances. Springer. doi:10.1007/978-3-642-00234-2_1

Dohnal, V., Gennaro, C., Savino, P., & Zezula, P. (2001). Separable Splits of Metric Data Sets. In SEBD (pp. 45-62). Academic Press.

Donahue, J., Jia, Y., Vinyals, O., Hoffman, J., Zhang, N., Tzeng, E., & Darrell, T. (2014). Decaf: A deep convolutional activation feature for generic visual recognition. *Proceedings of the 31th International Conference on Machine Learning*, 647–655.

Eghbali, S., Ashtiani, H., & Tahvildari, L. (2017). Online nearest neighbor search in binary space. In *2017 IEEE International Conference on Data Mining* (pp. 853-858). IEEE. 10.1109/ICDM.2017.104

Faloutsos, C., Barber, R., Flickner, M., Hafner, J., Niblack, W., Petkovic, D., & Equitz, W. (1994). Efficient and effective querying by image content. *Journal of Intelligent Information Systems*, 3(3-4), 231–262. doi:10.1007/BF00962238

Higuchi, N., Imamura, Y., Kuboyama, T., Hirata, K., & Shinohara, T. (2018). Nearest Neighbor Search using Sketches as Quantized Images of Dimension Reduction. *Proceedings of the 7th International Conference on Pattern Recognition Applications and Methods, ICPRAM*, 356-363. 10.5220/0006585003560363

Higuchi, N., Imamura, Y., Kuboyama, T., Hirata, K., & Shinohara, T. (2019). Fast nearest neighbor search with narrow 16-bit sketch. *Proceedings of the 8th International Conference on Pattern Recognition Applications and Methods, ICPRAM*, 540-547. 10.5220/0007377705400547

Hua, G., Yang, M. H., Learned-Miller, E., Ma, Y., Turk, M., Kriegman, D. J., & Huang, T. S. (2011). Introduction to the special section on real-world face recognition. *IEEE Transactions on Pattern Analysis and Machine Intelligence*, 33(10), 1921–1924. doi:10.1109/TPAMI.2011.182 PMID:26598769

Jafri, R., & Arabnia, H. R. (2009). A survey of face recognition techniques. *Journal of Information Processing Systems*, 5(2), 41-68.

Jegou, H., Douze, M., & Schmid, C. (2008). Hamming embedding and weak geometric consistency for large scale image search. In *European conference on computer vision, ECCV* (pp. 304-317). Springer. 10.1007/978-3-540-88682-2_24

Journaux, L., Destain, M. F., Miteran, J., Piron, A., & Cointault, F. (2008). Texture classification with generalized Fourier descriptors in dimensionality reduction context: An overview exploration. In *IAPR Workshop on Artificial Neural Networks in Pattern Recognition* (pp. 280-291). Springer. 10.1007/978-3-540-69939-2_27

Kittler, J., Hatef, M., Duin, R. P., & Matas, J. (1998). On combining classifiers. *IEEE Transactions on Pattern Analysis and Machine Intelligence, 20*(3), 226–239. doi:10.1109/34.667881

Kosman, E., & Leonard, K. J. (2005). Similarity coefficients for molecular markers in studies of genetic relationships between individuals for haploid, diploid, and polyploid species. *Molecular Ecology, 14*(2), 415–424. doi:10.1111/j.1365-294X.2005.02416.x PMID:15660934

Kraus, J. (2019). *Porovnanie binárnych skečov pre podobnostné vyhľadávanie v kosínusovom a euklidovskom priestore* (Bachelor Thesis). Masaryk University, Brno, Czech Republic.

Krissinel, E. (2012). Enhanced fold recognition using efficient short fragment clustering. *Journal of Molecular Biochemistry, 1*(2), 76. PMID:27882309

Krizhevsky, A., Sutskever, I., & Hinton, G. E. (2012). Imagenet classification with deep convolutional neural networks. Advances in Neural Information Processing Systems, 1097-1105.

LeCun, Y., Bengio, Y., & Hinton, G. (2015). Deep learning. *Nature, 521*(7553), 436–444. doi:10.1038/nature14539 PMID:26017442

Leskovec, J., Rajaraman, A., & Ullman, J. D. (2014). *Mining of massive data sets. Mining of Massive Datasets* (2nd ed.). Cambridge University Press. doi:10.1017/CBO9781139924801

Lowe, D. G. (1999). Object recognition from local scale-invariant features. *Proceedings of the seventh IEEE international conference on computer vision,* (2), 1150-1157. 10.1109/ICCV.1999.790410

Lv, Q., Charikar, M., & Li, K. (2004). Image similarity search with compact data structures. In *Proceedings of the thirteenth ACM International Conference on Information and Knowledge Management, CIKM* (pp. 208-217). 10.1145/1031171.1031213

Lv, Q., Josephson, W., Wang, Z., Charikar, M., & Li, K. (2006). Ferret: a toolkit for content-based similarity search of feature-rich data. *Proceedings of the 1st ACM SIGOPS/EuroSys European Conference on Computer Systems,* 317-330. 10.1145/1217935.1217966

Manber, U. (1994). Finding Similar Files in a Large File System. In *Proceedings of USENIX Winter 1994 Technical Conference (Vol. 94,* pp. 1-10). USENIX.

Mehrotra, H., Vatsa, M., Singh, R., & Majhi, B. (2013). Does iris change over time? *PLoS One, 8*(11), e78333.

Mic, V., Novak, D., Vadicamo, L., & Zezula, P. (2018c). Selecting sketches for similarity search. In *European Conference on Advances in Databases and Information Systems, ADBIS* (pp. 127–141). Springer.

Mic, V., Novak, D., & Zezula, P. (2016). Designing sketches for similarity filtering. In *IEEE 16th International Conference on Data Mining Workshops (ICDMW)* (pp. 655-662). IEEE.

Mic, V., Novak, D., & Zezula, P. (2017). Sketches with unbalanced bits for similarity search. In *International Conference on Similarity Search and Applications* (pp. 53-63). Springer.

Mic, V., Novak, D., & Zezula, P. (2018a) Binary Sketches for Secondary Filtering. *ACM Transactions on Information Systems, 37*(1), 1:1–1:28.

Mic, V., Novak, D., & Zezula, P. (2018b) Modifying Hamming Spaces for Efficient Search. *Proceedings of IEEE International Conference on Data Mining Workshops, ICDMW*, 945–953.

Mic, V., & Zezula, P. (2020). Accelerating Metric Filtering by Improving Bounds on Estimated Distances. In *International Conference on Similarity Search and Applications* (pp. 3-17). Springer.

Mitzenmacher, M., Pagh, R., & Pham, N. (2014). Efficient estimation for high similarities using odd sketches. *Proceedings of the 23rd international conference on World wide web*, 109-118.

Muller-Molina, A. J., & Shinohara, T. (2009). Efficient similarity search by reducing i/o with compressed sketches. In *2009 Second International Workshop on Similarity Search and Applications*, (pp. 30-38). IEEE.

Novak, D., Batko, M., & Zezula, P. (2011). Metric index: An efficient and scalable solution for precise and approximate similarity search. *Information Systems*, *36*(4), 721–733.

Novak, D., Kyselak, M., & Zezula, P. (2010). On locality-sensitive indexing in generic metric spaces. In *Proceedings of the Third International Conference on Similarity Search and Applications* (pp. 59-66). Academic Press.

Novak, D., & Zezula, P. (2016). PPP-codes for large-scale similarity searching. In *Transactions on Large-Scale Data-and Knowledge-Centered Systems XXIV* (pp. 61–87). Springer.

Ong, E. J., & Bober, M. (2016). Improved hamming distance search using variable length substrings. In *Proceedings of the IEEE Conference on Computer Vision and Pattern Recognition* (pp. 2000-2008). IEEE.

Oquab, M., Bottou, L., Laptev, I., & Sivic, J. (2014). Learning and transferring mid-level image representations using convolutional neural networks. *IEEE Conference on Computer Vision and Pattern Recognition, CVPR 2014*, 1717–1724.

Pola, I. R. V., Traina, C. Jr, & Traina, A. J. M. (2014). The nobh-tree: Improving in-memory metric access methods by using metric hyperplanes with non-overlapping nodes. *Data & Knowledge Engineering*, *94*, 65–88.

Rubner, Y., Tomasi, C., & Guibas, L. J. (2000). The earth mover's distance as a metric for image retrieval. *International Journal of Computer Vision*, *40*(2), 99–121.

Shirdhonkar, S., & Jacobs, D. W. (2008, June). Approximate earth mover's distance in linear time. In *2008 IEEE Conference on Computer Vision and Pattern Recognition*, (pp. 1-8). IEEE.

Sivic, J., & Zisserman, A. (2003, October). Video Google: A text retrieval approach to object matching in videos. In *9th IEEE International Conference on Computer Vision (ICCV 2003)* (pp. 1470–1477). IEEE.

Skala, M. (2005). Measuring the difficulty of distance-based indexing. In *International Symposium on String Processing and Information Retrieval* (pp. 103-114). Springer.

Skala, M. A. (2008). *Aspects of Metric Spaces in Computation* (PhD thesis). University of Waterloo.

Skopal, T. (2004). Pivoting M-tree: A Metric Access Method for Efficient Similarity Search. *Proceedings of the Dateso 2004, Annual International Workshop on DAtabases, TExts, Specifications and Objects*, 27-37.

Tiberio, P., & Zezula, P. (1993). Selecting signature files for specific applications. *Information Processing & Management*, *29*(4), 487–498.

Turaga, P., Chellappa, R., Subrahmanian, V. S., & Udrea, O. (2008). Machine recognition of human activities: A survey. *IEEE Transactions on Circuits and Systems for Video Technology*, *18*(11), 1473–1488.

Vadicamo, L., Mic, V., Falchi, F., & Zezula, P. (2019). Metric embedding into the hamming space with the n-simplex projection. In *International Conference on Similarity Search and Applications* (pp. 265-272). Springer.

Van Der Maaten, L., Postma, E., & Van den Herik, J. (2009). Dimensionality reduction: A comparative. *Journal of Machine Learning Research*, *10*(66-71), 13.

Wang, Z., Dong, W., Josephson, W., Lv, Q., Charikar, M., & Li, K. (2007). Sizing sketches: a rank-based analysis for similarity scarch. In *Proceedings of the 2007 ACM SIGMETRICS international conference on Measurement and modeling of computer systems* (pp. 157-168). ACM.

Yoshitaka, A., & Ichikawa, T. (1999). A survey on content-based retrieval for multimedia databases. *IEEE Transactions on Knowledge and Data Engineering*, *11*(1), 81–93.

Zezula, P., Amato, G., Dohnal, V., & Batko, M. (2006). Similarity Search – The Metric Space Approach. Springer.

ENDNOTES

[1]   http://disa.fi.muni.cz/profiset/
[2]   http://cophir.isti.cnr.it/

Chapter 6
Connectivity Management in Drone Networks:
Models, Algorithms, and Methods

Umut Can Çabuk
ⓘ https://orcid.org/0000-0002-5166-4670
Ege University, Turkey

Mustafa Tosun
Ege University, Turkey

Vahid Akram
Ege University, Turkey

Orhan Dagdeviren
Ege University, Turkey

ABSTRACT

Drone technologies have attracted the attention of many researchers in recent years due to their potential opportunities. Fleets of drones integrated with widely available relatively short-range communication technologies have various application areas such as wildlife monitoring, disaster relief, and military surveillance. One of the major problems in this manner is maintaining the connectivity of the drone network. In this chapter, the authors study the connectivity management issues in drone networks. Firstly, movement, communication, and channel models are described by the authors, along with the problem definition. The hardness of the problem is investigated by proving its NP-Hardness. Various algorithms proposed to solve the connectivity management problem and their variants are evaluated in detail. Lastly, for future directions, the authors present mathematical methods to solve the emerging problem in drone networks.

DOI: 10.4018/978-1-7998-4963-6.ch006

Figure 1. Drone Networks and Their Applications

INTRODUCTION

One of the most progressive technologies related to computer science and engineering and affected our daily lives dramatically is drone technology. Recently, various research institutes, universities, and companies have been dealing with drone projects for solving timely problems around the world. These studies can be investigated in a wide range of application areas such as disaster management, smart farming, military surveillance, wildfire tracking, civil security, photogrammetry, and power line inspection. A drone is a type of unmanned vehicle that is an aircraft without a human pilot, and it is generally composed of a flight controller, a battery, a transceiver, camera(s), a GPS module, and various sensors such as collision avoidance, accelerometer, and altimeter. Drones are unmanned aerial vehicles (UAVs) forming unmanned aircraft systems together with ground-based controllers and data transmission systems, which provide communication between these two parties. UAVs can be controlled remotely and manually by a human operator, whereas they can perform fully autonomous missions provided by onboard circuits that are integrated into the drone in advance.

The transmission capabilities and energy resources of the drones manufactured under the constraints of current technologies are generally limited for applications requiring a long lifetime. In many scenarios, a fleet of economic drones integrated with the communication devices such as IEEE 802.11 is designated instead of drones that are capable of communicating over long distances. An example network of drones is given in Figure 1.a, where 6 drones are connected in an ad hoc manner without any predefined infrastructure, and the transmission range of the base station only covers one of these drones. The use of a drone fleet or swarm can be much more advantageous in applications such as agriculture, meteorology, disaster detection, and search and rescue operations. For example, as given in Figure 1.b, the delivery of service among users who can be mobile in nature (military units on a battlefield, relief teams, or people using the internet service during a disaster) can be achieved with a drone swarm. As another example given in Figure 1.c, a network of these flying devices are assigned to accomplish a search and rescue operation. In this manner, drone swarms can scan the search area in detail and carefully, and they can send the required information to the base station over the backbone of drones after finding the target.

One of the most important requirements of multiple drone systems is initiating and maintaining communication between drones. If all drones in a swarm can access a base station or a central satellite system in a single hop manner, the communication between them can be done utilizing these infrastructures without providing multi-hop ad hoc network infrastructures (Bekmezci et al.,2013). However, this type of communication between drones can be very costly, even impossible in most scenarios. For this reason, in many applications, the communication between the control center and the remote drones should be provided by the intermediate drones. To cover a large area with drones and reach much further distances from the control center, the drones must have a reliable and continuous connection. Therefore, maintaining the connectivity between drones is one of the most important requirements in such systems (Sahingoz, 2014). In multiple drone-based systems, the number of studies conducted in the literature

Figure 2. A 2-Connected Network

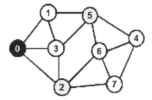

on maintaining connectivity between drones is limited and is emphasized by reputable publications that this problem is open to research (Erdelj&Natalizio,2016; Zhao et al.,2018).

One of the methods of strengthening connectivity in wireless networks is the deployment of k-connected networks (Cheng et al., 2008; Cornejo & Lynch, 2010; Han et al., 2010; Jorgic et al.,2007; Lloyd & Xue, 2007; Wang et al., 2011). The network must be at least 1-connected in order for nodes to communicate with each other. In 1-connected networks, malfunction of a single node can disrupt the integrity of the entire network, so 1-connectivity is not much desirable in terms of fault tolerance for various scenarios. In a 2-connected network, the failure of any node does not affect the system, but if 2 nodes are broken simultaneously, the connection of the network may be lost. In general, at least k nodes must fail to terminate the connectivity of a k-connected network. Figure 2 shows an example 2-connected network where malfunction of nodes 2 and 5 interrupts the connections between {4, 6, 7} and other nodes. The purpose of the k-connectivity restoration process is to maintain the current k value of the network at a constant level as much as possible by adding new nodes or moving existing nodes.

In this chapter, we study the connectivity management problem for drone networks from various perspectives in a comprehensive manner. Firstly, before formulating the movement-based connectivity management problem, we present the mobility model, communication model, and channel model for drone networks. After defining the problem formally, we provide the hardness analysis of the problem in terms of NP-Hardness proof. The algorithms aimed to solve this problem, and its similar versions are surveyed afterward. For future directions, mathematical methods are explained to tackle the connectivity management problem.

PROBLEM FORMULATION

This section defines the problem, its subproblem, and other preliminary information that should be known to the reader before focusing on the analyses.

Assumptions and Preliminaries

Drone network: A wireless ad-hoc network consisting of drones, flying robots, and other unmanned aerial vehicles as nodes. Non-flying mobile objects may be considered in rare cases. A stationary communication infrastructure may exist only in a limited sense, such as sustaining connectivity with a ground station; otherwise, the network is ad-hoc. The reasoning behind this design is the essential limitations of drones and similar objects, namely, limited energy (battery) sources and the restricted communication ranges.

Table 1. Symbols and definitions

Symbol	Meaning
|V|	The cardinality of set V
U \ V	Items in U that are not in V
$\mathbb{R}^2$	Two-dimensional Euclidean plane
$\mathbb{R}$	The set of real numbers

Graph representation of a drone network: A drone network can be represented as a graph G (V, E) (as defined by the Graph Theory), where V represents the set of drones (as nodes), and E represents the set of wireless links (as edges) between them.

Communication range: The radio range of the drones and other objects in the network. It can be different for all devices but typically accepted as uniform, at least for the same type of devices.

Communication range: The radio range of the drones and other objects in the network. It can be different for all devices but typically accepted as uniform, at least for the same type of devices.

Operating range: The active range in which a drone can do its sensing and/or actuating operations. It can be significantly larger or smaller than the radio range, depending on the sensors/actuators it is equipped with. Yet, it is not uncommon that it is accepted as equal to the radio range to simplify calculations.

Connected Graph: The graph (also the drone network) is connected if each vertex has a path to all other vertices in the graph.

Vertex Connectivity: The minimum number of required vertices, which makes the connected graph disconnected when they are removed, is the vertex connectivity of a graph. A k-connected graph means that the vertex connectivity of the graph is k.

Edge Connectivity: The minimum number of required edges, which makes the connected graph disconnected when they are removed, is the edge connectivity of a graph. A k-edge-connected graph means that the edge connectivity of the graph is k.

Coordinates and Localization: Drones are located in the 3-D Euclidean space ($\mathbb{R}^3$) and can keep track of their own coordinates continuously in real-time (i.e., with a GPS or similar equipment). In some cases, they can even learn their neighbors' locations via communication. 2-D Euclidean plane may be assumed instead of 3-D space, without loss of generality.

Movement Model

There are various mobility models for the drones' area coverage scenarios in the literature (Bujari et al., 2017). One well-known mobility model is the Distributed Pheromone Repel model (DPR) (Kuiper & Nadjm-Tehrani, 2006), which works by enforcing nodes to share a localized "pheromone" map that shows the scanning information of the area with each other. Although the speed of coverage of DPR is decent, it is also required to consider the connectivity of the drones in this context. The DPR model does not provide connectivity control, just like many other area coverage models in the literature. Several mobility models consider both area coverage and connectivity, such as in (Danoy et al., 2015; Yanmaz, 2012; Schleich et al., 2013; Messous et al., 2016). One of them is the Alpha-based mobility model proposed by Messous et al. (Messous et al., 2006), which takes the current energy levels of the drones into

Table 2. The α calculation table (Messous et al., 2006)

α	Neighbor Count		Distance to Base Station			
			0	**1,2**	**3,4,..**	**99**
Energy Level	<%25	1	Big	Medium	Medium	Big
		2,3	Medium	Small	Small	Medium
		>3	Small	Small	Small	Small
	%25-%70	1	Big	Big	Medium	Small
		2,3	Medium	Big	Medium	Small
		>3	Small	Medium	Small	Small
	>%70	1	Big	Big	Big	Big
		2,3	Medium	Small	Medium	Medium
		>3	Small	Small	Small	Small

account while providing the area coverage and connectivity. Therefore, it is more proper for the main concerns of drone operations within this context.

The drones in the model provide connectivity by following their neighbors, but without treating all neighbors equally. The drones calculate the "follow-up" coefficients known as α for each of their neighbors to determine the follow-up levels. The α has three levels, namely, "small", "medium", and "big". A "big" label indicates that this neighbor should be followed more, while neighbors with a "small" label should be followed to a lesser extent. The α is determined by using the neighbors' information, as shown in Table 2. The levels depend on the speed limit of the drones. "big" represents the maximum speed limit while "small" and "medium" represent 1 m/s and the average of the "big" and "small" levels, respectively.

After all the α values are computed, each neighbor's unit velocity vector is multiplied by its α value. Then the sum of the scaled vectors of all neighbors gives the next velocity vector of the drone. An example of the computation of the drone 1 is shown in Figure 3. In the example, the speed limit is taken 3 m/s, therefore "small", "medium", and "big" levels of α represent 1 m/s, 2 m/s, and 3 m/s, respectively. The $\alpha 1$, $\alpha 2$, and $\alpha 3$ are "big", "medium", and "small" respectively. $\overrightarrow{F_1}$, $\overrightarrow{F_2}$, $\overrightarrow{F_3}$ and $\overrightarrow{F_4}$ present the current velocities while $\overrightarrow{F_1'}$ shows the next velocity of the drone 1.

Figure 3. Example of calculation of the velocity (Messous et al., 2006)

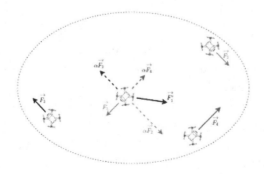

Due to the nature of the distributed computing paradigm, drones do not know nor care about their neighbors' state information. So, they need to send their information to each other periodically to let them compute their next velocity. How to send these messages in the system is discussed in the next section.

Communication Model

A routing protocol is the main component of a communication model. The routing protocols used in drone networks are classified under three main classes (Jiang & Han, 2018), which are, namely, "pro-active", "reactive", and "location-based" routing models. Firstly, pro-active models create and continuously update an active routing table by sending broadcast messages periodically. Therefore, when a node wants to send a message to another node, it already knows the shortest path for the transmission, anytime. However, periodically sending broadcast messages overloads the system (i.e., channels and hardware). Secondly, reactive protocols do not provide an updated routing table, unlike the pro-active protocols. Instead, they update the routing tables only when needed, by determining merely the path between the sender and the receiver. So, they do not create an unbearable load on the system, but there is a much higher delay compared to pro-active protocols since they wait until finding a valid path between the sender and receiver when a packet transmission is required. There are also hybrid protocols that combine reactive and pro-active protocols (Vasiliev et al., 2014). They aim to improve the routing performance with the expense of increasing the load on the system. Finally, in location-based protocols, all nodes know every other nodes' locations and determine the paths according to their locations.

One well known location-based protocol in ad hoc networks is the Greedy Perimeter Stateless Routing (GPSR) (Karp & Kung, 2000) protocol. In this protocol, messages are sent over the nodes that are closer to the receiver as location. For the GPSR protocol to work correctly, the network topology must be planar. However, it is impossible to provide planarity in applications that require high mobility, like area coverage applications. Ad-Hoc On-Demand Distance Vector (AODV) (RFC 3561) protocol is a widely used reactive protocol. Since the processes to find a path is carried on by the messages that are only sent on demand, instead of periodic transmission of broadcast messages, the packet load can be low in the AODV protocol. In the mobility model mentioned in the previous section, nodes periodically send their information, like hop distances to the sink. Therefore, the nodes always need to know the path information to the sink node, and since the reactive protocols do not provide an active routing table, the protocols like AODV may not be very suitable for connectivity management.

The Optimized Link State Routing (OLSR) (RFC 3626) protocol is the predecessor of the other pro-active protocols. In this protocol, the nodes broadcast their neighbors' information and routing tables. Accordingly, the nodes know their paths to other nodes and the nodes in their two-hop distances. They select Multi-Point Relay (MPR) nodes that dominate their two-hop neighbors among other neighbors. When a packet needs to be sent, it is solely sent through the MPR nodes. The main load is pushed over to the MPR nodes. The Mobility and Load aware OLSR (ML-OLSR) (Zheng et al., 2014) protocol is an improved version of the OLSR, which considers the high mobility and the load balancing on choosing the MPR nodes. Therefore, the ML-OLSR protocol seems to be more suitable for connectivity management operations.

Channel Model

Drone communications are indeed a particular sub-category of wireless communications due to their unique characteristics. Modern drones are complex devices with advanced computing capabilities and can be treated like mobile computers to some extent. So they may employ advanced radio technologies like WiFi, Bluetooth, or custom ones. However, their operation times are very limited; usually, 10 to 60 minutes for most commercial drones, owing to their battery constraints. Yet there are other differences, too. Drone communications can be analyzed under three cases, which may naturally co-exist in a drone network scenario. Namely, air-to-air (A2A) or drone-to-drone communications that imply flying ad-hoc networks (FANET), air-to-ground (A2G), and ground-to-air (G2A) communications. Among them, A2A communication is the most remarkable type. Because A2G and G2A communications include a fixed ground station with more resources and longer lifetime on one-side of the communication scheme, ground stations may even be connected to the power grid and another terrestrial (e.g., fiber optics) or a radio (e.g., satellite) network. Such cases, in which ground stations are disseminating or gathering information to or from fast-moving mobile devices, are researched intensively for different networking paradigms, like Global System for Mobile Communications (GSM), Universal Mobile Telecommunications System (UMTS), Long Term Evolution (LTE) and many others.

A2A communications, on the other hand, is a newer paradigm, especially considering drones. High mobility, short lifetime, quasi-short range, and need for fast transmission apply to all parties of the communication. The data to be transferred may or may not be large, depending on the application scenario. For example, a live camera broadcast or imagery data would likely be large, while plaintext sensory data or means of control commands would be smaller. In any case, the desired transfer rates can be assumed to be high since mobility is always high-level, and non-urgent data can occasionally be stored in the device memory to some extent. A short battery lifetime also limits the topological structures to be ad-hoc. Tree-shaped topologies and clustering are usually possible; however, when enforced as steady structures, these may force some drones to spend much more energy than the others, which is an undesired outcome for such limited devices. Finding optimal drone placement strategies require a good knowledge of the features of the air medium and the radio channel. For more flexible topologies, like many mesh variations, the characteristics of the radio channel should even be more thoroughly analyzed to achieve optimal data rates, broader coverage, and better performance.

The radio channels can be modeled with mathematical re-arrangements of some empirical measurements considering the effective path loss, a prevalent natural phenomenon that defines the attenuation of the radio signal depending on the distances and some environmental factors. The accuracy and applicability of these models are generally limited to the conditions in which their empirical measurements are based. The models can be extended to cover a broader range of parameters, but this may cause loss of accuracy in some cases. There are more than a few models in the literature. ITU-R Free Space (ITU-R, 2019), Egli (Egli, 1957), Longley-Rice (Kasampalis et al., 2014), Okumura (Okumura, 1968), Okumura-Hata (Hata, 1980), Hata-Davidson (Kasampalis et al., 2014), Cost 231 Hata, Cost 231 Walfisch-Ikegami (Mogensen & Wigard, 1999), Erceg (Erceg et al., 1999), and Stanford University Interim (SUI) (Sadec & Shellhammer, 2008; Erceg et al., 2001) models are among the most popular ones. They are already being used in the development and test of many advanced systems, some of which are even preferred in universal standards, such as GSM, LTE, and WiMAX. A decent comparison of these models is given in Table 3.

Nevertheless, these models usually aim to represent the characteristics of G2A or A2G channels in different environments (e.g., city centers, rural areas, etc.). None of these models directly aim at A2A networks and mostly do not include parameters nor boundaries to support the A2A scenarios. Furthermore, there is no mention of the Doppler shift and Doppler spread phenomena that exclusively affect the communication between the fast-moving parties of a wireless network.

Doppler shift briefly is the change of the main carrier frequency of a series of radio signals that are observed when at least one of the parties (e.g., receiver, transmitter, or both) of a communication link move(s) during the communication. There is no restriction on the direction of the movement, as long as the distance between the parties change. When this distance becomes smaller (i.e., parties come closer to each other), the carrier frequency increases; reciprocally, when the distance becomes larger (i.e., parties moving away from each other), the carrier frequency decreases. The degrading effects of such shifts make the existing path loss prediction models less reliable. Furthermore, these effects apply to all possible paths of the same signal in case of the existence of a multipath propagation (considering non-line-of-sight communications as well). Yet, the resulting shift of the frequency may be different for each path depending on the features of the path, like the total distance, reflection surfaces, air-medium conditions, etc. These shifts of frequency also shift the phase of the multipath components of the signal. Hence, when combined at the receiver, these components may eventually weaken (or even neutralize) each other, ultimately called the Doppler spread. That attenuative effect of the Doppler spread is usually minor and is classified as small-scale fading, whereas the path loss and shadowing are known as large-scale fadings. When the Doppler spread is large enough so that the channel characteristics change much faster than the speed of the baseband radio signal, which also means that the coherence time of the channel is much shorter than the symbol period of the radio signal, then fast-fading becomes dominant; otherwise slow-fading becomes dominant. More information on fading can be found elsewhere (Bai & Atiquzzaman, 2003). Some of the models mentioned above cover different types of small and large scale fading incidences, depending on their experimental setups. However, none of the models precisely cover the Doppler phenomena (especially the Doppler shift and the fast-fading caused by the Doppler spread). Fortunately, the fading caused by the Doppler effects can be neglected if the channel bandwidth is large enough, which is a realistic assumption when using modern wireless technologies like WiFi. However, given that the drones can move very fast (e.g., the world record as of 2017 is 73 m/s (Guinness; 2017)), drone communications, especially the A2A links, are prone to such degrading effects of the Doppler phenomena.

A recent study (Cabuk et al., 2020) has presented a comparative analysis among the mentioned path loss models to investigate their suitability and accuracy, particularly for drone networks containing independent A2A links. Per the results, the SUI model was found to be suitable for most drone network applications. What makes this model more applicable to drone networks than many others is its flexibility. It covers three different terrain types, allows receiver heights to be 2 to 10 m, allows transmitter heights to be 10 to 40 (some sources even claim 80) m, supports transmitter to transmitter or receiver to receiver links, works in frequencies from 1900 up to 11000 MHz. Moreover, a line-of-sight link may or may not exist. Though it is undoubtedly not the best fit, it still allows the modeling of many drones and swarm networking scenarios. The model can be defined as the following relations.

$$L = L_0 + \Delta L_f + \Delta L_h + s \tag{1}$$

The effective path loss L can be found in dB, as a sum of the coarse path loss L0, the frequency-dependent correction factor ΔLf and the height-dependent correction factor ΔLh. s is, on the other hand, an optional parameter that incorporates the loss caused by the shadowing and is only added when the

Table 3. Comparison of Path Loss estimation models

Model Name	Frequency Range (MHz)	BS Height Range (m)	Distance Range (km)	Environment Type	NLoS/Shadowing
ITU-R P.525-4 Free Space	No limit	No limit	No limit	No environment	Omitted
Longley-Rice	20 – 20000 [a]	0.5 - 3000	1 – 1000	Flat terrain, climate codes	Omitted
Egli	30 – 3000	2000 – 8000	£ 65	Flat, irregular terrain	Omitted
Okumura	150 – 1920 [b]	30 – 1000	1 – 100	Dense urban	Available
Okumura-Hata	100 – 1500	30 – 200	1 – 10	Dense urban, suburban, rural	Available
Hata-Davidson	30 – 1500	20 – 2500	1 – 300	Dense urban, suburban, rural	Available
COST 231 Hata	1500 – 2000 [c]	30 – 200	1 – 20	Dense urban, suburban, rural	Available
COST231 Walfish-Ikegami	300 – 3000	4 – 50	0.02 – 5	Flat terrain, custom urban parameters	Available
Erceg	1900	10 – 80	0.1 – 8	Flat, woody, hilly terrains, no urban	Omitted
SUI	1900 – 11000	15 – 40 [d]	0.1 – 10	Flat, woody, hilly terrains, no urban	Available

[a]Original model states up to 30 GHz, but later studies limited the range.
[b]Reported up to 3000 MHz with extrapolations.
[c]Some studies claim reliable up to 2600 MHz.
[d]Some documents claim reliable up to 80 m.

communication is maintained without a clear line-of-sight (LoS). Typical values of s are between 8.2 and 10.6 in dB.

$$L_0 = A + 10\gamma \log(d / d_o) \tag{2}$$

The coarse path loss can be obtained by a sum of the free-space path loss component A and a terrain-specific height-aware loss factor γ.

$$A = 20\log(4\pi d_o / \lambda) \tag{3}$$

The calculation of A is yet straightforward. λ is the carrier signal wavelength in meters that is deducted from $\lambda = C/f$, where C is the speed of light in m/s, and f is the carrier frequency in MHz, whereas d0 is predefined as 100 m.

$$\gamma = a - b h_t + c / h_t \tag{4}$$

Table 4. Parameters against Area Type

Parameters	Area Type A	Area Type B	Area Type C
a	4.6	4	3.6
b	0.0075	0.0065	0.005
c	12.6	17.1	20

γ includes references to the empirical measurements and is dependent on the terrain type on which the communication is going to be made. Type A refers to a mountainous, hilly, or forested area. Type B indicates a rugged area and/or a moderately covered woodland, and Type C expresses a plain and open field. Settlement areas could be represented by Type A or B, depending on their sizes. The corresponding values of a, b and c can be found from the given table. Further, h_t is the transmitter height in meters.

The values given in Table 4 were experimentally obtained when the carrier frequency was 2 GHz, and the receiver height hr was merely 2 m. Therefore, the following correction factors are required to be found.

$$\Delta L_f = 6\log(f / 2000) \tag{5}$$

$$\Delta L_h = \begin{cases} -10.8\log\left(h_r / 2\right), & \text{Area Type } A, B \\ -20\log\left(h_r / 2\right), & \text{Area Type } C \end{cases} \tag{6}$$

Once these factors are also calculated per effective frequency and heights, the effective path loss can finally be calculated. That path loss calculation lacks the fading caused by the Doppler shift and Doppler spread. Nevertheless, there are efforts to determine the attenuating effect of the Doppler shift on links between fast-moving objects. Wei et al. (Wei et al., 2011) have suggested a tuned free space path loss model for fast-moving objects by doing experiments on a high-speed train. Bok and Ryu (Bok & Ryn, 2014) have further revised that model by elaborating on the contribution of the Doppler shift as follows, where fd is the Doppler shift in the frequency.

$$L = 41.45 + 5\log_{10}(f_d) + 39.2\log_{10}(d) + 20\log_{10}(f) \tag{7}$$

Cabuk et al., in their later study (Cabuk et al., 2020), extracted the pure contribution of the Doppler shift and pointed it out as a separate factor to be used along with the SUI model instead of a free space-based model.

$$L_{Doppler} = -3.72 + 5\log_{10}(f_d) + 5.01\log_{10}(d) \tag{8}$$

Recognizing the attenuative effects within the path loss phenomena is crucially important in designing and implementing drone network applications. Because the path loss is directly correlated with the transmission delay (d_{trans}), which is a dominant factor in the total latency (d_{tot}) of the communication. The latency is briefly defined as follows:

$$d_{tot} = d_{proc} + d_{queue} + d_{prop} + d_{trans} \tag{9}$$

Where d_{proc} is the processing delay for each packet or stream (including security and integrity measures), d_{queue} is the queueing delay at both sides, and d_{prop} is the propagation delay depending on the medium and the signal characteristics. Issues related to such delays and techniques regarding mitigating them in FANETs are further discussed by Mukherjee et al. (Mukherjee, 2019).

Figure 4. Example scenario for the MBk-CM problem and solution

Problem Definition

Before explaining the details of the connectivity management problem in drone networks, it will be useful to consider the Steiner Tree Problem, which may lay a foundation for the given subject.

Steiner Tree Problem: A class of combinatorial optimization problems with various variants. All derivations of the problem essentially focus on interconnecting (some, if not all) objects within a given set of objects while considering a fundamentally defined objective function that is usually related to minimizing different cost metrics. The problem is frequently analyzed in graphs. In these cases, the edges are mostly undirected, and their weights are non-negative. Restoring the connectivity of a drone network may fit in the definitions of the Steiner Tree Problem under some circumstances.

Euclidean Steiner Tree: A well-known variant of the problem. The nodes are presumed to be placed on Euclidean planes and/or spaces, which adopted Euclidean geometric coordinates (Chung & Graham, 1985). The edge weights are usually associated with the corresponding Euclidean distances between the vertices that they connect. Yet, the objective function is minimizing the total length of the interconnecting edges. It is suitable for drone networks, which naturally makes use of Euclidean geometry.

Rectilinear Steiner Tree: A well-known restrictive case of the problem, commonly applied on top of the Euclidean Steiner Tree. But in this case, the distances between any pair of nodes are calculated using the rectilinear distance (also called the taxicab distance, the city-block distance, or the Manhattan distance) instead of the Euclidean distance (Hwang, 1976). This might be useful when the drones with predefined grid-like waypoints or ground robots with rail systems are in use for the given scenario and missions.

The connectivity management problem in drone networks can be analyzed under two categories: The movement-based connectivity management (MBCM) problem and the reinforcement-based connectivity management problem (RBCM).

The movement-based connectivity management (MBCM) problem is to make the disconnected drone network connected by replacing drones with minimum total replacement. In Figure 4 an example of the problem and its solution are given. At the beginning of the example, drones are disconnected; their communication range is 1 unit, and positions are (1,1,1), (2,3,2), and (3,2,3), respectively. The network can be made connected by moving drones like in Figure 4. After the movements, the new positions of the drones are (1.5,1.5,1.5), (2,2,2) and (2.5,2,2.5) respectively with a total of 2.56 unit replacement. In this example, desired vertex connectivity is 1. When the desired vertex connectivity is k, the problem evolves into the movement-based k-connectivity management (MBk-CM) problem.

Definition: Let a graph $G(V, E)$ represent a drone network. V is the set of drones and $E=\{(u, v)|\ u,v \in V$ and $\|u,v\| \geq r\}$ is the set of the connections between drones. The MBk-CM problem is to find match

Figure 5. Sample instance of Problem I

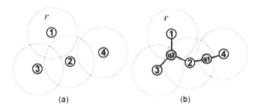

(a) (b)

$M : \mathbb{R}^3 \times \mathbb{R}^3 \to \mathbb{R}$ which makes the network k-connected with smallest $\Sigma_{v \in V}\ c(v,\ M(v))$, where $c : \mathbb{R}^3 \times \mathbb{R}^3 \to \mathbb{R}$ is the cost function.

Hardness of the Problem

The NP-Hardness of the movement assisted connectivity restoration of drone networks in $\mathbb{R}^3$ is proved by reduction of the Steiner Tree Problem with the Minimum number of Steiner Points and Bounded Edge Length (STP-MSPBEL)(Akram & Dagdeviren, 2018). The STP-MSPBEL is a known NP-Hard (Lin & Xue, 1999) problem which is formally defined as follow:

STP-MSPBEL Problem: Given a set V of n points in $\mathbb{R}^2$ and a positive integer r, the problem asks to establish a spanning tree to cover the point set $Q \supseteq V$ with a minimum number of Steiner points (points in $Q \backslash V$) such that the length of each edge in the tree is not greater than r.

Figure 5.a shows a sample instance of Problem STP-MSPBEL with $n=4$ and $V=\{1,2,3,4\}$. The big circles with dashed lines around each point show the maximum length of edges that originate from the point. The goal is creating a spanning tree that connects all points in V using the edges with the maximum length r and the minimum number of additional (Steiner) points. One of the optimal solutions to this problem has been presented in Figure 5.b, where two Steiner points $q1$ and $q2$ are used to create the spanning tree. So, we have $Q=\{1,2,3,4,q1,q2\}$ and it is impossible to find another solution with a smaller number of nodes.

STP-MSPBEL problem implies that connecting a set of nodes with limited communication range in a two-dimensional network by placing the minimum number of relay nodes is NP-Hard. Referring to this problem, various approximation algorithms have been proposed for connectivity restoration using relay nodes placement in the static wireless sensor and ad hoc networks (Cheng et al., 2008; Lloyd & Xue, 2006; Tang et al., 2006; Han et al., 2009; Henzinger et al., 2000). The movement-assisted connectivity restoration of drone networks is formally defined as follows; Let V be the set of v points in $\mathbb{R}^3$ and $E=\{(u,v)|\ u,v \in V$ and $|(u,v)| \geq r\}$ be the set of edges between the points with maximum distance r. Given a cost function $c : \mathbb{R}^3 \times \mathbb{R}^3 \to \mathbb{R}$, find a mapping $M : \mathbb{R}^3 \to \mathbb{R}^3$ such that $\sum_{v \in V} c(v, M(v))$ is minimum and $G=(M(V),E)$ is connected.

Figure 6.a shows a two-dimensional view of a sample instance of a restoration problem. In this figure, we have $V=\{1,2,3,4\}$ and $E = \varnothing$, which leads to a disconnected graph. Assume that the cost function is the distance between the points, so we have $\forall v,u \in V$: $c(u,v)= \|v,u\|$. The aim is to map the points to new locations such that the total cost is minimum and the resulting graph becomes connected. Figure 6.b shows a feasible solution to this problem as $M= \{(1:1),(2:2),(3:a),(4:b)\}$ with the cost $c= \|3,a\|+\|4,b\|$.

Figure 6. Sample instance of Problem II in $\mathbb{R}^2$

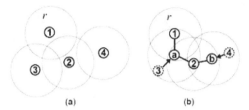

(a)   (b)

Let V be the set of n points in $\mathbb{R}^2$ which must be covered by a spanning tree in STP-MSPBEL problem and r be the maximum length of each edge in the spanning tree. If the set $Q \supseteq V$ is an optimum solution for STP-MSPBEL problem, then a proposed optimal algorithm for STP-MSPBEL problem should find the set $Q\backslash V = \{q_1, q_2, \dots, q_h\}$ of $h \geq 0$ Steiner points. Assume that we have an optimal algorithm $A(V,r,c)$ for connectivity restoration problem which finds a mapping with minimum cost (according to the cost function a) for creating a connected graph, defined by V and r. To prove the NP-Hardness of restoration problem, it is enough to show that algorithm A can produce an optimal solution for the STP-MSPBEL problem with an extra polynomial time computation.

The resulting optimum spanning tree in STP-MSPBEL problem can be considered as a connected graph $G=(Q,E)$ where $E= \{(u,v)| u,v \in Q$ and $\|u,v\| \geq r\}$ is the set of edges with the maximum length r. So, an optimal algorithm for STP-MSPBEL problem to find a connected graph $G=(Q,E)$ where $|Q|$ is minimum. Any instance of connectivity restoration problem can be transformed from $\mathbb{R}^3$ to $\mathbb{R}^2$ by setting the z coordinate of all points to 0 (Figure 7). So, if $A(V,r,c)$ can solve an instance of connectivity restoration problem in $\mathbb{R}^3$, it definitely solves any instance of the same problem in $\mathbb{R}^2$.

Since STP-MSPBEL problem is defined in $\mathbb{R}^2$, we assume that the z coordinate of all points in the connectivity restoration problem is always 0. The cost function of the algorithm A can be defined as follow:

$$c(v,u) = \begin{cases} 1 + \|v,u\| & \text{if } v \in V \\ 0 & \text{otherwise} \end{cases} \tag{9}$$

Figure 7. Transforming an instance of problem II in $\mathbb{R}^3$ *to* $\mathbb{R}^2$

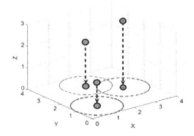

Figure 8. Covering a n×n plane using circles with radius r

Using the above function, if a point $v \in V$ maps to a location u, then the cost will be 1 plus their distance. So, the cost of mapping each node to its own location is 1. The cost of mapping any points out of V to any other point is always 0. Assuming that A returns the cost of mapping M, the following algorithm can find Q using A:

Algorithm **STP-MSPBEL**

```
1:    Q←V
2:    while A(Q,r,c)¹|V| do
3:      select an arbitrary point q ∉ Q.
4:      Q ← Q ∪ q
5:      return Q
```

The STP-MSPBEL algorithm repeatedly maps the points in Q to new locations until the cost of mapping becomes |V| which means that all points in V mapped to their own locations:

$$\forall v \in V : v = M(v) \rightarrow \sum_{v \in V} c(v, M(v)) = \sum_{v \in V} 1 + 0 = |V| \tag{10}$$

Considering that the resulting graph of A is always connected, and we add the Steiner points one by one, the $A(Q,r,c)=|V|$ condition is enough to decide about the correctness and optimality. If the points in Q are not sufficient for creating a connected graph, then A will map some points to new locations, and the cost will be higher than |V|:

$$\exists v \in V : v \neq M(v) \rightarrow c(v, M(v)) = (1 + \|v, u\|) > 1 \rightarrow \sum_{v \in V} c(v, M(v)) > |V| \tag{11}$$

The cost of mapping any point $q \notin V$ is 0; adding any Steiner point has no direct effect on cost except that it reduces the number of mapping with different source and target points in V. Finally, when there is enough (optimal) number of Steiner points in Q, all points in V will be mapped to their own locations, and the cost of mapping will be |V|. The maximum iteration of the loop is $|Q \backslash V|$ or the number of added Steiner points. For any $n \geq 0$, $r > 0$ and two-dimensional Euclidean plane ρ bounded by n, ρ can be completely covered by at most $((n/r)+1)2$ circles with radios r such that the distance between the center of neighboring circles is at most r and any point in ρ has a distance no greater than r to at least one circle

(Figure 8). Therefore $|Q\backslash V| < ((n/r)+1)2$ and the reduction is in polynomial time. So, the movement assisted connectivity restoration is an NP-Hard problem in both $\mathbb{R}^2$ and $\mathbb{R}^3$.

We prove that the connectivity management problem in 3-D space is NP-Hard as its similar version in 2-D space. Since there are many more alternative solution points for 3-D space, searching for the optimal solution will generally consume more time. On the other side, if we sacrifice the optimal solution, searching for a solution in 3-D space may be easier due to its large size.

ALGORITHMS

This section provides insight regarding existing and possible solutions to the defined problem.

Heuristic Methods

Simple heuristic algorithms can be used to reconnect the disconnected networks. They are mostly easy to implement and run, even distributed. However, the connection is established at the cost of total traveled distance (or energy consumption in a broader sense), which may or may not be acceptable. The problem with these simple heuristics is their complete ignorance of optimal, sub-optimal, or near-optimal solutions and also neglecting clever maneuvers that may save resources (e.g., energy). Anyway, their ease of use makes them worthwhile to consider in some cases. These can be grouped under two categories: swarm destination point estimation and individual destination point estimation. The first is the simpler one that proposes the group of drones (when still connected) to decide a trivial point of meet-up in case of disconnections. So, whenever a disconnection occurs, the (remaining) drones get to the meeting point to reconvene. An exemplary work can be found in (Kang & Park, 2016). The latter, however, can be knottier depending on the implementation. It proposes that all (or some) drones should follow their unique routes (or divert to a unique point) to get to their correct position to meet-up with others in case of disconnections. The routes or points should carefully be calculated before the deployment. These types of algorithms guarantee connectivity but usually cannot guarantee a significant rate of approximation.

The second group of heuristic methods that enforce individual destinations to all or some nodes can be designed to provide efficiency and even optimality to a considerable extent (i.e., near-optimality), under the assumption of failure only one node or a few trivial nodes. In (Senturk et al., 2012), Senturk et al. have proposed an efficient heuristic considering a similar assumption. They assumed that some node failures divide the original network topology into multiple partitions, yet the partitions are close enough to each other so that some "movable" drones can relocate themselves in between these partitions and act as relay nodes to connect the partitions while the other drones do not move at all. After the failures that partition the network, their algorithm initially calls another heuristic algorithm to find viable intermediate locations between the partitions for the potential relay nodes to be placed. When the relay node placement algorithm finishes, relay node candidates are selected considering their distances to the pre-calculated relay positions and their inclusion/exclusion of the connected dominating set (CDS) of the partition they are located in. For any relay node location, the algorithm tends to favor the closest non-CDS node as the relay node candidate. Thus, the distance to be traveled is somewhat minimized, and the connectivity of the partitions are preserved. Once the relay node candidates are nominated, they move to their pre-calculated positions and re-establish the connection between the partitions, therefore

Figure 9. A brief illustration of the algorithm in (Senturk et al., 2012). (Frames denote CDS) a) A failure creates two partitions; relay node positions' R1' and 'R2' are calculated. B) Drones' D' and 'F', the closest ones that are outside CDS, move and restore the connection

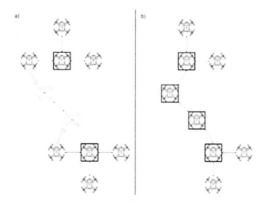

unify them. On the other hand, finding a CDS of a network partition can be costly in terms of time and message complexities.

An Evolutionary Algorithm for Search and Rescue Drone Networks

Müller et al. proposed a multiple drone-based search and rescue system. In this system, drones depart from a base station and start to search for a target in an area (Muller, 2012). An evolutionary algorithm is used to determine the coordinates of the drones which search and rescue by providing the connectivity of the network. According to the drones' communication range, the algorithm determines the coordinates that; each drone stays in the communication range of another neighboring drone. After the target is found, the drones form a line network towards the base station to transmit the info. When a drone lost the network connection, it returns to the base station, and its coordinates are determined again to provide network connectivity. This method can be very costly in terms of time and energy since the total traveled distance may be very high, depending on the scenario. Furthermore, the number of available drones can be a limiting factor.

A Neighborhood-Aware Substitution Algorithm

In multiple drone systems, including means of swarms, where there is a fixed or a mobile control station, a drone can be disconnected from the control station intentionally or unintentionally since the drones may perform continuous motions. Kim et al. proposed a simple method to provide a connection between the drones, which disconnected from the rest of the network as well as the station (Kim et al., 2016; Kim et al., 2017). In this method, drones send informative packets that contain their IDs and coordinates periodically. Therefore, each drone learns its neighbors' last coordinates. When a drone lost the connection to the rest of the network and the station, possibly due to an environmental effect, it then moves towards a "former" neighbor's last-known coordinates until the connection is re-constructed. But, although there is an undeniable chance of re-establishing the connection, this method cannot guarantee the connectivity at all. Because the swarms of drones may be moving as a group and may move unreliably fast. Thus, the chosen neighbor may not be in its last known coordinates anymore. Likewise, there may not be any other nodes nearby. The disconnected drone may try other neighbors' last-known locations to increase its chance after waiting with no contact. However, that does not provide any guarantee, either.

Role-based Connectivity Management for A2G Channels

Goddemeier et al., in their 2012 study (Goddemeier et al., 2012), have proposed a role-based connectivity maintenance approach for the particular case of the existence of a fixed ground station within a drone network. The solution method is suitable for spatial exploration, patrolling, or relaying scenarios, as well as area coverage applications to a limited extent, where the drones should maintain the connection with a base station. The management relies on the self-assigned roles of some drones becoming "relay nodes" or "articulation points" within the network. At least one drone declares itself as the relay node and does not leave the station's range. One of the outgoing drones become an articulation point and maintain its link to the relay node when its RSSI reaches a certain threshold. The number of articulation points increases as the swarm moves farther until, eventually, the network becomes a line topology. If that would not be enough to reach a distant destination point, then all the roles are revoked, and the swarm releases itself from the station for a temporary round-trip to the destination. Still, considering the enforced connection to a base station, such drone networks can no longer be called pure ad-hoc networks because the ground station acts as an infrastructure element, which limits the mobility and the potential spatial expansion of the drones in the field so that the underlying connectivity problem becomes less critical and easier to address with more intuitive (and cost-effective) solutions, especially the heuristics. Although their approach covers the management of both A2A and A2G links neatly, it does not entirely cover the restoration of the connectivity in case of failures.

Proactive Approaches: PCR, DCR, and RAM

For ad-hoc drone networks, instead of continuing the "normal" operation until a failure takes place and reacting to that failure to mitigate the issues only after it happens, some studies claim that having means of countermeasures or backup plans beforehand is a better strategy (Imran et al., 2010; Imran et al., 2012). They impose that reactive solutions require large-scale coordination among the healthy nodes (to avoid breaking any more links) and may cause considerable overhead. Imran et al. (Imran et al., 2012) have proposed PCR, partitioning detection, and connectivity restoration algorithm. It involves determining the drones that are possibly prone to failures by assessing their topological features (i.e., being a cut-vertex or not). Once these critical nodes are found, a backup node (that is preferably not critical itself) is then assigned to each such node among their neighbors. In case of the failure of a critical node, that will not be a surprise, and the backup node will replace it as soon as possible. If the relocation of the backup node would break other links (which is very likely), this node recursively causes a longer relocation process that involves other nodes, too. This behavior adds a reactive touch and makes the solution a "hybrid" one indeed. Nevertheless, the study assumes only one node failure at a time and no other failures during a recovery process, which degrade the serviceability of the algorithm. DCR (Imran et al., 2012) is an improved version of the PCR algorithm that enhances the backup selection criteria and allows the handling of multiple node failures through RAM extension. A more rigorous selection of backup nodes and the backup-of-backup logic allow restoring the connectivity even when multiple nodes fail. However, there are some topology formations, which prevent these methods from working.

While the mentioned studies suggest some apparent performance gains, there are also severe criticisms regarding proactive approaches, even if they are sort of hybrid (Imran et al.,2012-1). For example, in a crowded swarm with many critical nodes, the required number of (preferably non-critical" backup nodes must also be very high, which may not be possible in many scenarios. Likewise, for RAM to be useful, backup nodes must satisfy some hard-coded criteria, which may not be achievable in some missions.

Coverage-Aware Connectivity Restoration

Swarms that work on area coverage missions require extraordinary attention to their topology formations. In case of failures, the algorithms that perform means of restoration of the connection(s) should better be aware of the original formation and the area that it covered. It may naturally be impossible to sustain covering the same amount of area after re-establishing the connection with a fewer number of remaining nodes; however, the algorithms must employ spare nodes first, if any. Otherwise, they should aim to cover the largest possible area or sacrifice the smallest possible area by moving the least critical node among potential candidates.

Tamboli and Younis, in (Tamboli & Younis, 2010), have proposed a connectivity restoration algorithm that also pays regard to the area coverage, called C^3R. It requires each node to keep a record of its 1-hop or 2-hop neighbors (depending on the variation). This is done via "heartbeat" messages, broadcasted by all nodes. Within a connected network, whenever a node fails, say node 'F' for the sake of example, an action is taken whether 'F' is a cut-vertex or not. This design decision was made by the authors to prevent coverage-wholes. However, it would also be possible to take action only if this node was covering a mission-critical area and/or losing it caused disconnection. Anyway, in case of failures, all neighbors of node 'F' approach to its last-known position and establish a temporary connection to decide a recovery schedule, unless they are already participating in another failed nodes' recovery process. They agree on a time-based sentry-duty schedule and return to their initial positions (except the first one). From that point on, each node periodically visits the location of 'F' whenever the schedule forces them to do so, cover that area for a predefined time, hands the duty to the next node, and returns to its original position. In this way, the area of responsibility of the node 'F' shall be covered as well as the areas of the neighboring nodes, and thus, the swarm may continue its mission with little to no interruption. The scheme is undoubtedly useful in certain situations. However, three major drawbacks are evident. First, keeping the neighbor tables always up-to-date causes messaging overheads. Second, the number of tolerable failures is considerably limited as the loss of adjacent nodes is too tricky to be handled. Last but not least, in some topologies, a participating neighbor of a failed node 'F' may be a cut-vertex itself. Therefore, when it leaves its position to do the sentry-duty, the network would be disconnected, and the portion of the network that it connects to the rest of the network would be "offline" until it returns to its original position. In this case, the offline nodes would be unreachable by the other nodes (and vice versa), while there would be a significant need for buffering, which may or may not be possible. If the connectivity is preferred over coverage, then it would be better to exclude that node from the duty schedule.

Obstacle-Avoidant Connectivity Restoration

Physical obstacles of any kind, shape, and size are not rare to be encountered by drones during swarm missions. The existence of obstacles increases the difficulty of connectivity restoration problems, too. Such cases must be handled carefully to prevent additional failures. Mi et al.,(Mi et al., 2015) have pro-

Table 5. Different aspects of the discussed connectivity restoration algorithms.

Algorithm	Decision Making (Swarm/Individual)	Computation (Distributed/Central)	Guaranteed Restoration	Strategy (Proactive/ Reactive)	Coverage Aware	Obstacle Avoidant
Kang & Park, 2016	Swarm	Distributed	Yes	Reactive	No	No
Senturk et al., 2012	Individual	Distributed	Yes	Reactive	No	No
Muller, 2012	Individual	Central	Yes	Reactive	Yes	No
Kim et al., 2016	Individual	Distributed	No	Reactive	No	No
Kim et al., 2017	Individual	Distributed	No	Reactive	No	No
Goddemeier et al., 2012	Swarm	Distributed	Yes	Proactive	Yes	No
Imran et al., 2012	Individual	Central	Yes	Proactive	No	No
Imran et al.,2012-1	Individual	Central	Yes	Hybrid	No	No
Tamboli&Younis, 2010	Swarm	Distributed	Yes	Reactive	Yes	No
Mi et al., 2015	Individual	Central	Yes	Proactive	No	Yes

posed an algorithm that also considers obstacles when restoring the connectivity of a robotic network that faces a node failure. Their strategy involves the determination of cut-vertices in the network, and proactive assignment of one backup node exclusively for each cut-vertex node among their 1 or 2-hop neighbors. There is no backup for non-cut-vertex nodes, and no action is prescribed for the failure of non-cut-vertex nodes since the connectivity is not affected. In case of a cut-vertex failure, however, the backup node moves towards the failed node's (last-reported) position to replace it permanently, to maintain the connectivity of the network. A neighboring node is selected as the backup if and only if it has the smallest total node degree among these neighbors. In case of equality, the one with the shortest geographical distance is selected. Since there are no other criteria for backup selection, a cut-vertex may also be chosen as the backup of another cut-vertex. In this case, a cascading replacement procedure applies intuitively. Nevertheless, a node might be selected as the backup of multiple nodes. Though providing simplicity, this behavior limits the flexibility of the solution as it cannot be used to recover numerous node failures, where multiple nodes with the same backup node fail, or a node and its backup fail at the same time.

If any of the backup nodes encounter an obstacle during their movement, which can also be other nodes in this context, then the moving node tries to go around the obstacle by choosing a direction (left-hand-side or right-hand-side) considering the existing gyroscopic force that applies to the moving node. The go-around policy is enforced until the obstacle successfully circumnavigated. Possibly for the sake of simplicity, the algorithm only considers the closest obstacle if there are more than one. Likewise, the obstacles are presumed to be convex, simple, and are not extremely large. On the other hand, since the introduced circumnavigation algorithm is initially designed for land robots, it does not involve any means of fly-over policy, which can be done easily by drones. In some scenarios, this would be much more efficient in terms of energy, time, and traveled distance. Table 5 summarizes different aspects of the discussed algorithms in this section.

Figure 10. Formed layers in a sample drone network

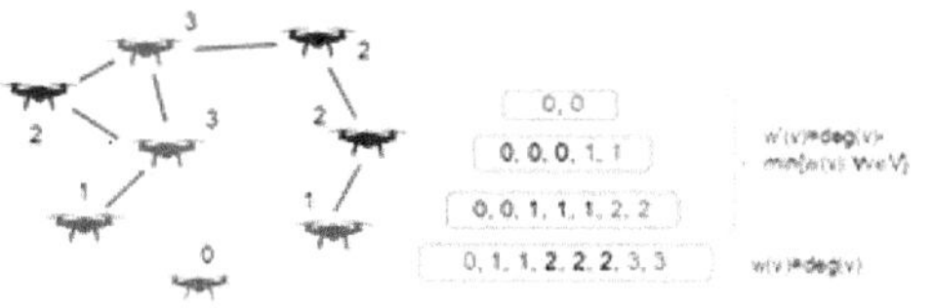

METHODS AND FUTURE DIRECTIONS

In this chapter, we will investigate the methods for future directions in order to cope with the problem.

Combinatorial algorithms

The intuitive methods are the simplest and most basic methods that can be used to solve the connectivity restoration problem. The purpose of intuitive methods is to get a result as fast as possible. By looking at only a few parameters, such as the number of drones or the distance between neighbor drones, algorithmic decisions are made; hence, the quality of the result can be compromised. In this method, the problem is divided into smaller parts, each part is solved separately, and then results are merged together. This method usually does not provide an approximation bound. Layering and parametric pruning techniques can be used to obtain convergence rates.

Layering

In the Layering method, a weight is assigned to each drone in the network using a weight function. Using these weights, target sets are generated. For example, let $G=(V,E)$ be a graph and $c>0$ be a constant value. We can define a function for each drone in the graph according to the degree of drones as $w(v)=c.\deg(v)$. In this function, the weight of drones with no neighbor becomes 0. Drones with a weight of 0 may have a lower moving cost than others because no connections will be lost by moving these drones. Thus, we can remove these drones from the list of drones that should remain in the initial place. In the second layer, we can change the constant value as $\forall v \in V$: $c=\min\{(w(v)/\deg(v)\}$. In this case, c will be equal to the lowest weight/degree value. After calculating this ratio in each layer, we can calculate the new weights of drones with the $\forall v \in V$: $t(v)=c.\deg(v)$ and $w'(v) = w(v)-t(v)$ functions. Thus, a new weight is calculated for each drone in each layer. Let D be the set of drones with degree 0 and W be the set of drones with weight 0. In each stage, if we remove $D \cup W$ from the graph, we will get the set of drones that should not move until a certain level. In this way, we can keep the drones in the last layer in their initial positions and move the other drones toward their nearest neighbor nodes.

Figure 10 shows the formed layers for a sample drone network where c = 1. The degree of each drone is written next to it, and the drones with different degrees are shown with different colors. As seen in Figure 10, the drones' weight changes in each layer and the number of drones that should be kept at the initial place decreases in each layer. According to these layers, green, blue, and then black nodes must move to their closest fixed neighbors.

For the case of c = 1, we can write the following sample movement function that can be used in the layers:

Figure 11. 2-connected network restoration with layering method

a) b) c) d)

$$M(v_i) = \begin{cases} w(v_i) > \min\{w(V)\}: i \\ other: \ i + \dfrac{i-j}{2} \ where \ \forall v_t \in V : \left\| v_i - v_j \right\| \leq \left\| v_i - v_t \right\| \end{cases} \qquad (12)$$

The above function reduces the distance between the nodes with the lowest weight and their closest neighbors to half in each layer. As another approach, we can move the drones that must be removed from the graph in each layer to the drones with a fixed position. One of the most important features of this method is that the approximation rate can be measured relatively easily. Therefore, the performance of the algorithms designed with this method can be evaluated more clearly. Figure 11 shows how we can use the layering method for 2-connected network restoration. In this example, the weights of drones in the first layer will be w (1) = 0, w (2) = 1, w (3) = 2 and w (4) = 1. In the first layer, the weight of drone 1 is less than other drones; hence this drone moves towards the nearest neighbor, which connects it to drones 2 and 3 (Figure 11.b). In the second layer, the weight of the drones is calculated as w (1) = 2, w (2) = 3, w (3) = 3 and w (4) = 1, and by moving toward closest neighbor (Figure 11.c) the network becomes 2-connected (Figure 11.d).

Parametric Pruning

In this method, the cost of the optimum solution to the problem is taking into account. The solutions that produce more cost than the optimal solution do not affect the result, so that we can remove them from the search space. In this way, we will narrow down the search area and reach an acceptable solution more quickly. The most important problem of this method is that the cost of the optimum solution can hardly be estimated. Therefore, in the parametric pruning method, one of the input parameters estimates the optimum solution. Using this input value, solutions with higher costs are deleted from the search space, and the search strategy is applied to the remaining solutions. Assume that I is a drone restoration problem, and I(t) is a restricted version o I after pruning by the parameter t. I(t) can be solved in 2 stages. In the first stage, we find the cost of an optimum solution as follow:

$$t^* = \sum_{v_i \in \frac{V}{v_b}} f\left(v_i, M_{opt}\left(v_i\right)\right) \qquad (13)$$

In the above formula, the node v_b is the base station, and M_{opt} is the optimum solution to the problem. In the second stage, we find an acceptable solution to the problem. To make a drone network-connected, we can move all drones toward the base station, but this method is not an optimum solution. Therefore,

Figure 12. 2-connected network restoration with parametric pruning method

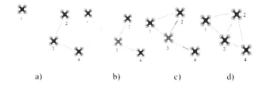

a)   b)   c)   d)

the following movement function can be a definite but not optimal solution to the connectivity restoration problem:

$$M(v_i) = \begin{cases} i = b: & i \\ \|i - b\| \le r: & i \\ other: & b + \dfrac{i-b}{|i-b|} \times r \end{cases} \qquad (14)$$

In the above motion function, the value of $b + \dfrac{i-b}{|i-b|} \times r$ moves node i to the communication boundary of node b. Suppose that in the optimum solution, each drone should move a certain amount towards the base station. For example, the following function moves the drone v_i and reduce the distance between v_i and v_b by half:

$$M(v_i) = \begin{cases} i = b: & i \\ \|i - b\| \le r: & i \\ other: & i + \dfrac{b-i}{2} \end{cases} \qquad (15)$$

Figure 12 shows the parametric pruning method for 2-connectivity restoration on an example topology. In this example, the total distance between all nodes and drone 3 is less than the same value for other drones. Hence, drone 3 is selected as the base station, and other drones move towards this drone. Drone 1 moves towards drone 3, and the network becomes 1-connected (Figure 12.b). If drones 2 and 4 moves towards drone 3 (Figure 12.c), they connect to each other, and the network becomes 2-connected (Figure 12.d).

Linear Programming Based Methods

Rounding or randomization techniques can be used to find a feasible solution for connectivity restoration in drone networks. In the rounding technique, the value found for the continuous variable in the LP feasible solution is converted to the nearest integer. In the randomization technique, an integer value is assigned randomly according to a certain probability distribution. For example, assume that variable x_i indicates whether the drone i moves or remains in its initial location. (If $x_i = 0$ the drone i will move and

Figure 13. 2-connected network restoration using LP-based method

if $x_i = 1$ the drone i will not move.). We can determine the value of this variable based on the number of neighbors. To drones with more neighbors have a higher probability of getting 1 in x_i because moving these nodes may disconnect more connections. If we show the number of neighbors of drone i by $|\Gamma_i|$ and the number of two hop neighbors with $\left|\Gamma_i^2\right|$, we can find an initial value for x_i as $x_i = \left|\Gamma_i\right|/\left|\Gamma_i^2\right|$. In this way, a movement function can be written as follows:

$$M\left(v_i\right) = \left(1 - \frac{\left|``_{v_i}\right|}{\left|``_{v_i}\right|^2}\right) \times \left(i + \frac{t-i}{2}\right) \ where \ t = 1/n \times \sum_{v_j \in V}\left(\left|``_{v_j}\right|/\left|``_{v_j}\right|^2 \times j\right) \tag{16}$$

In the above function, the average of the positions of the nodes that are likely to remain in their positions is calculated as a *t* value. (the nodes with higher probability have more effect on the average). Then, the distance between the nodes that are likely to move, and the position t is reduced by half. Figure 13 shows how this LP-based method can be used for the 2-connectivity restoration of the sample drone network. In this example, p_i shows the position of drone *i* (Figure 13.a) and variable x_i shows whether the drone *i* will move (Figure 13.b). Since the number of neighbors of drone 1 is 0, the x_i variable of this drone is 0. The number of neighbors of drones 2 and 4 is 1, and the number of their two-hop neighbors is 2. So, the x_i variable of these drones is 0.5. The number of neighbors of drone 3 is 2, and the number of its two-hop neighbors is also 2. So, the x_i variable of this drone is 1. So, drone 1, which has the lowest *xi* value, moves toward the middle of its two-hop neighbors. We can find the middle of the two-hop neighbors by calculating the average of their positions (Figure 13.c). Moving drone 1 to the (p2 + p3 + p4) / 3 position, creates a 2-connected network (Figure 13.d).

CONCLUSION

Drone technology is one of the most progressive technologies that affect our lives significantly and has many application areas such as smart farming, military surveillance, civil security, disaster management, and wildfire tracking. Drones are unmanned vehicles generally composed of batteries, flight controllers, transceivers, cameras, and various sensors. They can operate in a fully autonomous manner, while a human operator can also control them. Drones fabricated recently have limited capabilities in terms of energy sources and transmission capabilities for applications requiring a long lifetime and high coverage area. Drone swarms equipped with widely available relatively short-range communication protocols such as WiFi can be better alternatives for drones capable of long transmission in many scenarios such as relief teams in a disaster area, military units in a battlefield, and people experiencing an internet service in a tropical island through an ad hoc backbone. If a ground controller is in the transmission range of each drone forming a fleet, then maintaining an ad hoc routing architecture may not be meaningful. On the other hand, this situation can be impossible for various scenarios; thus, utilizing a multi-hop drone communication infrastructure is of utmost importance. The drones must be connected through a reliable and robust network for covering larger areas and for services with high quality. In order to achieve this objective, the connectivity between drones should be monitored carefully and restored if any communication link and drone hardware faults exist.

A network is k-connected if the network remains connected in case of k-1 node faults. Deployment of k-connected networks is an effective method to strengthen the connectivity of wireless networks. Maintaining the current k value of the network, namely k-connectivity restoration, aims to add new nodes or moving existing nodes. We study the connectivity management problems for drone networks from various perspectives in a comprehensive manner in this chapter. Firstly, we review the mobility models for drone fleets, especially point out the alpha-based mobility as it is appropriate for drone networking applications. Following this, we study the GPSR, AODV, and OLSR based communication models, and we show that ML-OLSR can be a good candidate for drone swarms. Among different reviewed channel models, we find that the SUI model is the most suitable for drone network applications. We provide NP-Hardness proof of our tackled problem by reduction of the Steiner tree problem with a minimum number of Steiner points and bounded edge length. We review heuristic methods, an evolutionary algorithm for search and rescue drone networks, a neighborhood-aware substitution algorithm, role-based connectivity management for A2G channels, proactive approaches, and coverage-aware connectivity restoration related to our problem and its variants. Combinatorial algorithms, layering, parametric pruning, and linear programming based methods are explained as the mathematical basis for future directions to deal with the problem. Besides, we assume that the positions of the nodes are already given before the execution of the connectivity management algorithms, but we know that positioning is a very important and hard problem, which is an important research topic for drone networks. Moreover, other important research issues such as flocking, consensus, rendezvous, and swarming are left open for drone networks.

REFERENCES

Akram, V. K., & Dagdeviren, O. (2018, June). On Hardness of Connectivity Maintenance Problem in Drone Networks. In *2018 IEEE International Black Sea Conference on Communications and Networking (BlackSeaCom)* (pp. 1-5). IEEE. 10.1109/BlackSeaCom.2018.8433713

Bai, H., & Atiquzzaman, M. (2003). Error modeling schemes for fading channels in wireless communications: A survey. *IEEE Communications Surveys and Tutorials*, *5*(2), 2–9. doi:10.1109/COMST.2003.5341334

Bekmezci, I., Sahingoz, O. K., & Temel, Ş. (2013). Flying ad-hoc networks (FANETs): A survey. *Ad Hoc Networks*, *11*(3), 1254–1270. doi:10.1016/j.adhoc.2012.12.004

Bok, J., & Ryu, H. G. (2014). Path loss model considering doppler shift for high speed railroad communication. In *16th International Conference on Advanced Communication Technology* (pp. 1-4). IEEE. 10.1109/ICACT.2014.6778910

Bujari, A., Palazzi, C. E., & Ronzani, D. (2017). FANET application scenarios and mobility models. In *Proceedings of the 3rd Workshop on Micro Aerial Vehicle Networks, Systems, and Applications* (pp. 43-46). ACM. 10.1145/3086439.3086440

Çabuk, U., Tosun, M., Jacobsen, R., & Dagdeviren, O. (2020). Path Loss Estimation of Air-to-Air Channels for FANETs over Rugged Terrains. *Proceedings of the 28th IEEE Signal Processing and Communication Applications (SIU).*

Cheng, X., Du, D. Z., Wang, L., & Xu, B. (2008). Relay sensor placement in wireless sensor networks. *Wireless Networks, 14*(3), 347–355. doi:10.100711276-006-0724-8

Chung, F. R. K., & Graham, R. L. (1985). A new bound for Euclidean Steiner minimal trees. *Annals of the New York Academy of Sciences, 440*(1), 328–346. doi:10.1111/j.1749-6632.1985.tb14564.x

Cornejo, A., & Lynch, N. (2010). Fault-tolerance through k-connectivity. In *Workshop on network science and systems issues in multi-robot autonomy: ICRA* (*Vol. 2*, p. 2010). Academic Press.

Danoy, G., Brust, M. R., & Bouvry, P. (2015). Connectivity stability in autonomous multi-level UAV swarms for wide area monitoring. In *Proceedings of the 5th ACM Symposium on Development and Analysis of Intelligent Vehicular Networks and Applications* (pp. 1-8). ACM. 10.1145/2815347.2815351

Egli, J. J. (1957). Radio propagation above 40 MC over irregular terrain. *Proceedings of the IRE, 45*(10), 1383–1391. doi:10.1109/JRPROC.1957.278224

Erceg, V., Greenstein, L. J., Tjandra, S. Y., Parkoff, S. R., Gupta, A., Kulic, B., Julius, A. A., & Bianchi, R. (1999). An empirically based path loss model for wireless channels in suburban environments. *IEEE Journal on Selected Areas in Communications, 17*(7), 1205–1211. doi:10.1109/49.778178

Erceg, V., Hari, K. V. S., Smith, M. S., Baum, D. S., Sheikh, K. P., Tappenden, C., … Trinkwon, D. (2001). *IEEE 802.16 Broadband Wireless Access WG: Channel Models for Fixed Wireless Applications.* IEEE.

Erdelj, M., & Natalizio, E. (2016). UAV-assisted disaster management: Applications and open issues. In *2016 international conference on computing, networking and communications (ICNC)* (pp. 1-5). IEEE.

Goddemeier, N., Daniel, K., & Wietfeld, C. (2012). Role-based connectivity management with realistic air-to-ground channels for cooperative UAVs. *IEEE Journal on Selected Areas in Communications, 30*(5), 951–963. doi:10.1109/JSAC.2012.120610

Guinness World Records Limited. (2017). *The Drone Racing League sets quadcopter speed record.* Retrieved from https://www.guinnessworldrecords.com/news/commercial/2017/7/the-drone-racing-league-builds-the-worlds-fastest-racing-drone-482701

Han, X., Cao, X., Lloyd, E. L., & Shen, C. C. (2009). Fault-tolerant relay node placement in heterogeneous wireless sensor networks. *IEEE Transactions on Mobile Computing, 9*(5), 643–656.

Hata, M. (1980). Empirical formula for propagation loss in land mobile radio services. *IEEE Transactions on Vehicular Technology, 29*(3), 317–325. doi:10.1109/T-VT.1980.23859

Henzinger, M. R., Rao, S., & Gabow, H. N. (2000). Computing vertex connectivity: New bounds from old techniques. *Journal of Algorithms, 34*(2), 222–250. doi:10.1006/jagm.1999.1055

Hwang, F. K. (1976). On Steiner minimal trees with rectilinear distance. *SIAM Journal on Applied Mathematics, 30*(1), 104–114. doi:10.1137/0130013

Imran, M., Younis, M., Haider, N., & Alnuem, M. A. (2012). Resource efficient connectivity restoration algorithm for mobile sensor/actor networks. *EURASIP Journal on Wireless Communications and Networking, 2012*(1), 347. doi:10.1186/1687-1499-2012-347

Imran, M., Younis, M., Said, A. M., & Hasbullah, H. (2010, December). Partitioning detection and connectivity restoration algorithm for wireless sensor and actor networks. In *2010 IEEE/IFIP International Conference on Embedded and Ubiquitous Computing* (pp. 200-207). IEEE. 10.1109/EUC.2010.37

Imran, M., Younis, M., Said, A. M., & Hasbullah, H. (2012). Localized motion-based connectivity restoration algorithms for wireless sensor and actor networks. *Journal of Network and Computer Applications, 35*(2), 844–856. doi:10.1016/j.jnca.2011.12.002

ITU-R. (2019). *Recommendation ITU-R P.525-4: Calculation of free-space attenuation.* Retrieved from https://www.itu.int/ITU-R/go/patents/en

Jiang, J., & Han, G. (2018). Routing protocols for unmanned aerial vehicles. *IEEE Communications Magazine, 56*(1), 58–63. doi:10.1109/MCOM.2017.1700326

Jorgic, M., Goel, N., Kalaichevan, K., Nayak, A., & Stojmenovic, I. (2007, August). Localized detection of k-connectivity in wireless ad hoc, actuator and sensor networks. In *2007 16th International Conference on Computer Communications and Networks* (pp. 33-38). IEEE. 10.1109/ICCCN.2007.4317793

Kang, J. H., & Park, K. J. (2016, July). Spatial retreat of net-drones under communication failure. In *2016 Eighth International Conference on Ubiquitous and Future Networks (ICUFN)* (pp. 89-91). IEEE. 10.1109/ICUFN.2016.7536989

Karp, B., & Kung, H. T. (2000). GPSR: Greedy perimeter stateless routing for wireless networks. In *Proceedings of the 6th annual international conference on Mobile computing and networking* (pp. 243-254). ACM. 10.1145/345910.345953

Kasampalis, S., Lazaridis, P. I., Zaharis, Z. D., Bizopoulos, A., Zettas, S., & Cosmas, J. (2014, June). Comparison of Longley-Rice, ITU-R P. 1546 and Hata-Davidson propagation models for DVB-T coverage prediction. In BMSB (pp. 1-4). Academic Press.

Kim, G. H., Mahmud, I., & Cho, Y. Z. (2017, December). Self-recovery scheme using neighbor information for multi-drone ad hoc networks. In *2017 23rd Asia-Pacific Conference on Communications (APCC)* (pp. 1-5). IEEE. 10.23919/APCC.2017.8303997

Kim, G. H., Nam, J. C., Mahmud, I., & Cho, Y. Z. (2016, July). Multi-drone control and network self-recovery for flying Ad Hoc Networks. In *2016 Eighth International Conference on Ubiquitous and Future Networks (ICUFN)* (pp. 148-150). IEEE.

Kuiper, E., & Nadjm-Tehrani, S. (2006). Mobility models for UAV group reconnaissance applications. In *2006 International Conference on Wireless and Mobile Communications (ICWMC'06)* (pp. 33-33). IEEE. 10.1109/ICWMC.2006.63

Lin, G. H., & Xue, G. (1999). Steiner tree problem with minimum number of Steiner points and bounded edge-length. *Information Processing Letters, 69*(2), 53–57. doi:10.1016/S0020-0190(98)00201-4

Lloyd, E. L., & Xue, G. (2006). Relay node placement in wireless sensor networks. *IEEE Transactions on Computers*, *56*(1), 134–138. doi:10.1109/TC.2007.250629

Messous, M. A., Senouci, S. M., & Sedjelmaci, H. (2016). *Network connectivity and area coverage for UAV fleet mobility model with energy constraint. In 2016 IEEE Wireless Communications and Networking Conference*. IEEE.

Mi, Z., Yang, Y., & Yang, J. Y. (2015). Restoring Connectivity of Mobile Robotic Sensor Networks While Avoiding Obstacles. *IEEE Sensors Journal*, *15*(8), 4640–4650. doi:10.1109/JSEN.2015.2426177

Mogensen, P. E., & Wigard, J. (1999). *Cost action 231: Digital mobile radio towards future generation system, final report*. Section 5.2: on Antenna and Frequency Diversity in Gsm. Section 5.3: Capacity Study of Frequency Hopping Gsm Network. Academic Press.

Mukherjee, A., Dey, N., Kumar, R., Panigrahi, B. K., Hassanien, A. E., & Tavares, J. M. R. S. (2019). Delay Tolerant Network assisted flying Ad-Hoc network scenario: Modeling and analytical perspective. *Wireless Networks*, *25*(5), 2675–2695. doi:10.100711276-019-01987-8

Müller, M. (2012). *Flying Ad-Hoc Networks*. Institute of Media Informatics Ulm University.

Okumura, Y. (1968). Field strength and its variability in VHF and UHF land-mobile radio service. *Rev. Electr. Commun. Lab.*, *16*, 825–873.

RFC 3561 (2003). *Ad hoc On-Demand Distance Vector Routing*.

RFC 3626 (2003). *Optimized Link State Routing*.

Sadek, A., & Shellhammer, S. (2008). *IEEE P802.19 Wireless Coexistence: SUI Path-Loss Model for Coexistence Study*. Academic Press.

Sahingoz, O. K. (2014). Networking models in flying ad-hoc networks (FANETs): Concepts and challenges. *Journal of Intelligent & Robotic Systems*, *74*(1-2), 513–527. doi:10.100710846-013-9959-7

Schleich, J., Panchapakesan, A., Danoy, G., & Bouvry, P. (2013). UAV fleet area coverage with network connectivity constraint. In *Proceedings of the 11th ACM international symposium on Mobility management and wireless access* (pp. 131-138). ACM. 10.1145/2508222.2508225

Senturk, I. F., Akkaya, K., & Senel, F. (2012). An effective and scalable connectivity restoration heuristic for Mobile Sensor/Actor Networks. *2012 IEEE Global Communications Conference (GLOBECOM)*. 10.1109/GLOCOM.2012.6503165

Tamboli, N., & Younis, M. (2010). Coverage-aware connectivity restoration in mobile sensor networks. *Journal of Network and Computer Applications*, *33*(4), 363–374. doi:10.1016/j.jnca.2010.03.008

Tang, J., Hao, B., & Sen, A. (2006). Relay node placement in large scale wireless sensor networks. *Computer Communications*, *29*(4), 490–501. doi:10.1016/j.comcom.2004.12.032

Vasiliev, D. S., Meitis, D. S., & Abilov, A. (2014). Simulation-based comparison of AODV, OLSR and HWMP protocols for flying Ad Hoc networks. In *International Conference on Next Generation Wired/Wireless Networking* (pp. 245-252). Springer. 10.1007/978-3-319-10353-2_21

Wang, S., Mao, X., Tang, S. J., Li, X., Zhao, J., & Dai, G. (2010). On "movement-assisted connectivity restoration in wireless sensor and actor networks". *IEEE Transactions on Parallel and Distributed Systems*, *22*(4), 687–694. doi:10.1109/TPDS.2010.102

Wei, H., Zhong, Z., Guan, K., & Ai, B. (2010, August). Path loss models in viaduct and plain scenarios of the high-speed railway. In *2010 5th International ICST Conference on Communications and Networking in China* (pp. 1-5). IEEE. 10.4108/iwoncmm.2010.3

Yanmaz, E. (2012, June). Connectivity versus area coverage in unmanned aerial vehicle networks. In *2012 IEEE International Conference on Communications (ICC)* (pp. 719-723). IEEE. 10.1109/ICC.2012.6364585

Zhao, T., Xie, Y., & Zhang, Y. (2018). Connectivity properties for UAVs networks in wireless ultraviolet communication. *Photonic Network Communications*, *35*(3), 316–324. doi:10.100711107-017-0753-5

Zheng, Y., Wang, Y., Li, Z., Dong, L., Jiang, Y., & Zhang, H. (2014). A mobility and load aware OLSR routing protocol for UAV mobile ad-hoc networks. In *2014 International Conference on Information and Communications Technologies (ICT 2014)*. IET Digital Library. 10.1049/cp.2014.0575

ADDITIONAL READING

Abbasi, A. A., Younis, M., & Akkaya, K. (2009, September). Movement-Assisted Connectivity Restoration in Wireless Sensor and Actor Networks. *IEEE Transactions on Parallel and Distributed Systems*, *20*(9), 1366–1379. doi:10.1109/TPDS.2008.246

Akram, V., & Dağdeviren, O. (2019). TAPU: Test and pick up-based k-connectivity restoration algorithm for wireless sensor networks. *Turkish Journal of Electrical Engineering and Computer Sciences*, *27*(2), 985–997. doi:10.3906/elk-1801-49

Akram, V. K., Dagdeviren, O., & Tavli, B. (2020). Distributed k-Connectivity Restoration for Fault Tolerant Wireless Sensor and Actuator Networks: Algorithm Design and Experimental Evaluations. *IEEE Transactions on Reliability*, 1–14. Advance online publication. doi:10.1109/TR.2020.2970268

Rabta, B., Wankmüller, C., & Reiner, G. (2018). A drone fleet model for last-mile distribution in disaster relief operations. *International Journal of Disaster Risk Reduction*, *28*, 107–112. doi:10.1016/j.ijdrr.2018.02.020

KEY TERMS AND DEFINITIONS

Area Coverage: Sensing and collecting meaningful data from the entirety or parts of a given mission area. Most drone applications involve means of area coverage.

Channel Model: A collection of empirical and/or theoretical relations that define the characteristics of the communication model, including but not limited to the path loss, shadowing, multi-path fading, noise, and Doppler effects.

Communication Model: A collection of rules of a set of nodes' behavior regarding establishing and maintaining their communication. It may enforce specific technologies and/or include allowable data rates, modulations, encoding, and link characteristics such as symmetricity, synchronization, ranges, etc.

Connectivity Restoration: Re-connecting a disconnected ad-hoc network by either moving the nodes to desired positions or manipulating the link characteristics.

Drone: An electric-powered rotating-wing unmanned aerial vehicle that also has a means of computing and sensing capabilities.

k-**Connectivity:** Also known as *k*-vertex-connectivity. A connected graph's ability to remain connected after removal of any fewer than *k* vertices.

Movement Model: A collection of rules and activities that apply to a swarm of unmanned aerial vehicles. It defines how the swarm collaboratively move to accomplish the given tasks. For instance, it may be enforced to visit (cover) a portion of an area exactly *k* times.

Neighborhood: For an arbitrary node, the set of surrounding nodes that it is directly connected to. A *k*-neighborhood may also include indirectly connected neighbors at most at its *k*-hop distance.

Obstacle Avoidance: Drone (as solo or as in swarms) ability to autonomously avoid colliding into any observed or unexpected objects that exist in their route to an arbitrary destination. Such a feature may comply with the mission requirements and should not cause termination of any task unless it is inevitable.

Path Loss: Attenuation and degradation of radio signals used due to the distance between communicating parties, signal's properties (e.g., frequency) and the environmental conditions.

Chapter 7
Exploring Cryptocurrency Sentiments With Clustering Text Mining on Social Media

Jiwen Fang
The University of Hong Kong, Hong Kong

Dickson K. W. Chiu
The University of Hong Kong, Hong Kong

Kevin K. W. Ho
ⓘ https://orcid.org/0000-0003-1304-0573
University of Guam, Guam

ABSTRACT

Social media has become a popular communication platform and aggregated mass information for sentimental analysis. As cryptocurrency has become a hot topic worldwide in recent years, this chapter explores individuals' behavior in sharing Bitcoin information. First, Python was used for extracting around one month's set of Tweet data to obtain a dataset of 11,674 comments during a month of a substantial increase in Bitcoin price. The dataset was cleansed and analyzed by the process documents operator of RapidMiner. A word-cloud visualization for the Tweet dataset was generated. Next, the clustering operator of RapidMiner was used to analyze the similarity of words and the underlying meaning of the comments in different clusters. The clustering results show 85% positive comments on investment and 15% negative ones to Bitcoin-related tweets concerning security. The results represent the generally bullish environment of the cryptocurrency market and general user satisfaction during the period concerned.

DOI: 10.4018/978-1-7998-4963-6.ch007

INTRODUCTION

Since the Bitcoin (BTC) was first released in 2008 and transacted in 2009 as the first cryptocurrency (see explanations of cryptocurrency and Bitcoin in the Terms and Definition section), the world has witnessed the revolutionary blockchain technology spread worldwide. Recently, Bitcoin has drawn big crowds into the market. Bitcoin price experienced a meteoric rise from around US$1,000 at the beginning of 2017 to almost US$20,000 at the end of the same year (see: http://coindesk.com). This phenomenon has made Bitcoin become one of the most discussed topics globally, and nearly 80% of Americans have heard of Bitcoin (De, 2018). The craze has boosted the market of cryptocurrencies and Initial Coin Offering (ICO). People and institutions turn their attention and investment from traditional financial instruments to the crypto market, which results in hypes of these cryptocurrencies. The CoinMarketCap website shows 1,845 cryptocurrencies already in the market, but "less than 1% of the world's population" has invested in cryptocurrencies (Palipea, 2018).

Based on these phenomena, this market will still draw huge potential investment and go through further technological development in the future, which appeals to much research and attention into this field. The emergence of Bitcoin may cause fundamental changes in people's lives without centralized monetary authorities in the future, which already brings the accounting profession's attention from different parts of the world (Tsuji & Hiraiwa, 2018). Bitcoin might be the first major cryptocurrency, developed by Satoshi Nakamoto, which depicted the decentralized blockchain feature that sprung up other blockchain technology (Brunton, 2019). Therefore, this chapter takes Bitcoin, with the largest market value and user base, as the case study to represent cryptocurrency in social media.

Furthermore, for the public, social media is one of the primary channels to search and acquire the latest news from the blockchain market (Choi *et al.*, 2020). We have undergone drastic changes in information search behaviors over the past couple of decades, with the various pervasive Internet applications (Hong *et al.*, 2007). This trend brings up social media to domination, with communication and interaction means completely altered to a new form, and many people use social media platforms to exchange information simultaneously (Lam et al., 2019; Fong et al., 2020). Lin and Lee (2004) claimed that people could get customized information with minimal effort and cost and obtain information to facilitate efficient decision-making within the Internet context. As social media provides "two-way conversations" between companies and clients to speed up market responsiveness and co-create value (See-To & Ho, 2014), companies from diffident industries realize the importance of social media, which is an excellent way to communicate and interact with their customers (Biederman, 2015). Twitter, as world-scale social media, brings significant impacts on individuals' daily lives, with monthly active users up to 336 million in the first quarter of 2019 (Clement, 2019). Twitter's position is highly ranked worldwide, not only among individuals, but companies and governments also employ Twitter as a platform to expand their influences, improve public relations, provide services, and attract potential customers (Himelboim *et al.*, 2014).

As a result, Twitter has generally been considered a powerful tool for observing cryptocurrency information searching behavior with much evidence. Firstly, the importance of cryptocurrency information on Twitter from users' viewpoints has high values and contributes to the growing community by creating millions of content (Kraaijeveld & De Smedt, 2020). Such content could be shared across different networking platforms at breath-taking speed, leading to heated debates about cryptocurrency and much concern for the public on a global scale. The cryptomarket cannot leave out social media, which increases awareness and improves transparency to the public, particularly for ICOs, marketing strategy, etc. Social media also feature a high volume of cryptocurrency information and never-ending conversations, which provide high value to users who need cryptocurrency information for financial decisions (Almatrafi *et al.*, 2018).

RESEARCH GAP AND CONTRIBUTION

Despite prior works on the investment information search behavior, there are scant studies about Bitcoin as compared with traditional financial instruments. With an increasing number of investors changed their investment direction into cryptocurrency, searching for Bitcoin social media is an interesting topic for further investigation. Thus, this study adopted a quantitative methodology to extract the information search behavior from Twitter to determine the influence of Bitcoin information on the public via social media. As such, this chapter aims to investigate the cryptocurrency-information search behavior of users on Twitter to figure out what kinds of information correlate with individual behaviors and decisions regarding Bitcoin. For extracting and structuring Bitcoin searching behaviors, this research adopts the method of clustering text-mining from opinions onTwitter from different user groups, and tries to address the following research questions (RQs):

RQ1. Are there significant differences in the sentiments among different groups of users on Twitter?
RQ2. What are the different attitudes and behaviors of users in these groups regarding Bitcoin information?

The rest of this chapter is organized as follows. We proceed with a review of related literature highlighting the research gap, followed by the methodology used in this research. Then we present our analysis and results on the keywords and clustering with RapidMiner. Finally, we conclude this chapter with discussions of our results and future work direction to address the limitations of this research.

LITERATURE REVIEW

Information Search and Sentiments

The concept of information search behavior originates from the market imperfections theory, and information search behavior has become an explanation for seeking values and benefits for customers (Lin & Lee, 2004). Wilson (2000) considered purposive seeking for information due to a need to satisfy some goals in mind, and Guo (2001) considered that information search is essential in making wise decisions. Indeed, few people could deny that more information searching could get better investment chances. Peterson and Merino (2003) further proposed that information searching behaviors are divided into two types: internal and external. Internal behaviors depend on individuals' memory, while external behaviors are determined by the goal or the problem-solving activities for reducing the uncertainty of risk. Lin and Lee (2004) pioneered in investigating information searching behavior related to making investment decisions, and they concluded that the extent and sources of information people used differ with purposes and other variables such as subjective knowledge, risk tolerance, age, educational level, income level, etc.

The differences in information search behavior depend significantly on demographic characteristics such as gender, age, education, marital status, employment status, and family size (Loibl & Hira, 2009), as well as phycological variables, including risk tolerance and subjective knowledge (Lin & Lee, 2004). Loibl and Hira (2009) also considered search antecedents into their research and identified five investor typologies by cluster analysis to explore the correlations with searching resources, demographic, and phycological factors. Other studies show that gender is also an important determinant. For example, Maghferat and Stock (2010) examined that men and women have different searching behaviors because of the characters of self-esteem and carefulness, and women possess the abilities of more complicated and comprehensive searching behavior. These influencers of information search behavior lay the fundamental for this research to analyze the connections between the Bitcoin information and users' behaviors.

The underlying reasons for user searching behaviors for cryptocurrency information may be curious about this new area, investment intention, research of this field, etc. Thus, by observing textual information on Twitter, we could discover common kinds of popular texts by dividing messages into different groups, finding similar words in each group, and then different posters' behaviors in different groups as inferred by clustering analysis.

Text-Mining in Social Media

Social media has proliferated in our daily lives and allows people to create and share their opinions anywhere, anytime. To manage the massive datasets in social media that can be multimedia with videos and images, many studies have been devoted to building retrieval systems such as MIRFlickr and NUS-WIDE, making social media data more accessible (Tang *et al.*, 2012). However, Bhisikar (2013) stressed that text mining is more appropriate for social media data analysis because an increasing volume of text data possess useful information. Thus, this study focuses on text information analysis.

Arbour *et al.* (2015) pointed out that statistical approaches are often necessary to handle the sheer volume of data on social networks. Then, measuring or extracting the text from these opinions becomes a big problem for text mining. Makhabel *et al.* (2017) proposed that sentiment analysis (also known as opinion analysis) could be a powerful tool to extract and analyze opinion information from the written language, which comprises various emotional un-structured formats. These sentiments and opinions are significant because they can be used to improve businesses' marketing and productivity (Li *et al.*, 2019). Taking online learning platforms as an example, as it is difficult for platforms to extract emergent information for response reason from the thousands of posts, questions, and comments, instructors need to design a model that can mine the written data (Almatrafi *et al.*, 2018). Therefore, this study utilized the text mining technique, instead of the qualitative methodology of distributed questionnaires, for obtaining Bitcoin information and mapping corresponding searching behaviors. The underlying meaning of structuring the opinions in social media can provide results to show correlations between text and searching behavior, which is easier for obtaining results about the influences of the social media in Bitcoin information.

Social Media Message Clustering

Text clustering belongs to one of the text mining applications that provides algorithms for processing and organizing textual data automatically (Tunali *et al.*, 2016). The clustering text mining method is featured

Table 1. Dataset view

	tweet_id	user_name	reply_num	like_num	retweet_num	text	post_time	user_id	avatar_url	tweet_url
0	10264906:	Bitcoin	128	594	213	Fun Fact: You can buy Coffee today with b	2018-08-06 23:30:11	Bitcoin	https://pbs.twin	/rogerkver/status/1026490629260333056
1	10265280:	Bitcoin Mag:	0	0	0	There are less than 4 million Bitcoins left to	2018-08-07 01:58:48	Bitcoin	https://pbs.twin	/officialmcafee/status/1026528029433061377
2	10264024:	Roger Ver	17	658	327	ICE, the firm that owns the NYSE, plans to la	2018-08-06 17:39:45	BitcoinMag	https://pbs.twin	/coindesk/status/1026402439220678656
3	10268109:	John McAfee	10	175	78	ATMs Now In The Thousands Around the W	2018-08-07 20:43:08	BitcoinMag	https://pbs.twin	/BTCTN/status/1026810973770924032
4	10268224:	CoinDesk	0	0	0	New BCash team line-up looks shit hot: All t	2018-08-07 21:28:54	rogerkver	https://pbs.twin	/DanDarkPill/status/1026822493468860416
5	10268396:	Bitcoin News	1	87	52	Uberâ€™s Biggest Shareholder Backs $15 Bi	2018-08-07 22:37:08	officialmca	https://pbs.twin	/CryptoCoinsNews/status/1026839664781668352
6	10268104:	dark pill	16	52	22	back above $7K and now over $2B in mark	2018-08-07 20:41:04	coindesk	https://pbs.twin	/CNBCFastMoney/status/1026810456030232582
7	10268047:	CCN	5	32	16	How to connect to the to tumble with 1	2018-08-07 20:18:17	BTCTN	https://pbs.twin	/3L10n/status/1026804722433445888
8	10267968:	CNBC's Fast M	0	0	0	Some select alts mooning at the same time :	2018-08-07 19:47:12	DanDarkPil	https://pbs.twin	/CryptoDonAlt/status/1026796898034835456
9	10268469:	ElectronLion	1	8	5	They were born after 2003: Facebook Twitt	2018-08-07 23:06:08	CryptoCoir	https://pbs.twin	/ValaAfshar/status/1026846962543468545

by grouping text into clusters, and each cluster has a large number of similarities among members but high dissimilarity among groups (Fung *et al.*, 2009).

Prior research developed various techniques and methodologies to conduct social media message clustering analyses. For example, Shreyas (2017) utilized clustering techniques to categorize users in social media, which helped companies find target users for marketing purposes by applying the constraint method for clustering to differentiate the incorporate and application-oriented users. The clustering results showed clear groups of users who are interested in different topics such as sports, entertainment, traveling, and others. This research showed that clustering techniques could serve as a powerful method for grouping comments demonstrated in social media applications into clusters, which would be useful for designing marketing strategies. Loibl and Hira (2009) also adopted clustering methods to group interviewed investors into five subsets according to similar information search behavior, which facilitated the presentation of different data sources and showed demographic and psychological influences as discusses earlier. To explore and extract text databases from a large volume of Web documents, Li *et al.* (2008) noted that groups the same topic of texts together for user search retrieval, which featured no training stage for labeled documents required. These studies have laid the foundation for analyzing a large volume of text data using the clustering mining method, which can extract opinions into different groups with similar characteristics.

METHODOLOGY

Data Resource

Data for this study retrieved with the keyword "Bitcoin" were extracted from Twitter with Python between July 10th and August 6th, 2018. The retrieved data comprised 11,674 items (see Table 1). The reason for choosing this period was that Bitcoin price just experienced the toughest time, dropping to around 5,850 USD, which is the lowest in the past two-year period, but then followed by a dramatic increase of about 45% at the end of July. Plus, Twitter allows followers to retweet the post for repeating messages, significantly increasing user connections and reaching more people to message one another. Thus, these phenomena raised significant attention or even panic to the public or investors who were active in social media to figure out what happened to Bitcoin. The massive tweet data could greatly reflect the Bitcoin information searching behavior, and the metadata is shown in Table 2.

Table 2. Metadata Description

Metadata	Description
tweet_id:	Every tweet has an ID number of 19 digits
user_name:	User name shows who post the tweet
reply_num	Twitter allows people to comment on the tweet to show their opinion and interact among users. More reply reflects more users paying attention to this tweet, and the content has more value for analysis.
like_num	Users can show their preference to the tweet, and they could tag this post to present their agreement to this tweet.
retweet_num	Users can share and post a tweet on their homepage. The retweet number also reflects the popularity of the same tweet.
text	Full text of a tweet that captures user opinion and sentiment.
post_time	The date and time of posting on Twitter.
user_id	Twitter gave an ID to users when they first registered, which can identify the user who posted a tweet.
avatar_url	Web address (URL) for locating the picture of the user in their profile directly.
tweet_url	Web address (URL) for locating a post directly.

Data Preparation Process

After extracting the dataset with the keyword 'Bitcoin' from Twitter, the data were pre-processed by RapidMiner to eliminate noisy data that affects the accuracy analysis before applying the clustering process (see Figure 1). First, some empty data should be excluded. Next, RapidMiner provides algorithms to extract and collate data in text strings for analysis. The operators used were the Tokenize

Figure 1. The inside process of Process Document operator

Figure 2. Word cloud visualization for the tweet dataset

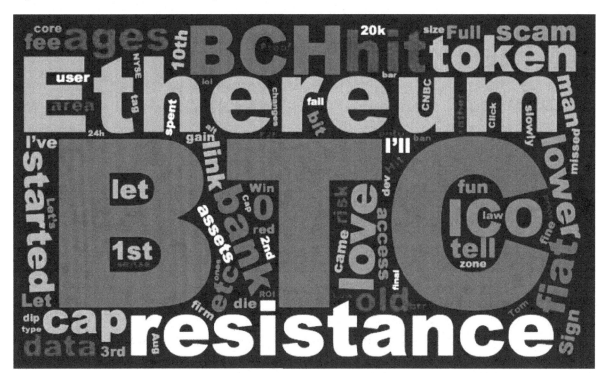

operator, Transform cases operator, Filter stopwords (English) operator, and Stem (snowball) operator. The Tokenize operator split the text into a sequence of tokens with specific splitting points and a proper linguistic character mode. Then, the Transform cases operator changed all words into lower cases in the document. After that, the Filter stopwords operator removed all stopwords such as interjections, pronouns, and conjunctions. Finally, the Stem (snowball) operator removed variations of the same root word and found the English root form.

ANALYSIS AND RESULTS

Keywords Analysis

Figure 2 shows that Bitcoin (BTC) is the most frequent word, followed by Ethereum and BCH, which are cryptocurrency names. The data showed the popularity of cryptocurrency by generating the frequently used words using size (bigger size for more popular words) and location (the more popular word would be located in the center). This word cloud visualization figure helps us figure out that the public still keeps a questionable attitude about this field because there are so many scams in ICOs. These words are displayed in the above visualization chart.

Figure 3. Clustering process using RapidMiner

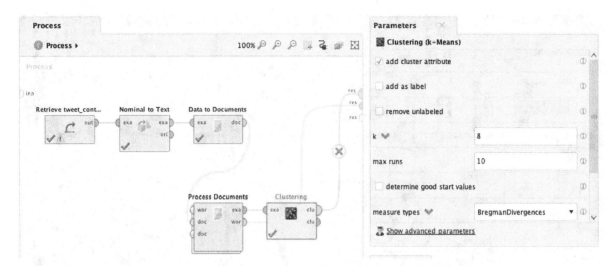

Clustering Analysis Using RapidMiner

The clustering operator of RapidMiner software was used to determine users' information search behavior on Twitter. After trying K equals 2, 6, 7, and 8, respectively, the most reasonable results of clustering group was obtained by setting K to 8, which is consistent with the settings of Harwati *et al.* (2017), who divided the messages into categories of positive attitude, negative attitude, service, interaction, etc. Figure 3 shows the detailed clustering process, and Table 3 summarizes the result.

More than half of the tweets extracted (59.1%) of the shared comments with dominating keywords such as "crypto," "trade," "token," "exchange," "invest," and "cash," and similar words are also found in the centroid table (see Table 4). People generally pay attention to crypto or token investment for market trading in exchanges. As the data collection period was selected when there was a dramatic increase of about 50% from the bottom price of 5,800 USD/Bitcoin, this phenomenon shows that the fluctuation in prices could raise attention or even the public's investment.

Table 3. Clustering values results

Index	Nominal value	Absolute count	Fraction
1	cluster_1	6898	0.591
2	cluster_4	1480	0.127
3	cluster_2	904	0.077
4	cluster_5	698	0.060
5	cluster_6	604	0.052
6	cluster_7	468	0.040
7	cluster_3	360	0.031
8	cluster_0	263	0.023

Table 4. Centroid Table in RapidMiner

Attribute	cluster_0	cluster_1	cluster_2	cluster_3	cluster_4	cluster_5	cluster_6	cluster_7 ↓
market	0	0.001	0.002	0.013	0.001	0.003	0.003	0.205
cap	0	0.000	0.000	0	0.000	0.002	0	0.047
crypto	0.001	0.011	0.008	0.015	0.016	0.005	0.015	0.041
bear	0	0.002	0.002	0.000	0.001	0.011	0	0.033
billion	0.001	0.002	0.001	0.006	0.002	0.001	0.003	0.028
bull	0	0.004	0.002	0.006	0.002	0.028	0.002	0.023

Cluster 4 with a percentage of 12.7% based on the word similarity of "blockchain," "secure," and "bank." As blockchain technology, which provides high security, is the foundation of cryptocurrency, comments about these words were, therefore, frequent. Users expressed their willingness to learn about this new knowledge. However, a high volume of words about "secure" and "bank" showed that the public was still worried about the security compared with the bank.

Cluster 2 (7.7%), cluster 5 (6%), cluster 6 (5.2%), cluster 7 (4%), cluster 3 (3.1%) were based on the word similarity of "love," "price," "future," "market," "ETF (Exchange-traded Fund)," respectively. The word of love could show that people were positive about Bitcoin's future, and taking investment strategies such as ETF was also dominant in their attitude.

Cluster 0, with only 2.3%, clustered around the word "history." The history of Bitcoin's price could affect the behavior. In this case, there was no historical record, which experienced the lowest price during the magical year of 2017 when the price soared 400%. When the prices were rising again, people were anxious and curious about it. Moreover, people preferred to use historical records as references when they decided to invest in Bitcoin at the historical low.

Overall, different clusters showed different user behaviors. The largest cluster, i.e., Cluster 1, was mainly about investment behavior and bullish feelings about this industry. During the target period, with the price increase, people showed a positive attitude in this market and were active in Bitcoin investment. However, some negative attitudes were also displayed clearly, such as the security worries and the dramatic volatility of Bitcoin's historical price range. Clusters 1 and 2,3,5,6,7 were positive about Bitcoin-related information (about 85%), while Clusters 0 and 4 were negative (about 15%).

DISCUSSION AND CONCLUSION

As the information on Twitter about Bitcoin is a huge dataset, it is an excellent resource to research the potential knowledge of users' behavior and the correlations between the information and searchers' attitude. Prior research has shown that the lexicon-based sentiment analysis approach is useful in analyzing Twitter data (Kraaijeveld & Smedt, 2020) and blog posts (Karalevicius, Degrande & De Weert, 2018) for predicting Bitcoin pricing. This study elaborated on the basic knowledge about related research fields in the literature review. For information behavior research, the data available is critical. Finally, with the combination of the information search behavior and social media mining, the K-means clustering method could map the different behavior about Bitcoin information on Twitter.

For RQ1, as the clustering method in RapidMiner has successfully divided the text into different groups, predicting the existence of significant differences in Bitcoin information searching behavior is supported. The differences among groups are significant because clustering results show that each cluster has its individual attributes and meanings.

For RQ2, the centroid table of RapidMiner shows word clusters that express the attitude of tweets, and different attitudes have led to different behavior. Under the environment of increased price, 85% of the comments belong to positive attitudes, such as the words "love," "future," "invest." A small percentage of about 15% show worries about this technology by the words "secure," "history," and "bank." Such information has provided a quick overview of users' attitudes that potentially affect their behaviors.

Through the tweet data clustering analysis, groups are divided into 8 clusters of user behaviors. A summary can be found in Table 5. Over half (59.1%) are grouped into Cluster 1 concerning "crypto," "trade," and "invest," which show a high willingness about the investment during that time, and we put them under the theme "Investment." Plus, the word indicators of "love" and "bullish" (Cluster 2) and other clusters (i.e., Clusters 3, 5, 6, and 7) formed a positive attitude of 85%. These clusters cover themes related to investment, desire to invest, investment vehicles, current price, prospect, and market situation (Mishev et al., 2020).

The two negative tweet clusters (i.e., Clusters 0 and 4) contain the keywords "secure," "bank," and "history." The users mainly worry on the security of blockchain technology and how this technology can provide secure transaction records, reflecting that many investors are not tech-savvy (Adhami, Giudici, & Martinazzi, 2018). Their worries are also grounded on Bitcoin's historical price volatility, reflecting many investors are not professional traders with limited knowledge on risk management of high-volatility financial instruments. Overall, as the percentage of negative tweets is much lower than the positive ones (15% vs. 85%), we can conclude that the market sentiment was bullish through the analysis.

Table 5. The theme of the clusters

Cluster	Percentage (Rank)	Attitude	Theme	Keywords
0	2.3% (8th)	Negative	Historical Record	History
1	59.1% (1st)	Positive	Investment	Crypto, Trade, Token, Exchange, Invest, Cash
2	7.7% (3rd)	Positive	Desire to Invest	Love, Bullish
3	3.1% (7th)	Positive	Investment vehicles	ETF
4	12.7% (2nd)	Negative	Technology	Blockchain, Secure, Bank
5	6.0% (4th)	Positive	Current Price	Price
6	5.2% (5th)	Positive	Prospect	Future
7	4.0 (6th)	Positive	Market situation	Market

Limitations and Future Work

In this research, we explored data in a critical month of shape rise in Bitcoin price. We are planning to analyze data of a more extended period data and other social media platforms (e.g., Facebook, Stocktwits), particularly a time-series analysis on the correlation of social media sentiments and Bitcoin price. Moreover, this study adopted K-means clustering, but the parameter K may need further experimentation for the text mining of social media. We are interested in the mining sentiments of other social and legal aspects of social media (Chiu *et al.*, 2011) and government processes (Wong *et al.*, 2007), as well as how the users using the information to formulate the valuation of cryptocurrencies (Tsuji, 2020). On the other hand, we are working on mining information about management policy from semi-structured interviews of managers of well-known librarians (Lo *et al.*, 2017; 2018) and social media usage metrics of libraries (Kong et al., 2016; Lam et al., 2019).

REFERENCES

Adhami, S., Giudici, G., & Martinazzi, S. (2018). Why do businesses go crypto? An empirical analysis of initial coin offerings. *Journal of Economics and Business*, *100*, 64–75. doi:10.1016/j.jeconbus.2018.04.001

Almatrafi, O., Johri, A., & Rangwala, H. (2018). Needle in a haystack: Identifying learner posts that require urgent response in MOOC discussion forums. *Computers & Education*, *118*, 1–9. doi:10.1016/j.compedu.2017.11.002

Arbour, M., Kaspar, R. W., & Teall, A. M. (2015). Strategies to promote cultural competence in distance education. *Journal of Transcultural Nursing*, *26*(4), 436–440. doi:10.1177/1043659614547201 PMID:25122626

Bhisikar, P. (2013). Overview of web mining and different technique for web personalisation. *International Journal of Engineering Research and Applications*, *3*(2), 543–545.

Biederman, A. (2015). Social media. *Franchising World*, *47*(10), 20–23.

Brunton, F. (2019). *Digital cash: The unknown history of the anarchists, utopians, and technologists who created cryptocurrency*. Princeton University Press.

Chiu, D. K. W., Kafeza, E., & Hung, P. C. (2011). ISF special issue on emerging social and legal aspects of information systems with Web 2.0. *Information Systems Frontiers*, *13*(2), 153–155. doi:10.100710796-009-9168-x

Choi, T. M., Guo, S., & Luo, S. (2020). When blockchain meets social-media: Will the result benefit social media analytics for supply chain operations management? *Transportation Research Part E, Logistics and Transportation Review*, *135*, 101860. doi:10.1016/j.tre.2020.101860

Clement, J. (2019). *Number of monthly active Twitter users worldwide from 1st quarter 2010 to 1st quarter 2019*. Retrieved from: https://www.statista.com/statistics/282087/number-of-monthly-active-twitter-users/

De, H. (2018). *Survey: Nearly 80% of Americans have heard of Bitcoin*. Retrieved from: https://www.coindesk.com/survey-nearly-80-of-americans-have-heard-of-bitcoin

Fong, K. C. H., Au, C. H., Lam, E. T. H., & Chiu, D. K. W. (2020). Social network services for academic libraries: A study based on social capital and social proof. *Journal of Academic Librarianship*, *46*(1), 102091. doi:10.1016/j.acalib.2019.102091

Fung, B. C., Wang, K., & Ester, M. (2009). Hierarchical document clustering. In J. Wang (Ed.), *Encyclopedia of Data Warehousing and Mining* (2nd ed., pp. 970–975). IGI Global. doi:10.4018/978-1-60566-010-3.ch150

Guo, C. (2001). A review on consumer external search: Amount and determinants. *Journal of Business and Psychology*, *15*(3), 505–519. doi:10.1023/A:1007830919114

Harwati, A., Mansur, A., & Karunia, A. (2017). Utilization of social media for consumer behavior clustering using text mining method. *Journal of Engineering and Applied Sciences (Asian Research Publishing Network)*, *12*(3), 6406–6411.

Himelboim, I., Golan, G. J., Moon, B. B., & Suto, R. J. (2014). A social networks approach to public relations on Twitter: Social mediators and mediated public relations. *Journal of Public Relations Research*, *26*(4), 359–379. doi:10.1080/1062726X.2014.908724

Hong, D., Chiu, D. K. W., Shen, V. Y., Cheung, S. C., & Kafeza, E. (2007). Ubiquitous enterprise service adaptations based on contextual user behavior. *Information Systems Frontiers*, *9*(4), 343–358. doi:10.100710796-007-9039-2

Karalevicius, V., Degrande, N., & De Weerdt, J. (2018). Using sentiment analysis to predict interday Bitcoin price movements. *The Journal of Risk Finance*, *19*(1), 56–75. doi:10.1108/JRF-06-2017-0092

Kong, E. W. S., Chiu, D. K. W., & Ho, K. K. W. (2016). Applications of social media in academic library services: A case of the Hong Kong Polytechnic University Library. *International Journal of Systems and Service-Oriented Engineering*, *6*(2), 53–65. doi:10.4018/IJSSOE.2016040103

Kraaijeveld, O., & De Smedt, J. (2020). The predictive power of public Twitter sentiment for forecasting cryptocurrency prices. *Journal of International Financial Markets, Institutions and Money*, *65*(C), 101188. doi:10.1016/j.intfin.2020.101188

Lam, E. T. H., Au, C. H., & Chiu, D. K. (2019). Analyzing the use of Facebook among university libraries in Hong Kong. *Journal of Academic Librarianship*, *45*(3), 175–183. doi:10.1016/j.acalib.2019.02.007

Li, Y., Chung, S. M., & Holt, J. D. (2008). Text document clustering based on frequent word meaning sequences. *Data & Knowledge Engineering*, *64*(1), 381–404. doi:10.1016/j.datak.2007.08.001

Li, Z., Fan, Y., Jiang, B., Lei, T., & Liu, W. (2019). A survey on sentiment analysis and opinion mining for social multimedia. *Multimedia Tools and Applications*, *78*(6), 6939–6967. doi:10.100711042-018-6445-z

Lin, Q., & Lee, J. (2004). Consumer information search when making investment decisions. *Financial Services Review*, *13*(4), 319–332.

Lo, P., Chiu, D., Cho, A., & Allard, B. (2018). *Conversations with Leading Academic and Research Library Directors: International Perspectives on Library Management*. Chandos Publishing.

Lo, P., Cho, A., & Chiu, D. K. (2017). *World's Leading National, Public, Monastery and Royal Library Directors: Leadership, Management, Future of Libraries.* Walter de Gruyter GmbH & Co KG. doi:10.1515/9783110533347

Loibl, C., & Hira, T. K. (2009). Investor information search. *Journal of Economic Psychology*, *30*(1), 24–41. doi:10.1016/j.joep.2008.07.009

Maghferat, P., & Stock, W. G. (2010). Gender-specific information search behavior. *Webology*, *7*(2), 1–15.

Makhabel, B., Mishra, P., Danneman, N., & Heimann, R. (2017). *R: Mining Spatial, Text, Web, and Social Media Data* (1st ed.). Packt Publishing.

Mishev, K., Gjorgjevikj, A., Vodenska, I., Chitkushev, L. T., & Trajanov, D. (2020). Evaluation of sentiment analysis in finance: From lexicons to transformers. *IEEE Access: Practical Innovations, Open Solutions*, *8*, 131662–131682. doi:10.1109/ACCESS.2020.3009626

Palipea, N. M. (2018). *How many people are currently investing in cryptocurrencies?* Retrieved from https://www.quora.com/How-many-people-are-currently-investing-in-cryptocurrencies

Peterson, R. A., & Merino, M. C. (2003). Consumer information search behavior and the Internet. *Psychology and Marketing*, *20*(2), 99–121. doi:10.1002/mar.10062

See-To, E. W. K., & Ho, K. K. W. (2014). Value co-creation and purchase intention in social network sites: The role of electronic Word-of-Mouth and trust–A theoretical analysis. *Computers in Human Behavior*, *31*, 182–189. doi:10.1016/j.chb.2013.10.013

Shreyas, S. (2017). A clustering technique for improving marketing strategy in social media using data mining approach. *International Journal of Engineering and Computer Science*, *6*(5), 21285–21288.

Tang, J., Wang, M., Hua, X.-S., & Chua, T.-S. (2012). Social media mining and search. *Multimedia Tools and Applications*, *56*(1), 1–7. doi:10.100711042-011-0822-1

Tsuji, M. (2020). The social psychology of Cryptocurrency: Do accounting standard-setters understand the users? *International Journal of Systems and Service-Oriented Engineering*, *10*(2), 1–12. doi:10.4018/IJSSOE.2020070101

Tsuji, M., & Hiraiwa, M. (2018). An analysis of the internal consistency of the new accounting standard for virtual currencies in Generally Accepted Japanese Accounting Principles: A virtual currency user perspective. *International Journal of Systems and Service-Oriented Engineering*, *8*(2), 30–40. doi:10.4018/IJSSOE.2018040103

Tunali, V., Bilgin, T., & Camurcu, A. (2016). An improved clustering algorithm for text mining: Multi-cluster spherical K-Means. *The International Arab Journal of Information Technology*, *13*(1), 12–19.

Wilson, T. D. (2000). Human information behavior. *Informing Science*, *3*(2), 49–55. doi:10.28945/576

Wong, J. Y., Chiu, D. K., & Mark, K. P. (2007, January). Effective e-Government process monitoring and interoperation: A case study on the removal of unauthorized building works in Hong Kong. In R. H. Sprague Jr. (Ed.), *Proceedings of the 40th Annual Hawaii International Conference on System Sciences* (pp. 101-101). IEEE. 10.1109/HICSS.2007.194

ADDITIONAL READING

Adamopoulos, P., Ghose, A., & Todri, V. (2018). The impact of user personality traits on word of mouth: Text-mining social media platforms. *Information Systems Research, 29*(3), 612–640. doi:10.1287/isre.2017.0768

Cao, N., Ji, S., Chiu, D. K. W., He, M., & Sun, X. (2020). A Deceptive Review Detection Framework: Combination of Coarse and Fine-grained Features. *Expert Systems with Applications, 156*, 113465. doi:10.1016/j.eswa.2020.113465

Chang, V., Chiu, D. K., Ramachandran, M., & Li, C. S. (2018). Internet of Things, Big Data and Complex Information Systems: Challenges, solutions and outputs from IoTBD 2016, COMPLEXIS 2016 and CLOSER 2016 selected papers and CLOSER 2015 keynote. *Future Generation Computer Systems, 79*(3), 973–974. doi:10.1016/j.future.2017.09.013

Chung, C., Chiu, D. K. W., Ho, K. K. W., & Au, C. H. (2020). Applying social media to environmental education: Is it more impactful than traditional media? *Information Discovery and Delivery, 48*(4), 255–266. doi:10.1108/IDD-04-2020-0047

Dhaoui, C., Webster, C. M., & Tan, L. P. (2017). Social media sentiment analysis: Lexicon versus machine learning. *Journal of Consumer Marketing, 34*(6), 480–488. doi:10.1108/JCM-03-2017-2141

Drobetz, W., Momtaz, P. P., & Schröder, H. (2019). Investor sentiment and initial coin offerings. *Journal of Alternative Investments, 21*(4), 41–55. doi:10.3905/jai.2019.1.069

Hofmann, M., & Klinkenberg, R. (Eds.). (2016). *RapidMiner: Data mining use cases and business analytics applications.* CRC Press. doi:10.1201/b16023

Ji, S., Zhang, Q., Li, J., Chiu, D. K. W., Xu, S., Yi, L., & Gong, M. (2020). A burst-based unsupervised method for detecting review spammer groups. *Information Sciences, 536*, 454–469. doi:10.1016/j.ins.2020.05.084

Kong, E. W. S., Chiu, D. K., & Ho, K. K. (2016). Applications of Social Media in Academic Library Services: A Case of the Hong Kong Polytechnic University Library. *International Journal of Systems and Service-Oriented Engineering, 6*(2), 53–65. doi:10.4018/IJSSOE.2016040103

Lau, R. Y., Liao, S. S., Wong, K. F., & Chiu, D. K. (2012). Web 2.0 Environmental Scanning and Adaptive Decision Support for Business Mergers and Acquisitions. *Management Information Systems Quarterly, 36*(4), 1239–1268. doi:10.2307/41703506

Liu, X., Sun, R., Wang, S., & Wu, Y. J. (2019). The research landscape of big data: A bibliometric analysis. *Library Hi Tech, 38*(2), 367–384. doi:10.1108/LHT-01-2019-0024

Rognone, L., Hyde, S., & Zhang, S. S. (2020). News sentiment in the cryptocurrency market: An empirical comparison with Forex. *International Review of Financial Analysis, 69*, 101462. doi:10.1016/j.irfa.2020.101462

Smuts, N. (2019). What Drives Cryptocurrency Prices? An Investigation of Google Trends and Telegram Sentiment. *Performance Evaluation Review, 46*(3), 131–134. doi:10.1145/3308897.3308955

KEY TERMS AND DEFINITIONS

Bitcoin: Is the first decentralized peer-to-peer cryptocurrency invented under the name Satoshi Nakamoto in 2008 with an open-source software implementation without support from any central bank or authority or any need for intermediaries. Transactions are recorded with blockchain technologies in public distributed manner and verified by network nodes through cryptography.

Cluster Analysis: Is used to classify objects or cases into groups called clusters, where no prior knowledge on cluster membership is required. Clustering procedures may be hierarchical or non-hierarchical, where the non-hierarchical methods in cluster analysis are often known as K-means clustering (employed in this research). Such procedures typically include problem formulation, distance measure selection, clustering procedure determination, choosing the number of clusters, cluster interpretation, and result validity assessment.

Cryptocurrency: Is a digital medium of exchange (normally without physical forms) in which strong cryptography is used to secure the database of transaction records, to record and control the coin ownership and creation, and to verify coin transfer. Cryptocurrencies typically have no central control and use blockchain as the technology to maintain public transactions in a peer-to-peer manner.

RapidMiner: Is an integrated data science software platform for data preparation, machine learning, deep learning, text mining, predictive analytics, result visualization, model validation, and optimization for a wide range of disciplines and applications, such as business, research, education, and application development (see: https://rapidminer.com/).

Sentiment Analysis (Opinion Mining): Uses natural language processing and machine learning to analyze and mining text to interpret, interpret, and classify emotions and subjective information (i.e., sentiment) from information sources. Sentiment analysis is widely applied to detect sentiments in social networks, news, websites, and other online conversations to estimate brand reputation, customer views, and different public opinions.

Social Media: Encompass a wide range of websites, apps, and interactive digital technologies that quickly facilitate users' creation and share content through virtual communities and networks. Such content includes text comments, digital photos, videos, user profiles, and usage data generated through web interactions. Social media encompasses. Some, like Twitter, specialize in sharing short written messages and links.

Text Mining: Attempts to discover new, high-quality information from text collected from various sources such as websites, social media, emails, publications, and reviews, by detecting patterns or trends. Text mining typically requires pre-processing text input to structured data, detecting patterns from structured data, and result interpretation.

Chapter 8
AI–Driven Big Healthcare Analytics:
Contributions and Challenges

Faiz Maazouzi

Department of Mathematics and Computer Science, University of Souk Ahras, Algeria

Hafed Zarzour

iD https://orcid.org/0000-0001-9441-4842

LIM Research, Department of Mathematics and Computer Science, University of Souk Ahras, Algeria

ABSTRACT

With the increased development of technology in healthcare, a huge amount of data is collected from healthcare organizations and stored in distributed medical data centers. In this context, such data quantities, called medical big data, which include different types of digital contents such as text, image, and video, have become an interesting topic tending to change the way we describe, manage, process, analyze, and visualize data in healthcare industry. Artificial intelligence (AI) is one of the sub-fields of computer science enabling us to analyze and solve more complex problems in many areas, including healthcare. AI-driven big healthcare analytics have the potential to predict patients at risk, spread of viruses like SARS-CoV-2, spread of new coronavirus, diseases, and new potential drugs. This chapter presents the AI-driven big healthcare analytics as well as discusses the benefits and the challenges. It is expected that the chapter helps researchers and practitioners to apply AI and big data to improve healthcare.

INTRODUCTION

The digital revolution is transforming our societies and our lives. Among other features, it generates the production of immense amounts of data. The combined effect of the exponential increase in the computing power and storage of computers allows public and private actors to have unparalleled means in history to analyze and disseminate their data. For many years healthcare, research and medical discovery have relied on the collection and analysis of data. Health professionals were trying to understand who gets

DOI: 10.4018/978-1-7998-4963-6.ch008

sick, how, and why. Today, thanks to the many sensors in smartphones and the increase in the quantity and quality of data, the possibilities for revolutionary discoveries are growing rapidly. Researchers are starting to compile this information into very useful databases that could change our understanding of the relationship between lifestyle and disease. Indeed, at present, the problem with many medical studies is that the patients surveyed report their behaviors and habits themselves. As a result, many of them tend to embellish their description to enhance their image.

On the contrary, thanks to smartphones and other connected objects, data such as the number of daily steps or heart rate are transmitted directly, impartially and objectively. As a result, the patient's ego or opinions never factor into the equation, allowing researchers to collect more and more accurate data than ever before.

The objective of healthcare analytics is to measure and track the health of the million of people around the world, while its main purpose is to keep each of patients healthy as it focuses on offering insights about hospital management, patient records, costs, diagnoses, and more.

The field of healthcare predictive analytics uses all types of data, statistical processes, and machine learning techniques to identify and provide an assessment about future outcomes based on data. Predictive models support preventive care by identifying and classifying patients based on major health conditions.

Today, technologies such as Artificial intelligence (AI), Big Data or connected health are on the way to evolve very quickly.

Many artificial intelligence and machine learning algorithms have been proposed in the past years in the healthcare analytics field, such as: machine learning with complex datasets (Wiens & Shenoy, 2018) machine learning algorithms in the processing of big data in the healthcare sector (Manogaran & Lopez, 2017), machine learning classifiers to assist healthcare-related decisions are proposed in (Pollettini et al., 2012). Decision support system for the electronic classification of patient records (Jiang., 2017). The machine learning techniques help in analyzing (X) unstructured, structured data, (Y) clustering of patients having similar medical symptoms, (Z) prediction of diseases.

The respective exponential growths of these technologies are about to meet, allowing each to develop even faster. The analytical technologies of Big Data in health will allow the development of medical treatments adapted to each person according to their genetic code. But in healthcare, big data alone is not enough. Therefore, it is necessary to use artificial intelligence in addition.

This chapter is organized as follows: Next section presents the BIG DATA. Section 3 describes the contribution of BIG DATA in healthcare analytics. A presentation of artificial intelligence and healthcare analytics is given in section 4. Challenges of Big Data and AI in healthcare analytics are presented in Section 4. Finally, a conclusion is done in Section 5.

BIG DATA

The term "Big data" seems to have been used for the first time in 1997 by Michael Cox and David Ellworth (Wang, Kung, & Byrd, 2018). It designates a system bringing together more than a trillion bytes (terabytes or 1012 bytes), or even petabytes (1015 bytes) or more which can include structured data, documents, images and sounds while also integrating specific search and search technologies. processing of these data.

In 2011, the health data stored around the world was estimated at 1017 bytes (Wang, Kung, & Byrd, 2018). We are now talking about 190x1018 bytes (Lajonchere, 2018).

In the last years, many studies have highlighted the utility of applying big data analysis to health informatics. For example, Asokan and Asokan (2015) discussed the importance of big data in improving the performance of the systems approach-based one health in the context of the health informatics science. In another study, Otero, Hersh, and Ganesh (2014) demonstrated how biomedical and health informaticians can work together in analytics and Big Data.

The economic magazine Forbes estimates that the global market of this sector will grow from 18.3 billion dollars in 2014 to 92.2 in 2026, which represents an annual growth of 14.4% (Columbus, 2017).

The field of big data is not defined only by the quantity stored. Generaly the reserchers use the acronym of 5V to summarize its extent: volume, velocity, variety, veracity, and value (Kim, & Groeneveld, 2017).

Figure 1. The 5V (Anuradha, 2015).

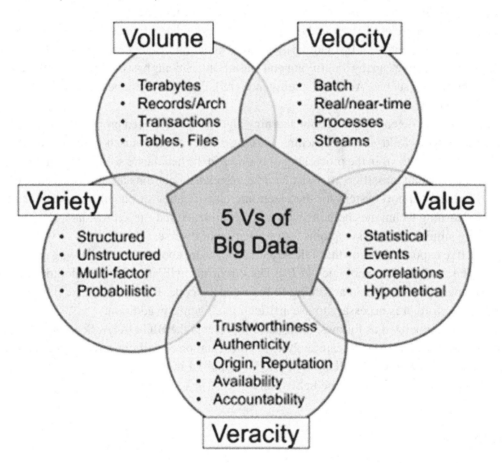

Volume: the development of IoT and the spread of geolocation or analytics have led to an explosion in the volume of medical data collected.

Velocity: Optimized Big Data must provide the right answer at the right time and through the right distribution channel. With such a wealth of medical data, it is necessary to process this data quickly to develop an appropriate response using high-performance software with great computing power. The flexibility and adaptability of AI and Machine Learning meet this need for performance in information processing.

The variety: Medical data have very heterogeneous formats. Technologies make it possible to analyze and cross-check unstructured medical data (Images, conversations, etc.) which represent at least 90% of the information collected.

Veracity: this is one of the major challenges in the exploitation of Big Data. spelling errors, fraud ... It is necessary to multiply the precautions (cross-checking and enrichment of medical data) to minimize the biases linked to the unreliability of Big Data.

The value: Surely the most important point of the 5 V! Big data storage and analytics technologies only make sense if they add value. The definition of goals will guide the use of Big Data.

The data must indeed be usable quickly and for certain applications, in real time. They must be "true": the researcher or operator must have confidence in these sources. The diversity of these and the volume of data constitute a real difficulty of analysis but make it a potential richness.

In order to process this "data", increasingly efficient computer programs are being developed based on "artificial intelligence". We distinguish:

- **Machine learning**, which is based on the acquisition of data and the development of algorithms based on it, algorithms that can determine the commonalities between two populations based on statistical methods. The use of learning on new data makes it possible to process a large number of variables and records (Manogaran & Lopez, 2017);
- **Deep learning**, which drives machine learning without initial rules, based on the concept of neural networks. These methods are based on probabilistic analysis modes, of the Bayesian type, already used, for example, in clinical research protocols to reinforce their power (Lajonchere, 2018).

Nowadays, facial and vocal recognition, are based on these deep learning techniques.

These two algorithmic technology approaches are inseparable from big data, of which they constitute an essential element: the heart of their processing. Thus, behind the term big data are grouped the concepts of mass storage, data from multiple sources, "5V", artificial intelligence allowing their exploitation, in order to answer a question posed on a field of analysis well determined (Lajonchere, 2018).

The Contribution of Big Data in Healthcare Analytics

In healthcare analytics, the objective of big data processing is to provide new information useful to society and to patients by guaranteeing citizens and researchers the best confidentiality and the best access to data (Chatellier, 2016).

Today, few examples from the literature illustrate what the use of big data and artificial intelligence software can bring:

The use of four self-learning algorithms has been compared to the recommendations of the American College of Cardiology. (ACC);

The experiment concerns 378,256 patients from the United Kingdom who were victims of cardiovascular accidents using data from 2005. The systems trained on 78% of the data and then estimated on the remaining 22% the chances of an incident occurring. cardiovascular. These results were compared to reality for the years after 2005. The ten-year predictive results obtained by the algorithms are better than those using the recommendations of the ACC. Out of the test sample of 83,000 patients, the best

Figure 2. Workflow of Big data Analytics. Data warehouses store massive amounts of data generated from various sources. This data is processed using analytic pipelines to obtain smarter and affordable healthcare options (Dash et al., 219).

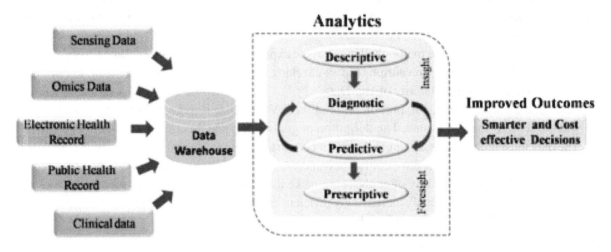

algorithm detects 7.6% more alerts and 1.6% fewer false alerts than recommendations. According to the authors, 355 patients could have been saved by the use of algorithms (Hutson, 2017).

In dermatology, the algorithmic analysis of 2,032 cases was compared with that of a group of 21 experts after training the machine on an image bank. The results obtained are comparable in terms of specificity and sensitivity, in most cases better for deep learning software. Thus, the prospects for using this algorithm, coupled with the use of smartphones, to collect images of skin abnormalities, suggests a significant extension of the prevention of dermatological cancers (Esteva et al., 2017);

In diabetes monitoring, the use of deep learning to detect diabetic retinopathies is already obtaining results that can be used in the clinic (Lajonchere, 2018). An algorithm was developed by Google in collaboration with a team at the University of Austin (Texas) from a test sample of 128,175 images of retinas from different origins. The validation was carried out on two samples of 9,963 and 1,748 images. The specificity on the second test was 96.2%, the sensitivity 93.9%, comparable to the results of the seven experts who also interpreted the images. The authors highlight the limits of the system at the current stage, such as the difficulty of using the algorithm on images from very different materials and the superiority of very experienced experts able to identify tiny lesions that the program cannot not detect (Lajonchere, 2018). But they also specify the advantage of reproducibility over humans, the software always having the same performance. Even if it remains to validate their routine use and the feasibility of applying these algorithms, the way is clear (Gulshan et al.,, 2016).

For several years, Google Flu Trends (GFT) has attempted to predict the spread of the influenza epidemic. The results of a study carried out on eight South American countries between 2012 and 2014 are not entirely conclusive. They are better in Mexico and the authors suggest that the correlation is higher in more temperate than subtropical countries (Pollett et al., 2016).

Monitoring the development of the AIDS epidemic and the consequences of prevention and treatment actions could, according to researchers, benefit from this work by using data from social networks in addition to data from health services (Young, 2016).

Figure 3. Publications associated with big data in healthcare. The numbers of publications in PubMed are plotted by year (Wang, Kung, & Byrd, 2018).

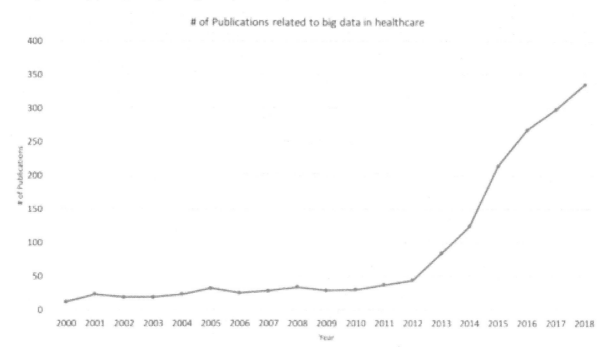

This list is not intended to be exhaustive. However, it shows the potentials of exploiting big data, in some cases already equivalent to human performance. But the state of progress of each project allows us to appreciate the road that still remains to be covered until it is used in routine. Mobilize researchers.

The use of health data for research purposes is largely based on their availability and accessibility, a notion called "open data", which aims to share them, for health, by hospitals, research organizations, administrations, companies, patient communities (Lajonchere, 2018).

In the last years, we have found several works in the field of big data in healthcare, especially in the years between 2014 – 2018, as shown in Figure 3.

Even big companies also offer big data in healthcare analytics services, as shown in Table 1.

For exemple the companie of IBM Watson Health presente a system of sharing clinical and health data to solve the volume problem by sharing and the variety problem by the different types of data it offers.

the same for other companies (MedeAnalytics, Health Fidelity, Flatiron Health,…). See table 1.

ARTIFICIAL INTELLIGENCE AND HEALTHCARE ANALYTICS

In medicine, the most promising areas of AI are related to image processing, radiology, dermatology, and ophthalmology. Even if we read everywhere that these tools are more efficient than doctors, their validity has yet to be demonstrated outside of studies, that is to say in a clinical situation.

When an innovation appears, we attribute a thousand virtues to it. But AI will at best be just one more tool available to healthcare professionals. When a doctor takes a blood test from a patient he suspects

Table 1. List of some of big companies which provide services on big data analysis in healthcare sector (Wang, Kung, & Byrd, 2018).

Company	Description	Website link
IBM Watson Health	Provides services on sharing clinical and health related data among hospital, researchers, and provider for advance researches	https://www.ibm.com/watson/healt h/index -1.html
MedeAnalytics	Provides performance management solutions, health systems and plans, and health analytics along with long track record facility of patient data	https://medea nalyt ics.com/
Health Fidelity	Provides management solution for risks assessment in workflows of healthcare organization and methods for optimization and adjustment	https://healt hfide lity.com/
Roam Analytics	Provides platforms for digging into big unstructured healthcare data for getting meaningful information	https://roama nalyt ics.com/
Flatiron Health	Provides applications for organizing and improving oncology data for better cancer treatment	https://flati ron.com/
Enlitic	Provides deep learning using large-scale data sets from clinical tests for healthcare diagnosis	https://www.enlit ic.com/
Digital Reasoning Systems	Provides cognitive computing services and data analytic solutions for processing and organizing unstructured data into meaningful data	https://digit alrea sonin g.com/
Ayasdi	Provides AI accommodated platform for clinical variations, population health, risk management and other healthcare analytics	https://www.ayasd i.com/
Linguamatics	Provides text mining platform for digging important information from unstructured healthcare data	https://www.lingu amati cs.com/
Apixio	Provides cognitive computing platform for analyzing clinical data and pdf health records to generate deep information	https://www.apixi o.com/
Roam Analytics	Provides natural language processing infrastructure for modern healthcare systems	https://roama nalyt ics.com/
Lumiata	Provides services for analytics and risk management for efficient outcomes in healthcare	https://www.lumia ta.com
OptumHealth	Provides healthcare analytics, improve modern health system's infrastructure and comprehensive and innovative solutions for the healthcare industry	https://www.optum.com/

has anemia, he believes the results the lab sends him, even without having counted the red blood cells myself. The same will be true for the AI, a help for the doctor.

The increase in the amount of data generated by the health care system will fundamentally change the way medicine is practiced in the future. We firmly believe that the doctor - patient relationship will remain the basis of medicine in the future, a relationship enriched by knowledge derived from machine learning (Rajkomar, Dean, & Kohane, 2019).

In addition to big data, the healthcare industry is undergoing a profound transformation thanks to machine learning and artificial intelligence. While robots are still far from replacing doctors and nurses, these technologies are shaking up the perception of health professionals.

Machine learning improves diagnostics, and makes it possible to make precise predictions about the evolution of a patient's health. In the near future, it will be sufficient to report the symptoms of pain or a health problem to a doctor. This will take care of entering these symptoms into a computer. The machine will then suggest the latest search matching the symptoms, so that the doctor can diagnose and treat the problem.

Combined with X-rays or MRIs, these computers will be able to detect problems too small to be seen by humans. Additionally, a computer can monitor medical and family records and compare them with recent research to suggest a tailored treatment protocol to the attending physician.

The Contribution of AI in Healthcare Analytics

Deployed in the medical sphere, artificial intelligence has many advantages:

Fewer errors: The main benefit of the integration of artificial intelligence is that it reduces the risk of errors due to its precision. Watson can, for example, analyze all patient data such as symptoms, medical consultations, family history and test results. In addition, he can engage in collaborative discussion with humans in order to support them in decision-making;

A perfect tool in oncology: This is the typical field of application for this application thanks to its immense capacity to compile a gigantic mass of data, to compare radiological images with millions of others and to formulate diagnostic and therapeutic hypotheses. relevant;

Tireless tools: Unlike humans, machines do not require frequent breaks or refreshments! They are programmed for long hours and can run continuously without flinching.

AI is not a threat to "human" healthcare analytics. The computer will not make a decision for the practitioner or the patient. It will offer leads, indications, statistical data and probabilities that will streamline decision making, minimizing the risk of error. AI is just another string to the medical profession and has tremendous potential for development and recruitment.

Challenges of Big Data and AI in Healthcare Analytics

Healthcare data heterogeneity: Due to the diversity of medical data including different formats from multiple sources, the data heterogeneity is become one of the big challenges to be tackled. A single artificial intelligence model may be not sufficient in this case, but a hybrid artificial intelligence model or a combination of several approaches could be quite simple and straightforward to perform accurate results without the need of using a data homogeneity process.

Healthcare data security and privacy: The security and privacy of medical data remain one of the biggest challenges that need to be considered when medical decision-making based on artificial intelligence is occurred. Data security issues are concerned since cybercriminals can attract sensitive information, while data privacy issues are concerned because the personal health records are distributed and accessed daily by the healthcare sectors. One possible way to tackle the challenge is to combine artificial intelligence techniques with the Blockchain technology to ensure the medical data security and privacy in healthcare systems. This combination could protect the healthcare data and use them appropriately.

Explainability of results: Many AI-based systems have been developed in last years to automate healthcare tasks and solve several problems related to early disease detection with high accuracy of results (Zarzour et al., 2020; Zarzour et al., 2018) .. However, there are only limited ways to support the explainability in order to understand the manner in which the results were generated. One possible way to tackle the explainability challenge is to focus on explainable artificial intelligence (Gunning, 2017). The explainable artificial intelligence aims to provide the evidence and transparency behind the prediction in AI -based systems for healthcare. Thus, such systems are not only accurate, but also highly explainable.

DISCUSSION AND IMPLICATIONS

Weak AI essentially aims to reproduce as faithfully as possible, using algorithms, the result of a specific behavior planned in advance, without any form of improvisation. This technology only performs scheduled tasks. In other words, it does what it is asked to do, nothing more, for example: identifying the risks of cardiovascular disease by scanning patients' retinas, writing short reports based on a thorough semantic analysis, or even answering questions asked by men orally thanks to the quantity of questions and answers recorded in the machine.

Unlike weak AI, strong AI is a computer program capable of reasoning, learning, and even problem-solving . As if it were "intelligent" in some way. The machines are capable of learning on their own from real-life situations, exactly like a child who ends up understanding by himself the logic of a game by dint of trying, making mistakes, correct the shot and then succeed. In 2020, strong AI is still in the experimental stage.

The introduction of Big Data in the healthcare sector represents a real revolution. Its fields of action and applications are numerous, whether they concern the care of patients, the development of treatments, or the contribution of new knowledge.

Big Data is already on the way to disrupting the field of clinical trials by reducing development costs, increasing the chances of success in terms of new discoveries, improving patient safety and reducing time to market. The more the number of objects connected to the Internet increases, the more the volume of accessible information grows with an increased complexity and links between the caches of health data.

CONCLUSION

In this chapter, we have presented the AI-driven big healthcare analytics and identified their benefits and challenges to improve healthcare systems. The contribution of big data in healthcare analytics was to provide useful information to both individual patient and society useful information with the best confidentiality, while the contribution of AI in healthcare analytics was to help in building smart solutions for healthcare by reducing the error risk as well as generating relevant diagnostic and therapeutic hypotheses. The main challenges consisted of healthcare data heterogeneity, Healthcare data security and privacy, and explainability of results.

An efficient healthcare analytics system should focus on multiple AI-based models to perform accurate results, combine artificial intelligence techniques with the Blockchain technology to ensure best protection of healthcare data, and use explainable artificial intelligence to guarantee evidence and transparency in the healthcare systems.

REFERENCES

Anuradha, J. (2015). A brief introduction on Big Data 5Vs characteristics and Hadoop technology. *Procedia Computer Science*, *48*, 319–324. doi:10.1016/j.procs.2015.04.188

Asokan, G. V., & Asokan, V. (2015). Leveraging "big data" to enhance the effectiveness of "one health" in an era of health informatics. *Journal of Epidemiology and Global Health*, *5*(4), 311–314. doi:10.1016/j.jegh.2015.02.001 PMID:25747185

Chatellier, G., Varlet, V., Blachier-Poisson, C., Beslay, N., Behier, J. M., Braunstein, D., ... Josseran, A. (2016). "Big data" and "open data": What kind of access should researchers enjoy? *Therapies*, *71*(1), 107–114. doi:10.1016/j.therap.2016.01.005 PMID:27080635

Columbus, L. (2016). Roundup Of Analytics, Big Data & BI Forecasts And Market Estimates, 2016. *Forbes: USA. Pristupljeno*, *12*, 2017.

Dash, S., Shakyawar, S. K., Sharma, M., & Kaushik, S. (2019). Big data in healthcare: Management, analysis and future prospects. *Journal of Big Data*, *6*(1), 54. doi:10.118640537-019-0217-0

Esteva, A., Kuprel, B., Novoa, R. A., Ko, J., Swetter, S. M., Blau, H. M., & Thrun, S. (2017). Dermatologist-level classification of skin cancer with deep neural networks. *Nature, 542*(7639), 115-118.

Gulshan, V., Peng, L., Coram, M., Stumpe, M. C., Wu, D., Narayanaswamy, A., ... Kim, R. (2016). Development and validation of a deep learning algorithm for detection of diabetic retinopathy in retinal fundus photographs. *Journal of the American Medical Association*, *316*(22), 2402–2410. doi:10.1001/jama.2016.17216 PMID:27898976

Gunning, D. (2017). Explainable artificial intelligence (xai). *Defense Advanced Research Projects Agency (DARPA), and Web, 2, 2.*

Hutson, M. (2017). Self-taught artificial intelligence beats doctors at predicting heart attacks. *Science*, 14. doi:10.1126cience.aal1058

Jiang, F., Jiang, Y., Zhi, H., Dong, Y., Li, H., Ma, S., Wang, Y., Dong, Q., Shen, H., & Wang, Y. (2017). Artificial intelligence in healthcare: Past, present and future. *Stroke and Vascular Neurology*, *2*(4), 230–243. doi:10.1136vn-2017-000101 PMID:29507784

Kim, J., & Groeneveld, P. W. (2017). *Big data, health informatics, and the future of cardiovascular medicine*. Academic Press.

Lajonchere, J. P. (2018). Role of Big Data in evolution of the medical practice. *Bulletin de l'Académie Nationale de Médecine*, *202*(1-2), 225–238.

Manogaran, G., & Lopez, D. (2017). A survey of big data architectures and machine learning algorithms in healthcare. *International Journal of Biomedical Engineering and Technology*, *25*(2-4), 182–211. doi:10.1504/IJBET.2017.087722

Otero, P., Hersh, W., & Ganesh, A. J. (2014). Big data: Are biomedical and health informatics training programs ready?: Contribution of the IMIA working group for health and medical informatics education. *Yearbook of Medical Informatics*, *9*(1), 177. PMID:25123740

Pollett, S., Boscardin, W. J., Azziz-Baumgartner, E., Tinoco, Y. O., Soto, G., Romero, C., ... Rutherford, G. W. (2016). Evaluating Google Flu Trends in Latin America: Important lessons for the next phase of digital disease detection. *Clinical Infectious Diseases*, ciw657. PMID:27678084

Pollettini, J. T., Panico, S. R., Daneluzzi, J. C., Tinós, R., Baranauskas, J. A., & Macedo, A. A. (2012). Using machine learning classifiers to assist healthcare-related decisions: Classification of electronic patient records. *Journal of Medical Systems*, *36*(6), 3861–3874. doi:10.100710916-012-9859-6 PMID:22592391

Rajkomar, A., Dean, J., & Kohane, I. (2019). Machine learning in medicine. *The New England Journal of Medicine*, *380*(14), 1347–1358. doi:10.1056/NEJMra1814259 PMID:30943338

Wang, Y., Kung, L., & Byrd, T. A. (2018). Big data analytics: Understanding its capabilities and potential benefits for healthcare organizations. *Technological Forecasting and Social Change*, *126*, 3–13. doi:10.1016/j.techfore.2015.12.019

Wiens, J., & Shenoy, E. S. (2018). Machine learning for healthcare: On the verge of a major shift in healthcare epidemiology. *Clinical Infectious Diseases*, *66*(1), 149–153. doi:10.1093/cid/cix731 PMID:29020316

Young, S. D. (2015). A "big data" approach to HIV epidemiology and prevention. *Preventive Medicine*, *70*, 17–18. doi:10.1016/j.ypmed.2014.11.002 PMID:25449693

Zarzour, H., Jararweh, Y., Hammad, M. M., & Al-Smadi, M. (2020, April). A long short-term memory deep learning framework for explainable recommendation. In 2020 11th International Conference on Information and Communication Systems (ICICS) (pp. 233-237). IEEE.

Zarzour, H., Maazouzi, F., Soltani, M., & Chemam, C. (2018, May). An improved collaborative filtering recommendation algorithm for big data. In *IFIP International Conference on Computational Intelligence and Its Applications* (pp. 660-668). Springer, Cham. 10.1007/978-3-319-89743-1_56

ADDITIONAL READING

Archenaa, J., & Anita, E. M. (2015). A survey of big data analytics in healthcare and government. *Procedia Computer Science*, *50*, 408–413. doi:10.1016/j.procs.2015.04.021

Faust, O., Hagiwara, Y., Hong, T. J., Lih, O. S., & Acharya, U. R. (2018). Deep learning for healthcare applications based on physiological signals: A review. *Computer Methods and Programs in Biomedicine*, *161*, 1–13. doi:10.1016/j.cmpb.2018.04.005 PMID:29852952

Ghassemi, M., Naumann, T., Schulam, P., Beam, A. L., Chen, I. Y., & Ranganath, R. (2019). Practical guidance on artificial intelligence for health-care data. *The Lancet. Digital Health*, *1*(4), e157–e159. doi:10.1016/S2589-7500(19)30084-6 PMID:33323184

Jiang, F., Jiang, Y., Zhi, H., Dong, Y., Li, H., Ma, S., Wang, Y., Dong, Q., Shen, H., & Wang, Y. (2017). Artificial intelligence in healthcare: Past, present and future. *Stroke and Vascular Neurology*, *2*(4), 230–243. doi:10.1136vn-2017-000101 PMID:29507784

Kambatla, K., Kollias, G., Kumar, V., & Grama, A. (2014). Trends in big data analytics. *Journal of Parallel and Distributed Computing*, *74*(7), 2561–2573. doi:10.1016/j.jpdc.2014.01.003

Khanna, D. (2018). *Use of Artificial Intelligence in Healthcare and Medicine*. International Journal Of Innovations in Engineering Research And Technology.

Panch, T., Szolovits, P., & Atun, R. (2018). Artificial intelligence, machine learning and health systems. *Journal of Global Health*, *8*(2), 020303. doi:10.7189/jogh.08.020303 PMID:30405904

Razzak, M. I., Imran, M., & Xu, G. (2020). Big data analytics for preventive medicine. *Neural Computing & Applications*, *32*(9), 4417–4451. doi:10.100700521-019-04095-y PMID:32205918

Sun, J., & Reddy, C. K. (2013, August). Big data analytics for healthcare. In *Proceedings of the 19th ACM SIGKDD international conference on Knowledge discovery and data mining* (pp. 1525-1525). 10.1145/2487575.2506178

Wang, Y., & Hajli, N. (2017). Exploring the path to big data analytics success in healthcare. *Journal of Business Research*, *70*, 287–299. doi:10.1016/j.jbusres.2016.08.002

Wang, Y., Kung, L., & Byrd, T. A. (2018). Big data analytics: Understanding its capabilities and potential benefits for healthcare organizations. *Technological Forecasting and Social Change*, *126*, 3–13. doi:10.1016/j.techfore.2015.12.019

Zarzour, H., Jararweh, Y., Hammad, M. M., & Al-Smadi, M. (2020, April). A long short-term memory deep learning framework for explainable recommendation. In *2020 11th International Conference on Information and Communication Systems (ICICS)* (pp. 233-237). IEEE.

Zarzour, H., Maazouzi, F., Soltani, M., & Chemam, C. (2018, May). An improved collaborative filtering recommendation algorithm for big data. In *IFIP International Conference on Computational Intelligence and Its Applications* (pp. 660-668). Springer, Cham. 10.1007/978-3-319-89743-1_56

KEY TERMS AND DEFINITIONS

Artificial Intelligence: A popular sub-field of computer science that aims to make machine intelligent as a human.

Big Data: A large volume of structured, semi-structured, and unstructured data that come from different sources with the difficulties of storage and analysis.

Big Data Analytics: A process of extracting useful information and pattern from big data.

Data Heterogeneity: A challenge that is caused during the process of data collection by unknown events.

Deep Learning: A specific part of machine learning models that employs multiple neural layers to solve more complex problems.

Explainablity: A mechanism that can help users in trusting and understanding the artificial intelligence applications they use.

Healthcare Analytics: A emerging technology helping hospitals and healthcare organizations to enhance the prediction of patients' outcomes and treatments as well as the quality of their services.

Machine Learning: A branch of artificial intelligence that is based on data acquisitions and algorithms developments to make decisions without explicit programs.

Chapter 9
Face Recognition and Face Detection Using Open Computer Vision Classifiers and Python

Priyank Jain
Indian Institute of Information Technology, Bhopal, India

Meenu Chawla
Maulana Azad National Institute of Technology, Bhopal, India

Sanskar Sahu
Indian Institute of Information Technology, Bhopal, India

ABSTRACT

Identification of a person by looking at the image is really a topic of interest in this modern world. There are many different ways by which this can be achieved. This research work describes various technologies available in the open-computer-vision (OpenCV) library and methodology to implement them using Python. To detect the face Haar Cascade are used, and for the recognition of face eigenfaces, fisherfaces, and local binary pattern, histograms has been used. Also, the results shown are followed by a discussion of encountered challenges and also the solution of the challenges.

1. INTRODUCTION

This work basically involves building a system for face detection followed by face recognition using several classifiers available in the open computer vision (OpenCV) library. Face recognition is a non-invasive identification system and faster than other systems since multiple faces can be analysed and recognized at the same time. The difference between face detection and identification is, face detection is to identify a face from given image and locate that face in that image. Face recognition basically involves

DOI: 10.4018/978-1-7998-4963-6.ch009

on comparing the face with the stored database and determining whose face is it. In this research work both of the techniques are accomplished using different techniques by using OpenCV and Python and are discussed below. The beginning of the reports consists of the brief history of face recognition. This is followed by the explanation of various algorithms used in the research work, i.e, HAAR-cascades, Eigenface, Fisherface and Local binary pattern histogram (LBPH). Next, the methodology, further modification and the results of the research are described. A discussion regarding the challenges faces and the resolutions are described. Finally, a conclusion is provided which finally concludes our report based on the research.

2. THE HISTORY OF FACE RECOGNITION

The first automated face recognition system was introduced by Kanade in the year 1977 using a feature vector of human faces. The principal component analysis (PCA) for feature extraction was introduced in the year 1983 by Sirovich and Kirby. Turk and Pentland Eigenface was developed in the year 1991 by using PCA and is considered a major milestone in technology. In 1994 Local binary pattern analysis for texture recognition was introduced and is improved upon for facial recognition later by incorporating Histograms (LBPH). Using Linear discriminant analysis (LDA) for dimensional reduction FisherFace was developed in 1996 which can identify faces in different illumination conditions which was a big issue in Eigenface method. Using HAAR cascades and ADA Boost Viola and Jones introduced a face detection technique. In 2007, Naruniec and Skarbek developed a face recognition technique using Gabor Jets that are similar to mammalian eyes. HAAR cascades are used in this research for the purpose of face detection and Eigenface, Fisherface and LBPH are used for face recognition.

3. FACE DETECTION USING HAAR-CASCADES

A mathematical function that produces square-shaped waves with a beginning and an end and used to create box shaped patterns to recognise signals with sudden transformations is called Haar wavelet as shown in an example in figure 1. A cascade can be created by combining several wavelets and that cascade can easily and efficiently identify edges, lines and circles with different colour intensities. These sets are used in Viola Jones face detection technique in 2001 and since then more patterns are introduced for object detection as shown in figure 1. To analyse an image using Haar cascades, target image is identified and a scale is selected smaller than the that image. The scale is then placed on the image. Then the average of the values of pixels in each section of the image is taken. A match is considered if the difference between two values is above a given threshold value. Face detection on a human face is performed similarly by matching a combination of different Haar like features. For example, forehead, eyebrows and eyes contrast as well as the nose with eyes as shown below in figure 2. Accurate face detection cannot be achieved by a single classifier, various different classifiers are combined to get an accurate result as shown in the block diagram in figure 3.

In this research, a similar methodology is used effectively which combines identification of faces and eyes thus involving accurate face detection. This is the same as used in the Viola Jones method where combination of several classifiers creates a stronger classifier. A machine learning algorithm called ADA boost tests out several weak classifiers on a certain selected location and chooses the most suit-

Figure 1. A Haar wavelet followed by resulting Haar like features

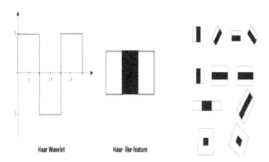

able classifier from the set and the algorithm can also reverse the direction of the classifier and extract improved and better results if necessary. Furthermore, to get better performance we can update Weight update steps only on misses which can improve the performance. In order to find different sized faces the scaling of the cascade is done by 1.25 and re-iterated. Using conventional loops and running the cascade on an image takes a huge amount of computing power and time.

To compute the matches fast Viola Jones used a summed area table (an integral image). The table was first developed in 1984, but became popular after 2001 when Viola Jones implemented Haar-cascades for face detection. By using a integral image enables matching features with a single pass over the image.

4. FACE RECOGNITION

The following sections describe the various face recognition algorithms and how they are implemented in OpenCV. The various algorithms are Eigenface, Fisherface, Local binary pattern histogram (LBPH).

4.1. Background on Face Recognition

When we look at an apple, our mind processes that image and immediately tells us: that it is an apple. This process is the simplest definition of recognition. So, what's facial recognition? The same process, but for faces, obviously.

Figure 2. Several Haar like features matched to the features of the face present in the image

Figure 3. Haar-cascade flow chart

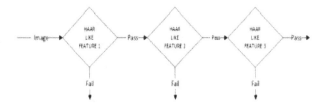

But here the real question arises: **How can a computer recognize a face?**

Let's take example: When you meet a person for first time you don't know who that person is? While he's talking to you or shaking your hand, you're analysing his face: eyes, nose, mouth, skin tone, etc. This is the process where our mind is gathering data and training for face recognition.

And if that person tells you that his name is Chris suppose. And your brain has already gathered his face data and it has also learned that the data belongs to Chris. The next time when we see Chris or see a picture of his face, our mind will follow this exact process:

- **Face Detection:** Detecting a face by looking at the picture.
- **Data Gathering:** Extraction of unique characteristics of Chris's face that it can use to differentiate him from another person, like eyes, mouth, nose, etc.
- **Data Comparison:** It will compare those unique features to all the features of all the people you know despite variations in light or expression.
- **Face Recognition:** The brain will then determine Who the individual is?
  Our mind's Face Recognition Process

Then, the more we meet Chris, the more data we will collect about him, and the quicker your mind will be able to recognize him. And one more interesting fact that our human brains are wired to do all these things automatically. In fact, we are very good at detecting faces almost everywhere as shown in figure A.

We need to teach this process to computers since they are not able to detect faces automatically.

Figure A

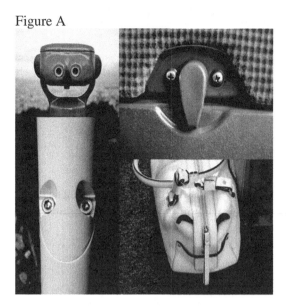

4.2. Theory of OpenCV Face Recognizers

Before beginning the coding part we probably assume that this is the most difficult part but thanks to OpenCV, coding facial recognition is now easier than ever. There are three easy steps to computer coding facial recognition and these steps are similar to the steps that our brains use for recognizing faces. These steps are:

Data Gathering: Gather data of the face of the persons we want to identify (face images in this case).

Train the Recognizer: Feed that face data along with the respective names of each face to the recognizer so that it can learn.

Recognition: Feed new faces of that person to the face recognizer we just trained and see that if it recognizes them.

It's that simple!

And once we finish coding this how our Face Recognizer will look like:

Figure 4. Pixels of the image are reordered to perform calculations for Eigenface

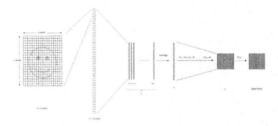

There are three built-in face recognizers in OpenCV we can use any of them just by changing a single line of code, thanks to its clean coding. Face recognizers and their calls in OpenCV are as follows:

1. EigenFaces cv2.face.createEigenFaceRecognizer()
2. FisherFaces cv2.face.createFisherFaceRecognizer()
3. Local Binary Patterns Histograms (LBPH) cv2.face.createLBPHFaceRecognizer()

Ok so we have to decide which Face Recognize we should use and below is the summary of each of them which will help us in deciding which one we should choose.

4.3. Eigenface

PCA classifies images to extract features using set of images and Eigenface is based on same technique. Same Lightning condition and eyes match in each image is really important for all images. And the images used must also contain the same number of pixels and in grayscale. Ok so now let's consider an image with n x n pixels for example as observed in figure 4. Resulting $1 \times n^2$ matrix is obtained, by concatenation of each raw to create a vector. A single matrix is used to store all the images in the dataset resulting a matrix with columns corresponding the number of images. Normalisation of the matrix is done to get an average human face. Unique features of each image is computed by subtracting the average face from each image vector. Each column in resulting matrix is represented as the difference of each face to the average human face. Figure 4 below shows the simplified illustration of the above explanation.

Then the covariance matrix is calculated from the result. Eigen analysis is performed using principal component analysis to obtain the Eigen vectors from the data.

The 1st Eigen vector is assigned to the highest variance and it is usually the diagonal in the resulting covariance matrix. And the next highest variance which is 90 degrees to the 1st vector is considered as the 2nd Eigen vector. Then the next highest variance will be the 3rd Eigen vector and so on. Each column is considered as a separate image and visualised, resembles a face and called Eigenfaces. Whenever we need to recognize a face, the image is imported and resized to match the same dimensions of the test data as mentioned above. Weights can be calculated by projecting extracted features on to each of the Eigenfaces. Similarity of the features extracted from the different image sets in the dataset to the features extracted from the input image is represented by these weights. The input image is identiðed as a face by comparing with the whole dataset. The image can be identiðed as to which person it belongs to by comparing it with each subset. Identiðcation can be controlled to eliminate false detection and recognition by applying a threshold detection. PCA assumes that the subspace is linear since it is sensitive to large numbers. It will mix then values when distribution is calculated and thus cannot effectively classify the images if the same face is analysed under different lighting conditions. Thus, features matching is a problem in different lightning conditions as they can change dramatically.

4.3.1. Eigenfaces Face Recognizer

In this algorithm not all parts of a face are equally important or useful for face recognition. We recognize a person by his distinct features like the eyes, nose, cheeks or forehead; and how they vary respect to each other.

We are focusing on the areas of maximum change. Like there is a significant change from eyes to the nose and from nose to mouth. Multiples faces are compared by observing these areas because one face can be differentiated from the other by catching maximum variations among those faces.

EigenFaces recognizer works in the same way. It tries to extract the components which are relevant and useful from the training images of all the people and discards the rest. These important features are what we call **principal components**.

We will use the terms such as principal components, variance, areas of high change and useful features indistinctly as they all mean the same

The variance extracted from a list of faces is shown in the image below.

EigenFaces Face Recognizer Principal Components. Source: <u>docs.opencv.org</u>

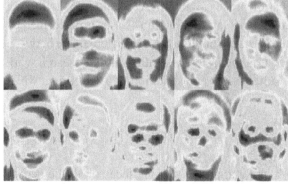

EigenFaces recognizer trains itself by extracting principal components and also keeps a record of which image belongs to which individual, so whenever a new image is introduced to the algorithm, it repeats the process as follows:

1. From the new picture extraction of principal components.
2. Comparison of the extracted features with the list of elements stored during training.
3. Find the ones with the best match.
4. Return the 'person' label associated with that best match component.

Figure 5. The first component of PCA and LDA. Classes in PCA looks more mixed than of LDA

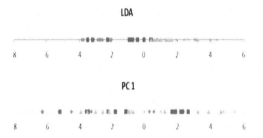

EigenFaces algorithm also considers illumination as an important feature. Lights and shadows are picked up by EigenFaces, which classifies them to be represented as a face. Face is recognized by picking up human things like two eyes, a mouth, a nose.

4.4 Fisherface

Fisherface technique is based on LDA derived from Ronald Fisher's linear discriminant technique used for pattern recognition and it is built upon EigenFaces. It uses labels for classes and data point information. PCA looks at the greatest variance when reducing dimension while LDA, uses labels and looks at an interesting dimension such that, when we research to that reduced dimension we maximise the difference between the mean of the classes normalised by their variance. The ratio between the class scatter and within-class scatter matrices are maximised by LDA and because of which different lighting conditions in images has a limited effect on the classification process using LDA technique. Maximizing the mean distance between different classes and minimizing the variation within classes is performed by Fisherface while Eigenface maximises the variations. And because of this LDA can differenciate between feature classes better than PCA as observed in figure 5. It is the fastest algorithm in the research work and it takes less amount of space. Thus, PCA is more suitable for representation of a set of data while LDA is suitable for classification.

4.4.1. Fisherfaces Face Recognizer

EigenFaces finds combined principal components by looking at all the training faces of all the people at once. Because of which it doesn't focus on the features that discriminate one individual from another. It concentrates on the ones that represent all the faces of all the people in the training data, as a whole. But let us consider change in lightning conditions as shown in below figure.

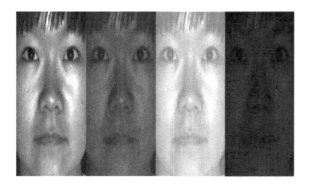

There will be issue for EigenFace as it also finds illumination as a useful component, it will find this variation very relevant for face recognition and may discard the features of the other people's faces, considering them less useful. The variance extracted by EigenFaces represents just one individual's facial features.

This issue can be fixed by using FisherFaces. We can use EigenFaces to extracts useful features from the faces of each person separately instead of extracting them from all the faces combined and if one person has high illumination changes, it will not affect the other people's features extraction process.

FisherFaces face recognizer algorithm is useful for extraction of principal components that differentiate one person from the others and therefore, individual's components do not dominate (become more useful) over the others.

Principal components using FisherFaces algorithm is shown in below image.

FisherFaces Face Recognizer Principal Components. Source: docs.opencv.org

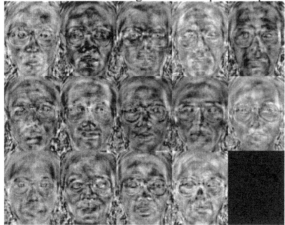

The features represent faces which receive the name of Fisher Faces.

FisherFaces still considers illumination changes as a useful feature as it only prevents features of one person from becoming dominant. So, we need to discard the light variation as it is not a part of actual face.

This problem can be solved by using Local Binary Pattern Histograms.

Figure 6. Local binary pattern histogram generating 8-bit number

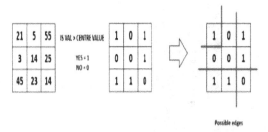

4.5. Local Binary Pattern Histogram

In 1990 Li Wang proposed Local binary patterns as classifiers in computer vision. In 2009 combination of LBP with histogram-oriented gradients was introduced that increased its performance in certain datasets. The image is divided into cells (4 x 4 pixels) for feature coding. Surrounding pixel values are compared with the central in either clockwise or counter-clockwise direction as shown in figure 6. Each neighbour pixel is compared with the centre pixel based on the value of intensity or luminosity. 1 or a 0 is assigned to the location depending if the difference is higher or lower than 0. 8-bit value is provided to the cell as a result. The advantage of this technique is the result is same as before even if the luminosity of the image

is changed as observed in figure 7. In larger cells to find the frequency of occurrences of values histograms are used to make the process faster. Edges can be detected by analysing the results in the cell as the values change. Feature vectors can be obtained by computing the values of all cells and concatenating the histograms. If ID is attached to the images we can use processing to classify them. And using the same process input images are classified and compared with the dataset and distance is obtained. Identification of known or unknown face can be done by setting up a threshold. The dominant features of the whole training set is computed by using EigenFaces and FisherFaces and by LBPH we can analyse them individually.

4.5.1. Local Binary Patterns Histograms (LBPH) Face Recognizer

Eigenfaces and Fisherfaces are both effected by light and obviously in real life we are not sure if we will get perfect light conditions. So here LBPH comes into play where we overcome this drawback by finding the local structure of the image by comparing each pixel to the neighbouring pixels

Figure 7. The results are same even if brightness is changed

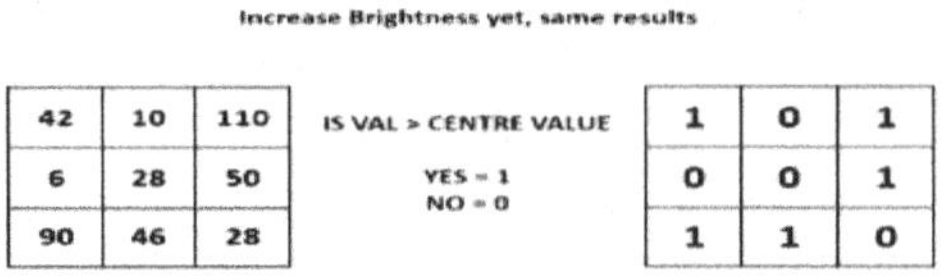

Increase Brightness yet, same results

42	10	110	IS VAL > CENTRE VALUE	1	0	1
6	28	50	YES = 1	0	0	1
90	46	28	NO = 0	1	1	0

4.5.2. The LBPH Face Recognizer Process

Take a 3×3 window and move it across one image. At each move (each local part of the picture), compare the pixel at the centre, with its surrounding pixels. Denote the neighbours with intensity value less than or equal to the centre pixel by 1 and the rest by 0.

After we read these 0/1 values under the 3×3 window in a clockwise order, we will have a binary pattern like 11100011 that is local to a particular area of the picture. When we finish doing this on the whole image, we will have a list of **local binary patterns**.

LBP conversion to binary. Source: López & Ruiz; Local Binary Patterns applied to Face Detection and Recognition.

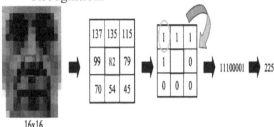

Now, after we get a list of local binary patterns, you convert each one into a decimal number using binary to decimal conversion (as shown in above image) and then we make a histogram of all of those decimal values. A sample histogram looks like this:

Histogram Sample.

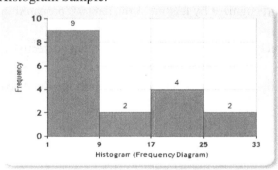

In the end, we will have one histogram for each face in the training data set. That means that if there were 100 images in the training data set then LBPH will extract 100 histograms after training and store them for later recognition. Remember, the algorithm also keeps track of which histogram belongs to which person.

Later during recognition, the process is as follows:

1. Feed a new image to the recognizer for face recognition.
2. The recognizer generates a histogram for that new picture.
3. It then compares that histogram with the histograms it already has.

4.   Finally, it finds the best match and returns the person label associated with that best match.

Below is a group of faces and their respective local binary patterns images. We can see that the LBP faces are not affected by changes in light conditions:

LBPH Face Recognizer Principal Components. Source: docs.opencv.org

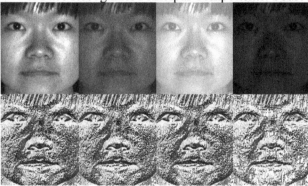

5. CODING FACE RECOGNITION USING PYTHON AND OPENCV

We are going to divide the Face Recognition process in this tutorial into three steps:

1.   **Prepare Training Data:** Read training images for each person/subject along with their labels, detect faces from each image and assign each detected face an integer label of the person it belongs.
2.   **Train Face Recognizer:** Train OpenCV's LBPH recognizer by feeding it the data we prepared in step 1.
3.   **Prediction:** Introduce some test images to face recognizer and see if it predicts them correctly.

Before we start the actual coding, we need to install the Code Dependencies and import the Required Modules:

Code Dependencies

Install the following dependencies:

1.   OpenCV 3.2.0
2.   Python v3.5
3.   NumPy that makes computing in Python easy. It contains a powerful implementation of N-dimensional arrays which we will use for feeding data as input to OpenCV functions.

**Required Modules

Import the following modules:

- **cv2:** This is the OpenCV module for Python used for face detection and face recognition.
- **os:** We will use this Python module to read our training directories and file names.
- **numpy:** This module converts Python lists to numpy arrays as OpenCV face recognizer needs them for the face recognition process.

In (Kanade, 1977)

#OpenCV module

import cv2

#os module for reading training data directories and paths

import os

#numpy to convert python lists to numpy arrays as it is needed by OpenCV face recognizers

import numpy as np

5.1. Prepare Training Data

The premise here is simple: The more images used in training, the better.

Being thorough with this principle is important because it is the only way for training a face recognizer so it can learn the different 'faces' of the same person; for example: with glasses, without glasses, laughing, sad, happy, crying, with a beard, without a beard, etc.

So, our training data consists of total two people with 12 images of each one. All training data is inside the folder: *training-data*.

This folder contains one subfolder for every individual, named with the format: **sLabel (e.g. s1, s2)** where **the label is the integer assigned to that person**. For example, the subfolder called **s1** means that it contains images for **person 1**.

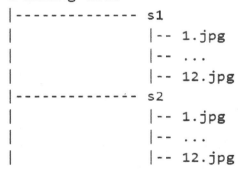

```
training-data
|-------------- s1
|                |-- 1.jpg
|                |-- ...
|                |-- 12.jpg
|-------------- s2
|                |-- 1.jpg
|                |-- ...
|                |-- 12.jpg
```

On the other hand, The folder test-data contains images that we will use to test our face recognition program after we have trained it successfully.

Considering that the OpenCV face recognizer only accepts labels as integers, we need to define a mapping between integer tags and the person's actual name. So, below I am defining the mapping of a person's integer labels and their respective names.

Note: As we have not assigned label 0 to anyone, the mapping for tag 0 is empty:

In (Sirovich & Kirby, 1987)

#there is no label 0 in our training data so subject name for index/label 0 is empty
subjects = ["", "Ramiz Raja", "Elvis Presley"]

5.2. Data Preparation for Face Recognition

Why we prepare data?

Well, to know which face belongs to which person, OpenCV face recognizer accepts information in a particular format. In fact, it receives two vectors:

- One is the faces of all the people.
- The second is the integer labels for each face.

For example, if we had two individuals and two images for each one:

```
PERSON-1      PERSON-2


img1          img1
img2          img2
```

Then, the data preparation step will produce following face and label vectors:

```
FACES                       LABELS


person1_img1_face             1
person1_img2_face             1
person2_img1_face             2
person2_img2_face             2
```

In detail, we can further divide this step into the following sub-steps:

1. Read all the sub folders names provided in the folder training-data. In this tutorial; we have folder names: s1, s2.
2. Extract label number. Remember that all the sub folders containing images of a person following the format: sLabel where Label is an integer representing each person. So for example, folder name: s1 means that the person has label 1, s2 means the person's label is 2, and so on. We will assign the integer extracted in this step to every face detected in the next one.
3. Read all the images of the person, and apply face detection to each one.
4. Add each face to face vectors with the corresponding person label (extracted in above step)

Let's code this part!
In (Turk & Pentland, 1991)

```
#function to detect face using OpenCV
def detect_face(img):
#convert the test image to gray scale as opencv face detector expects gray images
 gray = cv2.cvtColor(img, cv2.COLOR_BGR2GRAY)
 #load OpenCV face detector, I am using LBP which is fast
#there is also a more accurate but slow: Haar classifier
face_cascade = cv2.CascadeClassifier('opencv-files/lbpcascade_frontalface.xml')
 #let's detect multiscale images(some images may be closer to camera than others)
#result is a list of faces
faces = face_cascade.detectMultiScale(gray, scaleFactor-1.2, minNeighbors-5);
 #if no faces are detected then return original img
if (len(faces) == 0):
return None, None
 #under the assumption that there will be only one face,
#extract the face area
x, y, w, h) = faces()
 #return only the face part of the image
return gray[y:y+w, x:x+h], faces()
```

As you can see, we are using OpenCV's LBP face detector. To break it down:

- In line 4, we converted the image to grayscale because OpenCV mostly operates in gray scale.
- Then, in line 8, we loaded LBP face detector using classcv2.CascadeClassifier.
- After that, in line 12, we used classcv2.CascadeClassifier detectMultiScale method to detect all the faces in the image.
- Next, in line 20, from exposed faces, we only picked the first one, because in a person's portrait it is supposed to be only one face (under the assumption that there will be only one prominent face).
- As faces returned by the method detectMultiScaleare rectangles (x, y, width, height) and not actual faces images, we have to extract face area from the main image. So in line 23, we extracted face area from the gray picture and return both the face image area and face rectangle.

Now, you have a face detector. Also, we know the four steps to data preparation. And here is the main code:-
In (Dong-chen He & Li Wang, 1990)

```
#this function will read all persons' training images, detect face from each image
#and will return two lists of exactly same size, one list
#of faces and another list of labels for each face
def prepare_training_data(data_folder_path):
```

```
#------STEP-1--------
#get the directories (one directory for each subject) in data folder
dirs = os.listdir(data_folder_path)

#list to hold all subject faces
faces = []
#list to hold labels for all subjects
labels = []

#let's go through each directory and read images within it
for dir_name in dirs:

#our subject directories start with letter 's' so
#ignore any non-relevant directories if any
if not dir_name.startswith("s"):
continue;

#------STEP-2--------
#extract label number of subject from dir_name
#format of dir name = slabel
#, so removing letter 's' from dir_name will give us label
label = int(dir_name.replace("s", ""))

#build path of directory containing images for current subject subject
#sample subject_dir_path = "training-data/s1"
subject_dir_path = data_folder_path + "/" + dir_name

#get the images names that are inside the given subject directory
subject_images_names = os.listdir(subject_dir_path)

#------STEP-3--------
#go through each image name, read image,
#detect face and add face to list of faces
for image_name in subject_images_names:

#ignore system files like .DS_Store
if image_name.startswith("."):
continue;

#build image path
#sample image path = training-data/s1/1.pgm
image_path = subject_dir_path + "/" + image_name
#read image
image = cv2.imread(image_path)
```

```
#display an image window to show the image
cv2.imshow("Training on image...", image)
cv2.waitKey(100)

#detect face
face, rect = detect_face(image)

#------STEP-4--------
#for the purpose of this tutorial
#we will ignore faces that are not detected
if face is not None:
#add face to list of faces
faces.append(face)
#add label for this face
labels.append(label)

cv2.destroyAllWindows()
cv2.waitKey(1)
cv2.destroyAllWindows()

return faces, labels
```

We have defined a function that takes the path where it stores training subjects' folders as a parameter. This function follows the same data preparation sub steps that we reviewed previously:

(**step-1**) In line 8, we used the methodos.listdir to read names of all folders stored on the path, so they start functioning as a parameter.

In line 10-13 we defined labels and faces vectors.

(**step-2**) After that, we went through all subjects' folder names and from each one we extracted, in line 27, the label information. As folder names follow the sLabelnaming convention, just by removing the letters from folder name we will get the tag assigned to that subject.

(**step-3**) In line 34, we read all the current person's images, and in lines 39-66 we went through traverse those images one by one.

In lines 53-54, we used OpenCV's imshow(window_title, image) along with OpenCV's waitKey(interval) methods to display the current picture.

The methodwaitKey(interval) pauses the code flow for the given interval (milliseconds). So, we are using a 100ms interval so that we can view the image window for that time.

In line 57, we implemented face detection on the current picture.

(**step-4**) In lines 62-66, we added the detected face and label to their respective vectors.

But a function can't do anything unless we call it on some data that it has to prepare, right? Don't worry; I have got data for two faces. I am sure you will recognize at least one of them!

I'm pretty sure that The King is the ghost, so I've put his image into the face recognition step. We can recognize the faces.

Let's use these images of two individuals to prepare data for training of our Face Recognizer. Here is a simple code to do that:

In (Wang et al., 2009)

```
#let's first prepare our training data
#data will be in two lists of same size
#one list will contain all the faces
#and the other list will contain respective labels for each face
print("Preparing data...")
faces, labels = prepare_training_data("training-data")
print("Data prepared")
#print total faces and labels
print("Total faces: ", len(faces))
print("Total labels: ", len(labels))
```

```
Preparing data...
Data prepared
Total faces:  23
Total labels:  23
```

It's time to train our face recognizer so that, once trained, it can recognize new faces of the people it's been trained on. Ok then let's get training.

5.3. Train Face Recognizer

As we mentioned earlier, OpenCV comes equipped with three face recognizers.

1.   EigenFaces: cv2.face.createEigenFaceRecognizer()

2.   FisherFaces: cv2.face.createFisherFaceRecognizer()
3.   Local Binary Patterns Histogram (LBPH): cv2.face.LBPHFisherFaceRecognizer()

We are going to use now LBPH recognizer this time. It doesn't matter which of the OpenCV's face recognition programs we use because the code will remain the same. We just have to change one line, which is the face recognizer initialization line given below.

In (Belhumeur et al., 1997)

```
#create our LBPH face recognizer
face_recognizer = cv2.face.createLBPHFaceRecognizer()
#or use EigenFaceRecognizer by replacing above line with
#face_recognizer = cv2.face.createEigenFaceRecognizer()
#or use FisherFaceRecognizer by replacing above line with
#face_recognizer = cv2.face.createFisherFaceRecognizer()
Now that we have initialized our face recognizer and we also have pre-
pared our training data, it's time to train. We will do that by calling the
methodtrain(faces-vector, labels-vector) of face recognizer.
In (Viola & Jones, 2001)
#train our face recognizer of our training faces
face_recognizer.train(faces, np.array(labels))
Did you notice that instead of passing vectorlabels directly to face recogniz-
er, we are first converting it to numpy array? The reason is that OpenCV ex-
pects labels vector to be a numpyarray.
```

5.4. Prediction

This is where we get to see if our algorithm is recognizing our individual faces or not.

We're going to take one test image of each person, use face detection and then pass those faces to our trained face recognizer. Then we find out if our face recognition is successful.

Below are some utility functions that we will use for drawing bounding box (rectangle) around the face and putting the person's name near the face bounding box.

In (John, 1985)

```
#function to draw rectangle on image
#according to given (x, y) coordinates and
#given width and heigh
def draw_rectangle(img, rect):
    (x, y, w, h) = rect
    cv2.rectangle(img, (x, y), (x+w, y+h), (0, 255, 0), 2)

#function to draw text on give image starting from
#passed (x, y) coordinates.
def draw_text(img, text, x, y):
```

```
  cv2.putText(img, text, (x, y), cv2.FONT_HERSHEY_PLAIN, 1.5, (0, 255, 0),
2)
```

The first functiondraw_rectangle draws a rectangle on the image based on given coordinates. It uses OpenCV's built in functioncv2.rectangle(img, topLeftPoint, bottomRightPoint, rgbColor, lineWidth) to do so.

The second functiondraw_text uses OpenCV's built in functioncv2.putText(img, text, startPoint, font, fontSize, rgbColor, lineWidth) to draw text on the image.

Now that we have the drawing functions, we just need to call the face recognizer's predict(face) method to test our face recognizer on test images. The following function does the prediction for us:

In (Super Data Science, n.d.)

```
#this function recognizes the person in image passed
#and draws a rectangle around detected face with name of the
#subject
def predict(test_img):
#make a copy of the image as we don't want to change original image
img = test_img.copy()
#detect face from the image
face, rect = detect_face(img)
#predict the image using our face recognizer
label = face_recognizer.predict(face)
#get name of respective label returned by face recognizer
label_text = subjects[label]

#draw a rectangle around face detected
draw_rectangle(img, rect)
#draw name of predicted person
draw_text(img, label_text, rect[0], rect[1]-5)

return img
```

If we break this last code down:

- line-6 read the test image.
- line-7 detect the face from test image
- line-11 recognize the face by calling face recognizer's predict(face) method. This method will return a label.
- line-12 get the name associated with the tag.
- line-16 draw rectangle around the detected face.
- line-18 draw name of the predicted individual above face rectangle.

Now that we have the prediction function well defined, the next step is to call this function on our test images, display them to see if our face recognizer correctly performs face recognition.

In (IRJET, n.d.)

```
print("Predicting images...")
#load test images
test_img1 = cv2.imread("test-data/test1.jpg")
test_img2 = cv2.imread("test-data/test2.jpg")
#perform a prediction
predicted_img1 = predict(test_img1)
predicted_img2 = predict(test_img2)
print("Prediction complete")
#display both images
cv2.imshow(subjects[1], predicted_img1)
cv2.imshow(subjects[2], predicted_img2)
cv2.waitKey(0)
cv2.destroyAllWindows()
```

The face recognition worked! It can tell who Ramiz Raza is and who Elvis Presley is, so it's been trained correctly.

6. RESULTS

The following is the output of the research work. The research work shows the name of the individual whose images are trained. More the dataset for a individual more will be the accuracy of prediction and more will be the confidence. And no matter what if the individual image is not feeded in the dataset the research work will only detect its face. This process is followed when taking live input from webcam.

 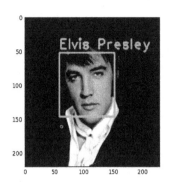

7. FURTHER MODIFICATIONS

1. Identification of eyes and telling details related to it.
2. Facial expression identification can be done.

8. CONCLUSION

This paper describes the research work for face recognition and face detection using OpenCV and Python. Next, it explains the technologies used in the research work and the methodology used. It also includes what all modules have been used while designing this research work and it also includes the code and step wise method. Further it includes the results of the research work and at last the modifications that can be done in future with using big data (Jain et al., 2020; Jain et al., 2016).

REFERENCES

Belhumeur, P. N., Hespanha, J. P., & Kriegman, D. J. (1997, July). Eigenfaces vs. fisherfaces: Recognition using class specific linear projection. *IEEE Transactions on Pattern Analysis and Machine Intelligence*, *19*(7), 711–720. doi:10.1109/34.598228

Dong-chen He, & Li Wang. (1990, July). Texture unit, texture spectrum, and texture analysis. *IEEE Transactions on Geoscience and Remote Sensing*, *28*(4), 509–512. doi:10.1109/TGRS.1990.572934

IRJET. (n.d.). https://www.irjet.net/archives/V5/i10/IRJET-V5I1089.pdf

Jain, Gyanchandani, & Khare. (2020). Improved k-Anonymize and l-Diverse Approach for Privacy Preserving Big Data Publishing Using MPSEC Dataset. *Computing and Informatics Journal, 39*(3), 537–567.

Jain, P., Gyanchandani, M., & Khare, N. (2016). Enhanced secured map-reduce layer for big data privacy and security. *Journal of Big Data, Springer, 6*.

John, G. (1985). Uncertainty relation for resolution in space, spatial frequency, and orientation optimized by two-dimensional visual cortical filters. *Journal of the Optical Society of America. A, Optics and Image Science*, *2*(7), 1160–1169. doi:10.1364/JOSAA.2.001160 PMID:4020513

Kanade, T. (1977). *Computer recognition of human faces* (Vol. 47). Birkh¨auser Basel. doi:10.1007/978-3-0348-5737-6

Sirovich, L., & Kirby, M. (1987). Low-dimensional procedure for the characterization of human faces. *Journal of the Optical Society of America. A, Optics and Image Science, 4*(3), 519–524. doi:10.1364/JOSAA.4.000519 PMID:3572578

Super Data Science. (n.d.). https://www.superdatascience.com/blogs/opencv-face-recognition

Turk, M., & Pentland, A. (1991, January). Eigenfaces for recognition. *Journal of Cognitive Neuroscience, 3*(1), 71–86. doi:10.1162/jocn.1991.3.1.71 PMID:23964806

Viola, P., & Jones, M. (2001). Rapid object detection using a boosted cascade of simple features. In *Proceedings of the 2001 IEEE Computer Society Conference on Computer Vision and Pattern Recognition. CVPR 2001* (vol. 1, pp. I–511–I–518). 10.1109/CVPR.2001.990517

Wang, X., Han, T. X., & Yan, S. (2009). An hog-lbp human detector with partial occlusion handling. In *2009 IEEE 12th International Conference on Computer Vision* (pp. 32–39). 10.1109/ICCV.2009.5459207

Section 3
Applications of Intelligent Analytics

Chapter 10
Big Data Analytics for Smart Airport Management

Desmond Narongou
 https://orcid.org/0000-0003-0815-025X
National Airports Corporation (NAC), Papua New Guinea

Zhaohao Sun
 https://orcid.org/0000-0003-0780-3271
Papua New Guinea University of Technology, Papua New Guinea

ABSTRACT

Smart airport management has drawn increasing attention worldwide for improving airport operational efficiency. Big data analytics is an emerging computing paradigm and enabler for smart airport management in the age of big data, analytics, and artificial intelligence (AI). This chapter will explore big data analytics for smart airport management from a perspective of PNG Jackson's International Airport. More specifically, this chapter first provides an overview of big data analytics and smart airport management and then looks at the impact of big data analytics on smart airport management. The chapter discusses how to apply big data analytics and smart airport management to upgrade PNG Jackson's International Airport in terms of safety and security, optimizing operational effectiveness, service enhancements, and customer experience. The approach proposed in this chapter might facilitate research and development of intelligent big data analytics, smart airport management, and customer relationship management.

INTRODUCTION

Smart airport management becomes increasingly important for developing smart airports worldwide. Based on the Grand View Research, the global smart airport market is expected to reach over US$ 25 billion by 2025 growing at a rate of 10% CAGR (Compound Annual Growth Rate) (Aviation Media, 2019). Smart airport management and technology are important for improving airport efficiency from operations facet to passenger experience (Mariani, Zmud, Krimmel, Sen, & Miller, 2019). Smart airport management shares and integrates key information and communication technology (ICT) systems, data,

DOI: 10.4018/978-1-7998-4963-6.ch010

and information to optimize performance and capacity, passenger experience, and customer service for the entire aviation ecosystem (Kershaw, 2013). Air traffic is at its busiest of all time (except the period of the worldwide COVID-19 pandemic), as there is an increasing demand for air travel over the world (Lee, Ng, Lv, & Taezoon, 2014). Smart airport management, therefore, not only helps provide a platform where not all processes can be automated using ICT, but also as an enabler for improving airport operational tasks, security, passenger experience and convenience (TAV Information Technologies, 2019). Smart airport management aims to integrate the currently segmented activities involved in check-in, boarding (Popovic, Kraal, & Kirk, 2009), and from arrival to disembarking and transiting. All airport operators need smart airport management solutions to expedite airport ground handling and passenger processing effectively without delays and long queues (Jaffer & Timbrell, 2014). Bouyakoub, et al, developed a smart airport management system based on the Internet of things (IoT) (Bouyakoub, Belkhir, Bouyakoub, & Guebli, 2017). However, airports are still facing several challenges for example, how to use big data analytics to make airport management smarter and more efficient; how to integrate big data analytics and smart airport management to improve the quality of services and customers' satisfaction. Based on the above brief analysis, the following issues are significant for smart airport management in general and Port Moresby International Airport (PMIA) in specific:

- How can the smart airport management be applied to improve PMIA operations?
- How to integrate big data analytics and smart airport management to improve the quality of Jackson's Airport in PNG?

This chapter will address the above-mentioned issues by exploring big data analytics for smart airport management from a perspective of PNG Jackson's International Airport. More specifically, this chapter first provides an overview of big data analytics and smart airport management, and then looks at the impacts of big data analytics on smart airport management. This chapter also discusses how to integrate big data analytics and smart airport management to improve the quality of services and customers' satisfaction of PMIA.

The remainder of this chapter is organized as follows: Section 2 explores the fundamentals of smart airport management. Section 3 discusses intelligent technologies for smart airport management. Sections 4 and 5 provide an overview of PMIA and its current infrastructure related to smart airport management systems and look at future smart airport systems and technologies for PMIA. Section 6 examines integrating big data analytics and smart airport management to improve the quality of services and customers experience and satisfaction and decision making of PMIA. Section 7 focuses on discussion and implications of this research. The final section provides a summary of the chapter and future research directions for this work.

FUNDAMENTALS OF SMART AIRPORT MANAGEMENT

This section looks at the fundamentals of smart airport management. It covers the following topics: What does smart, smart airport and smart airport management means? It also discusses a smart airport maturity model.

What Does Smart Means?

There are numerous definitions of the term smart available in the literature. For example, the Oxford Dictionary defines smart as "clean, intelligent, fashionable, and quick" (Oxford, 2008). Some states that smart means more productive, more creative, more interesting, more important, and more interested in a more general business environment (Deresiewicz, 2014, p. 14). From a business intelligence (BI) viewpoint, a system or tool or technology is smart means that it is available in the market with more favored functions to the customers and can meet the need of customers more satisfactorily (Sun, Sun, & Strang, 2018). Another considers that "being smart" relates to having intelligence or the ability to acquire and apply knowledge and skills. Smart also refers to connected, data-driven, technology that is sensor-based, and increasingly autonomous (making greater use of artificial intelligence (AI) (Vermeulen, 2017). Smart technologies include reactive technology, analytics, machine learning and AI (mySmart, 2019). Therefore, the term smart is characterized by having intelligent systems through internet-connected objects and devices.

Based on the above analysis, hereafter, we consider that something is smart means that it has more favored, satisfactory functions to the customers, developed by the advanced ICT technologies including intelligent technologies.

Smart Airport

Smart airport is an integrated system with a combination of airport processing solutions that provide for a most "efficient aviation ecosystem" (TAV Information Technologies, 2019). Smart airport manages, captures, and processes all airport activities including passenger experience and operations management in the aviation ecosystem. Smart airport means that airports are truly digitally connected through a variety of intelligent systems and technologies including IoT and big data analytics and opening up new opportunities that transcend legacy issues and realize a smart airport vision (Mariani, Johanna, Krimmel, Sen, & Miller, 2019).

A smart airport aims to integrate a variety of ICT systems (hardware, software, cloud, and processes) to provide better passenger and stakeholder experience and confidence, and a competitive advantage for all stakeholders and reduce costs (Jašari, 2015) (Nau & Benoit, 2017) (Mariani, Zmud, Krimmel, Sen, & Miller, 2019).

Therefore, a smart airport is an integrated airport environment that interconnects all ICT systems and related sources of data and information smartly for optimizing customer satisfaction, operational efficiency, strategic differentiation, and economic diversity, underpinned by advanced digital technologies and intelligent systems (Mariani, Zmud, Krimmel, Sen, & Miller, 2019).

Smart Airport Management

Smart airport management is an airport management platform that integrates and shares key ICT infrastructure and systems to optimize performance and capacity, passenger experience, and customer service for the entire aviation ecosystem (Nau & Benoit, 2017). Smart airport management is a slice of the bigger management process within the aviation industry that involves passenger experience and operations management taking into account the digital technologies that enable the flow of these operations (TAV Information Technologies, 2019).

General management functions of planning, organization, leading, and control (Terry, 1968) (Sun Z., 2019) are necessary for choosing sustainable technologies and systems that are capable to improve airport management (Mariani, Zmud, Krimmel, Sen, & Miller, 2019). Management as a social process has a great deal of responsibility for economical and effective planning, regulation of operations of an entity in fulfilling its functions. It is a dynamic process consisting of various elements and activities within an organization (Terry, 1968). Therefore, it is necessary to address smart airport from a management perspective (Sun Z., 2019).

To deliver sustainable business benefits through digital transformation, it is important to create a culture that drives innovation to practically accept and forecast future technological changes and invest in the capabilities and partnerships (Pell & Blondel, 2018). Because management deals with the art of getting things done through people, systems, and processes that are crucial for the operations (Terry, 1968). Therefore, smart airport management systems and technologies should incorporate these principles to define a solution that is customizable to an airport.

Smart Airport maturity Model

Smart airport maturity model is a roadmap depicted as an effort to summarize the average experience at the airport (Mariani, Zmud, Krimmel, Sen, & Miller, 2019). In the smart airport maturity model, the growth and development stages define the level of progression from one to another, as shown in Figure 1.

The smart airport maturity level of each airport globally depends on the type of ICT platform deployed (Nau & Benoit, 2017) as well as "the different priority that airports attribute to the potential benefits of digital technology" (Pell & Blondel, 2018).

Figure 1. A smart airport maturity model

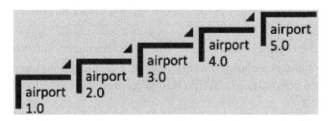

This simplified smart airport maturity model is designed to easily understand the progress from one stage to another, with key activities and milestone technological changes implemented, signifying the level of progress to reaching a smarter level of maturity. Based on Figure 1, the following paragraphs will look into each of the different levels of smart airport maturity model and briefly outline some key criteria that can be used to identify the level of smart airport development.

Airport 1.0 is the foundational start of the journey. Although with limited infrastructure, manual processes involving the handling of airport operations are prevalent with ICT systems and tools being used for operational safety and efficiency (Hong, Oh, & Lee, 2019).

Airport 2.0 focuses on revolutionizing the common-use terminal equipment (CUTE) and common-use self-service (CUSS) or common-use passenger processing systems (CUPPS) to minimize human intervention, while increasing process speed and time. Automated screening and passenger verification systems including check-in systems for example, are depicted in Airport 2.0 (Kershaw, 2019) (Bouyakoub, Belkhir, Bouyakoub, & Guebli, 2017).

Airport 3.0 focuses on mobile technology and cloud/web-based technologies and systems with more emphasis on self-services (Nau & Benoit, 2017) and more personalized services (Hong, Oh, & Lee, 2019). For example, according to an empirical analysis conducted for the self-service check-in implementation at the Changi airport, much attention is paid to ensuring that the flow of the entire process is efficient and smooth with many new techniques of checking-in have been introduced in recent years, such as online check-in (OCI) systems over the counter. The self-service check-in (SSCI) system has gained popularity at the terminal worldwide by the increasing popularity of SSCI booths at the terminal itself (Lee, Ng, Lv, & Taezoon, 2014).

Airport 4.0 uses Big Data, artificial intelligence (AI), IoT, Machine Learning to enhance passenger experience and enable the airport authority to increase revenue-oriented activities among others (Nau & Benoit, 2017). The Singapore Changi airport's smart airport vision is now moving ahead to Airport 4.0. The Changi Airport Group (CAG) has used ICT as a substitute for resources effectively and efficiently, leading to a lower cost of airport operations (Choudhury, 2015). At this stage, many intelligent technologies are deployed (Mariani, Johanna, Krimmel, Sen, & Miller, 2019) for improving customer satisfaction (Hong, Oh, & Lee, 2019). For example, passengers can use social media platforms to share and rate their experiences, receive flight notifications, as well as shopping hints so that they can enjoy the social interaction during their airport experience (TAV Information Technologies, 2019).

In addition to the four traditional phases, this chapter introduces Airport 5.0. This realizes the full maturity of the model together with the integration Internet of Things (IoT), AI, digitization, cloud computing, big data analytics and other intelligent technologies taking the center stage of the development and progression into full automation. This opens up new revenue streams and provides strategic differentiation and improvepassenger experience and with an increased customer base. According to CAG, the Changi airport terminal four (T4), using a fully automated departure process under the FAST initiative in 2015. It offers end-to-end self-service options by automating processes at check-in, bag drop, and integrates immigration and boarding with facial recognition technology (Changi Airport Group, 2018).

As the smart airport maturity model shifts from airport 1.0 to airport 5.0, the smart airport systems and technologies become more customer-centric. Airports now can integrate all smart airport management technologies and systems to provide value-added services and increase the participation of the stakeholders (Hong, Oh, & Lee, 2019).

The smart airport maturity model in Figure 1 can be used to identify key intelligent technologies for smart airport management that are essential to achieve one level and move on the another stage to reach a "digital front-line" (Pell & Blondel, 2018) in becoming a smarter airport. From Level 1 up, the focus is on business to business (B2B) concept whereby every attempt is to reduce manual processes. In level 4, more focus is being directed on business to consumer (B2C) approach whereby the attention is now drawn on business models for revenue generation within the aviation industry (Nau & Benoit, 2017). To address these commercial realities, airports must embrace the challenges and opportunities presented by digital technology and intelligent technology in a way that goes far beyond incremental process improvement (Pell & Blondel, 2018). As airport systems and technologies evolve to meet the growing demands and challenges, early adaption and integration are important to keep abreast of the changes to realign operations strategy and business model with the key functions of the airport ecosystems.

INTELLIGENT TECHNOLOGIES FOR SMART AIRPORT MANAGEMENT

Intelligent technologies for smart airport management can be classified into two categories: 1). Intelligent technologies for passenger experience; and 2). Intelligent technologies for operations management systems. The former focuses on intelligent providing mobility and intelligent self-service systems, for example, keeping passengers informed through flight information displays, self-check-in systems throughout the flow from check-in to boarding. The latter focuses on integrating all data and information from systems that impact and improve airport operational efficiency for informed decision making (TAV Information Technologies, 2019). The deployment of intelligent technologies for smart airport management systems as a service to the customer aids in improving legacy and redundant systems and processes, and system architectures with complex implications for ease of use to enhancing airport's operational efficiency (Pell & Blondel, 2018). This section will provide an overview of AI, intelligent big data analytics, IoT, and cloud computing as intelligent technologies for smart airport management.

Artificial Intelligence

Artificial Intelligence (AI) is intelligence exhibited by machines, in distinction to the natural intelligence possessed by human beings and animals that imitate cognitive functions associated with human awareness, such as learning, thinking, acting, and problem-solving (Russell & Norvig, 2010). AI has been termed as one of the most advanced technologies that human beings have ever had and will dominate the focus of technology for decades ahead. In the age of AI (Sun Z., 2019), people's lives have been improved significantly, specifically with the integration of AI technologies, ICT and IoT (Poola, 2017).

AI will be one of the most disruptive technologies during the next decade due to advances in computational power, big data, IoT, and advances in machine learning and deep neural networks (DNNs) (Pettey & van der Meulen, 2018). Then big characteristics of big data including big volume, big velocity, and big variety lay the foundation for supporting core AI technologies including machine learning, deep learning, natural language processing (NLP), and computer vision (SAS Institute Inc, 2019) (Sun, Strang, & Li, 2018). Furthermore,, statistics and modeling methods, data science and analytics with computing techniques (Davis, 2014) are the foundational functions and technologies for big data descriptive analytics and prescriptive analytics that will analyze the big data and IoT data from the various sensors. Insights from streaming analytics and AI will improve efficiency, convenience, and security of systems like smart airport management (SAS Institute Inc, 2019). According to the Community Roadpam for AI Researchers, business executives worldwide have seen AI technologies as a key to increase their competitiveness thus retaining their market share (Selman & Gil, 2019). AI proportionately has a huge capacity to proliferate big data and IoT's value by salvaging all the big data from smart connected devices to promote learning and collective intelligence of organizations and individuals.

Intelligent Big Data Analytics

Big data has not very big value without big data analytics, just as oil without the significant progress of the petrochemical industry (Sun, Sun, & Strang, 2018). However, the business value of big data becomes bigger and bigger with the processing, deep processing, smart processing, intelligent processing of big data. Big data analytics underpins processing, deep processing, second time processing, multi-processing of big data. Therefore, big data analytics is more important than big data. Intelligent big data analytics becomes a disruptive technology for healthcare, web services, service computing, cloud computing, and social networking computing (Laney & Jain, 2017). AI-derived business value is forecasted to increase to $US3.9 trillion in 2022 from $US1.2 trillion in 2018 (Pettey & van der Meulen, 2018). Therefore, intelligent big data analytics is an enabler for smart airport management and decision making in smart airports.

Intelligent big data analytics (IBA) is science and technology about collecting, organizing and analyzing big data to discover patterns, knowledge, and intelligence within the big data based on AI, and domain-specific mathematical and analytical models (Holsapplea, Lee-Postb, & Pakath, 2014)(Sun, Sun, & Strang, 2018) (Chen, Chiang, & Storey, 2012) (Davis, 2014). Currently, IBA can be classified into intelligent big data descriptive analytics, intelligent big data diagnostic analytics, big data predictive analytics, and big data prescriptive analytics (Sun, Sun, & Strang, 2018). All these mentioned should be improved through theoretical, technological, and methodological development to meet the global and social needs of different parties or individuals for intelligent big data analytics with applications.

Foundations of IBA consists of core foundations and supporting foundations. The core foundations include intelligent data warehousing, intelligent data mining, intelligent statistical modeling, machine learning including deep learning (Al-Jarrah, Yoo, Muhaidat, & Karagiannidis, 2015), intelligent visualization and optimization (Sun, Sun, & Strang, 2018). The supporting foundations include mathematics and statistics including descriptive and predictive statistical methods (Davis, 2014), computing and data science, AI and optimization, operations research, domain sciences including business and management science (Sun & Wang, 2017) (INFORMS, 2014).

Figure 2. A framework of intelligent big data analytics

Technologies of IBA include intelligent technology, computational technology, web technology and Internet technology, social networking technology, cloud technology (Erl, Mahmood, & Puttini, 2013), and management technology, to name a few (Laney & Jain, 2017). Gartner predicts that half of IT organizations will apply IBA or advanced analytics in application development to improve application quality and deliver speed (Laney & Jain, 2017).

Intelligent big data analytics is designed into intelligent systems and embedded in intelligent systems (Sun Z., 2019). This is an application form of intelligent big data analytics as an intelligent system. There are several intelligent big data analytics as an intelligent system in smart mobile phones, airplanes, supermarkets, and driverless cars. Intelligent big data analytics as an intelligent system has been accepted by the business, market, finance, banking, healthcare, and other industries (Sun Z., 2019). Recently, Woolworths and Coles, the K market in Australia have used intelligent machines with intelligent big data analytics. One scans what buying at the supermarket and pays the bill thereby clicks. No sales assistants work there anymore. Unmanned stores have become more and more in China nationwide. At Airports, one can check-in using a smartphone and get a boarding card automatically.

Successful organizations rely on effective utilization and organization of intelligent big data analytics because they show much power in innovation, competitive edges, and, ultimately, the overall productivity of an organization (Sun & Wang, 2017). This alleviates poor decision making thus giving an advantage over the use of the abundance of data to strategize the operational functions of an organization. Intelligent big data analytics is a leading frontier in bringing new big breakthroughs for enterprises in general and airports in specific (Sun, Zou, & Strang, 2015).

The Internet of Things

The Internet of Things (IoT) refers to a vast number of things that are connected to the Internet so they can share data with other things such as IoT applications, connected devices, industrial machines, and more (SAS Institute Inc, 2019). IoT consists of two interconnected terminologies: the first word is "Internet" and the second word is "Things". The "things" can be a living or non-living object, for example, a person, a computer, a smartphone, a device, a sensor, a switch, a fridge, gas stove, dog, furniture, and an electron gadget, etc. Each of them can interact with other things through the Internet (Madakam, Ramaswamy, & Tripathi, 2015). The number of IoT connected devices has been increased at the speed of 17% from 2018 onwards, as shown in Figure 3.

IoT is bringing together different enabling technologies in a specific way to do something smarter (Mariani, Johanna, Krimmel, Sen, & Miller, 2019). The IoT has been revolutionized multi-industry application technologies to provide real-time big data analytics, machine learning, sensors, and embedded systems. For example, in the aviation sector, digital chat boards can be deployed in the check-in, departure and arrival lounges to communicate relevant flight information, and navigation around the terminal (Choudhury, 2015). The growing presence of IoT has largely impacted how business models have been adjusted to meet these challenges, as seen in the "principal classes of benefits from deciding on the IoT capability or set of capabilities that are "right" for them that can deliver operational efficiency; strategic differentiation; and boosting new revenue streams (Mariani, Johanna, Krimmel, Sen, & Miller, 2019). We will address how to integrate intelligent big data analytics and IoT for smart airport management in Section 6.

Cloud Computing

Cloud computing has been at the forefront of organizations, individuals, government agencies in the 21st century. Cloud computing is the delivery of on-demand computing services - from applications to storage and processing power - typically over the Internet and on a pay-as-you-go basis (Ranger, 2018). The most common services provisioned by cloud computing are Infrastructure as a Service (IaaS), Platform as a Service (PaaS), and Software as Service (SaaS) (Erl, Mahmood, & Puttini, 2013), as shown in Figure 4.

Figure 3. IoT connected devices worldwide
(Source: https://iot-analytics.com/wp/wp-content/uploads/2018/08/Number-of-IoT-devices-worldwide-2015-2025.png).

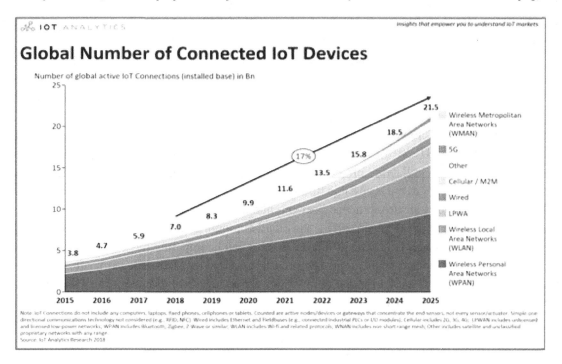

Figure 4. Cloud computing services

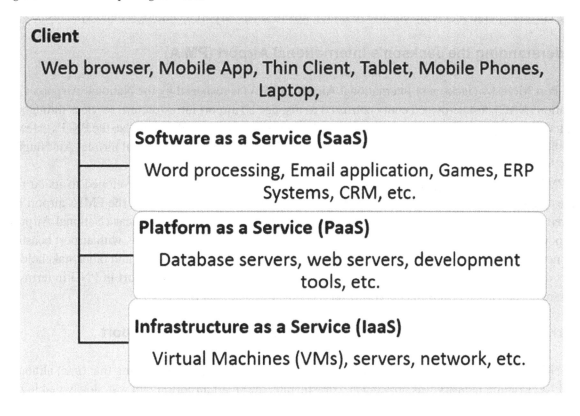

IaaS is the foundational service layer of cloud computing services (Ranger, 2018) (Erl, Mahmood, & Puttini, 2013). IaaS can provision processing, storage, networks, and other fundamental computing resources to the consumer (NIST, 2018). IaaS services also include backup and recovery, Compute, content delivery networks, services management, and storage (Liu, 2011).

PaaS is the next layer of cloud computing services. PaaS can deploy onto the cloud infrastructure consumer-created or acquired applications created using programming languages, libraries, services, and tools supported by the provider (Ranger, 2018) (NIST, 2018). PaaS services also include business intelligence, database, development and testing, integration, and application deployment (Liu, 2011).

SaaS is the top layer of cloud computing services. SaaS can use the provider's applications running on a cloud infrastructure (NIST, 2018). SaaS services include email and office productivity, billing, customer relationship management, collaboration tools, content management, social networks, etc. (Liu, 2011).

Cloud computing services are accessible through client devices, for example, a laptop, tablet, smartphone, and client application such as a web browser, and a thin client.

According to the research (Ranger, 2018), the cloud computing services revenue in 2016 was US$ 22.2 billion, and it will reach US$ 53.3 billion by 2021. Cloud computing has become an ideal way to deliver enterprise services and applications (Knorr, 2018). Google, Microsoft, Amazon, Tencent, and Alibaba are the industry leaders in cloud computing, which are revolutionizing our lives, work, and society through their cloud services.

PORT MORESBY INTERNATIONAL AIRPORT: AN INTRODUCTION

This section presents the Port Moresby International Airport (PMIA) and its developments by looking to its current operational setup and use, with regards to smart airport technologies and systems.

Understanding the Jackson's International Airport (PMIA)

The Port Moresby (Jackson's) International Airport (PMIA) is managed by the National Airports Corporation (NAC), a state-owned entity entrusted to manage all airport infrastructure services throughout Papua New Guinea (PNG). PMIA is one of the 22 airports managed by NAC. It is also the PNG's gateway to other international destinations through the air, and a home to PNG's national airline, Air Niugini. NAC's vision is to have 15 smart airports by 2030 (Collins Aerospace, 2018).

PMIA, founded during the Second World War and over time, has been developed to its current status. From the colonial period up to the time of PNG's independence in 1975, the PMIA airport has served as a major transit hub to other centers throughout the country and overseas (National Airports Corporation, 2017). Over time, major infrastructure development has taken place, with airport boasting few new modernized facilities to cater for passenger movement and processing, and other stakeholders at its domestic and international terminals. It is the largest and the busiest airport in PNG in terms of passengers and aircraft movements (Damarel Systems International Ltd, 2018).

Current Smart Airport Setup at the Jackson's International Airport

In PNG, the concept of the smart airports began around in the early 2000s. During that time, although the PNG aviation industry was growing at a drastic rate, the smart airport dream was slowly making its way into the scene when the NAC started embarking on its vision of having 15 smart airports by 2030. Having that vision as a guide, it started with automating some of its operations, processes, and a breakthrough came in 2013 when the Arinc vMUSE, an Arinc version of Common Use Passenger Processing System (CUPPS) was deployed at the PMIA (Collins Aerospace, 2017). Other related airport systems technologies like the baggage reconciliation system (BRS and VeriPax) were added in a few years later as part of the CUPPS agreement. Aeronautical Radio, Incorporated (ARINC), established in 1929, is a major provider of transport communications and systems engineering solutions for eight industries: aviation, airports, defense, government, healthcare, networks, security, and transportation (Wikipedia, 2020).

The NAC has renewed its contract with Rockwell Collins for ARINC Airport Solutions at Jackson's International Airport in Port Moresby. Under the contract, a range of solutions are provided to help NAC accommodate security requirements and IATA initiatives to deliver faster processing times for passengers. The passenger processing products included in the contract are ARINC vMUSE (common-use check-in), ARINC AirVue (enhanced flight information display systems), ARINC AirDB (optimized operational database), ARINC AirPlan (maximized scheduling and resource management), ARINC VeriPax (automated airport security screening), and Local DCS and baggage reconciliation (Collins Aerospace, 2018), as seen Figure 5.

Figure 5. Arinc-managed CUPPS deployed at PMIA

The PMIA has a modern CUPPS system from Arinc, which is deployed mostly for check-in and boarding, baggage tracking, flight information displays, and for capturing passenger movements out of PMIA.

Aircraft, passengers, and cargo movements in the aviation industry in PNG have been increasing rapidly in recent years. All these create an abundance of data and information flow. Smart Airport Management in PNG is beginning to gain momentum with large unstructured data and relatively few structured data from a managed data repository. Big data analytics is the driving force for smart airport management systems and technologies. It plays an important role in security, optimizing operational effectiveness, service enhancements, and customer experience within the aviation industry.

SMART AIRPORT MANAGEMENT FOR PMIA

This section proposes how PMIA can fully embrace the smart airport management and bring it as a core functional requirement to enhance operational efficiency at the airport. It also looks at the progress of the smart airport at PMIA and understanding the capabilities and functionalities of the current systems that will guide to developing a smart airport management model for PMIA in Section 6.

Progress of Smart airport management at PMIA

This subsection discusses the progress of smart airport management at PMIA.

The current smart airport systems at the PMIA aims to improve operational efficiency although more human effort is always needed at handling passengers' movement at the terminal, passenger processing at one hand is gaining speed and momentum by using these systems. PMIA as a smart airport model for PNG operates between level 1 and 2 of the smart airport maturity model. Coupled with limited infrastructure, the providence of general ICT services like Wifi and access to telephony services, CUTE equipment, and security processes and sytems aims at improving safety, security and operational efficiency at the airport indicate the growth from level 1 (Hong, Oh, & Lee, 2019). At level 2, the deployment of the common use passenger processing systems (CUPPS), passenger and baggage screening and verification systems (Collins Aerospace, 2017), including the 24-hour surveillance and monitoring systems like the close circuit television (CCTV) are evident. PMIA is now taking a step to reaching the level 2 of the model with CUPPS being deployed, and is now working towards meeting the challenges in level 3 of the smart airport maturity model with plans and work in progress to install and deploy the self-check-in kiosks. The deployment of CUPPS at PMIA has seen a great reduction in the manual process of handling passengers, reducing hardware costs for the airlines, and improving productivity and efficiency. PMIA is moving from Airport 2.0 to Airport 4.0, for example with the self-check-in kiosks and automated bag drop systems are still in their infant stages and will most likely be implemented towards the end of 2020. It achieves a smart airport by focusing on areas beyond tactical cost reduction or operational enhancement towards the holistic enhancement of airport value propositions (Pell & Blondel, 2018).

More collaboration and data sharing between the airport stakeholders (airport operators and the airlines) are key areas to achieve this transition. This provides strategic differentiation and at the same time working in partnership to balance operating and capital expenditures and maximum business value for all partners (Jaffer & Timbrell, 2014).

Future Smart Airport in PMIA and PNG

With the NAC's vision of operating 15 smart airports by 2030 (National Airports Corporation, 2017) and with PMIA as a smart airport model for other PNG airports, more burden has been placed on ICT capacity and process automation using the related technology including smart airport management systems.

Interestingly for reporting and billing purposes, current airport and ERP systems at NAC and PMIA do not integrate with each other. Different reports were generated independently on an ad hoc basis. For example, the Airport Operations Control Centre (AOCC) downloads daily aircraft movements and periodically send the figures to the management and government authorities. On the other hand, the IT team downloads the passenger movement counts and send it to finance for billing purposes. Finance, commercial, human resources, and other operational data and reports are handled by each respective division. Upon request by management, each functional data and report is then compiled for submission and presentation.

PMIA and NAC currently do not have a centralized Business Intelligence (BI) and analytics system with an airport data warehouse, which needs to be pushed forward too. This will streamline all exiting NAC systems (ERP system, maintenance systems, and airport systems) data into one central repository or datawarehouse for better analytics and management of information to help make decisions that are strategically aligned to the vision and maximizing value for the stakeholders (Lees, 2016).

A unified airport information system with intelligent big data analytics and IoT within the airport cloud is urgently developed or purchased to make PMIA a real smart airport in the world.

Integrating Big Data Analytics and Smart Airport Management for Improving Quality of Jackson's Airport

This section will propose PIASAM: a system architecture for integrating intelligent big data analytics (IBDA) with smart airport management to improve the quality of Jackson's Airport in PNG.

With big data analytics driving strategic decision making being dominant these days, PMIA will have to employ proper intelligent big data analytics with analytical tools that can integrate all sources of data and information flow within airport operations from resource allocation to management and decision making (Jian-bo, Chong-jun, & Hui-gang, 2012). The integration of big data analytics and BI system can analyze large data sets from all facets of airport operations will transform PMIA's operations management. With big data analytics, airport administrators can create meaningful interactive dashboard to monitor KPIs airport of operations and keeping people informed accordingly. A new passenger data analytics and information-based management is emerging as a promising tool to help airport managers to manage bottleneck challenges in airport finances, operations decision making, and strategically guide its way forward. The big data analytics can use data capture, analysis, and predictive modeling and performance optimization to make more strategic decisions based on highly detailed, trusted data and information (Lees, 2016).

Data Warehouse (DW), big data and analytics (BDA), and data services forms the central layer of the smart airport where there is collaboration, open access, and information sharing platform through the application programming interfaces (APIs). Data and information generated from all systems and technologies in the airport environment are captured in a centralized business intelligence system. This helps analyze data to provide better strategic advantage at the management and executive level of the airport stakeholders (Nau & Benoit, 2017). Customer service interactions is one key area that BDA can transform customer feedback and data into meaningful insights and supplying the data back to them keeps people informed and aware of their interactions within the airport.

PIASAM: A System Architecture for Integrating Intelligent Big Data Analytics With Smart Airport Management of PMIA

This section proposes PIASAM, a system architecture for integrating intelligent big data analytics with smart airport management of PMIA.

The PIASAM is made up of the IDA, the centralized Airport Data Warehouse (ADW), and the physical raw data capturing and storage systems from the airport operator. The IDA tool captures all loosely,

Figure 6. PIASAM: A system architecture for integrating IBDA with smart airport management for PMIA

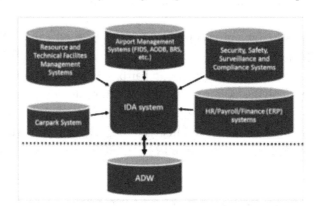

independent data from all sources within NAC and PMIA for example flight reports from AirDB, and other raw datasets. The main function of IDA is to extract, transform, and load (ETL) all data from all intelligent systems sources within the aviation ecosystem to boost intelligence (Oracle, 2012) (Sun, Sun, & Strang, 2018). ADW is a central repository or datawarehouse for airport operations data, weather conditions, airline information, market information, passenger information, aircraft data and air safety reports as well as flight tracking data (Larsen, 2013). It provides quick access to data, information, and reports for strategic, operational, and financial purposes related to airport operations.

Airport Management Systems (AMS) deals with providing flight and passenger details, and luggage tracking. It provides for daily operations aiding passenger movement and flight tracking with from one destination to another and vice versa as well as digital advertising platform with the flight information display systems (FIDS). The AMS also allocates and schedules aerodromes resources like parking bays and stands, counters and gates efficiently. Safety, security, surveillance, and compliance systems deals with all movement and activity from landside to the terminal and then the airside. Safety and security are key priority areas within the aviation sector. Timely risk and incident identification, reporting is vital to maintain a safe secure airport to mitigate risks and creating a safe airport environment. Vehicle tracking, allocation of parking lots, parking charges data helps to raise revenue while at the same time gives ease to the airport operator to alleviate and control issues happening around the airport. ERP systems comprise accounting, finance, HR, payroll systems, usually from the same vendor or integrated from a couple more vendors. Financial data, employee records are some of the key data generated from these systems. Resource and technical facilities management systems monitor facilities around landside, terminal, and the airside including apron and runway maintenance schedules, power consumption monitoring, and other related workflows.

PIASAM system architecture consisted of three integrated layers: the foundational layer, analytic layer and the presentation layer. The foundational layer is made up of different data sources for ADW, integrated through the IDA system (the analytics layer). The presentation layer focuses on Extract, Transforms, and Load (ETL) processes from the operational data sources to ADW. It also provided intelligent reports from the PIASAM system to the decision makers for decision making. This brings together the powerful capabilities for IDA to get real-time and strategic insights into passenger movement and growth and demand, revenues, expenditures, maintenance schedules, sales and marketing channels, and other airport systems activities. It will greatly benefit the airports by driving passengers and stakeholders' experience "through consolidating all data" into a centrally managed data repository to enable real-time and fast access to IDA for decision making (Oracle, 2012). From this point, big data analytics can play a significant role in improving the database and datawarehouse, using insight to help simplify and improve the operational difficulties and challenges faced by the sector" (Kohli, 2018).The PIASAM helps to identify and manage key airport data sets using an integrated ADW. IDA is used to discover knowledge, insights and intelligence from the datasets in ADW to solve operational problems, and support decision making in the airport management (Larsen, 2013).

Integrating Intelligent Big Data Analytics with IoT and Cloud Computing into PIASAM for Smart Airport Management

With the discovery of PIASAM and its key data flow and analytics processes, driving this further is the integration of intelligent big data analytics (IBA), IoT and cloud computing into the architecture to realize the true smart airport management for PMIA (Sun, Sun, & Strang, 2018).

IoT is the source for data collection and generation and supply into the data sources systems (ADW). Cloud computing will integrate with IoT because more and more devices in terms of IoT will be available in the cloud such as cloud database, cloud software, etc. (Erl, Mahmood, & Puttini, 2013). As soon as data available at ADW, IBA will mine the data from ADW and discover and visualize patterns and knowledge resulted from such mining. This gives an advantage to the airport executives to quantitatively and realistically design key indicators to monitor airport operations, customer satisfaction, and experience among other key measurable variables seamlessly based on the current and historical trends.

For example, CCTV cameras and other monitoring systems with embedded sensors that are installed around the airport to track and monitor movement and engagement with the airport services. These data can be related to a range of other information sources such as airline passenger data, FIDS, airline flight schedules, digital marketing advertisements, and retail points of sale. The data generated from these systems and devices will be eventually loaded into the ADW for further drilling and mining which is assessable by airport management. Through IDA, airport management can be able to interact with and understand the information trends better. With these available data analytics, airport managers can know the "root causes" behind an overcrowding inside a terminal at any point of a given time, and also know how many people were boarding a flight and other behaviors at the terminal (Lees, 2016). Furthermore, these data generated from CCTV and analyzed can be accessed seamlessly with ease by the airport management, regardless of wherever and whenever they may be at any point in time. The IDA can be hosted on a cloud platform (platform as a service) owned by a third party cloud service provider or the airport directly (Ranger, 2018). It will then allow the airport to access the services through the Internet as a kind of cloud service (Larsen, 2013). This truly simplifies how the smart airport management works when integrating intelligent big data analytics, IoT and cloud computing as it increases the flexibility to work from anywhere and access key data and reports for decision making. When going through security checks at the terminal, a smart security search helps to automate the screening processes. The results of each search plus alerts that arise from screening potential threats are viewed and recorded in real-time. Self-services data for web or mobile check-in, self-check-in/tagging/backdrop/ boarding, etc. are collected and analyzed by the PMIA to make airport processes smarter, supported by technologies such as automatic immigration, smart security search, and automatic AI-based baggage search (Hong, Oh, & Lee, 2019). Such information from these endpoints can be transformed into statiscal figures to help airport executives including government authortires to plan for further developments to enchance avaiton ecosystems. This serves to measure stakeholders and customer enagament within the sector appropriately.

Access to key data and the integration of key intelligent technologies from multiple sources are crucial for PMIA to enable smart airport management and effective strategic decision making (Manyika, Chui, & Bughin, 2011). Integrating IoT embedded systems around the airport as data sets and sources can support the IBA in PIASAM (Larsen, 2013). PIASAM will pave the way for integrating other smart airport technologies incrementally to reach the maturity of the level of 4.0 or 5.0, thus making PMIA a truly smart airport.

By hosting the replicas of all these systems on the cloud by a cloud-service provider, this increases their availability to account for real-time user access, alerts and processing.

DISCUSSION AND IMPLICATIONS

We have mentioned several scholarly research publications on intelligent big data analytics and smart airport management. In what follows, this section focuses on related work and discussion.

The core idea behind this is that research as a search is the basis for related work, discussion, and implications. Although there are a number of ways to collect scholarly data for this work, the authors chose to use Google scholar plus other available online sources to validate the ideas presented in this chapter. This was partly due to the availability of the abundance of high valued works by reputable authors published freely than other third-party research databases over the Internet that can be used for this purpose followed by lack of free hard copies of such related materials available for public consumption.

The authors searched Google scholar for "smart airport management" and found only five research publications (0.02 sec) on 31 March 2020. Then the authors read through each of them and found that only two of them are related to smart airport management in their papers. The first research developed smart airport management system as an IoT-based airport management system, which aims to automate passengers processing and flight management steps, to improve services, facilitate airport agents' tasks and offer passengers a pleasant and safe journey (Bouyakoub, Belkhir, Bouyakoub, & Guebli, 2017). The second research looks at airfield smart operations management and the application of shared services (Rui, 2020). Mobile smart airport management has been considered as an app system in the research.

The authors used Google Scholar to search for "smart airport" and it returns 762 results (0.05 sec) on 7 March 2020. The first two returned results showed smart airport automation system patents from 2005, and 2008 respectively (US Patent No. US 6950037B1, 2005) (US Patent No. US 7,385,527 B1, 2008). These two patents returned from the search on "smart airport" describing the smart airport automation processes. Another notable result from this search is a point of view from "Smart Airports: Transforming Passenger Experience To Thrive in the New Economy" (Fattah, Lock, Buller, & Kirby, 2009). This research focuses on thriving airport operations that are economically viable that can sustain the business by looking into other revenue generation models within the airport other than the traditional means for all stakeholders within the aviation ecosystems (Accenture, 2012). The authors also used Google Scholar to search for "smart airport management technology" and it "did not match any articles". The authors searched for "big data analytics for smart airport management" in Google Scholar and it "did not match any articles". This further implies that the proposed chapter topic has a huge potential to derive more research thus confirming its originality and will get more attention as it is driven further in academia, commerce, and technology areas.

Different areas of the implication that this research will pose on smart airport development using big data analytics with regards to technology, business, social, and other related fields of concern to people, systems, and processes.

Demand in air travel has been increasing rapidly since the last decade (Jaffer & Timbrell, 2014) which has also prompted for changes in the IT infrastructure landscape to meet up the challenges as airport operators look for better smarter solutions that can increase operational efficacy, increasing revenue streams, cutting down excessive costs and strengthening customer base, diversifying customer engagement whilst maintaining a high level of security and safety within the aviation ecosystem (Nau & Benoit, 2017). With the ever-changing world dominated by new intelligent systems and technologies, businesses are on the verge to cope up or die. This has been a growing challenge for airports to realign their strategy towards investing in more efficient smart technologies and systems to keep up to the changes and meeting customer needs and demands. "Shifting demographics, new corporate governance requirements, and emerging and maturing communications technologies are driving new travel patterns that will require innovative business models and strategies" (Fattah, Lock, Buller, & Kirby, 2009). Being a commercially viable airport environment is one of the biggest challenges most airports face. Some or even most have opted into a "public-private partnership (PPP)" scheme in a bid to increase demand for space and competition to sustain the business continuity and increase profitability as most airports are owned and managed by the government (National Airports Corporation, 2017).

One of the key take-away that this research does is to provide insights and understanding for operators, planners, and investors in an aviation industry, especially the airports that are climbing up the smart airport maturity model, for example, PMIA. Reducing human resources and effort where necessary while increasing passenger processing efficiency securely is why airports use digital innovation and automation tools, intelligent technologies within them can allow for passengers and stakeholders to rediscover the personalized airport experience (Stewart, 2016). With growing attention geared towards customer satisfaction and passenger experience, airports tend to create more flexible business processes that are highly influenced by AI, intelligent big data analytics, cloud computing and IoT which are aimed at increasing "service differentiation over completion" and improving decision making (Jašari, 2015).

To maintain sustainability and meet the growing challenges within the aviation sector, one research direction for future is that business and organizational models should be adopted and re-engineered to allow for airports to maximize and become truly smart.

CONCLUSION

The underlying objective of this chapter is to provide strategic guidance for applying big data analytics and its related intelligent technologies as a key enabler for smart airport management implementation at PMIA. These technologies have the potential to change PMIA operations by the deployment of AI, IoT, cloud computing, and big data analytics tools that will integrate all loosely sources of data within the aviation ecosystem. This will help to minimize bottlenecks faced in decision making strategically, financially, and operationally (Accenture, 2012). Intelligent big data analytics will drive smart airport technologies intelligently and provide an avenue to progress on with smart airport implementation at PMIA related to passenger processing, commercial viability, security, safety, and surveillance. As smart airport maturity shifted from 1.0 to 4.0 and finally to 5.0, "the services paradigm" is shifted from meeting "customer targeted benefits" towards integrating IoT, AI, and big data analytics to add value to the services (Hong, Oh, & Lee, 2019).

Self-check-in kiosks, CUPPS technologies, IoT, digital marketing and advertising, and intelligent data analytics will play a significant role for PMIA in its smart airport management and thus provide an operationally effective and efficient passenger processing and customer experience.

In the future, we will apply intelligent big data analytics to realize smart airport management for PMIA. By reviewing the shift using the intelligent technologies as mentioned herein, we will focus on the challenges of intelligent big data analytics and smart airport development and practical implementation and deployment realization.

REFERENCES

Accenture. (2012). *Airport Analytics*. Barcelona: Accenture. Retrieved January 12, 2020, from https://www.accenture.com/ae-en/~/media/accenture/conversion-assets/dotcom/documents/global/pdf/industries_10/accenture-airport-analytics-final.pdf

Al-Jarrah, O., Yoo, P. D., Muhaidat, S., & Karagiannidis, G. K. (2015). Effiicent machine learning for big data: A review. *Big Data Research*.

Aviation Media. (2019). *Smart Airports*. Retrieved 5 18, 2020, from Smart Airports South East Asia 2019: https://smart-airports.com/sea/

BONN HR. (2017, March 13). *National Airports Corporation*. Retrieved September 20, 2019, from National Airports Corporation: https://www.nac.com.pg/about-us/mission-and-vision/

Bouyakoub, S., Belkhir, A., Bouyakoub, F. M., & Guebli, W. (2017). Smart airport: an IoT-based Airport Management System. In *ICFNDS '17: Proceedings of the International Conference on Future Networks and Distributed Systems, July 2017 Article No.: 45* (pp. 1-7). ACM.

Changi Airport Group. (2018). *Annual report 2017/18*. Changi: Changi Airport Group. Retrieved December 7, 2019, from http://www.changiairport.com/content/dam/cacorp/publications/Annual%20Reports/2018/CAG%20AR201718%20Business%20and%20Operations%20Review.pdf

Chen, H., Chiang, R., & Storey, V. (2012, December). Business intelligence and analytics: From big data to big impact. *Management Information Systems Quarterly*, *36*(4), 1165–1188. doi:10.2307/41703503

Choudhury, A. R. (2015, March 30). *How IT helps Changi Airport to be smart, sweet and swift*. Retrieved January 3, 2020, from The Business Times: https://www.businesstimes.com.sg/focus/in-depth/cio-speaks/how-it-helps-changi-airport-to-be-smart-sweet-and-swift

Clavier, O. H., Schleicher, D. R., Houck, S. W., Sorensen, J. A., Davis, P. C., & Hunter, C. G. (2005, September 27). *US Patent No. US 6950037B1*. Retrieved April 7, 2020, from https://patents.google.com/patent/US6950037B1/en

Clavier, O. H., Schleicher, D. R., Houck, S. W., Sorensen, J. A., Davis, P. C., & Hunter, C. G. (2008, June 10). *US Patent No. US 7,385,527 B1*. Retrieved April 7, 2020, from https://patents.google.com/patent/US7385527B1/en

Collins Aerospace. (2017). *Papua New Guinea's National Airports Corporation closer to 2030 'smart airports' goal with Rockwell Collins contract renewal.* Retrieved October 30, 2019, from Collins Aerospace: https://www.rockwellcollins.com/Data/News/2018-Cal-Yr/IMS/20170207-NAC-ARINC-renewal.aspx

Collins Aerospace. (2018, June 15). *NAC Develops Smart Airports Goal.* Retrieved October 18, 2019, from Airport Technology: https://www.airport-technology.com/contractors/consult/arinc-airports/press-releases/nac-develops-smart-airports-goal/

Coronel, C., & Morris, S. (2015). *Database Systems: Design, Implementation, and Management* (11th ed.). Cengage Learning.

Damarel Systems International Ltd. (2018, July 26). *Damarel Systems International Ltd.* Retrieved October 30, 2019, from Damarel Systems International Ltd: https://www.damarel.com/news/l-dcs-becomes-part-of-smart-airports-initiative-in-papua-new-guinea/

Davis, C. K. (2014). Viewpoint Beyond Data and Analytics- Why business analytics and big data really matter for modern business organizations. *Communications of the ACM, 57*(8), 39–41. doi:10.1145/2602326

Deresiewicz, W. (2014). *Excellent Sheep: The Miseducation of the American Elite & the Way to Meaningful Life.* Free Press.

Erl, T., Mahmood, Z., & Puttini, R. (2013). *Cloud Computing: Concepts, Technology & Architecture.* Pearson.

Fattah, A., Lock, H., Buller, W., & Kirby, S. (2009). Smart Airports: Transforming Passenger Experience To Thrive in the New Economy. *Cisco Internet Business Solutions Group (IBSG)*, 1-16. Retrieved April &, 2020, from https://pdfs.semanticscholar.org/b579/1c0c4db633817f7c81f1bb0214081f1d3aa3.pdf

Holsapplea, C., Lee-Postb, A., & Pakath, R. (2014). A unified foundation for business analytics. *Decision Support Systems, 64*, 130–141. doi:10.1016/j.dss.2014.05.013

Hong, J., Oh, J., & Lee, H. (2019). Smart Airport and Next Generation Security Screening. *Electronics and Telecommunications Trend, 34*(2), 73–82. doi:10.22648/ETRI.2019.J.340208

INFORMS. (2014). Defining analytics a conceptual framework. *ORMS Today, 43*(3). Retrieved August 12, 2020, from INFORMS: https://www.informs.org/ORMS-Today/Public-Articles/June-Volume-43-Number-3/Defining-analytics-a-conceptual-framework

Jaffer, S., & Timbrell, G. (2014). Digital Strategy in Airports. *25 Australasian Conference on Information Systems-Digital Strategy in Airports* (pp. 1-11). Auckland: Australasian Conference on Information Systems (ACIS). doi:10292/8125

Jašari, A. (2015). Information Systems at the Airport. In *International Conference on Econmic and Social Studies* (pp. 8-13). Sarajevo: International Conference on Econmic and Social Studies. Retrieved October 30, 2019, from https://www.semanticscholar.org/paper/Information-Systems-at-the-Airport-Jasari/86c9d48f37c33453f6f9770f552c9144dd1eb603

Jian-bo, W., Chong-jun, F., & Hui-gang, F. (2012). Discussion on Airport Business Intelligence System Architecture. *International Journal of Business and Social Science, 3*(12), 134–138. Retrieved November 2019, from

Kershaw, D. (2019). *SMART Airports:Connecting airport, airline and aircraft.* ARINC International.

Knorr, E. (2018, October 2). *What is cloud computing? Everything you need to know now.* Retrieved April 08, 2020, from InforWorld: https://www.infoworld.com/article/2683784/what-is-cloud-computing.html

Kohli, D. (2018, November 2). *Big data facilitating the working towards a smart future.* Retrieved August 4, 2020, from International Airport Review: https://www.internationalairportreview.com/article/77340/working-towards-smart-future/

Laney, D., & Jain, A. (2017, June 20). *100 Data and Analytics Predictions Through.* Retrieved August 04, 2018, from Gartner: https://www.gartner.com/events-na/data-analytics/wp-content/uploads/sites/5/2017/10/Data-and-Analytics-Predictions.pdf

Larsen, T. (2013). Cross-platform aviation analytics using big-data methods. In *2013 Integrated Communications, Navigation and Surveillance Conference (ICNS)* (pp. 1-9). Herndon, VA: IEEE. doi:doi: 10.1109/ICNSurv.2013.6548579

Lee, C., Ng, Y., Lv, Y., & Taezoon, P. (2014). Empirical Analysis of Self-service Check-in Implementation in Singapore Changi Airport. *International Journal of Engineering Business Management, 6*(6), 33–44. doi:10.5772/56962

Lees, E. (2016). *A Better Way to Manage Airports: Passenger Analytics.* ICF International, Inc.

Liu, F. e. (2011). *NIST Cloud Computing Reference Architecture.* NIST.

Madakam, S., Ramaswamy, R., & Tripathi, S. (2015). Internet of Things (IoT): A Literature Review. *Journal of Computer and Communications, 3*(05), 164–173. doi:10.4236/jcc.2015.35021

Manyika, J., Chui, M., & Bughin, J. e. (2011, May). *Big data: The next frontier for innovation, competition, and productivity.* Retrieved from McKinsey Global Institute: https://www.mckinsey.com/business-functions/business-technology/our-insights/big-data-the-next-frontier-for-innovation

Mariani, J., Johanna, Z., Krimmel, E., Sen, R., & Miller, M. (2019, July 1). *Flying smarter: The smart airport and the Internet of Things.* Retrieved from Deloitte: https://www2.deloitte.com/us/en/insights/industry/public-sector/iot-in-smart-airports.html

Mariani, J., Zmud, J., Krimmel, E., Sen, R., & Miller, M. (2019). *Flying Smarter: The airport and the Internet of Things.* Deloitte Insights.

mySmart. (2019, April 12). *Smart Basics #4: What is 'smart' technology?* Retrieved March 05, 2020, from mySmart Intelligent Environment: https://mysmart.com.au/insights/smartbasics-what-is-smart-technology/

National Airports Corporation. (2017). *about-us/background/.* Retrieved December 16, 2019, from National Airports Corporation: https://www.nac.com.pg/about-us/background/

National Airports Corporation. (2017). *National Airports Corporation 2030 Growth Strategy.* National Airports Corporation.

Nau, J.-B., & Benoit, F. (2017). *Smart Airport: How Technology is shaping the future of airports.* Wavestone.

NIST. (2018, 1 08). *Final Version of NIST Cloud Computing Definition Published*. Retrieved 2 20, 2019, from https://www.nist.gov/news-events/news/2011/10/final-version-nist-cloud-computing-definition-published

Oracle. (2012, 12 12). Oracle Airline Data Model Overview. In *Oracle Airline Data Model: Business Overview Presentation*. Oracle. Retrieved 14 04, 2020, from https://www.oracle.com/technetwork/database/options/airlines-data-model/airlines-data-model-bus-overview-1451727.pdf

Oxford. (2008). *Oxford Advanced Learner's English Dictionary* (7th ed.). Oxford University Press.

Pell, R., & Blondel, M. (2018). *Airport Digital Transformation*. Boston: Arthur D Little. Retrieved December 2, 2019, from https://amadeus.com/documents/en/airports/research-report/airports-digital-transformation.pdf

Pcttcy, C., & van der Meulen, R. (2018, April 25). *Gartner Says Global Artificial Intelligence Business Value to Reach $1.2 Trillion in 2018*. Retrieved August 04, 2018, from Gartner: https://www.gartner.com/newsroom/id/3872933

Popovic, V., Kraal, B., & Kirk, P. (2009). Passenger Experience in an Airport: An Activity-centred Approach. In *IASDR 2009 Proceedings* (pp. 18-22). Retrieved 11 29, 2019, from https://www.researchgate.net/publication/42424464

Ranger, S. (2018, December 18). *What is cloud computing? Everything you need to know about the cloud, explained*. Retrieved April 08, 2020, from ZD Net: https://www.zdnet.com/article/what-is-cloud-computing-everything-you-need-to-know-from-public-and-private-cloud-to-software-as-a/

Rui, Z. (2020). Airfield Smart Operations Management and Application of Shared Services. In W. Wang, M. Baumann, & X. Jiang (Eds.), Green, Smart and Connected Transportation Systems. Lecture Notes in Electrical Engineering (vol. 617, pp. 1397-1408). Singapore: Springer. doi:10.1007/978-981-15-0644-4_105

Russell, S., & Norvig, P. (2010). *Artificial Intelligence: A Modern Approach* (3rd ed.). Prentice Hall.

SAS Institute Inc. (2019, December 2). *Internet of Things*. Retrieved April 08, 2020, from SAS Insights: https://www.sas.com/en_us/insights/big-data/internet-of-things.html

Selman, B., & Gil, Y. (2019). *A 20-Year Community Roadmap for Artificial Intelligence Research in the US*. Washington, DC: Computing Community Consortium. Retrieved April 29, 2020, from https://cra.org/ccc/wp-content/uploads/sites/2/2019/08/Community-Roadmap-for-AI-Research.pdf

Stewart, R. (2016, September 2). *Creating the 'Smart Airport' of the future*. Retrieved January 25, 2020, from International Airport Review: https://www.internationalairportreview.com/article/76136/smart-airport-future/

Sun, Z. (2019). Intelligent Big Data Analytics: A Managerial Perspective. In Z. Sun (Ed.), *Managerial Perspectives on Intelligent Big Data Analytics* (pp. 1–19). IGI-Global. doi:10.4018/978-1-5225-7277-0.ch001

Sun, Z. (2019). *Managerial Perspectives on Intelligent Big Data Analytics*. IGI-Global. doi:10.4018/978-1-5225-7277-0

Sun, Z., Strang, K., & Li, R. (2018). Big data with ten big characteristics. In *Proceedings of 2018 The 2nd Intl Conf. on Big Data Research (ICBDR 2018), October 27-29* (pp. 56-61). Weihai, China: ACM.

Sun, Z., Sun, L., & Strang, K. (2018). Big Data Analytics Services for Enhancing Business Intelligence. *Journal of Computer Information Systems*, *58*(2), 162–169. doi:10.1080/08874417.2016.1220239

Sun, Z., & Wang, P. (2017). Big Data, Analytics and Intelligence: An Editorial Perspective. *Journal of New Mathematics and Natural Computation*, *13*(2), 75–81. doi:10.1142/S179300571702001X

Sun, Z., Zou, H., & Strang, K. (2015). *Big Data Analytics as a Service for Business Intelligence. I3E2015, LNCS 9373*. Springer.

TAV Information Technologies. (2019). *Smart Airport: A comprehensive Concept to Carry Airports into a Smarter Era.* Istanbul: TAV Information Technologies. Retrieved 12 4, 2019, from http://www.tavtechnews.com/pdf/SMART-AIRPORT.pdf

Terry, G. R. (1968). *Principles of Management* (5th ed.). Richard D. Irwin, Inc.

Vermeulen, E. P. (2017, December 24). *What is "Smart" in Our New Digital World?* Retrieved March 05, 2020, from Hacker Noon: https://hackernoon.com/what-is-smart-in-our-new-digital-world-87e6426398

Wikipedia. (2020, April 8). *Arinc.* Retrieved April 10, 2020, from Wikipedia: https://en.wikipedia.org/wiki/ARINC

ADDITIONAL READING

Manyika, J., Chui, M., & Bughin, J. e. (2011, May). Big data: The next frontier for innovation, competition, and productivity. Retrieved from McKinsey Global Institute: https://www.mckinsey.com/business-functions/business-technology/our-insights/big-data-the-next-frontier-for-innovation

Stocking, C., DeLong, J., Braunagel, V., Healy, T., & Loper, S. (2009). Integrating Airport Information Systems. Washington, D.C.: Transportation Research Board. Retrieved January 6, 2020, from http://docplayer.net/11299277-Acrp-report-13-integrating-airport-information-systems-airport-cooperative-research-program-sponsored-by-the-federal-aviation-administration.html

Sun, Z., Strang, K., & Firmin, S. (2016). Business analytics-based enterprise information systems. *Journal of Computer Information Systems*, *56*(4), 74–84. doi:10.1080/08874417.2016.1183977

KEY TERMS AND DEFINITIONS

Artificial Intelligence (AI): Is science and technology concerned with imitating, extending, augmenting, automating intelligent behaviors of human being.

Big Data: Is data with at least one of the ten big characteristics consisting of big volume, big velocity, big variety, big veracity, big intelligence, big analytics, big infrastructure, big service, big value, and big market.

Cloud Computing: Is a computing paradigm based on the demand for resources and services in the cloud. It is a special distributed computing that introduces utilization models for remotely provisioning scalable and measured resources.

Data Science: Is a field that builds on and synthesizes a number of relevant disciplines and bodies of knowledge, including statistics, informatics, computing, communication, management, and sociology to translate data into information, knowledge, insight, and intelligence for improving innovation, productivity and decision making.

Intelligent Big Data Analytics: Is science and technology about collecting, organizing and analyzing big data to discover patterns, knowledge, and intelligence as well as other information within the big data based on artificial intelligence and intelligent systems.

Intelligent System: Is a system that can imitate, automate some intelligent behaviors of human beings. Expert systems and knowledge-based systems are examples of intelligent systems.

Internet of Things (IoT): Refers to systems that involve computation, sensing, communication, and actuation. It involves the connection between humans, non-human physical objects, and cyber objects, enabling monitoring, automation, and decision making.

PMIA: Port Moresby Jackson's International Airport (PMIA) is managed by the National Airports Corporation (NAC), a state-owned entity entrusted to manage all airport infrastructure services throughout Papua New Guinea (PNG).

Smart Airport Management: Is a special form of airport management that integrates and shares key Information Communication Technology (ICT) systems, data and information to optimize performance and capacity, passenger experience and customer service for the entire aviation ecosystem.

Chapter 11
A Big Data Analysis of the Factors Influencing Movie Box Office in China

Wentao Gao
The University of Hong Kong, Hong Kong

Ka Man Lam
The University of Hong Kong, Hong Kong

Dickson K. W. Chiu
The University of Hong Kong, Hong Kong

Kevin K. W. Ho
ⓘ https://orcid.org/0000-0003-1304-0573
University of Guam, Guam

ABSTRACT

A movie's economic revenue comes mainly from the movie box office, while the influencing factors of the movie box office are complex and numerous. This research explores the influencing factors of China's commercial movie box office by analyzing the top 100 box office movies released in Mainland China between 2013-2016, with a total of 400 movies. The authors analyzed the data collected using correlation analysis and decision tree analysis using RapidMiner, respectively. Based on the analysis results, they put forward suggestions for improving the box office of the movie industry.

INTRODUCTION

As an integrated art, movies can use various art forms such as music, dance, photography, etc., and trigger people's interest in aesthetics. With society's development, the material form and art form of movies are continually promoting and integrating development, and its social functions are gradually reflected and continuously strengthened. The movie industry has not only social and cultural attributes but also has

DOI: 10.4018/978-1-7998-4963-6.ch011

economic attributes. In this macro context, people have shown more concern about culture and its role in social and economic development (Lo et al., 2017; Jiang et al., 2019). In developed countries, such as Japan, the United States, and China, the movie culture industry has become an important national economy.

Even though the movie is an essential art form, there are many different types of revenues from a movie, including advertising and other revenue forms (Amit, 2015). In Mainland China, the movie industry had become a trendy and influential industry. Between 2013 and 2017, the box office sales escalated significantly from 22.2 billion Renminbi (1 USD=7 RMB approximately) in 2013 to a double of 55.9 billion in 2017. Due to the development and importance of the movie industry in Mainland China, we investigate the contributing factors for Chinese box offices in this research. From a macro perspective, this topic has much significance in exploring the development of the Chinese movie industry under the Chinese economy.

This study has several contributions to intelligent analytics research. First, with the expansion of the movie market, new profit-seekers have been entering the market to compete for market share, and the competition in the movie market has become increasingly fierce. A movie's profitability involves production, marketing, and distribution of the entire value chain, while each step has a significant impact on box office revenue. The high return of movies can attract a lot of capital, but the risks and uncertainties involved are also high. The study aims to improve the decision accuracy of movie companies and minimize the risk of their investments.

Secondly, movie marketing in the Big Data era involves a vast collection of consumer behavioral data through the Internet that helps marketers and producers find out the target audience for deciding the content, time, and form of the movie promotion. Such data analysis results affect the investment selection, planning, shooting, etc., in the production process based on the movie viewers' preferences. This research uses movie data as the box office's metrics to measure the influence factors for predicting movie success or failure.

LITERATURE REVIEW

Nowadays, the cultural industry is developing rapidly, and the bloom in the movie industry serves as a phenomenal benchmark. Therefore, the research on the movie industry has gradually become a topic of concern to scholars. As prior studies mainly focused on finding practical guidance at the micro-level discovering factors affecting the movie box office, it is meaningful for this research to study the increasing trend of movie box revenues and related prediction models macroscopically.

In the Big Data era, movie metadata and their box office can be readily retrieved for correlation analysis (Barbosu, 2016), providing excellent guidance for the development of China's domestic movie industry. The micro-level study of the factors affecting the box office revenue of a movie can be divided into three aspects: first, the impact of movie evaluation information on the box office revenue; second, the impact of movie content on the box office revenue; third, the release time of the movie (Einav, 2007).

Gallup (1992) summarized the factors affecting movie audience behavior into story content, actors, previews, marketing, and movie titles, and found that audience feedbacks on the Internet impact the movie box office, which will last from well before in theater till off-screen (Chen, Liu, & Zhang, 2012). Jo and Choi (2015) used a database comprising 41 movie stars (famous actors and actresses) and their presence in 467 movies to analyze whether famous actors and actresses influence the movie box office. Word of mouth (WOM) is one of the most critical factors to determine movie quality. For example, Kim, Park, and Park (2013) suggested that online WOM and expert reviews play a critical role in moviegoers' consumption behavior in the age of the Internet and social media. They also found that only the frequency of online WOM was a significant factor in international markets. Since WOM can also be posted by third-party as endorsements and quality signals, their impact on consumers is likely to depend on the consumer type and frequency of media choices (Koschat, 2012).

Due to the recent development of the movie industry, some data researchers and movie lovers pay more attention to the movie industry field. Thus, during the literature search, we noted three stages for analyzing the movie box office

Firstly, it involves the study of movie audiences. Handel (1996) divided this stage into pre-shooting tests (story test, actor test), shooting test (title test), and post-shooting tests (pre-screening research, publicity research, word-of-mouth research) according to the production process. The "correct identification index" in the promotion study is similar to the "penetration rate." The research method is also based on the interview method, in which the interviewer and the audiences are intensely visited to obtain feedback. Therefore, the studies in this stage still focus on the audiences' experiences to analyze the different responses during the different phases of the movie screening by the face to face interviews and questionnaires to understand how to increase the movie box office and which factors will influence the responses of the movie watchers.

Secondly, this stage can be described as exploring the contributing factors to the movie box office. In this stage, Litman is one of the representative researchers who explored the factors related to success in the motion picture industry and found that key factors include familiarity with actors/actresses, characters, and story, as well as kudos from reviewers and industry associations. Finally, Litman formulated a Barry Litman Model as the following formula (Litman & Kohl, 1989):

$$Y = -28.482 + 7.232 \text{ Famous Director} + 14.846 \text{ Famous Actor/Actresses} + 11.818 \text{ Science Fiction} + 13.858 \text{ Sequel} + 24.932 \text{ Oscar Nominations} - 4.966 \text{ Film Reviews} + 3.814 \text{ Big Publishing Company}$$

In Litman's model, the most influential factor in the box office is the Oscar nominations, followed by famous actors/actresses, sequels, science fiction, famous directors, movie reviews, and big publishing companies. Sochay (1994) further increased the number of factors to 22 based on the Litman model and suggested that market concentration and screen numbers have continued in later studies. Sharda and Delent (2006) first applied neural network data mining to complex predictive models. A total of 834 movies from 1998 to 2002 were used as a training set, and the black box was summed up by itself. A set of independent variable values was then compared with the obtained model conclusion to predict the gap between the box office result and the real result.

Thirdly, this stage can be described as the autonomously generated box office prediction model. With the popularity of the Internet and the birth of social media, viewers are increasingly inclined to express their feelings about movies through blogs, Twitter, and so on (Du, Xu, & Huang, 2012). At this stage, box office prediction models based on blogs, Twitter, Google search, Wikipedia, and news reports all use a single factor for box office prediction. Researchers pay attention to the audience's word of mouth and comments, and the established box office prediction model predicts with much-improved accuracy. Mishne and Glance (2006), based on relevant blog data, predict the emotional evaluation after movie release is lower than the total amount of blogs, reflecting word of mouth. However, this research only focused on the first week of the box office and introduced the number of theaters to avoid more box office problems due to the high number of screens.

Some researchers compared the effects of art movie reviews (Dutch newspapers) and mainstream movie reviews on movies and found that the size and number of movie reviews in Dutch newspapers can directly influence the box office (Gemser, 2007). Then, some researchers analyzed the movie released in the United States in 2003 and found that movie reviews impact movie box office revenue (King, 2007).

Many previous studies have explored various factors affecting the movie box office. However, scant studies use correlation analysis and decision tree methods to further analyze the influencing factors of the movie box office. The decision tree method is a simple but widely used classification technique because of its speed, easy-to-understand classification rules, and easy conversion into a database query language.

Meanwhile, the study of the influencing factors of the movie box office is a basis for predicting the movie box office. We can employ different ways to analyze these influencing factors from some excellent literature about predicting box office. Some researchers tried to apply neural networks to the contributing factors of movie box offices. For example, Sharda and Delen (2006) used this new research method and compared it with some traditional methods, such as discriminant analysis, to analyze the contributing factors of movie box offices. They used a traditional multilayer perceptron (MLP) and proposed a classification model for movie box office, and used the classification accuracy rate to evaluate the model's classification performance. Asur and Huberman (2010) from HP Labs introduced social data into influencing factors based on data information, analyzed user emotional tendency in different periods of the movie release, and predicted the box office by a regression method. Besides, Chang and Ki (2005) established a model that successfully predicted the box office in North America, significantly reducing the market risk of the movie industry.

RESEARCH QUESTIONS

Through the study of relevant research literature, the research methods, research conclusions that scholars summarized, and the dominant factors affecting the box office revenue of movies, this research analyzes the data of China's movie box office in a selected period of 4 years (2013-2016). The highest annual box office of 100 movies is selected for data analysis. After that, we use statistical methods to discretize the information of the contributing factors, determine the main factors affecting the box office revenue of movies, and then propose suggestions to increase the box office revenue for China's movie market. As such, this research uses two different methods and tools to analyze movie data, and the data's size is about 4,800 (400 items and 12 attributes). The research questions are:

RQ 1: What factors will influence the box office?
RQ 2: How can the box office revenue be increased using the conclusion of the data analysis for the role of moviemakers and the movie industry?

For the analysis, we used two statistics applications: SPSS and RapidMiner. In SPSS, correlation analysis was used to analyze contributing factors of movie box offices to understand whether different factors influence the box office, such as actors/actresses, directors, movie production budget, and audience scores. In RapidMiner, decision trees were used to analyze the relationships between different factors and the box office. The results of the decision tree could guide some suggestions for moviemakers and other stakeholders of the movie industry.

METHODOLOGY AND VARIABLES DESCRIPTION

Correlation Analysis

This part aims to find out what elements or factors will influence a movie's box office, and we first explore the correlation among different factors using the Pearson correlation (ρ) to establish whether these factors have correlations (through analyzing their ρ values) and whether those correlations are significant (through analyzing their p-values).

Decision Tree

A decision tree is a supervised classification algorithm for data classification in data mining. It establishes a classification function or classification model by learning sample sets. This function or classification model can map data records to a certain category to be used for data prediction classification.

A decision tree consists of decision nodes, branches, leaves, and the final classification results are represented by a tree structure (binary tree or multi-branch tree). Each node in the tree represents an attribute of the analysis object, and each branch represents a possible attribute value. Therefore, from the root node to the leaf node, there is a reasonable rule, and the whole tree corresponds to a group of reasonable and expression rules. The rules are usually described in the form of IF-THEN. The combination of attributes and attribute values formed the part of IF, along which the path from the root node of the decision tree constitutes. The category marked by the leaf node forms part of the conclusion of the rule. Constructing a decision tree model to extract valuable classification rules for helping decision-makers make accurate predictions has been applied in many fields.

VARIABLES DESCRIPTION

We use the top 100 movie data from the box office released in Mainland China between 2013 and 2016, with 400 movie data. To clearly understand which factors are related to the box office data, the research chose different influencing factors, such as the movie's budget, director, actor, movie's score, district, first release date, etc. All data in this project comes from these three professional and official movie websites in China, and their definitions are presented in Table 1:

- https://movie.douban.com/
- http://www.mtime.com/
- http://piaofang.maoyan.com/rankings/year?_v_=yes

Table 1. Definitions of variables

Variable	Definition
Box office	It originally referred to as the cinema ticket office, was later extended to the theaters' screening revenue or the movie screening revenue of a movie. The movie box office is the total revenue accumulated during a movie show and directly from the consumer's purchase of a movie product. The website's box office statistics include real-time box office, one-day box office, one-week box office, weekend box office, single-month box office, annual box office, global box office, historical box office, and cinema box office (Chang & Ki, 2005). The websites chosen in this research are official channels in China to release movie box office information, which guarantees the data authenticity. The research data in this paper is taken from the annual box office of history.
Adaptation/reshoot	It is to measure whether the movie is adapted from other forms of art, such as adapting popular pop elements in novels, animations, games, TV series, music, etc., into movie stories (Eliashberg, Hui, & Zhang, 2007).
Sequel	The sequel to the movie refers to the work in contact with and inherited from the first (also known as the "original movie") in terms of movie name, story development, plot design, and character settings. The sequel movie is different from the trilogy movie and the series. The trilogy movie emphasizes that the story content and narrative are coherent, and the series of movies not only includes the story theme in the mother movie. A sequel is a determinant of movie revenue earnings (Terry & De'Armond, 2008;).
Famous director / famous actor/actress	People may think that these (famous director/actor/actress) are the most critical factors for the movie box office (Wallace, Seigerman, & Holbrook, 1993). This type of data is chosen from Mtime.com. As there are no suitable data to measure whether a director or actor is famous or not, we use the data about whether the public likes the person, which is a rating value. For example, a famous director's name is Wen Jiang, and his rating is 89, which means 89 percent of raters like him and his movies. The data of famous actors/actresses are similar to famous directors and are represented by ratings.
Score	It refers to the content generated by network users. As mainstream Internet users, young people are used to publishing their own feelings and scoring movies through community, forums, movie review websites, such as Weibo and WeChat. Not only can movie scores influence the decision of the consumer to watch the movie in the early stage of the movie release, but it can also predict the audience's preference for a movie (Hsu, 2006). As an experiential entertainment product, the movie has a relatively high perceived risk. The movie viewer often takes the initiative to search for word-of-mouth information about the movie to reduce its perceived risk. The audience's score often reflects the quality of the movie. Such a score is usually measured on a 10-point scale. In global movie systems, movie critics are divided into professional movie critics and ordinary audiences. Professional movie reviews have a more significant impact on mainstream consumers' viewing decisions (Wyatt & Badger, 1987). China does not currently have a third-party professional movie critic system, so this article directly selects the professional movie website's movie score as the measurement.
Average ticket price	The average ticket price for movies with different production methods is different, which may often affect the box office.
Budget	In recent years, many moviemakers have spent a lot of money to make a great movie. Some movies that cost much money will receive excellent audience reviews, but some excellent movies only had low budgets. So studying the budget as a factor may lead to a more reasonable explanation.
District	In China, many people like non-Chinese movies. Thus, this project studies whether different districts influence the movies' box office.
Festival/ First release date/ first release date in China	These factors are all about the release time but are divided into different time dimensions. Some movies will be released first in some European countries before their release in China. Then from a time perspective, preliminary guesses may affect the box office revenue in different seasons.
No. of reviewers	It is the statistics about the number of reviewers of a specific movie, as we suspect it is related to the average ticket price and box office revenue (Gemser, Oostrum, & Leenders, 2006).

DATA ANALYSIS

Data Cleansing and Preprocessing

To preprocess data for the data analysis, we use SPSS and Excel to recode the data according to different data scope as a new dummy variable (see Table 2)

Table 2. Coding of the variables

Original Variables	Dummy Variables
Box office (in Millions of RMB)	0. < 100 1. 100-500 2. 500-1,000 3. >1,000
Adaptation/ reshoot	1. yes 0. no
Sequel	1. yes 0. no
District	0. China 1. The USA 2. The USA and China 3. China and other countries (except the USA) 4. The USA and other countries (except China) 5. Other countries
Time interval	0. Without time difference 1. Within half a month 2. Between half a month and a month 3. Between a month and two months 4. Between two months and half a year 5. Over half a year

Correlation Analysis

According to different contributing factors, some factors are related to the movie itself, such as the actors, directors, and movie scores. However, some contributing factors are related to the moviemakers as well. These factors are not on the contents, actors, or directors but are related to the movies' release or production. These factors may include the average ticket price, as well as the time interval between the first release date and the release date in the Chinese movie market.

As shown in Table 3, all p-values < 0.05, which illustrate that the box 'office's attribute is influenced by the movie budget, the popularity of directors, the popularity of actors/actresses, the movie score, and the average movie ticket price. In real life, the number of movie star fans is increasing. They watch a movie mainly because they like a particular movie star. For example, Tom Hanks is a famous movie star in the whole world, due to his handsome outward appearance and superb acting skills. So, each of his movies gets better box office revenue and viewer ratings. Therefore, these results are reasonable and in line with reality. Notably, both district code ($= 0.248$, $p > 0.05$) and festival ($= 0.761$ $p > 0.05$) had

Table 3. Correlation Table 1 from SPSS

Correlation Table 1		box office	budget	famous director	famousactor	score	average ticket price
box office	Pearson correlation	1	.289**	.197**	.100*	.244**	.354**
	Sig (2-tailed)		.000	.000	.045	.000	.000
	N	400	400	400	400	400	400
budget	Pearson correlation	.289**	1	.353**	.288**	.423**	.394**
	Sig (2-tailed)	.000		.000	.000	.000	.000
	N	400	400	400	400	400	400
famous director	Pearson correlation	.197**	.353**	1	.436**	.485**	.285**
	Sig (2-tailed)	.000	.000		.000	.000	.000
	N	400	400	400	400	400	400
famous actor	Pearson correlation	.100*	.288**	.436**	1	.285**	.202**
	Sig (2-tailed)	.045	.000	.000		.000	.000
	N	400	400	400	400	400	400
score	Pearson correlation	.244**	.423**	.485**	.285**	1	.162**
	Sig (2-tailed)	.000	.000	.000	.000		.001
	N	400	400	400	400	400	400
average ticket price	Pearson correlation	.354**	.394**	.285**	.202**	.162**	1
	Sig (2-tailed)	.000	.000	.000	.000	.001	
	N	400	400	400	400	400	400

**. Correlation is significant at the 0.01 level (2-tailed).
*. Correlation is significant at the 0.05 level (2-tailed).

Table 4. Correlation table 2 from SPSS

Correlation Table 2		box office	adaptation/ reshoot	sequel	district code	time interval	festival	No. of viewer showing
box office	Pearson correlation	1	.133**	.172**	-.058	-.101*	-.015	.667**
	Sig(2-Tailed)		.008	.001	.248	.044	.761	.000
	N	400	400	400	400	400	400	400
adaptation/ reshoot	Pearson correlation	.133**	1	.222**	-.016	-.132**	.120*	.189**
	Sig(2-Tailed)	.008		.000	.754	.008	.016	.000
	N	400	400	400	400	400	400	400
sequel	Pearson correlation	.172**	.222**	1	.034	.073	-.024	.095
	Sig(2-Tailed)	.001	.000		.499	.145	.626	.059
	N	400	400	400	400	400	400	400
district code	Pearson correlation	-.058	-.016	.034	1	.436**	-.262**	-.153**
	Sig(2-Tailed)	.248	.754	.499		.000	.000	.002
	N	400	400	400	400	400	400	400
time interval	Pearson correlation	-.101*	-.132**	.073	.436**	1	-.234**	-.169**
	Sig(2-Tailed)	.044	.008	.145	.000		.000	.001
	N	400	400	400	400	400	400	400
festival	Pearson correlation	-.015	.120*	-.024	-.262**	-.234**	1	.194**
	Sig(2-Tailed)	.761	.016	.626	.000	.000		.000
	N	400	400	400	400	400	400	400
No. of viewer showing	Pearson correlation	.667**	.189**	.095	-.153**	-.169**	.194**	1
	Sig(2-Tailed)	.000	.000	.059	.002	.001	.000	
	N	400	400	400	400	400	400	400

**. Correlation is significant at the 0.01 level (2-tailed).
*. Correlation is significant at the 0.05 level (2-tailed).

non-significant correlations, while there are significant correlations among adaptation reshoot, sequel, time interval, and the number of viewers with box office.

The results of the correlation analysis in SPSS have revealed some attributes that influence the box office. Then, we demonstrate these factors using more intuitive descriptive statistics.

1) Sequel: The sequel movie in contact with and inherited from the "original movie" in terms of movie names. For our dataset, there are 27% (108 movies) sequel movies. The box office receipts of these movies are related to the sequel or not because its mother movie influences the box office of a sequel movie. However, in the Chinese movie market, the series movies account for less market share.

2) Adaptation/reshoot: Many movies have been adapted from other forms of art, such as novels, dramas, etc. Such movies also depend on the popularity of the novels or dramas. We can see that 31.25% of movies are adapted, which is more than sequel movies. This result illustrates that a majority of the audience watch adapted or reshoot movies to enjoy works of novels in China's market.

3) Score code: Score is one of the most important indicators of whether a movie is popular. Because most of these indicators come from the masses who watched the movies, this indicator has great significance. As shown in Figure 1, only 8.25% of movies (33 movies) got a high score (over 4 on a 5-point scale). The data illustrate that the Chinese movie market still lacks excellent works in the viewers'" opinions. To a certain extent, if a movie got a relatively high rating, the box office will increase accordingly.

Figure 1. Bar chart of the score code

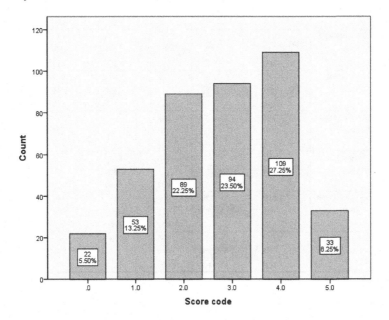

Figure 2. The process of building a decision tree in RapidMiner

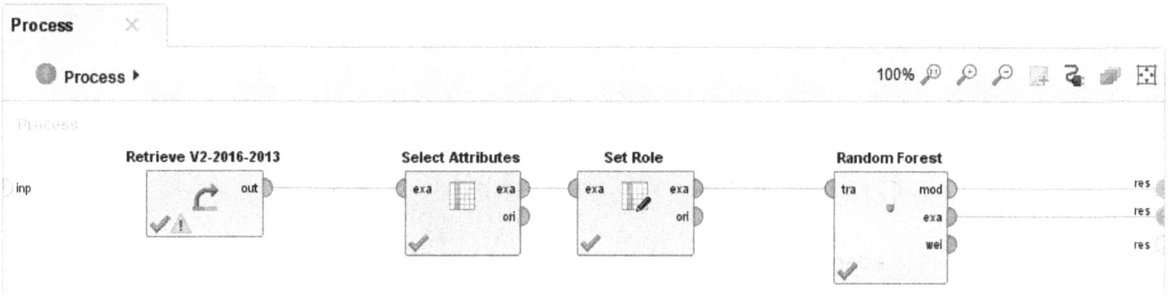

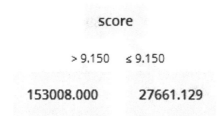

Decision Tree Analysis

After analyzing the different factors influencing the box office with correlation analysis, we apply decision trees of RapidMiner to validate our findings. We use the random forest method to explore more associational relationships among these different factors, which is a classifier for multiple decision trees without pruning. The steps to build a decision tree are as follows: (see Figure 2)

Step 1: Select Attributes - this is an essential operator that can select attributes to analyze. In this step, all factors are chosen for building different decision trees.

Step 2: Set Role - to explore the relationship between box office and other contributing factors. The role of the box office is set as "label."

Step 3: Add the Random Forest operator, connect "mod & exa" to res, and run it.

After running the operator of the decision tree, we can get some different trees and analyze them. As shown in Figure 3, if the *score* is greater than 9.15, then the box office is 1,530 million RMB (note the unit of Figure 3 is 10,000 RMB). However, if the *score* is smaller than 9.15, then the box office is 277 (Million RBM). Although it is difficult for a movie to score 9 points or more, the results show that the impact of the *score* on the box office is still huge.

As shown in Fig. 4, if the director's popularity is smaller than 90.5, then the box office is only 282 million RMB. However, if the director's popularity is greater than 90.5 and the actor/actress' popularity is smaller than 78, then the *box office* is 3,390 million RMB. If the popularity is greater than 78 and this is not an adaptation movie, then the *box office* is 826 million RMB. If this is an adaptation movie and the popularity is higher than 91.5, then the *box office* is 315 million RMB. From these results, we can

Figure 3. Decision Tree Level 1

score

\> 9.150   ≤ 9.150

153008.000   27661.129

Figure 4. Decision tree 2

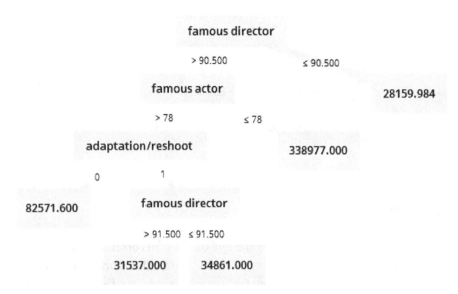

understand that the popularity of the directors and actors/actreesses exhibited a very significant influence on the movie box office.

According to Figure 5, the tree provides us some information about the influences of the budget, time interval, and festival for movie box offices. If the budget is higher than 142,500,000 and the time interval is smaller than 1.5 weeks, then the box office is 89.433.87, which is higher than the movie box office that time interval is more than 1.5 weeks. From this result, the impact of the festival on the box office is insignificant, but the interval between the first release date and the release date in China will impact

Figure 5. Decision Tree 3

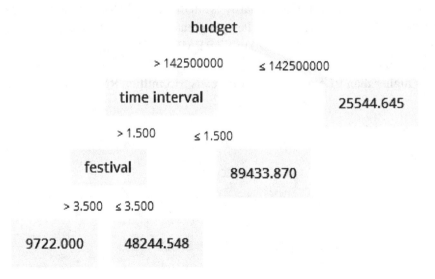

Figure 6. Relative plot of the result of the regression analysis

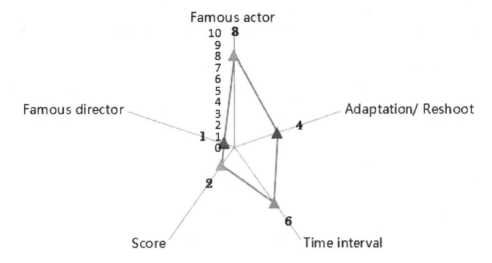

the box office. The smaller the interval of the movie, the higher the box office. Besides, the budget is a key factor that influences the box office significantly.

COMPARISON OF RESULTS

By comparing the regression analysis result with the decision tree result, we can further validate the impacts of the factors. Relative plots are handy for this purpose. Figure 6 illustrates that by sorting the influence of different influencing factors on the box office from the regression analysis result, this relative plot shows that *famous actor/actresses* and *time interval* significantly impact predicting the movie box office. However, Figure 7 illustrates that by sorting the influence of different contributing factors

Figure 7. Relative plot of the result of the decision trees

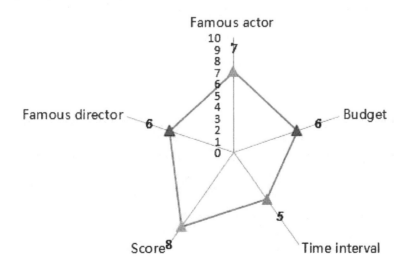

on the box office from the result of the decision tree, it can be seen the *score* and *famous actor* have relatively significant effects on the movie box office.

The reason for the difference between the two results from the two methods may be that the different parameters in the process of running the decision tree, and RapidMiner will pre-pruning these trees. Besides, before running it, preprocesses of data will be applied to replace some outliers. It also influences the results and produces some slight errors and differences. In short, the correlation relationships among these contributing factors can be verified by these two methods. These results can be used to make some proposals for the moviemakers to increase the movie box offices and improve the movie industry.

DISCUSSION

Movie Quality

The adaptation of the movie benefited from the huge crowd base behind the text adaptation. The moviemakers developed a targeted marketing distribution plan based on the characteristics of the target audience, then effectively improving the conversion rate of the ticket purchase, promoting the growth of the box office. Although the sequel movie is an extension of the brand, it is not a guarantee of a high box office and has little effect on the movie box office. However, the director is the commander of a movie, regardless of the predecessor director or the new director. Therefore, both the directors of commercial-oriented movies and famous high-quality actors influence the box office. Besides, the movie score reflects the audience's evaluation of the movie quality and impacts the movie box office.

Distribution

The issue of distribution has a positive influence on the box office of the movie. If the first release time is different from that in Mainland China, the time interval between the two dates will impact the box office revenue. If a popular movie is released in advance outside mainland China, the sooner the date is released in mainland China, the more significant the positive impact on the box office. The movie budget also largely determines the movie quality, which affects the movie box office. Although the average ticket price does not impact the box office much, its correlation with the box office indicates that the fare will still impact the box office.

RECOMMENDATIONS

Create a high-quality sequel series - Establishing the movie brand effect and expanding the influence of the movie are essential means to accumulate the core target audience. The extension of the brand is based on high-quality movie content. Moviemakers should dig deep into combining the audience's inner and cultural trends and deeply integrate popular elements and movie elements. They should also aim at creating world-influenced sequel movies like' Hollywood's Harry Potter, Speed and Passion, Spider-Man, and Lord of the Rings.

Focus on the matching of directors and actors - Directors often grasp the overall idea of a movie, manipulates the emotional route of the movie story, and determines the style of the movie. Usually, even with the same script, the effects produced by different directors are different, as directors with more production experience can better command the actors to play the script according to the story content. The acting and artistic style of the actor largely determines the expression of the movie on the script. A better actor is more likely to integrate between the script and the movie expression, thus ensuring the movie's effect on the script. It is undeniable that directors and actors strongly determine movie quality. Besides, due to the prevalence of the current fashion entertainment culture, some entertainment stars with fewer pre-productions but higher popularity index gradually enter the movie's production field. They often have a specific "viewer's edge" and can obtain a large amount of support to a certain extent. With admirers, this part of the actor also has the potential for box office appeal. Notably, in choosing a movie actor or actress, it is necessary to ensure the suitability of the script type and the performance style of the actor.

Time of movie release – Moviemakers should pay attention to the movie release time and choose the appropriate release period. The movie release time has a direct impact on the movie box office (Einav, 2007). As the time cost of watching movies during holidays is relatively low, the consumption resistance of movie products is relatively small, which is more conducive to ensuring the movie attendance rate. Therefore, if conditions permit, moviemakers can choose to release the movie during holiday seasons. If the competition is more intense, moviemakers can choose to release it before or after the holiday. In short, moviemakers may try to ensure that the movie's release period includes holidays, such as Spring Festival, May Day, Summer Holiday, National Day, and New Year's Day.

CONCLUSION

This paper analyzed movie data of 400 movies from the period between 2013 and 2016 in mainland China. Two analytic tools and methods were used in this study. First, correlation analysis was used to analyze what factors will influence the movie box office. Contributing factors include the movie budget, director popularity, viewer scores, average ticket price, adaptation/reshoot, sequel, and the number of viewers, with actor popularity and time interval being the two most significant factors. At the same time, districts and festivals do not have a significant correlation with the movie box office.

Second, in RapidMiner, decision trees were used to analyze how these contributing factors influenced the box office. Rules among attributes and box office values were generated and suggested that score is the most influential factor, followed by the popularity of actors/actresses and directors, budget, and time interval.

Furthermore, results from the two analytic methods were cross-validated, showing that the popularity of actors/actresses and time interval strongly affect the movie box office. Based on the data analysis results, this paper made recommendations to the movie industry: high-quality sequel series, experienced directors with famous/popular actors, the right timing of movie release during holiday seasons would help boost box office and revenues.

As for future work, we are looking into the general notion of reputation (Chiu, Leung, and Lam, 2009) on the movie box office. We are also interested in the authenticity and reputation attack of movie ratings (Ji et al., 2020; Wang et al., 2019).

REFERENCES

Amit, J. (2015). Movie stars and the volatility of movie revenues. *Journal of Media Economics*, *28*(4), 246–267. doi:10.1080/08997764.2015.1094079

Asur, S., & Huberman, B. A. (2010). Predicting the future with social media. *2010 IEEE/WIC/ACM International Conference on Web Intelligence and Intelligent Agent Technology*, 492–499. 10.1109/WI-IAT.2010.63

Barbosu, S. (2016). Big data on the big screen: Revealing latent similarity among movies and its effect on box office performance. SSRN *Electronic Journal*. doi:10.2139srn.2846821

Chang, B., & Ki, E. (2005). Devising a practical model for predicting theatrical movie success: Focusing on the experience good property. *Journal of Media Economics*, *18*(4), 247–269. doi:10.120715327736me1804_2

Chen, Y., Liu, Y., & Zhang, J. (2012). When do third-party product reviews affect firm value and what can firms do? The case of media critics and professional movie reviews. *Journal of Marketing*, *76*(2), 116–134. doi:10.1509/jm.09.0034

Chiu, D. K. W., Leung, H. F., & Lam, K. M. (2009). On the making of service recommendations: An action theory based on utility, reputation, and risk attitude. *Expert Systems with Applications*, *36*(2), 3293–3301. doi:10.1016/j.eswa.2008.01.055

Du, J., Xu, H., & Huang, X. (2014). Box office prediction based on microblog. *Expert Systems with Applications*, *41*(4), 1680–1689. doi:10.1016/j.eswa.2013.08.065

Einav, L. (2007). Seasonality in the US motion picture industry. *The RAND Journal of Economics*, *38*(1), 127–145. doi:10.1111/j.1756-2171.2007.tb00048.x

Eliashberg, J., Hui, S. K., & Zhang, Z. J. (2007). From story line to box office: A new approach for green-lighting movie scripts. *Management Science*, *53*(6), 881–893. doi:10.1287/mnsc.1060.0668

Gemser, G., Oostrum, M. V., & Leenders, M. A. (2006). The impact of movie reviews on the box office performance of art house versus mainstream motion pictures. *Journal of Cultural Economics*, *31*(1), 43–63. doi:10.100710824-006-9025-4

Handel, L. (1996). Hollywood looks at its audience. *Journalism Bulletin*, *28*(1), 109–110.

Hsu, G. (2006). Evaluative schemas and the attention of critics in the US movie industry. *Industrial and Corporate Change*, *15*(3), 467–496. doi:10.1093/icc/dtl009

Ji, S., Yang, W., Guo, S., Chiu, D. K. W., Zhang, C., & Yuan, X. (2020). Asymmetric response aggregation heuristics for rating prediction and recommendation. *Applied Intelligence*, *50*(5), 1416–1436. doi:10.100710489-019-01594-2

Jiang, T., Lo, P. C. P., Cheuk, M. K., & Chiu, K. W. D. (2019). *New Cultural Dialog: Interviews with Outstanding Librarians, Archivists, and Curators in Greater China*. Systech Publisher.

Jo, J., & Choi, S. H. (2015). Sentiment analysis of movie review for predicting movie rating. *Management & Information Systems Review*, *34*(3), 161–177. doi:10.29214/damis.2015.34.3.009

Kim, S. H., Park, N., & Park, S. H. (2013). Exploring the effects of online word of mouth and expert reviews on theatrical movies box office success. *Journal of Media Economics*, *26*(2), 98–114. doi:10.1080/08997764.2013.785551

King, T. (2007). Does movie criticism affect box office earnings? Evidence from movies released in the U.S. in 2003. *Journal of Cultural Economics*, *31*(3), 171–186. doi:10.100710824-007-9041-z

Koschat, M. A. (2012). The impact of movie reviews on box office: Media portfolios and the intermediation of genre. *Journal of Media Economics*, *25*(1), 35–53. doi:10.1080/08997764.2012.651063

Litman, B. R., & Kohl, L. S. (1989). Predicting financial success of motion pictures: The 80's experience. *Journal of Media Economics*, *2*(2), 35–50. doi:10.1080/08997768909358184

Lo, P., Chiu, D. K., & Cho, A. (2017). *Inside the World's Major East Asian Collections: One Belt, One Road, and Beyond*. Chandos Publishing.

Mishne, G., & Glance, N. S. (2006). Predicting movie sales from blogger sentiment. In *AAAI Spring Symposium: Computational Approaches to Analyzing Weblogs* (pp. 155–158). Academic Press.

Sharda, R., & Delen, D. (2006). Predicting box-office success of motion pictures with neural networks. *Expert Systems with Applications*, *30*(2), 243–254. doi:10.1016/j.eswa.2005.07.018

Sochay, S. (1994). Predicting the performance of motion pictures. *Journal of Media Economics*, *7*(4), 1–20. doi:10.120715327736me0704_1

Terry, N., & De'Armond, D. A. (2008). The determinants of movie rental revenue earnings. *Academy of Marketing Studies Journal*, *12*(2), 35–47.

Wallace, W. T., Seigerman, A., & Holbrook, M. B. (1993). The role of actors and actresses in the success of movies: How much is a movie star worth? *Journal of Cultural Economics*, *17*(1), 1–27. doi:10.1007/BF00820765

Wang, X., Ji, S. J., Liang, Y. Q., Leung, H. F., & Chiu, D. K. W. (2019). An unsupervised strategy for defending against multifarious reputation attacks. *Applied Intelligence*, *49*(12), 4189–4210. doi:10.100710489-019-01490-9

Wyatt, R. O., & Badger, D. P. (1987). To toast, pan or waffle: How movie reviews affect reader interest and credibility perception. *Newspaper Research Journal*, *8*(Summer), 19–30. doi:10.1177/073953298700800402

ADDITIONAL READING

Adamopoulos, P., Ghose, A., & Todri, V. (2018). The impact of user personality traits on word of mouth: Text-mining social media platforms. *Information Systems Research*, *29*(3), 612–640. doi:10.1287/isre.2017.0768

Cao, N., Ji, S., Chiu, D. K. W., He, M., & Sun, X. (2020). A Deceptive Review Detection Framework: Combination of Coarse and Fine-grained Features. *Expert Systems with Applications*, *156*, 113465. doi:10.1016/j.eswa.2020.113465

Chang, V., Chiu, D. K., Ramachandran, M., & Li, C. S. (2018). Internet of Things, Big Data and Complex Information Systems: Challenges, solutions and outputs from IoTBD 2016, COMPLEXIS 2016 and CLOSER 2016 selected papers and CLOSER 2015 keynote. *Future Generation Computer Systems*, *79*(3), 973–974. doi:10.1016/j.future.2017.09.013

Chiu, Y. L., Chen, K. H., Wang, J. N., & Hsu, Y. T. (2019). The impact of online movie word-of-mouth on consumer choice. *International Marketing Review*, *36*(6), 996–1025. doi:10.1108/IMR-06-2018-0190

Galvão, M., & Henriques, R. (2018). Forecasting movie box office profitability. *Journal of Information Systems Engineering and Management*, *3*(3), 22. doi:10.20897/jisem/2658

Hofmann, M., & Klinkenberg, R. (Eds.). (2016). *RapidMiner: Data mining use cases and business analytics applications*. CRC Press. doi:10.1201/b16023

Hu, Y. H., Shiau, W. M., Shih, S. P., & Chen, C. J. (2018). Considering online consumer reviews to predict movie box-office performance between the years 2009 and 2014 in the US. *The Electronic Library*, *36*(6), 1010–1026. doi:10.1108/EL-02-2018-0040

Hur, M., Kang, P., & Cho, S. (2016). Box-office forecasting based on sentiments of movie reviews and Independent subspace method. *Information Sciences*, *372*, 608–624. doi:10.1016/j.ins.2016.08.027

Ji, S., Zhang, Q., Li, J., Chiu, D. K. W., Xu, S., Yi, L., & Gong, M. (2020). A burst-based unsupervised method for detecting review spammer groups. *Information Sciences*, *536*, 454–469. doi:10.1016/j.ins.2020.05.084

Lee, J. H., Jung, S. H., & Park, J. (2017). The role of entropy of review text sentiments on online WOM and movie box office sales. *Electronic Commerce Research and Applications*, *22*, 42–52. doi:10.1016/j.elerap.2017.03.001

Lee, S., & Choeh, J. Y. (2018). The interactive impact of online word-of-mouth and review helpfulness on box office revenue. *Management Decision*, *56*(4), 849–866. doi:10.1108/MD-06-2017-0561

Liu, X., Sun, R., Wang, S., & Wu, Y. J. (2019). The research landscape of big data: A bibliometric analysis. *Library Hi Tech*, *38*(2), 367–384. doi:10.1108/LHT-01-2019-0024

KEY TERMS AND DEFINITIONS

Decision Tree: Builds classification models in the form of a tree structure by breaking down a dataset into smaller and smaller subsets, while at the same time, an associated decision tree is incrementally developed. The final result is a tree with decision nodes (having two or more branches) and leaf nodes (representing a classification or decision).

Pearson Correlation: (ρ) is a statistic that measures the linear correlation between two variables. It has a value between +1 and −1. A value of +1 is a total positive linear correlation, 0 is no linear correlation, and −1 is a total negative linear correlation.

Random Forest: Is an ensemble of a certain number of random trees that are created/trained on bootstrapped sub-sets of the input (see: https://docs.rapidminer.com/latest/studio/operators/modeling/predictive/trees/parallel_random_forest.html).

Random Forest "Mod & Exa": Mod is a port which delivers the model that is built by the operator, while exa is an example set input/output port (see: https://docs.rapidminer.com/9.4/studio/getting-started/important-terms.html).

Random Forest "Res": Is result set: distance or similarity between examples of the request set and reference set (see: https://docs.rapidminer.com/9.4/studio/getting-started/important-terms.html).

RapidMiner: Is an integrated data science software platform for data preparation, machine learning, deep learning, text mining, predictive analytics, result visualization, model validation, and optimization for a wide range of disciplines and applications, such as business, research, education, and application development (see: https://rapidminer.com/).

SPSS: Is a software platform that offers advanced statistical analysis, a vast library of machine learning algorithms, text analysis, open-source extensibility, integration with big data, and seamless deployment into applications (see: https://www.ibm.com/hk-en/analytics/spss-statistics-software).

Chapter 12
Evaluation of Hotel Web Pages According to User Suitability

Burak Efe
Necmettin Erbakan University, Turkey

Ömer Faruk Efe
(iD) https://orcid.org/0000-0001-8170-5114
Afyon Kocatepe University, Turkey

ABSTRACT

In recent years, with the development of the internet, there has been an increase in interest in the internet thanks to other technological developments. In the face of increased user demand, hotel webpages have to maintain high quality of service for a sustainable success. The authors present the Pythagorean fuzzy TOPSIS method to evaluate the hotel webpages. In this study, the most suitable hotel web page has been selected among the five hotel web page alternatives based on 13 criteria according to three experts' opinions. In contrast to precise numbers in TOPSIS method, the merit of fuzzy TOPSIS method is to handle the fuzzy numbers to evaluate the alternatives. Experts cannot express certain evaluations explicitly when using precise values during making decisions. However, the use of linguistic variables provides great success in decision making under uncertain environments. Pythagorean fuzzy number is used to define the weights of the criteria according to three experts' opinions. Five alternative hotel web pages are ranked by using Pythagorean fuzzy number.

INTRODUCTION

Advances in technology, which are effective in many sectors, present a lot of influence in the field of tourism. Companies need to adapt to these developments in order to ensure their continuity. Especially, advances in internet technology provide to meet the demands and needs of consumers to companies in the field of tourism (Şahin & Cıbıt, 2016). According to the internet and social media statistics prepared every year by "We are social" and "Hootsuit", Turkey Electronic Commerce statistics when evaluating results from 2019, has emerged that the highest spending is made in the travel category. Compared to

DOI: 10.4018/978-1-7998-4963-6.ch012

the previous year, the highest increase was in the category of travel expenditures with a rate of 9.7% (Bayrak, 2019). Hotel and holiday alternatives are easily accessible by helping the hotel and tour reservation websites of travel agencies. Consumers face many alternatives in hotel and holiday choices (Flavian et al., 2006).

It has become easier to present information in today's world, where communication has developed rapidly, distance has disappeared and the world has become smaller. Individuals or institutions share on the internet their information with their stakeholders via Web servers. While the information is presented via the Web, the features such as the format, color, placement of the screen, the structure of the characters used and the timeliness should be carefully designed. The performance of the web servers should be sufficient. Information requirements may not be met if a low-scale server is used and a high level of demand is received. This negatively affects users. Websites especially give businesses the opportunity to embody their products in terms of the service sector. Small hotel businesses, which cannot allocate large amounts of resources for marketing activities, can meet these needs at a much lower cost with a well-designed website over the Internet. Accommodation establishments should be followers in order to take maximum benefit of all the advantages provided by the Internet. They guide in organizing the web pages and updating their contents. Web pages must contain some information and have features (Geyik, 2010).

Users want to see room rates, available room categories, reservation policy and secure online reservation system from a hotel website. It is important for users to have the ability to view and change their reservations on the website after making their reservations. In addition, customers want all this information to be understandable and easily accessible on the website. The visual and audio technologies enable users to see hotel rooms and facilities such as a virtual tour. These are among the features that users want most to be found on hotel websites. When the features on the hotel websites are analyzed separately, it is observed that the mostly preferred features of hotel websites are address, telephone, fax, e-mail, room information, facility information, photo album, map, multiple language options and room prices regardless of the hotel category. It has been determined that online availability, online reservation and secure online sales features allow hotels to sell from their websites. The percentage of website features that give potential customers the opportunity to sell online is over 50% in 3-star hotels, 70% in 4-stars, and 90% in 5-stars. It shows that the hotels understand the importance of selling to the customer directly from their websites and they started to invest in their websites in this direction. Hotels should pay attention to give the best price guarantee to the potential customer. The best price guarantee is an important tool to encourage customers not only choosing any agency but also booking on the hotel's website (Ovalı, 2019).

Web pages published on the internet are interactive digital platforms used by institutions and organizations or individual users for information, advertising, promotion and communication. The visual elements used in the interface design of the web pages must be correctly interpreted and understood by the user. While preparing the web pages, the user can show individual differences in using the visual elements in the content of the web page effectively. When designing a web page, designers must ensure that the page is flexible, effective and organized. They must determine how the web content responds to the users' actions. Since web page content depends on visual communication principles, the interaction of page layout, formats, colors, fonts. Visual readability and usability of web pages have a great effect on communication with the user. The use of the Internet has also affected the formation of information dumps due to the storage of information in the web space because millions of users actively share. Therefore, distinctive features of web pages in terms of interface and usability should be developed. The prepared web page designs will allow the user to perceive the information more easily (Gözübüyükoğlu, 2019).

Multi criteria decision making (MCDM) methods address the decision-making process in the presence of multiple goals. A decision maker needs to choose between multiple criteria that are either measurable or not measurable. The best alternative is selected by making comparisons between alternatives based on each criterion (Efe, 2016).

MCDM methods are gaining importance as potential tools for analyzing and solving complex real life problems because of their ability to evaluate different alternatives based on various criteria. MCDM problems have a number of precedents such as the existence of multiple immeasurable and contradictory criteria, different units of measurement among the criteria, the presence of quite different alternatives. These decision-making problems, which define multi-dimensional situations, are solved by various MCDM methods. MCDM methods are primarily aimed at evaluating and sorting available alternatives. In some cases, different MCDM methods can give different results. The order of the same alternatives varies depending on the accepted methods. This is based on the use of different mathematical structures in the methods (Efe and Efe, 2018).

There are some studies in the literature about the evaluation of web sites by using multi criteria decision making methods. Chiou et al. (2010) examined to understand and improve website evaluation through the analysis of literature research. Kabir and Hasin (2012) have used multi-criteria decision making approach in evaluating the quality of travel agencies' websites according to the users 'perspective. Websites of five travel agencies were evaluated using TOPSIS (Technique for Order Preference by Similarity to Ideal Solution) and fuzzy TOPSIS methods. Qi et al. (2015) used modified fuzzy hierarchical TOPSIS model for hotel website evaluation. Soleymaninejad et al. (2016) have applied the analytic hierarchy process (AHP) based TOPSIS method to two major online travel agencies that are considered to be each other's main competitors in the USA. Ali (2016) presented hotel website quality by using 441 valid online questionnaires. Li et al. (2017) examined on the influence of economy hotel website quality on online booking intentions by collecting 298 samples from the users of three economy hotel websites. Roy et al. (2019) have integrated the weighted interval rough number (WIRN) method and the COPRAS (COmplex PRoportional ASsessment) technique to conduct a web based hotel evaluation and selection process in the tourism industry in India. Wong et al. (2020) handled 7 dimensions and 45 attributes of hotel mobile website from the perceptions of users.

The studies where hotel web pages are analyzed by using the Pythagorean fuzzy TOPSIS approach are limited according to literature review. Therefore, this study is a valuable study. Experts cannot express certain evaluations explicitly when using precise values during making decisions. However, the use of fuzzy logic linguistic variables provides great success in decision making in uncertain environments. Fuzzy logic has been used to assess the importance of criteria and evaluate experts on the basis of criteria in order to express their opinions as linguistic variables. In practice, Pythagorean fuzzy TOPSIS was evaluated alternative web pages based on criteria.

There are dozens of different web pages that provide information about the hotel. In evaluating hotel web pages, the criteria and the weight of these criteria should be determined. The measurement and evaluation of the choice of alternatives varies according to the individual. Therefore, an impartial and accurate evaluation process can be disrupted and lead to wrong decisions. Because many conflicting quantitative and qualitative criteria should be taken into account simultaneously. Fuzzy MCDM methods have been developed to solve these problems.

In this study, the Pythagorean fuzzy TOPSIS method was used to evaluate alternative hotel web pages. In recent years, Pythagorean fuzzy TOPSIS has been applied in different areas such as clean energy technology selection, supplier selection and airline assessment (Zhang & Xu, 2014; Gündoğdu et al., 2019; Yu et al., 2019).

THE PROPOSED APPROACH

Atanassov (1986) developed intuitionistic fuzzy set and many researchers employed it in different areas to handle uncertainty. Intuitionistic fuzzy set includes membership degree, non-membership degree and hesitancy degree. The total of these parameters equal to 1. However, this situation causes a problem when the total of the membership degree and non-membership degree exceeds to 1. Intuitionistic fuzzy set is insufficient to handle the uncertainty in this situation. Pythagorean fuzzy set developed by Yager (2013) handles more uncertainty than intuitionistic fuzzy sets. Pythagorean fuzzy set (PFS) ensures more robust and flexible solutions for uncertainty of problems. Zhang and Xu (2014) presented some definitions and operations for Pythagorean fuzzy set as follows:

Definition 1: X and P are a universe of discourse and a Pythagorean fuzzy number, respectively (Zhang and Xu, 2014).

$$P = \left\{ \left\langle x, P\left(\mu_P\left(x\right), v_P\left(x\right)\right)\right\rangle \middle| x \in X \right\} \tag{1}$$

Eq. (1) presents that $\mu_{P_{(}}x)$: X→[0,1] and $vP_{(}x$): X→[0,1] mean the membership degree and non-membership degree, respectively. The experts can want to present membership degree and non-membership degree about an evaluation. Eq. (1) ensures to handle the judgments of the experts for this situation. Eq. (2) shows that sum of squares of membership degree and non-membership degree cannot exceed to 1. This rule of pythagorean fuzzy set (PFS) ensures the difference from intuitionistic fuzzy set.

$$\mu P_{(}x)2 + vP_{(}x)2 \leq 1 \tag{2}$$

For any PFS in X, $x \in X$, $\pi P_{(}x)$ is called the degree of indeterminacy of x to P. Eq.(3) shows the hesitation degree.

$$\pi_P\left(x\right) = \sqrt{1 - \mu_P\left(x\right)^2 - v_P\left(x\right)^2} \tag{3}$$

Definition 2: Let $\beta_1 = P\left(\mu_{\beta_1}, v_{\beta_1}\right)$ and $\beta_2 = P\left(\mu_{\beta_2}, v_{\beta_2}\right)$ be two Pythagorean fuzzy numbers and $\lambda > 0$. Eqs. (4)-(7) presents the addition, multiplication, multiplication with crisp number k, and exponent operations. The operations on the two Pyhtagorean fuzzy numbers are defined in Eqs. (4)-(7) as follows: (Zhang and Xu, 2014).

$$\beta_1 \oplus \beta_2 = P\left(\sqrt{\mu_{\beta_1}^2 + \mu_{\beta_2}^2 - \mu_{\beta_1}^2 \mu_{\beta_2}^2}, v_{\beta_1} v_{\beta_2} \right) \tag{4}$$

$$\beta_1 \otimes \beta_2 = P\left(\mu_{\beta_1} \mu_{\beta_2}, \sqrt{v_{\beta_1}^2 + v_{\beta_2}^2 - v_{\beta_1}^2 v_{\beta_2}^2} \right) \tag{5}$$

$$k\beta = P\left(\sqrt{1 - \left(1 - \mu_\beta^2\right)^k}, \left(v_\beta\right)^k \right), k \geq 0 \tag{6}$$

$$\beta^k = P\left(\left(\mu_\beta\right)^k, \sqrt{1 - \left(1 - v_\beta^2\right)^k} \right), k \geq 0 \tag{7}$$

Definition 3: Let $\beta_1 = P\left(\mu_{\beta_1}, v_{\beta_1}\right)$ and $\beta_2 = P\left(\mu_{\beta_2}, v_{\beta_2}\right)$ be two Pythagorean fuzzy numbers, a nature quasi-ordering on the Pyhtagorean fuzzy numbers is definedin Eq. (8) as follows (Zhang and Xu, 2014):

$$\beta 1_{>} \beta 2 \text{ if and only if } \mu_{\beta_1} > \mu_{\beta_2} \text{ and } v_{\beta_1} < v_{\beta_2} \tag{8}$$

A score function is proposed to compare two Pythagorean fuzzy numbers in Eq. (9) as follows (Zhang and Xu, 2014):

$$s\left(\beta_1\right) = \left(\mu_{\beta_1}\right)^2 - \left(v_{\beta_1}\right)^2 \tag{9}$$

Definition 4: Based on the score functions proposed above, the following laws are defined to compare two Pythagorean fuzzy numbers in Eqs. (10)-(12) (Zhang and Xu, 2014):

(i) if $s\left(\beta_1\right) < s\left(\beta_2\right)$, then $\beta_1 \prec \beta_2$ \hfill (10)

(ii) if $s\left(\beta_1\right) > s\left(\beta_2\right)$, then $\beta_1 \succ \beta_2$ \hfill (11)

(iii) if $s(\beta 1_) = s(\beta 2)$, then $\beta 2 \sim \beta_2$ \hfill (1_2)

PFTOPSIS

The TOPSIS method proposed by Hwang and Yoon (1981) examines negative and positive ideal solutions when listing alternatives. In this study, fuzzy TOPSIS method was used while evaluating the alternatives for the otel web pages. Fuzzy logic approach is proposed to make decisions in uncertain environment. In recent years, the fuzzy TOPSIS method has been applied in different areas such as mobile phone selection, software selection (Efe, 2016; Efe, 2020).

Pythagorean fuzzy sets are an extension of usual and intuitionistic fuzzy sets. It provides more freedom to experts in expressing their opinions about the vagueness and uncertainty of considered problem. In Pythagorean fuzzy sets experts assign membership and non-membership degrees. On the other hand, TOPSIS method is applied to a variety of problems in the literature. It has many advantages as follows: It allows the experts to assign judgments by means of linguistic terms, which are better interpreted by humans, fuzzy in nature, and then transferred into Pythagorean fuzzy numbers. It has more capability in handling uncertainties, simultaneous consideration of the positive and negative ideal points, simple computation, and logical concept.

Based on definitions given above, in the following, PFTOPSIS algorithm is presented with its routine steps (Yücesan and Gül, 2020):

Step 1: Initially, decision matrix under Pythagorean fuzzy sets $R=(C_j(x_i))_{mxn}$ is constructed. Here, $C_j(j=1,2,...,n)$ and $x_i(i=1,2,...,m)$ refer to values of criteria and alternatives. Eq. (13) denotes the matrix form (Yücesan and Gül, 2020):

$$R = \left(C_J\left(x_i\right)\right)_{mxn} = \begin{pmatrix} P\left(\mu_{11},v_{11}\right) & P\left(\mu_{12},v_{12}\right) & \cdots & P\left(\mu_{1n},v_{1n}\right) \\ P\left(\mu_{21},v_{21}\right) & P\left(\mu_{22},v_{22}\right) & \cdots & P\left(\mu_{2n},v_{2n}\right) \\ \vdots & \vdots & \vdots & \vdots \\ P\left(\mu_{m1},v_{m1}\right) & P\left(\mu_{m2},v_{m2}\right) & \cdots & P\left(\mu_{mn},v_{mn}\right) \end{pmatrix} \tag{13}$$

Step 2: Secondly, Pythagorean fuzzy positive ideal solution (PIS) and negative ideal solutions (NIS) are determined using Eqs. (14-15) as follows (Yücesan and Gül, 2020):

$$x^+ = \left\{ C_j, \max_i \left\langle s\left(C_j\left(x_i\right)\right)\right\rangle | j=1,2,...,n\right\} = \left\{\left\langle C_1, P\left(\mu_1^+, v_1^+\right)\right\rangle, \left\langle C_2, P\left(\mu_2^+, v_2^+\right)\right\rangle, ..., \left\langle C_n, P\left(\mu_n^+, v_n^+\right)\right\rangle\right\} \tag{14}$$

$$x^- = \left\{ C_j, \min_i \left\langle s\left(C_j\left(x_i\right)\right)\right\rangle | j=1,2,...,n\right\} = \left\{\left\langle C_1, P\left(\mu_1^-, v_1^-\right)\right\rangle, \left\langle C_2, P\left(\mu_2^-, v_2^-\right)\right\rangle, ..., \left\langle C_n, P\left(\mu_n^-, v_n^-\right)\right\rangle\right\} \tag{15}$$

Let $\widetilde{A}_i = \mu_i, v_i, i = \left(1,2,...,n\right)$ be a collection of PFNs and w=$(w_1,w_2,...,w_n)^T$ be the weight vector of $\widetilde{A}_i, i=1,2,...,n)$ with $\sum_{i=1}^n w_i = 1$ then the Pyhtagorean fuzzy weighted power geometric (PFWPG) operator is in Eq. (16) (Yager and Abbasov, 2013):

$$\text{PFWPG}(\widetilde{A_1}, \widetilde{A_2}, ..., \widetilde{A_3}, = \left(1 - \prod_{i=1}^{n}\left(1 - \mu_i^2\right)^{w_i}\right)^{1/2}, \left(1 - \prod_{i=1}^{n}\left(1 - v_i^2\right)^{w_i}\right)^{1/2} \quad (16)$$

Step 3: Thirdly, distances from Pyhtagorean fuzzy PIS and NIS are determined using Eqs. (17-18) as follows (Yücesan and Gül, 2020):

$$D\left(x_i, x^+\right) = \sum_{j=1}^{n} w_j d\left(C_j\left(x_i\right), C_j\left(x^+\right)\right) = \frac{1}{2}\sum_{j=1}^{n} w_j \left(\left|\left(\mu_{ij}\right)^2 - \left(\mu_j^+\right)^2\right| + \left|\left(v_{ij}\right)^2 - \left(v_j^+\right)^2\right| + \left|\left(\pi_{ij}\right)^2 - \left(\pi_j^+\right)^2\right|\right) \quad (17)$$

$$D\left(x_i, x^-\right) = \sum_{j=1}^{n} w_j d\left(C_j\left(x_i\right), C_j\left(x^-\right)\right) = \frac{1}{2}\sum_{j=1}^{n} w_j \left(\left|\left(\mu_{ij}\right)^2 - \left(\mu_j^-\right)^2\right| + \left|\left(v_{ij}\right)^2 - \left(v_j^-\right)^2\right| + \left|\left(\pi_{ij}\right)^2 - \left(\pi_j^-\right)^2\right|\right) \quad (18)$$

i =1,2,..., n. In general, the smaller $D(x_i, x^+)$ the better the alternative x_i and the bigger $D(x_i, x^-)$ the better the alternative x_i and let

$$D_{\min}\left(x_i, x^+\right) = \min_{1 \leq i \leq m} D\left(x_i, x^+\right) \text{ and } D_{\max}\left(x_i, x^-\right) = \min_{1 \leq i \leq m} D\left(x_i, x^+\right)$$

Step 4: Fourthly, the revised closeness $\delta(xi_i$ of the alternative $(xi_i$ is computed using Eq. (19) as follows (Yücesan and Gül, 2020):

$$\xi\left(x_i\right) = \frac{D\left(x_i, x^-\right)}{D_{\max}\left(x_i, x^-\right)} - \frac{D\left(x_i, x^+\right)}{D_{\min}\left(x_i, x^+\right)} \quad (19)$$

Step 5: Finally, the best ranking order alternatives is determined. The alternative with the highest revised coefficient value is the best alternative (Yücesan and Gül, 2020).

APPLICATION

Hospitality businesses in the tourism sector must effectively and continuously promote the products and services they offer to existing and potential consumers in order to survive in an increasingly competitive environment. Since the tourism sector is a labor-intensive sector and it also has abstract features, they may have difficulty in reaching customers in promotional and marketing studies compared to other sectors. The Internet should be used as an effective tool for hotel businesses to carry out these activities. In addition to being an Internet mass media tool, it offers new opportunities to the marketing activities of hotel businesses. Hotel businesses, who want to take full advantage of all the advantages provided by

Table 1. Pythagorean fuzzy number and linguistic term

Linguistic term	Pythagorean fuzzy number (μ,v)
Very low (VL)	(0.1, 0.9)
Low (L)	(0.25, 0.75)
Medium (M)	(0.5, 0.4)
High (H)	(0.8, 0.2)
Very high (VH)	(0.95, 0.05)

the Internet, have taken their place on the Internet. The main thing here is not to have a hotel business website. The important thing is that hotel businesses choose the information that will be available on the website, they have the necessary criteria due to the presentation of this information and the nature of the sector (Gözübüyükoğlu, 2019).

With the development of the Internet, websites and mobile applications related to tourism and selling tourism products have made travel planning easier. Today, thanks to the internet and online tourism industry, people can make their travel plans individually without going to the agency. The online tourism industry mainly consists of review sites and tourism e-commerce sites. Review sites are platforms where travelers share hotels, restaurants, and other travel experiences. The revenue sources of these sites are mostly the advertisements they place on the websites. Tourism e-commerce sites sell tourism products such as air tickets and hotel rooms (Ovalı, 2019).

This study focuses on examining the hotel web pages according to user suitability. An expert team including three experts is established to evaluate the hotel web pages. E1, E2 and E3 decision makers defined thirteen criteria to assess the hotel web pages according to user suitability. These are hotel services text and photos (C1), room text and photos (C2), presence of price segmentation (C3), standard menu design (C4), structure localization information (C5), reservation system policy (C6), frequently asked questions menu (C7), secure credit card page (C8), customer retention (C9), accessibility (C10), navigability (C11), contact information (C12), advertising (C13). Decision makers presented their judgments by using Pythagorean fuzzy number about criteria and alternatives. Pythagorean fuzzy linguistic scale is shown in Table 1. For example, Table 1 presents very low linguistic term with (0.1, 0.9) Pythagorean fuzzy number. It means that the related evaluation has 0.1 membership degree and 0.9 nonmembership degree. Table 1 presents high linguistic term with (0.8, 0.2) Pythagorean fuzzy number. It means that the related evaluation has 0.8 membership degree and 0.2 nonmembership degree. Three decision makers introduce the importance degree of criteria for hotel web pages according to user suitability. Table 2 illustrates these importance degrees according to each expert. The importance degrees of E1, E2 and E3 decision makers are 0.4, 0.35 and 0.25, respectively. For example, expert 3 thinks high importance degree to C1 (hotel services text and photos) criterion in hotel website evaluation according to Table 2. Expert 2 thinks medium importance degree to C10 (accessibility) criterion in hotel website evaluation according to Table 2.

The opinions of three decision makers are aggregated by using the weights of three decision makers. The aggregated group opinion for the weights of criteria is presented in Table 3. C8 (secure credit card page) is the most important criterion for hotel website evaluation according to the results in Table 3. C13 (advertising) is the least important criterion for hotel website evaluation according to the results in Table 3.

Table 2. The importance degrees of criteria

	E1	E2	E3		E1	E2	E3		E1	E2	E3
C1	H	M	H	C6	H	H	VH	C11	L	VL	L
C2	H	H	M	C7	M	L	M	C12	M	L	M
C3	H	VH	VH	C8	VH	VH	VH	C13	VL	VL	L
C4	M	H	L	C9	VH	H	VH				
C5	L	L	M	C10	M	M	H				

TOPSIS approach is employed to evaluate the hotel web pages according to user suitability under Pythagorean fuzzy number. Three decision makers presented their opinions about criteria based alternative by using Pythagorean fuzzy number in Table 1. Five hotel web pages based on thirteen criteria according to the judgment of each expert are presented in Table 4. For example, expert 1 thinks low importance degree to C1 (hotel services text and photos) criterion for A1 hotel website alternative according to Table 4. Expert 3 thinks medium importance degree to C2 (room text and photos) criterion for A2 hotel website alternative according to Table 4. Pythagorean fuzzy number in Table 1 and the aggregation operator are used to aggregate the judgments of decision makers about criteria based alternative. The weighted decision matrix for criteria based alternative is introduced in Table 5.

Table 6 presents the Pythagorean fuzzy number positive ideal solution, Pythagorean fuzzy number negative ideal solution and the revised closeness coefficient of each alternative. According to the results of the proposed method, alternative 4 was defined the most significant alternative. The rankings of all alternatives are A4>A1>A2>A3>A5.

FUTURE RESEARCH DIRECTIONS

The service presentations of the hotel web pages increase its importance day by day. Customer expectations are increasing in this direction. For this reason, it will be important to determine the service quality of the web pages of the hotels that offer this service. As can be clearly seen, all the issues mentioned include thinking of more than one criterion to identify and solve these problems. Many different methods can be suggested for this, but hybrid fuzzy MCDM techniques are the most suitable techniques. Hybrid

Table 3. The weights of criteria

Criteria	Pythagorean fuzzy number	Criteria	Pythagorean fuzzy number
C1	(0.7311, 0.2895)	C8	(0.9500, 0.0500)
C2	(0.7533, 0.2674)	C9	(0.9198, 0.1257)
C3	(0.9141, 0.1329)	C10	(0.6130, 0.3626)
C4	(0.6218, 0.5023)	C11	(0.2108, 0.8205)
C5	(0.3367, 0.6964)	C12	(0.4348, 0.5757)
C6	(0.8604, 0.1754)	C13	(0.1530, 0.8752)
C7	(0.4348, 0.5757)		

Table 4. Evaluation data for criteria based alternative

	E1					E2					E3				
	A1	A2	A3	A4	A5	A1	A2	A3	A4	A5	A1	A2	A3	A4	A5
C1	L	L	M	M	L	VL	M	H	H	VL	L	L	M	H	L
C2	M	M	H	H	M	L	H	VH	H	H	H	M	M	VH	L
C3	H	H	M	H	M	M	VH	L	VH	L	M	H	M	M	M
C4	H	M	M	H	M	H	L	L	VH	M	M	M	M	H	L
C5	M	VH	H	H	H	L	H	M	H	M	H	H	H	M	H
C6	H	M	M	VH	M	H	M	L	H	L	M	L	M	VH	L
C7	H	H	H	H	M	H	H	H	H	L	M	M	M	VH	H
C8	H	M	H	VH	H	M	L	H	VH	H	H	L	M	H	M
C9	VH	H	M	VH	H	H	H	L	H	M	H	M	L	H	H
C10	M	H	VL	H	VL	L	VH	VL	M	VL	M	M	M	H	L
C11	VH	M	H	H	M	VH	M	M	VH	H	H	L	H	H	L
C12	M	VL	VL	VH	VL	L	VL	VL	H	L	L	L	L	VH	VL
C13	H	M	VH	H	M	VH	L	H	H	M	M	H	H	VH	L

fuzzy cluster theory and AHP, TOPSIS, PROMETHEE, WASPAS, and similar MCDM techniques help researchers find more effective results. In addition, Pythagorean fuzzy numbers are highly recommended for fuzzy MCDM methods and other techniques such as data envelopment analysis or target programming, applications and peer studies. In future studies, the authors can work integrating Pythagorean fuzzy numbers and different MCDM methods.

Table 5. The weighted decision matrix for criteria based alternative

	A1		A2		A3		A4		A5	
	μ	v	M	v	μ	v	μ	v	μ	v
C1	(0.1541	0.8371)	(0.2666	0.7045)	(0.4738	0.4400)	(0.5258	0.4077)	(0.1541	0.8371)
C2	(0.4295	0.5985)	(0.4882	0.4275)	(0.6420	0.3554)	(0.6482	0.3164)	(0.4684	0.5529)
C3	(0.6069	0.3600)	(0.8032	0.2103)	(0.3975	0.5859)	(0.7790	0.2750)	(0.3975	0.5859)
C4	(0.4684	0.5529)	(0.2704	0.7072)	(0.2704	0.7072)	(0.5464	0.5220)	(0.2829	0.6829)
C5	(0.1920	0.8025)	(0.2986	0.7057)	(0.2462	0.7268)	(0.2536	0.7224)	(0.2462	0.7268)
C6	(0.6482	0.3164)	(0.3914	0.5553)	(0.3741	0.5933)	(0.7914	0.2146)	(0.3249	0.6705)
C7	(0.3276	0.6159)	(0.3276	0.6159)	(0.3276	0.6159)	(0.3741	0.5933)	(0.2479	0.7334)
C8	(0.6946	0.2935)	(0.3587	0.6584)	(0.7157	0.2717)	(0.8835	0.1203)	(0.7157	0.2717)
C9	(0.8157	0.2014)	(0.6929	0.2936)	(0.3473	0.6641)	(0.8157	0.2014)	(0.6725	0.3135)
C10	(0.2665	0.6476)	(0.5224	0.4274)	(0.1694	0.8722)	(0.4482	0.4520)	(0.0938	0.8926)
C11	(0.1961	0.8229)	(0.0959	0.8757)	(0.1541	0.8371)	(0.1853	0.8259)	(0.1311	0.8693)
C12	(0.1642	0.7876)	(0.0665	0.9184)	(0.0665	0.9184)	(0.3999	0.5848)	(0.0737	0.9110)
C13	(0.1303	0.8830)	(0.0872	0.9155)	(0.1356	0.8785)	(0.1316	0.8793)	(0.0696	0.9127)

Table 6. Ranking orders of alternatives

	$D(X_i, X^+)$	$D(X_i, X^-)$	$\xi(X_i)$	Ranking order
A1	1,1772	1,2817	-16,108	2
A2	1,3700	1,1431	-18,894	3
A3	1,6291	0,8315	-22,691	4
A4	0,0707	2,3691	0	1
A5	1,9528	0,4805	-27,417	5

CONCLUSION

Web pages used on the internet are a communication area, so the availability of web interface designs by users requires the effective use of visual communication. When users visit web pages, they tend to leave without spending much time on the page in situations that require waiting. Therefore, the user interface and page availability on web pages is very important. Visual-weighted design, in which communication is highly effective on web pages, is important for the readability of the information on the page by the user. Web pages can be used visually and aurally as pictures, motion graphics, text information, video and audio etc. contains materials. The interface of the web pages prepared by the designer should be easy and understandable in terms of visuality. Visual communication elements such as photography, illustration, icon, typography, animation, video, sound used in the interface design correctly convey the message and determine how a user-oriented web page design should be. Web pages are very comprehensive in terms of content. For this reason, approaches to ensure the perception of the message information are important in the preparation of the page contents. Basic design principles are guiding in order to achieve the desired results in terms of visual design.

People mostly use social media to share their experiences and photos with their friends or other tourists after their travels. Before their travels, they use social media to determine the region they will visit and to get an idea about the tours. During their travels, they connect with their friends on social media and leave comments on the places they visit. People rely mostly on the comments of other tourists on the Internet and on social media after the opinions of their families and friends.

Hotel guests usually research about that area before going to a region. Information such as a list of places to visit in the region or dates of events in the city will guide the guest when planning their vacation and shortens the time spent by the guest for research. Having such information on the hotel website also allows the guest to spend more time on the hotel website. As the time spent on users' website increases, the probability of website leading up in search engines also increases.

The study aimed to evaluate hotel websites. To this end, a literature search was conducted to determine the criteria that affect the service process of hotel websites. In addition, feedbacks were received from experienced experts and the criteria were determined. Experts' opinions on these criteria were collected face to face and through interviews on the internet. Decision makers presented their decisions on the criteria and alternatives using the Pythagorean fuzzy number. As a result of these opinions, each criterion and alternative discussed was analyzed using the Pythagorean fuzzy TOPSIS method. According to the results of the method, the most important alternative 4 was found. The worst choice is alternative 5.

The contribution of the study to the literature can be defined as follows: (1) Pythagorean Fuzzy TOPSIS method has been adapted to the evaluation of hotel web pages; (2) The criteria are determined by literature review and expert opinions; (3) Hotel web pages are ranked according to service quality using TOPSIS method. The number of hotel websites handled for future studies can be increased, more criteria can be focused on, and more parameters can be taken into consideration by expanding the sub-criteria. Other fuzzy decision making methods or intuitive methods can be included in the problem in order to be strong in comparison. In addition, the proposed method can be applied in different decision making methods such as personnel selection, material selection, supplier selection, factory location selection, software selection.

REFERENCES

Ali, F. (2016). Hotel website quality, perceived flow, customer satisfaction and purchase intention. *Journal of Hospitality and Tourism Technology*, *7*(2), 213–228. doi:10.1108/JHTT-02-2016-0010

Atanassov, K. T. (1986). Intuitionistic fuzzy sets. *Fuzzy Sets and Systems*, *20*(1), 87–96. doi:10.1016/S0165-0114(86)80034-3

Bayrak, H. (2019). *Dijilopedi*. https://dijilopedi.com/2019-turkiye-internet-kullanim-ve-sosyal-medya-istatistikleri/

Chiou, W., Lin, C., & Perng, C. (2010). A strategic framework for website evaluation based on a review of the literature from 1995–2006. *Information & Management*, *47*(5-6), 282–290. doi:10.1016/j.im.2010.06.002

Efe, B. (2016). An integrated fuzzy multi criteria group decision making approach for ERP system selection. *Applied Soft Computing*, *38*, 106–117. doi:10.1016/j.asoc.2015.09.037

Efe, B., & Efe, Ö. F. (2018). Intuitionistic fuzzy number based group decision making approach for personnel selection. *Uludağ University Journal of The Faculty of Engineering*, *23*(3), 11–26. doi:10.17482/uumfd.338406

Efe, Ö. F. (2020). Hybrid Multi-Criteria Models: Joint Health and Safety Unit Selection on Hybrid Multi-Criteria Decision Making. In A. Behl (Ed.), *Multi-Criteria Decision Analysis in Management* (pp. 62–84). IGI Global. doi:10.4018/978-1-7998-2216-5.ch004

Flavian, C., Guinalıu, M., & Gurrea, R. (2006). The role played by perceived usability, satisfaction and consumer trust on website loyalty. *Information & Management*, *43*(1), 1–14. doi:10.1016/j.im.2005.01.002

Geyik, S. (2010). *Butik otellerin web sayfalarının içerik analiziyle değerlendirilmesi: karşılaştırmalı bir araştırma*. Yüksek Lisans Tezi. Balıkesir Üniversitesi Sosyal Bilimler Enstitüsü.

Gözübüyükoğlu, U. (2019). *Web sayfası tasarımında kullanıcı arayüzünün kullanılabilirliğinde görsel tasarımın önemi ve Atatürk Üniversitesi Güzel Sanatlar Fakültesi web sayfası tasarım örneği*. Yüksek Lisans Tezi. Atatürk Üniversitesi Güzel Sanatlar Enstitüsü.

Hwang, C. L., & Yoon, K. (1981). *Multiple attributes decision making methods and applications*. Springer-Verlag. doi:10.1007/978-3-642-48318-9

Kabir, G., & Hasin, M. (2012). Comparative Analysis Of TOPSIS and FUZZY TOPSIS for the Evaluation of Travel Website Service Quality. *International Journal of Qualitative Research*, *6*(3), 169–185.

Li, L., Peng, M., Jiang, N., & Law, R. (2017). An empirical study on the influence of economy hotel website quality on online booking intentions. *International Journal of Hospitality Management*, *63*, 1–10. doi:10.1016/j.ijhm.2017.01.001

Ovalı, P. N. (2019). *Otel web sitelerinin eMICA yöntemiyle analizi: İstanbul ve Antalya'daki 3, 4 Ve 5 yıldızlı otellere yönelik uygulama*. Doktora Tezi. İstanbul Üniversitesi Sosyal Bilimler Enstitüsü.

Qi, S., Law, R., & Buhalis, D. (2015). A modified fuzzy hierarchical TOPSIS model for hotel website evaluation. In *Hospitality, travel, and tourism: concepts, methodologies, tools, and applications* (pp. 263–283). IGI Global. doi:10.4018/978-1-4666-6543-9.ch017

Roy, J., Sharma, H. K., Kar, S., Zavadskas, E. K., & Saparauskas, J. (2019). An Extended COPRAS Model for Multi-Criteria Decision-Making Problems and Its Application in Web-Based Hotel Evaluation and Selection. *Economic Research- Ekonomska Istrazivanja*, *32*(1), 219–253. doi:10.1080/1331677X.2018.1543054

Şahin, B., & Cıbıt, Ö. (2016). Consumer perception towards relationship of mobile marketing and online shopping: A research towards travel agency customers. *The Journal of International Social Research*, *9*(44), 1221–1231.

Soleymaninejad, M., Shadifar, M., & Karimi, A. (2016). Evaluation of Two Major Online Travel Agencies of Us Using TOPSIS Method. *Digital Technologies*, *2*(1), 1–8.

Wong, E., Leung, R., & Law, R. (2020). Significance of the dimensions and attributes of hotel mobile website from the perceptions of users. *International Journal of Hospitality & Tourism Administration*, *21*(1), 15–37. doi:10.1080/15256480.2018.1429338

Yager, R. R. (2013). Pythagorean membership grades in multicriteria decision making. *IEEE Transactions on Fuzzy Systems*, *22*(4), 958–965. doi:10.1109/TFUZZ.2013.2278989

Yager, R. R., & Abbasov, A. M. (2013). Pythagorean membership grades, complex numbers, and decision making. *International Journal of Intelligent Systems*, *28*(5), 436–452. doi:10.1002/int.21584

Yu, C., Shao, Y., Wang, K., & Zhang, L. (2019). A group decision making sustainable supplier selection approach using extended TOPSIS under interval-valued Pythagorean fuzzy environment. *Expert Systems with Applications*, *121*, 1–17. doi:10.1016/j.eswa.2018.12.010

Yucesan, M., & Gul, M. (2020). Hospital service quality evaluation: An integrated model based on Pythagorean fuzzy AHP and fuzzy TOPSIS. *Soft Computing*, *24*(5), 3237–3255. doi:10.100700500-019-04084-2

Zhang, X. L., & Xu, Z. S. (2014). Extension of TOPSIS to multiple criteria decision making with Pythagorean fuzzy sets. *Int. J. Inter. Syst.*, *29*(12), 1061–1078. doi:10.1002/int.21676

KEY TERMS AND DEFINITIONS

Alternative (A): Different options in the context of certain actions, which are present for decision makers.

Criteria (C): Properties used to evaluate alternatives.

Fuzzy Set: A set of ordered pairs composed of the elements and corresponding degrees of membership to this set.

Multi-Criteria Decision Making (MCDM): MCDM is a research discipline that explicitly considers multiple criteria in decision-making process.

Pythagorean Fuzzy (PF): It was proposed by Yager (2013) and in some cases developed as a generalization to intuitive fuzzy sets.

Technique for Order Preference by Similarity to Ideal Solution (TOPSIS): It is a multi-criteria decision-making technique developed by Hwang and Yoon.

Chapter 13

The Impact of News on Public–Private Partnership Stock Price in China via Text Mining Method

Poshan Yu
Soochow University, China

Zhenyu Xu
Independent Researcher, China

ABSTRACT

In data analytics, the application of text analysis is always challenging, in particular, when performing the text mining of Chinese characters. This study aims to use the micro-blog data created by the users to conduct text mining and analysis of the impact of stock market performances in China. Based upon Li's instance labeling method, this chapter examines the correlation between social media information and a public-private partnership (PPP)-related company stock prices. The authors crawled the data from EastMoney platform via a web crawler and obtained a total of 79,874 language data from 10 January 2017 to 28 November 2019. The total material data obtained is 79,616, which the authors use for specific training in the financial corpus. The findings of this chapter indicate that the investor investment sentiment has a certain impact on the stock price movement of selected stocks in the PPP sector.

INTRODUCTION

Text mining is a process of extracting effective, novel, useful, comprehensible and valuable knowledge scattered in text files, and then using the knowledge to organize information better. At the end of 1998, the first batch of national key research and development projects in China clearly pointed out that text mining is an important part of "image, language, natural language understanding and knowledge mining". Text mining is a multidisciplinary field, covering a variety of technologies, including data mining

DOI: 10.4018/978-1-7998-4963-6.ch013

technology, information extraction, information retrieval, machine learning (ML), natural language processing (NLP), computational linguistics, statistical data analysis, linear geometry, probability theory and even graph theory.

In data analysis technology, the application of text analysis is always challenging, in particular, the text mining of Chinese characters. This study aims to use the micro-blog data created by the users to carry out text mining and analysis of the impact of stock market performances. Based upon Li's instance labeling method (Li et al., 2014), this paper examines the correlation between social media information and selected public-private partnership (PPP) related company's stock prices in China. This paper contributes by focusing upon the impact of user sentiment on stock prices via using user-generated data for Chinese micro-blogs for share performance analysis.

MARKET OVERVIEW OF CHINA'S ML INDUSTRY

Definition and Classification of ML

ML refers to the discipline that specializes in how computers simulate or implement human learning behaviors to acquire new knowledge or skills, allowing computers to reorganize the existing knowledge structure and continuously improve their performance. ML is based on data, searching for rules by studying sample data, and predicting future data based on the rules obtained. ML is the core of artificial intelligence (AI), a wide range of AI fields such as data mining, computer vision, NLP, and biometric recognition.

(1)   According to different learning modes, ML can be divided into supervised learning, unsupervised learning and reinforcement learning:

① The training data of supervised learning has classification labels. The higher the accuracy of the classification label, the higher the accuracy of the learning model. Supervised learning establishes a function model based on the given training data to realize the annotation mapping of the new data. Supervised learning algorithms include regression and classification, and application areas include NLP, information retrieval, text mining, handwriting recognition, spam detection, etc.

② Unsupervised learning uses unlabeled limited data to describe the structure or law hidden in the data. Its typical algorithm is clustering. Unsupervised learning does not need to use manually labeled data as training samples, and avoids classification errors caused by positive sample offset and negative sample offset. Application areas of unsupervised learning include economic forecasting, anomaly detection, data mining, image processing, pattern recognition, etc.

③ Reinforcement learning refers to a learning mode that maximizes the return of the subject in the process of interaction with the environment. The purpose of reinforcement learning is to achieve the best evaluation of the agent through the external environment. Reinforcement learning is widely used in robot control, unmanned driving, industrial control and other fields.

(2)   According to the depth of the algorithm network, ML can be divided into shallow learning and deep learning:

① The number of hidden layers of the shallow learning algorithm network is small, the algorithm framework is simple, and there is no need to extract multi-level abstract features. Typical shallow learning includes support vector machines, logistic regression and so on.

② Deep learning is a self-learning method based on multi-layer neural networks and large amounts of data as input rules. It relies on a large amount of actual behavior data provided to it, that is, the training data set, to adjust the parameters and rules in the rules. The deep learning algorithm network has many hidden layers and complex algorithms. Compared with shallow learning, deep learning pays more attention to the importance of feature learning. Typical deep learning algorithms include convolutional neural networks, recurrent neural networks and so on.

The Market Size of China's ML Industry

Since 2006, the promotion and application of deep learning has gradually accelerated, and the field of application has continued to expand, gradually becoming the mainstream algorithm in the field of ML. Driven by the development of deep learning, the proportion of ML in the AI application market rose from 9.6% in 2014 to 12.2% in 2018. The AI market has grown from 7.17 billion yuan in 2014 to 33.90 billion yuan in 2018, with a compound annual growth rate of 47.5%.

In the context of accelerating and increasing the proportion of ML applications, the development of ML has further accelerated.

ML is widely used in multiple vertical fields such as finance, education, healthcare, industry, retail, energy, etc. From 2014 to 2018, the average market price of ML application projects in each vertical field was between 5 million yuan and 5.8 million yuan. Calculating the average market price and the number of ML projects in each vertical field, the market size of China's ML industry has grown from 870 million yuan in 2014 to 5.25 billion yuan in 2018, with a compound annual growth rate of 56.7%. With the continuous improvement of ML algorithms, its application in various vertical fields will be further deepened, and ML application projects in various vertical fields will also continue to increase. It is estimated that by 2023, the ML market will reach 33.67 billion yuan. The compound annual growth rate in 2023 will reach 46.3%, according to Leadleo Institute.

Policies and Regulations Related to China's ML Industry

Clear policy orientation is an important driving factor for the development of China's ML industry. Many important industry plans issued by the Chinese government have put forward relevant development requirements and guidelines for the ML industry, which has strongly promoted the further development of the industry.

In July 2015, the State Council issued the "Guiding Opinions on Actively Promoting the "Internet +" Action", proposing the construction of a new type of computing cluster that supports ultra-large-scale deep learning, and building a massive training resource database including voice, image, video, and map data. The policy aims to strengthen the construction of innovative platforms such as basic AI resources and public services. In August 2015, the State Council issued the "Big Data Development Action Plan", proposing to support AI technology innovations such as natural language understanding, ML, and deep learning to improve data analysis and processing capabilities, knowledge discovery capabilities, and decision-making assistance capabilities.

In March 2016, the Ministry of Industry and Information Technology, the National Development and Reform Commission, and the Ministry of Finance jointly issued the "Robot Industry Development Plan (2016-2020)", proposing to focus on the research of basic and cutting-edge technologies such as AI and robotic deep learning. In the future, robots will realize the leapfrog development of the robot industry and breakthroughs in the universal control software platform for humans. Core technologies, such as machine coexistence, safety control, highly integrated joints, and dexterous hands were highlighted. In May 2016, the National Development and Reform Commission, the Ministry of Science and Technology, the Ministry of Industry and Information Technology, and the Central Cyberspace Administration jointly issued the "Internet +" AI three-year action implementation plan, proposing to build a new computing cluster sharing platform and cloud to meet deep learning and other intelligent computing needs. Basic resource service platforms, such as intelligent analysis and processing service platform, algorithm and technology open platform, intelligent security public service platform and the platform for basic identity authentication with multi-biometric identification function, are highligthed.

In July 2017, the State Council issued the "New Generation AI Development Plan", proposing to focus on breakthroughs in adaptive learning, autonomous learning and other theoretical methods, to achieve AI with high interpretability, and to break through the learning of quantum accelerators methods, as well as to establish a hybrid model of high-performance computing and quantum algorithms, forming an efficient, accurate and autonomous quantum AI system.

In November 2017, the State Council issued the "Guiding Opinions on Deepening the "Internet + Advanced Manufacturing" Development of the Industrial Internet", proposing that efforts should be made to improve the integration and innovation level of data analysis algorithms and industrial knowledge, mechanisms, and experience, and form product groups in different industries. Industrial field data analysis software and systems, and industrial intelligence software and solutions, using AI technologies, such as deep learning, are highlighted. In December 2017, the Ministry of Industry and Information Technology issued the "Three-year Action Plan for Promoting the Development of the New Generation of AI Industry (2018-2020)", proposing the use of ML technology to improve the accuracy and practicality of intelligent translation systems, and support the application of ML technology in smart home products will improve the level of intelligence of home appliances, smart network equipment and other products. It promotes to develop high-performance, high-scalability, and low-power cloud neural network chips for ML training.

In November 2018, the Ministry of Industry and Information Technology issued the "Work Plan for Announcement of Key Tasks for New Generation AI Industry Innovation." The tasks announced in the field of neural network chips are: the development of cloud neural network chips for ML training applications, the development of neural network chips for ML computing terminal applications, and the development of industrialized supporting tools, such as compilers, driver software, and development environments and other chips that support neural networks.

Based upon the above-mentioned policies, it demonstrates that Chinese government aims to promote the application of ML & AI to enhance the industrial development.

The Ethics of the Asset Management Industry Requires a "White Box" Model

Let's imagine if you are an investor, are you willing to hand over your assets to a group of unclear so-called "AI" algorithms for management and operation? The high complexity and low interpretability of ML algorithms determine that it is difficult for human beings to understand most of the time.

Table 1. Summary of Regulations about China's ML industry

Date	Authorities	Policy	Implications
July 2015	State Council.	"Guiding Opinions on Actively Promoting the "Internet +" Action".	Build a new computing cluster that supports ultra-large-scale deep learning, build a massive training resource library including voice, image, video, and map data, and strengthen the construction of innovative platforms, such as, AI basic resources and public services.
August 2015	State Council.	"Outline of Action to Promote the Development of Big Data".	Support AI technology innovations such as natural language understanding, ML, and deep learning, and improve data analysis and processing capabilities, knowledge discovery capabilities, and decision-making assistance capabilities.
March 2016	Jointly issued by the Ministry of Industry and Information Technology, the National Development and Reform Commission, and the Ministry of Finance.	"Robot Industry Development Plan (2016-2020)".	It is necessary to focus on the research of basic cutting-edge technologies such as AI and robot deep learning, and make breakthroughs in core technologies such as general robot control software platforms, human-machine coexistence, safety control, highly integrated joints, and dexterous hands.
May 2016	Jointly issued by the National Development and Reform Commission, the Ministry of Science and Technology, the Ministry of Industry and Information Technology, and the Central Cyberspace Administration of China.	"Internet +" AI Three-year Action Implementation Plan".	Build basic resource service platforms such as a new computing cluster sharing platform that meets the needs of intelligent computing such as deep learning, a cloud intelligent analysis and processing service platform, an algorithm and technology open platform, an intelligent security public service platform, and a basic identity authentication platform for multiple biometric identification.
July 2017	State Council.	"New Generation AI Development Plan".	It is necessary to focus on breakthroughs in theoretical methods such as adaptive learning and autonomous learning to realize AI with high interpretability and strong generalization ability. It is necessary to break through quantum-accelerated ML methods and establish a hybrid model of high-performance computing and quantum algorithms to form efficient and autonomous quantum AI system architecture.
November 2017	State Council.	"Guiding Opinions on Deepening "Internet + Advanced Manufacturing" and Developing Industrial Internet".	Efforts should be made to improve the integration and innovation level of data analysis algorithms and industrial knowledge, mechanism, and experience, and form a batch of industrial data analysis software and systems for different industrial scenarios, and industrial intelligent software and solutions with AI technologies such as deep learning.
December 2017	Ministry of Industry and Information Technology.	"Three-year Action Plan for Promoting the Development of the New Generation of AI Industry (2018-2020)".	It is necessary to use ML technology to improve the accuracy and practicability of the intelligent translation system, support the application of ML technology in smart home products, and improve the intelligence level of products, such as home appliances and smart network equipment.
November 2018	Ministry of Industry and Information Technology.	"Working plan for unveiling the key tasks of the new generation of AI industry innovation".	The task of unveiling the list in the field of neural network chips is: research and development of cloud neural network chips for ML training applications, development of terminal neural network chips suitable for ML calculations for terminal applications, research and development of compilers, driver software, and development for neural network chips Industrialization support tools such as the environment.

Sources: *State Council; Ministry of Industry and Information Technology; National Development and Reform Commission; Ministry of Finance and Central Cyberspace Administration of China*

This "black box" attribute of ML may not pose a problem in some industries. However, the particularity of the asset management industry is that asset managers are obliged to understand and inform the clients of the risks of their investment strategies. At this time, the interpretability of the model becomes particularly important. The ethics of the asset management industry requires an explainable "white box" model.

The urgent need to discover ML black boxes does not only exist in the asset management industry. In the medical field, doctors want to understand how ML algorithms "think", especially when the diagnosis they give is contrary to medical common sense. For instance, ML study uses 14,199 pneumonia patients as samples to explore pneumonia deaths. Patients with pneumonia and asthma have a lower risk of death than those without asthma. The abnormal conclusion that "asthma is a protective factor for patients with pneumonia". (Cabitza et al., 2017)

What is the reason for this abnormal conclusion? Subsequent, more in-depth studies have found that people with pneumonia and asthma are more likely than those without asthma to go directly to the intensive care unit (ICU) to prevent complications. This measure could reduce mortality by nearly half. However, ML algorithms do not characterize the probability of entering the ICU, but only data mining on the relationship between existing sample features and labels. If you don't open the black box of ML models and don't understand the "thinking" process of ML models, the diagnostic results of using ML directly can be more risky. (Cabitza et al., 2017)

In the final analysis, even in recent years, the current AI algorithms have been developed rapidly in the deep neural network and linear regression. There is no fundamental difference between them, but the sample feature x and label y are still fitted. The difference is that the ML model is more nonlinear. AI has no real intelligence. In the medical domain example above, the model can only understand the relationship between features and tags, but cannot mine causal relationships. The same is true for the health sector and the investment sector.

Scholars in the field of ML have noticed the explanatory nature of models, and in recent years researchers have proposed many ways to reveal the "black boxes" of ML models.

TEXT MINING AND ITS APPLICATION IN CHINA

Text Mining

Text mining is a branch of information mining, which is used for knowledge discovery based on text information. Text mining uses intelligent algorithms such as neural network, case-based reasoning, possibility reasoning, etc., and combines with word processing technology to analyze a large number of unstructured text sources (such as documents, spreadsheets, customer e-mails, question queries, web pages, etc.), extract or mark the concept of keywords and the relationship between words, and classify documents, according to their contents.

Get Useful Information, Knowledge and Information

Text mining is roughly composed of three parts: Consolidation is the basic field of text data mining, including ML, mathematical statistics and NLP; on this basis, it is the basic technology of text data mining. There are mainly five categories, including text information extraction, text classification, text clustering, text data compression, and text data processing; the above-mentioned basic technologies are two main application areas, including information acquisition and knowledge discovery.

Information acquisition includes information retrieval, information browsing, information filtering, information reporting, and knowledge discovery, including data analysis and data prediction. Among them, text information extraction and content classification require a lot of manpower and material resources. Especially for Chinese, keywords in different fields and industries are different. Therefore, it is particularly important to establish a keyword database suitable for different industries.

With the dynamic development of text mining in English, the application of text mining in Chinese has attracted more researcher's attention. Due to the particularity of Chinese text structure, more research on Chinese text mining is needed.

Characteristics of Chinese Text Mining

First of all, Chinese text is not separated like English word space, so it can not be directly like English that can directly use the simplest space and punctuation mark to complete word segmentation. Therefore, we generally need to use word segmentation algorithm to complete word segmentation when conducting Chinese text mining.

Second, the Chinese code is not UTF-8, but Unicode. This will lead to the word segmentation, compared with English, we have to deal with the coding problem.

Preprocessing Process of Chinese Text Mining

Data Collection

Before text mining, we need to get text data. There are generally two ways to get text data: Using corpora made by others and crawling their own corpus on the internet with crawlers.

For the first method, there are many commonly used text corpora on the internet. If you just study, you can download them directly for use. However, if it is a corpus of some special topics, such as the corpus related to "ML", this method will not work. We need to use the second method to obtain it.

For the second way to use crawlers, there are many open source tools. General crawlers generally use beautiful soup. However, we need some special corpus data. For example, the corpus related to "ML" mentioned above needs to be completed by using topic crawler (also known as focused crawler). Generally, ache, that is a web crawler for domain-specific search, is used. Ache allows us to use keywords or a classification algorithm to filter out the topic corpus we need, which is more powerful.

Focused Crawler

A focused crawler is a web crawler that selectively crawls pages related to predefined topics. It includes a page crawling module, page analysis module, link filtering module, page database, URL queue, initial URL set, and link evaluation module and content evaluation module are added.

Crawling strategy: evaluate the importance of page content and links

(1) Crawling strategy based on content evaluation:

Fish search algorithm

Fish Search algorithm is an algorithm that was created for efficient focused web crawler. This algorithm is one of the earliest focused crawling algorithms. Fish Search focused crawling algorithm that was implemented to dynamically search information on the internet. Searching system using fish search algorithm is more efficient than ordinary search systems as it uses a navigation strategy to automatically browse the web, according to Andas Amrin et al. (2015).

Fish search algorithm is based on using the calculation method of text similarity, the query words entered by users are regarded as the topic, and the pages containing query words are regarded as related to the topic. The limitation is that it is unable to evaluate the relevance between the page and the topic. As pointed out by Andas Amrin et al. (2015), Crawling and downloading web documents through the WWW may be significantly time consuming, which is unacceptable for users. The usage of resources of network is occasionally considered terrifically high. Compared to ordinary users visiting webpages and reading documents the fish search crawlers significantly loads not only network, also web servers. The algorithm can only retrieve documents for which URL's are found in other web pages. It means that this algorithm can not search documents from the "hidden" web.

Shark search algorithm

The shark search algorithm that is a content-based theme crawling algorithm uses the space vector model to calculate the relevance between the page and the topic.

(2) Crawler strategy based on link structure evaluation:

PageRank algorithm: the larger the PageRank value, the more important it is
HITS algorithm: by calculating the authority weight (authority type) and hub (center type) weight of each page to evaluate the importance of links

(3) The crawling strategy based on reinforcement learning introduces reinforcement learning into crawler, classifies hyperlinks according to the whole web page text and link text, and calculates the importance of each link.
(4) The crawling strategy based on context map is as follows

A ML system is trained by setting up context graph to learn the correlation between web pages. The distance between current page and related web page can be calculated by this system, and the closer the distance is, the better the link in the page will be visited first.

The crawler's definition of a topic is neither keyword nor weighted vector, but a set of web pages with the same theme.

It includes two important modules: classifier and purifier

Classifier: used to calculate the relevance between the crawled page and the topic to determine whether it is related to the topic

Purifier: used to identify central pages that are linked to a large number of related pages with fewer links

Remove non text parts of data

This step is mainly aimed at the corpus data collected by crawlers. Since there are many HTML tags in the crawled content, they need to be removed. A small amount of non text content can be directly removed with Python regular expression (RE), and complex content can be removed with beautiful soup that is a Python library designed for quick turnaround projects like screen-scraping. It is capable of pulling data out of HTML and XML files. After removing the non textual content, we can do real text preprocessing.

Dealing with Chinese coding

Because Python 2 does not support Unicode processing, the principle we need to follow when using Python 2 for Chinese text preprocessing is to use UTF-8 for storing data, and use GBK for Chinese encoding when reading out.

Chinese word segmentation

There are many commonly used Chinese word segmentation software, and we recommend stuttering segmentation. The installation is also very simple. For example, based on python, it can be completed with "PIP install Jieba". According to Data Science at New York University Shanghai, "Jieba" (Chinese for "to stutter") refers to Chinese text segmentation built to be the best Python Chinese word segmentation module.

```
import jieba

for i in range(3):
    with open('./doc%d.txt'%(i+1), 'r', encoding="utf-8") as f1:
        document = f1.read()
        document_cut = jieba.cut(document)
        result = ' '.join(document_cut)
        print(result)
        f1.close()
        with open('./result%d.txt'%(i+1), 'w', encoding="utf-8") as f2:
            f2.write(result)
            f2.close()
```

Introduction of stop words

When analysing text, there are many invalid words, such as "zhe", "he", and some punctuation marks, which we do not want to introduce in the text analysis, so we need to remove them. These words are stop words. Stop words uploaded to resources.

Feature processing

Now, we can use two methods of text preprocessing, namely, hashing and trilink. Vectorization is the most commonly used method, because it can be followed by TF-IDF feature processing. With the feature vector of TF-IDF of each text, we can use these data to establish classification model, clustering model, or topic model analysis.

Based on the dynamic semantic structure of Chinese text, it is important to analyze the text sets with different temporal characteristics, models and analyzes the understanding of content and dynamic evolution relationship, so as to strengthen the topic relevance and low redundancy of content, and improve the novelty and fluency of text content based on understanding.

For instance, the new securities law in China, effective as of 1 March, 2020, puts forward new requirements of "concise, clear and easy to understand" for information disclosure of listed companies, and puts forward higher requirements for the "readability" of information disclosure contents such as announcements of listed companies. It indicates that only relying on high-quality information form, information content can be transmitted to information users in an accurate, clear and concise way. High quality information forms thus help to break the shackles of information interpretation of information users, i.e. improving the decision-making quality of information users in the capital market and promoting the full flow of market elements and the effective allocation of resources. It is of great significance to realize investor protection, improve the efficiency of capital market operation and promote the high-quality development of economy.

In this connection, Dai et al. (2019) showed using the text data of online stock market forum and stock trading data, the composite index of investor sentiment in Shanghai stock exchange can improve the accuracy of stock index trend prediction, which is conducive to better decision-making of government, online platform, listed companies and investors. It is proved that the composite index model of investor sentiment based on SVM is more effective for stock index prediction. The same study, that constructs a data-based, scientific and dynamic professional vocabulary containing network language, uses structured interface design to record the structured data of network users, so as to cope with the immature situation of AI technology. However, the complexity of online emotion and the accuracy of emotional vocabulary quantification affect the scientificity of online emotion data measurement.

Wang et al. (2020) indicate that the readability of annual report has a significant positive correlation with stock liquidity. In the enterprises with high degree of marketization and social trust, the positive impact of annual report readability on stock liquidity is more obvious; under the role of institutional investors with strong governance function and information intermediary effect, annual report readability can significantly improve stock liquidity. Based upon the same study, the relationship between annual report readability and stock liquidity from the perspective of text mining would provide new evidence for the related research on the factors of stock liquidity, but the research is not deep enough.

Yang (2020) used emotional analysis to calculate the emotional orientation value of the text, provides a new influencing factor, and then studies the impact of tax incentives and entrepreneurs' market confidence on enterprise investment.

Text Mining Method on Traditional News Media

The use of text mining for text analysis is a popular research method at present. Qian et al. (2019) gets an efficient way to detect potential news events by splitting 14,556 data texts, grouping them to quantization, and inviting experts to annotate them. Katayama and Tsuda (2018) through an analysis of the Nikkei Telecon newsletter from 1963 to 2016, it explores what kinds of news can affect the share prices of listed companies and concludes that the emotional vocabulary on Polar dictionary has an impact on stock prices. Ruan et al. (2020), who used a deep analysis of 1,286,000 data from Sina Finance Channel's monthly issue, has established an investor sentiment index to pre-measure the stock market. Their findings showed that investors' forecasts of future cash flow will contribute to the accuracy of investor sentiment indicators.

De Fortuny et al. (2014) discusses the pros and cons of several widely used text-mining prediction models in the form of a literature review, and concludes that it is difficult to assess external effectiveness using some of these measures. Using a random forecast performance method, they selected 671,751 samples from the mainstream Flemish newspaper in the Netherlands to predict price movements in stocks, to avoid using a single method of forecasting, and suggested that future studies use the techniques of sentiment and technical indicators rather than simple composite performance indicators to validate the conclusions of the trading model. Yu et al. (2013) measured the text relevance of 6888 stocks with 3,236 Yahoo Finance's news, establishing a stock text entropy model based on an emotional keyword combination that can cover more emotional text words and further improve the level of vocabulary classification.

Hiransha et al. (2018) used four deep learning framework methods to analyze the 4861 days of Yahoo Finance's news with AI deep learning, and evaluated the different model effects of the National Stock Exchange of India and the New York Stock Exchange, concluding that the effect of using neural networks to estimate was much better than the ARIMA linear model. Lupiani-Ruiz et al. (2011) has established a search engine for financial news linguistics based on the linguistic web analytics engine, which allows users to make stock estimates by automatically crawling through online financial news and using knowledge entities in financial entities that match news content. The use of onto-the-body filler tools keeps financial subjects up-to-date, and the model is validated on the Spanish stock exchange, with stock data such as the IBEX35 index. Zhao (2019) used Baidu News and Baidu Index as a double demand and supply index, the results show that online news and search have a great impact on the indicator, online news and search and stock performance indicators are positively correlated, private information and turnover and volatility are negatively correlated.

Text Mining Method on Social Media

Social media text mining is a great way to get a direct look at the sentiments of ordinary investors. Zhang et al. (2018) captured 76,455 Chinese A-share news and 7284 Hong Kong stock data and 6,163,056 social media user data for 78 stocks by blocking 76,455 Shares and extracting users' emotions from social media. The common influence of coupling matrix and factor framework on stock price trend is studied, characterized by the prediction of multiple related stocks through commonality. Das et al. (2018) uses 56,0000 Tweets to analyze user data in real time, and user sentiment to predict user behavior, a classification model that self-corrects ongoing data to give a more accurate prediction of the stock price. Mele et al. (2019) used different news media over a four-month span to analyze time-release patterns on different platforms and their timeliness in reporting events, and established a detection model to predict future events, which showed that the model could more accurately and timely discover emerging news topics, and the study found that some news media were more likely to publish news on their official websites than social media platforms.

The study by Li et al. (2017), based on the twitter public sentiment numbers and the Dow Jones index, proposed a SMeDA-SA technique to mine and analyze Twitter data, and the article selected 200 million pieces of data for analysis, improving the accuracy of forecasts for many company stock movements by 70%. The Mahmoudi et al. (2018) study, which looked at the accuracy of emotional recognition patterns, compared the techniques in the latest emotional analysis literature with previous techniques, and used neural network methods to evaluate the results, showed that more accurate decision support systems could significantly improve the emotional classification performance of investors, while emoji inclusions significantly improved the emotional classification in traditional algorithms. Katayama et al. (2019) using the Deep Learning and Economic Corp. library, established the emotional model recognition model of the financial direction, and the results of the Japanese economic observer survey model show that the model is more likely to obtain more news emotional classification than using the traditional polar dictionary.

MORE DISCUSSION ABOUT TEXT MINING METHODS

Definition of NLP

NLP is a discipline that enables computers to automatically analyze and locally express human natural languages by constructing algorithms. NLP is the process by which computers understand and generate natural languages. NLP technology enables computers to recognize, analyze, understand, and generate natural language text (including words, words, sentences, and text). The mechanism of NLP includes two processes: natural language understanding and natural language generation: 1) Natural language understanding: computer understanding of natural language text thoughts and intentions; (2) Natural language generation: the computer uses natural language text to express ideas and intentions.

Natural language understanding and analysis is a hierarchical process, from lexical analysis, syntactic analysis, semantic analysis to pragmatic context analysis: (1) lexical analysis: analyzing every form of vocabulary to obtain language information; (2) synth analysis: analysis of the structure of sentences and phrases, determination of the role of each word and phrase in sentences and their relationships; (3) semantic analysis: find out the meaning of words, structure and the combined meaning of words and structures, determine the true meaning of language; (4) context analysis: analysis of the impact of the language's external environment on language users.

Self-Build NLP Tools

There are many methods of text mining, the more common methods are NLP and neural network text classification. The current market has also appeared a lot of AI-based emotional analysis software, these software can be text content classification, and quantitative processing, according to a large amount of data training or use of existing corpus training analysis. Stanford University opened up a natural language analysis software package in 2018. By using StanfordNLP, a Python language, that allows users to easily transform human natural text language into a list of sentences and words. StanfordNLP helps generate word attribute and lexical features for those words, which currently supports more than 70 human languages. It also provides 53 pre-trained human language neural model, thus greatly reduces the difficulty of the user to establish the NLP model and design algorithm. (Qi et al, 2018)

In addition, Stanford University has the open source tool Stanford CoreNLP, a Java language-based natural language management technology tool that is an upgrade to Stanford NLP, which includes features such as Standford NLP and word-to-word tag POS, and named entity recognizer NER parser. For emotional analysis, Stanford University officials provided users with six trained natural language packs, including English, Arabic, French, Chinese, German and Spanish. Users can localize the NLP of text locally or as a Web service, greatly improving the speed and efficiency of NLP. Manning, etc. (2014)

TextBlob is a Python-based open source text data processing library that uses NLTK and Pattern as basic support tools, and is very lightweight and can be used to drill down into tasks of NLP, such as word tagging, phrase extraction emotional analysis, classification and translation processing, which provides users with a simple API that users can easily call for NLP. (Loria, 2018) SnowNLP is an open source library based on Python's NLP class, unlike TextBlob, SnowNLP has developed its own core algorithm for NLP and provided Chinese text processing capabilities, SnowNLP also comes with a number of trained Chinese dictionaries for direct call, and users can also provide their own library for model training to achieve the function of NLP, thus providing Chinese words, Word labeling, emotional analysis, text classification, and extraction of text keywords and other related functions.

Commercial NLP Tools

Natural text processing has also become a commercial product of many Internet cloud computing service providers, especially Amazon, IBM Watson, Alibaba Cloud NLP, Tencent Cloud NLP and many other NLP tools that provide direct services by providing data input interfaces without the need to establish User's own NLP learning model. Users can use data for neural network learning, and only need to input data to receive corresponding processing content. Purchasing and billing are carried out according to the number of calls or according to the package, and the cost is relatively low, which is suitable for quickly realizing the function of natural language text analysis. The NLPIR Big Data Semantic Intelligent Analysis Platform is a NLP tool launched by the Big Data Search and Mining Laboratory of Beijing Institute of Technology, which integrates precise network collection, natural language understanding, text mining and network search technologies. It provides NLP tools for multiple platforms, multiple operating systems, and multiple languages, and provides services through free trials and commercial licenses. It is powerful and suitable for large enterprises and universities. (Zhou and Zhang, 2003)

NLP Technology Application

With the in-depth development of AI, the demand for NLP continues to increase in China. Many types of intelligent applications require NLP technology to help various sectors achieve intelligence. (1) search engines, information retrieval, machine translation, automatic summarization, and text classification in the text field, opinion mining, public opinion analysis, automatic examination system, information filtering and spam processing applications;

2) voice assistants, intelligent customer service, chat robots, automatic question and answer, intelligent commentary, and intelligent remote teaching applications in the voice field require NLP technology to understand or generate natural language.

PUBLIC PRIVATE PARTNERSHIP-RELATED STOCK PRICE CHANGE PREDICTION BASED ON TEXT MINING

Stock Data

We choose the stocks related to PPP concept plate of iFinD database for model training, and the selection is based on the share trading turnover, indicating the stock liquidity on the market. We refer to social media content as user-generated content (UGC) that contains an important part of communication via social media. We selected one of the important PPP-related stocks, namely China State Construction Engineering Corp Ltd (601668:Shanghai), as a proxy for our analysis. We crawled the data from East-Money platform (http://stock.eastmoney.com/) via a web crawler and obtained a total of 79,874 language data from 10 January, 2017 to 28 November, 2019. Regarding data cleaning, we removed data that didn't make any sense, including, pure numbers, pure punctuation, and other data rows. The total material data obtained is 79,616, which we will use for specific training in the financial corpus.

Classification Accuracy Calculation

Because the data through crawlers and sentiment analysis is relatively scattered, the work of data classification becomes particularly important. To ensure the accuracy of classification, we use a confusion matrix to evaluate the implementation of the model. This gives us a comprehensive view of how the classification model performs and the types of errors that are generated.

We used the confusion matrix calculation tool that comes with the Scikit Learn library for Python to calculate the classification accuracy of the model (Kotu and Deshpande, 2019). We started by splitting the data into prediction arrays and actual arrays.

We binarized the sentiment data and the changes in stock prices. Assuming that when the emotion is greater than a certain level, it is negative and recorded as 0; when the emotion is greater than that level, it is positive and recorded as 1.

By inputting two arrays of 0.5 (actual) and 0.04 (predicted) into Sklearn's confusion matrix calculation model, we get the following confusion matrix:

```
from sklearn.metrics import confusion_matrix
cm = confusion_matrix(array_actual,array_predict)
accuracy = 100-((FP+FN)*100/len(array_predict))

print("False Positive (Type I Error) :",cm[0][1])
print("False Negative (Type II Error):",cm[1][0])
print("Accuracy:" ,accuracy,'%')

# Output
[[545 145]
 [ 6 7 ]]
False Positive (Type I Error): 145
False Negative (Type II Error): 6
Accuracy: 78.52062588904694%
```

Type I error is 145, which means that the stock price is not actually rising, but the model predicts that the price will rise.

Type II error is 6, which means that the stock price has actually risen, but the model does not predict a rise.

Among the 703 predictions, the model made 151 incorrect predictions and 552 correct predictions. Therefore, the accuracy of the model is 78.52%, and the accuracy is 55.62 at the level of 0.5 (actual) and 0.04 (predicted). We believe that the classification is good enough for the text analysis.

Methodology

From a large number of texts, text mining is used to find interesting information (Cheng et al., 2015; Nguyen et al., 2015). Text mining is a method of mining valuable data from unstructured text. It is also known as knowledge discovery in text (KDT) or intelligent text analysis knowledge (Collier 2012). Text mining is a process of extracting data from structured and unstructured texts to discover interesting patterns (Feldman and Dagan, 1995). Text mining has served as one of the trend research fields and has been incorporated into various research areas including information retrieval, computational linguistics and data mining (Salloum et al. 2017).

In the text mining stage, we divide the task into several steps: the first step is word frequency analysis, so as to obtain the overall view of the stock at the macro level; The second is corpus training. The financial corpus is trained through artificial analysis of word segmentation data and SnowNLP's own sentiment analysis corpus, and the financial corpus sentiment analysis model that will be used for prediction is trained. The third part is empirical analysis. By using the self-built financial corpus sentiment analysis model, the sentiment analysis is performed on the stock review data of the existing PPP sector to obtain quantitative data, which is aligned with the stock price on the corresponding date. We used SPSS software to perform correlation analysis and regression analysis on the two, and drew an analysis of the impact of our PPP concept stock review on the PPP concept stock price.

Word Frequency Analysis

First, we use Python word frequency analysis to perform word frequency statistics on stock review data, so as to see the overall view of the stock from the macro, we first consolidated more than 70,000 comment data, used regular expressions to remove unwanted symbols, and used our own Chinese word dictionary, as shown in the figure.

We remove some words that look at individually and do not have any emotional expression, and finally we have more than 70,000 comment data for word-breaking and word frequency statistics, we counted the first 2000 words, these words are emotional-oriented words, we will use artificial labeling and natural language emotional analysis methods to classify the positivity and negativity of words in the next step, we have built a financial emotional database data. As shown in the figure.

We get the vocabulary before the frequency of 2000. Next we will use the financial corpus data for the corpus training

Language Library Training

We follow the word polarization classification in Zhang et al. (2017) and classify words in corpus data into several categories according to the norms of NLP: positive, neutral, and negative, and Wu (2018) using different data labeling methods, we use crowdsourced methods for positive and negative word labeling of their data. Crowdsourcing data processing speed is faster and simpler. The data processing can be controlled by multiple packet matching. We filtered 2000 data for preliminary use, removing the

Table 2. Self-built particle dictionary (partial)

的	千	需要	人	看	被	不	把
和	万	你	高	就	点	又	呢
是	亿	我	低	谁	将	还	这个
随着	不	啊	做	太	到	要	来
对于	来	也	给	得	想	元	个
对	去	有	出	前	让	大	走
等	让	就	比	后	才	小	上
能	才	吧	啦	与	没有	十	下
都	一	这	你们	或	年	百	为
会	二	吗	着	非	月	了	走
在	什么	如果	多	中	日	通常	少

more frequently used symbols, numbers, and other content, and finally obtained a total of 1985 preliminary vocabulary. We subcontracted it through the questionnaire website, which was divided into 19 small packages, each with three options: positive, neutral and negative, manually packaged in the form of paid questionnaires, collected 32 labels, consolidated in batches through Python's xlrd module, and eventually collected 361 positive words and 291 negative words in the financial sector, as shown in the figure.

We will use SnowNLP's own training module library training to generate files with marshall as an extension, and we will use the library model for emotional analysis of stock review data for China State Construction Engineering Corp Ltd (601668:Shanghai). SnowNLP's own emotional analysis method uses the simple Bayesian algorithm for emotional classification, simple Bayesian is an extension of Bayesian classification, suitable for document classification of common algorithms, its advantages are that in the case of having insufficient data can still be used. The disadvantage is that the input data is prepared in a more sensitive manner and requires nominal data for data training. Users can quickly get started SnowNLP, using self-built language library for emotional evaluation, here we call the already trained financial corpus for empirical analysis.

Table 3. Self-built Finance word corpus(partial)

1	中国	11	股	21	再	31	卖
2	建筑	12	好	22	股票	32	涨停
3	中建	13	主力	23	融资	33	开始
4	今天	14	就是	24	投资	34	快
5	跌	15	资金	25	价值	35	散户
6	买	16	砸	26	分红	36	现在
7	垃圾	17	股价	27	公司	37	这么
8	涨	18	买入	28	没	38	股市
9	明天	19	跑	29	业绩	39	一个
10	大盘	20	大笑	30	大家	40	可以

Table 4. Negative and positive word corpus(partial)

怂	坑		献花	龙头
假	骂		买进	收盘
拉圾	不要脸		大单	雄起
挂	没戏		涨停	风景
倒	套牢		利好	加油
不行	崩盘		消息	看好
余额	股灾		发	持有
差	连跌		鼓掌	希望
不知	补跌		红盘	涨点

Empirical Analysis

We first configured SnowNLP using a self-built financial library, performed an emotional analysis of 79874 comment data on a case-by-case basis, and obtained a data sheet with statement comments, release times, publishers, and emotional analysis. Due to the uneven volume of comment data per day, we will not use a single comment content here as an indicator of investor sentiment, and we use the emotional classification method in Li (2017) paper, which calculates the actual emotional tendency by calculating all comment data for each day as a whole, using the number of texts of positive or negative tendencies. We matched this nearly 80,000 pieces of data in chronological order, and then used the model designed in Li's paper to analyze the emotions of investors on each trading day, and obtained specific data on the emotional trends of investors on each trading day from 10 January, 2017 to 28 November, 2019. Since the Chinese stock market is trading in a T1 mode[1], we will use the t-day's emotional analysis data to align with the t+1-day stock ups and downs to assess the extent to which investor sentiment affects stock prices.

After aligning the data, we used SPSS software to analyze the correlation between 703 aligned investment sentiments and stock data, Our findings revealed that there was a significant correlation between

Table 5. Aligned sentiment and stock change data (partial)

Date	Sentiment	Up / Down
2018/10/23	0.411128	0.0174
2018/10/22	0.376446	-0.019
2018/10/21	0.318353	0.0394
2018/10/18	0.383544	0.0222
2018/10/17	0.375592	-0.0294
2018/10/16	0.432411	0.0139
2018/10/15	0.435698	-0.0098
2018/10/14	0.46891	-0.0136
2018/10/11	0.415748	0.0118

Figure 1. Quantitative emotion and stock fitting curve

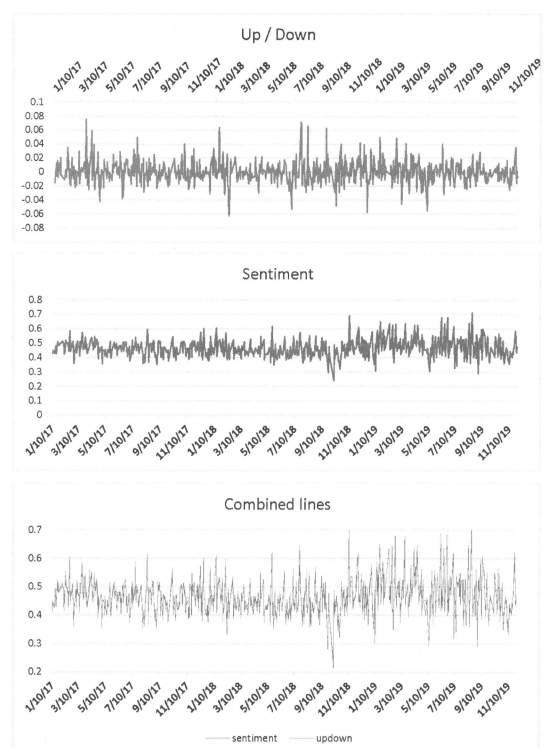

Table 6. SPSS descriptive and correlation statistical analysis

Descriptive Statistics			
	Average	Standard deviation	Number of cases
Sentiment	0.46120126	0.0584657	703
Up / down	-0.000181	0.0160929	703
Correlation			
		Sentiment	Up / down
Sentiment	Pearson Relevance	1	.121**
	Significance (2-tailed)	0.001	
	Sum of squares and cross product	2.4	0.08
	Covariance	0.003	0
	Number of cases	703	703
Up / Down	Pearson Relevance	.121**	1
	Significance (2-tailed)	0.001	
	Sum of squares and cross product	0.08	0.182
	Covariance	0	0
	Number of cases	703	703
At the 0.01 level (2-tailed), the correlation is significant.			

variables within the 0.01 significance range, i.e. investment sentiment had an effect on changes in share prices.

FUTURE RESEARCH DIRECTIONS

This paper studies the trading behavior of stocks by using user-built big data to explore the influence of investment sentiment on the stock price change of PPP. However, the following shortcomings remain in this study:

We need more data in the financial corpus. Subject to budget constraints, 80,000 pieces of metadata are not sufficient to build a complete financial sentiment library. Future research about corpus could further expand the number of crowdsourcing, reduce the corresponding crowd, and improve the accuracy of the corpus through manual screening. The potential problem of using Naive Bayes algorithm is the assumption of all predictors (or features) are independent that rarely occurs in real life. Naive Bayes algorithm faces a "zero frequency problem" of assigning zero probability to categories in the test dataset that are not available in the training dataset. As such, more sophisticated models natural language semantic processing algorithm for conducting the similar analysis could be developed. Future research could seek to overcome the limitations of this study via using more advanced algorithms to improve the accuracy of emotional recognition, such as recurrent neural network (Zhang, 2018).

CONCLUSION

This paper studies the impact of financial stock reviews on the stock's ups and downs. First, by capturing stockholder reviews as corpus metadata, using word segmentation software to segment them, afterwards we use subcontracting to perform artificial sentiment annotation to build a two-category financial corpus, and then use the Naive Bayes algorithm-based Python natural language learning tool extension SnowNLP to train data on a self-built corpus. We use the trained sentiment processing model to conduct stock reviews of China State Construction Engineering Corp Ltd (601668:Shanghai) from 10 January, 2017 to 28 November, 2019. Investment sentiment analysis was applied to obtain quantitative investment sentiment data, and then use this data to align with the stock rise and fall data corresponding to T+1 day requirement. Finally, we used SPSS software to analyze the correlation between the two variables, and the result was significantly correlated. Our findings indicated that the investor's investment sentiment has a certain impact on the stock price movement of China State Construction Engineering Corp Ltd stocks in the PPP sector.

REFERENCES

Amrin, A., Xia, C., & Dai, S. (2015). Focused Web Crawling Algorithms. *Journal of Computers*, *10*(4), 245–251. Advance online publication. doi:10.17706/jcp.10.4.245-251

Cabitza, F., Rasoini, R., & Gensini, G. F. (2017). Unintended consequences of machine learning in medicine. *Journal of the American Medical Association*, *318*(6), 517–518. doi:10.1001/jama.2017.7797 PMID:28727867

Cheng, Q., Lu, X., Liu, Z., & Huang, J. C. (2015). Mining research trends with anomaly detection models: The case of social computing research. *Scientometrics*, *103*(2), 453–469. doi:10.100711192-015-1559-9

Collier, N. (2012). Uncovering text mining: A survey of current work on web-based epidemic intelligence. *Global Public Health: An International Journal for Research, Policy and Practice*, *7*(7), 731–749. doi:10.1080/17441692.2012.699975 PMID:22783909

Dai, D., Lan, Y., Fan, T., & Zhao, M. (2019). Research on stock index prediction and decision-making based on text mining and machine learning. *China Soft Science*, *4*, 166–175.

Das, S., Behera, R. K., Kumar, M., & Rath, S. K. (2018). Real-Time Sentiment Analysis of Twitter Streaming data for Stock Prediction. *Procedia Computer Science*, *132*, 956–964. doi:10.1016/j.procs.2018.05.111

De Fortuny, E. J., De Smedt, T., Martens, D., & Daelemans, W. (2014). Evaluating and understanding text-based stock price prediction models. *Information Processing & Management*, *50*(2), 426–441. doi:10.1016/j.ipm.2013.12.002

Feldman, R., & Dagan, I. (1995). Knowledge discovery in textual databases (KDT). *First International Conference on Knowledge Discovery (KDD'95)*, 112-117.

Hiransha, M., Gopalakrishnan, E. A., Menon, V. K., & Soman, K. (2018). NSE stock market prediction using deep-learning models. *Procedia Computer Science*, *132*, 1351–1362. doi:10.1016/j.procs.2018.05.050

Katayama, D., Kino, Y., & Tsuda, K. (2019). A method of sentiment polarity identification in financial news using deep learning. *Procedia Computer Science*, *159*, 1287–1294. doi:10.1016/j.procs.2019.09.298

Katayama, D., & Tsuda, K. (2018). A method of measurement of the impact of japanese news on stock market. *Procedia Computer Science*, *126*, 1336–1343. doi:10.1016/j.procs.2018.08.084

Kotu, V., & Deshpande, B. (2019). *Data Science* (2nd ed.). Morgan Kaufmann.

Li, B., Chan, K. C., Ou, C., & Ruifeng, S. (2017). Discovering public sentiment in social media for predicting stock movement of publicly listed companies. *Information Systems*, *69*, 81–92. doi:10.1016/j.is.2016.10.001

Li, X., Xie, H., Chen, L., Wang, J., & Deng, X. (2014). News impact on stock price return via sentiment analysis. *Knowledge-Based Systems*, *69*, 14–23. doi:10.1016/j.knosys.2014.04.022

Loria, S. (2018). Textblob Documentation. *Release 0.15, 2*.

Lupiani-Ruiz, E., García-Manotas, I., Valencia-García, R., García-Sánchez, F., Castellanos-Nieves, D., Fernández-Breis, J. T., & Camón-Herrero, J. B. (2011). Financial news semantic search engine. *Expert Systems with Applications*, *38*(12), 15565–15572. doi:10.1016/j.eswa.2011.06.003

Mahmoudi, N., Docherty, P., & Moscato, P. (2018). Deep neural networks understand investors better. *Decision Support Systems*, *112*, 23–34. doi:10.1016/j.dss.2018.06.002

Manning, C. D., Surdeanu, M., Bauer, J., Finkel, J., Bethard, S. J., & McClosky, D. (2014). The Stanford CoreNLP natural language processing toolkit. Association for Computational Linguistics (Acl) System Demonstrations, 55–60. doi:10.3115/v1/P14-5010

Mele, I., Bahrainian, S. A., & Crestani, F. (2019). Event mining and timeliness analysis from heterogeneous news streams. *Information Processing & Management*, *56*(3), 969–993. doi:10.1016/j.ipm.2019.02.003

Nguyen, H. L., Woon, Y. K., & Ng, W. K. (2015). A survey on data stream clustering and classification. *Knowledge and Information Systems*, *45*(3), 535–569. doi:10.100710115-014-0808-1

Qi, P., Dozat, T., Zhang, Y., & Manning, C. D. (2018). Universal dependency parsing from scratch. *Proceedings of the CoNLL 2018 Shared Task: Multilingual Parsing from Raw Text to Universal Dependencies*, 160–170.

Qian, Y., Deng, X., Ye, Q., Ma, B., & Yuan, H. (2019). On detecting business event from the headlines and leads of massive online news articles. *Information Processing & Management*, *56*(6), 102086. doi:10.1016/j.ipm.2019.102086

Qiao, K., & Dam, L. (2020). The overnight return puzzle and the "T+1" trading rule in Chinese stock markets. *Journal of Financial Markets*, *50*, 100534. doi:10.1016/j.finmar.2020.100534

Ruan, Q., Wang, Z., Zhou, Y., & Lv, D. (2020). A new investor sentiment indicator (isi) based on artificial intelligence: A powerful return predictor in China. *Economic Modelling*, *88*, 47–58. doi:10.1016/j.econmod.2019.09.009

Salloum, S. A., Al-Emran, M., Monem, A. A., & Shaalan, K. (2017). A survey of text mining in social media: Facebook and Twitter perspectives. *Advances in Science. Technology and Engineering Systems*, *2*(1), 127–133. doi:10.25046/aj020115

Wang, Y., He, K., Wan, L., & Xie, X. (2020). Research on Annual Report Readability and Stock Liquidity Based on the Perspective of Text Mining. *Securities Market Herald*, *7*, 61–71.

Wu, Y. (2018). *Study and application on fine-grained sentiment analysis of financial microblog* (Master's thesis). South China University of Technology.

Yang, Y., & Yang, B. (2020). Tax incentives, entrepreneurial market confidence and corporate investment: An empirical study based on text mining of annual reports of listed companies. *Taxation Research*, *7*, 86–94.

Yu, L. C., Wu, J. L., Chang, P. C., & Chu, H. S. (2013). Using a contextual entropy model to expand emotion words and their intensity for the sentiment classification of stock market news. *Knowledge-Based Systems*, *41*, 89–97. doi:10.1016/j.knosys.2013.01.001

Zhang, X., Zhang, Y., Wang, S., Yao, Y., Fang, B., & Philip, S. Y. (2018). Improving stock market prediction via heterogeneous information fusion. *Knowledge-Based Systems*, *143*, 236–247. doi:10.1016/j.knosys.2017.12.025

Zhang, Z., Chen, Z., & Yan, H. (2017). *Stock prediction: A method based on extraction of news features and recurrent neural networks.* Papers 1707.07585, arXiv.org.

Zhang, D. (2018). *The application of sentiment analysis in finance corups* (Master's thesis). Jinan University.

Zhao, R. (2019). Inferring private information from online news and searches: Correlation and prediction in Chinese stock market. *Physica A*, *528*, 121450. doi:10.1016/j.physa.2019.121450

Zhou, L., & Zhang, D. (2003). NLPIR: A theoretical framework for applying natural language processing to information retrieval. *Journal of the American Society for Information Science and Technology*, *54*(2), 115–123. doi:10.1002/asi.10193

KEY TERMS AND DEFINITIONS

Artificial Intelligence (AI): It refers to a system or machine that imitates human intelligence to conduct tasks, and can continuously improve itself according to the collected information.

Crawler: Crawlers or web crawlers, also known as web spiders, are web bots that automatically allow users browse the World Wide Web. Web crawlers let users save the pages they visit so that search engines can generate indexes afterwards for use.

Deep Learning: It is a data-based learning algorithm based on artificial neural networks. Deep learning is an algorithm that represents learning based on data in ML.

Machine Learning (ML): ML is a branch of artificial intelligence. ML is a way to realize AI. By using ML, users may solve AI problems. ML theory is mainly about designing and analyzing algorithms that enable computers to "learn" automatically. ML algorithm, as a means, allow users to predict unknown data.

Natural Language Processing (NLP): NLP allows computer users to convert input languages into interesting symbols and relationships that are then processed for purpose. NLP helps users explore how to handle natural languages, which include many aspects and steps, including cognition, understanding, and generation. Natural language generation systems convert computer data into natural languages.

Public-Private Partnership (PPP): A co-operation between government and social capital is a public infrastructure project operation mode. Under this model, private enterprises, private capital and the government are encouraged to participate in the construction of public infrastructure. Broadly speaking, PPP refers to the participation of non-public sector resources in the provision of public products and services in the process of co-operation between the government and the private sector, which generates more beneficial results to partners than expected individual actions.

Text Mining: Text mining (also called text analysis) is the process of converting unstructured text data into meaningful and actionable information. Text mining uses different AI technologies to automatically process data and generate valuable insights, enabling companies to make data-driven decisions.

ENDNOTE

[1] T+1 trading is an asymmetric restriction that prohibits traders from selling the shares they bought on the same day, yet they are allowed to buy shares they sold earlier in the day. The rule was implemented immediately when the Shanghai Stock Exchange and the Shenzhen Stock Exchange were established in December 1990. The average overnight return in Chinese stock markets is negative, according to Qiao and Dam (2020).

Chapter 14
Ergonomic Criteria Based Material Handling Equipment Selection

Burak Efe
Necmettin Erbakan University, Turkey

ABSTRACT

Material handling refers to the processes of loading materials onto a material handling equipment, moving from one location to another location with the help of material handling equipment, and unloading the material from the transportation equipment to the relevant location. Non-ergonomic material handling equipment for the employee causes the increment of cycle time that does not add value to the product during transportation within the enterprise. The increase in cycle time causes an increase in fatigue and inefficiency in the employee. This study evaluates five material handling equipment based on eight ergonomic criteria by using interval type-2 fuzzy TOPSIS method. Interval type-2 fuzzy number provides to examine the fuzziness and the uncertainty more accurately than type-1 fuzzy number, which handles only one crisp membership degree. The opinions of experts are aggregated by employing interval type-2 fuzzy number operators.

INTRODUCTION

Globalization and technology have been very developed and serious recently. With the rapid development of technology, competition between companies is also increasing rapidly. Firms are working to reduce their costs and increase their profit shares in order to survive in this competitive environment and increase their market share. Reaching customers faster and providing better service are among the goals of the companies. With the rapid development of technology, it is now an imperative that factories switch to automation under difficult competitive conditions, increasing production speed, product quality and also reducing production costs. Employee health is very important because of the risk of injury if they bear heavy loads. The use of material handling equipment is important for businesses in this respect.

Kay (1998) examined the material handling equipment in 5 different categories.

DOI: 10.4018/978-1-7998-4963-6.ch014

1. Transport equipment: These are the equipment used to transport the material from one location to another location.
2. Positioning equipment: These are the equipment that enables management and positioning on one location of the material.
3. Unit load formation equipment: These are the limiting equipment that protects the integrity of the materials during transportation and stocking.
4. Storage equipment: These are the equipment used to store the material in a certain place for a while.
5. Identification and control equipment: These are the equipment used to coordinate and track the movements of materials within the facility between facilities, suppliers and customers.

Lifting, transporting heavy objects, performing some movements continuously, and realizing work in the inappropriate posture causes physical strain in workers. Many workers carry risks associated with the musculoskeletal system as they do not properly use body mechanics when lifting loads. Awareness can be raised on these workers with the right position lifting training. Ramazzini realized that some dangerous devices could enter the body through breathing and skin, and show harmful effects on the body, and noise could cause hearing loss. However, besides the physical and chemical properties of the study area, he also wrote that there is a large group of diseases related to posture, repetitive movements and heavy lifting. Musculoskeletal system diseases have a high impact on the individual's well-being and quality of life. Chronic pain associated with musculoskeletal diseases affect many aspects of life and reduces quality of life. It causes chronic pain due to musculoskeletal diseases and impaired physical and mental health causes impairment of social functions (Aslan, 2019; Franco, 1999).

Businesses want to reduce costs, keep workforce efficient, and keep equipment investment at a low level by keeping minimum level transactions with no added value. One of the most common transactions with no added value within the enterprise is the transportation of materials. Material handling operations prevent efficient utilization of the facility area and it also causes the additional costs for businesses. Material handling refers to the processes of loading materials onto a material handling equipment, moving from one location to another location with the help of material handling equipment, and unloading the material from the transportation equipment to the relevant location. The most important element of the material handling process is the equipment used in the process. When the equipment market is analyzed, it is seen that there is a wide variety of material handling equipment. As the variety of equipment increases, selection criteria also vary. When more than one criterion is considered in the selection of equipment, the selection of equipment can be evaluated as a multi-criteria decision making problem (Dur, 2019).

Reflecting customer / consumer demands on product design is not a new idea. After World War II, the European economy started to grow steadily, and new competitors from countries outside Europe were included in the market in the early 1970s. As a result of the competition created by Japanese enterprises, especially in the European market, the product range increased and the quality of the products increased. Customers were also affected by these developments, resulting in a selective customer profile with a high level of expectation. Thus, the manufacturer-oriented approach has lost its effect in product design and new approaches are being sought. As a result, the idea of customer / consumer oriented product design has gained importance since the early 1990s. Taking into account the customer / consumer requests during the design phase of the product will reduce the cost and provide the product to be largely free of usability problems by eliminating the usability problems that are difficult to return if it is detected later (Koç, 2009). In this competitive environment, production systems have become increasingly complex with the continuous development of technology. The complexity of production systems has increased the material flows within the system and has brought an increase in the time required to carry the material. Due to the importance of material transportation, academic studies on the subject have increased rapidly from past to present. The product will be ready for shipment in a timely manner and efficiency will be achieved by reducing the activities that do not create added value. The material transportation is carried out with a minimum resource consumption to minimize the risk of loss of life and property (Tunç, 2013).

New product design is a costly process. It is a set of processes that require effective market research. Research and development studies are carried out for successful design. In the present age, borders between countries have disappeared and a global market environment has been created. Due to the technological developments experienced in this process, the physical quality differences between the products have also disappeared. Customers who can choose from many product types with the same quality standards were also affected by these developments in the market. Today, a customer profile has emerged that "selects in purchasing" and "buys products that cater to their expectations". Therefore, in this market environment, businesses should listen to the voice of their customers and produce products that will meet their demands / needs in order to be "preferred". Taking into account customer requests in product design will (i) guide the creation of purchased / preferred products (ii) reduce the cost by providing usability problems. As a result, if businesses want to continue their lives in this global market environment, they should invest in the design of products that will meet the wishes and needs of customers, appeal to their perceptions / feelings, and create a sense of purchase in the customer (Koç, 2009). The requests, needs and feelings of customer/consumer are determined and products are designed accordingly in customer / consumer oriented product design. After product design, customer / consumers receive feedback about the product. This ensures that customer / consumers actively participate in the product design process.

Specifying a single value in the legislation on the subject will bring a simpler perspective to the problem and may cause other factors to be ignored. In addition, it would not be correct to give a fixed weight information due to the wide variety of employee profiles in different working conditions. The capacities of each employee are different from each other. However, a number of numerical data is also needed to obtain information about the general situation of the working activity. The weights of different heights will be depending on the distance from the body. It was created by assuming that the activity was carried out in a fixed body position with two hands (Ireland), 2005).

Chakraborty and Banik (2006) used AHP approach to select the best material handling equipment among alternatives. Mohamadghasemi et al. (2020) presented an integrated group fuzzy weighted average-ELECTRE III approach for material handling equipment selection. Tuzkaya et al. (2010) used fuzzy ANP to define the weights of criteria and fuzzy PROMETHEE method to rank material handling equipments. Karande and Chakraborty (2013) recommended the weighted utility additive theory to select the most suitable material handling equipment. Kausar et al. (2019) employed the modified fuzzy TOPSIS method to evaluate the best maintenance strategy of material handling equipment. Mathew and Sahu (2018) handled different multi criteria decision making methods to evaluate the material handling equipments. Nguyen et al. (2016) used fuzzy AHP approach to determine the importance degrees of criteria in conveyor selection problem. They presented fuzzy ARAS approach to rank the alternatives. Sen et al. (2017) introduced fuzzy AHP method for bulk material handling equipment selection. Mousavi et al. (2014) presented fuzzy grey approach for material handling equipment selection. Interval type-2 fuzzy number based TOPSIS method has been used in different areas such as mobile phone selection (Efe et al., 2020), website evaluation (Efe, 2019), measuring the innovation capacities of financial institutions (Jun et al., 2020), analysis of spiritual leadership and ethical climate for banking industry (Dinçer et al., 2020), Fine–Kinney-based occupational risk assessment (Gül et al., 2020).

Experts can express their opinions more easily and accurately using linguistic variables. Interval type-2 fuzzy number provides to examine the fuzziness and the uncertainty more accurately than type-1 fuzzy number, which handles only one crisp membership degree. TOPSIS approach is intuitive, easy to examine the opinions of the experts. The interval type-2 fuzzy number based TOPSIS method uses the interval type-2 fuzzy numbers to evaluate the alternatives in contrast to crisp numbers in TOPSIS method. The judgments of decision makers about the importance degrees of criteria and criteria based alternative are aggregated by using interval type-2 fuzzy number operators. This study evaluates five material handling equipments based on eight ergonomic criteria.

PRELIMINARIES

$\widetilde{\widetilde{A}}_1$ and $\widetilde{\widetilde{A}}_2$ are trapezoidal IT2F numbers (Chen and Lee, 2010), where

$$\widetilde{\widetilde{A}}_1 = (\tilde{A}_1^U, \tilde{A}_1^L) = ((a_{11}^U, a_{12}^U, a_{13}^U, a_{14}^U; H_1(\tilde{A}_1^U), H_2(\tilde{A}_1^U)), (a_{11}^L, a_{12}^L, a_{13}^L, a_{14}^L; H_1(\tilde{A}_1^L), H_2(\tilde{A}_1^L)))$$

and

$$\widetilde{\widetilde{A}}_2 = (\tilde{A}_2^U, \tilde{A}_2^L) = ((a_{21}^U, a_{22}^U, a_{23}^U, a_{24}^U; H_1(\tilde{A}_2^U), H_2(\tilde{A}_2^U)), (a_{21}^L, a_{22}^L, a_{23}^L, a_{24}^L; H_1(\tilde{A}_2^L), H_2(\tilde{A}_2^L))).$$

Eqs. (1)-(4) presents the addition, multiplication, multiplication with crisp number k, and exponent operations. These operations are presented as follows:

$$\widetilde{\widetilde{A}}_1 \oplus \widetilde{\widetilde{A}}_2 = (\tilde{A}_1^U, \tilde{A}_1^L) \oplus (\tilde{A}_2^U, \tilde{A}_2^L) = ((a_{11}^U + a_{21}^U, a_{12}^U + a_{22}^U, a_{13}^U + a_{23}^U, a_{14}^U + a_{24}^U; \\ \min\{H_1(\tilde{A}_1^U), H_2(\tilde{A}_1^U)\}), (a_{11}^L + a_{21}^L, a_{12}^L + a_{22}^L, a_{13}^L + a_{23}^L, a_{14}^L + a_{24}^L; \min\{H_1(\tilde{A}_1^L), H_2(\tilde{A}_1^L)\})) \tag{1}$$

$$\widetilde{\widetilde{A}}_1 \otimes \widetilde{\widetilde{A}}_2 = (\tilde{A}_1^U, \tilde{A}_1^L) \otimes (\tilde{A}_2^U, \tilde{A}_2^L) = ((a_{11}^U \times a_{21}^U, a_{12}^U \times a_{22}^U, a_{13}^U \times a_{23}^U, a_{14}^U \times a_{24}^U; \\ \min\{H_1(\tilde{A}_1^U), H_2(\tilde{A}_1^U)\}), (a_{11}^L \times a_{21}^L, a_{12}^L \times a_{22}^L, a_{13}^L \times a_{23}^L, a_{14}^L \times a_{24}^L; \min\{H_1(\tilde{A}_1^L), H_2(\tilde{A}_1^L)\})) \tag{2}$$

$$k \times \widetilde{\widetilde{A}}_1 = k \times (\tilde{A}_1^U, \tilde{A}_1^L) = ((k \times a_{11}^U, k \times a_{12}^U, k \times a_{13}^U, k \times a_{14}^U; H_1(\tilde{A}_1^U)), (k \times a_{11}^L, k \times a_{12}^L, k \times a_{13}^L, k \times a_{14}^L; H_1(\tilde{A}_1^L))) \tag{3}$$

where *k>0*.

$$(\widetilde{\widetilde{A}}_1)^k = (\tilde{A}_1^U, \tilde{A}_1^L)^k = (((a_{11}^U)^k, (a_{12}^U)^k, (a_{13}^U)^k, (a_{14}^U)^k; H_1(\tilde{A}_1^U)), ((a_{11}^L)^k, (a_{12}^L)^k, (a_{13}^L)^k, (a_{14}^L)^k; H_1(\tilde{A}_1^L))) \tag{4}$$

The rank calculation is presented in Eq. (5) as follows (Lee and Chen, 2008):

$$Rank\left(\tilde{\tilde{A}}_i\right) = M_1\left(\tilde{A}_i^U\right) + M_1\left(\tilde{A}_i^L\right) + M_2\left(\tilde{A}_i^U\right) + M_2\left(\tilde{A}_i^L\right) + M_3\left(\tilde{A}_i^U\right) + M_3\left(\tilde{A}_i^L\right) - \frac{1}{4}\left(S_1\left(\tilde{A}_i^U\right) + S_1\left(\tilde{A}_i^L\right) + S_2\left(\tilde{A}_i^U\right)\right. \tag{5}$$
$$\left. + S_2\left(\tilde{A}_i^L\right) + S_3\left(\tilde{A}_i^U\right) + S_3\left(\tilde{A}_i^L\right) + S_4\left(\tilde{A}_i^U\right) + S_4\left(\tilde{A}_i^L\right)\right) + H_1\left(\tilde{A}_i^U\right) + H_1\left(\tilde{A}_i^L\right) + H_2\left(\tilde{A}_i^U\right) + H_2\left(\tilde{A}_i^L\right)$$

$M_p\left(\tilde{A}_i^j\right)$ *shows the mean value.*

$$M_p\left(\tilde{A}_i^j\right) = \left(a_{ip}^j + a_{i(p+1)}^j\right)/2, \, 1 \le p \le 3.$$

$S_q\left(\tilde{A}_i^j\right)$ shows the standard deviation value.

$$S_q\left(\tilde{A}_i^j\right) = \sqrt{\frac{1}{2}\sum_{k=q}^{q+1}\left(a_{ik}^j - \frac{1}{2}\sum_{k=q}^{q+1}a_{ik}^j\right)^2}, \, 1 \le q \le 3,$$

$$S_4\left(\tilde{A}_i^j\right) = \sqrt{\frac{1}{4}\sum_{k=1}^{4}\left(a_{ik}^j - \frac{1}{4}\sum_{k=1}^{4}a_{ik}^j\right)^2}.$$

$H_p\left(\tilde{A}_i^j\right)$ shows the membership degree of the element $a_{i(q+1)}^j$ in $\tilde{A}_i^j, 1 \le p \le 2, j \in \{U, L\}$, and $1 \pounds i \pounds n$

The calculations of lower and upper possibility mean values are presented in Eqs. (6)-(7) as follows:

$$M_*(\tilde{A}) = \frac{1}{6}(a_1^U + 2a_2^U)h_U^2 + \frac{1}{6}(a_1^L + 2a_2^L)h_L^2 \tag{6}$$

$$M^*(\tilde{A}) = \frac{1}{6}(a_4^U + 2a_3^U)h_U^2 + \frac{1}{6}(a_4^L + 2a_3^L)h_L^2 \tag{7}$$

The possibility degree is calculated in Eq. (8) below (Gong et al., 2015):

$$p(\tilde{A}_1 \succ \tilde{A}_2) = \min\left\{\max\left(\frac{M^*(\tilde{A}_1) - M_*(\tilde{A}_2)}{M^*(\tilde{A}_1) - M_*(\tilde{A}_1) + M^*(\tilde{A}_2) - M_*(\tilde{A}_2)}, 0\right), 1\right\} \tag{8}$$

METHODOLOGY

This study used TOPSIS method developed by Hwang and Yoon (1981). The solution, known as the positive ideal solution in the method, maximizes the benefit criteria and minimizes the cost criteria. An ideal solution can also be defined as the collection of ideal levels (or degrees) in all the criteria considered. However, in general, the ideal solution cannot be reached and the decision maker should choose the one as close as possible to the ideal solution. Chen and Lee (2010) presented TOPSIS approach in Eqs. (9)-(21) as follows:

$$W_l = \left(\tilde{w}_i^l \right)_{1 \times m} = \begin{array}{cccc} f_1 & f_2 & \cdots & f_m \\ \left[\tilde{w}_1^l & \tilde{w}_2^l & \cdots & \tilde{w}_m^l \right] \end{array} \tag{9}$$

$$\tilde{\tilde{w}}_i = \sum_{l=1}^{k} w_l \tilde{w}_i^l \tag{10}$$

Eq. (9) presents that W_l shows the weight of the criteria. w_l is the weight of the decision maker D_l. Eq. (10) shows that $\tilde{w}_i^l$ is the weight of criteria f_i according to the expert D_l.

$$Y_l = (\tilde{f}_{ij}^l)_{m \times n} = \begin{array}{c} f_1 \\ f_2 \\ \vdots \\ f_m \end{array} \begin{bmatrix} \begin{array}{cccc} x_1 & x_2 & \cdots & x_n \end{array} \\ \tilde{f}_{11}^l & \tilde{f}_{12}^l & \cdots & \tilde{f}_{1n}^l \\ \tilde{f}_{21}^l & \tilde{f}_{22}^l & \cdots & \tilde{f}_{2n}^l \\ \vdots & \vdots & \vdots & \vdots \\ \tilde{f}_{m1}^l & \tilde{f}_{m2}^l & \cdots & \tilde{f}_{mn}^l \end{bmatrix} \tag{11}$$

$$\bar{Y} = (\tilde{\tilde{f}}_{ij})_{m \times n} \tag{12}$$

$$\tilde{\tilde{f}}_{ij} = \sum_{l=1}^{k} w_l \cdot \tilde{f}_{ij}^l \tag{13}$$

Eq. (11) means that Y_l shows the decision matrix of the expert D_l. Eq. (12) introduces that $\bar{Y}$ shows the average decision matrix. Eq. (13) presents that w_l is the weight of the expert D_l. $\tilde{f}_{ij}^l$ is the opinion of the expert D_l for $\tilde{\tilde{f}}_{ij}$.

$$\bar{W} = (\tilde{v}_{ij})_{m \times n} = \begin{array}{c} f_1 \\ f_2 \\ \vdots \\ f_m \end{array} \begin{bmatrix} \begin{array}{cccc} x_1 & x_2 & \cdots & x_n \end{array} \\ \tilde{v}_{11} & \tilde{v}_{12} & \cdots & \tilde{v}_{1n} \\ \tilde{v}_{21} & \tilde{v}_{22} & \cdots & \tilde{v}_{2n} \\ \vdots & \vdots & \vdots & \vdots \\ \tilde{v}_{m1} & \tilde{v}_{m2} & \cdots & \tilde{v}_{mn} \end{bmatrix} \tag{14}$$

where $\tilde{v}_{ij} = \tilde{w}_i \otimes \tilde{\tilde{f}}_{ij}, 1 \leq i \leq m$, and $1 £ j £ n$. $\bar{W}$ indicates the average weighted matrix in Eq. (14).

Let be $\tilde{v} = (\tilde{v}^U, \tilde{v}^L) = ((v_1^U, v_2^U, v_3^U, v_4^U; h_U), (v_1^L, v_2^L, v_3^L, v_4^L; h_L))$.: The approximate positive and negative ideal solution $x^+ = (v_1^+, v_2^+, ..., v_m^+)$ and $x^- = (v_1^-, v_2^-, ..., v_m^-)$ according to benefit (F_1) and cost criteria (F_2) are presented in Eqs. (15)-(16) as follows:

$$\tilde{v}_i^+ = \begin{cases} \overset{n}{\underset{j=1}{\vee}}\tilde{v}_{1ij}^L, \overset{n}{\underset{j=1}{\vee}}\tilde{v}_{2ij}^L, \overset{n}{\underset{j=1}{\vee}}\tilde{v}_{3ij}^L, \overset{n}{\underset{j=1}{\vee}}\tilde{v}_{4ij}^L, \overset{n}{\underset{j=1}{\wedge}}\left\{H(\tilde{A}_{ij}^L)\right\}, \overset{n}{\underset{j=1}{\vee}}\tilde{v}_{1ij}^U, \overset{n}{\underset{j=1}{\vee}}\tilde{v}_{2ij}^U, \overset{n}{\underset{j=1}{\vee}}\tilde{v}_{3ij}^U, \overset{n}{\underset{j=1}{\vee}}\tilde{v}_{4ij}^U, \overset{n}{\underset{j=1}{\wedge}}\left\{H(\tilde{A}_{ij}^U)\right\}, \; if\; f_i \in F_1 \\ \overset{n}{\underset{j=1}{\wedge}}\tilde{v}_{1ij}^L, \overset{n}{\underset{j=1}{\wedge}}\tilde{v}_{2ij}^L, \overset{n}{\underset{j=1}{\wedge}}\tilde{v}_{3ij}^L, \overset{n}{\underset{j=1}{\wedge}}\tilde{v}_{4ij}^L, \overset{n}{\underset{j=1}{\wedge}}\left\{H(\tilde{A}_{ij}^L)\right\}, \overset{n}{\underset{j=1}{\wedge}}\tilde{v}_{1ij}^U, \overset{n}{\underset{j=1}{\wedge}}\tilde{v}_{2ij}^U, \overset{n}{\underset{j=1}{\wedge}}\tilde{v}_{3ij}^U, \overset{n}{\underset{j=1}{\wedge}}\tilde{v}_{4ij}^U, \overset{n}{\underset{j=1}{\wedge}}\left\{H(\tilde{A}_{ij}^U)\right\}, \; if\; f_i \in F_2 \end{cases} \quad (15)$$

$$\tilde{v}_i^- = \begin{cases} \overset{n}{\underset{j=1}{\wedge}}\tilde{v}_{1ij}^L, \overset{n}{\underset{j=1}{\wedge}}\tilde{v}_{2ij}^L, \overset{n}{\underset{j=1}{\wedge}}\tilde{v}_{3ij}^L, \overset{n}{\underset{j=1}{\wedge}}\tilde{v}_{4ij}^L, \overset{n}{\underset{j=1}{\wedge}}\left\{H(\tilde{A}_{ij}^L)\right\}, \overset{n}{\underset{j=1}{\wedge}}\tilde{v}_{1ij}^U, \overset{n}{\underset{j=1}{\wedge}}\tilde{v}_{2ij}^U, \overset{n}{\underset{j=1}{\wedge}}\tilde{v}_{3ij}^U, \overset{n}{\underset{j=1}{\wedge}}\tilde{v}_{4ij}^U, \overset{n}{\underset{j=1}{\wedge}}\left\{H(\tilde{A}_{ij}^U)\right\}, \; if\; f_i \in F_1 \\ \overset{n}{\underset{j=1}{\vee}}\tilde{v}_{1ij}^L, \overset{n}{\underset{j=1}{\vee}}\tilde{v}_{2ij}^L, \overset{n}{\underset{j=1}{\vee}}\tilde{v}_{3ij}^L, \overset{n}{\underset{j=1}{\vee}}\tilde{v}_{4ij}^L, \overset{n}{\underset{j=1}{\wedge}}\left\{H(\tilde{A}_{ij}^L)\right\}, \overset{n}{\underset{j=1}{\vee}}\tilde{v}_{1ij}^U, \overset{n}{\underset{j=1}{\vee}}\tilde{v}_{2ij}^U, \overset{n}{\underset{j=1}{\vee}}\tilde{v}_{3ij}^U, \overset{n}{\underset{j=1}{\vee}}\tilde{v}_{4ij}^U, \overset{n}{\underset{j=1}{\wedge}}\left\{H(\tilde{A}_{ij}^U)\right\}, \; if\; f_i \in F_2 \end{cases} \quad (16)$$

Ú and Ù indicate max and min, respectively, and 1£i£m.

Eqs. (17)-(18) present lower and upper mean values, respectively. $p(\tilde{v}_i \succ \tilde{v}_i^+)$ and $p(\tilde{v}_i \succ \tilde{v}_i^-)$ are presented in Eqs. (19)-(20).

$$M_*(\tilde{v}_i) = \frac{1}{6}(v_{i1}^U + 2v_{i2}^U)H(\tilde{A}_i^U)^2 + \frac{1}{6}(v_{i1}^L + 2v_{i2}^L)H(\tilde{A}_i^L)^2 \quad (17)$$

$$M^*(\tilde{v}_i) = \frac{1}{6}(v_{i4}^U + 2v_{i3}^U)H(\tilde{A}_i^U)^2 + \frac{1}{6}(v_{i4}^L + 2v_{i3}^L)H(\tilde{A}_i^L)^2 \quad (18)$$

$$p(\tilde{v}_i \succ \tilde{v}_i^+) = \min\left\{\max\left(\frac{M^*(\tilde{v}_i) - M_*(\tilde{v}_i^+)}{M^*(\tilde{v}_i) - M_*(\tilde{v}_i) + M^*(\tilde{v}_i^+) - M_*(\tilde{v}_i^+)}, 0\right), 1\right\} \quad (19)$$

$$p(\tilde{v}_i \succ \tilde{v}_i^-) = \min\left\{\max\left(\frac{M^*(\tilde{v}_i) - M_*(\tilde{v}_i^-)}{M^*(\tilde{v}_i) - M_*(\tilde{v}_i) + M^*(\tilde{v}_i^-) - M_*(\tilde{v}_i^-)}, 0\right), 1\right\} \quad (20)$$

PC_i is calculated in Eq. (21) as follows:

$$PC_i = \frac{\sum_{j=1}^{m} p(\tilde{v}_i \succ \tilde{v}_i^-)}{\sum_{j=1}^{m}\left(p(\tilde{v}_i \succ \tilde{v}_i^-) + p(\tilde{v}_i \succ \tilde{v}_i^+)\right)} \quad (21)$$

Table 1. Linguistic scale

Linguistic term	IT2TrF numbers
Very low (VL)	(0.08,0.11,0.15,0.18;0.8), (0.04,0.09,0.17,0.22;1)
Low (L)	(0.20,0.25,0.33,0.36;0.8), (0.17,0.22,0.38,0.43;1)
Medium (M)	(0.40,0.45,0.54,0.57;0.8), (0.30,0.40,0.60,0.66;1)
High (H)	(0.77,0.80,0.86,0.90;0.8), (0.72,0.75,0.90,0.95;1)
Very high (VH)	(0.95,0.97,0.98,0.99;0.8), (0.92,0.96,0.99,1.00;1)

where 1£*i*£*n*.

APPLICATION OF ERGONOMIC MATERIAL HANDLING EQUIPMENT SELECTION

All of the problems and complications experienced in manufacturing systems are also seen in material handling systems because material handling systems are also part of manufacturing. Manufacturing systems and material handling systems cannot be considered separately. On the other hand, the vehicles to be used in material handling systems should be selected according to the production to be made. Every production has its own methods and processes. The aim of material handling equipment is to reduce the waiting times of the materials and the number of waiting materials. A number of systems have been developed to achieve this aim. Thanks to these systems, the timing of transport of the material is prepared to minimize waiting. The material arrives at the distribution station as soon as it is released. When it is processed or even taken, it is processed as soon as it arrives.

Eight criteria that affecting material handling equipment selection are defined according to the opinions of four experts so that these criteria are purchasing cost (C1), operating cost (C2), end of use value (C3), safety (C4), reliability (C5), ease of maintenance (C6), ergonomic ease of utilization (C7) and suitability of the purchasing goal (C8). TOPSIS approach is employed to evaluate the material handling equipments according to ergonomic criteria under interval type-2 fuzzy number. Four decision makers presented their opinions about the weights of criteria and criteria based alternative by using interval type-2 fuzzy number in Table 1. Five material handling equipments based on eight criteria according to the judgment of each expert are collected. An expert team including E1, E2, E3 and E4 experts is established to evaluate the material handling equipments and their weights are (0.20, 0.20, 0.25, 0.35), respectively.

Interval type-2 fuzzy linguistic scale is shown in Table 1. Four decision makers introduce the importance degree of ergonomic criteria for material handling equipments. Table 2 illustrates these importance degrees according to each expert.

The opinions of four decision makers are aggregated by using the weights of four decision makers. The aggregated group opinion for the weights of criteria is presented in Table 3.

TOPSIS method is employed to assess the material handling equipments according to ergonomic criteria under interval type-2 fuzzy number. Four decision makers presented their opinions about criteria based alternative by using interval type-2 fuzzy number in Table 1. Five material handling equipments based on eight criteria according to the judgment of each expert are presented in Table 4. The aggregated decision matrix for criteria based alternative is introduced in Table 5. Interval type-2 fuzzy number in

Table 2. The judgments of four decision makers about the weights of criteria.

Decision makers	Criteria							
	C1	C2	C3	C4	C5	C6	C7	C8
DM1	VH	H	M	M	M	H	H	M
DM2	H	VH	M	M	H	M	M	H
DM3	H	VH	M	H	M	M	M	H
DM4	VH	H	H	H	H	M	H	M

Table 3. Importance degrees of criteria

Criteria	IT2TrF numbers
C1	(0.8690,0.8935,0.9260,0.9495;0.8),(0.8300,0.8655,0.9495,0.9775;1.0)
C2	(0.8510,0.8765,0.9140,0.9405;0.8),(0.8100,0.8445,0.9405,0.9725;1.0)
C3	(0.5295,0.5725,0.6520,0.6855;0.8),(0.4470,0.5225,0.7050,0.7615;1.0)
C4	(0.6220,0.6600,0.7320,0.7680;0.8),(0.5520,0.6100,0.7800,0.8340;1.0)
C5	(0.6035,0.6425,0.7160,0.7515;0.8),(0.5310,0.5925,0.7650,0.8195;1.0)
C6	(0.4740,0.5200,0.6040,0.6360;0.8),(0.3840,0.4700,0.6600,0.7180;1.0)
C7	(0.6035,0.6425,0.7160,0.7515;0.8),(0.5310,0.5925,0.7650,0.8195;1.0)
C8	(0.5665,0.6075,0.6840,0.7185;0.8),(0.4890,0.5575,0.7350,0.7905;1.0)

Table 1 and the aggregation operator are employed to combine the opinions of experts about criteria based alternative. The weighted decision matrix for criteria based alternative is introduced in Table 6.

Table 4. Evaluation data of alternatives.

	E1					E2					E3					E4				
	A1	A2	A3	A4	A5	A1	A2	A3	A4	A5	A1	A2	A3	A4	A5	A1	A2	A3	A4	A5
C1	VH	H	L	L	H	VH	M	L	L	L	M	M	M	L	M	H	L	M	VL	M
C2	M	VL	M	M	VH	L	H	M	M	VH	L	L	M	M	VH	H	L	M	VL	L
C3	L	VH	M	M	VL	L	VH	H	H	H	M	H	H	H	VH	H	M	M	VL	VH
C4	M	L	M	L	VL	M	L	M	L	VL	M	L	M	L	VL	M	L	M	L	VL
C5	VH	M	L	L	VL	VH	M	L	L	VL	VH	M	L	L	VL	VH	M	L	L	VL
C6	M	VL	M	M	L	M	VL	M	M	L	M	VL	M	M	L	M	VL	M	M	L
C7	L	L	L	M	VL	L	L	L	M	VL	L	L	L	M	VL	L	L	L	M	VL
C8	M	M	L	M	L	M	M	L	M	L	M	M	L	M	L	M	M	L	M	L

Table 5. The aggregated decision matrix

A1	C1	(0.750,0.781,0.828,0.854;0.8),(0.695,0.747,0.861,0.898;1.0)
	C2	(0.440,0.483,0.558,0.591;0.8),(0.389,0.442,0.606,0.658;1.0)
	C3	(0.450,0.493,0.568,0.602;0.8),(0.395,0.451,0.617,0.670;1.0)
	C4	(0.400,0.450,0.540,0.570;0.8),(0.300,0.400,0.600,0.660;1.0)
	C5	(0.950,0.970,0.980,0.990;0.8),(0.920,0.960,0.990,1.000;1.0)
	C6	(0.400,0.450,0.540,0.570;0.8),(0.300,0.400,0.600,0.660;1.0)
	C7	(0.200,0.250,0.330,0.360;0.8),(0.170,0.220,0.380,0.430;1.0)
	C8	(0.400,0.450,0.540,0.570;0.8),(0.300,0.400,0.600,0.660;1.0)
A2	C1	(0.404,0.450,0.531,0.563;0.8),(0.339,0.407,0.583,0.638;1.0)
	C2	(0.290,0.332,0.400,0.432;0.8),(0.254,0.300,0.442,0.492;1.0)
	C3	(0.713,0.746,0.796,0.821;0.8),(0.653,0.712,0.831,0.869;1.0)
	C4	(0.200,0.250,0.330,0.360;0.8),(0.170,0.220,0.380,0.430;1.0)
	C5	(0.400,0.450,0.540,0.570;0.8),(0.300,0.400,0.600,0.660;1.0)
	C6	(0.080,0.110,0.150,0.180;0.8),(0.040,0.090,0.170,0.220;1.0)
	C7	(0.200,0.250,0.330,0.360;0.8),(0.170,0.220,0.380,0.430;1.0)
	C8	(0.400,0.450,0.540,0.570;0.8),(0.300,0.400,0.600,0.660;1.0)
A3	C1	(0.320,0.370,0.456,0.486;0.8),(0.248,0.328,0.512,0.568;1.0)
	C2	(0.400,0.450,0.540,0.570;0.8),(0.300,0.400,0.600,0.660;1.0)
	C3	(0.567,0.608,0.684,0.719;0.8),(0.489,0.558,0.735,0.791;1.0)
	C4	(0.400,0.450,0.540,0.570;0.8),(0.300,0.400,0.600,0.660;1.0)
	C5	(0.200,0.250,0.330,0.360;0.8),(0.170,0.220,0.380,0.430;1.0)
	C6	(0.400,0.450,0.540,0.570;0.8),(0.300,0.400,0.600,0.660;1.0)
	C7	(0.200,0.250,0.330,0.360;0.8),(0.170,0.220,0.380,0.430;1.0)
	C8	(0.200,0.250,0.330,0.360;0.8),(0.170,0.220,0.380,0.430;1.0)
A4	C1	(0.158,0.201,0.267,0.297;0.8),(0.125,0.175,0.307,0.357;1.0)
	C2	(0.288,0.331,0.404,0.434;0.8),(0.209,0.292,0.450,0.506;1.0)
	C3	(0.455,0.489,0.548,0.582;0.8),(0.398,0.449,0.585,0.637;1.0)
	C4	(0.200,0.250,0.330,0.360;0.8),(0.170,0.220,0.380,0.430;1.0)
	C5	(0.200,0.250,0.330,0.360;0.8),(0.170,0.220,0.380,0.430;1.0)
	C6	(0.400,0.450,0.540,0.570;0.8),(0.300,0.400,0.600,0.660;1.0)
	C7	(0.400,0.450,0.540,0.570;0.8),(0.300,0.400,0.600,0.660;1.0)
	C8	(0.400,0.450,0.540,0.570;0.8),(0.300,0.400,0.600,0.660;1.0)
A5	C1	(0.434,0.480,0.562,0.594;0.8),(0.358,0.434,0.616,0.672;1.0)
	C2	(0.688,0.718,0.753,0.770;0.8),(0.658,0.701,0.777,0.801;1.0)
	C3	(0.740,0.764,0.790,0.810;0.8),(0.704,0.744,0.808,0.834;1.0)
	C4	(0.080,0.110,0.150,0.180;0.8),(0.040,0.090,0.170,0.220;1.0)
	C5	(0.080,0.110,0.150,0.180;0.8),(0.040,0.090,0.170,0.220;1.0)
	C6	(0.200,0.250,0.330,0.360;0.8),(0.170,0.220,0.380,0.430;1.0)
	C7	(0.080,0.110,0.150,0.180;0.8),(0.040,0.090,0.170,0.220;1.0)
	C8	(0.200,0.250,0.330,0.360;0.8),(0.170,0.220,0.380,0.430;1.0)

Tables 7 and 8 present the ideal solutions and the mean values, respectively.

Table 9 presents the possibility degrees $p(\tilde{\tilde{v}}_i \succ \tilde{\tilde{v}}_i^+)$ and $p(\tilde{\tilde{v}}_i \succ \tilde{\tilde{v}}_i^-)$.

Table 6. The weighted aggregated decision matrix

A1	C1	(0.651,0.697,0.767,0.810;0.8),(0.577,0.646,0.818,0.877;1.0)
	C2	(0.374,0.423,0.510,0.556;0.8),(0.315,0.373,0.570,0.640;1.0)
	C3	(0.238,0.282,0.370,0.412;0.8),(0.177,0.235,0.435,0.510;1.0)
	C4	(0.249,0.297,0.395,0.438;0.8),(0.166,0.244,0.468,0.550;1.0)
	C5	(0.573,0.623,0.702,0.744;0.8),(0.489,0.569,0.757,0.820;1.0)
	C6	(0.190,0.234,0.326,0.363;0.8),(0.115,0.188,0.396,0.474;1.0)
	C7	(0.121,0.161,0.236,0.271;0.8),(0.090,0.130,0.291,0.352;1.0)
	C8	(0.227,0.273,0.369,0.410;0.8),(0.147,0.223,0.441,0.522;1.0)
A2	C1	(0.351,0.402,0.491,0.534;0.8),(0.281,0.352,0.554,0.623;1.0)
	C2	(0.247,0.291,0.366,0.406;0.8),(0.206,0.253,0.416,0.478;1.0)
	C3	(0.377,0.427,0.519,0.562;0.8),(0.292,0.372,0.586,0.661;1.0)
	C4	(0.124,0.165,0.242,0.276;0.8),(0.094,0.134,0.296,0.359;1.0)
	C5	(0.241,0.289,0.387,0.428;0.8),(0.159,0.237,0.459,0.541;1.0)
	C6	(0.038,0.057,0.091,0.114;0.8),(0.015,0.042,0.112,0.158;1.0)
	C7	(0.121,0.161,0.236,0.271;0.8),(0.090,0.130,0.291,0.352;1.0)
	C8	(0.227,0.273,0.369,0.410;0.8),(0.147,0.223,0.441,0.522;1.0)
A3	C1	(0.278,0.331,0.422,0.461;0.8),(0.206,0.284,0.486,0.555;1.0)
	C2	(0.340,0.394,0.494,0.536;0.8),(0.243,0.338,0.564,0.642;1.0)
	C3	(0.300,0.348,0.446,0.493;0.8),(0.219,0.291,0.518,0.602;1.0)
	C4	(0.249,0.297,0.395,0.438;0.8),(0.166,0.244,0.468,0.550;1.0)
	C5	(0.121,0.161,0.236,0.271;0.8),(0.090,0.130,0.291,0.352;1.0)
	C6	(0.190,0.234,0.326,0.363;0.8),(0.115,0.188,0.396,0.474;1.0)
	C7	(0.121,0.161,0.236,0.271;0.8),(0.090,0.130,0.291,0.352;1.0)
	C8	(0.113,0.152,0.226,0.259;0.8),(0.083,0.123,0.279,0.340;1.0)
A4	C1	(0.137,0.180,0.247,0.282;0.8),(0.103,0.151,0.291,0.348;1.0)
	C2	(0.245,0.290,0.369,0.408;0.8),(0.169,0.246,0.423,0.492;1.0)
	C3	(0.241,0.280,0.357,0.399;0.8),(0.178,0.235,0.412,0.485;1.0)
	C4	(0.124,0.165,0.242,0.276;0.8),(0.094,0.134,0.296,0.359;1.0)
	C5	(0.121,0.161,0.236,0.271;0.8),(0.090,0.130,0.291,0.352;1.0)
	C6	(0.190,0.234,0.326,0.363;0.8),(0.115,0.188,0.396,0.474;1.0)
	C7	(0.241,0.289,0.387,0.428;0.8),(0.159,0.237,0.459,0.541;1.0)
	C8	(0.227,0.273,0.369,0.410;0.8),(0.147,0.223,0.441,0.522;1.0)
A5	C1	(0.377,0.429,0.520,0.564;0.8),(0.297,0.376,0.585,0.657;1.0)
	C2	(0.585,0.629,0.688,0.724;0.8),(0.533,0.592,0.730,0.778;1.0)
	C3	(0.392,0.437,0.515,0.555;0.8),(0.315,0.389,0.570,0.635;1.0)
	C4	(0.050,0.073,0.110,0.138;0.8),(0.022,0.055,0.133,0.183;1.0)
	C5	(0.048,0.071,0.107,0.135;0.8),(0.021,0.053,0.130,0.180;1.0)
	C6	(0.095,0.130,0.199,0.229;0.8),(0.065,0.103,0.251,0.309;1.0)
	C7	(0.048,0.071,0.107,0.135;0.8),(0.021,0.053,0.130,0.180;1.0)
	C8	(0.113,0.152,0.226,0.259;0.8),(0.083,0.123,0.279,0.340;1.0)

Table 7. The approximate positive and negative ideal solutions.

Approximate positive ideal solution	C1	(0.137,0.180,0.247,0.282;0.8),(0.103,0.151,0.291,0.348;1.0)
	C2	(0.245,0.290,0.366,0.406;0.8),(0.169,0.246,0.416,0.478;1.0)
	C3	(0.392,0.437,0.519,0.562;0.8),(0.315,0.389,0.586,0.661;1.0)
	C4	(0.249,0.297,0.395,0.438;0.8),(0.166,0.244,0.468,0.550;1.0)
	C5	(0.573,0.623,0.702,0.744;0.8),(0.489,0.569,0.757,0.820;1.0)
	C6	(0.190,0.234,0.326,0.363;0.8),(0.115,0.188,0.396,0.474;1.0)
	C7	(0.241,0.289,0.387,0.428;0.8),(0.159,0.237,0.459,0.541;1.0)
	C8	(0.227,0.273,0.369,0.410;0.8),(0.147,0.223,0.441,0.522;1.0)
Approximate negative ideal solution	C1	(0.651,0.697,0.767,0.810;0.8),(0.577,0.646,0.818,0.877;1.0)
	C2	(0.585,0.629,0.688,0.724;0.8),(0.533,0.592,0.730,0.778;1.0)
	C3	(0.238,0.280,0.357,0.399;0.8),(0.177,0.235,0.412,0.485;1.0)
	C4	(0.050,0.073,0.110,0.138;0.8),(0.022,0.055,0.133,0.183;1.0)
	C5	(0.048,0.071,0.107,0.135;0.8),(0.021,0.053,0.130,0.180;1.0)
	C6	(0.038,0.057,0.091,0.114;0.8),(0.015,0.042,0.112,0.158;1.0)
	C7	(0.048,0.071,0.107,0.135;0.8),(0.021,0.053,0.130,0.180;1.0)
	C8	(0.113,0.152,0.226,0.259;0.8),(0.083,0.123,0.279,0.340;1.0)

The possibility degree based closeness coefficient PC_i for each alternative is shown in Table 10. A4 is the most suitable material handling equipment according to the results in Table 10.

CONCLUSION

Identification of work-related musculoskeletal diseases requires a certain degree of ergonomics knowledge and skills. Inadequate training prevents employees from identifying and reporting risks related to their job, but also prevents the necessary measures to be taken during the management phase. Ergonomic awareness training is an important step in this context. Education is an important element of effective

Table 8. The lower and upper possibility mean values.

	$M_*(A_{1i})$	$M^*(A_{1i})$	$M_*(A_{2i})$	$M^*(A_{2i})$	$M_*(A_{3i})$	$M^*(A_{3i})$	$M_*(A_{4i})$	$M^*(A_{4i})$	$M_*(A_{5i})$	$M^*(A_{5i})$
C1	0,530	0,669	0,287	0,450	0,229	0,394	0,121	0,238	0,306	0,476
C2	0,307	0,465	0,207	0,340	0,274	0,458	0,198	0,345	0,483	0,597
C3	0,193	0,353	0,304	0,476	0,240	0,421	0,193	0,337	0,317	0,465
C4	0,199	0,379	0,109	0,240	0,199	0,379	0,109	0,240	0,043	0,113
C5	0,465	0,618	0,193	0,371	0,106	0,235	0,106	0,235	0,042	0,111
C6	0,152	0,319	0,033	0,095	0,152	0,319	0,152	0,319	0,083	0,202
C7	0,106	0,235	0,106	0,235	0,106	0,235	0,193	0,371	0,042	0,111
C8	0,181	0,356	0,181	0,356	0,099	0,225	0,181	0,356	0,099	0,225

Table 9. The possibility degrees

	$p(\tilde{\tilde{v}}_{1i} \succ \tilde{\tilde{v}}_i^+)$	$p(\tilde{\tilde{v}}_{1i} \succ \tilde{\tilde{v}}_i^-)$	$p(\tilde{\tilde{v}}_{2i} \succ \tilde{\tilde{v}}_i^+)$	$p(\tilde{\tilde{v}}_{2i} \succ \tilde{\tilde{v}}_i^-)$	$p(\tilde{\tilde{v}}_{3i} \succ \tilde{\tilde{v}}_i^+)$	$p(\tilde{\tilde{v}}_{3i} \succ \tilde{\tilde{v}}_i^-)$	$p(\tilde{\tilde{v}}_{4i} \succ \tilde{\tilde{v}}_i^+)$	$p(\tilde{\tilde{v}}_{4i} \succ \tilde{\tilde{v}}_i^-)$	$p(\tilde{\tilde{v}}_{5i} \succ \tilde{\tilde{v}}_i^+)$	$p(\tilde{\tilde{v}}_{5i} \succ \tilde{\tilde{v}}_i^-)$
C1	1,000	0,500	1,000	0,000	0,969	0,000	0,500	0,000	1,000	0,000
C2	0,890	0,000	0,516	0,000	0,797	0,000	0,509	0,000	1,000	0,500
C3	0,112	0,528	0,480	0,896	0,305	0,701	0,065	0,501	0,481	0,932
C4	0,500	1,000	0,131	0,980	0,500	1,000	0,131	0,980	0,000	0,500
C5	0,500	1,000	0,000	1,000	0,000	0,974	0,000	0,974	0,000	0,500
C6	0,500	1,000	0,000	0,500	0,500	1,000	0,500	1,000	0,175	0,933
C7	0,136	0,974	0,136	0,974	0,136	0,974	0,500	1,000	0,000	0,500
C8	0,500	0,853	0,500	0,853	0,147	0,500	0,500	0,853	0,147	0,500

occupational safety and health programs. Training programs in the fight against work-related musculoskeletal diseases should lead managers, worker leaders and workers to identify risk factors in the workplace and become participants for necessary solutions. Musculoskeletal disorders involve muscles, joints and bone structures. Musculoskeletal diseases caused by work are mostly seen in waist, neck and hand and wrist body parts. Work-related musculoskeletal disease symptoms are pain, swelling, stiffness, lethargy, tingling, loss of coordination, loss of strength. Musculoskeletal system diseases have a high impact on the individual's well-being and quality of life. Chronic pain associated with musculoskeletal diseases affect many aspects of life and reduces quality of life. It causes chronic pain due to musculoskeletal diseases. The impaired physical and mental health causes impairment of social functions. Disruption in recreation activities and social relations of patients, side effects of the medications used, frequent visits to hospitals or clinics lead to limited time spent in the family. The effect of the load on the human body occurs in the form of the body bending forward as the load weight increases. Using ergonomic approaches, changes in the effect and posture on the body under different lifting conditions were carefully studied. The mechanical stretching was revealed by a biomechanical evaluation of the movements of people.

It is inevitable that design processes and understandings, which are a basic human phenomenon, are affected in process of change. The globalization has started to raise the technological developments after 1980s. This has caused a constant change on the life styles. Product designs, which interact with the individual, are examined in the historical process where the same plane is changing. With developing technology and increasing globalization, companies now have to compete with the whole world. Difficult competition conditions force businesses to differentiate in the market, while also reducing their costs. This competitive environment in favor of customers causes them to increase the quality standards of the products and services. In these conditions, it is obligatory for businesses to deliver the products that will meet the expectations of their customers with the most original designs, at the most affordable prices, in the shortest time possible. In order to meet these expectations, businesses face many product

Table 10. The possibility degree based closeness coefficient

	A1	A2	A3	A4	A5
PC_i	0,5859	0,6531	0,6056	0,6624	0,6090
Rank	5	2	4	1	3

design and manufacturing problems. The designed product should also meet customer tastes, cost and manufacturability constraints.

Material handling is defined as the supply of the foreseen material at the right time, in the right place, in the right order, in the right position, in the right conditions, at the desired cost with the right method. Although the time of emergence of material transportation is not known precisely, in the modern sense, the material transportation was born with the industrial revolution. The wooden boxes, which are the most important elements of material transportation until the twentieth century, were replaced by pallets. Equipments such as crates, barrels and barrels are used for storage. Another feature of the barrels is that they are rolled and used in material handling processes in the periods before material handling systems are developed. Drums are also preferred for the transportation of products such as textile products, flour, feed and legumes. Over time, with the progress of transportation, corrugated containers with cheaper and higher strength have been used instead of corrugated boxes.

Many companies attach importance to the selection of material handling equipment and aim to use the most suitable equipment for their processes. Proper handling equipment improves efficiency when moving materials onto production lines. When using unsuitable equipment, waiting times and error rates in production increase. The choice of material handling equipment is a strategic decision for many companies. There are many different material handling equipments in the equipment market and different criteria are evaluated for each type of equipment. This study presents interval type-2 fuzzy number based TOPSIS method for a multi-criteria decision making problem of ergonomic material handling equipment selection. Interval type-2 fuzzy number provides more reality than type-1 fuzzy number for the judgments of decision makers. Interval type-2 fuzzy number is useful to handle uncertainty of decision making problems. This number is used to evaluate the importance degrees of criteria and criteria based alternative by four decision makers. They present their judgments about these evaluations by using linguistic terms. Decision makers handle eight ergonomic criteria and determine the importance degrees of them. This study employs interval type-2 fuzzy number operations to aggregate the opinions of four decision makers so the weights of eight criteria are defined. These weights are used to rank the alternatives in interval type-2 fuzzy number based TOPSIS method. Four decision makers focus on ranking five alternatives according to eight criteria. They introduce their judgments about criteria based alternative by using interval type-2 fuzzy number. These judgments are aggregated by using interval type-2 fuzzy number operations. TOPSIS based on interval type-2 fuzzy number deals with ranking five ergonomic material handling equipments. In future papers, different multi-criteria decision making methods can be used to select the most suitable ergonomic criteria based handling equipment.

REFERENCES

Aslan, İ. H. (2019). *Yük Taşıyan İşçilerde Ergonomik Farkındalık Oluşturmaya Yönelik Verilen Eğitimin Vücut Farkındalığı, Postür Ve Yaşam Kalitesi Üzerine Etkisi* (Master of Science Thesis). İstanbul Okan University.

Chakraborty, S., & Banik, D. (2006). Design of a material handling equipment selection model using analytic hierarchy process. *International Journal of Advanced Manufacturing Technology, 28*(11-12), 1237–1245. doi:10.100700170-004-2467-y

Chen, S. M., & Lee, L. W. (2010). Fuzzy multiple attributes group decision-making based on the interval type-2 TOPSIS method. *Expert Systems with Applications*, *37*(4), 2790–2798. doi:10.1016/j.eswa.2009.09.012

Dinçer, H., Baykal, E., & Yüksel, S. (n.d.). Analysis of spiritual leadership and ethical climate for banking industry using an integrated IT2 fuzzy decision-making model. *Journal of Intelligent & Fuzzy Systems*, 1-13.

Dur, Z. (2019). *AHP'ye Dayalı Bulanık UTASTAR Yaklaşımı: Malzeme Taşıma Ekipmanı Uygulaması* (Master of Science Thesis). Hacettepe University.

Efe, B. (2019). Website Evaluation Using Interval Type-2 Fuzzy-Number-Based TOPSIS Approach. In Multi-Criteria Decision-Making Models for Website Evaluation (pp. 166-185). IGI Global. doi:10.4018/978-1-5225-8238-0.ch009

Efe, B., Yerlikaya, M. A., & Efe, Ö. F. (2020). Mobile phone selection based on a novel quality function deployment approach. *Soft Computing*, *24*(20), 1–15. doi:10.100700500-020-04876-x

Franco, G. (1999). Ramazzini and workers' health. *Lancet*, *354*(9181), 858–861. doi:10.1016/S0140-6736(99)80042-7 PMID:10485743

Gong, Y., Hu, N., Zhang, J., Liu, G., & Deng, J. (2015). Multi-attribute group decision making method based on geometric Bonferroni mean operator of trapezoidal interval type-2 fuzzy numbers. *Computers & Industrial Engineering*, *81*, 167–176. doi:10.1016/j.cie.2014.12.030

Gul, M., Mete, S., Serin, F., & Celik, E. (2020). Fine–Kinney-Based Occupational Risk Assessment Using Interval Type-2 Fuzzy VIKOR. In *Fine–Kinney-Based Fuzzy Multi-criteria Occupational Risk Assessment* (pp. 151–163). Springer.

Health and Safety Authority (Ireland). (2005). *Guidance on the Management of Manual Handling in the Workplace*. Author.

Hwang, C. L., & Yoon, K. (1981). *Multiple attributes decision making methods and applications*. Springer. doi:10.1007/978-3-642-48318-9

Jun, Q., Dinçer, H., & Yüksel, S. (2020). Stochastic hybrid decision-making based on interval type 2 fuzzy sets for measuring the innovation capacities of financial institutions. *International Journal of Finance & Economics*, ijfe.1805. doi:10.1002/ijfe.1805

Karande, P., Chakraborty, S. (2013). Material handling equipment selection using weighted utility additive theory. *Journal of Industrial Engineering*.

Kausar, A., Akram, S., Tabassum, M. F., Ahmad, A., & Khan, S. (2020). The Solution of Maintenance Strategy Selection Problem by using modified Fuzzy TOPSIS for of Material Handling Equipment. *Sukkur IBA Journal of Computing and Mathematical Sciences*, *3*(2), 46–54.

Kay, M. G. (1998). Material Handling Equipment. *Metal Finishing*, *96*(12), 67. doi:10.1016/S0026-0576(98)81337-8

Koç, E. (2009). *Kansei mühendisliği kullanılarak müşteri odaklı ürün tasarımı: Web sayfası tasarımında uygulanması* (Doctoral Dissertation). Eskişehir Osmangazi University.

Lee, L. W., & Chen, S. M. (2008) Fuzzy multiple attributes group decision-making based on the extension of TOPSIS method and interval type-2 fuzzy sets. In *Proceedings of the 2008 international conference on machine learning and cybernetic* (pp. 3260–3265). 10.1109/ICMLC.2008.4620968

Mathew, M., & Sahu, S. (2018). Comparison of new multi-criteria decision making methods for material handling equipment selection. *Management Science Letters*, *8*(3), 139–150. doi:10.5267/j.msl.2018.1.004

Mohamadghasemi, A., Hadi-Vencheh, A., Lotfi, F. H., & Khalilzadeh, M. (2020). An integrated group FWA-ELECTRE III approach based on interval type-2 fuzzy sets for solving the MCDM problems using limit distance mean. *Complex & Intelligent Systems*, 1-35.

Mousavi, S. M., Vahdani, B., Tavakkoli-Moghaddam, R., & Tajik, N. (2014). Soft computing based on a fuzzy grey group compromise solution approach with an application to the selection problem of material handling equipment. *International Journal of Computer Integrated Manufacturing*, *27*(6), 547–569. doi:10.1080/0951192X.2013.834460

Nguyen, H. T., Dawal, S. Z. M., Nukman, Y., Rifai, A. P., & Aoyama, H. (2016). An integrated MCDM model for conveyor equipment evaluation and selection in an FMC based on a fuzzy AHP and fuzzy ARAS in the presence of vagueness. *PLoS One*, *11*(4), e0153222. doi:10.1371/journal.pone.0153222 PMID:27070543

Sen, K., Ghosh, S., Sarkar, B. (2017). Comparison of customer preference for bulk material handling equipment through fuzzy-AHP approach. *Journal of The Institution of Engineers (India): Series C*, *98*(3), 367-377.

Tunç, T. (2013). *Analitik Hiyerarşi Sürecinin Malzeme Taşıma Sistemi Seçiminde Uygulanması* (Master of Science Thesis). Gazi University.

Tuzkaya, G., Gülsün, B., Kahraman, C., & Özgen, D. (2010). An integrated fuzzy multi-criteria decision making methodology for material handling equipment selection problem and an application. *Expert Systems with Applications*, *37*(4), 2853–2863. doi:10.1016/j.eswa.2009.09.004

ADDITIONAL READING

Qin, J., Liu, X., & Pedrycz, W. (2015). An extended VIKOR method based on prospect theory for multiple attribute decision making under interval type-2 fuzzy environment. *Knowledge-Based Systems*, *86*, 116–130. doi:10.1016/j.knosys.2015.05.025

Riaz, M., Hashmi, M. R., Kalsoom, H., Pamucar, D., & Chu, Y. M. (2020). Linear Diophantine Fuzzy Soft Rough Sets for the Selection of Sustainable Material Handling Equipment. *Symmetry*, *12*(8), 1215. doi:10.3390ym12081215

Zhong, L., & Yao, L. (2017). An ELECTRE I-based multi-criteria group decision making method with interval type-2 fuzzy numbers and its application to supplier selection. *Applied Soft Computing, 57*, 556–576. doi:10.1016/j.asoc.2017.04.001

KEY TERMS AND DEFINITIONS

Analytics Intelligence: Aims to present solutions that help firms for complex problems.

Interval Type-2 Fuzzy Number: Refers the interval between two type-1 fuzzy numbers.

Material Handling: Refers to the processes of loading materials onto a material handling equipment, moving from one location to another location with the help of material handling equipment, and unloading the material from the transportation equipment to the relevant location.

TOPSIS Method: Deals with maximizing the benefit criteria and minimizing the cost criteria.

Chapter 15
A Preliminary Framework to Fight Tax Evasion in the Home Renovation Market

Cataldo Zuccaro
University of Quebec in Montreal, Canada

Michel Plaisent
University of Quebec in Montreal, Canada

Prosper Bernard
University of Quebec in Montreal, Canada

ABSTRACT

This chapter presents a preliminary framework to tackle tax evasion in the field of residential renovation. This industry plays a major role in economic development and employment growth. Tax evasion and fraud are extremely difficult to combat in the industry since it is characterized by a large number of stakeholders (manufacturers, retailers, tradesmen, and households) generating complex transactional dynamics that often defy attempts to deploy transactional analytics to detect anomalies, fraud, and tax evasion. This chapter proposes a framework to apply transactional analytics and data mining to develop standard measures and predictive models to detect fraud and tax evasion. Combining big data sets, cross-referencing, and predictive modeling (i.e., anomaly detection, artificial neural network support vector machines, Bayesian network, and association rules) can assist government agencies to combat highly stealth tax evasion and fraud in the residential renovation.

INTRODUCTION

This article introduces the reader to the role of analytics and how governments can fight tax evasion in the construction and home improvement sector. According to the Institute for Operation Research and the Management Sciences (INFORMS, 2017), analytics aims at assisting organizations to fulfill their

DOI: 10.4018/978-1-7998-4963-6.ch015

objectives by using scientific and mathematical methods to analyze their data, describing and enlighten the meaning of past facts, forecasting and giving advice for future decision-making. The following sections will guide the reader on the economic importance of the home improvement market and its underground economies while presenting how analytics is already used in several contexts to combat tax evasion and to present a structured approach, inspired by CRISP–DM methodology (IBM, 2016), that can be applied to tackle the thorny problem of tax evasion in the home renovation industry. After identification of the main sources of data, a list of relevant studies helpful to fight tax evasion is presented.

The 'do-it-yourself' (DIY) home improvement and renovation markets overlap to constitute an important market which is expected to grow in the next years (Reportlinker, 2020). The major players in the market are the stores selling tools and goods (lumber, paint, structural material, electrical, plumbing and heating supplies), trades' people and individual households. To service the needs of its customers, hardware stores in the USA create roughly 668,459 jobs (IBISWord, 2019). On the consumer side, the Harvard's Joint Center for Housing Studies, estimated that roughly 400 billion was spent by homeowners for renovation supplies and equipment in 2017 (Hunter, 2020). A compilation in 2018 by Statista (2020) stated that sales in the home renovation market were already 394 billion USA dollars and in 2019 rose to almost 400 billion dollars. In addition, according to a study by Riquier (2019), the market was expected to grow to 450 billion dollars by 2023 and Bustanete (2018) predicted the market to reach 680 billion dollars by 2025. The retail hardware store market is largely dominated by Home Depot, Lowe's, Menard and McCoy (IBISWord, 2019). The 2018 sales for the main retailers of the USA were estimated (Statista, 2000) at 110 billion dollars for Home Depot, 72 billion dollars for Lowe's and a combined 38 billion dollars for Sherwin-William, Kingfisher and Fastenal (Statista, 2020).

In this very dynamic market, 80% of homeowners will hire someone to do the work according to Bustamante (2018) but only 51% of these would be licensed tradesmen and this is a major problem in detecting fraud and tax evasion in the home renovation market. An experiment conducted by Doeer & Necker (2018) with 2900 business illustrates the extend of this complicity in the home improvement in Germany, in which they found that 56% of businesses responding to an advertising asking for painting services, offered to evade tax payment. Bitzenis et al. (2016) summarize the situation by the fact that the shadow economy overlaps legal, illegal economy and household economy.

Fraud and tax evasion problems with construction are present in many countries that have seen the home renovation market grow dramatically during the last decade. For example, in Quebec, second most populated province of Canada, the market for home renovation is estimated to be nearly 50 billion Canadian dollars (Bedford, 2020) and according to tax and income department Revenu Quebec (2020), the construction industry is responsible for 40% of total tax evasion. In France, hidden work (undeclared but taxable) is responsible for between 6.8 and 8.4 billion euros (Chemin, 2019), and half of which was detected in construction (ACOSS, 2020).

Tax evasion and tax fraud can wreak havoc on the treasuries of most countries. The mean percentage for Europe was estimated to be 18.6% (Scheinder et al., 2015). Two clear examples of this are Italy and Greece where the shadow economy has been estimated respectively to be 22% of GDP and 20% while only 6% in the USA (Vousinas, 2017). In Australia, the shadow economy in the construction industry accounted for 10% for a similar period (Chancellor & Abbot, 2015). A previous study from Cebula & Feige (2012) based on time series from the International Monetary Fund estimated the shadow economy to 18–23% of a country's total revenues.

Obviously, it is impossible to eradicate fraud and tax evasion. There is a need to vigorously pursue and prosecute tax evaders with both the legal and technical tools available to governments. Legal remedies are specific to each country; however, today technical solutions are available to governments to reduce significantly fraud and tax evasion. This is how data mining can come to the rescue.

Data mining is frequently used, and in many cases, successfully, from fraud detection in e-commerce in the USA (Chuprina, 2020) to public purchase contracts of Brazil (Valesco et al., 2020). To tackle with tax evasion, France introduced an innovative approach to risk analysis by targeting companies with a high-risk profile for tax evasion and undeclared work (ACOSS, 2020) . This approach is centered on the use of specific sectorial models developed by exploitation of big data and data mining techniques. These models assign a score (statistically derived risk score) to each company along with the probability of generating a hidden or undeclared work offense (ACOSS, 2020). This approach has also been adopted by some US States (Texas) and many OECD countries (Wu et al., 2012). The American Internal Revenue Service (IRS), working with Teradata, has developed and is employing already powerful tools to fight fraud and tax evasion. Given their success, they intend to increase significantly the resources allocated to data analysis and modeling to improve fraud detection and tax evasion (Scannell, 2017). A study of Gonzalez & Velasquez (2013) mentions the tools used by height countries tax administrations to detect tax frauds (USA, Canada, Australia, UK, and four other). The main tools used are, according to them: neural networks (USA, Canada, and UK), decision trees, support vector machines (USA, Australia), logistic regression (USA, Australia and UK), and many others accordingly to each country's skills and needs. In Iran, tax administration officials combine multi-layer neural networks with support vector machines and logistic regression to detect corporate tax evasion in the food and textile sectors, including thousands of tax returns with 90% effectiveness (Rahimikia et al., 2017).

On a macro level of examination, Chancellor & Abbott (2015) state that many variables need to be examined as potential causes, such as income tax versus welfare payment, burden of regulations, high unemployment and household debt. A similar view is shared by Vousinas (2017) who states that determinants of tax evasion are to be found in the following causes: i) education level (lower-educated people who do not understand that taxes are needed for public services); ii) levels of tax burdens given an individual income; iii) the perceived fairness of tax burden; iv) the structure of the tax system (income versus VAT); v) the degree of market and economic organization. A study of the European situation shows a relation between culture and the shadow economy, concluding that low levels of shadow economies are found in individualistic societies (such as UK, Netherland, Belgium, Denmark), high masculinity (like Slovakia, Austria, UK, Switzerland), long-term orientation (Germany, Belgium, Netherland) and indulgent and happier society (as Sweden, Denmark, UK), while religious countries like Turkey have the worst record (Achim et al., 2019).

Both human nature and legal structures provide fertile ground for fraud and tax evasion (Doeer & Necker, 2018). On the individual level, many attempts have been made to understand the origin of fraud in psychological or economic motives. The motivation for fraud and tax is not a new phenomenon and has existed for millennia with the emergence of money and economies based on monetary systems, like insurance fraud in antique Greece (Ayres, 2019).

Nobel Prize Gary Becker links the perception by individuals that tax is unfair (in the case of incorrect assessment by the tax department), and more generally by tax rates and dissatisfaction toward government (Becker, 1968). Later on, the risk of being caught and the penalty level was included as potential factors, a view confirmed by a study by OECD (2012) who reports that the main factors are norms, opportunities, fairness, economics and interactions between the previous factors.

The US income tax comprises more than 10 000 pages (Simser, 2008) which suggests that tax complexity increases over the years which could lead to bona fide misinterpretation as well as tax evasion schemes. Main reasons to fail reporting of taxable work are mainly to avoid taxes such as social security contributions, income tax, value-added tax), and to avoid regulation of safety, work standards, reporting duties (Achim et al., 2019). An attempt to use the theory of reasoned action to explain tax evasion failed mainly due to the problems associated with self-reports of proscribed behavior (Hessing & Elffers, 1988). An interesting experimental study on the impact of gender attitudes shows that women are less inclined to commit tax evasion (and corruption) due to their gender attributes (cognitive and emotional) more than to the fact that they have fewer opportunities because of their lower power (Torgler & Valev, 2010). Finally, a unique explanation for Italy is presented by Hien (2020) who argued that the lack of intention to pay taxes did not originate from the 19th century Church–State conflict as rumored but rather grounded on the mistrust toward the state and the very low odds of being caught.

Tax evasion might be impossible to eradicate but thoughtful and innovative frameworks based on data and intelligent fraud detection algorithms can reduce substantially the crippling effects of fraud and tax evasion on advanced industrial economies (OECD, 2017, Wu et al., 2012). The authors will pursue the development of a framework for fraud detection in the home renovation market in the following pages.

BACKGROUND

The central element of the proposed framework is based on the CRISP-DM methodology (Cross Industry Standard Process for Data Mining) which was developed in 1996, but is still a de facto standard, especially for goal-directed and process-driven projects (Martinez-Plumed, 2019). It was improved by IBM under the name "*Analytics Solutions Unified Method* for Data Mining / Predictive Analytics (2016)". The ASUM model is based on the same six steps as the CRISP-DM model but it includes concerns about operational and deployment aspects of data mining projects. CRISP-DM methodology was preferred to ASUM because CRISP-DM is appropriate for the illustration of the use of analytics for a specific problem solution and that this text does not necessitate a step-by-step guide for an agile complete product implementation lifecycle.

Saltz & Shamshurin (2016) report 33 critical success factors for big data projects, Data (ability to store and access appropriate data) ●Governance (well-defined roles and responsibilities) ●Process (using a formal methodology such as Agile) ●Objectives (with measurable KPIs) ●Team (skills in data-driven decision-making) ●Tools (to enable data-derived insights) . Seen as a process, the CRISP-DM methodology relies on the following six steps. The description of the six steps is based on Pete Chapman's (2000) presentation of the *CRISP-DM User Guide*. Seen as a methodology, the CRISP-DM model enumerates the generic tasks normally associated with each phase of data modeling. These tasks are listed below with their expected output:

1. **Business Understanding:** determine business objectives; assess the situation; determine data mining goals; produce project plan
2. **Data Understanding:** collect initial data; describe data; explore data; verify data quality
3. **Data Preparation** (generally, the most time-consuming phase): select data; clean data; construct data; integrate data; format data
4. **Modeling:** select modeling technique; generate test design; build models; assess models
5. **Evaluation:** evaluate results; review process; determine next steps

6. **Deployment:** plan deployment; plan monitoring and maintenance; produce a final report; review project

The next section will provide the framework to be employed to undertake data modeling and data analytics to identify possible fraud and tax evasion in the Home Renovation Industry. Special emphasis will be placed on the first step of the CRISP-DM model, business understanding, since there is no implementation possible without a government authorization, facilitation and budget without a thorough understanding of the dynamics of fraud and tax evasion in this important economic sector.

Determining Business Objectives and Criteria

This paper focus on a special type of tax evasion committed on home improvements where customers are "partners in crime/accomplices" with an unreported construction entrepreneur, in order to do work "under the table" without adding GST/VAT or any government tax to customers thus allowing the entrepreneur to avoid declaring their labor as taxable income.

The customer saves the payment of these taxes to the government and the contractor avoids paying income tax and gest the benefits of deducting from his official revenue the cost of the goods and taxes paid on the goods. This unreported employment and cash-in-hand sales are qualified as tax evasion, a fraud, an illegal behavior, in opposition to tax avoidance, which relies on legal methods to avoid paying taxes. "Tax evasion occurs when an individual or business intentionally ignores Canadian tax laws. This includes falsifying records and claims, purposely not reporting income, or inflating expenses" (Canada Revenue Agency, 2019). Interestingly, Denis Healey, former UK Chancellor of the Exchequer, is credited with the following famous quote: *"The difference between tax avoidance and tax evasion is the thickness of a prison wall."* Tax evasion in the construction industry is part of the underground economy, dominated by cash payments, the absence of proven certification (mandatory in some areas (ex: electricity and plumber, etc.) and the absence or **obsolescence** of government license.

The construction industry is characterized by a great diversity according to the Quebec Construction Commission (2018). For a population of 8 million in Quebec, the construction industry represents 12% of GDP and a payroll of approximately 6 billion dollars given to 150,000 active employees working in several sectors of which one third in the residential sector. Among the registered companies, the 4,500 (82%) smallest enterprises (5 or fewer employees) pay 19% of wages, while the biggest pay 81% of wages. These numbers show that the absence of trade unions in the small companies has a great impact on wages. This opens the door to undeclared work and the absence of registered workers. Small companies avoid registering because a registered entrepreneur must pay his employees according to trade-union wages and a wide range of employee benefits such as paid vacations. This is one of the major incentives for unregistered work.

The home improvement sales and related work environments are characterized by high velocity, volume and variety characteristics of big data concern (Oracle, 2018). But in order to describe and understand the complexity of the task, one must take into consideration many other variables spread across many other intervening actors such as homeowners, the accredited evaluator, the enterprise database, the municipalities, government agencies and departments, judiciary decisions, advertising sites, newspapers, submission sites, and suppliers. Appendix 1 provides a detailed description of the relevance of different sources of information for modeling analytics in fraud and tax evasion detection.

OECD (2017) reports of countries taking actions to reduce fraud opportunities and increase detection capacities using one or more of four categories of data: behavioral data (such as tax return forms), transaction data (such as sales and payments), operational data (such as location, ownership) and open to public data such as advertising in newspapers or web sites:

- Russian Tax Service cross-match all transactions of VAT across all parties, almost in real time.
- Australia, offers pre-filled forms, matched with third parties, making it easier for compliers and harder for those who do not.
- New Zealand uses property transactions to select candidates for an audit.
- United Kingdom tax department uses credit and debit cards to compare with other businesses of the same size and location, in order to detect anomalies.
- In Peru the tax department linked loans to tax registration, putting under light almost 2 million informal businessmen.

According to OECD (2012), identifying authors of tax evasion create many challenges to Income Revenue Agencies:

- It is difficult to detect the activities given their disparities, their diverse nature and the fact that they are conducted secretly
- Many frauds committed by individuals deal with little amounts making the cost benefit approach difficult to apply
- Participants are not studious accountants and often are not even registered
- Assessing the unreported income may be difficult to do with legal concerns and collecting it even more difficult
- People who are rarely audited tend to change their tax evasion behavior
- Some people think taxes are not fair and don't see the need to comply with tax rules.

The main objective of this phase of CRISP-DM is to help the government revenue agency to develop predictive models "to ensure tax fairness and justice" (Revenu Quebec, 2020). In order to succeed despite the presence of serious fraud and tax evasion, the government is looking forward to implementing several measures to favor tax compliance, namely through tax audits. This entails the development of analytics and predictive models capable of identifying potential fraud cases and individuals. This is where bid data analytics can help most, given the huge quantity of income tax declarations and of purchase transactions by millions of taxpayers.

In the case of fighting tax fraud, establishing traditional enterprise or business objectives is not easily accomplished. Politicians are very sensitive to the fact that tax evaders are also electors and many politicians see adopting an aggressive approach to fraud dissuasion and tax evasion detection as detrimental to their election prospects (Skouras & Christodoulakis, 2014). This may induce governments to develop more indulgent policies toward fraud and tax evasion and persuade tax revenue employees to be more permissive when dealing with potential tax evaders.

In setting its business objectives, governments must consider that both qualitative and quantitative objectives must be pursued. Since that, by definition, fraud is hidden and varies according to the size of the enterprise, it is impossible to develop a wide range of qualitative and quantitative objectives. Quantitative objectives could be established targeting a reduction of the volume of fraud and tax evasion based on valid prior estimates for these two variables. In addition, governments could develop measures to reduce the number of people found guilty of fraud and tax evasion. Conversely, qualitative objectives could be established. For example, though big data analytics the government could refine the profile (socio-demographic and economic characteristics) of tax evaders and the most likely areas where this occurs most often. This information can be invaluable in targeting these segments with highly effective dissuasive messages through government advertising and social media campaigns.

The CRISP methodology suggests identifying the criteria to account for the success of predictive analytics and modeling. These objectives are established by the government. For example, one objective could be increasing tax evasion convictions by 10% annually or reducing the cost of tax auditing by improving analytical tools to detect fraud and tax evasion. Setting an objective is not satisfactory if no measurement is done to control effectiveness of the actions, that is why OECD (2017) recommends, as a golden rule, to use random samples in the sectors where audit will be done and compare it to another group (not audited) to measure the impact of their action.

Situation Assessment

Five deliverables should result from a detailed examination of issues related to the business or institutional objectives: inventory of resources, requirements, risk, terminology and cost/benefit.

Inventory of Resources

In the case of governments, proper funding for computers and software is usually available when correctly justified. The inventory of IT resources available includes hardware resources and software; data security resources; metadata on the origins and content descriptions of data files; evaluation of data volumes and history; analysis of the accessibility of external data via government agreement.

In addition, a rigorous evaluation must be conducted with regards to the availability and expertise of human resources. This is crucial because the availability of highly qualified personnel will facilitate the designing and implementation of tools for identifying cases of fraud and tax evasion. Among the resources, human expertise is a critical factor of success in enhancing the results since data-driven DM projects rely more on the efficiency of algorithms and the quality of data while domain (human)-driving projects benefit from human expertise and knowledge of their environment at the heart of the discovery (Kaddouri, 2011).

Requirements, Assumptions and Constraints

All three topics are intimately interlaced. The main requirement is access to a significant sample of all data in a sufficient short time to permit linkage of data. Also since the interrelation of data is necessary to build analytics models, these data must contain nominal information allowing for record associations among files. This brings a constraint of legality of divulgation and use of information. As an example, Medicare number, under actual law, cannot be used for other purposes than being provided for health services and medications. This also poses the challenge of a guarantee that the interrelated data will not be hacked. It is also assumed that for each record extracted from a file the information is updated to guarantee its validity.

Risks and Contingencies

The main risks in such a project are related to the confidentiality and security of data. As an example, federal income tax agency has seen 48,500 records compromised by cyber-incidents (Canada Revenue Agency, 2020) causing political damage to the government. The analytics project may hopefully rely on offline data, backup data, and older data than online data. Thus, the risk of interference with operations is low and highly manageable. The project manager can seek answers as to what happens if the project lasts longer than expected? Is the data quality is poor? Are the initial results disappointing?

Many countries use the invoice files in their data mining operation. The greatest attention should be given by Canadian and American readers to the legality and maybe the ethics of getting information on individuals from stores. The privacy and confidentiality of information provided by stores and credit card holders may prevent the government access to data in batch and making links with other files. This point has not yet been clarified and may limit the applicability of this project. The greatest caution should be observed in this regard.

Terminology

The Tax law is voluminous and has been completed by established case law. Identifying and understanding the laws and regulations relating to research in the fight against evasion is an important step. It is also important to understand the legal concept of tax evasion and disclosure obligations of taxpayers and partners. Some concepts need to be defined very precisely, namely the difference between cases of tax evasion and cases of tax avoidance. The terminology to be adopted must also define the concepts of fraud versus tax evasion. Knowledge elicitation from government experts will be needed to build a workable glossary of terms, characterized with enough precision to allow for automatic classification. Besides individual tax evasion business tax evasion and fraud, some businesses use cross-border and affiliated-transaction-based tax evasion (inter-subsidiaries or inter affiliates), a kind of suspicious economic behavior that Tian et al. (2016) can detect through their "colored network-based model. Another system, an interactive visual analytics named Tax Themis, which deals with heterogeneous tax-related data, is proposed by Lin et al. (2020).

Costs and Benefits

The project must also develop a detailed inventory of the following costs related to the development of analytic models for fraud and tax evasion detection: cost of personnel, costs for data coding, cleaning and modeling. As each new application generates new security concern, security costs should be included.

On the benefit column, one finds the opportunity to improve the effectiveness of fighting fraud and tax evasion from a legal perspective. The net benefit of increasing tax revenues computed as $9.06 recovered by invested dollars (Assnat, 2016) and the improvement of policies and procedures for developing intelligent systems to combat fraud and tax evasion.

Nonetheless, given the costs and benefits of pursuing an analytics strategy to combat fraud and tax evasion, it is important to mention that many factors can limit the effectiveness of the approach. According to Al-Khatib (2012) noise in the data (inaccurate or contradictory data), missing data and algorithm accuracy can negatively impact the costs and make it difficult to attain stated project objectives. In addition, poor prediction accuracy (detecting potential tax evaders) can affect costs of misclassification (the cost of minimizing the number of true positives and true negatives and minimizing false positives and false negatives).

INTELLIGENT TECHNIQUES FOR FIGHTING TAX EVASION

Oracle (2018) mentions three major steps, and the data-mining goals to attain when undertaking a data mining approach to problem solving this progression:

1. exploring data to discover patterns and trends; this step focuses on discovery; as an example the detection of anomalies among the records of income tax declarations;
2. developing models to explain the data and validate the data to select the best ones; these anomalies can give a hint of possible fraud (ex: should the cost of sales should be related to the wages paid and to the revenues, since the more one contractor buy material, the more he must hire employees to install it and thus, the greater should be his revenue from customers);
3. applying these models to make predictions, ex: a regression can determine what should be the "abnormality" in this relation (outlier) and help to identify possible tax evaders.

With regards to modeling tools; there are two main classes:

- **OLAP tools**, MOLAP (Multidimensional), ROLAP (relational MOLAP); these tools rely on the user to define analysis models either in EXCEL, PIVOT TABLE reports and other OLAP tools.
- **Data**-mining **tools** in which the analytics team chooses to define a model underlying the data, using various algorithms based on statistics. Once sufficient learning and expertise has been gained by the project team, automated procedures can be implemented to select the best predictive model to detect fraud and tax evasion. Simply, the algorithm (model) will discover the associations among the data. This approach facilitates predictions of the probable behavior of a company in the future, based on its historical data and behavior.

The analytics approach integrating predictive models can be of invaluable help in providing answers to the following questions, assuming that the project team has access to suppliers' data; what do contractors who have "defrauded" have in common? How are they different from those who have 'defrauded"? What volume of purchases and frequency determines their buying behavior? Is the purchase or rental of specialized tools (ex. mini concrete mixer) linked to the status of an entrepreneur? Are tax evaders' purchases related to their revenues, as compared to nonevaders? What are the normal coefficients for all items (lines) on the income tax form?

The modeling phase in the CRISP-DM framework will be critical in combining varied data sets to develop models to identify and predict fraud and tax evasion and to choose the appropriate tool. Indeed, over the years, many predictive models have been developed, but this paper will explain how the most useful techniques can be employed tax evasion detection.

Anomaly Detection

Anomaly detection develops models to identify outliers or atypical cases in the data. Many supervised statistical models (i.e., linear and logistic regression) possess rules that are employed to detect outliers. Unsupervised models such as anomaly detection do away with this structural rigidity and are able to detect patters of atypical behavior of the data. Being and unsupervised technique it does not need training set to develop detection rules. Contrary to several traditional methods, detection anomaly algorithms usually employ several variables at a time to detect trends and outliers and to identify clusters or peer groups with similar profiles. Each case can be compared to others in its cluster or peer group to identify possible anomalies. Each case is assigned an anomaly index and the larger the value of the index for a particular case, the greater the probability that it is an outlier in relation to its peer group. This approach has been successfully employed in fraud detection.

An example of the use of analytics in telecommunication network anomalies is given by Bhuyan et al. (2014) who surveyed the literature and found several approaches depending on the nature of the threat:

- **statistical** (parametric and nonparametric),
- **based on classification,**
- **based on clustering and outlier,**
- **soft computing** (Genetic algorithm, artificial neural network, ANN, Fuzzy set, rough set, Ant colony and artificial immune system),
- **based on knowledge** (rules and expert systems, ontology and logic-based),
- **combination** learners.

A good example of the utilization of anomaly detection is given by Mehta (2019) who analyzed a set of car dealers' sales, remittances, input and output taxes, purchase costs, credit/debit payments, buyers and vendor names. They constructed an index of the percentage of the value addition and effective tax rate ratio as indicators and by clustering, obtained a cluster of dealers with inconsistencies in their bills, participation in circular trade, number and amount of credit notes and debit notes issued. However, Thudumu et al. (2020) present many challenges in using anomaly detection with big data namely high dimensionality (limits the relevant attribute identification), velocity (affecting dynamic relationships) and volume (that brings uncertainty and limit performance).

Artificial Neural Network

Artificial neural networks are code-based algorithms that attempt to mimic the data processing by the brain. Most ANN models employ non-linear functions to derive complex relationships between variables. Artificial neural networks are composed of three layers; the input layer contains all the variables chosen to model a specific phenomenon, for example tax evasion. The hidden layer represents the weights for each variable in generating the values of the output variable, often a binary output. For example, in the case of tax evasion, the output variable could be either the person audited was found guilty or not guilty. Since it is a supervised technique, the network requires many cases or example in order to develop the variable weights to identify possible fraud or tax evasion in new cases. In this case, authors can obtain from the government and extensive set of people audited and found guilty or not guilty of tax evasion. The socio-demographic variables and other pertinent variables are integrated in the database and the neural net is trained to distinguish between the two groups. Once the model is able to detect the faulty cases from the correct ones, the network can be employed in new cases. The strength of the neural network resides in its capacity to employ linear and non-linear variables and a variety of link functions to generate the variable weights. Artificial neural networks employ either the multi-layer perceptron (MLP) or the radial basis functions (RBF).

SGNN (self-generating neutral network operates in two steps: first generating a tree from the sample and optimize it subsequently. Zhang et al. (2009) proposed an improvement to this method to detect tax fraud in an experiment with 71 attributes of 61 SMEs. By combining several SGNN into one ISGNN (iteration learning SGNN), slight improvement in the classification was attained but at a loss of price stability. Similarly, artificial neural networks have been employed to predict fraud and tax evasion. Mao et al. (2010) validate a model in which the ant colony algorithm was used to calibrate the weights of an artificial neural network to help China tax department to determine which person needs more audits. In Chile, Gonzales & Velasquez (2013) used several models to test empirically their usefulness by first, using neural network (self-organized map) to cluster and classify attributes of taxpayers with false invoices; then they used a decision tree to identify the variables potentially predictive of fraud and were able to attain a 90% success rate. Finally, Jang (2019) present an application of ANN to predict tax income based on past years of fiscal income in order to predict more accurately while taking into account the evolution of economic data such as GDP movements, the fluctuation of the real estate market and other potential factors.

Support Vector Machines (SVMs)

Support vector machines are part of the tools employed in statistical learning. Developed in the 1990s, support vector machines have become popular with researchers interested in developing high-performance models requiring very little tuning (adaptation to data). The objective of the technique is to find a hyper plane in a p-dimensional space (variables) that distinctly classify the data points of the target variable (binary classification variable of doing or not tax evasion). Support vectors are the data points most close to the hyper plane and influence the orientation of the hyper plane. The main idea is the calculation of the Kernel (model) to classify non-linearly separated data (variable to be predicted). The most popular kernel functions are linear, polynomial, radial basis and sigmoid. The support vector machines are popular because of their flexibility in handling different types of data (variables). Similar to artificial neural networks, they have been used in face detection, image classification, handwriting recognition, generalized predictive control and many other areas. This technique could also be employed in fraud detection and tax evasion control.

Bayesian Network

Bayesian networks are probabilistic models that relate a variety of variables to a target variable, often binary or multi-categories. The network establishes conditional dependencies between the input variables and the target, using a directed acyclic graph. The graph represents an event that occurred and predicting the likelihood that any one of several known variables was a contributing factor. For example, if someone were found to have engaged in tax evasion (tradesperson), the network could establish the probabilities that one of several variables could have contributed to the action (legal status of the person, declared income, age, or other explanatory variables). Being a supervised technique, it also requires a large training data set to be able to estimate the probabilities of fraud or tax evasion given a set of variables. This technique could also be employed to fraud detection. According to Ying et al., 2019), Bayesian network would be most appropriate for first procedures of inspection and case selection and present a 93.3% success when applying it to profitability, income growth rates, account receivable and inventory turnovers, liquidity and repayment capacity.

Association Rules

Association rules are derived by constructing a large transaction table where a zero represents the absence of an action and one the presence of an action. By employing association rules, one can discover useful relationships in large transactional data sets. The algorithm detects patters and rules based on the level of contingency between events. Originally employed in market basket analysis, it has been employed to study a wide variety of phenomena in economics, medicine, psychology and marketing. For example, in fraud detection, a transaction table can be set up to indicate the presence or absence of an action, for example, the use of cash to pay for construction materials, or the lack of a trade certification in the case of tax evasion conviction. A large data set of individuals convicted of tax evasion in the home renovation industry could be constructed with a wide range of transactional data to develop links between the two. The algorithm develops association rules between a set of events (transactional markers) and tax evasion conviction. These rules can then be applied to all the target population of tradespeople and estimate the probability of tax evasion. Those with a high probability could be the target of more detailed tax audit. In Taiwan, Wu et al. (2012) reports of the use of Association rules to detect value-added tax evaders among enterprises sampled and divided in two blocks each containing different attributes from the other but sharing information on past tax evasion, and after appropriate learning prediction of tax evader had only 5% error.

There are other tools to undertake predictive modeling such as discriminant analysis, logistic regression, Kohonen networks or regression trees. Useful as they may be, they are not designed for large and diversified data sets that need to be analyzed when developing models to detect fraud and tax evasion. The techniques presented above are very adaptable to a wide range of data and highly scalable and produce very similar results in terms of predictive precision. However, the models are only as good as the data. That is why in our framework for fraud and tax evasion detection, data preparation and data cleansing are extremely important phases in the development and implementation of a model for tax evasion.

The most important criterion for evaluating the performance of any predictive model is its predictive accuracy. The predictive accuracy is derived from a training sample of data. What this means is that the government agency generates a large sample of people in the same industry (renovation) that were audited and convicted of tax fraud and those not convicted of tax fraud. In addition, a wide range of variable is included to describe the transactional profiles of the two groups. The model will generate a set of parameters to classify the people in their respective group (convicted or not convicted of tax evasion). Typically, good models are able to classify at least 80% of the cases in their proper group. This means that the model can select at least 80% of people to be audited to be convicted of tax fraud. The level of model precision is not determined (based on statistical rules) but rather by the decision makers. A government agency may be happy with a 70% precision rate while another may want an 85% rate. This is probably the most important criterion in judging the quality and usability of a predictive model for fraud and tax evasion detection.

PRODUCTION OF A PROJECT PLAN

The establishment of a project framework or plan is thus extremely important. Given the complexity of the problem, it may be a difficult endeavor, but nonetheless, the effort must be undertaken to ensure that all the resources, human and data are in place or available. As in the CRISP-DM model, the project team might be forced to revisit previous steps in order to arrive at an possible strategy to fight fraud and tax evasion. Each of these can provide one or more of the indicators mentioned by Chancellor & Abbott (2015), namely cash advances on credit cards and change on property ownership and mortgages. Data Sources are very widespread.

Employees: some have qualifications governed by the Quebec Construction Commission, in which case the number of hours worked is compiled; they may or may not be members of unions which compiles data; they are submitted to government organizations which compile their worked hours. The wages paid by entrepreneurs should match those reported to government agencies.

Entrepreneurs: some are incorporated, others are registered and others are not registered as such. Business owners complete tax and other reports to government agencies (salary deductions per employee, etc.). They can be required to provide a detailed list of their purchases if they declare cost of sale purchases. These purchase receipts provide information on the payment modality (cash, credit/debit card). This can be cross-tabulated with home improvement stores who can be requested to prove their sales from a list of receipts. A link between seller and buyer can give the volume and nature of sales and reveal if all purchases have been used for declared sales.

Homeowners: they report renovation either when they sell their house (new price and renovation done available by REALTOR database for comparison with prior price given time; buyers who pay a price much higher than previous house evaluation receive a visit from an inspector to see what renovations have been made by the prior owner and by which contractor: ex. Renewing a kitchen costs between $10,000 to $25,000 to renovate, depending on the size, materials, etc. The observed differences between buying and selling may indicate improvements made by the contractor. Verification can be made on the declarations of the contractor to see if this job has been or not declared. Finally, owners have the possibility to reduce their tax for home renovations, if they have hired a contractor, whose name must be entered on their income tax declaration, allowing cross-computations with entrepreneur's declarations and purchases.

Registered appraisers have standard prices and property comparisons, based on technical characteristics of the buildings. These standard costs can be used to validate the business income declared for entrepreneurs in relation to the house they own.

Home Improvement giant stores like Home Depot offer special services and schedules to contractors; in order to be accepted as a contractor, one needs to spend a large amount per year, and generally will benefit from a discount by using the contractor card. The list of these contractors can be crossed-checked with government list of official contractors and their official revenues compared to their purchases.

Tools rental stores will provide to contractors special tools too expensive to buy example lifts or diamond drills with limited time usage that is not beneficial to buy for a contractor. Given the value of the tools, they will ask for a huge guarantee, generally a credit card that provide names and other useful information on the borrower. This information can be analyzed in regards to other information.

Municipalities issue building / renovation permits which include estimates for works; these estimates generally contain data generated by contractors; the file of permits can be cross-analyzed with purchases and revenues of contractors.

The Housing Building Office manages a list of certified contractors who pay annually for a permit; some do not renew it, some get their license revoked. These contractors removed from the list are skilled workers and undoubtedly asked for under the cover work. Their annual level of material purchases can be indicative of unregistered work and their revenue source if not replaced by a formal salary can be correlated to their house value and car price.

Civil courts of justice often decide on causes opposing consumers to more or less formal contractors. These decisions may be hints to detect who acts like a contractor and suggests cross-checking with income tax revenues.

The car immatriculation service has data on owners of trucks and trailers, useful for contractors. This file can be cross-analyzed with income tax and purchases to find out if the owner needs such a truck for personal or professional reasons, like carrying gyros or lumbers...which can also be linked to purchases. Analytics can describe the use of these types of vehicles in regards to the type of work.

Advertising sites like Buildzoom or contractors.com provides to consumers lists of contractors but these are not always certified or up to date with their permits, and thus maybe unregistered potential workers and contractors. A cross-analysis could reveal potential frauds.

Some Relevant Studies to be Done

Nota Bene: many of these studies rely on the fact that purchases will be done with a credit card but wise contractors who prefer shadow work for their business may pay in cash.

- What attributes (financial statement or socio-demographic elements) are most important in predicting tax evaders? Which of these characteristics are useful in fraud and tax evasion?
- Once the predictive characteristics are known, one can use the "classification" tool to apply to a new set of data.
- Clustering can be useful to discover groups of individuals based on unknown variables.
- Linear regression with these variables can be used to predict the volume of frauds or the tax amount that one should have declared
- Detecting anomalies among the buyers (ex a customer who buy 500 sheets of drywall is not renovation for a basement).
- Determining what is common to tax evaders in their buying behavior (ex. buy more infrastructure material, rent specialized and expensive equipment) using anomaly detection and association rules.
- How can one distinguish tax evaders from honest contractors? (Neural network, logistic regression).
- Are tax evaders' purchases related to their revenues, compared to nonevaders?
- How do tax evaders compared to nonevaders based on their relative tax form?
- File of purchases and municipal permits or transfers. What are the normal purchases of a consumer who renovates his house versus those of an entrepreneur?

SUBSEQUENT PHASES

The next step in CRISP-DM methodology is to focus on data: form understanding of preparation. The lines below list some key features to consider when describing data:

- Volume of data. In most modeling techniques, the volume of data leads to trade-offs. Large data sets can produce more accurate models, but also increase processing time. Government officials can discuss the issue with the project team to provide a representative set of data that is not too costly to build but is sufficient to provide answers to an acceptable level of trust and accuracy.

- Types of value. Data can be in several formats, such as categorical numeric (H / F), or Boolean (true / false) format.

- Coding methods. The values of a database often represent characteristics, such as gender or product types. For example, one set of data may use the letters M and F to mean masculine and feminine, while another will use numerical values 1 and 2. Some standardization will be desirable. Date variables must also be standardized, given their different formats. Decision must be made on suppression versus replacement of empty fields.

According to a New York Times survey of industry scientists (Lohr, 2014), big data cleansing is the most tedious and time-consuming to be undertaken by the analysts on the project team. Data cleansing can take the form of spelling corrections or changing literal word to numerical and to delete nonsense coding. The quality of modeling depends on the quality of data. A classic example is given by Shapira (2018) who cites the case of a large number of customers who were supposedly living in Schenectady (postal code 12,345), a very small city, because the registration form forced the entry of a 5-digit number and many customers were reluctant to do so. Another problem comes from the fact that most transactional data are produced in real time and human intervention cannot be applied to correct errors in the data and in some cases human intervention such as the manipulation of records may produce errors.

DISCUSSION AND IMPLICATIONS

This paper has shown that the governments can use the new capacities of data modeling and analytics tools in order to fight tax fraud and identify tax evaders. We have focused more on the easiest data to study, which are the invoices from home improvement stores. Despite the power of the algorithms and statistics, the success will always rely on access to appropriate data, proper codification and cleaning of data and the professional and educated use of tools. A systematic review of the relevant literature of critical success factor for big data projects identify 33 concerns grouped in six categories of concerns (Saltz & Shamshurin, 2016): i) objectives; ii) governance; iii) team; iv) process; v) data; vi) tools.

The growing use of big data and analytics raises the problem of privacy preservation as more and more disparate information can be merged into a single view of an individual, reducing the freedom that a person is allowed to preserve under separation of data into multiple silos. An illegal use of huge data on a single person can lead to abuse and bring "Big Brother" fears that would limit the use of facial recognition to solve potentially serious crimes. As a matter of fact, the use of facial recognition is actually under judicial scrutiny by civil liberty organisms. The development of the Internet of Things (IOT) is expected to generate more information on individuals while the role of cash in transactions is vanishing. Social media continue to develop and to generate information on persons and groups that can be combined increasing the risks of illegal or malicious use of data.

FUTURE RESEARCH DIRECTIONS

The use of analytics to prevent fraud in tax perception and identify tax evaders are only in its early age and will experience rapid development in the coming years. This will be amplified by the increased reliability and versatility of learning algorithms and AI to solve a wide variety of economic and managerial problems including fraud and tax detection. Seeing the positive results obtained by companies in fighting fraud with their customer transactions, governments will be more ready to integrate both project frameworks, such as CRISP-DM, and data modeling analytics in their policies and actions to fight fraud and tax evasion. Also, data-mining techniques will be refined leading to more precise predictive models with lower misclassification rates. However, this will not dissuade future citizens from evading taxes. New ways will be found by tax evaders. This is why, especially governments, must invest in personnel training and tool development to stay one step ahead of them. The future for the fight against fraud and tax evasion is very promising since many of the major software developers are investing heavily into the development of fraud detection models.

Big data and data analytics are here to stay. Most scientific fields and organizations have accepted their use and potential benefits with their use. Software developers such as IBM, SAS and Microsoft have developed highly user-friendly interface making these tools easily accessible even by the analyst not well versed in coding. In addition, these analytical and predictive tools will be combined with visualization tools greatly simplifying the interpretation of the results (i.e., Tableau visualization tool). Many universities are introducing big data and analytical modeling courses in faculties ranging from physics to political science and management.

Finally, future research must delve into the organizational dynamics associated with the integration of the CRISP-DM framework for data mining and the structural factors impeding and also facilitating its adoption. The problem is not with the lack of analytical techniques to analyze big data and develop predictive models, but rather, the problem is in measuring the contribution of such tools and techniques in improving organizational effectiveness. This is particularly important in governmental settings. Government is often more reticent in adopting new analytical techniques in solving public policy problems. Many are contented with the status quo. Obviously, these new tools and techniques can be extremely useful to government in fighting fraud and tax evasion. Some government agencies have been very open to their use while others have resisted their introduction. Future research should attempt to investigate the factors that facilitate and impede the adoption of data mining and analytical models by governments to fight fraud and tax evasion.

CONCLUSION

This paper has presented the complex problem of fraud and tax evasion in the home renovation industry and suggested that data mining could help government tax agencies identify tax evaders from their purchases and other files containing their relevant information. In order to apply data mining, a good understanding of the problem is needed, according to the CRISP –DM methodology before undertaking a data mining project to develop analytical tools to identify and predict fraud and tax evasion. The main elements of data mining were presented in order to demonstrate how useful data mining can be in order to deal with the problematic situation of fraud and uncover cases and individuals potentially deserving further examination by the tax revenue agency. However, it must be stated that even sophisticated analytical techniques will not prevent motivated persons from discovering new and innovative strategies for evading taxes. It is possible to increase fraud detection using analytics but there is a cost to do so and tax evaders will always find new ways to operate unless their accomplices (customers) realize that it is beneficial to their financial situation to demand invoices from their suppliers (construction companies and trades people). Bedford's law can be used to detect fraud and would work adequately for monetary data (Vani, 2019). How to change a civil culture will not be found by analytics. This requires intelligent communication and moral suasion. However, fraud detection using data analytics can provide the stimulus to engage in legal tax compliance with companies and customers knowing that it is easier for governments to detect and successfully prosecute fraud and tax evasion.

REFERENCES

Achim, M. V., Borlea, S. N., Găban, L. V., & Mihăilă, A. A. (2019). The Shadow Economy and Culture: Evidence in European Countries. *Eastern European Economics*, *57*(5), 352–374. doi:10.1080/001287 75.2019.1614461

Acoss. (2020). *Lutter contre la fraude au prélèvement social*. https://www.acoss.fr/home/nos-missions.html

Al-Khatib, A. M. (2012). Electronic Payment Fraud Detection Techniques. *World of Computer Science and Information Technology Journal*, *2*(4), 137–141.

Assnat. (2020). Objectif d'équité fiscale. *Bilan 2011-2016*.

Ayres, H. (2019). *5-infamous-fraud-cases-throughout-the-centuries*. ACFE insights. News and analysis on the global fight against fraud. https://www.acfeinsights.com/acfe-insights/5-infamous-fraud-cases-throughout-the-centuries

Becker, G. S. (1968). Crime and Punishment: an Economic Approach. In N. G. Fielding, A. Clarke, & R. Witt (Eds.), *The Economic Dimensions of Crime*. Palgrave Macmillan. doi:10.1007/978-1-349-62853-7_2

Bedford, E. (2020). *DIY and home improvement market in Canada - Statistics & Facts*. https://www.statista.com/topics/5188/diy-and-home-improvement-market-in-canada/

Bhuyan, M. H., Bhattacharyya, D. K., & Kalita, J. K. (2014). Network Anomaly Detection: Methods, Systems and Tools. IEEE Communications Surveys & Tutorials, 16(1), 303–336.

Bitzenis, A., Vlachos, V., & Schneider, F. (2016). An Exploration of the Greek Shadow Economy: Can Its Transfer into the Official Economy Provide Economic Relief Amid the Crisis? *Journal of Economic Issues*, *50*(1), 165–196. doi:10.1080/00213624.2016.1147918

Bustamante. (2018). *Home Improvement Industry Statistics*. https://ipropertymanagement.com/ research/home-improvement-industry-statistics

Canada Revenue Agency. (2019). *Combatting tax crimes: Tax evasion explained*. https:// www.canada.ca/en/revenue-agency/programs/about-canada-revenue-agency-cra/compliance/ combat-tax-crimes.html

Canada Revenue Agency. (2020). *Cyber-incidents*. https://www.canada.ca/en/revenue-agency/

Cebula, R. J., & Feige, E. L. (2012). America's unreported economy: Measuring the size, growth and determinants of income tax evasion in the U.S. *Crime, Law, and Social Change*, *57*(3), 265–285. doi:10.100710611-011-9346-x

Chancellor, W., & Abbott, M. (2015). The Australian construction industry: Is the shadow economy distorting productivity? *Construction Management and Economics*, *33*(3), 176–186. doi:10.1080/014 46193.2015.1028954

ChapmanP.ClintonJ.KerberR.KhabazaT.ReinartzT.ShearerC.WirthR. (2000);

Chemin, M.-C. (2019). *7,8 à 10 milliards d'euros de fraude sociale?* Fondation iFRAP. https://www. ifrap.org/budget-et-fiscalite/78-10-milliards-deuros-de-fraude-sociale-recap

Chuprina, R. (2020). *The In-depth 2020 Guide to E-commerce Fraud Detection*. www.datasciencecentral.com

CRISP-DM 1.0 Step-by-step data mining guides. (n.d.). ftp://ftp.software.ibm.com/software/analytics/ spss/support/Modeler/Documentation/14/UserManual/CRISP-DM.pdf

Doerr, A., & Necker, S. (2018). Toward an understanding of collaborative tax evasion: A natural field experiment with businesses. FreiburgerDiskussionspapiere zur Ordnungsökonomik, No. 18/13, Albert-Ludwigs-UniversitätFreiburg, Institute for Economic Research, University of Freiburg.

González, P. C., & Velásquez, J. D. (2013). Characterization and detection of taxpayers with false invoices using data mining techniques. *Expert Systems with Applications*, *40*(5), 1427–1436. doi:10.1016/j. eswa.2012.08.051

Hessing, D. J., Elffers, H., & Weigel, R. H. (1988). Exploring the limits of self-reports and reasoned action: An investigation of the psychology of tax evasion behavior. *Journal of Personality and Social Psychology*, *54*(3), 405–413. doi:10.1037/0022-3514.54.3.405

Hien, J. (2020). Culture and tax avoidance: The case of Italy. *Critical Policy Studies*, (August), 1–22. doi:10.1080/19460171.2020.1802318

Hunter, B. (2020). *Why the Home Improvement Industry is Worth Billions*. https://www.homeadvisor. com//r/why-home-improvement-industry-worth-billions/

IBISWord. (2019). *Home Improvement Stores in the US industry outlook (2019–2024)*. https://www. ibisworld.com/united-states/market-research-reports/home-improvement-stores-industry/

IBM. (2016). *Analytics Solutions Unified Method Implementations with Agile principles*. ftp://ftp.software.ibm.com/software/data/sw-library/services/ASUM.pdf

INFORMS. (2017). *Operations Research & Analytics*. https://www.informs.org/Explore/Operations-Research-Analytics

Jang, S. B. (2019). A Design of a Tax Prediction System based on Artificial Neural Network. *2019 International Conference on Platform Technology and Service (PlatCon)*, 1–4. 10.1109/PlatCon.2019.8669416

Kaddouri, A. (2011). *The role of human expertise in enhancing data mining* (Order No. 3481009). Available from ABI/INFORM Collection. (909541928)

Lin, Y., Wong, K., Wang, Y., Zhang, R., Dong, B., Qu, H., & Zheng, Q. (2020). TaxThemis: Interactive Mining and Exploration of Suspicious Tax Evasion Groups. IEEE Transactions on Visualization and Computer Graphics.

Lohr, S. (2014). *For Big-Data Scientists, "Janitor Work" Is Key Hurdle to Insights*. https://www.nytimes.com/2014/08/18/technology/for-big-data-scientists-hurdle-to-insights-is-janitor-work.html

Mao, S., Wanggen, W., Rui, W., & Yue, G. (2010). The application of ant colony algorithm and artificial neural network in tax assessment. *2010 IEEE International Conference on Audio, Language and Image Processing*. 10.1109/ICALIP.2010.5684375

Martínez-Plumed, F., Contreras-Ochando, L., Ferri, C., Flach, P., Hernández-Orallo, J., Kull, M., Lachiche, N., & Ramírez-Quintana, M. J. (2019). CRISP-DM Twenty Years Later: From Data Mining Processes to Data Science Trajectories. *IEEE Transactions on Knowledge and Data Engineering*, 1–14.

Mehta, P., Mathews, J., Visweswara, R., Kasi, S. V., Kumar, K. S., Suryamukhi, K., & Babu, C. S. (2019). Identifying Malicious Dealers in Goods and Services Tax. *2019 IEEE 4th International Conference on Big Data Analytics (ICBDA)*, 312–316. 10.1109/ICBDA.2019.8713211

OECD. (2012). Reducing Opportunities for Tax Non-compliance in the Underground Economy. *Forum on Tax Administration: SME Compliance Subgroup*. www.oecd.org/tax/forum-on-tax-administration/publications-and-products/sme/49427993.pdf

OECD. (2017). *Shining Light on the Shadow Economy - Opportunities and Threat*. https://www.oecd.org/tax/crime/shining-light-on-the-shadow-economy-opportunities-and-threats.pdf

Oracle. (2018). *What Is Big Data?* https://www.oracle.com/big-data/guide/what-is-big-data.html

Québec, R. (2020). *Ensuring Tax Compliance*. https://www.revenuquebec.ca/en/fair-for-all/ensuring-tax-compliance/tax-evasion/construction-sector/

Quebec Construction Commission. (2018). *L'industrie en chiffres*. https://www.ccq.org/fr-CA/En-tete/qui-sommes-nous/industrie-de-la-construction

Rahimikia, E., Mohammadi, S., Rahmani, T., & Ghazanfari, M. (2017). Detecting corporate tax evasion using a hybrid intelligent system: A case study of Iran. *International Journal of Accounting Information Systems*, *25*(May), 1–17. doi:10.1016/j.accinf.2016.12.002

Reportlinker. (2020). *DIY Home Improvement Market - Growth, Trends, and Forecasts (2020–2025)*. Author.

Riquier, A. (2019). *Home remodeling is a $450 billion market, and it is only going to get bigger*. https://www.marketwatch.com/story/home-remodeling-is-a-450-billion-market-and-its-only-going-to-get-bigger-2019-03-12

Saltz, J. S., & Shamshurin, I. (2016). Big data team process methodologies: A literature review and the identification of key factors for a project's success. *2016 IEEE International Conference on Big Data (Big Data)*, 2872–2879. 10.1109/BigData.2016.7840936

Scannell, K. (2017). The US intensifies fight against tax evasion by using data mining. *Financial Times*. https://www.ft.com/content/719544f6-529b-11e7-bfb8-997009366969

Schneider, F., Raczkowski, K., & Mróz, B. (2015). Shadow economy and tax evasion in the EU. *Journal of Money Laundering Control*, *18*(1), 34–51. doi:10.1108/JMLC-09-2014-0027

Shapira, G. (2018). The Seven Key Steps of Data Analysis. Oracle Corporation. *Profit Magazine*. http://www.oracle.com/us/corporate/profit/big-ideas/052313-gshapira-1951392.html

Simser, J. (2008). Tax evasion and avoidance typologies. *Journal of Money Laundering Control*, *11*(2), 123–134. doi:10.1108/13685200810867456

Skouras, S., & Christodoulakis, N. (2014). Electoral misgovernance cycles: Evidence from wildfires and tax evasion in Greece. *Public Choice*, *159*(3-4), 533–559. doi:10.100711127-013-0071-0

Statista. (2020). *Global Net Sales of the Home Depot from 2007–2019*. https://www.statista.com/statistics/240009/global-net-sales-of-the-home-depot/

Thudumu, S., Branch, P., Jin, J., & Jugdutt, S. (2020). A comprehensive survey of anomaly detection techniques for high dimensional big data. *Journal of Big Data*, *7*(42), 42. doi:10.118640537-020-00320-x

Tian, F., Lan, T., Chao, K. M., Godwin, N., Zheng, Q., Shah, N., & Zhang, F. (2016). Mining Suspicious Tax Evasion Groups in Big Data. *IEEE Transactions on Knowledge and Data Engineering*, *28*(10), 2651–2664. doi:10.1109/TKDE.2016.2571686

Torgler, B., & Valev, N. T. (2010). Gender and public attitudes toward corruption and tax evasion. *Contemporary Economic Policy*, *28*(4), 554–568. doi:10.1111/j.1465-7287.2009.00188.x

Vani, G. K. (2019). How to detect data collection fraud using System properties approach. *Multilogic in Science, 7*.

Velasco, R. B., Carpanese, I., Interian, R., Paulo, N., Octávio, C. G., & Ribeiro, C. (2020). A decision support system for fraud detection in public procurement. *International Transactions in Operational Research*, 1–21.

Vousinas, G. L. (2017). Shadow economy and tax evasion. The Achilles heel of Greek economy. Determinants, effects and policy proposals. *Journal of Money Laundering Control*, *20*(4), 386–404. doi:10.1108/JMLC-11-2016-0047

Wu, R. S., Ou, C. S., Lin, H. Y., Chang, S.-I., & Yen, D. C. (2012). Using data mining technique to enhance tax evasion detection performance. *Expert Systems with Applications*, *39*(10), 8769–8777. doi:10.1016/j.eswa.2012.01.204

Ying, Q., Xiaoxin, H., & Weige, J. (2019). Research on Tax Inspection Case Selection Model Based on Bayesian Network. In *Proceedings of the 2019. 2nd International Conference on Information Management and Management Sciences (IMMS 2019)*. Association for Computing Machinery. 10.1145/3357292.3357329

Zhang, K., Li, A., & Song, B. (2009). Fraud Detection in Tax Declaration Using Ensemble ISGNN. *2009 WRI World Congress on Computer Science and Information Engineering*, 237-240. 10.1109/CSIE.2009.73

ADDITIONAL READING

Becker, D. K. (2017). Predicting outcomes for big data projects: Big Data Project Dynamics (BDPD): Research in progress. *2017 IEEE International Conference on Big Data (Big Data)*, 2320-2330. 10.1109/BigData.2017.8258186

Biju, S. M., & Mathew, A. (2017). Comparative Analysis of Selected Big Data Analytics Tools. *Journal of International Technology and Information Management*, 26(2), 2–22.

Bortoli, S., Bouquet, P., Pompermaier, F., & Molinari, A. (2016). Semantic big data for tax assessment. In *Proceedings of the International Workshop on Semantic Big Data (SBD '16)*. Association for Computing Machinery, New York, NY, USA, Article 5, 1–6.

Columbus, L. (2017). IBM Predicts Demand for Data Scientists Will Soar 28% By 2020. *Forbes* from https://www.forbes.com/sites/louiscolumbus/2017/05/13/ibm-predicts-demand-for-data-scientists-will-soar-28-by-2020/#23002b457e3b

Hariri, R. H., Fredericks, E. M., & Bowers, K. M. (2019). Uncertainty in big data analytics: Survey, opportunities, and challenges. *Journal of Big Data*, 6(1), 1–16. doi:10.118640537-019-0206-3

Tang, J., & Karim, K. E. (2019). Financial fraud detection and big data analytics – implications on auditors' use of fraud. *Managerial Auditing Journal*, 34(3), 324–337. doi:10.1108/MAJ-01-2018-1767

KEY TERMS AND DEFINITIONS

Accuracy: The degree of proximity of a measurement in relation to the target true value. Sometimes called "trueness", it is often confounded with "precision" which refers to the variability of the results within one set of measurement.

Algorithm: A finite sequence of operating rules executed on data and which allow a result to be obtained. The sequence may comprise some cycles and conditional branching. In daily life, it compares to a recipe.

Anomaly Detection: Highlight, discovery, identification of an irregularity, a deviation from expectations arising from significant deviation (more or less) with a standard or a majority of cases a priori similar and potentially indicative of fraud, error or fault. Synonym for outlier detection.

Attribute: Characteristic attached to an entity (person, phenomenon, and situation) and used to describe it in a specific way, on a particular aspect. Information, normally considered as not decomposable, which determines and characterizes an entity.

Big Data: A huge and moving set of data of various varieties, structure, and format, produced by various sources, at various frequencies that must be processed quickly using specialized tools, other than common database management software.

Data Mining: Data analysis technique allowing extraction of new information, hidden correlations difficult to see under a mass of data, trends, anomalies, associations, mainly by the use of statistical processing, often in the context of big data.

Data Modeling: The development of a statistical or algorithmic model to describe, explain and predict a well-defined phenomenon or problem by employing a large variety of variables and observations (cases).

Fiscal Fraud: Subterfuge, illegal acts used by a taxpayer (individual or business) in order to evade the tax burden to which he would normally be submitted by the law as a result of generating personal income.

Methodology: Set of appropriate research methods and techniques applied to study a particular field or determined problems in order to find a solution or reach a goal. The CRISP-DM methodology is a sequenced list of tasks to be performed in order to reach conclusions on data.

Chapter 16
Development and Analysis of Virtual Laboratory as an Assistive Tool for Teaching Grade 8 Physical Science Classes

Maria Ndapewa Ntinda
University of Namibia, Namibia

Titus Haiduwa
University of Namibia, Namibia

Willbard Kamati
University of Namibia, Namibia

ABSTRACT

This chapter discusses the development of a virtual laboratory (VL) named "EduPhysics," an assistive software tailored around the Namibian Physical Science textbook for Grade 8 learners, and examines the viability of implementing VL in education. It further presented reviews on the role of computer simulations in science education and teachers' perspective on the use of EduPhysics in physical science classrooms. The chapter adopted a mixed method with an experimental research design and used questionnaires and interviews as data collection tools in high school physical science classes. The analysis found that there are limited resources in most physical science laboratories. Computer laboratories, however, are well equipped and have computing capacities to support the implementation of VL. It was concluded that virtual laboratories could be an alternative approach to hands-on practical work that is currently undertaken in resource-constrained physical science labs. For future work, augmented reality and logs will be incorporated within EduPhysics.

DOI: 10.4018/978-1-7998-4963-6.ch016

INTRODUCTION

Information and Communication Technology is one of the key enablers for digital transformation. Key trends in digital transformation involve the use of emerging technologies such as the Internet of Things (IoT), Virtual Reality (VR) and Artificial Intelligence (AI), and Machine Learning to digitize business processes to deliver exceptional Customer service and gain competitive advantage (Proctor, 2019; Salesforce, 2020). As technology become ubiquitous, however, learners become digital natives, and the education system gets intrinsically linked to emerging technologies to support and improve learning and teaching practices. It is undeniable that not all schools have enough infrastructure, facilities, and services to deliver science education. Hence, there is a need for research on whether the technology could be employed to complement or substitute limited resources in physical science laboratories in secondary schools.

Learning science courses using laboratory activities have been proven beneficial to learners (Forcino, 2013). Meanwhile, most schools in African countries, including those in Namibia, have a shortage of various resources needed to facilitate learning (Haidula, 2016). It has been also found that scientific experiments conducted in school laboratories are essential for the successful and comprehensive training of learners (Millennium Challenge Corporation, 2014). Normally, learners get first-hand experience on how to implement scientific concepts, theories, and understanding in school laboratories. In these laboratories learners mix materials, observe results and events to conclude certain experiments (Uğur, Savaş, & Erdal, 2010). However, this is not always possible in some schools due to a lack of resources in the laboratories. Lack of resources impedes laboratory experiments and this makes it difficult for learners to consolidate and implement the knowledge they have acquired from textbooks and traditional classroom teaching. This situation reduces the students' ability to learn and affects their academic performances negatively.

It is argued that the role of technology in science education in the 21st Century is inevitable. As a pedagogical tool, technology can lead to innovation in education, enhanced collaboration, and human-to-machine interaction in higher schools (Osakwe, Nomusa & Norbert, 2015). For instance, virtual and remote laboratories are one of the current trends in K-12 education and emerging technologies that will impact education in the next few years (Saga, 2013). With the advancement in technology, educational institutions and scientific organizations can, potentially, take full advantage of these technological advancements and introduce virtual laboratories in schools. Technology can be used to build virtual applications that can assist learners with their laboratory practical work. With virtual applications, experiments are conducted in virtual environments where the results of experiments can be simulated on a computer and evaluated in the absence of experimental equipment that would otherwise be essential (Uğur, Savaş, & Erdal, 2010). Schools with limited laboratory equipment could use virtual resources for practical work by introducing online laboratories and improve learners' experiences. Online laboratories allow users to investigate virtual materials and observe the effects of the manipulated material to gain insight into the experiment under observation (De Jong, Sotiriou, & Gillet, 2014). Indeed, virtual labs offer flexibility and allow learners to run experiments as many times as they can both in and out of school without much pressure. Also, learners remain safe even if they happen to make errors (Saga, 2013).

BACKGROUND

In the past, education at the secondary school level in Namibia was divided into two phases. The first phase was known as the junior secondary phase, consisting of grades 8-10, and the second phase was known as the senior secondary phase consisting of grades 10-12 (NIED, 2010). In 2017, a new curriculum was implemented for grade 8. The content of the new curriculum differs only slightly from that of the old curriculum. Under the old curriculum, grade 8 physical science offered the following topics: Scientific Processes, Matter and Materials, Environmental Chemistry, Mechanics, and Electricity & Magnetism (NIED, 2010). All the topics found in the old curriculum were carried over to the new curriculum except one: Electricity and Magnetism (NIED, 2015). Electricity and Magnetism topic was replaced with Experimental techniques. Thus, the new grade 8 physical science curriculum consists of the following five topics: Matter and Materials, Environmental chemistry, Mechanics, Scientific processes, and Experimental techniques (NIED, 2015).

Grade 8 physical science falls under the natural science area in the curriculum and has a thematic link to other subjects across the curriculum (NIED, 2015). Table 1 illustrates the cross-curricular issues dealt with in the physical science course.

Table 1. Cross-curricular issues dealt with in the physical science course

Cross-curricular issues	Grade 8
Environmental Learning	**Matter and Materials** Topic 2 Matter **Environmental chemistry** Topic 3 The gases of the air **Mechanics** Topic4 Forces
Information Communication Technology	**Scientific processes** **and experimental techniques** Topic 1 Scientific processes
Education for Human Rights and Democracy	**Experimental techniques** Topic 3 The Gases of the air

This curriculum is based on a paradigm of learner-centered education. At the end of grade 8, learners are expected to have some understanding of the physical and biological world at local, regional, and international levels. The final marks of the learners come from formative continuous assessments and summative assessments (NIED, 2015, p.52).

Formative continuous assessment is any assessment made during the school year to improve learning and to help shape and direct the teaching-learning process, while summative assessment is an assessment made at the end of the school year based on the accumulated total of the progress and achievements of the learner throughout the year in a given subject, together with any end-of-year tests or examinations. The result of the summative assessment is a single end-of-year promotion grade.

The curriculum recommends that every learner conduct a minimum of five practical investigations in the academic year. This is however not the case in all schools in Namibia due to the limited resources in school laboratories.

PROBLEM STATEMENT

Physical Science is one of the difficult and compulsory subjects offered to all Grade 8 learners in both public and private secondary schools in Namibia (NIED, 2015). At the end of each academic year, learners write a national examination where both their theoretical and practical skills are assessed (NIED, 2015). Although both theory and practical skills are assessed, practicals are not conducted at all in some schools. Especially in schools situated in remote and/or rural areas. Exposing learners to scientific experiments can assist them in retaining their knowledge permanently as experiments are carried out in their presence (National Research Council, 2006). Although conducting practical experiments in school laboratories strengthens students' learning (Forcino, 2013), regrettably, some schools in Namibia do not have physical science laboratories or have limited resources that cannot cater to all learners. School laboratories provide an environment for learners to test the validity of their intuitions, hunches, and ideas concerning the scientific viewpoints learned (Nghipandulwa, 2011).

As is pointed out by Vosniadou (n.d) and many others, students who are not exposed to first-hand practical experiments do not acquire hands-on experience and resort to memorizing theories and facts without having a concrete understanding of the subject matter. Although secondary schools in Namibia could utilize open-source VLs, curricula compatibility issues could impede its implementation. Therefore, if VLs are to be introduced into Namibian schools, the developed VLs need to be aligned to the Namibian curricula to overcome challenges experienced in schools with resource-constrained science laboratories but do have computer laboratories.

RATIONALE FOR THE CHAPTER

It was reported that more than 200 schools in Namibia had approximately 2000 computers installed in 2012 (Nampila, 2012). Amongst those, there were schools with computer laboratories that were only used for office practice lessons or administration purposes. Hence, is imperative that those schools use computer laboratories for physical science practical work by installing VLs. Although VLs are not physical, they can increase students' interest, motivation, and engagement in science, and they are recognized as pedagogically effective (Zervas, Kalimeris, & Sampson, 2014). To add, VLs might add particular value to learning in countries with resource-constrained science laboratories, and Namibia is no exception. It has been demonstrated that studying with the assistance of computers and multimedia applications can to some extent overcome the technical and instructive restrictions of classical hands-on laboratory courses in science teaching (Sassi, 2000). More research is therefore needed to understand the impact of using VLs in Namibian secondary schools to complement or substitute physical laboratories. However, before efforts to develop or purchasing VLs for use in Namibian secondary schools, there is a need to research and investigate the effective use of VLs in such schools.

Chapter Objectives

This chapter discusses the development of virtual laboratories and explores whether it is viable to implement VLs in Grade 8 physical science classes in Namibia to complement physical science practicals at schools with resource-constrained laboratories or substitute resources used during physical science practicals at schools with no physical science laboratories but have adequate computer laboratories.

According to Molohidis, Lefkos, Taramopoulos, Hatzikraniotis, and Psillos (2015), it is necessary to combine VLs with a proportional number of hands-on experiments for students' practical experiments. Thus, an *ad-hoc* online system, named "EduPhysics" was developed to assist learners with practical activities using simulations.

LITERATURE REVIEW

This section presents the review of related literature on simulations and virtual labs, an overview of physical science in Namibia, and the development of the EduPhysics VL.

Review of Related Studies

Virtual laboratories are defined as a way of learning or practicing experiments in a safe, online environment (Christina, 2020). A study by De Jong, Sotiriou, and Gillet (2014), indicated that online laboratories could be grouped into three categories: virtual laboratory (VL), remote laboratory, and dataset. These authors further differentiated the three categories, stating that learners can perform investigations either by using simulated (virtual) equipment in VL or can use physical equipment, operated on distance or can inspect the outcome of an investigation conducted by a third party such as a professional organization in a dataset. This chapter focuses on VLs, thus remote laboratory and datasets are not within the scope of this discussion. The advancement in technologies used to develop VL and the availability of computer laboratories in secondary schools create opportunities to introduce VLs in education, especially in developing countries where schools have limited resources in their science laboratories. The aim is not to replace physical science laboratories but rather to complement them.

As revealed in the literature above, simulation and virtual labs are commonly used in teaching and learning science curricula, namely: Chemistry, Physics, Biology, and Mathematics. In a controlled environment, learners can undertake laboratory activities using computers installed in the school laboratories or their mobile phones & gadgets. These laboratory experiments can significantly benefit learners in schools with deficiencies of learning materials and resources and eventually lead to increased interest in the course and an overall improvement of learners' academic performance (Nico, Wouter & Jan, 2011). Below is a summary of related studies and technologies used in other countries.

According to Saga (2013), Dr. David Yaron, an Associate Professor of Chemistry at Carnegie Mellon University in Russia created an engaging online resource platform called ChemCollective for chemistry education. Organized by a group of faculty and staff members at Carnegie Mellon University, these online resources for teaching and learning Chemistry consist of a collection of virtual labs, scenario-based learning activities, tutorials, and concept tests (Carnegie Mellon University, 2020). As an alternative to textbooks, teachers and learners use the Java version for offline use or the new HTML5 based version of the virtual lab to review and learn chemistry concepts using virtual labs, and simulations.

Saga (2013) further reported that, in Sweden, Lysekil, "high school students use virtual tools to explore the marine environment of Gullmar Fjord on the Swedish west coast". In this case, the Marine Biology students use a virtual ocean acidification laboratory to conduct their studies on the acidification of the marine environment.

Similarly, the high school Mathematics students at North Carolina State University used Geometer's Sketchpad to understand how theorems are developed (Saga, 2013). Such software is accessed through the university's virtual computing lab, an assistive, and interactive cloud-based learning environment for teachers to share software and research projects.

Zervas et al. (2014) also developed three VLs, namely laboratorio de quimica, physics-simulations, and earth & space, and summarised their functionalities. It was found that all these three VLs allowed users to execute an experiment, access multiple experiments, save the current state of an experiment to the mobile device, and modify different parameters for executing an experiment. It has been narrated that only the Laboratorio de quimica VL was able to load the current state of an experiment to the cloud. It has been also stated that it is important to follow design principles or methods when developing applications for mobile devices as content might not fit on the screens or might not be visible to the users.

Virtual and Physical laboratories in Education

Over the last few decades, Information Communication Technology (ICT) has gained prominence in education. As a result, various organizations embraced ICT tool to smoothen daily activities. ICT tools are any kind of device or object capable of facilitating communication. It could be but not limited to laptops, desktops, head projector, and software programs. Arguably, VLs are amongst ICT tools used in interactive classroom teaching. VLs were introduced in schools to attract and retain learners in Science, Technology, Engineering, and Mathematics (STEM) (Bak, Dandanell, & Bruun, n.d). VLs are interactive environments comprising of virtual materials and apparatus (De Jong, Linn, & Zacharias, 2013). In simple terms, VLs mimic physical laboratories on the screen of a computer (Molohidis, Lefkos, Taramopoulos, Hatzikraniotis, & Psillos, 2015). Physical laboratories, also known as traditional laboratories, are those that occupy real land, consist of real equipment, and require technical experts to function effectively (Budhu, 2002). Over the years, various countries adapted VLs for educational practices (Daineko & Dmitriyev, 2014) to complement or replace physical laboratories. As computing devices become ubiquitous, young children are exposed to technology at an early stage. Hence, acquiring digital competencies and becomes digital natives, also known as the NET generation. Net Generation simply refers to the generation of young people with access to several ICT devices and connected to the world via the Internet. Coined by Mark Prensky (2001), the term digital natives are people who grew up with unlimited access to ubiquitous technology (OECD et al., 2017; Prensky, 2001) and embraced technology. Hence, these learners are likely to adapt to educational technologies such as VLs as they grew up with unlimited access to modern information and communication technologies. VLs present learners with advanced educational materials and serve as an entertaining aspect of gamification that excites and motivates learners (Bak, Dandanell, & Bruun, n.d). Also, they enable students in resource-constrained traditional laboratories to design and conduct simulated experiments (Gomes, Coito, Costa, & Palma, 2007).

According to De Jong et al. (2013), introducing physical or virtual laboratories in education yields the same results as in physical laboratories, especially for students who do not have a previous relevant physical experience with the phenomenon or concept under study. Further, De Jong et al. (2013) found that both VLs and physical laboratories yield similar objectives such as exploring the nature of science, developing teamwork abilities, cultivating interest in science, promoting conceptual understanding, and developing inquiry skills. Mutually, virtual and physical laboratories support autonomous learning (Zervas et al., 2014). A study that compared students' learning in a virtual and physical unit operations laboratory found no significant difference in learning between the two instructional modes of teaching and learning (Wiesner & Lan, 2004).

On the other hand, some dissimilarities between virtual and physical laboratories have been reported. For instance, with VLs, disabled students, for example visually impaired students can conduct scientific experiments with the aid of screen reading software (Gomes & Garcia-Zubia, 2007) which is not possible in a physical laboratory. VLs also allow students who cannot get to physical laboratories to perform laboratory experiments online regardless of their location and time (Zervas et al. 2014).

In general, students can investigate experiments in VLs that cannot be conducted in physical laboratories due to the lack of materials available. Some dissimilarities between physical and virtual laboratories were also observed in the five human senses, namely sight, hearing, touch, taste, and smell (Suh & Lee, 2005). With VLs, students can only experience vision and hearing because most web-based applications use monitors and speakers (Suh & Lee, 2005) unlike in physical laboratories where students can use all five human senses. Moreover, experiments conducted in VLs require less time to set up and provide results of lengthy experiments instantaneously.

According to De Jong, Linn, and Zacharia (2013), students perform more experiments in an allocated time in VLs than in physical labs, thus obtaining more results in less time. De Jong et al. (2013, p.306) further indicated that "Physical experiments typically include authentic delays between trials that encourage careful planning and reflection of the next investigation". Although VLs have proven to offer teaching effectiveness, it is found to be ambiguous (Martinez, Naranjo, Perez, Suero, & Pardo, 2011). Especially, the value of VLs is to a certain extent contested by some researchers (De Jong, Linn, & Zacharia, 2013). However, in the context of this chapter, VLs would fill a critical void in education, especially to complement science experiments in physical laboratories.

Technologies used to Develop VLs

Various technologies such as Server-side databases, JavaScript, Java applets, and Macromedia flash (Desharnaise & Limson, 2007) have been used to develop VLs. Such technologies are selected depending on the speed, security, computing infrastructures, and users' proximity (Molohidis et al., 2015). Most VLs are accessible both on desktop computers and mobile phones and can be either web-based or standalone applications. Molohidis et al. (2015) developed a web-based VL for physics that embodied a complete physics micro-world. The aforementioned laboratory was deployed as Java applets with a minimum of requirements on the client-side and run in real-time. This laboratory adopted the Cosmos-Evidence-Ideas (CEI) framework, consists of large sets of virtual laboratories, and has three independent micro-world environments covering the following topics: optics, heat, and electricity for physics (Bak, Dandanell, & Bruun, n.d). The CEI framework assists students to understand concepts, theories, models, and representations of the material world as a social and physical environment (Molohidis et al., 2015). Java technologies were used to develop the Optilab, a virtual lab in Java3D that covers Geometric and Wave Optics (Molohidis et al., 2015).

The proliferation of mobile devices amongst learners gave rise to the use of mobile VLs in education (Zervas et al., 2014). Mobile VL is defined as the performance of virtual experiments using mobile devices. Mobile VLs were developed to provide mobile access to existing open-source virtual laboratories. For example, ASK-MVL provides mobile access to existing open-source virtual labs provided by the PhET repository of virtual Labs (Zervas et al., 2014). ASK-MVL enables users to execute experiments and modify different parameters for executing an experiment (Zervas et al., 2014). ASK-MVL was developed to run on an Android operating system and has been developed using PhoneGap, a framework for mobile phone development (Zervas et al., 2014). Bottentuit and Coutinho (2007) developed a virtual chemistry laboratory for 7th-grade learners enrolled in organic chemistry.

System Design and Implementation

This section describes the conversion of the system requirement specification into a fully functional system.

In terms of the software development processes model, the development of EduPysics adopted a Rapid Application Development (RAD) model. RAD model is based on prototyping and iterative and Incremental model. It works well where little planning and requirement analysis is required. In the RAD model, the project is divisible into smaller modules hence accelerating the systems development process. According to Sommerville (2011), RAD is mainly aimed at rapid development and delivery of the working porotype, a "trial-and-error" approach for discovering and demonstrating how a system can operate. The system development went through the following distinct phases of system development life cyc planning and requirement analysis, design, development, testing, implementation, support, and maintenance.

Figure 1. RAD Model

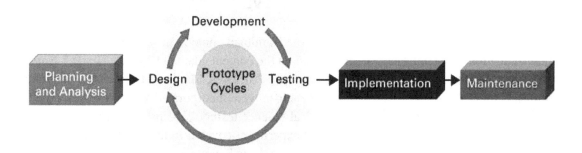

The planning and analysis phase involved identifying the development team, resource allocation, requirement gathering, and detailed analysis (studying the current teaching system and prioritizing the project requests). The team then progress to design and development were architectural, interface and database design happen. After that, the system goes through the stages of software testing. Unit, integration, system, and acceptance testing were performed before implementation. After deployment support has been extended to the system users (Sommerville, 2011).

Disciplines' Content Demonstrated in VLs

The degree of reality simulated in VL environments differ, ranging from showing different dimensional images, demonstrating principles to using Virtual Reality modeling languages' interfacing (Budhu, 2002). The use of 3D models was exemplified in software named Labster that caters to different subjects in the natural science field at the university level (Daineko & Dmitriyev, 2014). Existing VLs were developed in alignment either with specific course content or with a large set of virtual laboratories that demonstrated different disciplines such as STEM and robotics (Budhu, 2002; Colorado, 2018; Daineko & Dmitriyev, 2014). PhET simulations and Labster are examples of VLs catering to different fields such as Physics, Biology, Chemistry, Mathematics, and Earth science (Daineko & Dmitriyev, 2014; McKagan, 2018).

The open design software was implemented at all levels of education ranging from primary schools to higher education institutions and catered for different individuals, for either personal homework or large classes (McKagan, 2018). Wikiversity (2020) defined open design as a design that "consists of software and hardware components". PhET simulations are an example of an open design that allows online laboratory owners to plug in their online labs and offer students an opportunity to conduct scientific experiments using different online labs (De Jong, Sotiriou, & Gillet, 2014; De Jong et al., 2013). Go-Lab is another example of an open interface that allows teachers to add scaffolds and tools to inquiry learning (De Jong et al., 2014). Go-Lab has a wiki-like interface that uses a drag and drops feature and consists of different discipline labs (De Jong et al., 2014).

As discussed in the literature above, it is evident that VLs could be used in every discipline and multiple disciplines can be incorporated in one VL. Open design could be employed to cater for multiple courses. In Namibia, VLs have not yet been developed therefore studies are needed to develop VLs for specific courses before employing open-ended designs.

THE PROPOSED SOLUTION: EDUPHYSICS VL

EduPhysics is an *ad-hoc* system tailored around the Namibian content, developed specifically for the Namibian educational system. The system is based on the content adapted from the Grade 8 Namibian Physical Science textbook. The topics such as Scientific Processes, Matter and Materials, Environmental Chemistry, Mechanics, and Electricity & Magnetism were incorporated within the developed VL. These topics came from the recommended Physical Science textbook to ensure that the content found on EduPhysics mimics the outcome of the actual experiment covered in the Grade 8 physical science syllabus. EduPhysics was developed using HyperText Makeup Languages, Cascaded Style Sheet, JavaScript, Bootstrap, jQuery, and Base64. The aim of employing different technologies was to ensure that the application is accessible through different web browsers. There is an enormous increase in the use of mobile devices amongst learners in Namibia and this has made them a choice of technology for learning (Osakwe, Dlodlo, & Jere, 2017). Thus, EduPhysics is co-designed and developed for both mobile devices and desktop computers (see Figure 3) because of the ubiquity of mobile devices and users' computer literacy. During this phase, the bandwidth and network coverage in Namibia was considered, thus EduPhysics was designed in the simplest way to cater to learners with low-end processing computers and internet-enabled mobile devices. This section presents and describes the interface design of EduPhysics.

The interface on the left in Figure 2 illustrates an example of an **(A)** interface of a desktop computer while the interface on the right illustrates an example of a **(B)** interface for mobile phones.

Functionalities discussed by Kalimeris, Sampson, and Zervas (2014) were adopted and three were incorporated in the EduPhysics. These functionalities are: (1) Execute an experiment (2) Access multiple experiments, and (3) Load/Save the current state of an experiment to the mobile device or a computer. Although EduPhysics consists of all topics covered in the Grade 8 physical science textbook, only two will be discussed in full in this chapter.

Figure 2. Desktop Computer and Mobile phone interfaces

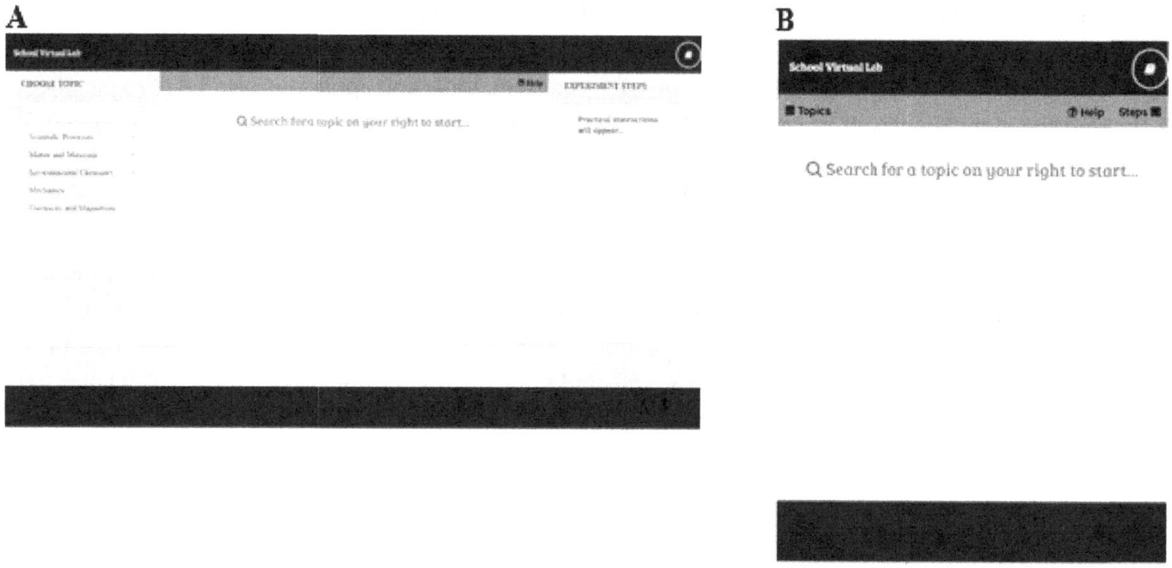

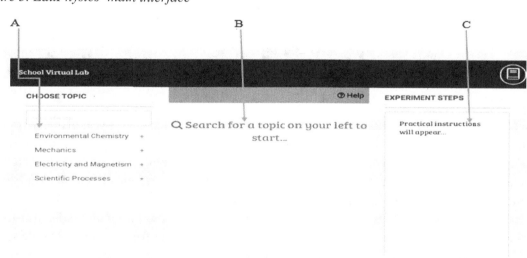

Description of EduPhysics' Main User Interface (UI)

The EduPhysics system consists of three sections, labeled from A to C. The first section (A) on the left allows users to decide on the practical experiment they wish to undertake, either by selecting the practical topic or by searching for the topic in the search box. Users can search for different practical topics provided which as found in the Grade 8 physical science syllabus. Upon completion, the searched topic will then appear in the dropdown menu for selection. Apart from using the search box, topics can also

Figure 3. EduPhysics' main interface

be located using the dropdown menu directly. Once the user selects a topic, all practical under that topic will appear underneath as illustrated in Figure 3 section (A).

When a practical experiment is selected, iconic tools and apparatus are displayed in the second section (B) (see Figure 3). The user then drags the icons, for example, tools and apparatus needed to experiment, following the steps displayed in section (C) as illustrated in Figure 3. The last section (C) as shown in Figure 3 presents instructions to the users on how to conduct a selected practical experiment, which the user selected in section (A).

EduPhysics was designed to allow users to follow the steps in the order presented to them. This ensured that users conduct practical work as they would in a physical laboratory. During the practical, users can make use of the Help option for assistance, as shown in Figure 4. The Help option assists users with steps, detailing the process of how to experiment within the EduPhysics environment. When a user selects a topic, experiments that are part of the selected topic are displayed beneath the topic. Thereafter, the user selects the experiment they wish to conduct.

Figure 4. Demonstrates the search option

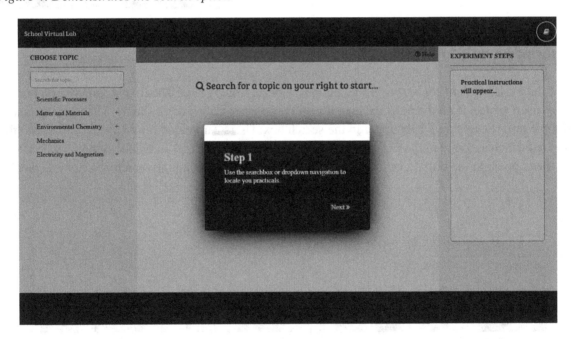

Tools to be used and instructions to be followed during the experiment then appear in their respective sections as shown in Figure 5.

All experiments' output conducted within the EduPhysics environment are simulated when being conducted. EduPhysics also forces users to follow the steps provided gradually to ensure that learners grasp the concepts as they would in a traditional laboratory.

To experiment, the user drags the icons to the middle section. The user then follows the instructions as displayed in the third section (see Figure 5). Thereafter, the user drags the icons to the middle section to simulate an experiment.

Figure 5. Lab tools and instructions generated

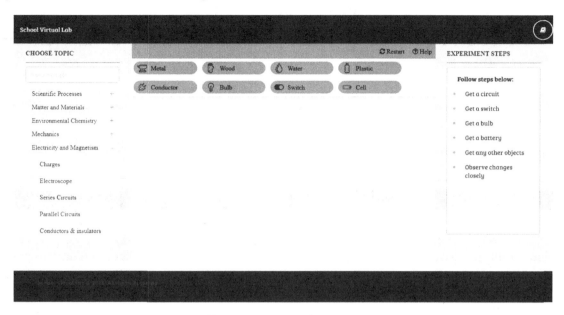

Figure 6 illustrates an example of a completed practical conducted from the Electricity and Magnetism topic, showing an example of a conductor's and insulator's simulated output.

The conductors and insulators experiment enables users to test the conductivity of different materials such as water, plastic, metal, and wood on an electrical circuit.

Figure 6. Conductors and Insulators simulated output

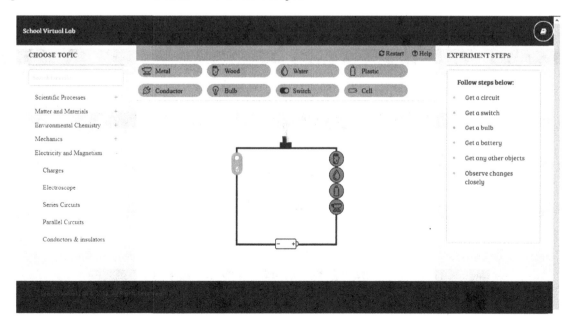

Figure 7. Series circuit and Parallel circuit experiment

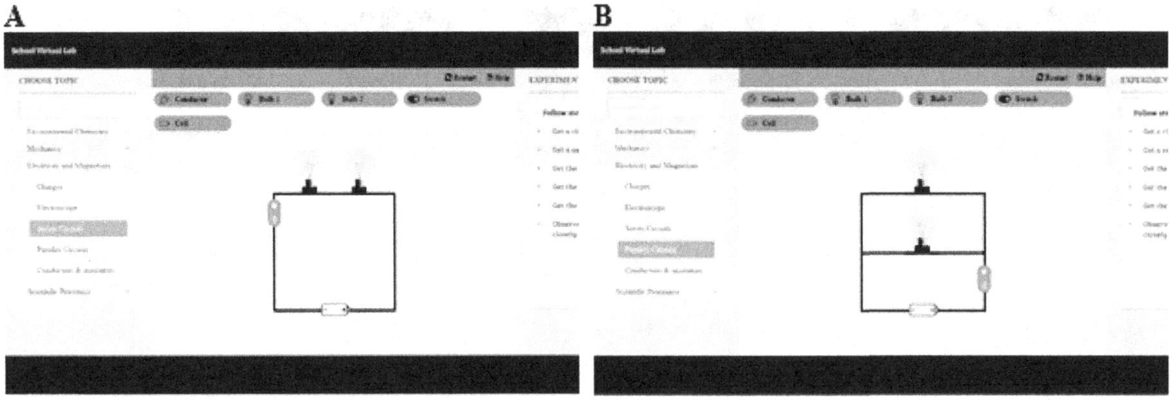

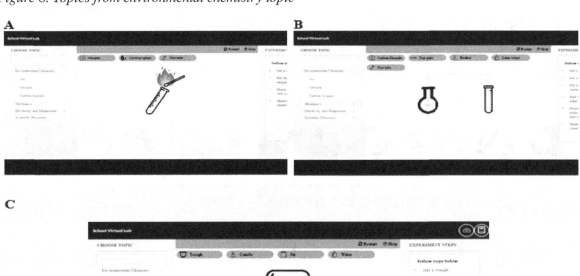

Figure 7 illustrates an example of an (A) series and (B) parallel circuit simulated output. This practical allows users to test their knowledge of electricity and observe when the bulb lights depending on the location of the batteries.

Figure 8 illustrates an example of a practical experiment contained in the environmental chemistry topic. In the first example (A), the experiment simulates how oxygen supports combustion. In the second

Figure 8. Topics from environmental chemistry topic

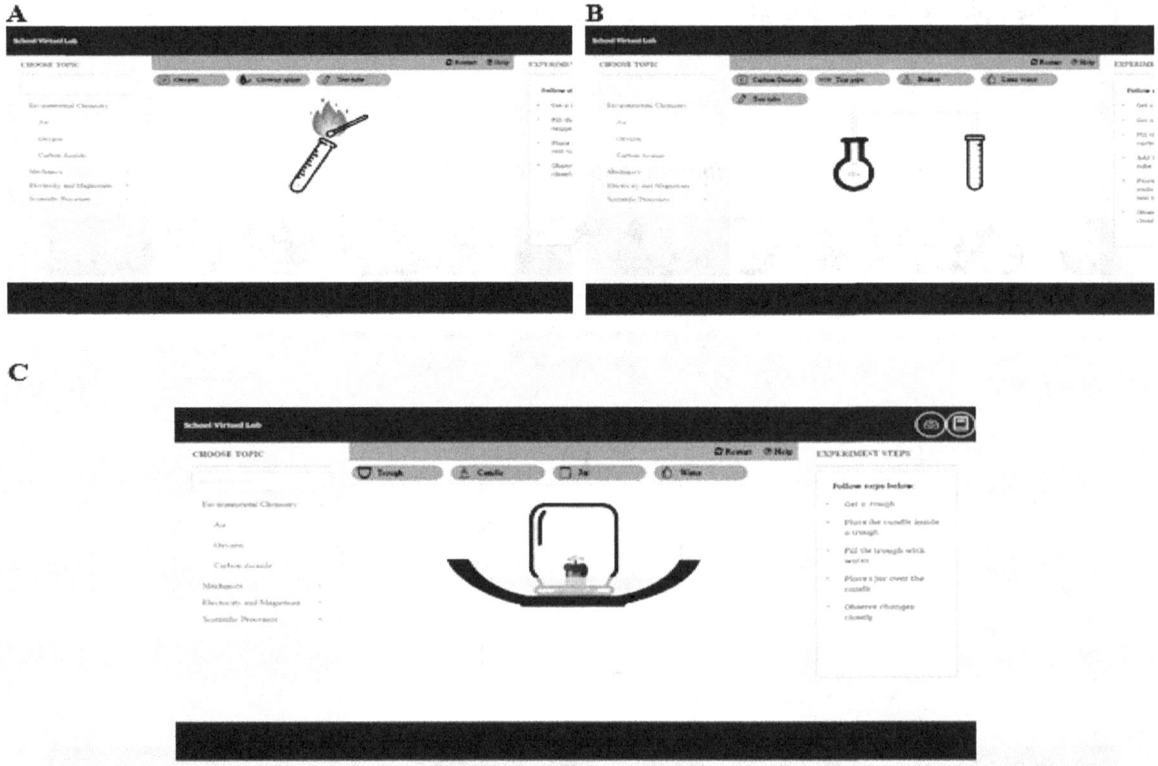

example (B), the experiment proves that carbon dioxide changes the color of limewater to milky white, and the last example (C) shows that fire dies out slowly when the oxygen supply becomes exhausted.

METHODOLOGY

Research Design

This chapter employed a mixed research method with an experimental research design. The quantitative research focused on reporting the numerical results of using the program whilst the qualitative research has highlighted the research findings on the impact of simulations and virtual labs in education as well as the two groups' perspectives, comments, and reactions to the pilot use of the EduPhysics Virtual Laboratory in a secondary school in Windhoek, Namibia. The quantitative data has been gathered in physical science laboratories whereas qualitative data came from analyzing documents and related literature as well as semi-structured semi-interviews. Making use of both, quantitative and qualitative methods allows researchers to have a broader understanding of the topic under discussion (Gülsüm & Didem, 2017).

Population and Sampling

The target population of this study was teachers in secondary schools in Namibia. Participants were selected from various secondary schools and a purposive sampling technique was employed to ensure a manageable amount of data since studying the entire population is practical, not possible (Osakwe, Dlodlo & Jere, 2017). Thirty (30) teachers participated in the study, fifteen of the total participants were physical science teachers and the other 15 were office practice teachers (Computer studies). Physical science teachers were selected because the chapter aimed to determine whether EduPhysics could be introduced to complement traditional physical science labs. At the same time, office practice teachers were selected as the chapter involved technology and the researchers wanted to assess technology-related issues. Hence, a purposive sampling technique ensured the inclusion of both judgmental and expert sample. The research findings are divided into four categories: Teachers' perceptions of the use of EduPhysics in physical science classrooms, Teachers' computer literacy skills, and computer laboratories *versus* science laboratories in schools.

Data Collection Instruments

Questionnaires with open-ended questions were distributed to teachers in various schools in the capital city, Windhoek where the experiment was conducted amongst grade 8 learners in Secondary School. Questionnaires were used as they are relatively cheap and quick to gather data from a larger sample (Creswell, 2012). In addition, semi-structured interviews were used as data collection tools amongst teachers. Researchers directly observed learners' reactions to the VL and the conditions of computer and physical science laboratories. The analysis found that there are limited resources in most physical science laboratories.

Data Analysis

Microsoft Excel was used as a statistical software package to analyze the data gathered from respondents. Data gathered from related literature was also used to inform the study.

Procedure

The project was carried out in different phases. In the first phase, the curriculum was reviewed and Edu-Physics was developed, whereafter the system was presented to the teachers. The teachers' perceptions of the system were then obtained and their suggestions were incorporated in the systems development. The results obtained from the teachers are presented in the section below.

RESULTS

This section presents data collected in February 2019 amongst fifteen secondary schools in the Khomas region, Windhoek, Namibia.

Teachers' Perceptions of the Use of EduPhysics in Physical Science Classrooms

Teachers' perspectives on their use and understanding of VLs, specifically EduPhysics, in science teaching, especially in carrying out virtual science experiments, have been examined. The qualitative data, gathered from participant questionnaire responses under this section were examined in two categories: positive and negative outlook. The findings suggest that most teachers overwhelmingly recognize the educational benefits of virtual laboratories.

The use of EduPhysics was demonstrated to the participants. The researcher explained the functions of the system, exemplifying a few experiments from each topic. Participants were then asked whether they would use EduPhysics if introduced at their schools. One participant was quoted saying, *EduPhysics might assist learners to improve their scientific concepts as the learners will have access to EduPhysics regardless of their location and time.* Another participant was quoted saying, "*EduPhysics will smoothen the process of conducting the experiments and if implemented, the physical science laboratory maintenance costs might reduce.* These comments reflected a positive outlook on the use of VLs as an alternative pedagogical approach to science education. The use of VL as an alternative to traditional hands-on laboratory sessions is possible not only because it is cost-effective but also because of its ability to increase learners' knowledge and understanding of their subject. Also, some participants felt that the use of computers in teaching is a reinforcement to learners.

Whilst the above provides evidence that VLs are effective in increasing student knowledge and understanding of the science content, VLs cannot fully replace traditional laboratories. Lewis (2014, p. 8) argued that:

Virtual laboratories do not provide students with opportunities to develop key practical or technical skills, for example, the setting up of experimental preparations or the use of specific items of equipment. They do not provide students with exposure to, and experience of, analysis of uncharacteristic or incorrect data. They always work, creating the false impression that this is always the case in "real"

Figure 9. Teachers' computer literacy skills

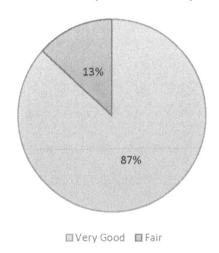

Teachers' computer literacy skills

13%

87%

☐ Very Good   ☐ Fair

scientific research. Therefore, if the development of these skills forms part of the learning outcomes for the course, these cannot be achieved using virtual laboratory tools.

While the use of and benefits of virtual laboratories are well documented, it would be naïve to suggest that hands-on traditional laboratories should be completely replaced by VLs. VL also has its limitations, and there are some situations in which it is not useful. For instance, VLs do not provide hands-on experience of individual techniques or training in the use of individual items of equipment, health, and safety or promote awareness of ethical issues (Lewis, 2014) However, due to the scarcity of laboratory materials in most schools in Namibia, VL can potentially be an alternative pedagogical tool that needs to be explored.

Teachers' Computer Literacy Skills

Insight on teachers and learners' computer skills was examined. The selected participants (teachers) were asked to rate their computer literacy skills and the rate of their learners' computer literacy skills using a Likert-scale based questionnaire. Although not all learners enroll for office practice, a course that introduces learners to ICT in secondary schools, the results revealed that all learners had a fair understanding of computers. All the participants rated their learners' computer literacy skills as fair. Though not surprising, these results are in agreement with the argument raised by Williams, Crittenden, Keo, and McCarty (2012), who claimed that millennials and post-millennials are digital natives. This is promising as learners are already accustomed to technology, VLs could be implemented with less support and learners might embrace the use of VLs.

On the other hand, regarding the teachers' computer literacy skills, 87% of participants rated their computer literacy skills as very good, while 17% of participants rated their computer literacy as fair. See Figure 8.

Although the majority of participants assessed themselves as computer literate, teachers are yet to feel comfortable integrating computers in their curriculum (Cawthera, n.d).

Figure 10. Number of learners per teacher

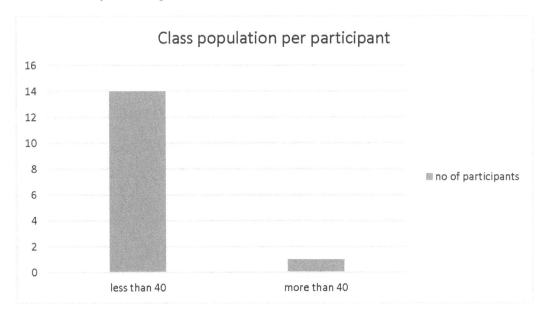

The State of Computer Laboratories versus Science Laboratories in Schools in Namibia

This section compares the availability of science equipment found in physical science laboratories and the availability of equipment in computer laboratories at schools. The results revealed that physical science labs lack the required equipment and resources for conducting science experiments. On the other hand, computer labs have sufficient equipment to support learner interaction with science materials. Thus, computer labs can be used by learners to observe, investigate, and understand the natural world from a click of a mouse.

Since computer equipment is needed for the successful implementation of VLs; participants were asked to indicate whether the schools had enough computer labs with sufficient equipment and to indicate the learner-to-computer ratio. The results revealed that all schools that participated had computer labs. Seven of the schools had computer labs specifically for grade 8 learners only. At schools with fewer computer labs, computer labs are shared amongst two to five grades. Although there are some schools where learners shared computer labs, it was also found that computer labs were well equipped with computers, printers, Internet connectivity, and projectors. With the average of 1:2 learner-to-computer ratio, implementing VLs in secondary schools in Windhoek might not be a challenge, but it might pose a challenge to most schools in rural areas in Namibia due to lack of electricity, network connectivity, computers, etc.

In a normal traditional laboratory with sufficient resources, each learner conducts his or her practice. However, this is not always the case in large classes, especially in resource-constrained traditional laboratories.

Participants were asked to indicate the number of learners in their classrooms and the results are given in Figure 9. It was found that 14 participants had fewer than 40 learners in their classrooms, and one participant had more than 40. This is probably the case in sub-Saharan countries generally (Wallet,

Figure 11. Number of practical attended by students per week

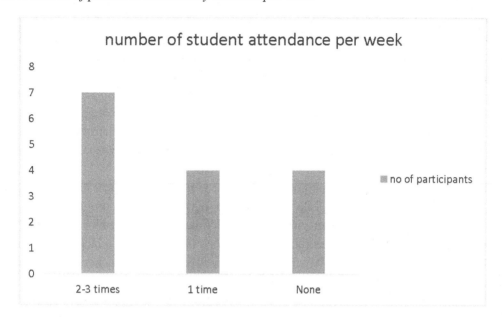

2015). The high number of registered learners and the limited resources pose a challenge for teachers to carry out practical work (Mba & Uba, 2012).

Participants were also asked to indicate whether there were sufficient resources for use during practical experiments. Eleven participants indicated that physical science laboratories had insufficient resources. Chemicals, apparatus, taps, sink were some of the resources reported missing.

In the Namibian curriculum, it is compulsory for learners to at least conduct practical investigations (NIED, 2015). Participants were asked to indicate the number of hours that learners attend practical sessions per week, and their responses are shown in Figure 10.

Seven participants indicated that learners attend practical sessions 2-3 times a week, four participants indicated that learners attend practical sessions once a week, and four participants indicated that the learners do not attend practical sessions at all.

However, it also occurred that there are schools where learners do not conduct practical experiments. Instead, teachers use textbooks to explain practical concepts, as noted by one participant saying, "*I use books to explain practical concepts because we do not have a physical science laboratory*". Some participants indicated that they improvised laboratory apparatus by using the available resources. Improvising resources does not always yield the same results as would be obtained by using resources meant specifically for certain experiments.

SOLUTIONS AND RECOMMENDATIONS

Though the participants generally embraced the use of VL, it posits formidable implications for and challenges to education. This section discusses some of the issues to emerge from the participants' responses, which are perceived to pose challenges to VL. These challenges are related to both teachers and learners. The challenge issues are embedded in the curriculum and structural design, teachers' and learners' practices, and attitudes toward VL.

From the questionnaires, it became evident that some teachers did not wholeheartedly welcome the use of VL as an alternative to hands-on traditional experimentation. For instance, one participant noted that: *it will be difficult to use VL because it is time-consuming and at the same time learners might be doing different things on the computer that are not related to the lesson. Our students are so fascinated by computers and I do not think we as teachers are ready to use VL.* The use of EduPhysics and VL, in particular, will be a difficult task, unless a well-planned and supportive teacher training programme is in place. Teachers are likely to resist changes from traditional teaching to a virtual environment if they are not properly trained.

The success of EduPhysics depends a great deal on the confidence teachers have in their ability to use computers and related technology. Likewise, learners may find virtual programs to be a bit of a technological burden, especially if a given virtual program comes with the need for a lot of technological manipulation (Ngoyi, 2013). Teachers in this chapter agreed that there was a lack of IT- related skills among learners and teachers. As a result, participants suggested that both teachers and learners should be trained on how to use EduPhysics.

On the last note. It is worth noting that Virtual labs are beneficial to learners. A study on the impact of the virtual laboratory experiences on attitudes towards physics laboratories at the Near East University, revealed that virtual laboratory experiences had positive effects on the students' attitudes (A!ıksoy & Islek,2017). During the experiments with the EduPhysics VL program, researchers observed that learners were enthusiastic about the use of the VL in their lab practices. In schools where there were not enough resources used during physical science practical, EduPhysics complimented the physical laboratories. . According to the teachers who participated in this study, they observed a change in the attitude of learners who initially had a negative attitude toward the physical science subject. In addition, the cost of resources used in physical laboratories has been cut and the virtual environment ensured safety for those who are allergic to certain materials and shortened time needed to complete a particular task. Teachers also observed an increase in the progress of conducting practical experiments amongst slow learners.

This chapter recommends the following to successfully implement VLs in education. 1). There is a need to involve stakeholders from all the regions countrywide. These stakeholders include teachers, Ministry of Education officials, learners, and developers. 2). Incorporation of augmented reality and logs in EduPhysics. Logs create a platform for teachers to monitor learners' activities and enable teachers to assist learners on subjects they are struggling with. 3). Integrating EduPhysics with an open interface option for software developers to extend EduPhysics. The open interface option allows the incorporation of other science courses in EduPhysics. 4). EduPhysics should be dynamic to allow teachers to set up different activities and exercises to encourage inquiry-based learning amongst learners. The work reported in this chapter was based on the previous curriculum and a few selected schools, therefore EduPhysics needs to be revised and the content from the new curriculum needs to be integrated into EduPhysics. EduPhysics also needs to be implemented in different schools countrywide to ascertain its viability. This will determine whether the use of EduPhysics will improve the academic performance of the learners.

FUTURE RESEARCH DIRECTIONS

For future research directions, the project intends to incorporate augmented reality and logs within EduPhysics. In addition, the application may consider the Gamification of experiments by creating 3D virtual lab-based games to encourage and support learning. Artificial intelligence techniques will be added to EduPhysics to create a virtual laboratory that allows intelligent analytics of learners' data such as progress with the experiments and possible 360° visuals of materials being simulated. Furthermore, the researchers will also research the possible integration of EduPhysics within Learning Management Systems (LMS) such as Moodle to achieve a remote presence environment.

CONCLUSIONS

In summary, there is no doubt that technology could be utilized to complement services, especially in countries with limited resources. This chapter discussed the development and introduced EduPhysics, a virtual laboratory for teaching grade 8 Physical science classes in Namibian secondary schools. It further interpreted and reported on data collected amongst participants using a questionnaire on the use of VLs in secondary schools in Windhoek, Namibia. Participants' response has been used to evaluate designs and the viability of the virtual laboratories. The central assumption that guided this chapter was the limited resources in most physical science laboratories, while most computer laboratories in schools are adequately equipped. Hence, was found that there is a need to provide learners from schools with resource-constrained physical science labs with an alternative approach to hands-on practical work. This could be using VLs such as EduPhysics. As a result, EduPhysics was developed based on the grade 8 Namibian curriculum and introduced to participants to ascertain their perception of the use of VLs in Education. Participants generally welcomed the use of VLs and supported its introduction as an alternative approach for teaching and learning in resource-constrained schools. Although participants strongly welcome the use of VLs, it was observed that some participants lacked the required skills to operate them. Therefore, thorough training on the use of VLs is required before its implementation.

REFERENCES

Bak, L. K., Dandanell, G., & Bruun, C. V. (n.d.). *The Implementation of Labster Virtual Labs at Copenhagen University. A Case Study.* Retrieved November 23, 2018, from https://www.elearningmedia.es/sites/default/files/pdfs/The_implementation_of_Labster_at_Copenhagen_University_A_case_study_final.pdf

Bottentuit, J. B., & Coutinho, C. P. (2007). *Virtual Laboratories and M-Learning: learning with mobile devices.* Retrieved December 02, 2018, from https://core.ac.uk/download/pdf/55607753.pdf

Budhu, M. (2002). Virtual laboratories for engineering education. *International Conference on Engineering Education*, 12-18. Retrieved December 30, 2018, from https://pdfs.semanticscholar.org/660e/6763061bb695d5560dd684720d0f2bb29ff7.pdf

Carnegie Mellon University. (2020). *ChemCollective: Online Resources for Teaching and Learning Chemistry.* Retrieved November 29, 2020, from http://chemcollective.org/

Cawthera, A. (n.d.). *Computers in secondary schools in developing countries, costs, and other issues.* The Department For International Development (DFID). World Links For Development (WorLD): a part of the World Bank Institute. The Human Development Network of the World Bank. Retrieved February 07, 2019, from https://ageconsearch.umn.edu/bitstream/12831/1/er010043.pdf

Christina, P. (2020). *What are virtual laboratories and how do they work in eLearning?* Retrieved November 29, 2020, from https://www.talentlms.com/blog/virtual-laboratories-elearning/

Colorado, U. O. (2018). *Simulations.* Retrieved December 12, 2018, from https://phet.colorado.edu/en/simulations/category/new

Creswell, J. W. (2012). Qualitative inquiry and research design: Choosing among five traditions. *Sage (Atlanta, Ga.).*

Daineko, Y., & Dmitriyev, V. (2014). Software module" virtual physics laboratory" in higher education. *Application of Information and Communication Technologies (AICT). IEEE 8th International Conference on. IEEE.* Retrieved November 30, 2018, from https://ieeexplore.ieee.org/abstract/document/7036005

De Jong, T., Linn, M. C., & Zacharia, Z. C. (2013). Physical and virtual laboratories in science and engineering education. *Science, 340*(6130), 305–308. doi:10.1126cience.1230579 PMID:23599479

De Jong, T., Sotiriou, S., & Gillet, D. (2014). Innovations in STEM education: The Go-Lab federation of online labs. *Smart Learning Environments, 1*(1), 3. doi:10.118640561-014-0003-6

Desharnaise, R. A., & Limson, M. (2007). Designing and Implementing virtual Courseware to promote inquiry-based learning. *Journal of Online Learning and Teaching, 3*(1), 30–39.

Forcino, F. L. (2013). The Importance of a Laboratory Section on Student Learning. *Journal of Geoscience Education, 6*(2), 213–221. doi:10.5408/12-412.1

Gomes, L., & Garcia-Zubia, J. (2007). *In a traditional under resourced science laboratory.* Deusto.

Gülsüm, A., & Didem, I. (2017). *The Impact of the Virtual Laboratory on Students' Attitudes in a General Physics Laboratory.* doi:10.3991/ijoe.v13i04.6811

Haidula, T. (2016, January 8). *Lack of resources blurs pupils' vision.* Retrieved May 01, 2018, from https://www.namibian.com.na/print.php?id=145923&type=2

Martinez, G., Naranjo, F. L., Perez, A. L., Suero, M. I., & Pardo, P. J. (2011). Comparative study of the effectiveness of three learning environments: Hyper-realistic virtual simulations, traditional schematic simulations, and traditional laboratory. *Physical Review Special Topics. Physics Education Research, 7*(2), 020111.

Mba, S. I., & Uba, I. I. (2012). The Effect of laboratory works in teaching and learning of physics in onitsha north, Anambra state. *Journal of Science and Arts, 12*(1), 75–84. Retrieved November 29, 2020, from https://www.researchgate.net/profile/Ikemefuna_Uba/publication/265581923_the_effect_of_laboratory_works_in_teaching_and_learning_of_physics_in_onitsha_north_anambra_state/links/55ee12b008aedecb68fc71d6.pdf

McKagan, S. (2018). *Resources for using PhET simulations in class-PhEt Activities Database*. Retrieved December 12, 2018, from https://serc.carleton.edu/49131

Millennium Challenge Corporation. (2014). *Poverty reduction through economic growth*. Retrieved May 01, 2018, from https://www.mcanamibia.org/files/files/OshanaFact%20Sheet(1).pdf

Molohidis, A., Lefkos, I., Taramopoulos, A., Hatzikraniotis, E., & Psillos, D. (2015). Web-based Virtual Labs. In *Proceedings of the 7th International Conference on Computer Supported Education-Volume 1* (pp. 418-423). SCITEPRESS-Science and Technology Publications, Lda.

Nampila, J. (2012). *Development of a Computer-Assisted School Information System for Namibian Schools*. Retrieved May 01, 2018, from http://ir.polytechnic.edu.na/bitstream/handle/10628/383/Nampila.%20 MIT.%20Dev%20of%20a%20computer-assisted%20school%20info%20system%20for%20Namibian%20 schools.pdf?sequence=1&isAllowed=y

National Research Council. (2006). *America's lab report: Investigations in high school science*. National Academies Press.

New Era. (2017, December 8). *Education minister says providing infrastructure a major challenge*. Retrieved December 17, 2018, from https://neweralive.na/posts/education-minister-says-providing-infrastructure-a-major-challenge

New Era. (2017, December 21). *Slight improvement in Grade 10 exam results*. Retrieved November 21, 2018, from https://neweralive.na/posts/slight-improvement-in-grade-10-exam-results

Nghipandulwa, L. (2011). *Secondary school teachers' perceptions of the importance of practical work in biology in Oshana educational region* (Doctoral dissertation). University of Namibia, Windhoek.

Nico, R., Wouter R. V., & Jan T. D. (2011). The learning effects of computer simulations in science education. *Computers & Education, 58*, 136–153.

NIED. (2010). *Physical Science Junior Secondary Syllabus Grades 8-10*. Okahandja: NIED. Retrieved March 22, 2019, from http://www.nied.edu.na

NIED. (2015). *Junior Secondary Phase*. Okahandja: NIED. Retrieved January 23, 2019, from http://www.nied.edu.na/assets/documents/02Syllabuses/04JuniorSecondary/PhysicalScience/JSC_Syllabuses_PS_Sep2016.pdf

NIED. (n.d.). *Improving civic participation of the Youth in Namibia through the use*. Namibia Institute for Democracy (NID). Retrieved May 10, 2018, from https://www.unicef.org/namibia/NID-UNICEF_2011_Listen_Loud_Final_Report.pdf

OECD. (2017). Assessing complex problem solving in the classroom: Meeting challenges and opportunities. In B. Csapó & J. Funke (Eds.), *The Nature of Problem Solving: Using Research to Inspire 21st Century Learning*. OECD Publishing., doi:10.1787/9789264273955-12-

Osakwe, J., Dlodlo, N., & Jere, N. (2017). Where learners and teachers' perceptions on mobile learning meet: A case of Namibian secondary schools in the Khomas region. *Technology in Society, 49*, 16–30. doi:10.1016/j.techsoc.2016.12.004

Osakwe, J. O., Nomusa, D., & Norbert, J. (2015). A Preliminary Framework for the Adoption of Mobile Learning Technology in Namibian High Schools: A Case of the Erongo Region. International Journal of Science and Research.

Prensky, M. (2001). *Digital Natives, Digital Immigrants*. Retrieved 30 November 2020, from https://www.marcprensky.com/writing/Prensky%20-%20Digital%20Natives,%20Digital%20Immigrants%20-%20Part1.pdf

Proctor, J. (2019). *Digital Transformation Enablers - Artificial Intelligence & Machine Learning*. Retrieved December 6, 2020, from https://www.inteqgroup.com/blog/digital-transformation-enablers-part-1-artificial-intelligence-machine-learning

Saga, B. (2013). *10 Emerging Educational Technologies and How They Are Being Used Across the Globe*. Retrieved 29 November 2020, from https://www.opencolleges.edu.au/informed/features/the-ten-emerging-technologies-in-education-and-how-they-are-being-used-across-the-globe/

Salesforce. (2020). *What Is Digital Transformation*. Retrieved December 6, 2020, from https://www.salesforce.com/products/platform/what-is-digital-transformation/

Sassi, E. (2000). Computer supported lab-work in physics education: advantages and problems. *International Conference on Physics Teacher Education beyond 2000*.

Sommerville, I. (2011). *Software Engineering* (9th ed.). Retrieved 29 November 2020, from http://index-of.co.uk/Engineering/Software%20Engineering%20 (9th%20Edition).pdf

Suh, K.-S., & Lee, Y. E. (2005). *The effects of virtual reality on consumer learning: An empirical investigation*. Management Information Systems Research Center. Retrieved November 22, 2018, from https://www.jstor.org/stable/25148705

Uğur, M., Savaş, K., & Erdal, H. (2010). An internet-based real-time remote automatic control laboratory for control education. *Procedia: Social and Behavioral Sciences*, 2(2), 5271–5275. doi:10.1016/j.sbspro.2010.03.859

Vosniadou, S. (n.d.). *How children learn*. International Academy of Education. Retrieved December 20, 2018, from http://www.ibe.unesco.org/fileadmin/user_upload/archive/Publications/educationalpractices-seriespdf/prac07e.pdf

Wallet, P. (2015). *Information and communication technology: A comparative analysis of basic e-readiness in schools*. The UNESCO Institute for Statistics (UIS). Retrieved February 07, 2019, from http://uis.unesco.org/sites/default/files/documents/information-and-communication-technology-ict-in-education-in-sub-saharan-africa-2015-en.pdf

Wiesner, T. F., & Lan, W. (2004). Comparison of student learning in physical and simulated unit operations experiments. *Journal of Engineering Education*, 93(3), 195–204. doi:10.1002/j.2168-9830.2004.tb00806.x

Wikiversity. (2020). *Open design*. Retrieved 30 November 2020, from https://en.wikiversity.org/wiki/Open_design

Williams, D. L., Crittenden, V. L., Keo, T., & McCarty, P. (2012). The use of social media: An exploratory study of usage among digital natives. *Journal of Public Affairs*, *12*(2), 127–136. doi:10.1002/pa.1414

Zervas, P., Kalimeris, I., & Sampson, D. G. (2014). A Method for Developing Mobile Virtual Laboratories. In *2014 IEEE 14th International Conference on Advanced Learning Technologies* (pp. 8-10). IEEE. 10.1109/ICALT.2014.12

ADDITIONAL READING

Azar, A., & Şengüleç, Ö. A. (2011). Computer-assisted and laboratory-assisted teaching methods in physics teaching: The effect on student physics achievement and attitude towards physics. International Journal of Physics & Chemistry Education, 3(SI), 43-50.

Carroll, J. M., Chin, G., Rosson, M. B., & Neale, D. C. (2000, August). The development of cooperation: Five years of participatory design in the virtual school. In Proceedings of the 3rd conference on Designing interactive systems: processes, practices, methods, and techniques (pp. 239-251).

Çelik, H., Sarı, U., & Harwanto, U. N. (2015). Developing and evaluating physics teaching material with Algodoo (Phun) in virtual environment: Archimedes' Principle. International Journal of Innovation in Science and Mathematics Education (formerly CAL-laborate International), 23(4).

De Magistris, M. (2005). A MATLAB-based virtual laboratory for teaching introductory quasi-stationary electromagnetics. *IEEE Transactions on Education*, *48*(1), 81–88. doi:10.1109/TE.2004.832872

Lewis, D. I. (2014). The pedagogical benefits and pitfalls of virtual tools for teaching and learning laboratory practices in the biological sciences. The Higher Education Academy: STEM.

Yang, K. Y., & Heh, J. S. (2007). The impact of internet virtual physics laboratory instruction on the achievement in physics, science process skills and computer attitudes of 10th-grade students. *Journal of Science Education and Technology*, *16*(5), 451–461. doi:10.100710956-007-9062-6

KEY TERMS AND DEFINITIONS

EduPhysics: Is a virtual laboratory, which was developed in this study to simulate virtual experiments.

Simulation: Is an approximate imitation of the operation of a process or system that represents its operation over time.

Virtual Laboratory: Is a computer-based activity where students interact with an experimental apparatus or other activity via a computer interface.

Compilation of References

Accenture. (2012). *Airport Analytics.* Barcelona: Accenture. Retrieved January 12, 2020, from https://www.accenture.com/ae-en/~/media/accenture/conversion-assets/dotcom/documents/global/pdf/industries_10/accenture-airport-analytics-final.pdf

Achim, M. V., Borlea, S. N., Găban, L. V., & Mihăilă, A. A. (2019). The Shadow Economy and Culture: Evidence in European Countries. *Eastern European Economics, 57*(5), 352–374. doi:10.1080/00128775.2019.1614461

ACM/IEEE/AIS. (2019). *Computing Curricula.* Retrieved from https://computingcurricula.com/

Acoss. (2020). *Lutter contre la fraude au prélèvement social.* https://www.acoss.fr/home/nos-missions.html

Adhami, S., Giudici, G., & Martinazzi, S. (2018). Why do businesses go crypto? An empirical analysis of initial coin offerings. *Journal of Economics and Business, 100*, 64–75. doi:10.1016/j.jeconbus.2018.04.001

Adomavicius, G., & Tuzhilin, A. (2005). Toward the next generation of recommender systems: A survey of the state-of-the-art and possible extensions. *IEEE Transactions on Knowledge and Data Engineering, 17*(6), 734–749. doi:10.1109/TKDE.2005.99

Ahkmedzhanov, N. M., Zhukotcky, A. V., Kudrjavtcev, V. B., Oganov, R. G., Rastorguev, V. V., Ryjov, A. P., & Stogalov, A. S. (2003). System for evaluation and monitoring of risks of cardiovascular disease [in Russian]. *Intelligent Systems, 7*, 5–38.

Akram, V. K., & Dagdeviren, O. (2018, June). On Hardness of Connectivity Maintenance Problem in Drone Networks. In *2018 IEEE International Black Sea Conference on Communications and Networking (BlackSeaCom)* (pp. 1-5). IEEE. 10.1109/BlackSeaCom.2018.8433713

Ali, F. (2016). Hotel website quality, perceived flow, customer satisfaction and purchase intention. *Journal of Hospitality and Tourism Technology, 7*(2), 213–228. doi:10.1108/JHTT-02-2016-0010

Al-Jarrah, O., Yoo, P. D., Muhaidat, S., & Karagiannidis, G. K. (2015). Effiicent machine learning for big data: A review. *Big Data Research.*

Al-Khatib, A. M. (2012). Electronic Payment Fraud Detection Techniques. *World of Computer Science and Information Technology Journal, 2*(4), 137–141.

Almatrafi, O., Johri, A., & Rangwala, H. (2018). Needle in a haystack: Identifying learner posts that require urgent response in MOOC discussion forums. *Computers & Education, 118*, 1–9. doi:10.1016/j.compedu.2017.11.002

Amit, J. (2015). Movie stars and the volatility of movie revenues. *Journal of Media Economics, 28*(4), 246–267. doi:10.1080/08997764.2015.1094079

Amrin, A., Xia, C., & Dai, S. (2015). Focused Web Crawling Algorithms. *Journal of Computers*, *10*(4), 245–251. Advance online publication. doi:10.17706/jcp.10.4.245-251

Anuradha, J. (2015). A brief introduction on Big Data 5Vs characteristics and Hadoop technology. *Procedia Computer Science*, *48*, 319–324. doi:10.1016/j.procs.2015.04.188

Apache Spark. (n.d.). https://spark.apache.org/docs/latest/index.html

Apache. (n.d.). https://spark.apache.org/docs/latest/cluster-overview.html

Arbour, M., Kaspar, R. W., & Teall, A. M. (2015). Strategies to promote cultural competence in distance education. *Journal of Transcultural Nursing*, *26*(4), 436–440. doi:10.1177/1043659614547201 PMID:25122626

Ashby, W. R. (1956). *An Introduction to Cybernetics*. Chapman and Hall. doi:10.5962/bhl.title.5851

Ashley, K. D. (1991). Reasoning with cases and hypotheticals in HYPO. *International Journal of Man-Machine Studies*, *34*(6), 753–796. doi:10.1016/0020-7373(91)90011-U

Aslan, İ. H. (2019). *Yük Taşıyan İşçilerde Ergonomik Farkındalık Oluşturmaya Yönelik Verilen Eğitimin Vücut Farkındalığı, Postür Ve Yaşam Kalitesi Üzerine Etkisi* (Master of Science Thesis). İstanbul Okan University.

Asokan, G. V., & Asokan, V. (2015). Leveraging "big data" to enhance the effectiveness of "one health" in an era of health informatics. *Journal of Epidemiology and Global Health*, *5*(4), 311–314. doi:10.1016/j.jegh.2015.02.001 PMID:25747185

Assnat. (2020). Objectif d'équité fiscale. *Bilan 2011-2016*.

Asur, S., & Huberman, B. A. (2010). Predicting the future with social media. *2010 IEEE/WIC/ACM International Conference on Web Intelligence and Intelligent Agent Technology*, 492–499. 10.1109/WI-IAT.2010.63

Atanassov, K. T. (1986). Intuitionistic fuzzy sets. *Fuzzy Sets and Systems*, *20*(1), 87–96. doi:10.1016/S0165-0114(86)80034-3

Atkinson, K., Bench-Capon, T., & Bollegala, D. (2020). Explanation in AI and law: Past, present and future. *Artificial Intelligence*, *289*, 103387. Advance online publication. doi:10.1016/j.artint.2020.103387

Aviation Media. (2019). *Smart Airports*. Retrieved 5 18, 2020, from Smart Airports South East Asia 2019: https://smart-airports.com/sea/

Ayres, H. (2019). *5-infamous-fraud-cases-throughout-the-centuries*. ACFE insights. News and analysis on the global fight against fraud. https://www.acfeinsights.com/acfe-insights/5-infamous-fraud-cases-throughout-the-centuries

Bai, H., & Atiquzzaman, M. (2003). Error modeling schemes for fading channels in wireless communications: A survey. *IEEE Communications Surveys and Tutorials*, *5*(2), 2–9. doi:10.1109/COMST.2003.5341334

Bak, L. K., Dandanell, G., & Bruun, C. V. (n.d.). *The Implementation of Labster Virtual Labs at Copenhagen University. A Case Study*. Retrieved November 23, 2018, from https://www.elearningmedia.es/sites/default/files/pdfs/The_implementation_of_Labster_at_Copenhagen_University_A_case_study_final.pdf

Barbosu, S. (2016). Big data on the big screen: Revealing latent similarity among movies and its effect on box office performance. SSRN *Electronic Journal*. doi:10.2139srn.2846821

Barredo Arrieta, A., Díaz-Rodríguez, N., Del Ser, J., Bennetot, A., Tabik, S., Barbado, A., Garcia, S., Gil-Lopez, S., Molina, D., Benjamins, R., Chatila, R., & Herrera, F. (2020). Explainable Explainable Artificial Intelligence (XAI): Concepts, taxonomies, opportunities and challenges toward responsible AI. *Information Fusion*, *58*, 82–115. doi:10.1016/j.inffus.2019.12.012

Batko, M., Gennaro, C., Savino, P., & Zezula, P. (2004). *DigitalLibrary Architectures: Peer-to-Peer, Grid, and Service-Orientation, Pre-proceedings of the Sixth Thematic Workshop of the EU Network of Excellence DELOS*. Edizioni Libreria Progetto.

Batko, M., Falchi, F., Lucchese, C., Novak, D., Perego, R., Rabitti, F., Sedmidubsky, J., & Zezula, P. (2010). Building a web-scale image similarity search system. *Multimedia Tools and Applications*, *47*(3), 599–629. doi:10.100711042-009-0339-z

Batko, M., Kohoutkova, P., & Novak, D. (2009). Cophir image collection under the microscope. In *Second International Workshop on Similarity Search and Applications* (pp. 47-54). IEEE. 10.1109/SISAP.2009.25

Bayrak, H. (2019). *Dijilopedi*. https://dijilopedi.com/2019-turkiye-internet-kullanim-ve-sosyal-medya-istatistikleri/

Becker, G. S. (1968). Crime and Punishment: an Economic Approach. In N. G. Fielding, A. Clarke, & R. Witt (Eds.), *The Economic Dimensions of Crime*. Palgrave Macmillan. doi:10.1007/978-1-349-62853-7_2

Bedford, E. (2020). *DIY and home improvement market in Canada - Statistics & Facts*. https://www.statista.com/topics/5188/diy-and-home-improvement-market-in-canada/

Bekmezci, I., Sahingoz, O. K., & Temel, Ş. (2013). Flying ad-hoc networks (FANETs): A survey. *Ad Hoc Networks*, *11*(3), 1254–1270. doi:10.1016/j.adhoc.2012.12.004

Belhumeur, P. N., Hespanha, J. P., & Kriegman, D. J. (1997, July). Eigenfaces vs. fisherfaces: Recognition using class specific linear projection. *IEEE Transactions on Pattern Analysis and Machine Intelligence*, *19*(7), 711–720. doi:10.1109/34.598228

Bhisikar, P. (2013). Overview of web mining and different technique for web personalisation. *International Journal of Engineering Research and Applications*, *3*(2), 543–545.

Bhuyan, M. H., Bhattacharyya, D. K., & Kalita, J. K. (2014). Network Anomaly Detection: Methods, Systems and Tools. IEEE Communications Surveys & Tutorials, 16(1), 303–336.

Biederman, A. (2015). Social media. *Franchising World*, *47*(10), 20–23.

Bitzenis, A., Vlachos, V., & Schneider, F. (2016). An Exploration of the Greek Shadow Economy: Can Its Transfer into the Official Economy Provide Economic Relief Amid the Crisis? *Journal of Economic Issues*, *50*(1), 165–196. doi:10.1080/00213624.2016.1147918

Bok, J., & Ryu, H. G. (2014). Path loss model considering doppler shift for high speed railroad communication. In *16th International Conference on Advanced Communication Technology* (pp. 1-4). IEEE. 10.1109/ICACT.2014.6778910

BONN HR. (2017, March 13). *National Airports Corporation*. Retrieved September 20, 2019, from National Airports Corporation: https://www.nac.com.pg/about-us/mission-and-vision/

Bostrom, N., & Yudkowsky, E. (2018). The Ethics of Artificial Intelligence. In *Cambridge Handbook of Artificial Intelligence*. Cambridge University Press.

Bottentuit, J. B., & Coutinho, C. P. (2007). *Virtual Laboratories and M-Learning: learning with mobile devices*. Retrieved December 02, 2018, from https://core.ac.uk/download/pdf/55607753.pdf

Bouyakoub, S., Belkhir, A., Bouyakoub, F. M., & Guebli, W. (2017). Smart airport: an IoT-based Airport Management System. In *ICFNDS '17: Proceedings of the International Conference on Future Networks and Distributed Systems, July 2017 Article No.: 45* (pp. 1-7). ACM.

Broder, A. Z. (1997). On the resemblance and containment of documents. Proceedings of Compression and Complexity of SEQUENCES 1997, 21-29.

Broersen, J. (2014). Responsible intelligent systems. *KI-Künstliche Intelligenz*, *28*(3), 209–214. doi:10.100713218-014-0305-4

Brunton, F. (2019). *Digital cash: The unknown history of the anarchists, utopians, and technologists who created cryptocurrency*. Princeton University Press.

Buckley, J. J. (1985). Fuzzy hierarchical analysis. *Fuzzy Sets and Systems*, *17*(3), 233–247. doi:10.1016/0165-0114(85)90090-9

Budhu, M. (2002). Virtual laboratories for engineering education. *International Conference on Engineering Education*, 12-18. Retrieved December 30, 2018, from https://pdfs.semanticscholar.org/660e/6763061bb695d5560dd684720d0f2bb29ff7.pdf

Bujari, A., Palazzi, C. E., & Ronzani, D. (2017). FANET application scenarios and mobility models. In *Proceedings of the 3rd Workshop on Micro Aerial Vehicle Networks, Systems, and Applications* (pp. 43-46). ACM. 10.1145/3086439.3086440

Bustamante. (2018). *Home Improvement Industry Statistics*. https://ipropertymanagement.com/ research/home-improvement-industry-statistics

Cabitza, F., Rasoini, R., & Gensini, G. F. (2017). Unintended consequences of machine learning in medicine. *Journal of the American Medical Association*, *318*(6), 517–518. doi:10.1001/jama.2017.7797 PMID:28727867

Çabuk, U., Tosun, M., Jacobsen, R., & Dagdeviren, O. (2020). Path Loss Estimation of Air-to-Air Channels for FANETs over Rugged Terrains. *Proceedings of the 28th IEEE Signal Processing and Communication Applications (SIU)*.

Canada Revenue Agency. (2019). *Combatting tax crimes: Tax evasion explained*. https:// www.canada.ca/en/revenue-agency/programs/about-canada-revenue-agency-cra/compliance/ combat-tax-crimes.html

Canada Revenue Agency. (2020). *Cyber-incidents*. https://www.canada.ca/en/revenue-agency/

Cao, Y., Qi, H., Zhou, W., Kato, J., Li, K., Liu, X., & Gui, J. (2018). Binary hashing for approximate nearest neighbor search on big data: A survey. *IEEE Access: Practical Innovations, Open Solutions*, *6*, 2039–2054. doi:10.1109/ACCESS.2017.2781360

Carnegie Mellon University. (2020). *ChemCollective: Online Resources for Teaching and Learning Chemistry*. Retrieved November 29, 2020, from http://chemcollective.org/

Cawthera, A. (n.d.). *Computers in secondary schools in developing countries, costs, and other issues*. The Department For International Development (DFID). World Links For Development (WorLD): a part of the World Bank Institute. The Human Development Network of the World Bank. Retrieved February 07, 2019, from https://ageconsearch.umn.edu/bitstream/12831/1/er010043.pdf

Cebula, R. J., & Feige, E. L. (2012). America's unreported economy: Measuring the size, growth and determinants of income tax evasion in the U.S. *Crime, Law, and Social Change*, *57*(3), 265–285. doi:10.100710611-011-9346-x

Chaffey, D. (2009). *E-business and E-commerce Management*. Prentice Hall.

Chakraborty, S., & Banik, D. (2006). Design of a material handling equipment selection model using analytic hierarchy process. *International Journal of Advanced Manufacturing Technology*, *28*(11-12), 1237–1245. doi:10.100700170-004-2467-y

Chancellor, W., & Abbott, M. (2015). The Australian construction industry: Is the shadow economy distorting productivity? *Construction Management and Economics*, *33*(3), 176–186. doi:10.1080/01446193.2015.1028954

Chang, B., & Ki, E. (2005). Devising a practical model for predicting theatrical movie success: Focusing on the experience good property. *Journal of Media Economics*, *18*(4), 247–269. doi:10.120715327736me1804_2

Changi Airport Group. (2018). *Annual report 2017/18*. Changi: Changi Airport Group. Retrieved December 7, 2019, from http://www.changiairport.com/content/dam/cacorp/publications/Annual%20Reports/2018/CAG%20AR201718%20Business%20and%20Operations%20Review.pdf

ChapmanP.ClintonJ.KerberR.KhabazaT.ReinartzT.ShearerC.WirthR. (2000);

Charikar, M. S. (2002). Similarity estimation techniques from rounding algorithms. *Proceedings on 34th Annual ACM Symposium on Theory of Computing*, 380-388.

Chatellier, G., Varlet, V., Blachier-Poisson, C., Beslay, N., Behier, J. M., Braunstein, D., ... Josseran, A. (2016). "Big data" and "open data": What kind of access should researchers enjoy? *Therapies*, *71*(1), 107–114. doi:10.1016/j.therap.2016.01.005 PMID:27080635

Chávez, E., Figueroa, K., & Navarro, G. (2008). Effective Proximity Retrieval by Ordering Permutations. *IEEE Transactions on Pattern Analysis and Machine Intelligence*, *30*(9), 1647–1658. doi:10.1109/TPAMI.2007.70815 PMID:18617721

Chemin, M.-C. (2019). *7,8 à 10 milliards d'euros de fraude sociale?* Fondation iFRAP. https://www.ifrap.org/budget-et-fiscalite/78-10-milliards-deuros-de-fraude-sociale-recap

Chen, C. P., & Zhang, C.-Y. (2014). Data-intensive applications, challenges, techniques and technologies: A survey on Big Data. *Information Sciences*, *275*, 314–347. doi:10.1016/j.ins.2014.01.015

Cheng, Q., Lu, X., Liu, Z., & Huang, J. C. (2015). Mining research trends with anomaly detection models: The case of social computing research. *Scientometrics*, *103*(2), 453–469. doi:10.100711192-015-1559-9

Cheng, X., Du, D. Z., Wang, L., & Xu, B. (2008). Relay sensor placement in wireless sensor networks. *Wireless Networks*, *14*(3), 347–355. doi:10.100711276-006-0724-8

Chen, H., Chiang, R., & Storey, V. (2012, December). Business intelligence and analytics: From big data to big impact. *Management Information Systems Quarterly*, *36*(4), 1165–1188. doi:10.2307/41703503

Chen, K., Li, X., & Wang, H. (2015). On the model design of integrated intelligent big data analytics systems. *Industrial Management & Data Systems*, *115*(9), 1666–1682. doi:10.1108/IMDS-03-2015-0086

Chen, L. M., Su, Z. X., & Jiang, B. (2015). *Mathematical Problems in Data Science*. Springer. doi:10.1007/978-3-319-25127-1

Chen, S. M., & Lee, L. W. (2010). Fuzzy multiple attributes group decision-making based on the interval type-2 TOPSIS method. *Expert Systems with Applications*, *37*(4), 2790–2798. doi:10.1016/j.eswa.2009.09.012

Chen, Y., Liu, Y., & Zhang, J. (2012). When do third-party product reviews affect firm value and what can firms do? The case of media critics and professional movie reviews. *Journal of Marketing*, *76*(2), 116–134. doi:10.1509/jm.09.0034

Chiou, W., Lin, C., & Perng, C. (2010). A strategic framework for website evaluation based on a review of the literature from 1995–2006. *Information & Management*, *47*(5-6), 282–290. doi:10.1016/j.im.2010.06.002

Chiu, C. Y., Wang, H. M., & Chen, C. S. (2010). Fast min-hashing indexing and robust spatio-temporal matching for detecting video copies. *ACM Transactions on Multimedia Computing Communications and Applications*, *6*(2), 1–23. doi:10.1145/1671962.1671966

Chiu, D. K. W., Kafeza, E., & Hung, P. C. (2011). ISF special issue on emerging social and legal aspects of information systems with Web 2.0. *Information Systems Frontiers*, *13*(2), 153–155. doi:10.100710796-009-9168-x

Chiu, D. K. W., Leung, H. F., & Lam, K. M. (2009). On the making of service recommendations: An action theory based on utility, reputation, and risk attitude. *Expert Systems with Applications*, *36*(2), 3293–3301. doi:10.1016/j.eswa.2008.01.055

Choi, T. M., Guo, S., & Luo, S. (2020). When blockchain meets social-media: Will the result benefit social media analytics for supply chain operations management? *Transportation Research Part E, Logistics and Transportation Review*, *135*, 101860. doi:10.1016/j.tre.2020.101860

Choudhury, A. R. (2015, March 30). *How IT helps Changi Airport to be smart, sweet and swift*. Retrieved January 3, 2020, from The Business Times: https://www.businesstimes.com.sg/focus/in-depth/cio-speaks/how-it-helps-changi-airport-to-be-smart-sweet-and-swift

Christina, P. (2020). *What are virtual laboratories and how do they work in eLearning?* Retrieved November 29, 2020, from https://www.talentlms.com/blog/virtual-laboratories-elearning/

Chung, F. R. K., & Graham, R. L. (1985). A new bound for Euclidean Steiner minimal trees. *Annals of the New York Academy of Sciences*, *440*(1), 328–346. doi:10.1111/j.1749-6632.1985.tb14564.x

Chuprina, R. (2020). *The In-depth 2020 Guide to E-commerce Fraud Detection*. www.datasciencecentral.com

Ciaccia, P., Patella, M., & Zezula, P. (1997). M-tree: An Efficient Access Method for Similarity Search in Metric Spaces. *Proceedings of the 23rd VLDB Conference*, 426-435.

Clavier, O. H., Schleicher, D. R., Houck, S. W., Sorensen, J. A., Davis, P. C., & Hunter, C. G. (2005, September 27). *US Patent No. US 6950037B1*. Retrieved April 7, 2020, from https://patents.google.com/patent/US6950037B1/en

Clavier, O. H., Schleicher, D. R., Houck, S. W., Sorensen, J. A., Davis, P. C., & Hunter, C. G. (2008, June 10). *US Patent No. US 7,385,527 B1*. Retrieved April 7, 2020, from https://patents.google.com/patent/US7385527B1/en

Clement, J. (2019). *Number of monthly active Twitter users worldwide from 1st quarter 2010 to 1st quarter 2019*. Retrieved from: https://www.statista.com/statistics/282087/number-of-monthly-active-twitter-users/

Collier, N. (2012). Uncovering text mining: A survey of current work on web-based epidemic intelligence. *Global Public Health: An International Journal for Research, Policy and Practice*, *7*(7), 731–749. doi:10.1080/17441692.2012.699975 PMID:22783909

Collins Aerospace. (2017). *Papua New Guinea's National Airports Corporation closer to 2030 'smart airports' goal with Rockwell Collins contract renewal*. Retrieved October 30, 2019, from Collins Aerospace: https://www.rockwellcollins.com/Data/News/2018-Cal-Yr/IMS/20170207-NAC-ARINC-renewal.aspx

Collins Aerospace. (2018, June 15). *NAC Develops Smart Airports Goal*. Retrieved October 18, 2019, from Airport Technology: https://www.airport-technology.com/contractors/consult/arinc-airports/pressreleases/nac-develops-smart-airports-goal/

Colorado, U. O. (2018). *Simulations*. Retrieved December 12, 2018, from https://phet.colorado.edu/en/simulations/category/new

Columbus, L. (2016). Roundup Of Analytics, Big Data & BI Forecasts And Market Estimates, 2016. *Forbes: USA. Pristupljeno*, *12*, 2017.

Connor, R., Cardillo, F. A., Vadicamo, L., & Rabitti, F. (2017b). Hilbert exclusion: Improved metric search through finite isometric embeddings. *ACM Transactions on Information Systems*, *35*(3), 1–27. doi:10.1145/3001583

Connor, R., Vadicamo, L., & Rabitti, F. (2017a). High-dimensional simplexes for supermetric search. In *Similarity Search and Applications – 10th International Conference, SISAP 2017, Proceedings*, 96–109.

Cornejo, A., & Lynch, N. (2010). Fault-tolerance through k-connectivity. In *Workshop on network science and systems issues in multi-robot autonomy: ICRA* (*Vol. 2*, p. 2010). Academic Press.

Coronel, C., & Morris, S. (2015). *Database Systems: Design, Implementation, and Management* (11th ed.). Cengage Learning.

Creswell, J. W. (2012). Qualitative inquiry and research design: Choosing among five traditions. *Sage (Atlanta, Ga.)*.

CRISP-DM 1.0 Step-by-step data mining guides. (n.d.). ftp://ftp.software.ibm.com/software/analytics/ spss/support/Modeler/Documentation/14/UserManual/CRISP-DM.pdf

Cromzigt, L. (2016). Strawson's take on responsibility applied to AI. *Student Undergraduate Research E-journal!, 2.*

Daft, R., & Marcic, D. (2008). *Management: The New Workplace*. China Cengage Learning.

Dahl, G. E., Yu, D., Deng, L., & Acero, A. (2011). Context-dependent pre-trained deep neural networks for large-vocabulary speech recognition. *IEEE Transactions on Audio, Speech, and Language Processing, 20*(1), 30–42. doi:10.1109/TASL.2011.2134090

Dai, D., Lan, Y., Fan, T., & Zhao, M. (2019). Research on stock index prediction and decision-making based on text mining and machine learning. *China Soft Science, 4*, 166–175.

Daineko, Y., & Dmitriyev, V. (2014). Software module" virtual physics laboratory" in higher education. *Application of Information and Communication Technologies (AICT). IEEE 8th International Conference on. IEEE.* Retrieved November 30, 2018, from https://ieeexplore.ieee.org/abstract/document/7036005

Damarel Systems International Ltd. (2018, July 26). *Damarel Systems International Ltd.* Retrieved October 30, 2019, from Damarel Systems International Ltd: https://www.damarel.com/news/l-dcs-becomes-part-of-smart-airports-initiative-in-papua-new-guinea/

Danoy, G., Brust, M. R., & Bouvry, P. (2015). Connectivity stability in autonomous multi-level UAV swarms for wide area monitoring. In *Proceedings of the 5th ACM Symposium on Development and Analysis of Intelligent Vehicular Networks and Applications* (pp. 1-8). ACM. 10.1145/2815347.2815351

DARPA. (2018). *AI Next Campaign*. Retrieved from https://www.darpa.mil/work-with-us/ai-next-campaign

Dash, S., Shakyawar, S. K., Sharma, M., & Kaushik, S. (2019). Big data in healthcare: Management, analysis and future prospects. *Journal of Big Data, 6*(1), 54. doi:10.118640537-019-0217-0

Das, S., Behera, R. K., Kumar, M., & Rath, S. K. (2018). Real-Time Sentiment Analysis of Twitter Streaming data for Stock Prediction. *Procedia Computer Science, 132*, 956–964. doi:10.1016/j.procs.2018.05.111

Daugman, J. (2003). The importance of being random: Statistical principles of iris recognition. *Pattern Recognition, 36*(2), 279–291. doi:10.1016/S0031-3203(02)00030-4

Davis, C. K. (2014). Viewpoint Beyond Data and Analytics- Why business analytics and big data really matter for modern business organizations. *Communications of the ACM, 57*(8), 39–41. doi:10.1145/2602326

De Fortuny, E. J., De Smedt, T., Martens, D., & Daelemans, W. (2014). Evaluating and understanding text-based stock price prediction models. *Information Processing & Management, 50*(2), 426–441. doi:10.1016/j.ipm.2013.12.002

De Jong, T., Linn, M. C., & Zacharia, Z. C. (2013). Physical and virtual laboratories in science and engineering education. *Science*, *340*(6130), 305–308. doi:10.1126cience.1230579 PMID:23599479

De Jong, T., Sotiriou, S., & Gillet, D. (2014). Innovations in STEM education: The Go-Lab federation of online labs. *Smart Learning Environments*, *1*(1), 3. doi:10.118640561-014-0003-6

De, H. (2018). *Survey: Nearly 80% of Americans have heard of Bitcoin*. Retrieved from: https://www.coindesk.com/survey-nearly-80-of-americans-have-heard-of-bitcoin

Dean, J., & Ghemawat, S. (2008). Map-Reduce: Simplified data processing on large clusters. *Communications of the ACM*, *51*(1), 107–113. doi:10.1145/1327452.1327492

Delena, D., & Demirkanb, H. (2013). Data, information and analytics as services. *Decision Support Systems*, *55*(1), 359–363. doi:10.1016/j.dss.2012.05.044

Deresiewicz, W. (2014). *Excellent Sheep: The Miseducation of the American Elite & the Way to Meaningful Life*. Free Press.

Descartes, R. (1637). Discourse on the Methods of the Rightly Conducting the Reason, and Seeking Truth in the Sciences. *GlobalGrey 2018*. Retrieved from https://www.globalgreyebooks.com/index.html

Desharnaise, R. A., & Limson, M. (2007). Designing and Implementing virtual Courseware to promote inquiry-based learning. *Journal of Online Learning and Teaching*, *3*(1), 30–39.

Deza, M. M., & Deza, E. (2009). Encyclopedia of distances. Springer. doi:10.1007/978-3-642-00234-2_1

Dickson, B. (2017) *What is the difference between artificial and augmented intelligence?* Retrieved from https://bdtech-talks.com/2017/12/04/what-is-the-difference-between-ai-and-augmented-intelligence/

Dinçer, H., Baykal, E., & Yüksel, S. (n.d.). Analysis of spiritual leadership and ethical climate for banking industry using an integrated IT2 fuzzy decision-making model. *Journal of Intelligent & Fuzzy Systems*, 1-13.

Dixit, V. V., Chand, S., & Nair, D. J. (2016). Autonomous vehicles: Disengagements, accidents and reaction times. *PLoS One*, *11*(12), e0168054. doi:10.1371/journal.pone.0168054 PMID:27997566

Doerr, A., & Necker, S. (2018). Toward an understanding of collaborative tax evasion: A natural field experiment with businesses. FreiburgerDiskussionspapiere zur Ordnungsökonomik, No. 18/13, Albert-Ludwigs-UniversitätFreiburg, Institute for Economic Research, University of Freiburg.

Dohnal, V., Gennaro, C., Savino, P., & Zezula, P. (2001). Separable Splits of Metric Data Sets. In SEBD (pp. 45-62). Academic Press.

Donahue, J., Jia, Y., Vinyals, O., Hoffman, J., Zhang, N., Tzeng, E., & Darrell, T. (2014). Decaf: A deep convolutional activation feature for generic visual recognition. *Proceedings of the 31th International Conference on Machine Learning*, 647–655.

Dong-chen He, & Li Wang. (1990, July). Texture unit, texture spectrum, and texture analysis. *IEEE Transactions on Geoscience and Remote Sensing*, *28*(4), 509–512. doi:10.1109/TGRS.1990.572934

Doshi-Velez, F., Kortz, M., Budish, R., Bavitz, C., Gershman, S., O'Brien, D., . . . Wood, A. J. a. p. a. (2017). *Accountability of AI under the law: The role of explanation*. Academic Press.

Du, J., Xu, H., & Huang, X. (2014). Box office prediction based on microblog. *Expert Systems with Applications*, *41*(4), 1680–1689. doi:10.1016/j.eswa.2013.08.065

Dur, Z. (2019). *AHP'ye Dayalı Bulanık UTASTAR Yaklaşımı: Malzeme Taşıma Ekipmanı Uygulaması* (Master of Science Thesis). Hacettepe University.

Efe, B. (2019). Website Evaluation Using Interval Type-2 Fuzzy-Number-Based TOPSIS Approach. In Multi-Criteria Decision-Making Models for Website Evaluation (pp. 166-185). IGI Global. doi:10.4018/978-1-5225-8238-0.ch009

Efe, B. (2016). An integrated fuzzy multi criteria group decision making approach for ERP system selection. *Applied Soft Computing, 38*, 106–117. doi:10.1016/j.asoc.2015.09.037

Efe, B., & Efe, Ö. F. (2018). Intuitionistic fuzzy number based group decision making approach for personnel selection. *Uludağ University Journal of The Faculty of Engineering, 23*(3), 11–26. doi:10.17482/uumfd.338406

Efe, B., Yerlikaya, M. A., & Efe, Ö. F. (2020). Mobile phone selection based on a novel quality function deployment approach. *Soft Computing, 24*(20), 1–15. doi:10.100700500-020-04876-x

Efe, Ö. F. (2020). Hybrid Multi-Criteria Models: Joint Health and Safety Unit Selection on Hybrid Multi-Criteria Decision Making. In A. Behl (Ed.), *Multi-Criteria Decision Analysis in Management* (pp. 62–84). IGI Global. doi:10.4018/978-1-7998-2216-5.ch004

Eghbali, S., Ashtiani, H., & Tahvildari, L. (2017). Online nearest neighbor search in binary space. In *2017 IEEE International Conference on Data Mining* (pp. 853-858). IEEE. 10.1109/ICDM.2017.104

Egli, J. J. (1957). Radio propagation above 40 MC over irregular terrain. *Proceedings of the IRE, 45*(10), 1383–1391. doi:10.1109/JRPROC.1957.278224

Eiloart, J. (2018, Dec 2). *Top five business analytics intelligence trends for 2019*. Retrieved from https://www.information-age.com/business-analytics-intelligence-123477004/

Einav, L. (2007). Seasonality in the US motion picture industry. *The RAND Journal of Economics, 38*(1), 127–145. doi:10.1111/j.1756-2171.2007.tb00048.x

Eliashberg, J., Hui, S. K., & Zhang, Z. J. (2007). From story line to box office: A new approach for green-lighting movie scripts. *Management Science, 53*(6), 881–893. doi:10.1287/mnsc.1060.0668

Engelbart, D. C. (1962). *Augmenting human intellect: a conceptual framework*. Retrieved from https://www.dougengelbart.org/pubs/augment-3906.html

Erceg, V., Hari, K. V. S., Smith, M. S., Baum, D. S., Sheikh, K. P., Tappenden, C., ... Trinkwon, D. (2001). *IEEE 802.16 Broadband Wireless Access WG: Channel Models for Fixed Wireless Applications*. IEEE.

Erceg, V., Greenstein, L. J., Tjandra, S. Y., Parkoff, S. R., Gupta, A., Kulic, B., Julius, A. A., & Bianchi, R. (1999). An empirically based path loss model for wireless channels in suburban environments. *IEEE Journal on Selected Areas in Communications, 17*(7), 1205–1211. doi:10.1109/49.778178

Erdelj, M., & Natalizio, E. (2016). UAV-assisted disaster management: Applications and open issues. In 2016 international conference on computing, networking and communications (ICNC) (pp. 1-5). IEEE.

Erl, T., Mahmood, Z., & Puttini, R. (2013). *Cloud Computing: Concepts, Technology & Architecture*. Pearson.

Esteva, A., Kuprel, B., Novoa, R. A., Ko, J., Swetter, S. M., Blau, H. M., & Thrun, S. (2017). Dermatologist-level classification of skin cancer with deep neural networks. *Nature, 542*(7639), 115-118.

Explainable artificial intelligence. (2020). In *Wikipedia*. https://en.wikipedia.org/wiki/Explainable_artificial_intelligence

Faloutsos, C., Barber, R., Flickner, M., Hafner, J., Niblack, W., Petkovic, D., & Equitz, W. (1994). Efficient and effective querying by image content. *Journal of Intelligent Information Systems*, *3*(3-4), 231–262. doi:10.1007/BF00962238

Fan, S., Lau, R. Y., & Zhao, J. L. (2015). Demystifying Big Data Analytics for Business Intelligence Through theLens ofMarketing Mix. *Big DataResearch*, *2*, 28–32.

Fattah, A., Lock, H., Buller, W., & Kirby, S. (2009). Smart Airports:Transforming Passenger Experience To Thrive in the New Economy. *Cisco Internet Business Solutions Group (IBSG)*, 1-16. Retrieved April &, 2020, from https://pdfs.semanticscholar.org/b579/1c0c4db633817f7c81f1bb0214081f1d3aa3.pdf

Feldman, R., & Dagan, I. (1995). Knowledge discovery in textual databases (KDT). *First International Conference on Knowledge Discovery (KDD'95)*, 112-117.

Flavian, C., Guinalıu, M., & Gurrea, R. (2006). The role played by perceived usability, satisfaction and consumer trust on website loyalty. *Information & Management*, *43*(1), 1–14. doi:10.1016/j.im.2005.01.002

Fong, K. C. H., Au, C. H., Lam, E. T. H., & Chiu, D. K. W. (2020). Social network services for academic libraries: A study based on social capital and social proof. *Journal of Academic Librarianship*, *46*(1), 102091. doi:10.1016/j.acalib.2019.102091

Fon, V., & Parisi, F. (2006). Judicial precedents in civil law systems: A dynamic analysis. *International Review of Law and Economics*, *26*(4), 519–535. doi:10.1016/j.irle.2007.01.005

Forcino, F. L. (2013). The Importance of a Laboratory Section on Student Learning. *Journal of Geoscience Education*, *6*(2), 213–221. doi:10.5408/12-412.1

Forge. (n.d.). https://forge.fiware.org/plugins/mediawiki/wiki/fiware/index.php/FIWARE.OpenSpecification.Data.BigData

Franco, G. (1999). Ramazzini and workers' health. *Lancet*, *354*(9181), 858–861. doi:10.1016/S0140-6736(99)80042-7 PMID:10485743

Fung, B. C., Wang, K., & Ester, M. (2009). Hierarchical document clustering. In J. Wang (Ed.), *Encyclopedia of Data Warehousing and Mining* (2nd ed., pp. 970–975). IGI Global. doi:10.4018/978-1-60566-010-3.ch150

Gandomi, A., & Haider, M. (2015). Beyond the hype: Big data concepts, methods, and analytics. *International Journal of Information Management, 35*, 137–144.

Gartner. (2020a). *Augmented analytics.* Retrieved August 13, 2020, from Gartner Glossary: https://www.gartner.com/en/information-technology/glossary/augmented-analytics

Gartner. (2020b). *Diagnostic Analytics.* Retrieved August 12 2020, from Gartner: https://www.gartner.com/en/information-technology/glossary/diagnostic-analytics

Geeks for Geeks. (n.d.). https://www.geeksforgeeks.org/difference-between-cloud-computing-and-cluster-computing/

Gemser, G., Oostrum, M. V., & Leenders, M. A. (2006). The impact of movie reviews on the box office performance of art house versus mainstream motion pictures. *Journal of Cultural Economics*, *31*(1), 43–63. doi:10.100710824-006-9025-4

Géron, A. (2019). *Hands-on machine learning with Scikit-Learn, Keras, and TensorFlow: Concepts, tools, and techniques to build intelligent systems.* O'Reilly Media.

Geyik, S. (2010). *Butik otellerin web sayfalarının içerik analiziyle değerlendirilmesi: karşılaştırmalı bir araştırma.* Yüksek Lisans Tezi. Balıkesir Üniversitesi Sosyal Bilimler Enstitüsü.

Goddemeier, N., Daniel, K., & Wietfeld, C. (2012). Role-based connectivity management with realistic air-to-ground channels for cooperative UAVs. *IEEE Journal on Selected Areas in Communications*, *30*(5), 951–963. doi:10.1109/JSAC.2012.120610

Gomes, L., & Garcia-Zubia, J. (2007). *In a traditional under resourced science laboratory*. Deusto.

Gong, Y., Hu, N., Zhang, J., Liu, G., & Deng, J. (2015). Multi-attribute group decision making method based on geometric Bonferroni mean operator of trapezoidal interval type-2 fuzzy numbers. *Computers & Industrial Engineering*, *81*, 167–176. doi:10.1016/j.cie.2014.12.030

González, P. C., & Velásquez, J. D. (2013). Characterization and detection of taxpayers with false invoices using data mining techniques. *Expert Systems with Applications*, *40*(5), 1427–1436. doi:10.1016/j.eswa.2012.08.051

Goodfellow, I., Bengio, Y., & Courville, A. (2016). *Deep Learning*. MIT Press.

Gözübüyükoğlu, U. (2019). *Web sayfası tasarımında kullanıcı arayüzünün kullanılabilirliğinde görsel tasarımın önemi ve Atatürk Üniversitesi Güzel Sanatlar Fakültesi web sayfası tasarım örneği*. Yüksek Lisans Tezi. Atatürk Üniversitesi Güzel Sanatlar Enstitüsü.

Guinness World Records Limited. (2017). *The Drone Racing League sets quadcopter speed record*. Retrieved from https://www.guinnessworldrecords.com/news/commercial/2017/7/the-drone-racing-league-builds-the-worlds-fastest-racing-drone-482701

Gul, M., Mete, S., Serin, F., & Celik, E. (2020). Fine–Kinney-Based Occupational Risk Assessment Using Interval Type-2 Fuzzy VIKOR. In *Fine–Kinney-Based Fuzzy Multi-criteria Occupational Risk Assessment* (pp. 151–163). Springer.

Gulshan, V., Peng, L., Coram, M., Stumpe, M. C., Wu, D., Narayanaswamy, A., ... Kim, R. (2016). Development and validation of a deep learning algorithm for detection of diabetic retinopathy in retinal fundus photographs. *Journal of the American Medical Association*, *316*(22), 2402–2410. doi:10.1001/jama.2016.17216 PMID:27898976

Gülsüm, A., & Didem, I. (2017). *The Impact of the Virtual Laboratory on Students' Attitudes in a General Physics Laboratory*. doi:10.3991/ijoe.v13i04.6811

Gunning, D. (2017). Explainable artificial intelligence (xai). *Defense Advanced Research Projects Agency (DARPA), and Web, 2*, 2.

Guo, C. (2001). A review on consumer external search: Amount and determinants. *Journal of Business and Psychology*, *15*(3), 505–519. doi:10.1023/A:1007830919114

Haidula, T. (2016, January 8). *Lack of resources blurs pupils' vision*. Retrieved May 01, 2018, from https://www.namibian.com.na/print.php?id=145923&type=2

Handel, L. (1996). Hollywood looks at its audience. *Journalism Bulletin*, *28*(1), 109–110.

Han, X., Cao, X., Lloyd, E. L., & Shen, C. C. (2009). Fault-tolerant relay node placement in heterogeneous wireless sensor networks. *IEEE Transactions on Mobile Computing*, *9*(5), 643–656.

Harwati, A., Mansur, A., & Karunia, A. (2017). Utilization of social media for consumer behavior clustering using text mining method. *Journal of Engineering and Applied Sciences (Asian Research Publishing Network)*, *12*(3), 6406–6411.

Hata, M. (1980). Empirical formula for propagation loss in land mobile radio services. *IEEE Transactions on Vehicular Technology*, *29*(3), 317–325. doi:10.1109/T-VT.1980.23859

Health and Safety Authority (Ireland). (2005). *Guidance on the Management of Manual Handling in the Workplace*. Author.

Henke, N., & Bughin, J. (2016, December). *The Age of Analytics: Competing in a Data Driven World.* McKinsey Global Institute.

Henzinger, M. R., Rao, S., & Gabow, H. N. (2000). Computing vertex connectivity: New bounds from old techniques. *Journal of Algorithms*, *34*(2), 222–250. doi:10.1006/jagm.1999.1055

Herrera, M., Pérez-Hernández, M., Kumar Parlikad, A., & Izquierdo, J. (2020). Multi-Agent Systems and Complex Networks: Review and Applications in Systems Engineering. *Processes (Basel, Switzerland)*, *8*(3), 312. doi:10.3390/pr8030312

Hessing, D. J., Elffers, H., & Weigel, R. H. (1988). Exploring the limits of self-reports and reasoned action: An investigation of the psychology of tax evasion behavior. *Journal of Personality and Social Psychology*, *54*(3), 405–413. doi:10.1037/0022-3514.54.3.405

Hien, J. (2020). Culture and tax avoidance: The case of Italy. *Critical Policy Studies*, (August), 1–22. doi:10.1080/19460171.2020.1802318

Higuchi, N., Imamura, Y., Kuboyama, T., Hirata, K., & Shinohara, T. (2018). Nearest Neighbor Search using Sketches as Quantized Images of Dimension Reduction. *Proceedings of the 7th International Conference on Pattern Recognition Applications and Methods, ICPRAM*, 356-363. 10.5220/0006585003560363

Higuchi, N., Imamura, Y., Kuboyama, T., Hirata, K., & Shinohara, T. (2019). Fast nearest neighbor search with narrow 16-bit sketch. *Proceedings of the 8th International Conference on Pattern Recognition Applications and Methods, ICPRAM*, 540-547. 10.5220/0007377705400547

Himelboim, I., Golan, G. J., Moon, B. B., & Suto, R. J. (2014). A social networks approach to public relations on Twitter: Social mediators and mediated public relations. *Journal of Public Relations Research*, *26*(4), 359–379. doi:10.1080/1062726X.2014.908724

Hiransha, M., Gopalakrishnan, E. A., Menon, V. K., & Soman, K. (2018). NSE stock market prediction using deep-learning models. *Procedia Computer Science*, *132*, 1351–1362. doi:10.1016/j.procs.2018.05.050

Holsapplea, C., Lee-Postb, A., & Pakath, R. (2014). A unified foundation for business analytics. *Decision Support Systems*, *64*, 130–141. doi:10.1016/j.dss.2014.05.013

Hong, D., Chiu, D. K. W., Shen, V. Y., Cheung, S. C., & Kafeza, E. (2007). Ubiquitous enterprise service adaptations based on contextual user behavior. *Information Systems Frontiers*, *9*(4), 343–358. doi:10.100710796-007-9039-2

Hong, J., Oh, J., & Lee, H. (2019). Smart Airport and Next Generation Security Screening. *Electronics and Telecommunications Trend*, *34*(2), 73–82. doi:10.22648/ETRI.2019.J.340208

Howson, C., Richardson, J., Sallam, R., & Kronz, A. (2019). *Magic Quadrant for Analytics and Business Intelligence Platforms.* Retrieved 7 7, 2019, from Gartner: https://cadran-analytics.nl/wp-content/uploads/2019/02/2019-Gartner-Magic-Quadrant-for-Analytics-and-Business-Intelligence-Platforms.pdf

Howson, C., Sallam, R. L., & Richa, J. L. (2018, Feb 26). *Magic Quadrant for Analytics and Business Intelligence Platforms.* Retrieved Aug 16, 2018, from Gartner: www.gartner.com

Hsu, G. (2006). Evaluative schemas and the attention of critics in the US movie industry. *Industrial and Corporate Change*, *15*(3), 467–496. doi:10.1093/icc/dtl009

Hua, G., Yang, M. H., Learned-Miller, E., Ma, Y., Turk, M., Kriegman, D. J., & Huang, T. S. (2011). Introduction to the special section on real-world face recognition. *IEEE Transactions on Pattern Analysis and Machine Intelligence*, *33*(10), 1921–1924. doi:10.1109/TPAMI.2011.182 PMID:26598769

Hunter, B. (2020). *Why the Home Improvement Industry is Worth Billions*. https://www.homeadvisor.com//r/why-home-improvement-industry-worth-billions/

Hutson, M. (2017). Self-taught artificial intelligence beats doctors at predicting heart attacks. *Science*, 14. doi:10.1126cience.aal1058

Hwang, C. L., & Yoon, K. (1981). *Multiple attributes decision making methods and applications*. Springer-Verlag. doi:10.1007/978-3-642-48318-9

Hwang, F. K. (1976). On Steiner minimal trees with rectilinear distance. *SIAM Journal on Applied Mathematics*, *30*(1), 104–114. doi:10.1137/0130013

IBISWord. (2019). *Home Improvement Stores in the US industry outlook (2019–2024)*. https://www.ibisworld.com/united-states/market-research-reports/home-improvement-stores-industry/

IBM. (2016). *Analytics Solutions Unified Method Implementations with Agile principles*. ftp://ftp.software.ibm.com/software/data/sw-library/services/ASUM.pdf

IBM. (2018). *Cognitive computing. Preparing for the Future of Artificial Intelligence*. Retrieved from https://research.ibm.com/cognitive-computing/ostp/rfi-response.shtml

IDC. (2019). *IDC Forecasts Revenues for Big Data and Business Analytics Solutions will Reach $189.1 Billion This Year with Double-Digit Annual Growth Through 2022*. Retrieved 1 23, 2020, from IDC: https://www.idc.com/getdoc.jsp?containerId=prUS44998419

IDC. (2019, March 11). *Worldwide Spending on Artificial Intelligence Systems Will Grow to Nearly $35.8 Billion in 2019*. Retrieved August 11, 2020, from New IDC Spending Guide: https://www.idc.com/getdoc.jsp?containerId=prUS44911419

Imran, M., Younis, M., Haider, N., & Alnuem, M. A. (2012). Resource efficient connectivity restoration algorithm for mobile sensor/actor networks. *EURASIP Journal on Wireless Communications and Networking*, *2012*(1), 347. doi:10.1186/1687-1499-2012-347

Imran, M., Younis, M., Said, A. M., & Hasbullah, H. (2010, December). Partitioning detection and connectivity restoration algorithm for wireless sensor and actor networks. In *2010 IEEE/IFIP International Conference on Embedded and Ubiquitous Computing* (pp. 200-207). IEEE. 10.1109/EUC.2010.37

Imran, M., Younis, M., Said, A. M., & Hasbullah, H. (2012). Localized motion-based connectivity restoration algorithms for wireless sensor and actor networks. *Journal of Network and Computer Applications*, *35*(2), 844–856. doi:10.1016/j.jnca.2011.12.002

INFORMS. (2014). Defining analytics a conceptual framework. *ORMS Today, 43*(3). Retrieved August 12, 2020, from INFORMS: https://www.informs.org/ORMS-Today/Public-Articles/June-Volume-43-Number-3/Defining-analytics-a-conceptual-framework

INFORMS. (2017). *Operations Research & Analytics*. https://www.informs.org/Explore/Operations-Research-Analytics

Intelligent agent. (2020). In *Wikipedia*. https://en.wikipedia.org/wiki/Intelligent_agent

IRJET. (n.d.). https://www.irjet.net/archives/V5/i10/IRJET-V5I1089.pdf

ITU-R. (2019). *Recommendation ITU-R P.525-4: Calculation of free-space attenuation*. Retrieved from https://www.itu.int/ITU-R/go/patents/en

Jaffer, S., & Timbrell, G. (2014). Digital Strategy in Airports. *25 Australasian Conference on Information Systems-Digital Strategy in Airports* (pp. 1-11). Auckland: Australasian Conference on Information Systems (ACIS). doi:10292/8125

Jafri, R., & Arabnia, H. R. (2009*)*. A survey of face recognition techniques. *Journal of Information Processing Systems, 5*(2), 41-68.

Jain, Gyanchandani, & Khare. (2020). Improved k-Anonymize and l-Diverse Approach for Privacy Preserving Big Data Publishing Using MPSEC Dataset. *Computing and Informatics Journal, 39*(3), 537–567.

Jain, P., Gyanchandani, M., & Khare, N. (2016). Enhanced secured map-reduce layer for big data privacy and security. *Journal of Big Data, Springer, 6.*

Jang, S. B. (2019). A Design of a Tax Prediction System based on Artificial Neural Network. *2019 International Conference on Platform Technology and Service (PlatCon)*, 1–4. 10.1109/PlatCon.2019.8669416

Jašari, A. (2015). Information Systems at the Airport. In *International Conference on Econmic and Social Studies* (pp. 8-13). Sarajevo: International Conference on Econmic and Social Studies. Retrieved October 30, 2019, from https://www.semanticscholar.org/paper/Information-Systems-at-the-Airport-Jasari/86c9d48f37c33453f6f9770f552c9144dd1eb603

Jegou, H., Douze, M., & Schmid, C. (2008). Hamming embedding and weak geometric consistency for large scale image search. In *European conference on computer vision, ECCV* (pp. 304-317). Springer. 10.1007/978-3-540-88682-2_24

Jian-bo, W., Chong-jun, F., & Hui-gang, F. (2012). Discussion on Airport Business Intelligence System Architecture. *International Journal of Business and Social Science, 3*(12), 134–138. Retrieved November 2019, from

Jiang, F., Jiang, Y., Zhi, H., Dong, Y., Li, H., Ma, S., Wang, Y., Dong, Q., Shen, H., & Wang, Y. (2017). Artificial intelligence in healthcare: Past, present and future. *Stroke and Vascular Neurology, 2*(4), 230–243. doi:10.1136vn-2017-000101 PMID:29507784

Jiang, J., & Han, G. (2018). Routing protocols for unmanned aerial vehicles. *IEEE Communications Magazine, 56*(1), 58–63. doi:10.1109/MCOM.2017.1700326

Jiang, T., Lo, P. C. P., Cheuk, M. K., & Chiu, K. W. D. (2019). *New Cultural Dialog: Interviews with Outstanding Librarians, Archivists, and Curators in Greater China.* Systech Publisher.

Ji, S., Yang, W., Guo, S., Chiu, D. K. W., Zhang, C., & Yuan, X. (2020). Asymmetric response aggregation heuristics for rating prediction and recommendation. *Applied Intelligence, 50*(5), 1416–1436. doi:10.100710489-019-01594-2

John, G. (2013). *The Age of Artificial Intelligence.* Retrieved from TEDxLondonBusinessSchool: https://www.youtube.com/watch?v=0qOf7SX2CS4

John, G. (1985). Uncertainty relation for resolution in space, spatial frequency, and orientation optimized by two-dimensional visual cortical filters. *Journal of the Optical Society of America. A, Optics and Image Science, 2*(7), 1160–1169. doi:10.1364/JOSAA.2.001160 PMID:4020513

Johnsonbaugh, R. (2013). *Discrete Mathematics* (7th ed.). Pearson Education Limited.

Jo, J., & Choi, S. H. (2015). Sentiment analysis of movie review for predicting movie rating. *Management & Information Systems Review, 34*(3), 161–177. doi:10.29214/damis.2015.34.3.009

Jorgic, M., Goel, N., Kalaichevan, K., Nayak, A., & Stojmenovic, I. (2007, August). Localized detection of k-connectivity in wireless ad hoc, actuator and sensor networks. In *2007 16th International Conference on Computer Communications and Networks* (pp. 33-38). IEEE. 10.1109/ICCCN.2007.4317793

Journaux, L., Destain, M. F., Miteran, J., Piron, A., & Cointault, F. (2008). Texture classification with generalized Fourier descriptors in dimensionality reduction context: An overview exploration. In *IAPR Workshop on Artificial Neural Networks in Pattern Recognition* (pp. 280-291). Springer. 10.1007/978-3-540-69939-2_27

Jun, Q., Dinçer, H., & Yüksel, S. (2020). Stochastic hybrid decision-making based on interval type 2 fuzzy sets for measuring the innovation capacities of financial institutions. *International Journal of Finance & Economics*, ijfe.1805. doi:10.1002/ijfe.1805

Kabir, G., & Hasin, M. (2012). Comparative Analysis Of TOPSIS and FUZZY TOPSIS for the Evaluation of Travel Website Service Quality. *International Journal of Qualitative Research*, 6(3), 169–185.

Kaddouri, A. (2011). *The role of human expertise in enhancing data mining* (Order No. 3481009). Available from ABI/INFORM Collection. (909541928)

Kamdar, R., Paliwal, P., & Kumar, Y., & Computers. (2018). A state of art review on various aspects of multi-agent system. *Journal of Circuits. Systems*, 27(11), 1830006.

Kanade, T. (1977). *Computer recognition of human faces* (Vol. 47). Birkh"auser Basel. doi:10.1007/978-3-0348-5737-6

Kang, J. H., & Park, K. J. (2016, July). Spatial retreat of net-drones under communication failure. In *2016 Eighth International Conference on Ubiquitous and Future Networks (ICUFN)* (pp. 89-91). IEEE. 10.1109/ICUFN.2016.7536989

Kantardzic, M. (2011). *Data Mining: Concepts, Models, Methods, and Algorithms*. Wiley & IEEE Press. doi:10.1002/9781118029145

Kaplan, J. (2016). *Artificial intelligence: What everyone needs to know*. Oxford University Press. doi:10.1093/wentk/9780190602383.001.0001

Karalevicius, V., Degrande, N., & De Weerdt, J. (2018). Using sentiment analysis to predict interday Bitcoin price movements. *The Journal of Risk Finance*, 19(1), 56–75. doi:10.1108/JRF-06-2017-0092

Karande, P., Chakraborty, S. (2013). Material handling equipment selection using weighted utility additive theory. *Journal of Industrial Engineering*.

Karp, B., & Kung, H. T. (2000). GPSR: Greedy perimeter stateless routing for wireless networks. In *Proceedings of the 6th annual international conference on Mobile computing and networking* (pp. 243-254). ACM. 10.1145/345910.345953

Kasampalis, S., Lazaridis, P. I., Zaharis, Z. D., Bizopoulos, A., Zettas, S., & Cosmas, J. (2014, June). Comparison of Longley-Rice, ITU-R P. 1546 and Hata-Davidson propagation models for DVB-T coverage prediction. In BMSB (pp. 1-4). Academic Press.

Katayama, D., Kino, Y., & Tsuda, K. (2019). A method of sentiment polarity identification in financial news using deep learning. *Procedia Computer Science*, 159, 1287–1294. doi:10.1016/j.procs.2019.09.298

Katayama, D., & Tsuda, K. (2018). A method of measurement of the impact of japanese news on stock market. *Procedia Computer Science*, 126, 1336–1343. doi:10.1016/j.procs.2018.08.084

Kausar, A., Akram, S., Tabassum, M. F., Ahmad, A., & Khan, S. (2020). The Solution of Maintenance Strategy Selection Problem by using modified Fuzzy TOPSIS for of Material Handling Equipment. *Sukkur IBA Journal of Computing and Mathematical Sciences*, 3(2), 46–54.

Kay, M. G. (1998). Material Handling Equipment. *Metal Finishing*, 96(12), 67. doi:10.1016/S0026-0576(98)81337-8

Kershaw, D. (2019). *SMART Airports:Connecting airport, airline and aircraft*. ARINC International.

Kim, G. H., Mahmud, I., & Cho, Y. Z. (2017, December). Self-recovery scheme using neighbor information for multi-drone ad hoc networks. In *2017 23rd Asia-Pacific Conference on Communications (APCC)* (pp. 1-5). IEEE. 10.23919/APCC.2017.8303997

Kim, J., & Groeneveld, P. W. (2017). *Big data, health informatics, and the future of cardiovascular medicine.* Academic Press.

Kim, G. H., Nam, J. C., Mahmud, I., & Cho, Y. Z. (2016, July). Multi-drone control and network self-recovery for flying Ad Hoc Networks. In *2016 Eighth International Conference on Ubiquitous and Future Networks (ICUFN)* (pp. 148-150). IEEE.

Kim, S. H., Park, N., & Park, S. H. (2013). Exploring the effects of online word of mouth and expert reviews on theatrical movies box office success. *Journal of Media Economics, 26*(2), 98–114. doi:10.1080/08997764.2013.785551

King, T. (2007). Does movie criticism affect box office earnings? Evidence from movies released in the U.S. in 2003. *Journal of Cultural Economics, 31*(3), 171–186. doi:10.100710824-007-9041-z

Kittler, J., Hatef, M., Duin, R. P., & Matas, J. (1998). On combining classifiers. *IEEE Transactions on Pattern Analysis and Machine Intelligence, 20*(3), 226–239. doi:10.1109/34.667881

Knorr, E. (2018, October 2). *What is cloud computing? Everything you need to know now.* Retrieved April 08, 2020, from InforWorld: https://www.infoworld.com/article/2683784/what-is-cloud-computing.html

Koç, E. (2009). *Kansei mühendisliği kullanılarak müşteri odaklı ürün tasarımı: Web sayfası tasarımında uygulanması* (Doctoral Dissertation). Eskişehir Osmangazi University.

Kohli, D. (2018, November 2). *Big data facilitating the working towards a smart future.* Retrieved August 4, 2020, from International Airport Review: https://www.internationalairportreview.com/article/77340/working-towards-smart-future/

Kong, E. W. S., Chiu, D. K. W., & Ho, K. K. W. (2016). Applications of social media in academic library services: A case of the Hong Kong Polytechnic University Library. *International Journal of Systems and Service-Oriented Engineering, 6*(2), 53–65. doi:10.4018/IJSSOE.2016040103

Koschat, M. A. (2012). The impact of movie reviews on box office: Media portfolios and the intermediation of genre. *Journal of Media Economics, 25*(1), 35–53. doi:10.1080/08997764.2012.651063

Kosman, E., & Leonard, K. J. (2005). Similarity coefficients for molecular markers in studies of genetic relationships between individuals for haploid, diploid, and polyploid species. *Molecular Ecology, 14*(2), 415–424. doi:10.1111/j.1365-294X.2005.02416.x PMID:15660934

Kotu, V., & Deshpande, B. (2019). *Data Science* (2nd ed.). Morgan Kaufmann.

Kraaijeveld, O., & De Smedt, J. (2020). The predictive power of public Twitter sentiment for forecasting cryptocurrency prices. *Journal of International Financial Markets, Institutions and Money, 65*(C), 101188. doi:10.1016/j.intfin.2020.101188

Kraus, J. (2019). *Porovnanie binárnych skečov pre podobnostné vyhľadávanie v kosínusovom a euklidovskom priestore* (Bachelor Thesis). Masaryk University, Brno, Czech Republic.

Krissinel, E. (2012). Enhanced fold recognition using efficient short fragment clustering. *Journal of Molecular Biochemistry, 1*(2), 76. PMID:27882309

Krizhevsky, A., Sutskever, I., & Hinton, G. E. (2012). Imagenet classification with deep convolutional neural networks. Advances in Neural Information Processing Systems, 1097-1105.

Kuiper, E., & Nadjm-Tehrani, S. (2006). Mobility models for UAV group reconnaissance applications. In *2006 International Conference on Wireless and Mobile Communications (ICWMC'06)* (pp. 33-33). IEEE. 10.1109/ICWMC.2006.63

Kumar, G. B. (2015). An encyclopedic overview of 'Big Data' Analytics. *International Journal of Applied Engineering Research: IJAER, 10*(3), 5681–5705.

Lajonchere, J. P. (2018). Role of Big Data in evolution of the medical practice. *Bulletin de l'Académie Nationale de Médecine, 202*(1-2), 225–238.

Lam, E. T. H., Au, C. H., & Chiu, D. K. (2019). Analyzing the use of Facebook among university libraries in Hong Kong. *Journal of Academic Librarianship, 45*(3), 175–183. doi:10.1016/j.acalib.2019.02.007

Laney, D., & Jain, A. (2017, June 20). *100 Data and Analytics Predictions Through*. Retrieved August 04, 2018, from Gartner: https://www.gartner.com/events-na/data-analytics/wp-content/uploads/sites/5/2017/10/Data-and-Analytics-Predictions.pdf

Lang, S. (2002). *Algebra, Graduate Texts in Mathematics 211* (Revised third ed.). Springer-Verlag.

LaPlante, A. (2019). *What Is Augmented Analytics? Powering Your Data with AI*. Boston: O' Realy. Retrieved from https://go.oracle.com/LP=84622

Larsen, T. (2013). Cross-platform aviation analytics using big-data methods. In *2013 Integrated Communications, Navigation and Surveillance Conference (ICNS)* (pp. 1-9). Herndon, VA: IEEE. doi:doi: 10.1109/ICNSurv.2013.6548579

Laudon, K. G., & Laudon, K. C. (2016). *Management Information Systems: Managing the Digital Firm* (14th ed.). Pearson.

Lebedev, A. A., & Ryjov, A. P. (2009). Design team capability and project progress evaluation based on information monitoring technology. In *Proceedings of the 5th International Conference on Soft Computing, Computing with Words and Perceptions in System Analysis, Decision and Control*. Famagusta, Cyprus: IEEE. 10.1109/ICSCCW.2009.5379492

LeCun, Y., Bengio, Y., & Hinton, G. (2015). Deep learning. *Nature, 521*(7553), 436–444. doi:10.1038/nature14539 PMID:26017442

Lee, C., Ng, Y., Lv, Y., & Taezoon, P. (2014). Empirical Analysis of Self-service Check-in Implementation in Singapore Changi Airport. *International Journal of Engineering Business Management, 6*(6), 33–44. doi:10.5772/56962

Lee, L. W., & Chen, S. M. (2008) Fuzzy multiple attributes group decision-making based on the extension of TOPSIS method and interval type-2 fuzzy sets. In *Proceedings of the 2008 international conference on machine learning and cybernetic* (pp. 3260–3265). 10.1109/ICMLC.2008.4620968

Lees, E. (2016). *A Better Way to Manage Airports: Passenger Analytics*. ICF International, Inc.

Leskovec, J., Rajaraman, A., & Ullman, J. D. (2014). *Mining of massive data sets. Mining of Massive Datasets* (2nd ed.). Cambridge University Press. doi:10.1017/CBO9781139924801

Lessig, L. (2009). *Code: And other laws of cyberspace*: ReadHowYouWant. com.

Li, B., Chan, K. C., Ou, C., & Ruifeng, S. (2017). Discovering public sentiment in social media for predicting stock movement of publicly listed companies. *Information Systems, 69*, 81–92. doi:10.1016/j.is.2016.10.001

Licklider, J. C. R. (1960). Man-Computer Symbiosis. *IRE Transactions on Human Factors in Electronics, HFE-1*, 4-11. Retrieved from http://groups.csail.mit.edu/medg/people/psz/Licklider.html

Li, L., Peng, M., Jiang, N., & Law, R. (2017). An empirical study on the influence of economy hotel website quality on online booking intentions. *International Journal of Hospitality Management, 63*, 1–10. doi:10.1016/j.ijhm.2017.01.001

Lin, Y., Wong, K., Wang, Y., Zhang, R., Dong, B., Qu, H., & Zheng, Q. (2020). TaxThemis: Interactive Mining and Exploration of Suspicious Tax Evasion Groups. IEEE Transactions on Visualization and Computer Graphics.

Lin, G. H., & Xue, G. (1999). Steiner tree problem with minimum number of Steiner points and bounded edge-length. *Information Processing Letters, 69*(2), 53–57. doi:10.1016/S0020-0190(98)00201-4

Lin, Q., & Lee, J. (2004). Consumer information search when making investment decisions. *Financial Services Review*, *13*(4), 319–332.

Litman, B. R., & Kohl, L. S. (1989). Predicting financial success of motion pictures: The 80's experience. *Journal of Media Economics*, *2*(2), 35–50. doi:10.1080/08997768909358184

Liu, F. e. (2011). *NIST Cloud Computing Reference Architecture*. NIST.

Liu, H.-Y., Maas, M., Danaher, J., Scarcella, L., Lexer, M., & Van Rompaey, L. (2020). Artificial intelligence and legal disruption: A new model for analysis. *Law, Innovation and Technology*, *12*(2), 1–54. doi:10.1080/17579961.2020.1815402

Li, X., Xie, H., Chen, L., Wang, J., & Deng, X. (2014). News impact on stock price return via sentiment analysis. *Knowledge-Based Systems*, *69*, 14–23. doi:10.1016/j.knosys.2014.04.022

Li, Y., Chung, S. M., & Holt, J. D. (2008). Text document clustering based on frequent word meaning sequences. *Data & Knowledge Engineering*, *64*(1), 381–404. doi:10.1016/j.datak.2007.08.001

Li, Z., Fan, Y., Jiang, B., Lei, T., & Liu, W. (2019). A survey on sentiment analysis and opinion mining for social multimedia. *Multimedia Tools and Applications*, *78*(6), 6939–6967. doi:10.100711042-018-6445-z

Lloyd, E. L., & Xue, G. (2006). Relay node placement in wireless sensor networks. *IEEE Transactions on Computers*, *56*(1), 134–138. doi:10.1109/TC.2007.250629

Lohr, S. (2012, February 11). The Age of Big Data. *The New York Times*, 1-5.

Lohr, S. (2014). *For Big-Data Scientists, "Janitor Work" Is Key Hurdle to Insights*. https://www.nytimes.com/2014/08/18/technology/for-big-data-scientists-hurdle-to-insights-is-janitor-work.html

Loibl, C., & Hira, T. K. (2009). Investor information search. *Journal of Economic Psychology*, *30*(1), 24–41. doi:10.1016/j.joep.2008.07.009

Lo, P., Chiu, D. K., & Cho, A. (2017). *Inside the World's Major East Asian Collections: One Belt, One Road, and Beyond*. Chandos Publishing.

Lo, P., Chiu, D., Cho, A., & Allard, B. (2018). *Conversations with Leading Academic and Research Library Directors: International Perspectives on Library Management*. Chandos Publishing.

Lo, P., Cho, A., & Chiu, D. K. (2017). *World's Leading National, Public, Monastery and Royal Library Directors: Leadership, Management, Future of Libraries*. Walter de Gruyter GmbH & Co KG. doi:10.1515/9783110533347

Loria, S. (2018). Textblob Documentation. *Release 0.15, 2*.

Lowe, D. G. (1999). Object recognition from local scale-invariant features. *Proceedings of the seventh IEEE international conference on computer vision*, (2), 1150-1157. 10.1109/ICCV.1999.790410

Lupiani-Ruiz, E., García-Manotas, I., Valencia-García, R., García-Sánchez, F., Castellanos-Nieves, D., Fernández-Breis, J. T., & Camón-Herrero, J. B. (2011). Financial news semantic search engine. *Expert Systems with Applications*, *38*(12), 15565–15572. doi:10.1016/j.eswa.2011.06.003

Lv, Q., Charikar, M., & Li, K. (2004). Image similarity search with compact data structures. In *Proceedings of the thirteenth ACM International Conference on Information and Knowledge Management, CIKM* (pp. 208-217). 10.1145/1031171.1031213

Lv, Q., Josephson, W., Wang, Z., Charikar, M., & Li, K. (2006). Ferret: a toolkit for content-based similarity search of feature-rich data. *Proceedings of the 1st ACM SIGOPS/EuroSys European Conference on Computer Systems*, 317-330. 10.1145/1217935.1217966

Madakam, S., Ramaswamy, R., & Tripathi, S. (2015). Internet of Things (IoT): A Literature Review. *Journal of Computer and Communications*, *3*(05), 164–173. doi:10.4236/jcc.2015.35021

Maghferat, P., & Stock, W. G. (2010). Gender-specific information search behavior. *Webology*, *7*(2), 1–15.

Mahmoudi, N., Docherty, P., & Moscato, P. (2018). Deep neural networks understand investors better. *Decision Support Systems*, *112*, 23–34. doi:10.1016/j.dss.2018.06.002

Makhabel, B., Mishra, P., Danneman, N., & Heimann, R. (2017). *R: Mining Spatial, Text, Web, and Social Media Data* (1st ed.). Packt Publishing.

Manber, U. (1994). Finding Similar Files in a Large File System. In *Proceedings of USENIX Winter 1994 Technical Conference* (*Vol. 94*, pp. 1-10). USENIX.

Manning, C. D., Surdeanu, M., Bauer, J., Finkel, J., Bethard, S. J., & McClosky, D. (2014). The Stanford CoreNLP natural language processing toolkit. Association for Computational Linguistics (Acl) System Demonstrations, 55–60. doi:10.3115/v1/P14-5010

Manogaran, G., & Lopez, D. (2017). A survey of big data architectures and machine learning algorithms in healthcare. *International Journal of Biomedical Engineering and Technology*, *25*(2-4), 182–211. doi:10.1504/IJBET.2017.087722

Manyika, J., Chui, M., & Bughin, J. e. (2011, May). *Big data: The next frontier for innovation, competition, and productivity*. Retrieved from McKinsey Global Institute: https://www.mckinsey.com/business-functions/business-technology/our-insights/big-data-the-next-frontier-for-innovation

Mao, S., Wanggen, W., Rui, W., & Yue, G. (2010). The application of ant colony algorithm and artificial neural network in tax assessment. *2010 IEEE International Conference on Audio, Language and Image Processing*. 10.1109/ICALIP.2010.5684375

Mariani, J., Johanna, Z., Krimmel, E., Sen, R., & Miller, M. (2019, July 1). *Flying smarter: The smart airport and the Internet of Things*. Retrieved from Deloitte: https://www2.deloitte.com/us/en/insights/industry/public-sector/iot-in-smart-airports.html

Mariani, J., Zmud, J., Krimmel, E., Sen, R., & Miller, M. (2019). *Flying Smarter: The airport and the Internet of Things*. Deloitte Insights.

Martinez, G., Naranjo, F. L., Perez, A. L., Suero, M. I., & Pardo, P. J. (2011). Comparative study of the effectiveness of three learning environments: Hyper-realistic virtual simulations, traditional schematic simulations, and traditional laboratory. *Physical Review Special Topics. Physics Education Research*, *7*(2), 020111.

Martínez-Plumed, F., Contreras-Ochando, L., Ferri, C., Flach, P., Hernández-Orallo, J., Kull, M., Lachiche, N., & Ramírez-Quintana, M. J. (2019). CRISP-DM Twenty Years Later: From Data Mining Processes to Data Science Trajectories. *IEEE Transactions on Knowledge and Data Engineering*, 1–14.

Mathew, M., & Sahu, S. (2018). Comparison of new multi-criteria decision making methods for material handling equipment selection. *Management Science Letters*, *8*(3), 139–150. doi:10.5267/j.msl.2018.1.004

Mayorga, R. V., & Perlovsky, L. (2018). Sapience, Consciousness, and Knowledge Instinct. In Toward artificial sapience. Principles and methods for wise systems (pp. 1-24). Academic Press.

Mba, S. I., & Uba, I. I. (2012). The Effect of laboratory works in teaching and learning of physics in onitsha north, Anambra state. *Journal of Science and Arts*, *12*(1), 75–84. Retrieved November 29, 2020, from https://www.researchgate.net/profile/Ikemefuna_Uba/publication/265581923_the_effect_of_laboratory_works_in_teaching_and_learning_of_physics_in_onitsha_north_anambra_state/links/55ee12b008aedecb68fc71d6.pdf

McAfee, A., & Brynjolfsson, E. (2017). *Machine, platform, crowd: Harnessing our digital future*. WW Norton & Company.

McKagan, S. (2018). *Resources for using PhET simulations in class-PhEt Activities Database*. Retrieved December 12, 2018, from https://serc.carleton.edu/49131

McKinsey Global Institute. (2013). *Disruptive technologies: Advances that will transform life, business, and the global economy*. Retrieved from https://www.mckinsey.com/insights/business_technology/disruptive_technologies

McKinsey. (2011, May). *Big data: The next frontier for innovation, competition, and productivity*. Retrieved from McKinsey Global Institute: https://www.mckinsey.com/business-functions/business-technology/our-insights/big-data-the-next-frontier-for-innovation

Mehrotra, H., Vatsa, M., Singh, R., & Majhi, B. (2013). Does iris change over time? *PLoS One*, *8*(11), e78333.

Mehta, P., Mathews, J., Visweswara, R., Kasi, S. V., Kumar, K. S., Suryamukhi, K., & Babu, C. S. (2019). Identifying Malicious Dealers in Goods and Services Tax. *2019 IEEE 4th International Conference on Big Data Analytics (ICBDA)*, 312–316. 10.1109/ICBDA.2019.8713211

Mele, I., Bahrainian, S. A., & Crestani, F. (2019). Event mining and timeliness analysis from heterogeneous news streams. *Information Processing & Management*, *56*(3), 969–993. doi:10.1016/j.ipm.2019.02.003

Mesarovich, M. D., Macko, D., & Takahara, Y. (1970). *Theory of hierarchical multilevel systems*. Academic Press.

Messous, M. A., Senouci, S. M., & Sedjelmaci, H. (2016). *Network connectivity and area coverage for UAV fleet mobility model with energy constraint. In 2016 IEEE Wireless Communications and Networking Conference*. IEEE.

Mic, V., Novak, D., & Zezula, P. (2016). Designing sketches for similarity filtering. In *IEEE 16th International Conference on Data Mining Workshops (ICDMW)* (pp. 655-662). IEEE.

Mic, V., Novak, D., & Zezula, P. (2018a) Binary Sketches for Secondary Filtering. *ACM Transactions on Information Systems*, *37*(1), 1:1–1:28.

Mic, V., Novak, D., Vadicamo, L., & Zezula, P. (2018c). Selecting sketches for similarity search. In *European Conference on Advances in Databases and Information Systems, ADBIS* (pp. 127–141). Springer.

Mic, V., Novak, D., & Zezula, P. (2017). Sketches with unbalanced bits for similarity search. In *International Conference on Similarity Search and Applications* (pp. 53-63). Springer.

Mic, V., Novak, D., & Zezula, P. (2018b) Modifying Hamming Spaces for Efficient Search. *Proceedings of IEEE International Conference on Data Mining Workshops, ICDMW*, 945–953.

Mic, V., & Zezula, P. (2020). Accelerating Metric Filtering by Improving Bounds on Estimated Distances. In *International Conference on Similarity Search and Applications* (pp. 3-17). Springer.

Millennium Challenge Corporation. (2014). *Poverty reduction through economic growth*. Retrieved May 01, 2018, from https://www.mcanamibia.org/files/files/OshanaFact%20Sheet(1).pdf

Minelli, M., Chambers, M., & Dhiraj, A. (2013). *Big Data, Big Analytics: Emerging Business Intelligence and Analytic Trends for Today's Businesses* (Chinese Edition 2014). Wiley & Sons. doi:10.1002/9781118562260

Mishev, K., Gjorgjevikj, A., Vodenska, I., Chitkushev, L. T., & Trajanov, D. (2020). Evaluation of sentiment analysis in finance: From lexicons to transformers. *IEEE Access: Practical Innovations, Open Solutions*, 8, 131662–131682. doi:10.1109/ACCESS.2020.3009626

Mishne, G., & Glance, N. S. (2006). Predicting movie sales from blogger sentiment. In *AAAI Spring Symposium: Computational Approaches to Analyzing Weblogs* (pp. 155–158). Academic Press.

Mitzenmacher, M., Pagh, R., & Pham, N. (2014). Efficient estimation for high similarities using odd sketches. *Proceedings of the 23rd international conference on World wide web*, 109-118.

Mi, Z., Yang, Y., & Yang, J. Y. (2015). Restoring Connectivity of Mobile Robotic Sensor Networks While Avoiding Obstacles. *IEEE Sensors Journal*, 15(8), 4640–4650. doi:10.1109/JSEN.2015.2426177

Mogensen, P. E., & Wigard, J. (1999). *Cost action 231: Digital mobile radio towards future generation system, final report*. Section 5.2: on Antenna and Frequency Diversity in Gsm. Section 5.3: Capacity Study of Frequency Hopping Gsm Network. Academic Press.

Mohamadghasemi, A., Hadi-Vencheh, A., Lotfi, F. H., & Khalilzadeh, M. (2020). An integrated group FWA-ELECTRE III approach based on interval type-2 fuzzy sets for solving the MCDM problems using limit distance mean. *Complex & Intelligent Systems*, 1-35.

Molohidis, A., Lefkos, I., Taramopoulos, A., Hatzikraniotis, E., & Psillos, D. (2015). Web-based Virtual Labs. In *Proceedings of the 7th International Conference on Computer Supported Education-Volume 1* (pp. 418-423). SCITEPRESS-Science and Technology Publications, Lda.

Mousavi, S. M., Vahdani, B., Tavakkoli-Moghaddam, R., & Tajik, N. (2014). Soft computing based on a fuzzy grey group compromise solution approach with an application to the selection problem of material handling equipment. *International Journal of Computer Integrated Manufacturing*, 27(6), 547–569. doi:10.1080/0951192X.2013.834460

Mukherjee, A., Dey, N., Kumar, R., Panigrahi, B. K., Hassanien, A. E., & Tavares, J. M. R. S. (2019). Delay Tolerant Network assisted flying Ad-Hoc network scenario: Modeling and analytical perspective. *Wireless Networks*, 25(5), 2675–2695. doi:10.100711276-019-01987-8

Müller, M. (2012). *Flying Ad-Hoc Networks*. Institute of Media Informatics Ulm University.

Muller-Molina, A. J., & Shinohara, T. (2009). Efficient similarity search by reducing i/o with compressed sketches. In *2009 Second International Workshop on Similarity Search and Applications*, (pp. 30-38). IEEE.

Multi-agent system. (2020). In *Wikipedia*. https://en.wikipedia.org/wiki/Multi-agent_system

mySmart. (2019, April 12). *Smart Basics #4: What is 'smart' technology?* Retrieved March 05, 2020, from mySmart Intelligent Environment: https://mysmart.com.au/insights/smartbasics-what-is-smart-technology/

Nampila, J. (2012). *Development of a Computer-Assisted School Information System for Namibian Schools*. Retrieved May 01, 2018, from http://ir.polytechnic.edu.na/bitstream/handle/10628/383/Nampila.%20MIT.%20Dev%20of%20a%20computer-assisted%20school%20info%20system%20for%20Namibian%20schools.pdf?sequence=1&isAllowed=y

National Airports Corporation. (2017). *about-us/background/*. Retrieved December 16, 2019, from National Airports Corporation: https://www.nac.com.pg/about-us/background/

National Airports Corporation. (2017). *National Airports Corporation 2030 Growth Strategy*. National Airports Corporation.

National Research Council. (2006). *America's lab report: Investigations in high school science*. National Academies Press.

Nau, J.-B., & Benoit, F. (2017). *Smart Airport: How Technology is shaping the future of airports*. Wavestone.

New Era. (2017, December 21). *Slight improvement in Grade 10 exam results.* Retrieved November 21, 2018, from https://neweralive.na/posts/slight-improvement-in-grade-10-exam-results

New Era. (2017, December 8). *Education minister says providing infrastructure a major challenge.* Retrieved December 17, 2018, from https://neweralive.na/posts/education-minister-says-providing-infrastructure-a-major-challenge

Nghipandulwa, L. (2011). *Secondary school teachers' perceptions of the importance of practical work in biology in Oshana educational region* (Doctoral dissertation). University of Namibia, Windhoek.

Nguyen, H. L., Woon, Y. K., & Ng, W. K. (2015). A survey on data stream clustering and classification. *Knowledge and Information Systems, 45*(3), 535–569. doi:10.100710115-014-0808-1

Nguyen, H. T., Dawal, S. Z. M., Nukman, Y., Rifai, A. P., & Aoyama, H. (2016). An integrated MCDM model for conveyor equipment evaluation and selection in an FMC based on a fuzzy AHP and fuzzy ARAS in the presence of vagueness. *PLoS One, 11*(4), e0153222. doi:10.1371/journal.pone.0153222 PMID:27070543

Nico, R., Wouter R. V., & Jan T. D. (2011). The learning effects of computer simulations in science education. *Computers & Education, 58*, 136–153.

NIED. (2010). *Physical Science Junior Secondary Syllabus Grades 8-10.* Okahandja: NIED. Retrieved March 22, 2019, from http://www.nied.edu.na

NIED. (2015). *Junior Secondary Phase.* Okahandja: NIED. Retrieved January 23, 2019, from http://www.nied.edu.na/assets/documents/02Syllabuses/04JuniorSecondary/PhysicalScience/JSC_Syllabuses_PS_Sep2016.pdf

NIED. (n.d.). *Improving civic participation of the Youth in Namibia through the use.* Namibia Institute for Democracy (NID). Retrieved May 10, 2018, from https://www.unicef.org/namibia/NID-UNICEF_2011_Listen_Loud_Final_Report.pdf

NIST. (2018, 1 08). *Final Version of NIST Cloud Computing Definition Published.* Retrieved 2 20, 2019, from https://www.nist.gov/news-events/news/2011/10/final-version-nist-cloud-computing-definition-published

Norusis, M. J. (1997). *SPSS: SPSS 7.5 Guide to Data Analytics.* Prentice Hall.

Novak, D., Kyselak, M., & Zezula, P. (2010). On locality-sensitive indexing in generic metric spaces. In *Proceedings of the Third International Conference on Similarity Search and Applications* (pp. 59-66). Academic Press.

Novak, D., Batko, M., & Zezula, P. (2011). Metric index: An efficient and scalable solution for precise and approximate similarity search. *Information Systems, 36*(4), 721–733.

Novak, D., & Zezula, P. (2016). PPP-codes for large-scale similarity searching. In *Transactions on Large-Scale Data-and Knowledge-Centered Systems XXIV* (pp. 61–87). Springer.

NSF. (2019 a). *NSF's 10 Big Ideas.* Retrieved from https://www.nsf.gov/news/special_reports/big_ideas/index.jsp

NSF. (2019 b). *NSF's 10 Big Ideas. Future of Work at the Human-Technology Frontier.* Retrieved from https://www.nsf.gov/news/special_reports/big_ideas/human_tech.jsp

OECD. (2012). Reducing Opportunities for Tax Non-compliance in the Underground Economy. *Forum on Tax Administration: SME Compliance Subgroup.* www.oecd.org/tax/forum-on-tax-administration/publications-and-products/sme/49427993.pdf

OECD. (2017). Assessing complex problem solving in the classroom: Meeting challenges and opportunities. In B. Csapó & J. Funke (Eds.), *The Nature of Problem Solving: Using Research to Inspire 21st Century Learning.* OECD Publishing., doi:10.1787/9789264273955-12-

OECD. (2017). *Shining Light on the Shadow Economy - Opportunities and Threat.* https://www.oecd.org/tax/crime/shining-light-on-the-shadow-economy-opportunities-and-threats.pdf

Okumura, Y. (1968). Field strength and its variability in VHF and UHF land-mobile radio service. *Rev. Electr. Commun. Lab., 16*, 825–873.

Ong, E. J., & Bober, M. (2016). Improved hamming distance search using variable length substrings. In *Proceedings of the IEEE Conference on Computer Vision and Pattern Recognition* (pp. 2000-2008). IEEE.

Oquab, M., Bottou, L., Laptev, I., & Sivic, J. (2014). Learning and transferring mid-level image representations using convolutional neural networks. *IEEE Conference on Computer Vision and Pattern Recognition, CVPR 2014*, 1717–1724.

Oracle. (2012, 12 12). Oracle Airline Data Model Overview. In *Oracle Airline Data Model: Business Overview Presentation*. Oracle. Retrieved 14 04, 2020, from https://www.oracle.com/technetwork/database/options/airlines-data-model/airlines-data-model-bus-overview-1451727.pdf

Oracle. (2018). *What Is Big Data?* https://www.oracle.com/big-data/guide/what-is-big-data.html

Osakwe, J. O., Nomusa, D., & Norbert, J. (2015). A Preliminary Framework for the Adoption of Mobile Learning Technology in Namibian High Schools: A Case of the Erongo Region. International Journal of Science and Research.

Osakwe, J., Dlodlo, N., & Jere, N. (2017). Where learners and teachers' perceptions on mobile learning meet: A case of Namibian secondary schools in the Khomas region. *Technology in Society, 49*, 16–30. doi:10.1016/j.techsoc.2016.12.004

Otero, P., Hersh, W., & Ganesh, A. J. (2014). Big data: Are biomedical and health informatics training programs ready?: Contribution of the IMIA working group for health and medical informatics education. *Yearbook of Medical Informatics, 9*(1), 177. PMID:25123740

Ovalı, P. N. (2019). *Otel web sitelerinin eMICA yöntemiyle analizi: İstanbul ve Antalya'daki 3, 4 Ve 5 yıldızlı otellere yönelik uygulama.* Doktora Tezi. İstanbul Üniversitesi Sosyal Bilimler Enstitüsü.

Oxford. (2008). *Oxford Advanced Learner's English Dictionary* (7th ed.). Oxford University Press.

Palipea, N. M. (2018). *How many people are currently investing in cryptocurrencies?* Retrieved from https://www.quora.com/How-many-people-are-currently-investing-in-cryptocurrencies

Payrovnaziri, S. N., Chen, Z., Rengifo-Moreno, P., Miller, T., Bian, J., Chen, J. H., Liu, X., & He, Z. (2020). Explainable artificial intelligence models using real-world electronic health record data: A systematic scoping review. *Journal of the American Medical Informatics Association: JAMIA, 27*(7), 1173–1185. doi:10.1093/jamia/ocaa053 PMID:32417928

Pell, R., & Blondel, M. (2018). *Airport Digital Transformation.* Boston: Arthur D Little. Retrieved December 2, 2019, from https://amadeus.com/documents/en/airports/research-report/airports-digital-transformation.pdf

Peterson, R. A., & Merino, M. C. (2003). Consumer information search behavior and the Internet. *Psychology and Marketing, 20*(2), 99–121. doi:10.1002/mar.10062

Pettey, C., & van der Meulen, R. (2018, April 25). *Gartner Says Global Artificial Intelligence Business Value to Reach $1.2 Trillion in 2018.* Retrieved August 04, 2018, from Gartner: https://www.gartner.com/newsroom/id/3872933

Planetb. (n.d.). http://www.planetb.ca/syntax-highlight-word

Pola, I. R. V., Traina, C. Jr, & Traina, A. J. M. (2014). The nobh-tree: Improving in-memory metric access methods by using metric hyperplanes with non-overlapping nodes. *Data & Knowledge Engineering, 94*, 65–88.

Pollettini, J. T., Panico, S. R., Daneluzzi, J. C., Tinós, R., Baranauskas, J. A., & Macedo, A. A. (2012). Using machine learning classifiers to assist healthcare-related decisions: Classification of electronic patient records. *Journal of Medical Systems*, *36*(6), 3861–3874. doi:10.100710916-012-9859-6 PMID:22592391

Pollett, S., Boscardin, W. J., Azziz-Baumgartner, E., Tinoco, Y. O., Soto, G., Romero, C., ... Rutherford, G. W. (2016). Evaluating Google Flu Trends in Latin America: Important lessons for the next phase of digital disease detection. *Clinical Infectious Diseases*, ciw657. PMID:27678084

Popovic, V., Kraal, B., & Kirk, P. (2009). Passenger Experience in an Airport: An Activity-centred Approach. In *IASDR 2009 Proceedings* (pp. 18-22). Retrieved 11 29, 2019, from https://www.researchgate.net/publication/42424464

Prakken, H. (2017). On the problem of making autonomous vehicles conform to traffic law. *Artificial Intelligence Law. Innovation and Technology*, *25*(3), 341–363.

Prensky, M. (2001). *Digital Natives, Digital Immigrants*. Retrieved 30 November 2020, from https://www.marcprensky.com/writing/Prensky%20-%20Digital%20Natives,%20Digital%20Immigrants%20-%20Part1.pdf

Proctor, J. (2019). *Digital Transformation Enablers - Artificial Intelligence & Machine Learning*. Retrieved December 6, 2020, from https://www.inteqgroup.com/blog/digital-transformation-enablers-part-1-artificial-intelligence-machine-learning

Qian, Y., Deng, X., Ye, Q., Ma, B., & Yuan, H. (2019). On detecting business event from the headlines and leads of massive online news articles. *Information Processing & Management*, *56*(6), 102086. doi:10.1016/j.ipm.2019.102086

Qiao, K., & Dam, L. (2020). The overnight return puzzle and the "T+1" trading rule in Chinese stock markets. *Journal of Financial Markets*, *50*, 100534. doi:10.1016/j.finmar.2020.100534

Qi, P., Dozat, T., Zhang, Y., & Manning, C. D. (2018). Universal dependency parsing from scratch. *Proceedings of the CoNLL 2018 Shared Task: Multilingual Parsing from Raw Text to Universal Dependencies*, 160–170.

Qi, S., Law, R., & Buhalis, D. (2015). A modified fuzzy hierarchical TOPSIS model for hotel website evaluation. In *Hospitality, travel, and tourism: concepts, methodologies, tools, and applications* (pp. 263–283). IGI Global. doi:10.4018/978-1-4666-6543-9.ch017

Quebec Construction Commission. (2018). *L'industrie en chiffres*. https://www.ccq.org/fr-CA/En-tete/qui-sommes-nous/industrie-de-la-construction

Québec, R. (2020). *Ensuring Tax Compliance*. https://www.revenuquebec.ca/en/fair-for-all/ensuring-tax-compliance/tax-evasion/construction-sector/

Rahimikia, E., Mohammadi, S., Rahmani, T., & Ghazanfari, M. (2017). Detecting corporate tax evasion using a hybrid intelligent system: A case study of Iran. *International Journal of Accounting Information Systems*, *25*(May), 1–17. doi:10.1016/j.accinf.2016.12.002

Rajkomar, A., Dean, J., & Kohane, I. (2019). Machine learning in medicine. *The New England Journal of Medicine*, *380*(14), 1347–1358. doi:10.1056/NEJMra1814259 PMID:30943338

Ranger, S. (2018, December 18). *What is cloud computing? Everything you need to know about the cloud, explained*. Retrieved April 08, 2020, from ZD Net: https://www.zdnet.com/article/what-is-cloud-computing-everything-you-need-to-know-from-public-and-private-cloud-to-software-as-a/

Raviteja, T. (2020). An introduction of autonomous vehicles and a brief survey. *Journal of Critical Reviews*, *7*(13), 196–202.

Reddy, C. K. (2014). A survey of platforms for big data analytics. *Journal of Big Data (Springer)*, *1*(8), 1–20.

Reportlinker. (2020). *DIY Home Improvement Market - Growth, Trends, and Forecasts (2020–2025).* Author.

RFC 3561 (2003). *Ad hoc On-Demand Distance Vector Routing.*

RFC 3626 (2003). *Optimized Link State Routing.*

Riquier, A. (2019). *Home remodeling is a $450 billion market, and it is only going to get bigger.* https://www.marketwatch.com/story/home-remodeling-is-a-450-billion-market-and-its-only-going-to-get-bigger-2019-03-12

Rostamy, A. A. A., Meysam, S., Behnam, A., & Bakhshi, T. F. (2012). Using fuzzy analytical hierarchy process to evaluate main dimensions of business process reengineering. *Journal of Applied Operational Research, 4*(2), 69–77.

Rouse, M. (2017, July). *Augmented intelligence.* Retrieved from https://whatis.techtarget.com/definition/augmented-intelligence

Roy, J., Sharma, H. K., Kar, S., Zavadskas, E. K., & Saparauskas, J. (2019). An Extended COPRAS Model for Multi-Criteria Decision-Making Problems and Its Application in Web-Based Hotel Evaluation and Selection. *Economic Research- Ekonomska Istrazivanja, 32*(1), 219–253. doi:10.1080/1331677X.2018.1543054

Ruan, Q., Wang, Z., Zhou, Y., & Lv, D. (2020). A new investor sentiment indicator (isi) based on artificial intelligence: A powerful return predictor in China. *Economic Modelling, 88*, 47–58. doi:10.1016/j.econmod.2019.09.009

Rubner, Y., Tomasi, C., & Guibas, L. J. (2000). The earth mover's distance as a metric for image retrieval. *International Journal of Computer Vision, 40*(2), 99–121.

Rui, Z. (2020). Airfield Smart Operations Management and Application of Shared Services. In W. Wang, M. Baumann, & X. Jiang (Eds.), Green, Smart and Connected Transportation Systems. Lecture Notes in Electrical Engineering (vol. 617, pp. 1397-1408). Singapore: Springer. doi:10.1007/978-981-15-0644-4_105

Russell, S., & Norvig, P. (2010). *Artificial Intelligence: A Modern Approach* (3rd ed.). Prentice Hall.

Ryjov, A. (2004). Information Monitoring Systems as a Tool for Strategic Analysis and Simulation in Business. In *Proceeding of the International Conference on Fuzzy Sets and Soft Computing in Economics and Finance.* Saint-Petersburg, Russia: RFSA.

Ryjov, A., Belenki, A., Hooper, R., Pouchkarev, V., Fattah, A., & Zadeh, L. A. (1998). Development of an Intelligent System for Monitoring and Evaluation of Peaceful Nuclear Activities (DISNA). Vienna: IAEA, STR-310.

Ryjov, A. (1988). *The principles of fuzzy set theory and measurement of fuzziness* [in Russian]. Dialog-MSU Publishing.

Ryjov, A. (2001). On information aggregation in fuzzy hierarchical systems [in Russian]. *Intelligent Systems, 6*, 341–364.

Ryjov, A. (2003). Fuzzy Linguistic Scales: Definition, Properties and Applications. In L. Reznik & V. Kreinovich (Eds.), *Soft Computing in Measurement and Information Acquisition* (pp. 23–38). Springer. doi:10.1007/978-3-540-36216-6_3

Ryjov, A. (2004). *Models of information retrieval in a fuzzy environment* [in Russian]. MSU Publishing.

Ryjov, A. (2012). Modeling and Optimization of Information Retrieval for Perception-Based Information. In F. Zanzotto, S. Tsumoto, N. Taatgen, & Y.Y. Yao (Eds), *Proceedings of the International Conference on Brain Informatics 2012* (pp. 140-149). Berlin: Springer. 10.1007/978-3-642-35139-6_14

Ryjov, A. (2013). Systems for evaluation and monitoring of complex processes and their applications [in Russian]. *Intelligent Systems, 17*(1-4), 104–117.

Ryjov, A. (2014a). Human-centric systems for evaluating the status and monitoring the progress for socio-political processes. In *Proceedings of the 8th International Conference on Theory and Practice of Electronic Governance*. New York: ACM Conference Publications. 10.1145/2691195.2691285

Ryjov, A. (2014b). Personalization of Social Networks: Adaptive Semantic Layer Approach. In W. Pedrycz & S.-M. Chen (Eds.), *Social Networks: A Framework of Computational Intelligence* (pp. 21–40). Springer International Publishing Switzerland. doi:10.1007/978-3-319-02993-1_2

Ryjov, A. (2015). Towards an optimal task-driven information granulation. In W. Pedrycz & S.-M. Chen (Eds.), *Information Granularity, Big Data, and Computational Intelligence* (pp. 191–208). Springer International Publishing Switzerland.

Saaty, T. L. (1980). *The analytic hierarchy process*. McGraw-Hill.

Sabherwal, R., & Becerra-Fernandez, I. (2011). *Business Intelligence: Practices, Technologies, and Management*. John Wiley & Sons, Inc.

Sadek, A., & Shellhammer, S. (2008). *IEEE P802.19 Wireless Coexistence: SUI Path-Loss Model for Coexistence Study*. Academic Press.

Saga, B. (2013). *10 Emerging Educational Technologies and How They Are Being Used Across the Globe*. Retrieved 29 November 2020, from https://www.opencolleges.edu.au/informed/features/the-ten-emerging-technologies-in-education-and-how-they-are-being-used-across-the-globe/

Şahin, B., & Cıbıt, Ö. (2016). Consumer perception towards relationship of mobile marketing and online shopping: A research towards travel agency customers. *The Journal of International Social Research*, 9(44), 1221–1231.

Sahingoz, O. K. (2014). Networking models in flying ad-hoc networks (FANETs): Concepts and challenges. *Journal of Intelligent & Robotic Systems*, 74(1-2), 513–527. doi:10.100710846-013-9959-7

Salesforce. (2020). *What Is Digital Transformation*. Retrieved December 6, 2020, from https://www.salesforce.com/products/platform/what-is-digital-transformation/

Salloum, S. A., Al-Emran, M., Monem, A. A., & Shaalan, K. (2017). A survey of text mining in social media: Facebook and Twitter perspectives. *Advances in Science. Technology and Engineering Systems*, 2(1), 127–133. doi:10.25046/aj020115

Saltz, J. S., & Shamshurin, I. (2016). Big data team process methodologies: A literature review and the identification of key factors for a project's success. *2016 IEEE International Conference on Big Data (Big Data)*, 2872–2879. 10.1109/BigData.2016.7840936

Samek, W., & Müller, K.-R. (2019). Towards explainable artificial intelligence. In *Explainable AI: interpreting, explaining and visualizing deep learning* (pp. 5–22). Springer. doi:10.1007/978-3-030-28954-6_1

Sample, I. (2017). Computer says no: why making AIs fair, accountable and transparent is crucial. *The Guardian*.

SAS Institute Inc. (2019, December 2). *Internet of Things*. Retrieved April 08, 2020, from SAS Insights: https://www.sas.com/en_us/insights/big-data/internet-of-things.html

Sassi, E. (2000). Computer supported lab-work in physics education: advantages and problems. *International Conference on Physics Teacher Education beyond 2000*.

Sathi, A. (2013). Big data analytics: Disruptive technologies for changing the game. Boise, ID: MC Press, IBM Corporation.

Scannell, K. (2017). The US intensifies fight against tax evasion by using data mining. *Financial Times*. https://www.ft.com/content/719544f6-529b-11e7-bfb8-997009366969

Schleich, J., Panchapakesan, A., Danoy, G., & Bouvry, P. (2013). UAV fleet area coverage with network connectivity constraint. In *Proceedings of the 11th ACM international symposium on Mobility management and wireless access* (pp. 131-138). ACM. 10.1145/2508222.2508225

Schneider, F., Raczkowski, K., & Mróz, B. (2015). Shadow economy and tax evasion in the EU. *Journal of Money Laundering Control, 18*(1), 34–51. doi:10.1108/JMLC-09-2014-0027

See-To, E. W. K., & Ho, K. K. W. (2014). Value co-creation and purchase intention in social network sites: The role of electronic Word-of-Mouth and trust–A theoretical analysis. *Computers in Human Behavior, 31*, 182–189. doi:10.1016/j.chb.2013.10.013

Selman, B., & Gil, Y. (2019). *A 20-Year Community Roadmap for Artificial Intelligence Research in the US.* Washington, DC: Computing Community Consortium. Retrieved April 29, 2020, from https://cra.org/ccc/wp-content/uploads/sites/2/2019/08/Community-Roadmap-for-AI-Research.pdf

Sen, K., Ghosh, S., Sarkar, B. (2017). Comparison of customer preference for bulk material handling equipment through fuzzy-AHP approach. *Journal of The Institution of Engineers (India): Series C, 98*(3), 367-377.

Senturk, I. F., Akkaya, K., & Senel, F. (2012). An effective and scalable connectivity restoration heuristic for Mobile Sensor/Actor Networks. *2012 IEEE Global Communications Conference (GLOBECOM).* 10.1109/GLOCOM.2012.6503165

Shapira, G. (2018). The Seven Key Steps of Data Analysis. Oracle Corporation. *Profit Magazine.* http://www.oracle.com/us/corporate/profit/big-ideas/052313-gshapira-1951392.html

Sharda, R., & Delen, D. (2006). Predicting box-office success of motion pictures with neural networks. *Expert Systems with Applications, 30*(2), 243–254. doi:10.1016/j.eswa.2005.07.018

Sharda, R., Delen, D., & Turba, E. (2018). *Business Intelligence and Analytics: Systems for Decision Support* (10th ed.). Pearson.

Shirdhonkar, S., & Jacobs, D. W. (2008, June). Approximate earth mover's distance in linear time. In *2008 IEEE Conference on Computer Vision and Pattern Recognition,* (pp. 1-8). IEEE.

Shreyas, S. (2017). A clustering technique for improving marketing strategy in social media using data mining approach. *International Journal of Engineering and Computer Science, 6*(5), 21285–21288.

Simser, J. (2008). Tax evasion and avoidance typologies. *Journal of Money Laundering Control, 11*(2), 123–134. doi:10.1108/13685200810867456

Sirovich, L., & Kirby, M. (1987). Low-dimensional procedure for the characterization of human faces. *Journal of the Optical Society of America. A, Optics and Image Science, 4*(3), 519–524. doi:10.1364/JOSAA.4.000519 PMID:3572578

Sivic, J., & Zisserman, A. (2003, October). Video Google: A text retrieval approach to object matching in videos. In *9th IEEE International Conference on Computer Vision (ICCV 2003)* (pp. 1470–1477). IEEE.

Skala, M. A. (2008). *Aspects of Metric Spaces in Computation* (PhD thesis). University of Waterloo.

Skala, M. (2005). Measuring the difficulty of distance-based indexing. In *International Symposium on String Processing and Information Retrieval* (pp. 103-114). Springer.

Skopal, T. (2004). Pivoting M-tree: A Metric Access Method for Efficient Similarity Search. *Proceedings of the Dateso 2004, Annual International Workshop on DAtabases, TExts, Specifications and Objects,* 27-37.

Skouras, S., & Christodoulakis, N. (2014). Electoral misgovernance cycles: Evidence from wildfires and tax evasion in Greece. *Public Choice, 159*(3-4), 533–559. doi:10.100711127-013-0071-0

Sochay, S. (1994). Predicting the performance of motion pictures. *Journal of Media Economics*, 7(4), 1–20. doi:10.120715327736me0704_1

Soleymaninejad, M., Shadifar, M., & Karimi, A. (2016). Evaluation of Two Major Online Travel Agencies of Us Using TOPSIS Method. *Digital Technologies*, 2(1), 1–8.

Sommerville, I. (2011). *Software Engineering* (9th ed.). Retrieved 29 November 2020, from http://index-of.co.uk/Engineering/Software%20Engineering%20 (9th%20Edition).pdf

Stack Exchange. (n.d.). https://dsp.stackexchange.com/questions/23662/k-means-for-2d-point-clustering-in-python

Stack Overflow. (n.d.). https://stackoverflow.com/questions/36232334/plotting-3d-decision-boundary-from-linear-svm

Statista. (2020). *Global Net Sales of the Home Depot from 2007–2019.* https://www.statista.com/ statistics/240009/global-net-sales-of-the-home-depot/

Stewart, R. (2016, September 2). *Creating the 'Smart Airport' of the future.* Retrieved January 25, 2020, from International Airport Review: https://www.internationalairportreview.com/article/76136/smart-airport-future/

Stranieri, A., & Zeleznikow, J. (1998). *The Role of Open Texture and Stare Decisis in Data Mining Discretion.* Academic Press.

Stranieri, A., & Zeleznikow, J. (2006). Knowledge discovery from legal databases—Using neural networks and data mining to build legal decision support systems. In *Information Technology and Lawyers* (pp. 81–117). Springer. doi:10.1007/1-4020-4146-2_4

Stranieri, A., Zeleznikow, J., Gawler, M., & Lewis, B. (1999). A hybrid rule–neural approach for the automation of legal reasoning in the discretionary domain of family law in Australia. *Artificial Intelligence and Law*, 7(2-3), 153–183. doi:10.1023/A:1008325826599

Strawson, P. F. (1962). Freedom and Resentment in Free Will. Oxford UP.

Suh, K.-S., & Lee, Y. E. (2005). *The effects of virtual reality on consumer learning: An empirical investigation.* Management Information Systems Research Center. Retrieved November 22, 2018, from https://www.jstor.org/stable/25148705

Sun, Z. (2017a). *Delegation intelligence-The Next Frontier for Making Business Success* (BAIS No. 17007). https://www.researchgate.net/publication/318813383_Delegation_Intelligence_The_Next_Frontier_for_Making_Business_Success

Sun, Z., & Finnie, G. (2010). Intelligent Techniques in E-Commerce: A Case-based Reasoning Perspective. Berlin: Springer-Verlag.

Sun, Z., & Huo, Y. (2019). A Managerial Framework for Intelligent Big Data Analytics. In *ICBDSC 2019, January 10-13, Proceedings of ICBDSC 2019*. Bali, Indonesia: ACM.

Sun, Z., & Huo, Y. (2019). The spectrum of big data analytics. *Journal of Computer Information Systems*. doi:10.1080/08874417.2019.1571456

Sun, Z., Han, J., & Dong, D. (2008). *Five Perspectives on Case Based Reasoning.* Paper presented at the ICIC2008, Shanghai, China. 10.1007/978-3-540-85984-0_50

Sun, Z., Strang, K., & Li, R. (2018). Big data with ten big characteristics. *Proceedings of 2018 The 2nd Intl Conf. on Big Data Research (ICBDR 2018), Weihai, China, Oct. 27-29, 2018, ACM International Conference Proceeding Series*, 56-61.

Sun, Z. (2017b). A logical approach to experience-based reasoning. *Journal of New Mathematics and Natural Computation*, 13(1), 21–40. doi:10.1142/S179300571750003X

Sun, Z. (2018). 10 Bigs: Big Data and Its Ten Big Characteristics. *PNG UoT BAIS*, *3*(1), 1–10. doi:10.13140/RG.2.2.31449.62566

Sun, Z. (2018). Intelligent Big Data Analytics. *Foundations and Applications.*, *3*(4). Advance online publication. doi:10.13140/RG.2.2.11037.41441

Sun, Z. (2019). Intelligent Big Data Analytics: A Managerial Perspective. In Z. Sun (Ed.), *Managerial Perspectives on Intelligent Big Data Analytics* (pp. 1–19). IGI-Global. doi:10.4018/978-1-5225-7277-0.ch001

Sun, Z. (2019). *Managerial Perspectives on Intelligent Big Data Analytics*. IGI-Global. doi:10.4018/978-1-5225-7277-0

Sun, Z., & Finnie, G. (2007). A fuzzy logic approach to experience based reasoning. *International Journal of Intelligent Systems*, *22*(8), 867–889. doi:10.1002/int.20220

Sun, Z., Finnie, G., & Weber, K. (2005a). Abductive case-based reasoning. *International Journal of Intelligent Systems*, *20*(9), 957–983. doi:10.1002/int.20101

Sun, Z., & Huo, Y. (2020). Intelligence without Data. *Global Journal of Computer Science and Technology C*, *20*(1), 25–35. doi:10.34257/GJCSTCVOL20IS1PG25

Sun, Z., Strang, K., & Li, R. (2018). Big data with ten big characteristics. In *Proceedings of 2018 The 2nd Intl Conf. on Big Data Research (ICBDR 2018), October 27-29* (pp. 56-61). Weihai, China: ACM.

Sun, Z., Sun, L., & Strang, K. (2018). Big Data Analytics Services for Enhancing Business Intelligence. *Journal of Computer Information Systems*, *58*(2), 162–169. doi:10.1080/08874417.2016.1220239

Sun, Z., & Wang, P. (2017). Big Data, Analytics and Intelligence: An Editorial Perspective. *Journal of New Mathematics and Natural Computation*, *13*(2), 75–81. doi:10.1142/S179300571702001X

Sun, Z., & Wang, P. P. (2017). A Mathematical Foundation of Big Data. *Journal of New Mathematics and Natural Computation*, *13*(2), 8–24.

Sun, Z., & Xiao, J. (1994). *Essentials of Discrete Mathematics, Problems and Solutions*. Hebei University Press.

Sun, Z., Zou, H., & Strang, K. (2015). *Big Data Analytics as a Service for Business Intelligence. I3E2015, LNCS 9373*. Springer.

Super Data Science. (n.d.). https://www.superdatascience.com/blogs/opencv-face-recognition

Tableau. (2015). *Top 8 Trends for 2016: Big Data*. Retrieved from www.tableau.com/Big-Data

Tamboli, N., & Younis, M. (2010). Coverage-aware connectivity restoration in mobile sensor networks. *Journal of Network and Computer Applications*, *33*(4), 363–374. doi:10.1016/j.jnca.2010.03.008

Tang, J., Hao, B., & Sen, A. (2006). Relay node placement in large scale wireless sensor networks. *Computer Communications*, *29*(4), 490–501. doi:10.1016/j.comcom.2004.12.032

Tang, J., Wang, M., Hua, X.-S., & Chua, T.-S. (2012). Social media mining and search. *Multimedia Tools and Applications*, *56*(1), 1–7. doi:10.100711042-011-0822-1

TAV Information Technologies. (2019). *Smart Airport: A comprehensive Concept to Carry Airports into a Smarter Era*. Istanbul: TAV Information Technologies. Retrieved 12 4, 2019, from http://www.tavtechnews.com/pdf/SMART-AIRPORT.pdf

Terry, G. R. (1968). *Principles of Management* (5th ed.). Richard D. Irwin, Inc.

Terry, N., & De'Armond, D. A. (2008). The determinants of movie rental revenue earnings. *Academy of Marketing Studies Journal, 12*(2), 35–47.

The Economic Times. (2016). *Human-machine super-intelligence may tackle world's problems.* Retrieved from http://articles.economictimes.indiatimes.com/2016-01-01/news/69448299_1_systems-hci-problems

Thudumu, S., Branch, P., Jin, J., & Jugdutt, S. (2020). A comprehensive survey of anomaly detection techniques for high dimensional big data. *Journal of Big Data, 7*(42), 42. doi:10.118640537-020-00320-x

Tian, F., Lan, T., Chao, K. M., Godwin, N., Zheng, Q., Shah, N., & Zhang, F. (2016). Mining Suspicious Tax Evasion Groups in Big Data. *IEEE Transactions on Knowledge and Data Engineering, 28*(10), 2651–2664. doi:10.1109/TKDE.2016.2571686

Tiberio, P., & Zezula, P. (1993). Selecting signature files for specific applications. *Information Processing & Management, 29*(4), 487–498.

Torgler, B., & Valev, N. T. (2010). Gender and public attitudes toward corruption and tax evasion. *Contemporary Economic Policy, 28*(4), 554–568. doi:10.1111/j.1465-7287.2009.00188.x

Torra, V. (2002). A review of the construction of hierarchical fuzzy systems. *International Journal of Intelligent Systems, 17*(5), 531–543. doi:10.1002/int.10036

Toulmin, S. (1958). *The Uses of Argument.* Cambridge University Press.

Tsai, C., Lai, C., Chao, H., & Vasilakos, A. (2015). Big data analytics: A survey. *Journal of Big Data, 2*(1), 31–62. doi:10.118640537-015-0030-3 PMID:26191487

Tsuji, M. (2020). The social psychology of Cryptocurrency: Do accounting standard-setters understand the users? *International Journal of Systems and Service-Oriented Engineering, 10*(2), 1–12. doi:10.4018/IJSSOE.2020070101

Tsuji, M., & Hiraiwa, M. (2018). An analysis of the internal consistency of the new accounting standard for virtual currencies in Generally Accepted Japanese Accounting Principles: A virtual currency user perspective. *International Journal of Systems and Service-Oriented Engineering, 8*(2), 30–40. doi:10.4018/IJSSOE.2018040103

Tunali, V., Bilgin, T., & Camurcu, A. (2016). An improved clustering algorithm for text mining: Multi-cluster spherical K-Means. *The International Arab Journal of Information Technology, 13*(1), 12–19.

Tunç, T. (2013). *Analitik Hiyerarşi Sürecinin Malzeme Taşıma Sistemi Seçiminde Uygulanması* (Master of Science Thesis). Gazi University.

Turaga, P., Chellappa, R., Subrahmanian, V. S., & Udrea, O. (2008). Machine recognition of human activities: A survey. *IEEE Transactions on Circuits and Systems for Video Technology, 18*(11), 1473–1488.

Turban, E., & Volonino, L. (2011a). *Information Technology for Management: Improving Performance in the Digital Economy* (8th ed.). John Wiley & Sons.

Turban, E., & Volonino, L. (2011b). *Information Technology for Management: Improving Strategic and Operational Performance* (8th ed.). Wiley & Sons.

Turek, M. (2020). Explainable Artificial Intelligence (XAI). *DARPA.* https://www.darpa.mil/program/explainable-artificial-intelligence

Turing, A. (1950). Computing Machinery and Intelligence. *Mind, 49*(236), 433–460. doi:10.1093/mind/LIX.236.433

Turk, M., & Pentland, A. (1991, January). Eigenfaces for recognition. *Journal of Cognitive Neuroscience, 3*(1), 71–86. doi:10.1162/jocn.1991.3.1.71 PMID:23964806

Tutorials Point. (n.d.). https://www.tutorialspoint.com/python/index.htm

Tuzkaya, G., Gülsün, B., Kahraman, C., & Özgen, D. (2010). An integrated fuzzy multi-criteria decision making methodology for material handling equipment selection problem and an application. *Expert Systems with Applications, 37*(4), 2853–2863. doi:10.1016/j.eswa.2009.09.004

Uğur, M., Savaş, K., & Erdal, H. (2010). An internet-based real-time remote automatic control laboratory for control education. *Procedia: Social and Behavioral Sciences, 2*(2), 5271–5275. doi:10.1016/j.sbspro.2010.03.859

Ukeneru-Steve & Coulibaly. (2019). *Application of K-Means Clustering Algorithmic for the Classification between Gross Domestic Product and Food Consumption in the World.* University of The District of Columbia.

University of Reading. (2014). *Turing test success marks milestone in computing history.* Retrieved from http://www.reading.ac.uk/news-and-events/releases/PR583836.aspx

Vadicamo, L., Mic, V., Falchi, F., & Zezula, P. (2019). Metric embedding into the hamming space with the n-simplex projection. In *International Conference on Similarity Search and Applications* (pp. 265-272). Springer.

Van Der Maaten, L., Postma, E., & Van den Herik, J. (2009). Dimensionality reduction: A comparative. *Journal of Machine Learning Research, 10*(66-71), 13.

Vani, G. K. (2019). How to detect data collection fraud using System properties approach. *Multilogic in Science, 7.*

Vasiliev, D. S., Meitis, D. S., & Abilov, A. (2014). Simulation-based comparison of AODV, OLSR and HWMP protocols for flying Ad Hoc networks. In *International Conference on Next Generation Wired/Wireless Networking* (pp. 245-252). Springer. 10.1007/978-3-319-10353-2_21

Velasco, R. B., Carpanese, I., Interian, R., Paulo, N., Octávio, C. G., & Ribeiro, C. (2020). A decision support system for fraud detection in public procurement. *International Transactions in Operational Research*, 1–21.

Vermeulen, E. P. (2017, December 24). *What is "Smart" in Our New Digital World?* Retrieved March 05, 2020, from Hacker Noon: https://hackernoon.com/what-is-smart-in-our-new-digital-world-87e6426398

Viola, P., & Jones, M. (2001). Rapid object detection using a boosted cascade of simple features. In *Proceedings of the 2001 IEEE Computer Society Conference on Computer Vision and Pattern Recognition. CVPR 2001* (vol. 1, pp. I–511–I–518). 10.1109/CVPR.2001.990517

Vosniadou, S. (n.d.). *How children learn.* International Academy of Education. Retrieved December 20, 2018, from http://www.ibe.unesco.org/fileadmin/user_upload/archive/Publications/educationalpracticesseriespdf/prac07e.pdf

Vousinas, G. L. (2017). Shadow economy and tax evasion. The Achilles heel of Greek economy. Determinants, effects and policy proposals. *Journal of Money Laundering Control, 20*(4), 386–404. doi:10.1108/JMLC-11-2016-0047

Wachter, S., Mittelstadt, B., & Floridi, L. (2017). Why a right to explanation of automated decision-making does not exist in the general data protection regulation. *International Data Privacy Law, 7*(2), 76–99. doi:10.1093/idpl/ipx005

Wallace, W. T., Seigerman, A., & Holbrook, M. B. (1993). The role of actors and actresses in the success of movies: How much is a movie star worth? *Journal of Cultural Economics, 17*(1), 1–27. doi:10.1007/BF00820765

Wallet, P. (2015). *Information and communication technology: A comparative analysis of basic e-readiness in schools.* The UNESCO Institute for Statistics (UIS). Retrieved February 07, 2019, from http://uis.unesco.org/sites/default/files/documents/information-and-communication-technology-ict-in-education-in-sub-saharan-africa-2015-en.pdf

Wang, F.-Y. (2012). A big-data perspective on AI: Newton, Merton, and Analytics Intelligence. *IEEE Intelligent Systems, 27*(5), 2-4.

Wang, X., Han, T. X., & Yan, S. (2009). An hog-lbp human detector with partial occlusion handling. In *2009 IEEE 12th International Conference on Computer Vision* (pp. 32–39). 10.1109/ICCV.2009.5459207

Wang, S., Mao, X., Tang, S. J., Li, X., Zhao, J., & Dai, G. (2010). On "movement-assisted connectivity restoration in wireless sensor and actor networks". *IEEE Transactions on Parallel and Distributed Systems, 22*(4), 687–694. doi:10.1109/TPDS.2010.102

Wang, X., Ji, S. J., Liang, Y. Q., Leung, H. F., & Chiu, D. K. W. (2019). An unsupervised strategy for defending against multifarious reputation attacks. *Applied Intelligence, 49*(12), 4189–4210. doi:10.100710489-019-01490-9

Wang, Y., He, K., Wan, L., & Xie, X. (2020). Research on Annual Report Readability and Stock Liquidity Based on the Perspective of Text Mining. *Securities Market Herald, 7*, 61–71.

Wang, Y., Kung, L., & Byrd, T. A. (2018). Big data analytics: Understanding its capabilities and potential benefits for healthcare organizations. *Technological Forecasting and Social Change, 126*, 3–13. doi:10.1016/j.techfore.2015.12.019

Wang, Z., Dong, W., Josephson, W., Lv, Q., Charikar, M., & Li, K. (2007). Sizing sketches: a rank-based analysis for similarity search. In *Proceedings of the 2007 ACM SIGMETRICS international conference on Measurement and modeling of computer systems* (pp. 157-168). ACM.

Wasserstrom, R. A. (1961). *The judicial decision: Toward a theory of legal justification.* Stanford University Press.

Wei, H., Zhong, Z., Guan, K., & Ai, B. (2010, August). Path loss models in viaduct and plain scenarios of the high-speed railway. In *2010 5th International ICST Conference on Communications and Networking in China* (pp. 1-5). IEEE. 10.4108/iwoncmm.2010.3

Weiss, G. (2013). *Multiagent systems* (2nd ed.). MIT Press.

WH. (2019). *The National Artificial Intelligence Research and Development Strategic Plan: 2019 update.* Retrieved from https://www.whitehouse.gov/wp-content/uploads/2019/06/National-AI-Research-and-Development-Strategic-Plan-2019-Update-June-2019.pdf?fbclid=IwAR3QZaL_1w3Y4I7pEva8J8qIfjc_azzbSnyBjD63dZO5xqMAwYUA_dQ1IQ0

Wiens, J., & Shenoy, E. S. (2018). Machine learning for healthcare: On the verge of a major shift in healthcare epidemiology. *Clinical Infectious Diseases, 66*(1), 149–153. doi:10.1093/cid/cix731 PMID:29020316

Wiesner, T. F., & Lan, W. (2004). Comparison of student learning in physical and simulated unit operations experiments. *Journal of Engineering Education, 93*(3), 195–204. doi:10.1002/j.2168-9830.2004.tb00806.x

Wiki-Descartes. (2020). *Rene_Descartes.* Retrieved August 05, 2020, from Wikipedia: https://en.wikipedia.org/wiki/Rene_Descartes

Wikipedia. (2020, April 8). *Arinc.* Retrieved April 10, 2020, from Wikipedia: https://en.wikipedia.org/wiki/ARINC

Wikipedia-EAI. (2020, November 5). *Explainable artificial intelligence.* Retrieved November 13, 2020, from Wikipedia: https://en.wikipedia.org/wiki/Explainable_artificial_intelligence

Wikipedia-IA. (2020, November 11). *Intelligent agent.* Retrieved November 13, 2020, from Wikipedia: https://en.wikipedia.org/wiki/Intelligent_agent

Wikipedia-MAS. (2020, November 9). *Multi-agent system.* Retrieved November 13, 2020, from Wikipedia: https://en.wikipedia.org/wiki/Multi-agent_system

Wikiversity. (2020). *Open design*. Retrieved 30 November 2020, from https://en.wikiversity.org/wiki/Open_design

Williams, D. L., Crittenden, V. L., Keo, T., & McCarty, P. (2012). The use of social media: An exploratory study of usage among digital natives. *Journal of Public Affairs*, *12*(2), 127–136. doi:10.1002/pa.1414

Wilson, T. D. (2000). Human information behavior. *Informing Science*, *3*(2), 49–55. doi:10.28945/576

Wong, E., Leung, R., & Law, R. (2020). Significance of the dimensions and attributes of hotel mobile website from the perceptions of users. *International Journal of Hospitality & Tourism Administration*, *21*(1), 15–37. doi:10.1080/1525 6480.2018.1429338

Wong, J. Y., Chiu, D. K., & Mark, K. P. (2007, January). Effective e-Government process monitoring and interoperation: A case study on the removal of unauthorized building works in Hong Kong. In R. H. Sprague Jr. (Ed.), *Proceedings of the 40th Annual Hawaii International Conference on System Sciences* (pp. 101-101). IEEE. 10.1109/HICSS.2007.194

Wooldridge, M. (2002). *An Introduction to MultiAgent Systems*. John Wiley & Sons.

Wu, Y. (2018). *Study and application on fine-grained sentiment analysis of financial microblog* (Master's thesis). South China University of Technology.

Wu, R. S., Ou, C. S., Lin, H. Y., Chang, S.-I., & Yen, D. C. (2012). Using data mining technique to enhance tax evasion detection performance. *Expert Systems with Applications*, *39*(10), 8769–8777. doi:10.1016/j.eswa.2012.01.204

Wyatt, R. O., & Badger, D. P. (1987). To toast, pan or waffle: How movie reviews affect reader interest and credibility perception. *Newspaper Research Journal*, *8*(Summer), 19–30. doi:10.1177/073953298700800402

Yager, R. R. (2013). Pythagorean membership grades in multicriteria decision making. *IEEE Transactions on Fuzzy Systems*, *22*(4), 958–965. doi:10.1109/TFUZZ.2013.2278989

Yager, R. R., & Abbasov, A. M. (2013). Pythagorean membership grades, complex numbers, and decision making. *International Journal of Intelligent Systems*, *28*(5), 436–452. doi:10.1002/int.21584

Yang, Y., & Yang, B. (2020). Tax incentives, entrepreneurial market confidence and corporate investment: An empirical study based on text mining of annual reports of listed companies. *Taxation Research*, *7*, 86–94.

Yanmaz, E. (2012, June). Connectivity versus area coverage in unmanned aerial vehicle networks. In *2012 IEEE International Conference on Communications (ICC)* (pp. 719-723). IEEE. 10.1109/ICC.2012.6364585

Ying, Q., Xiaoxin, H., & Weige, J. (2019). Research on Tax Inspection Case Selection Model Based on Bayesian Network. In *Proceedings of the 2019. 2nd International Conference on Information Management and Management Sciences (IMMS 2019)*. Association for Computing Machinery. 10.1145/3357292.3357329

Yoshitaka, A., & Ichikawa, T. (1999). A survey on content-based retrieval for multimedia databases. *IEEE Transactions on Knowledge and Data Engineering*, *11*(1), 81–93.

Young, S. D. (2015). A "big data" approach to HIV epidemiology and prevention. *Preventive Medicine*, *70*, 17–18. doi:10.1016/j.ypmed.2014.11.002 PMID:25449693

Yu, C., Shao, Y., Wang, K., & Zhang, L. (2019). A group decision making sustainable supplier selection approach using extended TOPSIS under interval-valued Pythagorean fuzzy environment. *Expert Systems with Applications*, *121*, 1–17. doi:10.1016/j.eswa.2018.12.010

Yucesan, M., & Gul, M. (2020). Hospital service quality evaluation: An integrated model based on Pythagorean fuzzy AHP and fuzzy TOPSIS. *Soft Computing*, *24*(5), 3237–3255. doi:10.100700500-019-04084-2

Yu, L. C., Wu, J. L., Chang, P. C., & Chu, H. S. (2013). Using a contextual entropy model to expand emotion words and their intensity for the sentiment classification of stock market news. *Knowledge-Based Systems*, *41*, 89–97. doi:10.1016/j.knosys.2013.01.001

Zadeh, L. A. (1975). The concept of a linguistic variable and its application to approximate reasoning. Part 1,2,3. Information Sciences, 8, 199-249. doi:10.1016/0020-0255(75)90036-5

Zadeh, L. A. (1965). Fuzzy set. *Information and Control*, *8*(3), 338–353. doi:10.1016/S0019-9958(65)90241-X

Zarzour, H., Jararweh, Y., Hammad, M. M., & Al-Smadi, M. (2020, April). A long short-term memory deep learning framework for explainable recommendation. In 2020 11th International Conference on Information and Communication Systems (ICICS) (pp. 233-237). IEEE.

Zarzour, H., Maazouzi, F., Soltani, M., & Chemam, C. (2018, May). An improved collaborative filtering recommendation algorithm for big data. In *IFIP International Conference on Computational Intelligence and Its Applications* (pp. 660-668). Springer, Cham. 10.1007/978-3-319-89743-1_56

Zervas, P., Kalimeris, I., & Sampson, D. G. (2014). A Method for Developing Mobile Virtual Laboratories. In *2014 IEEE 14th International Conference on Advanced Learning Technologies* (pp. 8-10). IEEE. 10.1109/ICALT.2014.12

Zezula, P., Amato, G., Dohnal, V., & Batko, M. (2006). Similarity Search – The Metric Space Approach. Springer.

Zhang, D. (2018). *The application of sentiment analysis in finance corups* (Master's thesis). Jinan University.

Zhang, Z., Chen, Z., & Yan, H. (2017). *Stock prediction: A method based on extraction of news features and recurrent neural networks*. Papers 1707.07585, arXiv.org.

Zhang, K., Li, A., & Song, B. (2009). Fraud Detection in Tax Declaration Using Ensemble ISGNN. *2009 WRI World Congress on Computer Science and Information Engineering*, 237-240. 10.1109/CSIE.2009.73

Zhang, X. L., & Xu, Z. S. (2014). Extension of TOPSIS to multiple criteria decision making with Pythagorean fuzzy sets. *Int. J. Inter. Syst.*, *29*(12), 1061–1078. doi:10.1002/int.21676

Zhang, X., Zhang, Y., Wang, S., Yao, Y., Fang, B., & Philip, S. Y. (2018). Improving stock market prediction via heterogeneous information fusion. *Knowledge-Based Systems*, *143*, 236–247. doi:10.1016/j.knosys.2017.12.025

Zhao, R. (2019). Inferring private information from online news and searches: Correlation and prediction in Chinese stock market. *Physica A*, *528*, 121450. doi:10.1016/j.physa.2019.121450

Zhao, T., Xie, Y., & Zhang, Y. (2018). Connectivity properties for UAVs networks in wireless ultraviolet communication. *Photonic Network Communications*, *35*(3), 316–324. doi:10.100711107-017-0753-5

Zheng, Y., Wang, Y., Li, Z., Dong, L., Jiang, Y., & Zhang, H. (2014). A mobility and load aware OLSR routing protocol for UAV mobile ad-hoc networks. In *2014 International Conference on Information and Communications Technologies (ICT 2014)*. IET Digital Library. 10.1049/cp.2014.0575

Zhou, L., & Zhang, D. (2003). NLPIR: A theoretical framework for applying natural language processing to information retrieval. *Journal of the American Society for Information Science and Technology*, *54*(2), 115–123. doi:10.1002/asi.10193

About the Contributors

Zhaohao Sun is currently a full professor of Information Technology, Department of Business Studies, Director of Research Centre of Big Data Analytics and Intelligent Systems (BAIS). PNG University of Technology, Prof. Dr Zhaohao Sun graduated from Bond University Australia, University of Ballarat, Brandenburg Technical University Cottbus (TU Cottbus), Germany and Hebei University, China with PhD, Graduate Cert. of Edu., MSc (Dipl.-Math.), MSc, and BSc respectively. He previously held the academic posotions of an adjunct professor of the Federation University Australia, chair professor of Hebei University of Science & Technology, professor of Hebei Normal University and other academic positions at Hebei University, China; RWTH Aachen, TU Cottbus, Germany; Bond University and the University of Wollongong, Australia. Dr Sun is a world renowned scholar in many research fields such as big data, data science, e-commerce, case based reasoning, and intelligent systems. He has 7 books and 160+ peer-reviewed research paper publications, completed 20+ research grants, supported by the Chinese Government, German Government, Australian Government, USA Government and PNG Government, and lectured 46+ different courses for undergraduate and postgraduate students of IT, IS, CS and EMBA in universities of Australia, China and PNG. The taught courses include Big data Analytics and Artificial Intelligence, Business Intelligence and Analytics, Cloud Computing, Data Management Systems, Information Systems Management, and Management Information Systems. He is an editor and/or associate editor of five international journals. His research has appeared in Journal of Computer Information Systems, Intelligent Journal of Intelligent Systems, Information Sciences, Knowledge-Based Systems, etc. His current research interests include big data, big data analytics, data science, artificial intelligence, cloud computing, business intelligence, e-commerce, and intelligent systems. He is a senior member of ACS, and a member of AIS and IEEE (MAIS and MIEEE). He can be contacted at zhaohao. sun@gmail.com.

* * *

Vahid Khalilpour Akram received the BSc and the MSc degrees in Computer Engineering from Azad University in 2002 and 2005, respectively. He received PhD degree from Ege University, International Computer Institute in 2017 and currently is an assistant professor at Ege University, Izmir, Turkey. His research interests include wireless ad hoc networks, distributed algorithms, and parallel computing.

Prosper Bernard has a solid multidisciplinary academic background, with a Ph.D. in Business Administration from the City University of New York and an MBA from St-John's University in New York. He also holds a B.A. from the University of Montreal, Summa Cum Laude, and a B.Sc. from

McGill, a CDP in Data processing, a CMC in Management consulting, and an Adm. A. in Management. He has published several books and articles. Dr. Prosper M. Bernard is an internationally respected lecturer and consultant with extensive experience in Business Strategy, Project Management, Management of Information Systems, International Business/Marketing, and International Business Education. Prof. Bernard served as vice-president at the University of Québec at Montreal, Dean of the School of Business, one of the largest in North America, as Director of the Executive MBA program, president of the graduate studies committee, and director of the PhD program in Business run in a Consortium of the four Montreal Universities. He has lectured and has acted as a visiting professor at many universities, including McGill University, the University of Alberta, St-John's University in New York, Ecole Polytechnique, Barry University in Miami, the University of Southern California, the Fundacão Getulio Vargas, São Paulo, Brazil, The University of Sarasota, INCAE in Costa Rica, the University Claude Bernard in Lyon, France, and many others. Dr. Bernard also acts as a Management Consultant for many organisations in the fields of International Business, Project Management, Business Planning, Business Education, and Information Systems. He has held managerial positions in Information Systems in the fields of banking, insurance, education, and transportation. He is/was on the board of directors of some companies (private and public) such as UQAM, Virtual Universe Corporation as one of the founders (Calgary Stock Exchange), and International Data Share (Toronto Stock Exchange).

Umut Can Çabuk received his B.Sc. degree in electronics engineering from Uludağ University (Bursa, Turkey) in 2012, and his M.Sc. degree in information technology engineering from Aarhus University (Aarhus, Denmark) in 2015. He is currently conducting his Ph.D. thesis studies at the International Computer Institute of Ege University (Izmir, Turkey), where he also works as a research assistant. His research interests include mobile and wireless networks, the internet of things, computer security, and graph theory. He has co-authored over 25 scholarly publications and issued two patent applications.

Li Chen is a professor at the Department of Computer Science and Information Technology, University of the District of Columbia, USA.

Dickson K. W. Chiu received the B.Sc. (Hons.) degree in Computer Studies from the University of Hong Kong in 1987. He received the M.Sc. (1994) and the Ph.D. (2000) degrees in Computer Science from the Hong Kong University of Science and Technology (HKUST). He started his own computer company while studying part-time. He has also taught at several universities in Hong Kong. His teaching and research interests are in Information Management, Service Computing, Library Science, and E-learning with a cross-disciplinary approach, involving workflows, software engineering, information technologies, agents, information system research, and databases. The results have been widely published in over 250 international publications (most of them indexed by SCI, SCI-E, EI, and SSCI), including many practical taught master and undergraduate project results. He received a best paper award in the 37th Hawaii International Conference on System Sciences in 2004. He is the founding Editor-in-chief of the International Journal on Systems and Service-Oriented Engineering, and serves on the editorial boards of several international journals. He is an editor(-in-chief) of Library Hi Tech, a prestigious journal indexed by SSCI (impact factor 1.256). He co-founded several international workshops and co-edited several journal special issues. He also served as a program committee member for around 250 international conferences and workshops. Dr. Chiu is a Senior Member of both the ACM and the IEEE, and a life member of the Hong Kong Computer Society. According to Google Scholar, he has nearly 4,000 citations, h-index 34, i-10 index 85; ranked worldwide 2nd in the category of "e-services," 9th in "library science," and 11th in "e-business."

Orhan Dagdeviren received the BSc and the MSc degrees in Computer Engineering from Izmir Institute of Technology. He received PhD degree from Ege University, International Computer Institute. He is an associate professor and is the head of Network Engineering Science and Technology (NETOS) Laboratory in International Computer Institute. His interests lie in the distributed computing, fault tolerance, applied graph theory and computer networking areas.

Burak Efe graduated from Gazi University, Department of Industrial Engineering in 2011. He received the M.Sc. degree in Industrial Engineering from Gazi University. He received Ph.D. degree in Industrial Engineering from Gazi University. His research interests are Multi-criteria decision making, fuzzy logic, ergonomics, occupational health and safety. He has been working as an Assistant Professor in Necmettin Erbakan University.

Ömer Faruk Efe graduated from Selçuk University, Department of Industrial Engineering in 2008. He received an M.Sc. degree in Industrial Engineering from Selçuk University. He received a Ph.D. degree in Industrial Engineering from Sakarya University. His research interests are Multi-criteria decision making, fuzzy logic, lean production, ergonomics, occupational health, and safety. He has been working as an Assistant Professor at Afyon Kocatepe University.

Jiwen Fang received the Master's degree in Library and Information Management at the University of Hong Kong in 2018. This chapter mainly derives from his graduation project. Her research interests are in Data Science and Financial Information Systems.

Wentao Gao received the MSc degree in Library and Information Management in 2018 at the University of Hong Kong and previously a bachelor's degree in Finance from mainland China. He has work experience in banking, e-commerce, and real-estate development. This article is adapted from his graduation project. His research interests are on big data analysis, financial intelligence, and marketing quantitative methods.

Titus Haiduwa is a Lecturer in the Department of Information Technology, School of Computing, University of Namibia. He is currently a doctoral degree student at the University of Namibia. His research interest includes ICT4D, HCI, AI, Software Development and Information Security.

Kevin K. W. Ho is a Professor at the School of Business and Public Administration, University of Guam. Kevin's research interests include electronic service, information systems strategy, social media, green information systems, sustainability management, and electronic government. He is an associate editor in International Journal of Systems and Service-Oriented Engineering, and editor board member in International Journal of Social and Organizational Dynamics in Information Technology, International Journal of Technology and Human Interaction, and Journal of Communication and Education. Starting Jan 2020, he will take over as an editor(-in-chief) of Library Hi Tech, a prestige journal indexed by SSCI. His research has been published in Computers in Human Behavior, Decision Support Systems,

Information & Management, Internet Research, Journal of Electronic Commerce Research, Journal of Global Information Management, among others.

Priyank Jain is working as an Assistant Professor in IIIT Bhopal. He has more than ten years of experience as an Assistant Professor and Research Scholar. His Ph.D. is in the "Big Data" field. He has experience from the Indian Institute of Management, Ahmedabad, India (IIM-A) in the research field. His Educational Qualification is M.Tech & BE in Information Technology. Dr. Priyank Jain areas of specialization are Big Data, Big Data Privacy & Security, data mining, Privacy-Preserving, & Information Retrieval. Dr. Priyank Jain has publications in various International Conference, International SCI, SCIE, and Scopus Journals & National Conference. He is a member of HIMSS.

Willbard Kamati is a currently pursuing his Masters of Science in Information Technology at the University of Namibia and holds a Bachelors of Science(honours) in Information Technology. He works as a Data Entry although passionate about software development.

Ka Man Lam received her BEng in Computer Engineering, MPhil and PhD degrees in Computer Science and Engineering from The Chinese University of Hong Kong. She received Excellent Teaching Assistantship Award from the Department of Computer Science and Engineering, The Chinese University of Hong Kong in 2005 and 2006. She has also received the Best Teaching Award from the Department of Computer Science in 2011 and 2018 and Faculty Performance Award in Teaching in 2017 when she worked as a Lecturer at Hong Kong Baptist University. Currently, Dr. Lam is a Lecturer at the Department of Computer Science, The University of Hong Kong.

Faiz Maazouzi received the bachelor's, master's, and Ph.D. degrees from Badji Mokhtar–Annaba University, Algeria, in 2007, 2009, and 2014, respectively, all in computer science. He has been an Assistant Professor with the Department of Mathematics and Computer Science, University of Souk Ahras, Algeria, since 2014. His research interests include data mining and intrusion detection systems. He has served as an Organizing Committee Member in numerous international conferences.

Vladimir Mic is a post-doctoral researcher at Masaryk University, Brno, Czech Republic. He received his Ph.D. in computer science at the same university in 2020. His research is focused on the similarity searching in metric spaces, not only using transformations of search space into Hamming space. His published research also addresses the convex transforms of similarity distance functions and improving tightness of bounds given by triangle inequalities in metric space similarity models.

Desmond Narongou currently works as an Airport Systems Officer with the National Airports Corporation (NAC) at the Port Moresby (Jackson's) International Airport since September 2018. He graduated with a Bachelors Degree of Commerce in Information Technology (with merit) from PNG University of Technology in 2017. He's passionate about exploring new technologies and systems, research, and writing.

Maria Ndapewa Ntinda is a lecturer in the Computer Science Department, School of Computing at the University of Namibia. She has an interest in Educational Technologies, Augmented Reality, Tourism, and aligning curriculum with the industry demands. Maria is pursuing her Ph.D. in Computer Science at the University of Turku, Finland.

Michel Plaisent is a full professor in the University of Québec in Montréal (Canada). After a bachelor in Information technology, a M.Sc. in project management and a Ph.D. in Information Technology Management, he joined the Business school in 1980 where he held different position while developing his research career as professor, namely IT program director for 6 years. His doctoral research was pioneer as he studied the use of computer mediated communication systems by CEO. Since then, Dr. Plaisent's researches continue to focus human factors of IT, namely cognitive ergonomics, learning problems and personal productivity tools for managers. Among his new researches lets mention: Education 4.0 concepts and tools, and more broadly the impact of internet on life and society. He has published more than 25 books and more than one hundred of articles in international conferences and academic indexed journals. On International dimension, he is engaged in China MBA program and he manages for UQAM research collaboration protocols with three South-Asia universities.

Alexander P. Ryzhov is a professor at Department of Mathematical Foundations of Intelligent Systems, Faculty of Mechanics and Mathematics, Lomonosov Moscow State University, and professor and Head of the Department of Business Processes Management Systems at School of IT Management, Institute of Economics, Mathematics and Information Technologies, Russian Presidential Academy of National Economy and Public Administration. Alexander has a Ph.D. in Mathematics, and D.Sc. in Engineering, Executive MBA from Bled School of Management. He has more than 30 years of the combined business, advanced research, and teaching experience, more than 100 scientific publications including 5 books and chapters in 14 books. More information on http://www.intsys.msu.ru/en/staff/ryzhov/

Andrew Stranieri is an Associate Professor in the Centre for Informatics and Applied Optimisation at Federation University, Ballarat, Australia. He adapted his training in psychology to inform research into cognitive models of argumentation and artificial intelligence. This was instrumental in modelling decision making in refugee law, copyright law, eligibility for legal aid, sentencing and research ethics developed by a spin-out company he managed. His research in health informatics spans data mining in health, telemedicine and intelligent decision support systems. He has published three books and is the author of over 160 peer reviewed journal and conference proceedings papers.

Mustafa Tosun received his B.Sc. and M.Sc. degree in computer engineering from Pamukkale University (Denizli, Turkey) in 2015 and 2018. He is currently conducting his Ph.D. thesis studies at the International Computer Institute of Ege University (Izmir, Turkey), where he also works as a research assistant. His research interests include algorithms, mobile and wireless networks, the internet of things, distributed systems, distributed algorithms, and graph theory.

Zhenyu (Andrew) Xu is a Suzhou-based independent researcher. His research interests include fintech, startups, big data, machine learning, deep learning, artificial intelligence, NLP, sentiment analysis, and Python programming.

Poshan (Sam) Yu is a Lecturer in Accounting & Finance at Soochow University international cooperative education program. He is also an External Professor of FinTech & Finance at SKEMA Business School (China). Sam leads FasterCapital (Dubai, UAE) as Regional Partner (China). His research interests include FinTech, RegTech, Public-Private Partnership (PPP), M&A, Private Equity, Venture Capital, Startups, Art Finance & China's "One Belt, One Road" policy.

Hafed Zarzour received his Ph.D degree in Computer Science from Annaba University, Algeria. He is currently an associate professor of Computer Science at Souk Ahras University, Algeria. He has published several research papers in International Journals and Conferences of high repute including IEEE,Springer, Elsevier, Wiley, ACM, Taylor and Francis, IGI Global, Inderscience, etc. His research focuses on Deep Learning, Artificial Intelligence, and Educational Technology.

Pavel Zezula is professor of computer science at Masaryk University, Brno, Czech Republic. His professional interests focus on techniques for big data analysis such as content-based data retrieval, large-scale similarity search, or mechanisms to improve the findability of the data. He is a co-author of a highly cited metric-based similarity search structure M-Tree and a pioneering book on "Similarity Search".

Cataldo Zuccaro obtained a Ph.D. in marketing at the University of Quebec in Montreal in 1999. He is a professor of marketing at the University of Quebec in Montreal. He had been a director of the MBA Research and the chair of the department of business strategies. Dr. Cataldo Zuccaro is a specialist in Data Analysis, Business Analytics and Marketing. His areas of research are marketing research methods, business modeling, customer scoring and segmentation, business analytics and research methods. He has taught and continues to teach in the university's Executive MBA program in such countries as Romania, Poland, France, Morocco, Algeria, Tunisia, Lebanon, Mexico and Peru. He has also consulted for large multinational corporations and government agencies. Dr. Zuccaro has published his research in such journals as Recherches sociologiques Revue des sciences administratives du Canada, Journal of the market research society Journal of social psychology, International journal of market research, Journal of modelling management, International journal of bank marketing, Social research indicators and the Journal of Economics and Economic Education Research. He is the winner, in 2010, of the silver medal for the best paper in the International Journal of Market Research.

Index

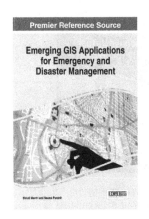

IGI Global Author Services

Providing a high-quality, affordable, and expeditious service, IGI Global's Author Services enable authors to streamline their publishing process, increase chance of acceptance, and adhere to IGI Global's publication standards.

Benefits of Author Services:

- **Professional Service:** All our editors, designers, and translators are experts in their field with years of experience and professional certifications.
- **Quality Guarantee & Certificate:** Each order is returned with a quality guarantee and certificate of professional completion.
- **Timeliness:** All editorial orders have a guaranteed return timeframe of 3-5 business days and translation orders are guaranteed in 7-10 business days.
- **Affordable Pricing:** IGI Global Author Services are competitively priced compared to other industry service providers.
- **APC Reimbursement:** IGI Global authors publishing Open Access (OA) will be able to deduct the cost of editing and other IGI Global author services from their OA APC publishing fee.

Author Services Offered:

English Language Copy Editing
Professional, native English language copy editors improve your manuscript's grammar, spelling, punctuation, terminology, semantics, consistency, flow, formatting, and more.

Scientific & Scholarly Editing
A Ph.D. level review for qualities such as originality and significance, interest to researchers, level of methodology and analysis, coverage of literature, organization, quality of writing, and strengths and weaknesses.

Figure, Table, Chart & Equation Conversions
Work with IGI Global's graphic designers before submission to enhance and design all figures and charts to IGI Global's specific standards for clarity.

Translation
Providing 70 language options, including Simplified and Traditional Chinese, Spanish, Arabic, German, French, and more.

Hear What the Experts Are Saying About IGI Global's Author Services

"Publishing with IGI Global has been **an amazing experience** *for me for sharing my research. The* **strong academic production** *support ensures quality and timely completion."* – **Prof. Margaret Niess, Oregon State University, USA**

"The service was **very fast, very thorough, and very helpful** *in ensuring our chapter meets the criteria and requirements of the book's editors. I was* **quite impressed and happy** *with your service."* – **Prof. Tom Brinthaupt, Middle Tennessee State University, USA**

www.igi-global.com

Publisher of Peer-Reviewed, Timely, and Innovative Academic Research Since 1988

IGI Global's Transformative Open Access (OA) Model:
How to Turn Your University Library's Database Acquisitions Into a Source of OA Funding

Well in advance of Plan S, IGI Global unveiled their OA Fee Waiver (Read & Publish) Initiative. Under this initiative, librarians who invest in IGI Global's InfoSci-Books and/or InfoSci-Journals databases will be able to subsidize their patrons' OA article processing charges (APCs) when their work is submitted and accepted (after the peer review process) into an IGI Global journal.

How Does it Work?

Step 1: **Library Invests in the InfoSci-Databases:** A library perpetually purchases or subscribes to the InfoSci-Books, InfoSci-Journals, or discipline/subject databases.

Step 2: **IGI Global Matches the Library Investment with OA Subsidies Fund:** IGI Global provides a fund to go towards subsidizing the OA APCs for the library's patrons.

Step 3: **Patron of the Library is Accepted into IGI Global Journal (After Peer Review):** When a patron's paper is accepted into an IGI Global journal, they option to have their paper published under a traditional publishing model or as OA.

Step 4: **IGI Global Will Deduct APC Cost from OA Subsidies Fund:** If the author decides to publish under OA, the OA APC fee will be deducted from the OA subsidies fund.

Step 5: **Author's Work Becomes Freely Available:** The patron's work will be freely available under CC BY copyright license, enabling them to share it freely with the academic community.

Note: This fund will be offered on an annual basis and will renew as the subscription is renewed for each year thereafter. IGI Global will manage the fund and award the APC waivers unless the librarian has a preference as to how the funds should be managed.

Hear From the Experts on This Initiative:

"I'm very happy to have been able to make one of my recent research contributions *freely available* along with having access to the *valuable resources* found within IGI Global's InfoSci-Journals database."

— **Prof. Stuart Palmer,**
Deakin University, Australia

"Receiving the support from IGI Global's OA Fee Waiver Initiative *encourages me to continue my research work without any hesitation.*"

— **Prof. Wenlong Liu,** College of Economics and Management at Nanjing University of Aeronautics & Astronautics, China

For More Information, Scan the QR Code or Contact:
IGI Global's Digital Resources Team at eresources@igi-global.com.

Printed in the United States
By Bookmasters